BARNES' NOTES

A Commentary on The Book of Genesis

James G. Murphy

BakerBooks
A Division of Baker Book House Co
Grand Rapids, Michigan 49516

Barnes' Notes

Heritage Edition

Fourteen Volumes 0834-4

1.	Genesis (Murphy)	0835-2	8.	Minor Prophets (Pusey)	0842-5
2.	Exodus to Esther (Cook)	0836-0	9.	The Gospels	0843-3
3.	Job	0837-9	10.	Acts and Romans	0844-1
4.	Psalms	0838-7	11.	I Corinthians to Galatians	0846-8
5.	Proverbs to Ezekiel (Cook)	0839-5	12.	Ephesians to Philemon	0847-6
6.	Isaiah	0840-9	13.	Hebrews to Jude	0848-4
7.	Daniel	0841-7	14.	Revelation	0849-2

When ordering by ISBN (International Standard Book Number), numbers listed above should be preceded by 0-8010-.

Reprinted from the 1847 edition published
by Blackie & Son, London

Reprinted 2005 by Baker Books
a division of Baker Book House Company
P.O. Box 6287, Grand Rapids, MI 49516-6287

Printed in the United States of America

For information about academic books, resources for Christian leaders, and all new releases available from Baker Book House, visit our web site:
http://www.bakerbooks.com/

INTRODUCTION

The Commentary of Professor Murphy on Genesis has been in the hands of scholars for several years, and has won a high place in their regard. Indeed, there is reason to believe that no recent exposition of Genesis has been consulted with more frequency or profit by the clergy of England and America, than this — a circumstance which affords good evidence of its intrinsic worth, though not, perhaps, of its adaptation to the minds and culture of the people. To the latter point I would therefore call attention; for this work will be found, I think, as well fitted to meet the wants of the English reader as it is to meet those of the Hebrew scholar. The two features which might be supposed to restrict its usefulness to persons acquainted with the Hebrew language, are these: it is founded on the Hebrew text, examined in the light of the best modern scholarship, and it introduces each paragraph with a list and explanation of the principal Hebrew words which are met for the first time in that paragraph.

Of these two features, the former is plainly a great excellence; for it brings the reader, along with the expositor, into more intimate and living contact with the inspired record. Think of a man undertaking to expound the dialogues of Plato, with nothing but a good translation to guide him! How often would he long to know, by a careful study of the original, whether the version of an obscure passage before him was the only natural one! How often would he be in just a little doubt whether he had apprehended the exact shade of thought which the translator meant to express! A doubt which might be removed by a single glance at the words of Plato himself. And how often would the original set his mind upon inquiries, leading to a deeper view of the writer's aim and spirit! The same may be said of Shakespeare. Who would think of expounding his plays by the help of a German translation, merely? If it were possible to ascertain in this way the leading thought of every line, how much of the flavor and aroma of the sentiment would nevertheless be lost! And how much of the delight, enthusiasm, and confidence which a study of the very words of Shakespeare would inspire, must be wanting! So too, at a great, if not an equal disadvantage must an interpreter of Genesis be placed, who is unacquainted with the Hebrew original. No man, indeed, can explain the Scriptures in the best manner possible, on the basis of a translation. The exposition must lack, to a degree, the freshness and life, the breadth and freedom, the richness and depth, which would distinguish an equally faithful commentary, founded on a good knowledge of the inspired text. And, other things being equal, the more thorough one's knowledge of that text, the more perfect his mastery of every idiom and allusion, by so much the more will his work excel in the qualities just named. But these are the very qualities which touch the reader's heart and make the study of God's Word a delight. These are the qualities which transport the reader into the past and the distant, causing him to live and move, to think and feel, with "holy men of old." They are the charm of a work for the people, making it attractive as well as instructive.

These qualities do not, however, belong to every commentary prepared by a good scholar. The benefit of great learning is often lost to the world for want of fit expression. What reader can pass from the pages of Delitzsch on the Psalms, to those of Perowne on the same book, without a sense of relief and delight, akin to that which he would feel in emerging from the depths of a tangled forest upon a fair and open lawn, "shaven by the scythe and levelled by the roller"? If the works of biblical students are to live, and mould the views of intelligent men, they must excel in form as well as in substance, in style as well as in thought. The friends of the Bible would do well to bear this in mind, and even take a lesson from some of its foes ; for the latter, whatever may be said of their knowledge and treatment of the orignal Word, are masters of their own language, and are careful to give their opinions the best utterance possible. This is an important reason why their writings are sought by men of average culture. Whatever is written is written well, the views advocated are put in the most favorable light, and if there be any weakness or obscurity of thought, it is at least relieved by beauty of style. Their care in this respect is worthy of praise, and devout scholars, who study the holy oracles with life-long zeal, should go and do likewise, sparing no effort to give their knowledge to others in a captivating form. A commentary is useless unless it is read, and a commentary is not read by the people unless it is couched in "acceptable words." A profound acquaintance with divine truth ought to fill the expositor's soul with the very life and light of that truth, so that these will radiate from his pen in forms of beauty and of power.

Now the Commentary of Professor Murphy on the book of Genesis excels in this respect. The style fitly expresses the thought, and the thought is rich, clear, and vigorous. It is a most readable work, and at the same time very instructive. Rarely does a Hebrew word appear in the expositon. In reading the Commentary, one feels that it must have been intended for the use of the people, even more than for scholars; and I am quite certain that the people will delight to use it, when its fitness to meet their wants and increase their interest in the study of God's Word is known to them. It cannot fail of being, in the end, a popular commentary.

For I may now add, that the few lines before each paragraph devoted to the explanation of the leading Hebrew words, are by no means necessary to the completeness of the work. The analysis, the translation, and the interpretation of the text, section by section, are a perfect whole, without the lines referred to, and I am therefore satisfied that the English student will be neither annoyed nor confused by them. For they stand by themselves, and can be passed over, with no real loss to the common reader, while yet their presence may be convenient to the Hebrew scholar.

In directing special attention to the style of this work, it has been my object to commend it to the masses of the people, who are in danger of turning away from its interesting and instructive pages, because they contain a small number of foreign words. To do this would be a serious mistake, for I am convinced by a fresh perusal of the work that it has rare qualities adapting it to the people. There is scarcely a heavy or obscure sentence in the whole book. It bears one along from page to page with ever-growing delight, and if, now and then, the interpreter's view of a difficult passage may be called in question, it will never be found unworthy of close examination. Such a work on the first book of the Bible will be eagerly sought, when it is sufficiently known, and the use of it by Sabbath-school teachers and their pupils will be of inestimable advantage to them both.

ALVAH HOVEY.

NEWTON CENTRE, Nov. 12, 1872.

PREFACE

TO THE AMERICAN EDITION

In introducing to the American public Dr. Murphy's Commentary on Genesis, I would commend it as a timely antidote to much of the negative and destructive criticism upon the Pentateuch which has so largely obtained in Germany, and of late in England also, rather than as a complete solution of the many and vexed questions in language, in science, and in history which pertain to the so-called "Books of Moses." The merits of Dr. Murphy's work are a nice critical analysis of the text, a candid consideration of all alleged difficulties, a common-sense view of the principles of interpretation, and a philosophical clearness and comprehensiveness in the statement of inference or of doctrine. It consists of an exact literal translation of such passages as contain either verbal or grammatical difficulties, and of a critical and exegetical commentary, based upon the grammatical construction of the text, and framed in view of the best lights of modern criticism and science. Thus, in the narratives of the creation and the deluge, our author unfolds step by step the literal meaning of the sacred writer, and evolves from the Hebrew a sense which well accords with the facts of astronomical and geological science. The philological considerations that, in describing the creation, the sacred writer "presents each change as it would appear to an ordinary spectator standing on the earth," that he notes "only obvious results," and "touches merely the heads of things," are the key to a method of interpretation which leaves the largest freedom to scientific inquiry. The author's use of the term "day," though too much restricted by literalism in his comment upon verse 5 of chapter i., finds all reasonable expansion in the principle laid down under verse 12, that "there is a due proportion between the action and the time of the action, the creation to be developed and the time of the development."

In treating of the deluge, Dr. Murphy shows that all the requirements of the Hebrew text are met by the supposition of a flood which covered the portion of the earth's surface then known to man; and that "the sobriety and historical veracity of the narrative are strikingly exhibited in the moderate height to which the waters are said to have risen above the ancient hills." It is doubtful, however, whether it would relieve the difficulties pertaining to the account of the creation, were we there to limit the earth to "so much of the surface of our globe as was known by observation" in the time of Moses. This notion was pressed to an extreme by Dr. Pye Smith, in the supposition of a partial chaos in the region of the land of Eden. I do not understand Dr. Murphy, however, to limit the term "earth," in Gen. i. 2, any further than by insisting that "the desolation and disorder are limited in their range to the *land*, and do not extend to the skies." He lays down a true principle of interpretation when he says, further, that "along with the sky and its conspicuous objects, the land then known to the primeval man formed the sum total of the observable universe. These two terms — the heavens and the earth — have not even yet arrived at their full complement of meaning; and it was not the object or the effect of divine revelation to anticipate science on these points."

It is enough for the purpose of silencing scientific, or rather *un*scientific cavils against the inspiration of Genesis, that we show there is no real contradiction, but a substantial agreement, between the Mosaic cosmogony and the established truths of physical science. Professor Dana has shown conclusively, in the closing chapter of his "Manual of Geology," that "the order of events in the Scripture cosmogony corresponds essentially" with that which is deduced from the observations of science upon the crust of the earth. Yet while this general harmony of Genesis with geology is established, we may safely affirm, with another Christian scientist, that "the classification of the rocks is not yet in a condition to warrant us to believe it likely that any scheme will be found satisfactory, which claims to have discovered a *complete* parallelism between the ages of nature, as revealed to us in the fossiliferous strata, and the days of creation described in the first chapter of Genesis."[1] In this indeterminate state of the question, it is enough that Dr. Murphy has established a reasonable harmony between his interpretation of the history of creation by Moses and the schedule of creation as furnished by geology.

The sententious philosophy of the author is strikingly apparent in his comments upon "the great introductory sentence" of Genesis: "This simple sentence denies atheism; for it assumes the being of God. It denies polytheism, and among its various forms the doctrine of two eternal principles, the one good and the other evil; for it confesses the one eternal Creator. It denies materialism; for it asserts the creation of matter. It denies pantheism; for it assumes the existence of God before all things, and apart from them. It denies fatalism; for it involves the freedom of the Eternal Being." A writer who is capable of such clear and discriminating thought expressed in language so strong and compact, will be welcomed by American students of theology.

The laws of interpretation laid down by Dr. Murphy in his Introduction, commend themselves equally by their simplicity and their good sense. It is the boast of the destructive criticism that it subjects the Old Testament to the same tests which it applies to other ancient documents; but in point of fact, this criticism applies to the Bible the most arbitrary and exceptional

[1] Dr. John Duns; Biblical Natural Science, I. 48.

methods. How many difficulties raised by Bishop Colenso against the authenticity of the Pentateuch would have been obviated by the simple principle that "we cannot found the slightest inference on a passage which we do not understand, or affirm a single discrepancy until we have made all reasonable inquiry whether it really exists, and what is its precise nature and amount"! Thus Colenso's objection to Lev. viii. 1–4, that the court of the tabernacle could not have contained the whole congregation, betrays his want of familiarity with Hebrew terms.

"The *congregation* is simply a multitude assembled, a gathering or collection of people, without reference to organization or special appointment. With the definite article, it generally meant the whole body of the people. Hence every assembly was a congregation; but every congregation was not an assembly. We may say the congregration of the assembly, but we do not say in Scripture language the assembly of the congregation.

"The word *mo'ed* means appointed or stated meeting time, and an appointed festival or convention held at that time. It is the word constantly used in the phrase 'tabernacle of the congregation,' which is the tent of appointment or meeting, at the door of which all civil and sacred meetings were by appointment held. Now, putting the true equivalents for the three words *edah*, *qahal*, and *mo'ed* where they occur, the passage quoted stands thus: 'And gather thou all the assembly to the door of the tent of meeting. And Moses did as Jehovah commanded him, and the assembly was gathered into the door of the tent of the meeting.' Here, then, it appears the term in the original is the assembly, a select body, containing, not certainly the women and children, unless as idle spectators, nor even the main part of the able-bodied men of twenty years old and upwards, but the princes of tribes, the chiefs of houses, the elders, and probably the 'officers' and some of the higher judges, and including a proportion of the priestly tribe under these designations. The number of those who were regular members of this assembly, or of those who were actually in attendance on this occasion, *we do not know.* And thus it is utterly impossible for us to create an impossibility here, do or suppose what we will."[1]

Dr. Murphy reminds his readers that a meeting of parishioners is summoned and held in the vestry of the parish church, and legally transacts the parish business, though according to the Bishop of Natal "the vestry would only hold six abreast, and at that rate the parishioners would extend perhaps ten miles into space!" Applying this common-sense view to the case in hand, he says:

"Let us recollect that the court was fifty cubits wide, and that its gate was twenty cubits — twice the width of the door of the tent — or thirty-six feet wide. Now, with a tent-door of eighteen feet, and a court-entrance of thirty-six feet, only ninety feet apart, and a laver and an altar in the interval, what will a reasonable man, with some little practical experience in public meetings, understand by being assembled 'at the door of the tent of meeting?' Obviously he will suppose such an assembly may be in any part of the square within the court or of the space in front of it which may be required for the convenience of the assembly. If you are told that a man is at your door, you suppose him, no doubt, to be within a foot or two of it; but if you are told that a mob is *at your door*, you presently imagine that they may occupy not only the area, but the whole of the opposite street. How much more, if your door were eighteen feet wide, your area-gate thirty-six, and the multitude tenfold greater! We read in Acts xiii. 44, that the next Sabbath-day came almost *the whole city* together to hear the Word of God; and in xvii. 5, that

[1] The nineteen alleged impossibilities of Colenso on the Pentateuch shown to be possible. By the Rev. James G. Murphy, LL.D., T.C.D. London, James Nisbit & Co. pp. 15, 16.

they set *all the city* in an uproar, and assaulted the house of Jason. Here all the city was at the door of one house." [1]

These examples, taken from another work of our author, illustrate the principle laid down above, and expose the fallacy of much of the hypothetical criticism upon the Pentateuch. "In fact," says Dr. Murphy, "the argument of the school of critics to which Dr. Colenso belongs is built up of a series of surmises upon the ground of certain difficulties which they cannot solve. This is a beguiling sort of argument. He that deals in it is prone to forget the difference between the bearing of a probability or presumption on a supposition and on a conclusion. A second or third presumption in favor of a supposition adds to its probability. But if one probable premise enter into our reasoning, the remotest conclusion can never rise above that probability. If two premises are only probable, every after-conclusion is less probable than either of them. On the other hand, an established fact outweighs a whole host of adverse presumptions, and ninety-nine undisputed statements are abundantly sufficient to sustain one that admits of some dispute." [2]

This general reasoning Dr. Murphy afterwards presses with the *argumentum ad hominem* against Colenso's alleged incongruities in the account of the passover.

"The Bishop knows a little of Hebrew; but he is not what we should call a Hebrew scholar. He does not understand, or he does not know how to apply, the laws of Hebrew composition. When the sacred writer spoke of midnight in the previous chapter [Exodus xi.] he was, let us admit, arrived at the 14th Abib in one line of the history. But then he had another to carry on, and so he goes back in the twelfth chapter to the 1st Abib to bring up this second line. And in the twelfth verse 'this night' means the night after the 14th Abib mentioned in the sixth verse. For the Hebrew writer always imagines himself at the time and place of the scene

[1] Ibid. p. 17. [2] Ibid. p. 81.

described, and therefore naturally uses *this* night in reference to the 14th day at which he has arrived in his directions. And besides, if this night were the night of the 14th, as the Bishop insists, how could directions be given on the 14th about what was to be done on the 10th? Here is a man who is ignorant of three common laws of Hebrew composition, or does not know how to apply them, presuming to criticize Moses, and only betraying the shallowness of his own knowledge or the precipitancy of his own judgment."

Dr. Colenso's arithmetical difficulties with regard to the duties and the apportionments of the priests are disposed of by Dr. Murphy with a combination of logic, learning, and wit that leaves the Bishop of Natal but little ground to stand upon. The following spicy paragraph concludes that portion of the discussion:

"It seems a strange thing for a bishop to object to thirteen cities being given to the priestly family. Has he never heard of bishops' lands with towns built on them? Surely, if they could not inhabit all the houses, they could let them to solvent tenants. This is the most frivolous objection we have ever met with, and especially from such a quarter. Most of our readers are acquainted with such things as bishops' palaces, revenues, lands, rentals, etc., and will not therefore be greatly astonished at thirteen towns with their suburbs for the whole future priesthood of Israel."

A second general principle laid down by Dr. Murphy is, that "presumed contradictions or discrepancies in the book lie as well against the theory of a mechanical compilation from heterogeneous materials by a final redactor as against an original unity of authorship." The favorite argument of the destructive school of critics is, that the discrepancies between the so-called Jehovistic and Elohistic elements in the Pentateuch forbid the supposition of unity of authorship; and hence the hypothesis that the Books of Moses were a compilation from distinct documents and traditions, to which an uncertain date is assigned, somewhere in the period between the Judges and the Babylonish exile. But even if the alleged discrepancies could be established — which Dr. Murphy by no means admits — the fact would weigh as well against unity of editorship as against an original unity of authorship. Indeed, a compiler or redactor of a later age might be expected to correct discrepancies which had crept into the original composition. And Dr. Murphy reasons conclusively that any possible hypothesis for the solution of the difficulties inherent in an ancient history which bears the general marks of antiquity, is sufficient to remove the objection that the narrative is self-contradictory. We owe much to a writer whose critical learning is guided and applied by such strong common sense.

Dr. Murphy has condensed his theory of inspiration into this pithy aphorism, — that the Bible is the Word of God, "with all the peculiarities of man and all the authority of God." This same thought he has amplified in the pamphlet so often quoted, —

"The inspiration of the written Word of God we consider simply explained by the following words from Rev. ii. 1: "Unto the angel of the church of Ephesus, *write*." Here the Lord dictates, and John writes. The *mode* in which this takes place is not our concern; the *fact* is. The thoughts, purposes, commands, doctrines, promises of God, pass through the channel of John's mind, and come to expression by his tongue or by his pen. Hence the Scriptures are for the matter and the form in one respect the Word of God, — displaying the unity, harmony, and infallibility of its lofty source, — and in another respect the word of man — exhibiting all the peculiarities of his mother tongue and his individual mind. The simple development of this proposition will explain all those phenomena of Scripture by which it proves itself to be in the primary sense the Word of God, and at the same time, in the secondary sense, the word of the actual writer."

But it is not within the province of this brief Introduction to analyze all the principles of the author, nor to discuss his opinions upon disputed questions. It only remains to add a few words concerning the author himself.

Dr. Murphy was born in 1808, in the village of Comber, County Down, about seven miles from Belfast. After the usual scholastic training he entered Trinity College, Dublin, where he soon attained the technical rank of a "scholar," which entitled him to certain important privileges. In 1836 he was ordained to the ministry in the Presbyterian Church, and commenced his parochial labors in the town of Ballyshannon, County Donegall, where he remained till 1841, when he removed to Belfast as Head Master of the Royal Academical Institution. He was no less distinguished as a mathematician than for his classical attainments.

In 1847 he was appointed by the General Assembly of the Presbyterian Church to his present office as Professor of Hebrew in the Assembly's College at Belfast. This college, which nearly corresponds to an American theological seminary, has a Faculty consisting of Dr. Cooke, Professor of Sacred Rhetoric and Catechetics; Dr. Edgar, Professor of Systematic Theology; Dr. Killen, Professor of Church History and Pastoral Theology; Dr. Murphy, Professor of Hebrew and other Oriental Languages; Dr. Gibson, Professor of Natural Theology and Christian Ethics; and Dr. J. L. Porter, Professor of Biblical Literature. Several of these gentlemen are well known in the United States. Drs. Edgar and Gibson have visited this country, and Dr. Gibson's narrative of the "Year of Grace in Ireland," published by Messrs. Gould & Lincoln, has had an extensive circulation; Dr. Killen's volume on "The Ancient Church" has been republished by Mr. Scribner of New York; Dr. Porter, formerly of Damascus, has contributed several articles to the Bibliotheca Sacra and to various Biblical encyclopedias.

The Assembly's College has, upon an average, about one hundred students in theology in its several classes. It is under the jurisdiction of the General Assembly, though each Professor receives an endowment from the government of two hundred and fifty pounds in addition to students' fees.

Adjacent to this institution is Queen's College, which has an average of four hundred students, in arts, medicine, law, and agriculture. This college furnishes yearly a large number of students to the theological college; the two institutions working in entire harmony.

Dr. Murphy received from Trinity College the honorary degree of LL.D. He is thoroughly Irish in birth, in education, in ecclesiastical offices, and in literary labors and honors. In addition to the volume on Genesis herewith presented to the public, he has published a Hebrew Grammar for the use of his students, and has translated Keit's Commentary on Kings for Clark's Foreign Theological Library. He has now nearly completed his Commentary on Exodus. His view upon the most important point of Egyptian chronology is foreshadowed in a private note to the subscriber, as follows: "Adhering still to the Hebrew or Masoretic text of the Old Testament, I am constrained to stand by the Hebrew chronology until I meet with some *experimentum crucis* that will prove or disprove it."

In character, Dr. Murphy has the simplicity of the true scholar and the devout and humble spirit of the true disciple of Christ. In introducing him to American students at the present period, it is not unimportant to add that he has shared the sympathy of his colleague, Dr. Gibson, for the United States during our struggle with the rebellion, and that as a friend of freedom and of the progress of humanity, he desires, "the prosperity of this country in all its noble and beneficent enterprises."

JOSEPH P. THOMPSON.

NEW YORK, Nov. 1865.

AUTHOR'S PREFACE

An ancient writing, purporting to be continuous and handed down to us as the work of one author, is to be received as such unless we have good and solid reasons for the contrary. The Pentateuch is a book exactly of this description, continuous in its form, and coming down to us as in the main the work of Moses. We may not give up this *prima facie* evidence without cause. In particular, we should require strong and cogent arguments to convince us that this interesting monument of antiquity is, as some say, a dry and bare compilation, not even of document after document, but of selections from several later works all going over nearly the same ground, dovetailed into one another by a still later hand to form a factitious whole. For at first sight this seems to be a mere stretch of fancy, in which criticism has overmastered philosophy. A scheme so intricate in form and fantastic in conception cannot be accepted, unless it stand on impregnable grounds.

The main grounds on which this theory rests appear to be two, — first, certain discrepancies and difficulties that are supposed to be adverse to the unity and early origin of the work; and second, certain characteristics of style, by which the selections are detected and restored to their original authors, who are then seen to be consistent in themselves, though still inconsistent with one another. And the result to which this theory leads, is, that the Pentateuch is neither given by inspiration of God nor historically valid, but rather a mechanical compilation of a later age from heterogeneous materials, the discrepancies of which the compiler had not either the sense to perceive or the tact to eliminate.

Before we accept a conclusion fraught with such results, it is obvious that we are bound to be fully assured, both that the premises are in themselves true, and that they are able to bear all the weight that is laid on them. Hence three questions come before us for adjudication. 1. Of what nature must the difficulties of statement and style be to constrain us to the adoption of this theory? 2. What is the amount of the difficulties actually involved in the statements of the book, and what are the peculiarities of style that characterize its different parts? 3. Are these difficulties of statement and diversities of style of such a nature that they could only arise from a medley of the kind supposed? Do the former disturb the unity and early origin of the book, as well as its historical value and divine authority? Do the latter enable us to assign its several parts to their respective authors?

The first of these is the question of principle. It involves the axioms or postulates on which the whole discussion turns. It is freely granted that the presence of plain contradictions or impossibilities is sufficient to overturn the historical credit or the early origin of a work. But they do not prove the diversity of authorship propounded in the above theory. It is acknowledged on all sides that some one l and at length put the Pentateuch together in its ultimate form. And if a final redactor did not see the presumed contradictions or did not regard them, neither might the original author. This part of the theory, therefore, has no support from the supposed existence of impossibilities.

The appearance, however, of discrepancies or difficulties that fall short of the contradictory or impossible, cannot be allowed to have these effects. So far from seeming strange, they are to be expected in a work more than three thousand years old, containing a brief history of at least twenty-two centuries, and dealing, not in abstract or general assertions, but in concrete and definite statements. They rather confirm than weaken its claim to antiquity and genuineness, so long as they stand within the bounds of possibility. If there be any possible mode of reconciling the seemingly incompatible statements, the contradiction is removed. If a second mode can be pointed out, the contradiction is still more remote. For several solutions of an apparent contradiction are so far from counteracting that they sustain one another in repelling it to a vanishing distance. Not one of them may be the real missing link in the chain of facts, which by hypothesis, be it remembered, is unknown; but they all combine to show that the events in question may occur, not in one, but in a variety of ways.

It must, we think, be conceded that all the diversities of style that have been or can be discovered, apart from contradictions or impossibilities, do not suffice to prove a work to be a medley from different authors. They cannot in the nature of things have the force of demonstration. Having the authors, we may make out characteristics of style. Having a foregone conclusion as to certain passages, we may trace and tabulate their peculiarities. But all this may proceed from diversity of topic, mental state or design in the same author, and scarcely affords the color of a presumption for the intermingling of pieces from different authors.

The full discussion of this question belongs to another place. But meanwhile we conclude, that, as contradictions may occur in the work of one author, and certain diversities in the use of words may appear in different pieces of the same writer, these phenomena are not sufficient of themselves to substantiate the whole theory under consideration. The existence, however, of absolute contradictions or impossibilities in its statements deprives a work of independent historical value or great antiquity of origin.

The second question regards the actual contents of the book. What are the difficulties it actually presents, and the diversities of style it exhibits? To ascertain these facts, we must examine the book, and determine as far as possible its real meaning. This is especially necessary in a work that has come down to us from a hoary antiquity, composed in a language that has not been spoken for eighteen centuries, and in a style which, though regular and systematic, is yet remarkably simple and primitive. We shall be doing great wrong to this venerable document, if we ascribe to it statements for which its own words, fairly interpreted, do not vouch. We cannot found the slightest inference on a passage which we do not understand, or affirm a single discrepancy until we have made all reasonable inquiry whether it really exists, and what is its precise nature and amount.

The following work is a contribution towards this important branch of the inquiry. It is an attempt to apply the laws of interpretation to the first book of the Pentateuch. The interest attached to the book of Genesis can hardly be exaggerated. It contains the records of the present condition of the earth and of the human race from its origin to the time of Moses. It answers the fundamental questions of theology, of physics, of ethics, and of philology. The difficulty of its exposition is proportioned to the antiquity of its origin and the loftiness of its theme. The present attempt to elucidate its meaning is neither perfect in its execution nor exhaustive in its results. But it makes some important advances in both these directions, as the author conceives; and therefore it has been submitted to public examination.

The work consists of a translation of the original, and a critical and exegetical commentary, the whole forming a full interpretation of the sacred text. With the exception of the first chapter, which is extremely literal, the translation is a revision of the authorized version. On a close comparison of this version with the original, we find everything to admire in the purity of the English, and little to amend in the faithfulness of the rendering. The emendations introduced aim at a nearer approach to the original meaning in some passages, and in others to the original mode of thought and expression. Alterations of the former kind are of essential moment; in making which the author has endeavored to divest his mind of any questionable preconception that might warp his judgment. The minor changes consist chiefly in adhering more closely to the original order of words, in rendering the same word in Hebrew as often as possible by the same word in English, and in occasionally substituting a word of English origin for one derived from the Latin. In expressing the sense of the original, the author has been greatly aided by the English version, and is fully persuaded that no independent version more adapted to the genius of the English lauguage will ever be produced. Nevertheless, even this part of his work will, he hopes, be found to have thrown considerable light on the meaning of the book that did not appear in the English version.

The commentary is the complement of the translation. It is critical and exegetical; but so far as these qualities are distinct, much more attention has been paid to the latter. The formation of an improved text is not within the scope of the present work. The edition of Van der Hooght, the *textus receptus* of the Old Testament, is sufficient for all ordinary passages, and has been followed here. Peculiarities of form and syntax have been only sparingly discussed, as they are all noted and explained in our grammars and lexicons. The higher criticism, or the interpretation of the text, has been the chief study of the author, to which all other matters have been made subsidiary. It has been his endeavor to bring out the meaning of the original according to the philosophy of language, thought, and history.

For this purpose a few general principles of interpretation have been laid down, which, it is hoped, will meet with universal acceptance. These have been applied to elicit as far as possible the precise meaning of the sacred writer, the order of thought, and the order of time. A careful study of the method of composition has enabled him to throw much light on the logical order of the narrative, and the physical order of the events related.

Many difficulties of great magnitude, such as those respecting the six days' creation and the deluge, have disappeared in the mere process of interpretation. None of any importance known to the author are left without a solution. Other solutions might in some cases have proved more acceptable to some minds. But he has acted to the best of his judgment in presenting what seemed to him most probable, and has contented himself with the reflection that a possible solution serves to remove the appearance of contradiction, while it is in itself of no historical value.

Variety of style has been certainly found in the different parts of the book; but then it has been only such as the same author might display according to the subdivisions of his plan and subject. It cannot be demonstrably or even probably ascribed to a medley of passages from different authors.

If these results stand the test of impartial criticism, the scheme of a congeries of pieces put together by a later hand with all its consequences falls to the ground, so far as the book of Genesis is concerned. The right interpretation of the remaining books of the Pentateuch will, the author believes, be attended with the same result. The fundamental proposition regarding the Pentateuch, with which we started, will then remain undisturbed in all its integrity, before even a single particle of the positive evidence by which it is supported has been adduced.

The fair interpretation of these books, however, serves much more than the mere negative purpose of obviating difficulties. It presents before the mind in its native connection the wonderful harmony of this ancient book with itself, with history, and with physical and metaphysical science. It proves a volume, extant long before science was born, and couched in the language of common life, to be in no respect at variance with the conclusions of astronomy and geology, while it is the fountain-head of theological and ethical philosophy. These disclosures are the meet sequel of the external evidence by which its genuineness, credibility, and divine authority are attested. This body of external and internal evidence demonstrates that it is, what it purports in every page to be, the revelation of the early ways of God with man.

The growing sense of the fundamental concord that must subsist between the book of revelation and the book of nature renders the just interpretation of the earliest portion of the former a matter of the deepest interest to the man of scientific and reverent spirit. The records of that last creation, limited in time and space, to which we ourselves belong, of that moral declension in the history of man described as the fall, of that mental revolution known as the confusion of tongues, of those physical changes connected with the deluge and the overthrow of Sodom and Amorah, can never cease to engage the attention of the reflective mind.

Whether the author will be permitted to proceed any further in the interesting field of investigation which he has traced in the preceding pages, depends entirely on the will of Providence. Meanwhile the present work is complete in itself; and the author commits it to the world, humbly praying that a blessing may attend its perusal, and sincerely thanking the God of all grace for that measure of health which has enabled him to complete his task.

J. G. M.

INTRODUCTION

THE BIBLE

I.—ITS CONTENTS

THE Bible, or the Book of God, is a collection of writings commenced not later than 1500 B.C., and completed about 100 A.C. It is called by Irenaeus (b. 120 A.C.) θεῖαι γραφαὶ, *Divine Writings*, and by Clemens Alexandrinus (d. 220 A.C.) γραφαὶ, αἱ θεόπνευστοι γραφαὶ, *Scriptures, the God-inspired Scriptures.* Hence it has been designated the Canon, or the Canonical Scriptures, because, including all and only the writings given by inspiration of God, it is the canon or rule of faith and practice for man. It is divided into the Old and New Testaments, ἡ παλαιὰ διαθήκη and ἡ καινὴ δ. The former is written in Hebrew proper (except Jer. x. 11; Ezra iv. 8, vi. 18; vii. 12–26; and Dan. ii. 4, vii., which are in Chaldee); the latter in Greek. There are sixty-six pieces in the Bible, of which thirty-nine are in the Old Testament, and twenty-seven in the New. The Jews, however, reckon twenty-two books in the Old Testament, corresponding to the number of letters in the Hebrew alphabet, according to the following arrangement: Genesis, Exodus, Leviticus, Numbers, Deuteronomy; Joshua, Judges with Ruth, Samuel (I. and II.), Kings (I. and II.), Isaiah, Jeremiah with Lamentations, Ezekiel, the twelve minor prophets (Hosea, Joel, Amos, Obadiah, Jonah, Mikah, Nahum, Habaccuc, Zephaniah, Haggai, Zekariah, Malaki); Psalms, Proverbs, Job, Song of Songs, Ecclesiastes, Esther, Daniel, Ezra with Nehemiah, and Chronicles (I. and II.). The books of the New Testament are the Gospels of Matthew, Mark, Luke, and John, the Acts of the Apostles; the fourteen epistles of Paul (to the Romans, Corinthians I. and II., Galatians, Ephesians, Philippians, Colossians, Thessalonians I. and II., Timothy I. and II., Titus, Philemon and the Hebrews), that of James, the two of Peter, the three of John, that of Jude; and the Revelation of John.

Besides the division of the Old Testament into twenty-two books, there is another very important distribution of it into three groups of writings, called in the New Testament the Law, the Prophets, and the Psalms or the remaining sacred writings, ὁ νόμος καὶ προφῆται καὶ Ψαλμοὶ, תּוֹרָה נְבִיאִים וּכְתוּבִים. The Law contains the five books of Moses, the five fifths of the law, חֲמִשָּׁה חוּמְשֵׁי הַתּוֹרָה, corresponding to which is the Greek πεντάτευχος, *Pentateuch*, the five-volumed book. The Prophets contain eight books: the former prophets נְבִיאִים רִאשׁוֹנִים, the writers of Joshua, Judges, Samuel, and Kings; the latter נ׳ אַחֲרוֹנִים, Isaiah, Jeremiah, Ezekiel, and the twelve minor prophets. The remaining books, called by the Greek fathers ἁγιόγραφα, *Hagiographa*, or *Holy Writings*, are the three poetical books, Psalms, Proverbs, and Job, the five מְגִלּוֹת, rolls, Song of Songs, Ruth, Lamentations, Ecclesiastes, Esther; the prophet Daniel; and the historical books, Ezra, Nehemiah, and Chronicles. This threefold division of the Old Testament Canon is a historical, not a logical, distribution of its contents. It exhibits three successive collections of sacred documents: the first, formed and indeed mainly composed by Moses; the second, containing the earlier and latter prophets, made in the time of Jeremiah, and probably under his direction, with the exception of the last three of the minor prophets, which were added to this class of writings afterwards, because they were strictly prophets of Judah; the third, consisting of the remaining sacred books, and formed in the main by Ezra. This collection contains two books, Ruth and Lamentations, which, though reckoned in the Jewish enumeration of books as appendages of Judges and Jeremiah respectively, are put here either for the convenience of being grouped with the other three of the five rolls, or because, like some other books of this collection, they were not before formally introduced into the Canon. The prophet Daniel appears in this class, probably, because he spent all his life in the court of Babylon.

II.—ITS SUBJECT.

The whole Bible is a record of the ways of God with man. Hence it begins with the creation of man, traces the development and points out the destiny of the race. In order to be so compendious, and at the same time remarkable for the minuteness of its details, it deals largely in the enunciation of general principles and the statement of leading facts. It dwells with becoming fulness on God's gracious and merciful dealings and bearings with man. And hence the scene of the narrative, which at the beginning was coextensive with man, gradually narrows to Sheth, to Noah, to Shem, to Abraham, to Isaac, to Jacob, almost to Judah, and then suddenly rebounds to its original universality of extent.

The ways of God with man take the particular form of a covenant. A covenant is an agreement between two parties, with conditions to be fulfilled and corresponding benefits to be realized on both sides. The very nature of a covenant implies that the parties to it are intelligent; and the very existence of two rational beings in sensible relation with each other involves a covenant expressed or understood. Hence the Bible is fittingly termed the testament or covenant, *testamentum fœdus*, διαθήκη, בְּרִית. It exhibits the relation between God and man, the essentially intelligent and the naturally intelligent, the natural condition of this great covenant, and the conduct of the two parties concerned. This covenant, which is originally a covenant of works, securing to man the benefit on performance of the condition, has soon to become a covenant of grace, guaranteeing the blessing, notwithstanding the breach of the compact, that some, at least, of the fallen race may reap the benefit of its provisions. It becomes, in sooth, a *promise*, wherein God, the one party, remaining faithful to his side of the covenant, sees to it that it is upheld in the integrity of its rewards and even its conditions, notwithstanding, and even on account of, the failure of the other party. Hence the covenant takes a special form, the provisions of which are narrowed to the seed of Abraham. Now the book of the covenant at its opening takes broad ground, but in consequence of the privileges of Israel, it is sometimes supposed to have become exclusive in its offers of mercy. This, however, cannot be the true state of the case, for two reasons: First, we find ourselves again at the close of the book on the common ground of all humanity having an invitation to return to God. And this very issue is distinctly expressed in all the forms of the covenant with Abraham, Isaac, and Jacob. Thus it is written, "In thee, and in thy seed, shall *all the families of the earth be blessed*" (Gen. xii. 3; xxii. 18; xxvi. 4; xxviii. 14). Secondly, God never revoked his covenant with Adam or with Noah: it remains in force still; and the special covenant with Israel, so far from annulling it, was expressly designed to make it available again for the whole human family. The Old Testament, therefore, maintains its universality throughout, though in sad succession the Cainites, the Gentiles, the Shemites, the Ishmaelites, the Edomites retired into forgetfulness and abandonment of that covenant of mercy which was made for them, and thereby soon ceased to have a place in the record of God's intercourse with man. A sentence or a paragraph suffices to dismiss from notice these wilful breakers of the covenant. The stream of the narrative is thus straitened, not in God, but in man. But at length, by virtue of the atoning work of Christ and the renewing work of his Spirit, the old covenant emerges again as the new covenant, in all its primeval and perpetual universality, and with such new powers and provisions as to carry the offer and ultimately the possession of salvation to the whole human race.

III.—ITS STRUCTURE.

The Bible is a book of growth. It is a tree of knowledge. It grows from a seed to a full-sized plant. In this way alone is it suited to man. For as the individual advances from infancy to full-grown manhood, so the race of Adam had its infancy, its boyhood, its manhood, and will have its ripe and full age. Such a progress of the human race required a progressive book of lessons. Hence we are not to expect every truth to be fully revealed in the earliest books of Scripture, but only such germs of truth as will gradually develope themselves into a full body of revealed doctrine, and in such measure as man can receive and may require at each stage of his career. The Bible, therefore, grows not only in the continual accessions made to its matter, but also in the doctrines which it adds from time to time to the system of sacred truth, and in the more and more developed state in which all its doctrines are presented.

The Old Testament is as clearly distinguished in point of matter from the New as in regard to time. The one was closed at least four hundred years before the other was commenced. The former contains an exposition of the dealings of God with man down to the times of Malaki, together with a remarkable series of predictions concerning the destiny of the human race, and especially concerning the coming of the Messiah to accomplish by his own obedience unto death the redemption of man from the curse of sin, and so eventually, by the quickening of his Spirit, raise the objects of his redeeming love to the light, life, and liberty of the children of God. The latter records the fulfilment of this prophecy by the coming of our Lord Jesus Christ, his standing in the stead of man, rendering a perfect obedience for him, undergoing the sentence of death for him, rising again and entering upon eternal life, and making all-prevalent intercession on his behalf. It further indicates the realization of another set of predictions in the calling and qualifying of his apostles and evangelists, and the reconstruction of his church under these new circumstances in a new form and with new life and power of expansion. It then opens up with greater clearness, in a new series of prophetic announcements, the future history of the church, and especially the second coming of the Messiah, to raise the dead, judge the quick and the dead, and so close the development of the present world.

As the whole Bible is divided into the Old and the New Testaments, so the Old Testament itself naturally falls into two parts. The history of man in relation with God is carried on from the beginning of Genesis to the end of the second book of Kings, where it is brought to an end with an account of the downfall of the last remnant of the chosen people. As the thread is here clearly broken off, no less in sorrow, indeed, than in anger, the sacred writer who recounts the events subsequent to this point of time, in order to give a connected view of the course of affairs, goes back to the beginning of human things, and draws out another thread of history, which is continued to the close of the Old Testament times. This we have in the book of Chronicles, which begins with the words, Adam, Sheth, Enosh, gives a rapid sketch of the narrative already furnished, with some additional particulars, and then dwells with great minuteness on the history of David's line and kingdom. These are now traced through the captivity, and for some time after, in the books of Ezra and Nehemiah, which form the continuation of Chronicles. This new line of history is contained in the Hagiographa, where also we find the historical book of Esther, belonging to the same period. This may, therefore, be called the second volume of Old Testament history.

The state of things during this period is marked by two characteristic features, — the dependence of the people of God on a heathen power, and the approach on the part of the heathen to some acknowledgment of the true God. From the date of the captivity, 606 B.C., the people of God remained in subjection to the universal monarchy of the day. After the lapse of seventy years in exile they were permitted by this power to return to their own country, and govern themselves according to the laws of their national polity. Under the Maccabees they asserted their independence for a time; but they were soon obliged to seek the alliance and acknowledge the supremacy of the Roman empire. In consequence of this state of dependence on the one hand and protection on the other, the old antagonism between Israel and the nations was in some measure broken down. The heathen power was induced to recognize, to some extent, the true God, and pay some respect to his people. A preparation was thus made for the reception of the nations into the church of God on the advent of the Messiah. The transactions of the period, therefore, form a moment in the progress of things from the separation of the Jew and the Gentile to the breaking down of the partition between them in the New Testament times. They are the natural sequel of the unfaithfulness of the peculiar people, and the meet preparative for the calling of the Gentiles.

The previous portion, again, of the Old Testament is naturally and historically divided into the Law and the Prophets. But these two parts are more closely connected with each other than the whole which they compose with the remainder of the Old Testament. The Pentateuch describes the constitution, the Prophets the development, of the people rendered peculiar by special covenant with God. They form a complete whole, in which the Pentateuch is the basis, the early prophets the historic, and the later prophets the prophetic development, until the end corresponds in scope and grandeur with the beginning.

Of the Pentateuch itself, the first book, Genesis, is preparatory to the other four. These record the growth of the family of Jacob, or Israel, into the peculiar people; the constitution of the theocracy; the giving of a code of laws moral, ritual, and civil; the conquest of part of the land promised to the forefathers of the nation; and the completion of the institutions and enactments needed for a settled condition. For this order of things the first book furnishes the occasion.

IV. — ITS STYLE.

Another striking feature of this literature is its style. It is written in the language of common life. It was designed for the whole race of man. In its earliest period there was no philosophic activity, and therefore no scientific style. If it had been then composed in a newly-invented diction, it would have had no intelligent reader. Even in the palmiest days of philosophy, a work in the philosophic form of expression would have been available only for a very limited class of readers. Moreover, if the Spirit that animated the sacred writers had deviated, for the sake of superior accuracy, or bare literality of statement, from the language of common life, he would have chosen, not the phraseology of philosophy, — which varies necessarily with the progress of discovery, and, philosophers themselves being witnesses, is but an inadequate and provisional vehicle for thought or truth, — but the tongue of angels, which alone would have been adequate to express the absolute truth of things. But if he had done so, even the philosophic student, not to speak of the ordinary reader, would have been incompetent to understand, and indisposed to accept, a mode of thought and speech so far transcending the feeble idioms of his own mind and voice. Men versed in the dialects of the schools have been slow to make full acknowledgment of the necessity and the wisdom of the popular style in the composition of the Bible; and no small amount of the misinterpretation to which it has been exposed, has arisen from neglecting the usage of speech among the people for whom it was written, and insensibly applying to it a usage with which our modern education has made us familiar. It ought not to be forgotten that the early written language of the Greeks and Romans was not philosophical, but popular.

V.—ITS AUTHOR.

This body of literature is unparalleled in the history of the world for the majesty of its subject, the symmetry of its structure, the harmony of its parts, and the slow march of its growth. The subject, we have seen, is the history of the dealings of God with man. It is therefore altogether unique in its kind. Other ancient records have commenced with the age of gods; but they have soon subsided into the every-day doings of ordinary mortals. But the one sacred topic is here pursued with undeviating consistency throughout the whole volume. Even the collateral books of Psalms, Proverbs, Job, Canticles, and Ecclesiastes contribute to the elucidation of this lofty theme. No other literature in the world has invariably adhered to the same high argument. The wonderful symmetry of its structure is obvious even from the general analysis we have now given of its contents. But it becomes more and more conspicuous as we examine more minutely into the details of the whole fabric. And yet there is a native artlessness, an unlabored simplicity, in its manner, which enhances the charm of regularity. It is not the starched precision of dry science or art, but the substantial unity of nature and life. The harmony of parts which the Holy Scripture exhibits, results from the harmony of the reality which it faithfully portrays. The productions of different authors are almost equally different in their topics; and even when they expatiate on the same theme, they only display the idiosyncrasies of the several minds from which they proceed, and are incapable of being harmonized in their contents, or arranged into a uniform system. Even the collected works of a single human author are found to betray marks of inconsistency, vacillation, and disorder. But the truths, which the Scripture presents in a natural or historical form, have proved as capable of methodical treatment and systematic arrangement as the facts of the physical and metaphysical world. The gradual advance by which the Bible has grown to its full maturity is no less in contrast with the miscellaneous accumulations of human literature. Consisting of sixty-six pieces, composed by no less than forty authors, scattered over a period of at least sixteen hundred years, partly in the language of Shem, and partly in that of Japheth, among an eastern people of agricultural and pastoral habits, not distinguished for philosophic attainments, yet rising to the loftiest theme of human thought, exhibiting at every stage of its progress a uniform plan, and maintaining a constant unanimity of testimony and doctrine, this volume proves itself to be the result of no mere human authorship.

(a) This antecedent indication of a divine authorship, arising from the inspection of the book itself, is found to be accompanied with all the subsequent evidences of the fact, which are naturally to be expected. (b) The uniform testimony of the honest and intelligent fathers and members of the Christian church, from the times of the apostles down to the present day, is embodied in the phrases, "Divine Writings," "God-inspired Writings," which we have already quoted from Irenaeus and Clemens Alexandrinus. Gainsayers have appeared, and still do appear, who take exception to the dogma of inspiration in itself, or in some of the forms in which it has been presented by theologians. But, taken even as a whole, their adverse judgment must be acknowledged to be of small account against the preponderating testimony of ecclesiastical writers of all ages. (c) This collection of writings also uniformly claims to be the Word of God, both in direct terms and incidental statements. The Great Prophet and Teacher says, "Search the Scriptures; for in them ye think ye have eternal life: and they are they which testify of me" (John v. 39). He opened the understandings of his disciples, "that they might understand the Scriptures" (Luke xxiv. 45). Paul designates the Old Testament "the oracles of God" (Rom. iii. 2), and Peter declares that "the prophecy came not in old time by the will of man, but holy men of God spake as they were moved by the Holy Ghost" (2 Peter i. 21). Paul says of himself, "If any man think himself to be a prophet or spiritual, let him acknowledge that the things that I write unto you are the commandments of the Lord" (1 Cor. xiv. 37). And John solemnly affirms, "If any man shall add unto these things, God shall add unto him the plagues that are written in this book; and if any man shall take away from the words of the book of this prophecy, God shall take away his part out of the book of life, and out of the holy city, and from the things which are written in this book" (Rev. xx. 18, 19). These, and similar passages out of this book, calmly and deliberately place us in a dilemma from which there is no escape. Either the Scriptures are the word of God, or they are not. If they be not, then the writers of these Scriptures, who directly and indirectly affirm their divine origin, are false witnesses; and if they have proved unworthy of credit on this fundamental point, they can be of no authority on other equally important matters. But neither before examination, nor after an examination of eighteen centuries, have we the slightest reason for doubting the veracity of these men; and their unanimous evidence is in favor of the divine authorship of the Bible. (d) All that we have learned of the contents of these books accords with their claim to be the word of God. The constant harmony of their statements, when fairly interpreted, with one another, with general history, and with physical and metaphysical truth, affords an incontestable proof of their divine origin. The statements of other early writers have invariably come into conflict with historical or scientific truth. But, still further, these books communicate to us matters concerning God, the origin and the future destiny of man, which are of vital importance in themselves, and yet are absolutely beyond the reach of human intuition, observation, or deduction. It is impossible, therefore, for mere human beings, apart from divine instruction and authority, to attest these things to us at all. Hence these books, if they were not traceable ultimately to a Divine Author, would absolutely fail us in the very points that are essential to be known; namely, the origin of our being, the relation in which we stand to God, and the way to eternal happiness, on which neither science nor history affords us any light. But they yield a clear, definite, and consistent light and help, meeting the very askings and longings of our souls on these momentous topics. The wonderful way in which they convince the reason, probe the conscience, and apply a healing balm to the wounded spirit, is in itself an independent attestation to their divine origin. (e) The peculiar structure of this volume of writings, the general acknowledgment of the Jewish and Christian church in all ages, the account which it naturally furnishes of its own origin and the nature of its contents, are the sure and only grounds of evidence in regard to authorship; and these concur in ascribing it to an ultimate divine source. And we have only to add that there has not yet been, and we do not expect there will be, any tenable objection to this vast and growing array of evidence.

The nature of inspiration can only be learned from Scripture itself. To it, therefore, we apply for a definition of this important term. The Apostle Paul in writing to Timothy, a pastor and teacher in the church of God, makes use of the following expressions concerning Scripture: Τὰ ἱερὰ γράμματα τὰ δυνάμενά σε σοφίσαι εἰς σωτηρίαν, and Πᾶσα γραφὴ θεόπνευστος καὶ ὠφέλιμος πρὸς διδασκαλίαν. "The holy *scripta* able to make thee wise unto salvation," and "Every scripture given by inspiration of God, and profitable for doctrine." From these expressions we gather the following order of doctrine concerning the origin and character of the Bible. 1. It is given by inspiration of God. 2. It is first holy; second, able to make wise unto salvation; and, third, profitable for doctrine and other purposes of edification. In these elements of the doctrine of inspiration, the following points are worthy of remark: 1. It is a *writing*, not a writer, of which the character is here given. The thing said to be inspired is not that which goes into the mind of the author, but that which comes out of his mind by means of his pen. It is not the material on which he is to exercise his mind, but the result of that mental exercise which is here characterized. Hence it has received all the impress, not merely of man in general, but even of the individual author in particular, at the time when it is so designated. It is that piece of composition which the human author has put into a written form which is described as inspired. This is the true warrant for, and the proper meaning of, the phrase *verbal inspiration.* 2. To be inspired of God, is to be communicated from God, who is a spirit, to the mind of man. The *modus operandi,* mode of communication, we do not pretend to explain. But the possibility of such communication we cannot for a moment doubt. The immediate author of a merely human book may not be the ultimate author of a single sentiment it contains. He may have received every fact from trustworthy witnesses, who are after all the real vouchers for all that it records. And the very merit of the immediate author may consist in judiciously selecting the facts, faithfully adhering to his authorities, and properly arranging his materials for the desired effect. Analogous to this is the divine authorship of the sacred volume. By the inspiration of the Almighty, the human author is made to perceive certain things divine and human, to select such as are to be revealed, and to record these with fidelity in the natural order and to the proper end. The result is a writing given by inspiration of God, with all the peculiarities of man, and all the authority of God. 3. Such a written revelation is "holy." The primary holiness of a writing is its *truth*. God's part in it secures its veracity and credibility. Even man often tells the truth, where he is a disinterested witness; and we believe not only his sincerity, but his competence. God, who cannot lie, is able to secure his scribes from error intentional or unintentional. The secondary holiness of a writing appears in the two following particulars: 4. It is also "able to make wise unto salvation." This refers to the kind of truth contained in the book of God. It is a revelation of mercy, of peace on earth and good-will to man. This, at the same time, imparts an unspeakable interest to the book, and points out the occasion warranting the divine interference for its composition. 5. It is also "profitable for doctrine." It tends to holiness. It is moral as well as merciful in its revelations. It contains truth, mercy, and righteousness. It reflects, therefore, the holiness of God. It is in all respects worthy of its high original.

VI. — ITS INTERPRETATION.

It is impossible to forget that we live in the world of the fall. Hence it must needs be that offences come, stumblings at certain facts or doctrines of the word of God. If it were not for this, the business of interpretation would be comparatively easy. The Bible shines by its own light, and only needs preservation, translation, and illustration by human and natural history. But as things now are, the art of interpretation presupposes difficulties, even to the comparatively earnest and sincere, in the way of understanding and accepting its revelations. And the interpreter must not unfrequently allude to the misconceptions which he endeavors to remove. The reader must not be surprised, therefore, if, in a world of darkness, objections have occurred to other minds which have never struck his own. The aim of an exposition of the Word of God is expressly to obviate difficulties, and elucidate as far as possible the ways of God with man. In the course of exposition, therefore, passages that present obstacles to the mind, or relate to the things of God, must be treated at length, while those that are plain in themselves, or collateral to the grand topic, may almost be left to speak for themselves.

It follows, from this consideration, that the laws of interpretation, to be of any avail for the conviction of men, must be above question. It is necessary, therefore, to start with some fundamental fact, broad enough to be the basis of a system of exegetical maxims. *The Bible,* then, *is the word of God concerning the ways of God with man, put into a written form by men during a period of sixteen hundred years; the Old Testament in the Hebrew language, the New Testament in the Greek.* This pregnant fact is the sum of what we have already stated concerning the Scriptures, and it will be convenient to resolve it into its elementary parts, in order to display the several grounds for the general laws of interpretation.

1. The Bible is written *by men.* This is admitted on all hands. Hence it is subject to the ordinary rules of interpretation which apply to all human writings; not to rules arbitrary in their nature, modern in their invention, or unexampled in the days of the writer. Still further, the Bible is written *for men,* and accordingly, in the language of common life, not in the special terminology of science or art. Hence the following rules are obvious:

Rule I. The usage of common life determines the meaning of a word or phrase; not that of philosophy.

Rule II. The usage of the time and place of the writer determines the meaning; not that of any other time; not modern usage.

Rule III. If a word or phrase had several meanings, the context determines which it bears in a given passage. The more common meaning of the writer's day is to be preferred, provided it suit the passage; not that more common in our day.

Rule IV. If the author have occasion to employ a new word, or an old word in a new signification, his definition or his usage must determine the meaning; not any other author's usage.

Rule V. The direct or literal sense of a sentence is the meaning of the author, when no other is indicated; not any figurative, allegorical, or mystical meaning.

Rule VI. Passages bearing a direct, literal, or fully ascertained sense go to determine what passages have another sense than the literal, and what that other sense is; not our opinions.

2. The Bible treats of God in relation with man. It is obvious that this circumstance will afford occasion for new words and phrases, and new applications of the old ones. It brings into view such peculiar figures of speech as are called anthropomorphism and anthropopathism. It gives a new expansion to all the previous rules. It is needful to specify only one additional rule here, —

Rule VII. A word, phrase, or sentence belonging primarily to the things of man, must be understood, when applied to the things of God, in a sense consistent with his essential nature; not in a sense contradictory of any known attribute of that nature.

3. There is a growth in the Bible in two respects. 1. There is a growth in the adding of document to document for at least sixteen hundred years. Hence the simple or primary meaning of any part of speech will appear in the earlier documents; the more expanded and recondite may come out only in the later. 2. There is a growth also in adding fact to fact, and truth to truth, whereby doctrines that at first come out only in the bud are in the end expanded into full blow. At its commencement the Bible chooses and points out the all-sufficient root from which all doctrine may germinate. That root is God. In him inhere all the virtues that can create and uphold a world, and therefore in the knowledge of him are involved all the doctrines that can instruct and edify the intelligent creature. Hence the elementary form of a doctrine will be found in the older parts of Scripture; the more developed form in the later books. This gives rise to two similar rules of interpretation, —

Rule VIII. The meaning of a word or phrase in a later book of Scripture is not to be transferred to an earlier book, unless required by the context.

Rule IX. The form of a doctrine in a subsequent part of the Bible must not be taken to be as fully developed in a preceding part without the warrant of usage and the context.

4. The Old Testament was composed in Hebrew, the New in

Greek. Each must be interpreted according to the genius of the language in which it was originally written. The interpreter must therefore be familiar with the grammar of each, in which the particulars which constitute its genius are gathered into a system. The writers of the New Testament were, moreover, Hebrews by birth and habit, with the possible exception of Luke. Their Greek therefore bears a Hebrew stamp; and their words and phrases are employed to express Hebrew things, qualities, customs, and doctrines. Hence they must receive much of their elucidation from the Hebrew parts of speech of which they are the intended equivalents. Two rules of interpretation come under this head, —

Rule X. The sense of a sentence, and the relation of one sentence to another, must be determined according to the grammar of the language in which it is written.

Rule XI. The meaning of New Testament words and phrases must be determined in harmony with Old Testament usage; not by Greek against Hebrew usage.

5. The Bible is the word of God. All the other elements of our fundamental postulate are plain on the surface of things, and therefore unanimously admitted. This, however, some interpreters of the Bible do not accept, at least without reserve. But notwithstanding their rejection of this dogma, such interpreters are bound to respect the claims of this book to be the Word of God. This they can only do by applying to its interpretation such rules as are fairly deducible from such a characteristic. In doing so they put themselves to no disadvantage. They only give the claimant a fair stage, and put its high claim to a reasonable test. Now God is a God of truth. His word is truth. Hence all Scripture must be consistent with truth and with itself. It contains no real contradiction. This gives rise to the following rules:

Rule XII. All Scripture is true historically and metaphysically; not mythical or fallible.

Rule XIII. In verbally discordant passages that sense is to be adopted which will explain or obviate the discrepancy; not a sense that makes a contradiction. To explain is positively to show the harmony of the passage; to obviate is negatively to show that there is no contradiction.

Rule XIV. Scripture explains Scripture. Hence the clear and

plain passages elucidate the dark and abstruse; not anything foreign to Scripture in time, place, or sentiment; not our philosophy.

Rule XV. Of rules that cross one another, the higher sets aside or modifies the lower.

VII. — THE PENTATEUCH.

I. Its Author. — The Pentateuch is a work presenting at first sight all the ordinary marks of unity. Its five parts stand in a natural relation to one another. Genesis contains the origin of the present constitution of nature, of man, of the Sabbath, of many of the primary arts and customs of human society, of the covenant of works, of sin, of the covenant of grace, of the promise, and of the chosen people. Exodus records the growth of the chosen family into a nation, the departure of Israel from Egypt, the giving of the law, the directions for the construction of the tabernacle and its appurtenances, and the carrying of these directions into effect. Leviticus treats of the ritual under the heads of the various offerings, the consecration of the priests, the removal of uncleanness, the means of purification, and the regulations concerning festivals and vows. Numbers recounts the first census of the people, the sojourning in the wilderness, the conquest of the country east of the Jordan, the second census, and certain other arrangements preparatory to the crossing of the Jordan. Deuteronomy contains a recapitulation of the great deliverance the people had experienced, an admonitory address to them by Moses on the eve of his departure, with certain additional pieces designed for their instruction and encouragement. The book is then closed with a chapter giving an account of the death of Moses, which is due to the continuator of the sacred history. A literary work exhibiting such marks of connection and order it is natural to ascribe to one author. Moses was a man of learning (Acts vii. 22), a writer (Exod. xvii. 14, xxiv. 4), a poet (Exod. xv.; Deut. xxxii.), a lawgiver, and a public leader. He was also a witness and a chief mover in all the events recounted from the second chapter of Exodus to the last of Deuteronomy. It is therefore antecedently most probable that he was the author of the Pentateuch.

Close and critical examiners, however, of this work have found certain passages, sentences, and words which seem to come from a later hand. Various modes of explaining this appearance have been adopted, according to the circumstances of the interpreter. Either the divinely authorized reviser, transcriber, and continuator of the sacred volume, made, by the divine direction, the needful additions in writing to the written work of Moses, or the author must have been as late as the supposed latest event or allusion recorded in the book. Either of these suppositions is possible. But the antecedent probability is in favor of the former. Apart from the few passages which have the appearance of a later date, the work remains still a perfect whole from the beginning to the death of Moses, *when it closes.* It is also expressly affirmed in the book itself that Moses wrote certain parts of it, if not the whole (Exod. xvii. 14, xxiv. 4; Num. xxxiii. 2; Deut. xxxi. 9, 22, 24–26). Hence the probability is, that the whole work, being complete in itself, is the production of him to whom great part of it is by itself ascribed. As the whole book is also the first part of a progressive work, to be continued for many ages, it is natural that certain explanatory notes may have been inserted by the direction of the Divine Author. As Moses may have elucidated the documents that came down to him by a few verbal changes and additions, so may his continuator have added a few notes of explanation to his finished work for the benefit of a later generation. But the date of a work is that of the first edition, so to speak; not that of its final retouching. Though an author may have lived to publish ten editions of his work, with slight modifications in each, yet the date of it is at least as far back as that of the first edition. So, though the Almighty may have employed a subsequent prophet to add the last chapter of Deuteronomy, and insert a few explanatory clauses or parentheses, yet the book of the law is still to be dated from its first complete draft by the original author.

Some critics also find discrepancies of statement and style in the Pentateuch, and have endeavored to explain these phenomena by distributing the work among several authors, each of whom contributed his own part to the whole performance. If this were carried merely to the extent of presuming that certain historical pieces of composition came down to Moses, which he retouched and fitted into the first part of his own work, and that this again was retouched by a subsequent sacred writer, it could do no harm, and might be attended with some advantage to the interpretation of the book. But the hypothesis that a work with obvious marks of substantial unity was fabricated out of several works of different authors and ages is improbable in itself. It rests mainly on an over-refinement of critical acumen, and has proved a failure in other instances of its application. And it is unavailing as a means of explaining discrepancies of statement, since it merely succumbs to these difficulties, leaves them where it found them, thinks only of adding to their number and force, and simply ascribes their occurrence to the inadvertence of the compiler. This is a mode of dealing with a work of antiquity to which we are not warranted in resorting, until it has been proved contradictory to itself, to the acknowledged facts of observation, or the intuitive principles of reason. A fair examination of this work will show the very reverse of this to be the fact. It is the only key to the history of the human race, the chief voucher for many of its important facts; and it presents an astonishing harmony with its own statements, and with the main deductions of reason and observation concerning the origin and nature of man. The supposed discrepancies are due either to our misconception of its meaning, or to our ignorance of the circumstances in which it was written. Such discrepancies can never affect either the unity or the authenticity of the work. They leave in all its force the antecedent probability of its composition by Moses.

This probability is turned into an established certainty, by testimony of the most satisfactory kind, as soon as we go beyond the work itself into the succeeding portions of Sacred Scripture. In the very first chapter of the book of Joshua we read of the book of the law, which is plainly ascribed to Moses (i. 7, 8). Other references to the book of the law by Moses are found in subsequent passages of Joshua (viii. 31–34, xxiii. 6, xxiv. 26). Similar testimonies are extant in the following books: 1 Kings ii. 3; 2 Kings xiv. 6, xxiii. 25; 2 Chron. xxv. 4, xxxiv. 14, xxxv. 12; Ezra vi. 18; Neh. viii. 1, xiii. 1. We close this evidence by an incidental statement of our Lord after his resurrection, — "These are the words which I spake unto you while I was yet with you, that all things must be fulfilled which were written *in the law of Moses*, and in the prophets, and in the Psalms concerning me" (Luke xxiv. 44). It is only needful to say that the law of Moses here means the Pentateuch, and that this passage is only a single sample out of the concurrent testimony of the New Testament to the Mosaic authorship of this book.

II. Its written form. — The Pentateuch contains six hundred and sixty-nine פָּרָשִׁיּוֹת or paragraphs, distinguished into פְּתוּחוֹת open and סְתוּמוֹת closed. Those in which a new line was commenced were called open; those in which the same line after an interval was continued were said to be closed. The former were marked with a פ standing in the space between the paragraphs; the latter with a ס. These may be represented by ¶ and §. The former were intended to mark greater distinctions in the matter; the latter, less. The same paragraph divisions are also found in the prophets and Hagiographa. They were in existence anterior to the Talmud, as they are noticed in the Mishna; while in the Gemara they are declared to be inviolable rules of sacred orthography, and ascribed to Moses. According to Keil, they may have proceeded from the authors of the sacred books.

Besides these paragraphs, the division into פְּסוּקִים, *verses*, was found in the poetical books from an early period. These verses are by the accents subdivided into κῶλα and κόμματα. In the oldest MSS. these verses were written separately, though this arrangement has been laid aside in the Masoretic MSS. A similar division of the sentences in the other books is mentioned in the Mishna, and this was at all events the foundation of our present verse system. This was first introduced into editions of the Hebrew Bible by Athias, a learned Jew of Amsterdam, in 1661, A.C. It was adopted in the Vulgate so early as 1558.

The present division into chapters originated with the Christians in the thirteenth century, being ascribed by some to Cardinal Hugo, by others to Stephen Langton, Archbishop of Canterbury. It was first used in a concordance to the Vulgate, and adopted in the fifteenth century by R. Nathan for a concordance of the Hebrew Bible.

The Pentateuch was also divided into fifty-four larger parashoth or lessons, for reading in the worship of the synagogue. By this distribution the whole Pentateuch was read over at a section every Sabbath in the Jewish intercalary year, which contained fifty-four weeks. In the ordinary year, which contained not more than fifty-one weeks, two of the shorter sections were read together on several Sabbaths so as to complete the reading. In the spaces where the lesson for the Sabbath and the paragraph end together, instead of one פ or ס, as the case may be, we find three inserted.

Corresponding to these sections of the law were the הַפְטָרוֹת divisions or lessons of the prophets, which are mentioned in the Mishna. Elias Levita says that these were introduced by the Jews, when Antiochus Epiphanes forbade the reading of the law. This, however, is a mere conjecture; and it is more probable that these sections were added to the service of the synagogue in order to render it more complete. A table of the haphtaroth as well as the parashoth is given in Van der Hooght's Bible at the end of the Hagiographa.

The Masoretic text is the basis of the following translation and commentary. Important deviations from it are noted.

VIII. — GENESIS.

The book of Genesis is separable into eleven documents or pieces of composition, most of which contain other subordinate divisions. The first of these has no introductory phrase; the third begins with זֶה סֵפֶר תּוֹלְדֹת 'this is the book of the generations;' and the others with אֵלֶּה תּוֹלְדוֹת 'these are the generations.'

The subordinate pieces, however, of which these primary documents consist, are as distinct from each other, as complete in themselves, and as clearly owing each to a separate effort of the composer, as the wholes which they go to constitute. The history of the fall, Gen. iii., the family of Adam, iv., the description of the vices of the antediluvians, vi. 1–8, and the confusion of tongues, xi. 1–9, are as distinct efforts of composition, and as perfect in themselves, as any of the primary divisions. The same holds good throughout the entire book. Even these subordinate pieces contain still smaller passages, having an exact and self-contained finish, which enables the critic to lift them out and examine them, and makes him wonder if they have not been inserted in the document as in a mould previously fitted for their reception. The memoranda of each day's creative work, of the locality of Paradise, of each link in the genealogy of Noah and of Abraham, are striking examples of this. They sit, each in the narrative, like a stone in its setting.

Whether these primary documents were originally composed by Moses, or came into his hands from earlier sacred writers, and were by him revised and combined into his great work, we are not informed. By revising a sacred writing, we mean replacing obsolete or otherwise unknown words or modes of writing by such as were in common use in the time of the reviser, and putting in an explanatory clause or passage when necessary for the men of a later day. The latter of the above suppositions is not inconsistent with Moses being reckoned the responsible author of the whole collection. We hold it to be more natural, satisfactory, and accordant with the phenomena of Scripture. It is satisfactory to have the recorder, if not an eye-witness, yet as near as possible to the events recorded. And it seems to have been a part of the method of the Divine Author of the Scripture to have a constant collector, conservator, authenticator, reviser, and continuator of that book which he designed for the spiritual instruction of successive ages. We may disapprove of one writer tampering with the work of another ; but we must allow the Divine Author to adapt his own work, from time to time, to the necessities of coming generations. This implies, however, that writing was in use from the origin of man.

We are not able to say when writing of any kind was invented, or when syllabic or alphabetic writing came into use. But we meet with the word סֵפֶר *sêpher*, a writing, from which we have our English *cipher*, so early as the fifth chapter of Genesis. And many things encourage us to presume a very early invention of writing. It is, after all, only another form of speech, another effort of the signing faculty in man. Why may not the hand gesticulate to the eye, as well as the tongue articulate to the ear? We believe the former was concurrent with the latter in early speech, as it is in the speech of all lively nations to the present day. We have only another step to writing. Let the gestures of the hand take a permanent form by being carved in lines on a smooth surface, and we have a written character.

This leads us to the previous question of human speech. Was it a gradual acquisition after a period of brute silence? Apart from history, we argue it was not. We conceive that speech leaped at once from the brain of man a perfect thing, — perfect as the new-born infant, — yet capable of growth and development. This has been the case with all inventions and discoveries. The pressing necessity has come upon the fitting man, and he has given forth a complete idea, which after ages can only develope. The Bible record confirms this theory. Adam comes to be, and then by the force of his native genius speaks. And in primitive times we have no doubt the hand moved as well as the tongue. Hence we hear so soon of "the book."

2. On the supposition that writing was known to Adam, Gen. i.–iv., containing the first two of these documents, formed the Bible of Adam's descendants, or the antediluvians. Gen. i.–xi. 9, being the sum of these two and the following three, constitutes the Bible of the descendants of Noah. The whole of Genesis may be called the Bible of the posterity of Jacob; and, we may add, that the five books of the law, of which the last four at least are immediately due to Moses, were the first Bible of Israel as a nation.

3. Genesis is purely a historical work. It serves as the narrative preamble to the legislation of Moses. It possesses, however, a much higher and broader interest than this. It is the first volume of the history of man in relation with God. It consists of a main line of narrative, and one or more collateral lines. The main line is continuous, and relates to the portion of the human race that remains in communication with God. Side by side with this is a broken line, or rather several successive lines, which are linked on, not to one another, but to the main line. Of these, two come out in the primary documents of Genesis; namely, Gen. xxv. 12–18, and Gen. xxxvi., containing the respective records of Ishmael and Esau. When these are placed side by side with those of Isaac and Jacob, the stages in the main line of narrative are found to be nine, or two less than the primitive documents.

These great lines of narrative, in like manner, include minor lines, whenever the history falls into several threads, which must all be taken up one after another, in order to carry on the whole concatenation of events. These come out in paragraphs, and even shorter passages, which necessarily overlap one another in point of time. The striking peculiarity of Hebrew composition is aptly illustrated by the successive links in the genealogy of the fifth chapter, where the life of one patriarch is brought to a close before that of the next is taken up, though they actually run parallel for the greater part of the predecessor's life It furnishes a key to much that is difficult in the narrative.

4. This book is naturally divided into two great parts, — the first narrating the creation; the second, the development of the things created from the beginning to the deaths of Jacob and Joseph.

The first part is equal in value to the whole record of what may take place to the end of time, and therefore to the whole of the Bible, not only in its historical, but in its prophetical aspect. A created system of things contains in its bosom the whole of that which may be unfolded from it.

The second great part of Genesis consists of two main divisions, — the one detailing the course of events before the deluge, the other after it. These divisions may be distributed into sections in the following way: The stages of the narrative marked off in the primary documents are nine; in consequence, however, of the transcendent importance of the primeval events, we have broken up the second document into three sections, and the fourth into two, and have thus divided the contents of the book into twelve great sections. All these matters of arrangement are set forth to view in the following

TABLE OF CONTENTS.

		SECTIONS.	CHAPTERS.	DOCUMENTS.			
I. Creation.		I. Creation,	i.–ii. 3.	I.	1st Bible.	2d Bible.	3d Bible.
II. Development.	Before.	II. The Man,	ii. 4–25.	II.			
		III. The Fall,	iii.				
		IV. The Race,	iv.				
		V. Line to Noah,	v.–vi. 8.	III.			
	After the Deluge.	VI. The Deluge,	vi. 9–viii.	IV.			
		VII. The Covenant,	ix.				
		VIII. The Nations,	x.–xi. 9.	V.			
		IX. Line to Abram,	xi. 10–26.	VI.			
		X. Abraham,	xi. 27–xxv. 11.	VII.			
		XI. Isaac,	xxv. 12–18.	VIII.			
			xxxv. 19–xxv.	IX.			
		XII. Jacob,	xxxvi.	X.			
			xxxvii.–l.	XI.			

COMMENTARY

PART I

SECTION I.—THE CREATION

I. THE ABSOLUTE CREATION.—Gen. i. 1.

רֵאשִׁית *head-part, beginning*, of a thing, in point of time (Gen. x. 10), or value (Prov. i. 7). Its opposite is אַחֲרִית (Isa. xlvi. 10). בְּרֵאשִׁית *in the beginning*, is always used in reference to time. Here only is it taken absolutely.

בָּרָא *create, give being to something new.* It has God always for its subject. Its object may be anything: matter (Gen. i. 1); animal life (Gen. i. 21); spiritual life (Gen. i. 27). Hence creation is not confined to a single point of time. Whenever anything absolutely new—that is, not involved in anything previously extant—is called into existence, there is creation (Num. xvi. 30). Any thing or event also may be said to be created by Him, who created the whole system of nature to which it belongs (Mal. ii. 10). The verb in its simple form occurs forty-eight times (of which eleven are in Genesis, fourteen in the whole Pentateuch, and twenty-one in Isaiah), and always in one sense.

אֱלֹהִים. GOD. The noun אֱלוֹהַּ or אֱלֹהַּ is found in the Hebrew scriptures fifty-seven times in the singular (of which two are in Deuteronomy, and forty-one in the book of Job), and about three thousand times in the plural, of which seventeen are in Job. The Chaldee form אֱלָהּ occurs about seventy-four times in the singular, and ten in the plural. The letter ה is proved to be radical, not only by bearing mappiq, but also by keeping its ground before a formative ending. The Arabic verb, with the same radicals, seems rather to borrow from it than to lend the meaning *coluit, worshipped*, which it sometimes has. The root probably means to be *lasting, binding, firm, strong.* Hence the noun means the Everlasting, and in the plural, the Eternal Powers. It is correctly rendered God, the name of the Eternal and Supreme Being in our language, which perhaps originally meant lord or ruler. And, like this, it is a common or appellative noun. This is evinced by its direct use and indirect applications.

Its direct use is either proper or improper, according to the object to which it is applied. Every instance of its proper use manifestly determines its meaning to be the Eternal, the Almighty, who is himself without beginning, and has within himself the power of causing other things, personal and impersonal, to be, and on this event is the sole object of reverence and primary obedience to his intelligent creation.

Its improper use arose from the lapse of man into false notions of the object of worship. Many real or imaginary beings came to be regarded as possessed of the attributes, and therefore entitled to the reverence belonging to Deity, and were in consequence called gods by their mistaken votaries, and by others who had occasion to speak of them. This usage at once proves it to be a common noun, and corroborates its proper meaning. When thus employed, however, it immediately loses most of its inherent grandeur, and sometimes dwindles down to the bare notion of the supernatural or the extramundane. In this manner it seems to be applied by the witch of Endor to the unexpected apparition that presented itself to her (1 Sam. xxviii. 13).

Its indirect applications point with equal steadiness to this primary and fundamental meaning. Thus it is employed in a relative and well-defined sense to denote one appointed of God to stand in a certain divine relation to another. This relation is that of authoritative revealer or administrator of the will of God. Thus we are told (John x. 34) that "he called them gods, to whom the word of God came." Thus Moses became related to Aaron as God to his prophet (Exod. iv. 16), and to Pharaoh as God to his creature (Exod. vii. 1). Accordingly, in Ps. lxxxii. 6, we find this principle generalized: "*I* had said, gods are ye, and sons of the Highest all of you." Here the divine authority vested in Moses is expressly recognized in those who sit in Moses' seat as judges for God. They exercised a function of God among the people, and so were in God's stead to them. Man, indeed, was originally adapted for ruling, being made in the image of God, and commanded to have dominion over the inferior creatures. The parent also is instead of God in some respect to his children, and the sovereign holds the relation of patriarch to his subjects. Still, however, we are not fully warranted in translating אֱלֹהִים *judges* in Exod. xxi. 6, xxii. 7, 8, 27 (8, 9, 28), because a more easy, exact, and impressive sense is obtained from the proper rendering.

The word מַלְאָךְ *angel*, as a relative or official term, is sometimes applied to a person of the Godhead; but the process is not reversed. The Seventy indeed translate אֱלֹהִים in several instances by ἄγγελοι (Ps. viii. 6; xcvii. 7; cxxxviii. 1). The correctness of this is seemingly supported by the quotations in Heb. i. 6. and ii. 7. These, however, do not imply that the renderings are absolutely correct, but only sufficiently so for the purpose of the writer. And it is evident they are so, because the original is a highly imaginative figure, by which a class is conceived to exist, of which in reality only one of the kind is or can be. Now the Seventy, either imagining, from the occasional application of the official term 'angel' to God, that the angelic office somehow or sometimes involved the divine nature, or viewing some of the false gods of the heathen as really angels, and therefore seemingly wishing to give a literal turn to the figure, substituted the word ἄγγελοι as an interpretation for אֱלֹהִים. This free translation was sufficient for the purpose of the inspired author of the epistle to the Hebrews, inasmuch as the worship of all angels (Heb. i. 6) in the Septuagint sense of the term was that of the highest rank of dignitaries under God; and the argument in the latter passage (Heb. ii. 7) turns not on the words, "thou madest him a little lower than the angels," but upon the sentence, "thou hast put all things under his feet." Moreover, the Seventy are by no means consistent in this rendering of the word in similar passages (see Ps. lxxxii. 1, xcvii. 1; 1 Sam. xxviii. 13).

With regard to the use of the word, it is to be observed that the plural of the Chaldee form is uniformly plural in sense. The English version of בַּר־אֱלָהִין *the Son of God* (Dan. iii. 25) is the only exception to this. But as it is the phrase of a heathen, the real meaning may be, *a son of the gods*. On the contrary, the plural of the Hebrew form is generally employed to denote the one God. The singular form, when applied to the true God, is naturally suggested by the prominent thought of his being the only one. The plural, when so applied, is generally accompanied with singular conjuncts, and conveys the predominant conception of a plurality in the one God, — a plurality which must be perfectly consistent with his being the only possible one of his kind. The explanations of this use of the plural — namely, that it is a relic of polytheism, that it indicates the association of the angels with the one God in a common or collective appellation, and that it expresses the multiplicity of attributes subsisting in him — are not satisfactory. All we can say is, that it indicates such a plurality in the only one God as makes his nature complete and creation possible. Such a plurality in unity must have dawned upon the mind of Adam. It is afterwards, we conceive, definitely revealed in the doctrine of the Father, the Son, and the Holy Ghost.

שָׁמַיִם *skies, heavens,* being the *high* (שמי *be high,* Arab.) or the *airy* region ; the overarching dome of space, with all its revolving orbs.

אֶרֶץ *land, earth,* the *low* or the *hard.* The underlying surface of land.

The verb is in the perfect form, denoting a completed act. The adverbial note of time, "in the beginning," determines it to belong to the past. To suit our idiom it may, therefore, be strictly rendered "had created." The skies and the land are the universe divided into its two natural parts by an earthly spectator. The absolute beginning of time, and the creation of all things, mutually determine each other.

I. 1. In the beginning had God created the heavens and the earth.

This great introductory sentence of the book of God is equal in weight to the whole of its subsequent communications concerning the kingdom of nature.

It assumes the existence of God; for it is he who in the beginning creates. It assumes his eternity; for he is before all things: and as nothing comes from nothing, he himself must have always been. It implies his omnipotence; for he creates the universe of things. It implies his absolute freedom; for he begins a new course of action. It implies his infinite wisdom; for a *kosmos,* an order of matter and mind, can only come from a being of absolute intelligence. It implies his essential goodness; for the Sole, Eternal, Almighty, All-wise, and All-sufficient Being has no reason, no motive, and no capacity for evil. It presumes him to be beyond all limit of time and place; as he is before all time and place.

It asserts the creation of the heavens and the earth; that is, of the universe of mind and matter. This creating is the omnipotent act of giving existence to things which before had no existence. This is the first great mystery of things; as the end is the second. Natural science observes things as they are, when they have already laid hold of existence. It ascends into the past as far as observation will reach, and penetrates into the future as far as experience will guide But it does not touch the beginning or the end. This first sentence of revelation, however, records the beginning. At the same time it involves the progressive development of that which is begun, and so contains within its bosom the whole of what is revealed in the book of God. It is thus historical of the beginning, and prophetical of the whole of time. It is, therefore, equivalent to all the rest of revelation taken together, which merely records the evolutions of one sphere of creation, and nearly and more nearly anticipates the end of present things.

This sentence assumes the being of God, and asserts the beginning of things. Hence it intimates that the existence of God is more immediately patent to the reason of man than the creation of the universe. And this is agreeable to the philosophy of things; for the existence of God is a necessary and eternal truth, more and more self-evident to the intellect as it rises to maturity. But the beginning of things is, by its very nature, a contingent event, which once was not and then came to be contingent on the free will of the Eternal, and, therefore, not evident to reason itself, but made known to the understanding by testimony and the reality of things. This sentence is the testimony, and the actual world in us and around us is the reality. Faith takes account of the one, observation of the other.

It bears on the very face of it the indication that it was written by man, and for man; for it divides all things into the heavens and the earth. Such a division evidently suits those only who are inhabitants of the earth. Accordingly, this sentence is the foundation-stone of the history, not of the universe at large, of the sun, of any other planet, but of the earth, and of man its rational inhabitant. The primeval event which it records may be far distant, in point of time, from the next event in such a history; as the earth may have existed myriads of ages, and undergone many vicissitudes in its condition, before it became the home of the human race. And, for ought we know, the history of other planets, even of the solar system, may yet be unwritten, because there has been as yet no rational inhabitant to compose or peruse the record. We have no intimation of the interval of time that elapsed between the beginning of things narrated in this prefatory sentence and that state of things which is announced in the following verse.

With no less clearness, however, does it show that it was dictated by superhuman knowledge. For it records the beginning of things of which natural science can take no cognizance. Man observes certain laws of nature, and, guided by these, may trace the current of physical events backwards and forwards, but without being able to fix any limit to the course of nature in either direction. And not only this sentence, but the main part of this and the following chapter communicates events that occurred before man made his appearance on the stage of things; and therefore before he could either witness or record them. And in harmony with all this, the whole volume is proved by the topics chosen, the revelations made, the views entertained, the ends contemplated, and the means of information possessed, to be derived from a higher source than man.

This simple sentence denies atheism; for it assumes the being of God. It denies polytheism, and, among its various forms, the doctrine of two eternal principles, the one good and the other evil; for it confesses the one Eternal Creator. It denies materialism; for it asserts the creation of matter. It denies pantheism; for it assumes the existence of God before all things, and apart from them. It denies fatalism; for it involves the freedom of the Eternal Being.

It indicates the relative superiority, in point of magnitude, of the heavens to the earth, by giving the former the first place in the order of words. It is thus in accordance with the first elements of astronomical science.

It is therefore pregnant with physical and metaphysical, with ethical and theological instruction for the first man, for the predecessors and contemporaries of Moses, and for all the succeeding generations of mankind.

This verse forms an integral part of the narrative, and not a mere heading as some have imagined. This is abundantly evident from the following reasons: 1. It has the form of a narrative, not of a superscription. 2. The conjunctive particle connects the second verse with it; which could not be if it were a heading. 3. The very next sentence speaks of the earth as already in existence, and therefore its creation must be recorded in the first verse. 4. In the first verse the heavens take precedence of the earth; but in the following verses all things, even the sun, moon, and stars seem to be but appendages to the earth. Thus, if it were a heading, it would not correspond with the narrative. 5. If the first verse belong to the narrative, order pervades the whole recital; whereas, if it be a heading, the most hopeless confusion enters. Light is called into being before the sun, moon, and stars. The earth takes precedence of the heavenly luminaries. The stars, which are co-ordinate with the sun, and pre-ordinate to the moon, occupy the third place in the narrative of their manifestation.

For any or all of these reasons it is obvious that the first verse forms a part of the narrative.

As soon as it is settled that the narrative begins in the first verse, another question comes up for determination; namely, whether the heavens here mean the heavenly bodies that circle in their courses through the realms of space, or the mere space itself which they occupy with their perambulations. It is manifest that the heavens here denote the heavenly orbs themselves, — the celestial mansions with their existing inhabitants, — for the following cogent reasons: 1. Creation implies something created, and not mere space, which is nothing, and cannot be said to be created. 2. As the earth here obviously means the substance of the planet we inhabit, so, by parity of reason, the heavens must mean the substance of the celestial luminaries, the heavenly hosts of stars and spirits. 3. The heavens are placed before the earth, and therefore must mean that reality which is greater than the earth; for if they meant space, and nothing real, they ought not to be before the earth. 4. The heavens are actually *mentioned* in the verse, and therefore must mean a real thing; for if they meant nothing at all, they ought not to be mentioned. 5. The heavens must denote the heavenly realities, because this imparts a rational order to the whole chapter; whereas an unaccountable derangement appears if the sun, moon, and stars do not come into existence till the fourth day, though the sun is the centre of light and the measurer of the daily period. For any or all of these reasons, it is undeniable that the heavens in the first verse mean the fixed and planetary orbs of space; and, consequently, that these uncounted tenants of the skies, along with our own planet, are all declared to be in existence before the commencement of the six days' creation.

Hence it appears that the first verse records an event antecedent to those described in the subsequent verses. This is the absolute and aboriginal creation of the heavens and all that in them is, and of the earth in its primeval state. The former includes all those resplendent spheres which are spread before the wondering eye of man, as well as those hosts of planets and of spiritual and angelic beings which are beyond the range of his natural vision. This brings a simple and unforced meaning out of the whole chapter, and discloses a beauty and a harmony in the narrative which no other interpretation can afford. In this way the subsequent verses reveal a new effort of creative power, by which the pre-adamic earth, in the condition in which it appears in the second verse, is fitted up for the residence of a fresh animal creation, including the human race. The process is represented as it would appear to primeval man in his infantile simplicity, with whom his own position would naturally be the fixed point to which everything else was to be referred.

II. THE LAND.—Gen. i. 2.

הָיָה *be.* It is to be noted, however, that the word has three meanings, two of which now scarcely belong to our English *be.* 1. *Be*, as an event, *start into being, begin to be, come to pass.* This may be understood of a thing beginning to be, יְהִי אוֹר *be light*; or of an event taking place, וַיְהִי מִקֵּץ יָמִים *and it came to pass* from the end of days. 2. *Be*, as a change of state, *become.* This is applied to that which had a previous existence, but undergoes some change in its properties or relations; as וַתְּהִי נְצִיב מֶלַח *and she became* a pillar of salt. 3. *Be*, as a state. This is the ultimate meaning to which the verb tends in all languages. In all its meanings, especially in the first and second, the Hebrew speaker presumes an onlooker, to whom the object in question appears coming into being, becoming or being, as the case may be. Hence it means to be manifestly, so that eye-witnesses may observe the signs of existence.

תֹּהוּ וָבֹהוּ *a waste and a void.* The two terms denote kindred ideas, and their combination marks emphasis. Besides the present passage בֹּהוּ occurs in only two others (Is. xxxiv. 11; Jer. iv. 23), and always in conjunction with תֹּהוּ. If we may distinguish the two words, בֹּהוּ refers to the matter, and תֹּהוּ to the form, and therefore the phrase combining the two denotes a state of utter confusion and desolation, an absence of all that can furnish or people the land.

חֹשֶׁךְ *darkness*, the absence of light.

פָּנִים *face, surface.* פָּנָה *face, look, turn towards.*

תְּהוֹם *roaring deep, billow.* הוּם *hum, roar, fret.*

רוּחַ *breath, wind, soul, spirit.*

רָחַף *be soft, tremble.* Pi. *brood, flutter.*

וְהָאָרֶץ *and the earth.* Here the conjunction attaches the noun, and not the verb, to the preceding statement. This is therefore a connection of objects in space, and not of events in time. The present sentence, accordingly, may not stand closely conjoined in point of time with the preceding one. To intimate sequence in time the conjunction would have been prefixed to the verb in the form וַתְּהִי *then was.*

אֶרֶץ means not only *earth*, but *country*, *land*, a portion of the earth's surface defined by natural, national, or civil boundaries ; as, *the land* of Egypt, *thy land* (Ex. xxiii. 9, 10).

Before proceeding to translate this verse, it is to be observed that the state of an event may be described either definitely or indefinitely. It is described definitely by the three states of the Hebrew verb, — the perfect, the current, and the imperfect. The latter two may be designated in common the imperfect state. A completed event is expressed by the former of the two states, or, as they are commonly called, tenses of the Hebrew verb ; a current event, by the imperfect participle ; an incipient event, by the second state or tense. An event is described indefinitely when there is neither verb nor participle in the sentence to determine its state. The first sentence of this verse is an example of the perfect state of an event, the second of the indefinite, and the third of the imperfect or continuous state.

2. And the earth had become a waste and a void, and darkness was upon the face of the deep ; and the Spirit of God was brooding upon the face of the water.

After the undefined lapse of time from the first grand act of creation, the present verse describes the state of things on the land immediately antecedent to the creation of a new system of vegetable and animal life, and, in particular, of man, the intelligent inhabitant, for whom this fair scene was now to be fitted up and replenished.

Here "the earth" is put first in the order of words, and therefore, according to the genius of the Hebrew language, set forth prominently as the subject of the sentence ; whence we conclude that the subsequent narrative refers to the land — the skies from this time forward coming in only incidentally, as they bear upon its history. The disorder and desolation, we are to remember, are limited in their range to the land, and do not extend to the skies ; and the scene of the creation now remaining to be described is confined to the land, and its superincumbent matter in point of space, and to its present geological condition in point of time.

We have further to bear in mind that the land among the antediluvians, and down far below the time of Moses, meant so much of the surface of our globe as was known by observation, along with an unknown and undetermined region beyond ; and observation was not then so extensive as to enable men to ascertain its spherical form or even the curvature of its surface. To their eye it presented merely an irregular surface bounded by the horizon. Hence it appears that, so far as the current significance of this leading term is concerned, the scene of the six days' creation cannot be affirmed on scriptural authority alone to have extended beyond the surface known to man. Nothing can be inferred from the mere words of Scripture concerning America, Australia, the islands of the Pacific, or even the remote parts of Asia, Africa, or Europe, that were yet unexplored by the race of man. We are going beyond the warrant of the sacred narrative, on a flight of imagination, whenever we advance a single step beyond the sober limits of the usage of the day in which it was written.

Along with the sky and its conspicuous objects the land then known to the primeval man formed the sum total of the observable universe. It was as competent to him with his limited information, as it is to us with our more extensive but still limited knowledge, to express the all by a periphrasis consisting of two terms that have not even yet arrived at their full complement of meaning: and it was not the object or the effect of divine revelation to anticipate science on these points.

Passing now from the subject to the verb in this sentence, we observe it is in the perfect state, and therefore denotes that the condition of confusion and emptiness was not in progress, but had run its course and become a settled thing, at least at the time of the next recorded event. If the verb had been absent in Hebrew, the sentence would have been still complete, and the meaning as follows: "And the land was waste and void." With the verb present, therefore, it must denote something more. The verb הָיָה *be* has here, we conceive, the meaning *become;* and the import of the sentence is this: "And the land had become waste and void." This affords the presumption that the part at least of the surface of our globe which fell within the cognizance of primeval man, and first received the name of land, may not have been always a scene of desolation or a sea of turbid waters, but may have met with some catastrophe by which its order and fruitfulness had been marred or prevented.

This sentence, therefore, does not necessarily describe the state of the land when first created, but merely intimates a change that may have taken place since it was called into existence. What its previous condition was, or what interval of time elapsed between the absolute creation and the present state of things, is not revealed. How many transformations it may have undergone, and what purpose it may have heretofore served, are questions that did not essentially concern the moral well-being of man, and are therefore to be asked of some other interpreter of nature than the written word.

This state of things is *finished* in reference to the event about to be narrated. Hence the settled condition of the land, expressed by the predicates "a waste and a void," is in studied contrast with the order and fulness which are about to be introduced. The present verse is therefore to be regarded as a statement of the wants that have to be supplied in order to render the land a region of beauty and life.

The second clause of the verse points out another striking characteristic of the scene. "And darkness was upon the face of the deep": Here again the conjunction is connected with the noun. The time is the indefinite past, and the circumstance recorded is merely appended to that contained in the previous clause. The darkness, therefore, is connected with the disorder and solitude which then prevailed on the land. It forms a part of the physical derangement which had taken place on this part at least of the surface of our globe.

It is further to be noted that the darkness is described to be on the face of the deep. Nothing is said about any other region throughout the bounds of existing things. The presumption is, so far as this clause determines, that it is a local darkness confined to the face of the deep. And the clause itself stands between two others which refer to the land, and not to any other part of occupied space. It cannot therefore be intended to describe anything beyond this definite region.

The deep, the roaring abyss, is another feature in the pre-adamic scene. It is not now a region of land and water, but a chaotic mass of turbid waters, floating over, it may be, and partly laden with, the ruins of a past order of things; at all events not at present possessing the order of vegetable and animal life.

The last clause introduces a new and unexpected element into the scene of desolation. The sentence is, as heretofore, coupled to the preceding one by the noun or subject. This indicates still a conjunction of things, and not a series of events. The phrase רוּחַ אֱלֹהִים means the spirit of God, as it is elsewhere uniformly applied to spirit, and as רִחֵף *brooded*, does not describe the action of wind. The verbal form employed is the imperfect participle, and therefore denotes a work in the actual process of accomplishment. The brooding of the spirit of God is evidently the originating cause of the reorganization of things on the land, by the creative work which is successively described in the following passage.

ntimated that God is a spirit. For "the spirit of God" o "God who is a spirit." This is that essential charac- Everlasting which makes creation possible. Many -, ancient and modern, have felt the difficulty of proceeding from the one to the many; in other words, of evolving the actual multiplicity of things out of the absolutely one. And no wonder. For the absolutely one, the pure monad that has no internal relation, no complexity of quality or faculty, is barren, and must remain alone. It is, in fact, nothing; not merely no *thing*, but absolutely naught. The simplest possible existent must have BEING, *and* THAT to which this being belongs, *and*, moreover, some specific or definite CHARACTER by which it is what it is. This character seldom consists of one quality; usually, if not universally, of more than one. Hence in the Eternal One may and must be that CHARACTER which is the concentration of all the causative antecedents of a universe of things. The first of these is WILL. Without free choice there can be no beginning of things. Hence matter cannot be a creator. But will needs, cannot be without, WISDOM to plan and POWER to execute what is to be willed. These are the three essential attributes of SPIRIT. The manifold wisdom of the Eternal Spirit, combined with his equally manifold power, is adequate to the creation of a manifold system of things. Let the free behest be given, and the universe starts into being.

It would be rash and out of place to speculate on the nature of the brooding here mentioned further than it is explained by the event. We could not see any use of a mere wind blowing over the water, as it would be productive of none of the subsequent effects. At the same time, we may conceive the spirit of God to manifest its energy in some outward effect, which may bear a fair analogy to the natural figure by which it is represented. Chemical forces, as the prime agents, are not to be thought of here, as they are totally inadequate to the production of the results in question. Nothing but a creative or absolutely initiative power could give rise to a change so great and fundamental as the construction of an Adamic abode out of the luminous, aerial, aqueous, and terrene materials of the preëxistent earth, and the production of the new vegetable and animal species with which it was now to be replenished.

Such is the intimation we gather from the text, when it declares that "the spirit of God was brooding upon the face of the waters." It means something more than the ordinary power put forth by the Great Being for the natural sustenance and development of the universe which he has called into existence. It indicates a new and special display of omnipotence for the present exigencies of this part of the realm of creation. Such an occasional, and, for ought we know, ordinary though supernatural interposition, is quite in harmony with the perfect freedom of the Most High in the changing conditions of a particular region, while the absolute impossibility of its occurrence would be totally at variance with this essential attribute of a spiritual nature.

In addition to this, we cannot see how a universe of moral beings can be governed on any other principle; while, on the other hand, the principle itself is perfectly compatible with the administration of the whole according to a predetermined plan, and does not involve any vacillation of purpose on the part of the Great Designer.

We observe, also, that this creative power is put forth on the face of the waters, and is therefore confined to the land mentioned in the previous part of the verse and its superincumbent atmosphere.

Thus this primeval document proceeds, in an orderly way, to portray to us in a single verse the state of the land antecedent to its being fitted up anew as a meet dwelling-place for man.

III. THE FIRST DAY. — Gen. i. 3–5.

3. אָמַר *say, bid.* After this verb comes the thing said in the words of the speaker, or an equivalent expression. In this respect it corresponds with our English *say.*

אוֹר *light.* Light is simply that which makes a sensible impression on the organs of vision. It belongs to a class of things which occasionally produce the same effect.

וַיֹּאמֶר *then said.* Here we have come to the narrative or the record of a series of events. The conjunction is prefixed to the verb, to indicate the connection of the event it records with that which precedes. There is here, therefore, a sequence in the order of time. In a chain of events, the narrative follows the order of occurrence. Collateral chains of events must of necessity be recorded in successive paragraphs. The first paragraph carries on one line of incidents to a fit resting-place. The next may go back to take up the record of another line. Hence a new paragraph beginning with a conjoined verb is to be connected in time, not with the last sentence of the preceding one, but with some sentence in the preceding narrative more or less distant from its terminating point (see on ver. 5, and ii. 3). Even a single verse may be a paragraph in itself referring to a point of time antecedent to the preceding sentence.

A verb so conjoined in narrative is in Hebrew put in the incipient or imperfect form, as the narrator conceives the events to grow each out of that already past. He himself follows the incidents step by step down the pathway of time, and hence the initial aspect of each event is towards him, as it actually comes upon the stage of existence.

As the event now before us belongs to past time, this verb is well enough rendered by the past tense of our English verb. This tense in English is at present indefinite, as it does not determine the state of the event as either beginning, continuing, or concluded. It is not improbable, however, that it originally designated the first of these states, and came by degrees to be indefinite. The English present also may have denoted an incipient, and then an imperfect or indefinite.

3. רָאָה *see* (ὁράω?) אוֹר *emit light,* רָאָה *see by light.*
טוֹב *good.* Opp. רָע.

4. קָרָא *cry, call.*

עֶרֶב *evening, sunset.* A space of time before and after sunset. עַרְבַּיִם *two evenings,* a certain time before sunset, and the time between sunset and the end of twilight. בֵּין הָעַרְבַּיִם the interval between the two evenings, from sunset to the end of twilight, according to the Karaites and Samaritans; from sun declining to sunset, according to the Pharisees and Rabbinists. It might be the time from the beginning of the one to the beginning of the other, from the end of the one to the end of the other, or from the beginning of the one to the end of the other. The last is the most suitable for all the passages in which it occurs. These are ten in number, all in the law (Ex. xii. 6, xvi. 12, xxix. 31, 41, xxx. 8; Lev. xxiii. 5; Num. ix. 3, 5, 8, xxviii. 4). The slaying of the evening lamb and of the passover lamb, the eating of the latter and the lighting of the lamps, took place in the interval so designated.

At the end of this portion of the sacred text we have the first פ. This is explained in the Introduction, Section VII.

3. Then said God, Let there be light; and there was light. 4. Then saw God the light that it was good: then divided God between the light and between the darkness. 5. Then called

God to the light, day, and to the darkness he called night. Then was evening,' then was morning, day one. ¶ 1.

The first day's work is the calling of light into being. Here the design is evidently to remove one of the defects mentioned in the preceding verse, — "and darkness was upon the face of the deep." The scene of this creative act is therefore coincident with that of the darkness it is intended to displace. The interference of supernatural power to cause the presence of light in this region, intimates that the powers of nature were inadequate to this effect. But it does not determine whether or not light had already existed elsewhere, and had even at one time penetrated into this now darkened region, and was still prevailing in the other realms of space beyond the face of the deep. Nor does it determine whether by a change of the polar axis, by the rarefaction of the gaseous medium above, or by what other means, light was made to visit this region of the globe with its agreeable and quickening influences. We only read that it did not then illuminate the deep of waters, and that by the potent word of God it was then summoned into being. This is an act of creative power; for it is a calling into existence that which had previously no existence in that place, and was not owing to the mere development of nature. Hence the act of omnipotence here recorded is not at variance with the existence of light among the elements of that universe of nature, the absolute creation of which is affirmed in the first verse.

3. *Then said God.* In this verse God speaks. From this we learn that he not only is, but is *such* that he can express his will and commune with his intelligent creatures. He is manifest not only by his creation, but by himself. If light had come into existence without a perceptible cause, we should still have inferred a first Causer by an intuitive principle which demands an adequate cause for anything making its appearance which was not before. But when God says, "Be light," in the audience of his intelligent creatures, and light forthwith comes into view, they perceive God commanding, as well as light appearing.

Speech is the proper mode of spiritual manifestation. Thinking, willing, acting are the movements of spirit, and speech is the index of that which is thought, willed, and done. Now, as the essence of God is the spirit which thinks and acts, so the form of God is that in which the spirit speaks, and otherwise meets the observations of intelligent beings. In these three verses, then, we have God, the spirit of God, and the word of God. And as the term *spirit* is transferred from an inanimate thing to signify an intelligent agent, so the term *word* is capable of receiving a similar change of application.

Inadvertent critics of the Bible object to God being described as *speaking*, or performing any other act that is proper only to the human frame or spirit. They say it is anthropomorphic or anthropopathic, implies a gross, material, or human idea of God, and is therefore unworthy of him and of his word. But they forget that great law of thought and speech by which we apprehend analogies, and with a wise economy call the analogues by the same name. Almost all the words we apply to mental things were originally borrowed from our vocabulary for the material world, and therefore really figurative, until by long habit the metaphor was forgotten, and they became to all intents and purposes literal. And philosophers never have and never will have devised a more excellent way of husbanding words, marking analogies, and fitly expressing spiritual things. Our phraseology for mental ideas, though lifted up from a lower sphere, has not landed us in spiritualism, but enabled us to converse about the metaphysical with the utmost purity and propriety.

And as this holds true of human thoughts and actions, so does it apply with equal truth to the divine ways and works. Let there be in our minds right notions of God, and the tropical language we must and ought to employ in speaking of divine things will derive no taint of error from its original application to their human analogues. Scripture communicates those adequate notions of the most High God which are the fit corrective of its necessarily metaphorical language concerning the things of God. Accordingly the intelligent perusal of the Bible has never produced idolatry; but, on the other hand, has communicated even to its critics the just conceptions they have acquired of the spiritual nature of the one true God.

It ought to be remembered, also, that the very principle of all language is the use of signs for things, that the trope is only a special application of this principle according to the law of parsimony, and that the East is peculiarly addicted to the use of tropical language. Let not western metaphysics misjudge, lest it be found to misunderstand eastern æsthetics.

It is interesting to observe in the self-manifesting God the great archetypes of which the semblances are found in man. Here we have the sign-making or signifying faculty in exercise. Whether there were created witnesses present at the issue of this divine command, we are not here informed. Their presence, however, was not necessary to give significance to the act of speech, any more than to that of self-manifestation. God may manifest himself and speak, though there be none to see and hear.

We see, too, here the name in existence before the thing, because it primarily refers to the thing as contemplated in thought.

The self-manifesting God and the self-manifesting act of speaking are here antecedent to the act of creation, or the coming of the thing into existence. This teaches us that creation is a different thing from self-manifestation or emanation. God is; he manifests himself; he speaks; and lastly he puts forth the power, and the thing is done.

Let there be light. The word *be* simply denotes the *existence* of the light, by whatever means or from whatever quarter it comes into the given locality. It might have been by an absolute act of pure creation or making out of nothing. But it may equally well be effected by any supernatural operation which removes an otherwise insurmountable hinderance, and opens the way for the already existing light to penetrate into the hitherto darkened region. This phrase is therefore in perfect harmony with preëxistence of light among the other elementary parts of the universe from the very beginning of things. And it is no less consonant with the fact that heat, of which light is a species or form, is, and has from the beginning been, present in all those chemical changes by which the process of universal nature is carried on through all its innumerable cycles.

4. *Then saw God the light that it was good.* God contemplates his work, and derives the feeling of complacence from the perception of its excellence. Here we have two other archetypal faculties displayed in God, which subsequently make their appearance in the nature of man, the understanding, and the judgment.

The perception of things external to himself is an important fact in the relation between the Creator and the creature. It implies that the created thing is distinct from the creating Being, and external to him. It therefore contradicts pantheism in all its forms.

The judgment is merely another branch of the apprehensive or cognitive faculty, by which we note physical and ethical relations and distinctions of things. It comes immediately into view on observing the object now called into existence. God saw "that it was good." That is good in general which fulfils the end of its being. The relation of good and evil has a place and an application in the physical world, but it ascends through all the grades of the intellectual and the moral.

That form of the judgment which takes cognizance of moral distinctions is of so much importance as to have received a distinct name,—the conscience, or moral sense.

Here the moral rectitude of God is vindicated, inasmuch as the work of his power is manifestly good. This refutes the doctrine of the two principles, the one good and the other evil, which the Persian sages have devised in order to account for the presence of moral and physical evil along with the good in the present condition of our world.

Divided between the light and between the darkness. God then separates light and darkness, by assigning to each its relative position in time and space. This no doubt refers to the vicissitudes of day and night, as we learn from the following verse:

5. *Called to the light, day, etc.* After separating the light and the darkness, he gives them the new names of day and night, according to the limitations under which they were now placed. Before this epoch in the history of the earth there was no rational inhabitant, and therefore no use of naming. The assigning of names, therefore, is an indication that we have arrived at that stage in which names for things will be necessary, because a rational creature is about to appear on the scene.

Naming seems to be designating according to the specific mode in which the general notion is realized in the thing named. This is illustrated by several instances which occur in the following part of the chapter. It is the right of the maker, owner, or other superior to give a name; and hence the receiving of a name indicates the subordination of the thing named to the namer. Name and thing correspond: the former is the sign of the latter; hence in the concrete matter-of-fact style of Scripture the name is often put for the thing, quality, person, or authority it represents.

The designations of day and night explain to us what is the meaning of dividing the light from the darkness. It is the separation of the one from the other, and the orderly distribution of each over the different parts of the earth's surface in the course of a night and a day. This could only be effected in the space of a diurnal revolution of the earth on its axis. Accordingly, if light were radiated from a particular region in the sky, and thus separated from darkness at a certain meridian, while the earth performed its daily round, the successive changes of evening, night, morning, day, would naturally present themselves in slow and stately progress during that first great act of creation.

Thus we have evidence that the diurnal revolution of the earth took place on the first day of the last creation. We are not told whether it occurred before that time. If ever there was a time when the earth did not revolve, or revolved on a different axis or according to a different law from the present, the first revolution or change of revolution must have produced a vast change in the face of things, the marks of which would remain to this day, whether the impulse was communicated to the solid mass alone, or simultaneously to all the loose matter resting on its surface. But the text gives no intimation of such a change.

At present, however, let us recollect we have only to do with the land known to antediluvian man, and the coming of light into existence over that region, according to the existing arrangement of day and night. How far the breaking forth of the light may have extended beyond the land known to the writer, the present narrative does not enable us to determine.

We are now prepared to conclude that the entrance of light into this darkened region was effected by such a change in its position or in its superincumbent atmosphere as allowed the interchange of night and day to become discernible, while at the same time so much obscurity still remained as to exclude the heavenly bodies from view. We have learned from the first verse that these heavenly orbs were already created. The luminous element that plays so conspicuous and essential a part in the process of nature, must have formed a part of that original creation. The removal of darkness, therefore, from the locality mentioned, is merely owing to a new adjustment by which the preëxistent light was made to visit the surface of the abyss with its cheering and enlivening beams.

In this case, indeed, the real change is effected, not in the light itself, but in the intervening medium which was impervious to its rays. But it is to be remembered, on the other hand, that the actual result of the divine interposition is still the diffusion of light over the face of the watery deep, and that the actual phenomena of the change, as they would strike an onlooker, and not the invisible springs of the six days' creation, are described in the chapter before us.

Then was evening, then was morning, day one. The last clause of the verse is a resumption of the whole process of time during this first work of creation. This is accordingly a simple and striking example of two lines of narrative parallel to each other and exactly coinciding in respect of time. In general we find the one line overlapping only a part of the other.

The day is described, according to the Hebrew mode of narrative, by its starting-point, "the evening." The first half of its course is run out during the night. The next half in like manner commences with "the morning," and goes through its round in the proper day. Then the whole period is described as "one day." The point of termination for the day is thus the evening again, which agrees with the Hebrew division of time (Lev. xxiii. 32).

To make "the evening" here the end of the first day, and so "the morning" the end of the first night, as is done by some interpreters, is therefore equally inconsistent with the grammar of the Hebrews and with their mode of reckoning time. It also defines the diurnal period, by noting first its middle point and then its termination, which does not seem to be natural. It further defines the period of sunshine, or the day proper, by "the evening," and the night by the morning; a proceeding equally unnatural. It has not even the advantage of making the event of the latter clause subsequent to that of the former. For the day of twenty-four hours is wholly spent in dividing the light from the darkness; and the self-same day is described again in this clause, take it how we will. This interpretation of the clause is therefore to be rejected.

The days of this creation are natural days of twenty-four hours each. We may not depart from the ordinary meaning of the word without a sufficient warrant either in the text of Scripture or in the law of nature. But we have not yet found any such warrant. Only necessity can force us to such an expedient. Scripture, on the other hand, warrants us in retaining the common meaning by yielding no hint of another, and by introducing "evening, night, morning, day," as its ordinary divisions. Nature favors the same interpretation. All geological changes are of course subsequent to the great event recorded in the first verse, which is the beginning of things. All such changes, except the one recorded in the six days' creation, are with equal certainty antecedent to the state of things described in the second verse. Hence no lengthened period is required for this last creative interposition.

"Day one" is here used for the first day, the cardinal one being not usually employed for the ordinal in Hebrew (Gen. viii. 13; Exod. xl. 2). It cannot indicate any emphasis or singularity in the day, as it is in no respect different from the other days of creation. It implies that the two parts before mentioned make up one day. But this is equally implied by all the ordinals on the other days.

This day is in many ways interesting to us. It is the first day of the last creation; it is the first day of the week; it is the day of the resurrection of the Messiah; and it has become the Christian Sabbath.

The first five verses form the first parashah or section of the Hebrew text. If this division come from the author, it indicates that he regarded the first day's work as the body of the narrative, and the creation of the universe, in the first verse, and the condition of the earth, in the second, as mere preliminaries to introduce and elucidate his main statement. If, on the contrary, it proceed from some transcriber of a subsequent period, it may indicate that he considered the creative work of the first day to consist of two parts,—first, an absolute creation; and, second, a supplementary act, by which the primary universe was first enlightened.

IV. THE SECOND DAY.—Gen. i. 6–8.

6. רָקִיעַ *expanse;* στερέωμα, רָקַע *spread out* by beating, as leaf gold. This expanse was not understood to be solid, as the fowl is said to fly on the face of it (Gen. i. 21). It is also described as luminous (Dan. xii. 3), and as a monument of divine power (Ps. cl. 1).

7. עָשָׂה *work* on, *make* out of already existing materials.

6. Then said God, Let there be an expanse in the midst of the water, and let it be dividing between water to water. 7. Then made God the expanse, and divided between the water which was from above to the expanse, and between the water which was from beneath to the expanse: and it was so. 8. Then called God to the expanse, heaven: then was evening, then was morning, day second. ¶ 2.

The second act of creative power bears upon the deep of waters, over which the darkness had prevailed, and by which the solid crust was still overlaid. This mass of turbid and noisy water must be reduced to order, and confined within certain limits, before the land can be reached. According to the laws of material nature, light or heat must be an essential factor in all physical changes, especially in the production of gases and vapors. Hence its presence and activity are the first thing required in instituting a new process of nature. Air naturally takes the next place, as it is equally essential to the maintenance of vegetable and animal life. Hence its adjustment is the second step in this latest effort of creation.

6. *Let there be an expanse in the midst of the water.* For this purpose God now calls into existence the expanse. This is that interval of space between the earth on the one side and the birds on the wing, the clouds and the heavenly bodies on the other, the lower part of which we know to be occupied by the air. This will appear more clearly from a comparison of other passages in this chapter (Gen. 1. 14, 20).

And let it be dividing between water and water. It appears that the water in a liquid state was in contact with another mass of water, in the shape of dense fogs and vapors; not merely overhanging, but actually resting on the waters beneath. The object of the expanse is to divide the waters which are under it from those which are above it. Hence it appears that the thing really done is, not to create the space that extends indefinitely above our heads (which, being in itself no thing, but only room for things, requires no creating), but to establish in it the intended disposition of the waters in two separate masses, the one above, and the other below the intervening expanse. This we know is effected by means of the atmosphere, which receives a large body of water in the state of vapor, and bears up a visible portion of it in the form of clouds. These ever-returning and ever-varying piles of mist strike the eye of the unsophisticated spectator; and when the dew is observed on the grass, or the showers of rain, hail, and snow are seen falling on the ground, the conclusion is obvious, that above the expanse, be the distance small or great, is laid up an unseen and inexhaustible treasury of water, by which the earth may be perpetually bedewed and irrigated. The aqueous vapor is itself, as well as the element with which it is mingled, invisible and impalpable; but when condensed by cold it becomes apparent to the eye in the form of mists and clouds, and, at a certain point of coolness, begins to deposit itself in the palpable form of dew, rain, hail, or snow. As soon as it becomes obvious to the sense it receives distinguishing names, according to its varying forms. But the air being invisible, is unnoticed by the primitive observer until it is put in motion, when it receives the name of wind. The space it occupies is merely denominated the expanse; that is, the interval between us and the various bodies that float above and hang upon nothing, or nothing perceptible to the eye.

The state of things before this creative movement may be called one of disturbance and disorder, in comparison with the present condition of the atmosphere. This disturbance in the relations of air and water was so great that it could not be reduced to the present order without a supernatural cause. Whether any other gases, noxious or innocuous, entered into the constitution of the previous atmosphere, or whether any other ingredients were once held in solution by the watery deep, we are not informed. Whether any volcanic or plutonic violence had disturbed the scene, and raised a dense mass of gaseous damp and fuliginous matter into the airy region, is not stated. How far the disorder extended we cannot tell. We are merely certain that it reached over all the land known to man during the interval between this creation and the deluge. Whether this disorder was temporary or of long standing, and whether the change was effected by altering the axis of the earth's rotation, and thereby the climate of the land of primeval man, or by a less extensive movement confined to the region under consideration, are questions on which we receive no instruction, because the solution does not concern our well-being. As soon as human welfare comes to be in any way connected with such knowledge, it will by some means be made attainable.

The introduction of the expanse produced a vast change for the better on the surface of the earth. The heavy mass of murky damp and aqueous steam commingling with the abyss of waters beneath is cleared away. The fogs are lifted up to the higher regions of the sky, or attenuated into an invisible vapor. A leaden mass of clouds still overshadows the heavens. But a breathing space of pure pellucid air now intervenes between the upper and lower waters, enveloping the surface of the earth, and fitted for the respiration of the flora and fauna of a new world.

Let it be noted that the word *be* is here again employed to denote the commencement of a new adjustment of the atmosphere. This, accordingly, does not imply the absolute creation on the second day of our present atmosphere: it merely indicates the constitution of it out of the materials already at hand, — the selecting and due apportionment of the proper elements; the relegation of all now foreign elements to their own places; the dissipation of the lazy, deadening damps, and the establishment of a clear and pure air fit for the use of the future man. Any or all of these alterations will satisfy the form of expression here adopted.

7. *Then made God the expanse.* Here the distinction between command and execution is made still more prominent than in the third verse. For the word of command stands in one verse, and the effect realized is related in the next. Nay, we have the doing of the thing and the thing done separately expressed. For, after stating that God made the expanse, it is added, "and it was so." The work accomplished took a permanent form, in which it remained a standing monument of divine wisdom and power.

8. *Then called God to the expanse, heaven.* This expanse is, then, the proper and original skies. We have here an interesting and instructive example of the way in which words expand in their significance from the near, the simple, the obvious, to the far and wide, the complex and the inferential. The heaven, in the first instance, meant the open space above the surface in which we breathe and move, in which the birds fly and the clouds float. This is the atmosphere. Then it stretches away into the seemingly boundless regions of space, in which the countless orbs of luminous and of opaque surfaces circumambulate. Then the heavens come to signify the contents of this indefinitely augmented expanse, — the celestial luminaries themselves. Then, by a still further enlargement of its meaning, we rise to the heaven of heavens, the inexpressibly grand and august presence-chamber of the Most High, where the cherubim and seraphim, the innumerable company of angels, the myriads of saints, move in their several grades and spheres, keeping the charge of their Maker, and realizing the joy of their being. This is the third heaven (2 Cor. xii. 2) to the conception of which the imaginative capacity of the human mind rises by an easy gradation. Having once attained to this majestic conception, man is so far prepared to conceive and compose that sublime sentence with which the book of God opens, — "In the beginning God created *the heavens* and the earth."

The expanse, or aerial space, in which this arrangement of things has been effected, having received its appropriate name, is recognized as an accomplished fact, and the second day is closed.

V. THE THIRD DAY. — Gen. i. 9-13.

9. קָוָה *turn, bind, gather, expect.*
יַבָּשָׁה *the dry, the ground.* יָבֵשׁ *be dry.* בּוֹשׁ *be abashed.*
11. דֶּשֶׁא *green thing, grass.*
עֵשֶׂב *herb.*
זֶרַע *seed.* זָרַע *sow,* sero.
פְּרִי *fruit.* פָּרָה *bear,* fero, φέρω.

9. Then said God, Gathered be the water from under the skies unto one place, and let the ground appear: and it was so. 10. Then called God to the ground, land; and to the gathering of the water called he seas: then saw God that it was good.

11. Then said God, Grow let the land grass, herb yielding seed, fruit tree bearing fruit after its kind, in which is its seed, upon the land: and it was so. 12. Then brought the land forth grass, herb yielding seed after its kind, and tree bearing fruit, in which was its seed after its kind: then saw God that it was good. 13. Then was evening, then was morning, day third. ¶ 3.

The work of creation on this day is evidently twofold, — the distribution of land and water, and the creation of plants. The former part of it is completed, named, reviewed, and approved before the latter is commenced. All that has been done before this, indeed, is preparatory to the introduction of the vegetable kingdom. This may be regarded as the first stage of the present creative process.

9. *Let the water be gathered to one place; let the ground appear.* This refers to the yet overflowing deep of waters (v. 2) under the expanse. They must be confined within certain limits. For this purpose the order is issued, that they be gathered into one place; that is, evidently, into a place apart from that designed for the land.

10. *Then called God to the ground, land.* We use the word *ground* to denote the dry surface left after the retreat of the waters. To this the Creator applies the term אֶרֶץ *land, earth.* Hence we find that the primitive meaning of this term was land, the dry solid surface

of matter on which we stand. This meaning it still retains in all its various applications (see on v. 2). As it was soon learned by experience that the solid ground was continuous at the bottom of the water-masses, and that these were a mere superficial deposit gathering into the hollows, the term was, by an easy extension of its meaning, applied to the whole surface, as it was diversified by land and water. Our word *earth* is the term to express it in this more extended sense. In this sense it was the meet counterpart of the heavens in that complex phrase by which the universe of things is expressed.

And to the gathering of the waters called he seas. In contradistinction to the land, the gathered waters are called seas; a term applied in Scripture to any large collection of water, even though seen to be surrounded by land; as, the salt sea, the sea of Kinnereth, the sea of the plain or valley, the fore sea, the hinder sea (Gen. xiv. 3; Num. xxxiv. 11; Deut. iv. 49; Joel ii. 20; Deut. xi. 24). The plural form "seas" shows that the "one place" consists of several basins, all of which taken together are called the place of the waters.

The Scripture, according to its manner, notices only the palpable result; namely, a diversified scene of "land" and "seas." The sacred singer possibly hints at the process in Ps. civ. 6–8: "The deep as a garment thou didst spread over it; above the mountains stood the waters. At thy rebuke they fled; at the voice of thy thunder they hasted away. They go up the mountains; they go down the valleys; unto the place that thou hast founded for them." This description is highly poetical, and therefore true to nature. The *hills* are to rise out of the waters above them. The agitated waters dash up the stirring mountains, but, as these ascend, at length sink into the valleys, and take the place allotted for them. Plainly the result was accomplished by lowering some and elevating other parts of the solid ground. Over this inequality of surface, the waters, which before overspread the whole ground, flowed into the hollows, and the elevated regions became dry land. This is a kind of geological change which has been long known to the students of nature. Such changes have often been sudden and violent. Alterations of level, of a gradual character, are known to be going on at all times.

This disposition of land and water prepares for the second step, which is the main work of this day; namely, the creation of plants. We are now come to the removal of another defect in the state of the earth, mentioned in the second verse,—its deformity, or rude and uncouth appearance.

11. *Let the land grow.* The plants are said to be products of the land, because they spring from the dry ground, and a margin round it where the water is so shallow as to permit the light and heat to reach the bottom. The land is said to grow or bring forth plants; not because it is endowed with any inherent power to generate plants, but because it is the element in which they are to take root, and from which they are to spring forth.

Grass, herb yielding seed, fruit tree bearing fruit. The plants now created are divided into three classes,— grass, herb, and tree. In the first, the seed is not noticed, as not obvious to the eye; in the second, the seed is the striking characteristic; in the third, the fruit, "in which is its seed," in which the seed is enclosed, forms the distinguishing mark. This division is simple and natural. It proceeds upon two concurrent marks, — the structure and the seed. In the first, the green leaf or blade is prominent; in the second, the stalk; in the third, the woody texture. In the first, the seed is not conspicuous; in the second, it is conspicuous; in the third, it is enclosed in a fruit which is conspicuous. This division corresponds with certain classes in our present systems of botany. But it is much less complex than any of them, and is founded upon obvious characteristics. The plants that are on the margin of these great divisions may be arranged conveniently enough under one or another of them, according to their several orders or species.

After its kind. This phrase intimates that like produces like, and therefore that the "kinds" or species are fixed, and do not run into one another. In this little phrase the theory of one species being developed from another is denied.

12. Here the fulfilment of the divine command is detailed, after being summed up in the words "it was so," at the close of the previous verse. This seems to arise from the nature of growth, which has a commencement, indeed, but goes on without ceasing in a progressive development. It appears from the text that the full plants, and not the seeds, germs, or roots, were created. The land sent forth grass, herb, tree, each in its fully developed form. This was absolutely necessary, if man and the land animals were to be sustained by grasses, seeds, and fruits.

Thus the land begins to assume the form of beauty and fertility. Its bare and rough soil is set with the germs of an incipient verdure. It has already ceased to be "a waste." And now, at the end of this third day, let us pause to review the natural order in which everything has been thus far done. It was necessary to produce light in the first place, because without this potent element water could not pass into vapor, and rise on the wings of the buoyant air into the region above the expanse. The atmosphere must in the next place be reduced to order, and charged with its treasures of vapor, before the plants could commence the process of growth, even though stimulated by the influence of light and heat. Again, the waters must be withdrawn from a portion of the solid surface before the plants could be placed in the ground, so as to have the full benefit of the light, air, and vapor in enabling them to draw from the soil the sap by which they are to be nourished. When all these conditions are fulfilled, then the plants themselves are called into existence, and the first cycle of the new creation is completed.

Could not the Eternal have accomplished all this in one day? Doubtless he might. He might have effected it all in an instant of time. And he might have compressed the growth and development of centuries into a moment. He might even by possibility have constructed the stratifications of the earth's crust with all their slips, elevations, depressions, unconformities, and organic formations in a day. And, lastly, he might have carried on to completion all the evolutions of universal nature that have since taken place or will hereafter take place till the last hour has struck on the clock of time. But what then? What purpose would have been served by all this speed? It is obvious that the above and such like questions are not wisely put. The very nature of the ETERNAL shows the futility of such speculations. Is the commodity of time so scarce with him that he must or should for any good reason sum up the course of a universe of things in an infinitesimal portion of its duration? May we not, rather, must we not, soberly conclude that there is a due proportion between the action and the time of the action, the creation to be developed and the time of development. Both the beginning and the process of this latest creation are to a nicety adjusted to the preëxistent and concurrent state of things. And the development of that which is created not only displays a mutual harmony and exact coincidence in the progress of all its other parts, but is at the same time finely adapted to the constitution of man, and the natural, safe, and healthy ratio of his physical and metaphysical movements.

VI. THE FOURTH DAY.—Gen. i. 14–19.

14. מָאוֹר *a light, luminary,* centre of radiant light.
מוֹעֵד *set time, season.*

Words beginning with a formative מ usually signify that in which the simple quality resides or is realized. Hence they often denote place.

17. נָתַן *give, hold out, show.* תן *stretch, hold out.* Tendo, teneo, τείνω.

14. Then said God, Let there be lights in the expanse of the heavens, to divide between the day and between the night; and let them have been for signs and for seasons, and for days and years. 15. And let them have been for lights in the expanse of the heavens, to shine upon the earth: and it was so. 16. Then made God the two great lights, the great light to rule the day, the little light to rule the night, and the stars. 17. Then gave them God in the expanse of the heavens, to shine upon the earth. 18. And to rule over the day and over the night, and to divide between the light and between the darkness: then saw God that it was good. 19. Then was evening, then was morning, day fourth. ¶ 4.

The darkness has been removed from the face of the deep, its waters have been distributed in due proportions above and below the expanse; the lower waters have retired and given place to the emerging land, and the wasteness of the land thus exposed to view has begun to be adorned with the living forms of a new vegetation. It only remains to remove the "void" by peopling this now fair and fertile world with the animal kingdom. For this purpose the Great Designer begins a new cycle of supernatural operations.

14, 15. *Lights.* The work of the fourth day has much in common with that of the first, which, indeed it continues and completes. Both deal with light, and with dividing between light and darkness, or day and night. *Let there be.* They agree also in choosing the word *be*, to express the nature of the operation which is here performed. But the fourth day advances on the first. It brings into view the luminaries, the light radiators, the source, while the first only indicated the stream. It contemplates the far expanse, while the first regards only the near.

For signs and for seasons, and for days and years. While the first day refers only to the day and its twofold division, the fourth refers to signs, seasons, days, and years. These lights are for "signs." They are to serve as the great natural chronometer of man, having its three units, — the day, the month, and the year, — and marking the divisions of time, not only for agricultural and social purposes, but also for meeting out the eras of human history and the cycles of natural science. They are signs of place as well as of time, — topometers, if we may use the term. By them the mariner has learned to mark the latitude and longitude of his ship, and the astronomer to determine with any assignable degree of precision the place as well as the time of the planetary orbs of heaven. The "seasons" are the natural seasons of the year, and the set times for civil and sacred purposes which man has attached to special days and years in the revolution of time.

As the word "day" is a key to the explanation of the first day's work, so is the word "year" to the interpretation of that of the fourth. As the cause of the distinction of day and night is the diurnal rotation of the earth on its axis in conjunction with a fixed source of light, which streamed in on the scene of creation as soon as the natural hinderance was removed, so the vicissitudes of the year are owing, along with these two conditions, to the annual revolution of the earth in its orbit round the sun, together with the obliquity of the ecliptic. To the phenomena so occasioned are to be added incidental variations arising from the revolution of the moon round the earth, and the small modifications caused by the various other bodies of the solar system. All these celestial phenomena come out from the artless simplicity of the sacred narrative as observable facts on the fourth day of that new creation. From the beginning of the solar system the earth must, from the nature of things, have revolved around the sun. But whether the rate of velocity was ever changed, or the obliquity of the ecliptic was now commenced or altered, we do not learn from this record.

15. *To shine upon the earth.* The first day spreads the shaded gleam of light over the face of the deep. The fourth day unfolds to the eye the lamps of heaven, hanging in the expanse of the skies, and assigns to them the office of "shining upon the earth." A threefold function is thus attributed to the celestial orbs, — to divide day from night, to define time and place, and to shine on the earth. The word

of command is here very full, running over two verses, with the exception of the little clause, "and it was so," stating the result.

16–19. This result is fully particularized in the next three verses. *Made.* This word corresponds to the word "be" in the command, and indicates the disposition and adjustment to a special purpose of things previously existing. *The two great lights.* The well known ones, great in relation to the stars, as seen from the earth. *The great light,* in comparison with the *little* light. *The stars,* from man's point of view, are insignificant, except in regard to number (Gen. xv. 5). 17. *God gave them.* The *absolute* giving of the heavenly bodies in their places was performed at the time of their actual creation. The *relative* giving here spoken of is that which would appear to an earthly spectator, when the intervening veil of clouds would be dissolved by the divine agency, and the celestial luminaries would stand forth in all their dazzling splendor. 18. *To rule.* From their lofty eminence they regulate the duration and the business of each period. The whole is inspected and approved as before.

Now let it be remembered that the *heavens* were created at the absolute beginning of things recorded in the first verse, and that they included all other things except the earth. Hence, according to this document, the sun, moon, and stars were in existence simultaneously with our planet. This gives simplicity and order to the whole narrative. *Light* comes before us on the first and on the fourth day. Now, as two distinct causes of a common effect would be unphilosophical and unnecessary, we must hold the one cause to have been in existence on these two days. But we have seen that the one cause of the day and of the year is a fixed source of radiating light in the sky, combined with the diurnal and annual motions of the earth. Thus the recorded preëxistence of the celestial orbs is consonant with the presumptions of reason. The "making" or reconstitution of the atmosphere admits their light so far that the alternations of day and night can be discerned. The *making* of the lights of heaven, or the display of them in a serene sky by the withdrawal of that opaque canopy of clouds that still enveloped the dome above, is then the work of the fourth day.

All is now plain and intelligible. The heavenly bodies become the lights of the earth, and the distinguishers not only of day and night, but of seasons and years, of times and places. They shed forth their unveiled glories and salutary potencies on the budding, waiting land. How the higher grade of transparency in the aerial region was effected, we cannot tell; and, therefore, we are not prepared to explain why it is accomplished on the fourth day, and not sooner. But from its very position in time, we are led to conclude that the constitution of the expanse, the elevation of a portion of the waters of the deep in the form of vapor, the collection of the subaerial water into seas, and the creation of plants out of the reeking soil, must all have had an essential part, both in retarding till the fourth day, and in then bringing about the dispersion of the clouds and the clearing of the atmosphere. Whatever remained of hinderance to the outshining of the sun, moon, and stars on the land in all their native splendor, was on this day removed by the word of divine power.

Now is the proximate cause of day and night made palpable to the observation. Now are the heavenly bodies made to be signs of time and place to the intelligent spectator on the earth, to regulate seasons, days, months, and years, and to be the luminaries of the world. Now, manifestly, the greater light rules the day, as the lesser does the night. The Creator has withdrawn the curtain, and set forth the hitherto undistinguishable brilliants of space for the illumination of the land and the regulation of the changes which diversify its surface. This bright display, even if it could have been effected on the first day with due regard to the forces of nature already in operation, was unnecessary to the unseeing and unmoving world of vegetation, while it was plainly requisite for the seeing, choosing, and moving world of animated nature which was about to be called into existence on the following days.

The terms employed for the objects here brought forward, — "lights, the great light, the little light, the stars;" for the mode of their manifestation, "be, make, give;" and for the offices they discharge, "divide, rule, shine, be for signs, seasons, days, years," — exemplify the admirable simplicity of Scripture, and the exact adaptation of its style to the unsophisticated mind of primeval man. We have no longer, indeed, the naming of the various objects, as on the former days; probably because it would no longer be an important source of information for the elucidation of the narrative. But we have more than an equivalent for this in variety of phrase. The several words have been already noticed: it only remains to make some general remarks.

(1.) The sacred writer notes only obvious results, such as come before the eye of the observer, and leaves the secondary causes, their modes of operation, and their less obtrusive effects, to scientific inquiry. The progress of observation is from the foreground to the background of nature, from the physical to the metaphysical, and from the objective to the subjective. Among the senses, too, the eye is the most prominent observer in the scenes of the six days. Hence the "lights," they "shine," they are for "signs" and "days," which are in the first instance objects of vision. They are "given," held or shown forth in the heavens. Even "rule" has probably the primitive meaning *to be over.* Starting thus with the visible and the tangible, the Scripture in its successive communications advance with us to the inferential, the intuitive, the moral, the spiritual, the divine.

(2.) The sacred writer also touches merely the heads of things in these scenes of creation, without condescending to minute particulars or intending to be exhaustive. Hence many actual incidents and intricacies of these days are left to the well-regulated imagination and sober judgment of the reader. To instance such omissions, the moon is as much of her time above the horizon during the day as during the night. But she is not then the conspicuous object in the scene, or the full-orbed reflector of the solar beams, as she is during the night. Here the better part is used to mark the whole. The tidal influence of the great lights, in which the moon plays the chief part, is also unnoticed. Hence we are to expect very many phenomena to be altogether omitted, though interesting and important in themselves, because they do not come within the present scope of the narrative.

(3.) The point from which the writer views the scene is never to be forgotten, if we would understand these ancient records. He stands on earth. He uses his eyes as the organ of observation. He knows nothing of the visual angle, of visible as distinguishable from tangible magnitude, of relative in comparison with absolute motion on the grand scale: he speaks the simple language of the eye. Hence his earth is the meet counterpart of the heavens. His sun and moon are great, and all the stars are a very little thing. Light comes to be, to him, when it reaches the eye. The luminaries are held forth in the heavens, when the mist between them and the eye is dissolved.

(4.) Yet, though not trained to scientific thought or speech, this author has the eye of reason open as well as that of sense. It is not with him the science of the tangible, but the philosophy of the intuitive, that reduces things to their proper dimensions. He traces not the secondary cause, but ascends at one glance to the great first cause, the manifest act and audible behest of the Eternal Spirit. This imparts a sacred dignity to his style, and a transcendent grandeur to his conceptions. In the presence of the high and lofty One that inhabiteth eternity, all things terrestrial and celestial are reduced to a common level. Man in intelligent relation with God comes forth as the chief figure on the scene of terrestrial creation. The narrative takes its commanding position as the history of the ways of God with man. The commonest primary facts of ordinary observation, when recorded in this book, assume a supreme interest as the monuments of eternal wisdom and the heralds of the finest and broadest generalizations of a consecrated science. The very words are instinct with a germinant philosophy, and prove themselves adequate to the expression of the loftiest speculations of the eloquent mind.

VII. THE FIFTH DAY. — Gen. i. 20-23.

20. שָׁרַץ *crawl, teem, swarm, abound.* An intransitive verb, admitting, however, an objective noun of its own or a like signification.

נֶפֶשׁ *breath, soul, self.* This noun is derived from a root signifying to breathe. Its concrete meaning is, therefore, *that which breathes,* and consequently has a body, without which there can be no breathing; hence, *a breathing body,* and even a body that once had breath (Num. vi. 6). As breath is the accompaniment and sign of life, it comes to denote *life,* and hence, a living body, *an animal.* And as life properly signifies animal life, and is therefore essentially connected with feeling, appetite, thought, נֶפֶשׁ, denotes also these qualities, and that which possesses them. It is obvious that it denotes the vital principle not only in man but in the brute. It is therefore a more comprehensive word than our *soul,* as commonly understood.

21. תַּנִּין *long creature,* a comprehensive genus, including vast fishes, serpents, dragons, crocodiles; r. *stretch.*

22. בָּרַךְ *break, kneel; bless.*

20. Then said God, Let the waters abound with the crawler that has breath and life, and let fowl fly above the earth, upon the face of the expanse of the skies. 21. Then created God the great fishes and every living breathing thing that creepeth, with which the waters abounded after their kind, and every bird of wing after its kind: then saw God that it was good. 22. Then blessed them God, saying, Be fruitful, and multiply, and fill the waters in the seas, and let the fowl multiply in the land. 23. Then was evening, then was morning, day fifth. ¶ 5

The solitude (בֹּהוּ), the last and greatest defect in the state of the earth, is now to be removed by the creation of the various animals that are to inhabit it and partake of its vegetable productions.

On the second day the Creator was occupied with the task of reducing the air and water to a habitable state. And now on the corresponding day of the second three he calls into existence the inhabitants of these two elements. Accordingly the animal kingdom is divided into three parts in reference to the regions to be inhabited, — fishes, birds, and land animals. The fishes and birds are created on this day. The fishes seem to be regarded as the lowest type of living creatures.

They are here subdivided only into the monsters of the deep and the smaller species that swarm in the waters.

20. *The crawler* (שֶׁרֶץ) includes apparently all animals that have short or no legs, and are therefore unable to raise themselves above the soil. The aquatic and most amphibious animals come under this class. *The crawler of living breath*, having breath, motion, and sensation, the ordinary indications of animal life. *Abound with.* As in the 11th verse we have, Let the earth grow grass (תַּדְשֵׁא דֶּשֶׁא), so here we have, Let the waters crawl with the crawler (יִשְׁרְצוּ שֶׁרֶץ) ; the verb and noun having the same root. The waters are here not the cause but the element of the fish, as the air of the fowl. *Fowl*, every thing that has wings. *The face of the expanse.* The expanse is here proved to be aerial or spatial ; not solid, as the fowl can fly on it.

21. *Created.* Here the author uses this word for the second time. In the selection of different words to express the divine operation, two considerations seem to have guided the author's pen, — variety and propriety of diction. The diversity of words appears to indicate a diversity in the mode of exercising the divine power. On the first day (v. 3) a new admission of light into a darkened region, by the partial rarefaction of the intervening medium, is expressed by the word " be." This may denote that which already existed, but not in that place. On the second day (v. 6, 7) a new disposition of the air and the water is described by the verbs " be " and " make." These indicate a modification of that which already existed. On the third day (v. 9, 11) no verb is directly applied to the act of divine power. This agency is thus understood, while the natural changes following are expressly noticed. In the fourth (v. 14, 16, 17) the words " be," " make," and " give " occur, where the matter in hand is the manifestation of the heavenly bodies and their adaptation to the use of man. In these cases it is evident that the word " create " would have been only im-

properly or indirectly applicable to the action of the Eternal Being. Here it is employed with propriety; as the animal world is something new and distinct summoned into existence. It is manifest from this review that variety of expression has resulted from attention to propriety.

Great fishes. Monstrous crawlers that wriggle through the water or scud along the banks. *Every living, breathing thing that creeps.* The smaller animals of the water and its banks. *Bird of wing.* Here the wing is made characteristic of the class, which extends beyond what we call birds. The Maker inspects and approves his work.

22. *Blessed them.* We are brought into a new sphere of creation on this day, and we meet with a new act of the Almighty. To bless is to wish, and, in the case of God, to will some good to the object of the blessing. The blessing here pronounced upon the fish and the fowl is that of abundant increase. *Bear.* This refers to the propagation of the species. *Multiply.* This notifies the abundance of the offspring. *Fill the waters.* Let them be fully stocked. *In the seas.* The sea of Scripture includes the lake, and, by parity of reason, the rivers, which are the feeders of both. This blessing seems to indicate that, whereas in the case of some plants many individuals of the same species were simultaneously created, so as to produce a universal covering of verdure for the land and an abundant supply of aliment for the animals about to be created, — in regard to these animals a single pair only, at all events of the larger kinds, was at first called into being, from which, by the potent blessing of the Creator, was propagated the multitude by which the waters and the air were peopled.

VIII. THE SIXTH DAY. — Gen. i. 24–31.

24. בְּהֵמָה *cattle, dumb, tame beasts.*

רֶמֶשׂ *creeping, small or low animals.*

חַיָּה *living thing, animal.*

חַיַּת־הָאָרֶץ *wild beast.*

26. אָדָם *man, mankind; r. be red.* A collective noun, having no plural number, and therefore denoting either an individual of the kind, or the kind or race itself. It is connected in etymology with אֲדָמָה *the red soil,* from which the human body was formed (Gen. ii. 7). It therefore marks the earthly aspect of man.

צֶלֶם *shade, image,* in visible outline.

דְּמוּת *likeness,* in any quality.

רָדָה *tread, rule.*

24. Then said God, Let the land bring forth living breathing thing after its kind, cattle, and creeper, and beast of the land after its kind: and it was so. 25. Then made God the beast of the land after its kind, and the cattle after their kind, and every creeper of the soil after its kind: then saw God that it was good.

26. Then said God, Let us make man in our image after our likeness: and let them rule over the fish of the sea, and over the fowl of the skies, and over the cattle, and over all the land, and over every creeper that creepeth upon the land.
27. Then created God the man in his image: in the image of God created he him: male and female created he them. 28.
Then blessed them God, and said unto them God, Be fruitful, and multiply, and fill the land, and subdue it; and rule over the fish of the sea, and over the fowl of the skies, and over every living thing that creepeth upon the land. 29. Then
said God, Lo, I have given you every herb yielding seed, which is upon the face of all the land, and every tree, in which is the fruit of a tree yielding seed: to you shall it be for food. 30.
And to every beast of the land, and to every fowl of the skies, and to every thing that creepeth upon the land, wherein is living breath, every green herb for food: and it was so. 31.
Then saw God everything that he had made, and lo, it was very good. Then was evening, then was morning, day the sixth. ¶ 6.

This day corresponds with the third. In both the land is the sphere of operation. In both are performed two acts of creative power. In the third the land was clothed with vegetation: in the sixth it is peopled with the animal kingdom. First, the lower animals are called into being, and then, to crown all, man.

24, 25. This branch of the animal world is divided into three parts. "Living breathing thing" is the general head under which all these are comprised. "Cattle" denotes the animals that dwell with man, especially those that bear burdens. The same term in the original, when there is no contrast, when in the plural number or with the specification of "the land," the "field," is used of wild beasts. "Creeping things" evidently denote the smaller animals, from which the cattle are distinguished as the large. The quality of creeping is, however, applied sometimes to denote the motion of the lower animals with the body in a prostrate posture, in opposition to the erect posture of man (Ps. civ. 20). The "beast of the land" or the field signifies the wild rapacious animal that lives apart from man. The word חַיָּה *beast* or *animal*, is the general term employed in these verses for the whole animal kind. It signifies wild animal with certainty only when it is accompanied by the qualifying term "land" or "field," or the epithet "evil" (רָעָה). From this division it appears that animals that prey on others were included in this latest creation. This is an extension of that law by which the organic living substances of the vegetable kingdom form the sustenance of the animal species. 25. The execution of the divine mandate is then recorded, and the result inspected and approved.

26, 27. Here we evidently enter upon a higher scale of being. This is indicated by the counsel or common resolve to create, which is now for the first time introduced into the narrative. When the Creator says, "Let us make man," he calls attention to the work as one of preëminent importance. At the same time he sets it before himself as a thing undertaken with deliberate purpose. Moreover, in the former mandates of creation his words had regard to the thing itself that was summoned into being; as, "Let there be *light;*" or to some preëxistent object that was physically connected with the new creature; as, "Let the *land* bring forth grass." But now the language of the fiat of creation ascends to the Creator himself: Let US make man. This intimates that the new being in its higher nature is associated not so much with any part of creation as with the Eternal Uncreated himself.

The plural form of the sentence raises the question, With whom took he counsel on this occasion? Was it with himself, and does he here simply use the plural of majesty? Such was not the usual style of monarchs in the ancient East. Pharaoh says, "*I* have dreamed a dream" (Gen. xli. 15). Nebuchadnezzar, "*I* have dreamed" (Dan. ii. 3). Darius the Mede, "*I* make a decree" (Dan. vi. 26). Cyrus, "The Lord God of heaven hath given *me* all the kingdoms of the earth" (Ezra i. 2). Darius, "*I* make a decree" (Ezra vi. 8). We have no ground, therefore, for transferring it to the style of the heavenly King. Was it with certain other intelligent beings in existence before man that he took counsel? This supposition cannot be admitted; because the expression "let us *make*" is an invitation *to create*, which is an incommunicable attribute of the Eternal One, and because the phrases, "our image, our likeness," when transferred into the third person of narrative, become "*his* image, the image *of God*," and thus limit the pronouns to God himself. Does the plurality, then, point to a plurality of attributes in the divine nature? This cannot be, because a plurality of qualities exists in everything, without at all leading to the application of the plural number to the individual, and because such a plurality does not warrant the expression, "let *us* make." Only a plurality of persons can justify the phrase. Hence we are forced to conclude that the plural pronoun indicates a plurality of persons or hypostases in the Divine Being. (See p. 27.)

26. *Man.* Man is a new species, essentially different from all other kinds on earth. *In our image, after our likeness.* He is to be allied to heaven as no other creature on earth is. He is to be related to the Eternal Being himself. This relation, however, is to be not in matter, but in form; not in essence, but in semblance. This precludes all pantheistic notions of the origin of man. "Image" is a word taken from sensible things, and denotes likeness in outward form, while the material may be different. "Likeness" is a more general term, indicating resemblance in any quality, external or internal. It is here explanatory of image, and seems to show that this term is to be taken in a figurative sense, to denote not a material but a spiritual conformity to God. The Eternal Being is essentially self-manifesting. The appearance he presents to an eye fitted to contemplate him is his image. The union of attributes which constitute his spiritual nature is his character or likeness.

We gather from the present chapter that God is a spirit (Gen. i. 2), that he thinks, speaks, wills, and acts (Gen. i. 3, 4, etc.). Here, then, are the great points of conformity to God in man, namely, reason, speech, will, and power. By reason we apprehend concrete things in perception and consciousness, and cognize abstract truth, both metaphysical and moral. By speech we make certain easy and sensible acts of our own the signs of the various objects of our contemplative faculties to ourselves and others. By will we choose, determine, and resolve upon what is to be done. By power we act, either in giving expression to our concepts in words, or effect to our determinations in deeds. In the reason is evolved the distinction of good and evil (Gen. i. 4, 31), which is in itself the approval of the former and the disapproval of the latter. In the will is unfolded that freedom of action which chooses the good and refuses the evil. In the spiritual being that exercises reason and will resides the power to act, which presupposes both these faculties, — the reason as informing the will, and the will as directing the power. This is that form of God in which he has created man, and condescends to communicate with him.

And let them rule. The relation of man to the creature is now stated. It is that of sovereignty. Those capacities of right thinking, right willing, and right acting, or of knowledge, holiness, and righteousness, in which man resembles God, qualify him for dominion, and constitute him lord of all creatures that are destitute of intellectual and moral endowments. Hence, wherever man enters he makes his sway to be felt. He contemplates the objects around him, marks their qualities and relations, conceives and resolves upon the end to be attained, and endeavors to make all things within his reach work together for its accomplishment. This is to rule on a limited scale. The field of his dominion is "the fish of the sea, the fowl of the skies, the cattle, the whole land, and every thing that creepeth on the land." The order here is from the lowest to the highest. The fish, the fowl, are beneath the domestic cattle. These again are of less importance than the land, which man tills and renders fruitful in all that can gratify his appetite or his taste. The last and greatest victory of all is over the wild animals, which are included under the class of creepers that are prone in their posture, and move in a creeping attitude over the land. The primeval and prominent objects of human sway are here brought forward after the manner of Scripture. But there is not an object within the ken of man which he does not aim at making subservient to his purposes. He has made the sea his highway to the ends of the earth, the stars his pilots on the pathless ocean, the sun his bleacher and painter, the bowels of the earth the treasury from which he draws his precious and useful metals and much of his fuel, the steam his motive power, and the lightning his messenger. These are proofs of the evergrowing sway of man.

27. *Created.* Man in his essential part, the image of God in him, was entirely a new creation. We discern here two stages in his creation. The general fact is stated in the first clause of the verse, and then the two particulars. "In the image of God created he him." This is the primary act, in which his relation to his Maker is made prominent. In this his original state he is actually one, as God in whose image he is made is one. "Male and female created he

them." This is the second act or step in his formation. He is now no longer one, but two, — the male and the female. His adaptation to be the head of a race is hereby completed. This second stage in the existence of man is more circumstantially described hereafter (Gen. ii. 21–25).

28. The divine blessing is now pronounced upon man. It differs from that of the lower animals chiefly in the element of supremacy. Power is presumed to belong to man's nature, according to the counsel of the Maker's will (v. 26). But without a special permission he cannot exercise any lawful authority. For the other creatures are as independent of him as he is of them. As creatures he and they are on an equal footing, and have no natural right either over the other. Hence it is necessary that he should receive from high heaven a formal charter of right over the things that were made for man. He is therefore authorized, by the word of the Creator, to exercise his power in subduing the earth and ruling over the animal kingdom. This is the meet sequel of his being created in the image of God. Being formed for dominion, the earth and its various products and inhabitants are assigned to him for the display of his powers. The subduing and ruling refer not to the mere supply of his natural wants, for which provision is made in the following verse, but to the accomplishment of his various purposes of science and beneficence, whether towards the inferior animals or his own race. It is the part of intellectual and moral reason to employ power for the ends of general no less than personal good. The sway of man ought to be beneficent.

29, 30. Every herb bearing seed and tree bearing fruit is granted to man for his sustenance. With our habits it may seem a matter of course that each should at once appropriate that which he needs of things at his hand. But in the beginning of existence it could not be so. Of two things proceeding from the same creative hand neither has any original or inherent right to interfere in any way whatever with the other. The absolute right to each lies in the Creator alone. The one, it is true, may need the other to support its life, as fruit is needful to man. And therefore the just Creator cannot make one creature dependent for subsistence on another without granting to it the use of that other. But this is a matter between Creator and creature, not by any means between creature and creature. Hence it was necessary to the rightful adjustment of things, whenever a rational creature was ushered into the world, that the Creator should give an express permission to that creature to partake of the fruits of the earth. And in harmony with this view we shall hereafter find an exception made to this general grant (Gen. ii. 17). Thus, we perceive, the necessity of this formal grant of the use of certain creatures to moral and responsible man lies deep in the nature of things. And the sacred writer here hands down to us from the mists of a hoary antiquity the primitive deed of conveyance, which lies at the foundation of the the *common property* of man in the earth, and all that it contains.

The whole vegetable world is assigned to the animals for food. In the terms of the original grant the herb bearing seed and the tree bearing fruit are especially allotted to man, because the grain and the fruit were edible by man without much preparation. As usual in Scripture the chief parts are put for the whole, and accordingly this specification of the ordinary and the obvious covers the general principle that whatever part of the vegetable kingdom is convertible into food by the ingenuity of man is free for his use. It is plain that a vegetable diet alone is expressly conceded to man in this original conveyance, and it is probable that this alone was designed for him in the state in which he was created. But we must bear in mind that he was constituted master of the animal as well as of the vegetable world; and we cannot positively affirm that his dominion did not involve the use of them for food.

30. The whole of the grasses and the green parts or leaves of the herbage are distributed among the inferior animals for food. Here, again, the common and prominent kind of sustenance only is specified. There are some animals that greedily devour the fruits of trees and the grain produced by the various herbs; and there are others that derive the most of their subsistence from preying on the smaller and weaker kinds of animals. Still, the main substance of the means of animal life, and the ultimate supply of the whole of it, are derived from the plant. Even this general statement is not to be received without exception, as there are certain lower descriptions of animals that derive sustenance even from the mineral world. But this brief narrative of things notes only the few palpable facts, leaving the details to the experience and judgment of the reader.

31. Here we have the general review and approval of everything God had made, at the close of the six days' work of creation. Man, as well as other things, was very good when he came from his Maker's hand; but good as yet untried, and therefore good in capacity rather than in victory over temptation. It remains yet to be seen whether he will be good in act and habit.

This completes, then, the restoration of that order and fulness the absence of which is described in the second verse. The account of the six days' work, therefore, is the counterpart of that verse. The six days fall into two threes, corresponding to each other in the course of events. The first and fourth days refer principally to the darkness on the face of the deep; the second and fifth to the disorder and emptiness of the aerial and aqueous elements; and the third and sixth to the similar condition of the land. Again, the first three days refer to a lower, the second three to a higher order of things. On the first the darkness on the face of the earth is removed; on the fourth that on the face of the sky. On the second the water is distributed above and below the expanse; on the fifth the living natives of these regions are called into being. On the third the plants rooted in the soil are made; on the sixth the animals that move freely over it are brought into existence.

This chapter shows the folly and sin of the worship of light, of sun, moon, or star, of air or water, of plant, of fish or fowl, of earth, of cattle, creeping thing or wild beast, or, finally, of man himself; as all these are but the creatures of the one Eternal Spirit, who, as the Creator of all, is alone to be worshipped by his intelligent creatures.

This chapter is also to be read with wonder and adoration by man; as he finds himself to be constituted lord of the earth, next in rank under the Creator of all, formed in the image of his Maker, and therefore capable not only of studying the works of nature, but of contemplating and reverently communing with the Author of nature.

In closing the interpretation of this chapter, it is proper to refer to certain first principles of hermeneutical science. First, that interpretation only is valid which is true to the meaning of the author. The very first rule on which the interpreter is bound to proceed is to assign to each word the meaning it commonly bore in the time of the writer. This is the prime key to the works of every ancient author, if we can only discover it. The next is to give a consistent meaning to the whole of that which was composed at one time or in one place by the author. The presumption is that there was a reasonable consistency of thought in his mind during one effort of composition. A third rule is to employ faithfully and discreetly whatever we can learn concerning the time, place, and other circumstances of the author to the elucidation of his meaning.

And, in the second place, the interpretation now given claims acceptance on the ground of its internal and external consistency with truth.

1st. It exhibits the consistency of the whole narrative in itself. It acknowledges the narrative character of the first verse. It assigns an essential significance to the words, "the heavens," in that verse. It attributes to the second verse a prominent place and function in the arrangement of the record. It places the special creative work of the six days in due subordination to the absolute creation recorded in the first verse. It gathers information from the primitive meanings of the names that are given to certain objects, and notices the subsequent development of these meanings. It accounts for the manifestation of light on the first day, and of the luminaries of heaven on the fourth, and traces the orderly steps of a majestic climax throughout the narrative. It is in harmony with the usage of speech as far as it can be known to us at the present day. It assigns to the words "heavens," "earth," "expanse," "day," no greater latitude of meaning than was then customary. It allows for the diversity of phraseology employed in describing the acts of creative power. It sedulously refrains from importing modern notions into the narrative.

2d. The narrative thus interpreted is in striking harmony with the dictates of reason and the axioms of philosophy concerning the essence of God and the nature of man. On this it is unnecessary to dwell.

3d. It is equally consistent with human science. It substantially accords with the present state of astronomical science. It recognizes, as far as can be expected, the relative importance of the heavens and the earth, the existence of the heavenly bodies from the beginning of time, the total and then the partial absence of light from the face of the deep, as the local result of physical causes. It allows, also, if it were necessary, between the original creation, recorded in the first verse, and the state of things described in the second, the interval of time required for the light of the most distant discoverable star to reach the earth. No such interval, however, could be absolutely necessary, as the Creator could as easily establish the luminous connection of the different orbs of heaven as summon into being the element of light itself.

4th. It is also in harmony with the elementary facts of geological knowledge. The land, as understood by the ancient author, may be limited to that portion of the earth's surface which was known to antediluvian man. The elevation of an extensive tract of land, the subsidence of the overlying waters into the comparative hollows, the clarifying of the atmosphere, the creation of a fresh supply of plants and animals on the newly-formed continent, compose a series of changes which meet the geologist again and again in prosecuting his researches into the bowels of the earth. What part of the land was submerged when the new soil emerged from the waters, how far the shock of the plutonic or volcanic forces may have been felt, whether the alteration of level extended to the whole solid crust of the earth, or only to a certain region surrounding the cradle of mankind, the record before us does not determine. It merely describes in a few graphic touches, that are strikingly true to nature, the last of those geologic changes which our globe has undergone.

5th. It is in keeping, as far as it goes, with the facts of botany, zoology, and ethnology.

6th. It agrees with the cosmogonies of all nations, so far as these are founded upon a genuine tradition and not upon the mere conjectures of a lively fancy.

Finally, it has the singular and superlative merit of drawing the diurnal scenes of that creation to which our race owes its origin in the simple language of common life, and presenting each transcendent change as it would appear to an ordinary spectator standing on the earth. It was thus sufficiently intelligible to primeval man, and remains to this day intelligible to us, as soon as we divest ourselves of the narrowing preconceptions of our modern civilization.

IX. THE SEVENTH DAY.—Gen. ii. 1-3.

1. צָבָא *a host in marching order*, a company of persons or things in the order of their nature and the progressive discharge of their functions. Hence it is applied to the starry host (Deut. iv. 19), to the angelic host (1 Kings xxii. 19), to the host of Israel (Exod. xii. 41), and to the ministering Levites (Num. iv. 23). *κόσμος*.

2. הַשְּׁבִיעִי. Here הַשִּׁשִּׁי is read by Sam., LXX., Syr., and Josephus. The Masoretic reading, however, is preferable, as the sixth day was completed in the preceding paragraph: to finish a work on the seventh day is, in Hebrew phrase, not to do any part of it on that day, but to cease from it as a thing already finished; and "resting," in the subsequent part of the verse, is distinct from "finishing," being the positive of which the latter is the negative.

שָׁבַת *rest.* יָשַׁב *sit.*

3. קָדַשׁ *be separate, clean, holy, set apart for a sacred use.*

II. 1. Then were finished the heavens and the earth and all the host of them. 2. Then finished God on the seventh day his work which he had made; and rested on the seventh day from all his work which he had made. 3. Then blessed God the seventh day and hallowed it; because in it he had rested from all his work, which created had God to make. ¶ 7.

In this section we have the institution of the day of rest, the Sabbath (שַׁבָּת), on the cessation of God from his creative activity.

1. *And all the host of them.* All the array of luminaries, plants, and animals by which the darkness, waste, and solitude of sky and land were removed, has now been called into unhindered action or new existence. The whole is now finished; that is, perfectly fitted at length for the convenience of man, the high-born inhabitant of this fair scene. Since the absolute beginning of things the earth may have undergone many changes of climate and surface before it was adapted for the residence of man. But it has received the finishing touch in these last six days. These days accordingly are to man the only period of creation, since the beginning of time, of special or personal interest. The preceding interval of progressive development and periodical creation is, in regard to him, condensed into a point of time. The creative work of the six days is accordingly called the "making," or fitting up for man of "the skies and the land and the sea, and all that in them is" (Exod. xx. (11) 10).

2. *Then finished.* To finish a work, in Hebrew conception, is to cease from it, to have done with it. *On the seventh day.* The seventh day is distinguished from all the preceding days by being itself the subject of the narrative. In the absence of any work on this day, the Eternal is occupied with the day itself, and does four things in reference to it. *First*, he ceased from his work which he had made. *Secondly*, he rested. By this was indicated that his undertaking was accomplished. When nothing more remains to be done, the purposing agent rests contented. The resting of God arises not from weariness, but from the completion of his task. He is refreshed, not by the recruiting of his strength, but by the satisfaction of having before him a finished good (Exod. xxxi. 17).

3. *Thirdly*, he blessed the seventh day. Blessing results in the bestowment of some good on the object blessed. The only good that can be bestowed on a portion of time is to dedicate it to a noble use,

a peculiar and pleasing enjoyment. Accordingly, *in the fourth place*, he hallowed it or set it apart to a holy rest. This consecration is the blessing conferred on the seventh day. It is devoted to the rest that followed, when God's work was done, to the satisfaction and delight arising from the consciousness of having achieved his end, and from the contemplation of the good he has realized. Our joy on such occasions is expressed by mutual visitation, congratulation, and hospitality. None of these outward demonstrations is mentioned here, and would be, so far as the Supreme Being is concerned, altogether out of place. But our celebration of the Sabbath naturally includes the holy convocation or solemn meeting together in joyful mood (Lev. xxiii. 3), the singing of songs of thanksgiving in commemoration of our existence and our salvation (Exod. xx. 11 (10); Deut. v. 15), the opening of our mouths to God in prayer, and the opening of God's mouth to us in the reading and preaching of the Word. The sacred rest which characterizes the day precludes the labor and bustle of hospitable entertainment. But the Lord at set times spreads for us his table laden with the touching emblems of that spiritual fare which gives eternal life.

The solemn act of blessing and hallowing is the institution of a perpetual order of seventh-day rest: in the same manner as the blessing of the animals denoted a perpetuity of self-multiplication, and the blessing of man indicated further a perpetuity of dominion over the earth and its products. The present record is a sufficient proof that the original institution was never forgotten by man. If it had ceased to be observed by mankind, the intervening event of the fall would have been sufficient to account for its discontinuance. It is not, indeed, the manner of Scripture, especially in a record that often deals with centuries of time, to note the ordinary recurrence of a seventh-day rest, or any other periodical festival, even though it may have taken firm hold among the hereditary customs of social life. Yet incidental traces of the keeping of the Sabbath are found in the record of the deluge, when the sacred writer has occasion to notice short intervals of time. The measurement of time by weeks then appears (Gen. viii. 10, 12). The same division of time again comes up in the history of Jacob (Gen. xxix. 27, 28). This unit of measure is traceable to nothing but the institution of the seventh-day rest.

This institution is a new evidence that we have arrived at the stage of rational creatures. The number of days employed in the work of creation shows that we are come to the times of man. The distinction of times would have no meaning to the irrational world. But apart from this consideration, the seventh-day rest is not an ordinance of nature. It makes no mark in the succession of physical things. It has no palpable effect on the merely animal world. The sun rises, the moon and the stars pursue their course; the plants grow, the flowers blow, the fruit ripens; the brute animal seeks its food and provides for its young on this as on other days. The Sabbath, therefore, is founded, not in nature, but in history. Its periodical return is marked by the numeration of seven days. It appeals not to instinct, but to memory, to intelligence. A reason is assigned for its observance; and this itself is a step above mere sense, an indication that the era of man has begun. The reason is thus expressed: "Because in it he had rested from all his work." This reason is found in the procedure of God; and God himself, as well as all his ways, man alone is competent in any measure to apprehend.

It is consonant with our ideas of the wisdom and righteousness of God to believe that the seventh-day rest is adjusted to the physical nature of man and of the animals which he domesticates as beasts of labor. But this is subordinate to its original end, the commemoration of the completion of God's creative work by a sacred rest, which has a direct bearing, as we learn from the record of its institution, on metaphysical and moral distinctions.

The rest here, it is to be remembered, is God's rest. The refreshment is God's refreshment, which arises rather from the joy of achievement than from the relief of fatigue. Yet the work in which God was engaged was the creation of man and the previous adaptation of the world to be his home. Man's rest, therefore, on this day is not only an act of communion with God in the satisfaction of resting after his work was done, but, at the same time, a thankful commemoration of that auspicious event in which the Almighty gave a noble origin and a happy existence to the human race. It is this which, even apart from its divine institution, at once raises the Sabbath above all human commemorative festivals, and imparts to it, to its joys and to its modes of expressing them, a height of sacredness and a force of obligation which cannot belong to any mere human arrangement.

In order to enter upon the observance of this day with intelligence, therefore, it was necessary that the human pair should have been acquainted with the events recorded in the preceding chapter. They must have been informed of the original creation of all things, and therefore of the eternal existence of the Creator. They must further have been instructed in the order and purpose of the six days' creation, by which the land and sky were fitted up for the residence of man. They must in consequence have learned that they themselves were created in the image of God, and intended to have dominion over all the animal world. This information would fill their pure and infantile minds with thoughts of wonder, gratitude, and complacential delight, and prepare them for entering upon the celebration of the seventh-day rest with the understanding and the heart. It is scarcely needful to add that this was the first full day of the newly-created pair in their terrestrial home. This would add a new historical interest to this day above all others. We cannot say how much time it would take to make the parents of our race aware of the meaning of all these wondrous events. But there can be no reasonable doubt that he who made them in his image could convey into their minds such simple and elementary conceptions of the origin of themselves and the creatures around them as would enable them to keep even the first Sabbath with propriety. And these conceptions would rise into more enlarged, distinct, and adequate notions of the reality of things along with the general development of their mental faculties. This implies, we perceive, an oral revelation to the very first man. But it is premature to pursue this matter any further at present.

The recital of the resting of God on this day is not closed with the usual formula, "and evening was, and morning was, day seventh." The reason of this is obvious. In the former days the occupation of the Eternal Being was definitely concluded in the period of the one day. On the seventh day, however, the rest of the Creator was only commenced, has thence continued to the present hour, and will not be fully completed till the human race has run out its course. When the last man has been born and has arrived at the crisis of his destiny, then may we expect a *new creation*, another putting forth of the divine energy, to prepare the skies above and the earth beneath for a new stage of man's history, in which he will appear as a race no longer in process of development, but completed in number, confirmed in moral character, transformed in physical constitution, and so adapted for a new scene of existence. Meanwhile, the interval between the creation now recorded and that prognosticated in subsequent revelations from heaven (Is. lxv. 17; 2 Pet. iii. 13; Rev. xxi. 1) is the long Sabbath of the Almighty, so far as this world is concerned, in which he serenely contemplates from the throne of his providence the strange workings and strivings of that intellectual and moral race he has called into being, the ebbings and flowings of ethical and physical good in their checkered history, and the final destiny to which each individual in the unfettered exercise of his moral freedom is incessantly advancing.

Hence we gather some important lessons concerning the primeval design of the Sabbath. It was intended, not for God himself, whose Sabbath does not end till the consummation of all things, but for man, whose origin it commemorates and whose end it foreshadows (Mark ii. 27). It not obscurely hints that work is to be the main business of man in the present stage of his existence. This work may be either an exhilerating exercise of those mental and corporeal faculties with which he is endowed, or a toilsome labor, a constant struggle for the means of life, according to the use he may make of his inborn liberty.

But between the sixfold periods of work is interposed the day of rest, a free breathing time for man, in which he may recall his origin from and meditate on his relationship to God. It lifts him out of the routine of mechanical or even intellectual labor into the sphere of conscious leisure and occasional participation with his Maker in his perpetual rest. It is also a type of something higher. It whispers into his soul an audible presentiment of a time when his probationary career will be over, his faculties will be matured by the experience and the education of time, and he will be transformed and translated to a higher stage of being, where he will hold uninterrupted fellowship with his Creator in the perpetual leisure and liberty of the children of God. This paragraph completes the first of the eleven documents into which Genesis is separable, and the first grand stage in the narrative of the ways of God with man. It is the keystone of the arch in the history of that primeval creation to which we belong. The document which it closes is distinguished from those that succeed in several important respects:

First, it is a diary; while the others are usually arranged in generations or life-periods.

Secondly, it is a complete drama, consisting of seven acts with a prologue. These seven stages contain two triads of action, which match each other in all respects, and a seventh constituting a sort of epilogue or completion of the whole.

Though the Scripture takes no notice of any significance or sacredness inherent in particular numbers, yet we cannot avoid associating them with the objects to which they are prominently applied. The number one is peculiarly applicable to the unity of God. Two, the number of repetition, is expressive of emphasis or confirmation, as the two witnesses. Three marks the three persons or hypostases in God. Four notes the four quarters of the world, and therefore reminds us of the physical system of things, or the *cosmos*. Five is the *half* of ten. *the whole*, and the basis of our decimal numeration. Seven, being composed of twice three and one, is peculiarly fitted for sacred uses; being the sum of three and four, it points to the communion of God with man. It is, therefore, the number of sacred fellowship. Twelve is the product of three and four, and points to the reconciliation of God and man: it is therefore the number of the church. Twenty-two and eleven, being the *whole* and the *half* of the Hebrew alphabet, have somewhat the same relation as ten and five. Twenty-four points to the New Testament, or completed church.

The other documents do not exhibit the sevenfold structure, though they display the same general laws of composition. They are arranged according to a plan of their own, and are all remarkable for their simplicity, order, and perspicuity.

Thirdly, the matter of the first differs from that of the others. The first is a record of creation; the others of development. This is sufficient to account for the diversity of style and plan. Each piece is admirably adapted to the topic of which it treats.

Fourthly, the first document is distinguished from the second by the use of the term אֱלֹהִים only for the Supreme Being. This name is here appropriate, as the Everlasting One (p. 26) here steps forth from the inscrutable secrecy of his immutable perfection to crown the latest stage of our planet's history with a new creation adapted to its present conditions. Before all creation he was the Everduring, the Unchangeable, and therefore the blessed and only Potentate, dwelling with himself in the unapproachable light of his own essential glory (1 Tim. vi. 15). From that ineffable source of all being came forth the free fiat of creation. After that transcendent event, He who was from everlasting to everlasting may receive new names expressive of the various relations in which he stands to the universe of created being. But before this relation was established these names could have no existence or significance.

Neither this last nor any of the former distinctions affords any argument for diversity of authorship. They arise naturally out of the diversity of matter, and are such as may proceed from an intelligent author judiciously adapting his style and plan to the variety of his topics. At the same time, identity of authorship is not essential to the historical validity or the divine authority of the elementary parts that are incorporated by Moses into the book of Genesis. It is only unnecessary to multiply authorship without a cause.

PART II

THE DEVELOPMENT

SECTION II. — THE MAN

X. THE FIELD. — Gen. ii. 4-7.

4. תּוֹלְדוֹת *generations, products, developments.* That which comes from any source, as the child from the parent, the record of which is *history.*

יְהוָה This word occurs about six thousand times in Scripture. It is obvious from its use that it is, so to speak, the proper name of God. It never has the article. It is never changed for construction with another noun. It is never accompanied with a suffix. It is never applied to any but the true God. This sacred exclusiveness of application, indeed, led the Jews to read always in place of it אֲדוֹנָי, or, if this preceded it, אֱלֹהִים, to intimate which the vowel points of one of these terms were subscribed to it. The root of this name is הָוָה, an older variety of הָיָה, which, as we have seen (p. 25), has three meanings, — *be* in the sense of coming into existence, *be* in that of becoming, and *be* in that of merely existing. The first of these meanings has no application to God, who had no beginning of existence. The last applies to God, but affords no distinctive characteristic, as it belongs equally to all objects that have existence. The second is proper to God in the sense, not of acquiring any new attribute, but of becoming active from a state of repose. But he becomes active to the eye of man only by causing some new effect to be, which makes its appearance in the world of sensible things. He becomes, then, only by causing to be or to become. Hence he that becomes, when applied to the Creator, is really he that causes to be. This name, therefore, involves the active or causative force of the root from which it springs, and designates God in relation with the system of things he has called into being, and especially with man, the only intelligent observer of him or of his works in this nether world. It distinguishes him as the Author of being, and therefore the Creator, the worker of miracles, the performer of promise, the keeper of covenant. Beginning with the י of personality, it points out God as the person whose habitual character it has become to cause his purpose to take place. Hence אֱלֹהִים designates God as the Everlasting, the Almighty, in his unchangeable essence, as he is before as well as after creation. יְהֹוָה distinguishes him as the personal Self-existent, and Author of all existing things, who gives expression and effect to his purpose, manifests himself thereby as existing, and maintains a spiritual intercourse with his intelligent creatures.

The vowel marks usually placed under the consonants of this word are said to belong to אֲדֹנָי; and its real pronunciation, which is supposed to be lost, is conjectured to have been יַהְוֶה. This conjecture is supported by the analogy of the supposed antique third singular masculine imperfect of the verb הָוָה, and by the Greek forms IAΩ and IABE which are found in certain authors (Diod. Sic. i. 19; Macrob. Saturn i. 18; Theodoret, Quaest. xv. ad Exod.). It is true, indeed, when it has a prefix all its vowels coincide with those of אֲדֹנָי. But otherwise the vowel under the first letter is different, and the qamets at the end is as usual in proper names ending in ה as in others. יְהֹוָה also finds an anology in the word יְרֹחָם. In the forms IAΩ and IABE the Greek vowels doubtless represent the Hebrew consonants, and not any vowel points. ה is often represented by the Greek *α*. From יַהְוֶה we may obtain יָהוּ at the end of compounds, and therefore, expect יָהוּ at the beginning. But the form at the beginning is יְהוֹ or יוֹ, which indicates the pronunciation יְהֹוָה as current with the punctuators. All this countenances the suggestion that the casual agreement of the two nouns Jehovah and Adonai in the principal vowels was the circumstance that facilitated the Jewish endeavor to avoid uttering the proper name of God except on the most solemn occasions. יַהְוֶה, moreover, rests on precarious grounds. The Hebrew analogy would give יִהְוֶה not יַהְוֶה for the verbal form. The middle vowel cholem may indicate the intensive or active force of the root, but we lay no stress on the mode of pronunciation, as it cannot be positively ascertained.

5. שָׂדֶה *plain, country, field,* for pasture or tillage, in opp. to גַּן, *garden, park.*

7. נְשָׁמָה *breath,* applied to God and man only.

We meet with no division again in the text till we come to Gen. iii.

15, when the first minor break in the narrative occurs. This is noted by the intervening space being less than the remainder of the line. The narrative is therefore so far regarded as continuous.

We are now entering upon a new plan of narrative, and have therefore to notice particularly that law of Hebrew composition by which one line of events is carried on without interruption to its natural resting-point; after which the writer returns to take up a collateral train of incidents, that are equally requisite for the elucidation of his main purpose, though their insertion in the order of time would have marred the symmetry and perspicuity of the previous narrative. The relation now about to be given is posterior, as a whole, to that already given as a whole; but the first incident now to be recorded is some time prior to the last of the preceding document.

Hitherto we have adhered closely to the form of the original in our rendering, and so have made use of some inversions which are foreign to our prose style. Hereafter we shall deviate as little as possible from the authorized version.

4. These are the generations of the heavens and the earth on their being created, in the day that the LORD God made earth and heaven. 5. And not a plant of the field was yet in the land, and not an herb of the field yet grew; for the LORD God had not caused it to rain upon the land, and there was no man to till the ground. 6. And a mist went up from the land and watered the whole face of the soil. 7. And the LORD God formed the man of dust from the soil, and breathed into his nostrils the breath of life: and man became a living soul.

The document upon which we are now entering extends from Gen. ii. 4 to Gen. iv. In the second and third chapters the author uses the combination יְהוָֹה אֱלֹהִים *the* LORD *God*, to designate the Supreme Being; in the fourth he drops אֱלֹהִים *God*, and employs יְהוָֹה *the* LORD, alone. So far, then, as the divine appellation is concerned, the fourth chapter is as clearly separable from the second and third as the first document is from the present. If diversity of the divine name were a proof of diversity of authorship, we should here have two documents due to different authors, each of them different also from the author of the first document. The second and third chapters, though agreeing in the designation of God, are clearly distinguishable in style.

The general subject of this document is the history of man to the close of the line of Cain and the birth of Enosh. This falls into three clearly marked sections, — the origin, the fall, and the family of Adam. The difference of style and phraseology in its several parts will be found to correspond with the diversity in the topics of which it treats. It reverts to an earlier point of time than that at which we had arrived in the former document, and proceeds upon a new plan, exactly adapted to the new occasion.

The present section treats of the process of nature which was simultaneous with the latter part of the supernatural process described in the preceding document. Its opening paragraph refers to the field.

4. This verse is the title of the present section. It states the subject of which it treats, — *the generations of the skies and the land.* The generations are the posterity or the progress of events relating to the posterity of the party to whom the term is applied (Gen. v. 1, vi. 9, x. 1, xi. 10, xxxvii. 2). The development of events is here presented under the figure of the descendants of a parental pair; the skies and the land being the metaphorical progenitors of those events, which are brought about by their conjunct operation.

It then notes the *date* at which the new narrative commences. *In their being created.* This is the first or general date; namely, after the primary creation and during the course of the secondary. As the latter occupied six days, some of the processes of nature began before these days had elapsed. Next, therefore, is the more special date, — *in the day of Jehovah God's making land and skies.* Now, on looking back at the preceding narrative, we observe that the skies were adjusted and named on the second day, and the land on the third. Both, therefore, were completed on the third day, which accordingly is the opening date of the second branch of the narrative.

The peculiarity of the present section, therefore, is, that it combines the creative with the preservative agency of God. Creation and progress here go hand in hand for a season. The narrative here, then, overlaps half the time of the former, and at the end of the chapter has not advanced beyond its termination.

Jehovah Elohim, the LORD God. This phrase is here for the first time introduced. Elohim, as we have seen, is the generic term denoting God as the Everlasting, and therefore the Almighty, as he was before all worlds, and still continues to be, now that he is the sole object of supreme reverence to all intelligent creatures. Jehovah is the proper name of God to man, self-existent himself, the author of existence to all persons and things, and manifesting his existence to those whom he has made capable of such knowledge.

Hence the latter name is appropriate to the present stage of our narrative. God has become active in a way worthy of himself, and at the same time peculiar to his nature. He has put forth his creative power in calling the universe into existence. He has now reconstituted the skies and the land, clothed the latter with a new vegetation, and peopled it with a new animal kingdom. Especially has he called into being an inhabitant of this earth made in his own image, and therefore capable of understanding his works and holding intercourse with himself. To man he has now *come to be* in certain acts by which he has discovered himself and his power. And to man he has accordingly become known by a name which signalizes that new creative process of which man forms a prominent part. Jehovah — he who causes the successive events of time to come to pass in the sight and in the interest of man — is a name the peculiar significance of which will come out on future occasions in the history of the ways of God with man.

The union of these two divine names, then, indicates him who was before all things, and by whom now all things consist. It also implies that he who is now distinguished by the new name Jehovah is the same who was before called Elohim. The combination of the names is specially suitable in a passage which records a concurrence of creation and development. The apposition of the two names is continued by the historian through this and the following chapter. The abstract and aboriginal name then gives way to the concrete and the historical.

The skies and the land at the beginning of the verse are given in order of their importance in nature, the skies being first as grander and higher than the land; at the end, in the order of their importance in the narrative, the land being before the skies, as the future scene of the events to be recorded.

This superscription, we see, presupposes the former document, as it alludes to the creation in general, and to the things made on the second and third days in particular, without directly narrating these events. This mode of referring to them implies that they were well known at the time of the narrator, either by personal observation or by testimony. Personal observation is out of the question in the present case. By the testimony of God, therefore, they were already known, and the preceding record is that testimony. The narrator of the second passage, therefore, even if not the same as that of the former, had to a moral certainty the first before his mind when composing the second.

5. This verse corresponds to the second verse of the preceding narrative. It describes the field or arable land in the absence of certain conditions necessary to the progress of vegetation. Plant and herb here comprise the whole vegetable world. Plants and herbs of the field are those which are to be found in the open land. A different statement is made concerning each.

Not a plant of the field was yet in the land. Here it is to be remembered that the narrative has reverted to the third day of the preceding creation. At first sight, then, it might be supposed that the vegetable species were not created at the hour of that day to which the narrative refers. But it is not stated that young trees were not in existence, but merely that plants *of the field* were not yet in the land. Of the herbs it is only said that they had not yet sent forth a bud or blade. And the actual existence of both trees and herbs is implied in what follows. The reasons for the state of things above described are the want of rain to water the soil, and of man to cultivate it. These would only suffice for growth if the vegetable seeds, at least, were already in existence. Now, the plants were made before the seeds (Gen. i. 11, 12), and therefore the first full-grown and seed-bearing sets of each kind were already created. Hence we infer that the state of things described in the text was this: The original trees were confined to a centre of vegetation, from which it was intended that they should spread in the course of nature. At the present juncture, then, there was not a tree *of the field*, a tree of propagation, in the land; and even the created trees had not sent down a single root of *growth* into the land. And if they had dropped a seed, it was only on the land, and not in the land, as it had not yet struck root.

And not an herb of the field yet grew. The herbage seems to have been more widely diffused than the trees. Hence it is not said that they were not in the land, as it is said of field trees. But at the present moment not an herb had exhibited any signs of growth or sent forth a single blade beyond the immediate product of creative power.

Rain upon the land, and man to till it, were the two wants that retarded vegetation. These two means of promoting vegetable growth differed in their importance and in their mode of application. Moisture is absolutely necessary, and where it is supplied in abundance the shifting wind will in the course of time waft the seed. The browsing herds will aid in the same process of diffusion. Man comes in merely as an auxiliary to nature in preparing the soil and depositing the seeds and plants to the best advantage for rapid growth and abundant fruitfulness. The narrative, as usual, notes only the chief things. Rain is the only source of vegetable sap; man is the only intentional cultivator.

6. As in the former narrative, so here, the remaining part of the chapter is employed in recording the removal of the two hinderances to vegetation. The first of these is removed by the institution of the natural process by which rain is produced. The atmosphere had been adjusted so far as to admit of some light. But even on the third day a dense mass of clouds still shut out the heavenly bodies from view. But on the creation of plants the Lord God caused it to rain on the land. This is described in the verse before us. *A mist* went *up from the land.* It had been ascending from the steaming, reeking land ever since the waters retired into the hollows. The briny moisture which could not promote vegetation is dried up. And now he causes the accumulated masses of cloud to burst forth and dissolve themselves in copious showers. Thus the mist *watered the whole face of the soil.* The face of the sky is thereby cleared, and on the following day the sun shone forth in all his cloudless splendor and fostering warmth.

On the fourth day, then, a second process of nature commenced. The bud began to swell, the tender blade to peep forth and assume its tint of green, the gentle breeze to agitate the full-sized plants, the first seeds to be shaken off and wafted to their resting-place, the first root to strike into the ground, and the first shoot to rise towards the sky.

This enables us to determine with some degree of probability the season of the year when the creation took place. If we look to the ripe fruit on the first trees we presume that the season is autumn. The scattering of the seeds, the falling of the rains, and the need of a cultivator intimated in the text, point to the same period. In a genial climate the process of vegetation has its beginnings at the falling of the early rains. Man would be naturally led to gather the abundant fruit which fell from the trees, and thus even unwittingly provide a store for the unbearing period of the year. It is probable, moreover, that he was formed in a region where vegetation was little interrupted by the coldest season of the year. This would be most favorable to the preservation of life in his state of primeval inexperience.

These presumptions are in harmony with the numeration of the months at the deluge (Gen. vii. 11), and with the outgoing and the turn of the year at autumn (Exod. xxiii. 16, xxxiv. 22).

7. The second obstacle to the favorable progress of the vegetable kingdom is now removed. *And the Lord God formed the man of dust from the soil.* This account of the origin of man differs from the former on account of the different end the author has in view. There his creation as an integral whole is recorded with special reference to his higher nature, by which he was fitted to hold communion with his Maker, and exercise dominion over the inferior creation. Here his constitution is described with marked regard to his adaptation to be the cultivator of the soil. He is a compound of matter and mind. His material part is dust from the soil, out of which he is *formed* as the potter moulds the vessel out of the clay. He is אָדָם *Adam*, the man of the soil, אֲדָמָה *adamah*. His mission in this respect is to draw out the capabilities of the soil to support by its produce the myriads of his race.

His mental part is from another source. *And breathed into his nostrils the breath of life.* The word נְשָׁמָה is invariably applied to God or man, never to any irrational creature. The "breath of life" is peculiar to this passage. It expresses the spiritual and principal element in man, which is not formed, but breathed by the Creator into the bodily form of man. This rational part is that in which he bears the image of God, and is fitted to be his vicegerent on earth. As the earth was prepared to be the dwelling, so was the body to be the organ of that breath of life which is his essence, himself.

And the man became a living soul. This term "living soul" is also applied to the water and land animals (Gen. i. 20, 21, 24). As by his body he is allied to earth and by his soul to heaven, so by the vital union of these he is associated with the whole animal kingdom, of which he is the constituted sovereign. This passage, therefore, aptly describes him as he is fitted to dwell and rule on this earth. The height of his glory is yet to come out in his relation to the future and to God.

The line of narrative here reaches a point of repose. The second want of the teeming soil is here supplied. The man to till the ground is presented in that form which exhibits his fitness for this appropriate and needful task. We are therefore at liberty to go back for another train of events which is essential to the progress of our narrative.

XI. THE GARDEN. — Gen. ii. 8–14.

8. גַּן *garden, park,* παράδεισος, an enclosed piece of ground. עֵדֶן *Eden, delight.* קֶדֶם *fore-place, east; foretime.*

11. פִּישׁוֹן Pishon; r. *flow over, spread, leap.* חֲוִילָה Chavilah. חוֹל *sand.* חֶבֶל *region.*

12. בְּדֹלַח ἄνθραξ, *carbuncle,* (LXX.) βδέλλιον, a gum of eastern countries, Arabia, India, Media (Josephus, etc.). The pearl (Kimchi). שֹׁהַם πράσινος, *leeklike,* perhaps the beryl (LXX.), ὄνυξ, *onyx, sardonyx,* a precious stone of the color of the nail (Jerome).

13. גִּיחוֹן Gichon; r. *break forth.* כּוּשׁ Kush; r. *heap, gather?*

14. חִדֶּקֶל דִּגְלָא Dijlah, *Tigris.* חָדַק *be sharp. rapidus,* פְּרָת Frat, Euphrates. The *sweet* or *broad* stream. Old P. *frata,* Sansc. *prathu,* πλατύς.

8. And the Lord God planted a garden in Eden to the east; and put there the man whom he had formed.

9. And the Lord God made to grow out of the soil every tree likely for sight and good for food; and the tree of life in the midst of the garden, and the tree of the knowledge of good and evil. 10. And a river was going out of Eden to water the garden: and thence it was parted and became four heads. 11. The name of the one was Pishon; it is that compassing the whole land of Havilah, in which was gold. 12. And the gold of that land was good; there were the bdellium and the onyx stone. 13. And the name of the second river was Gihon; it is that compassing the whole land of Kush. 14. And the name of the third river was Hiddekel: it is that going east of Asshur. And the fourth river was Perath.

This paragraph describes the planting of the garden of Eden, and determines its situation. It goes back, therefore, as we conceive, to the third day, and runs parallel with the preceding passage.

8. *And the Lord God planted a garden in Eden to the east.* It is evident that the order of thought is here observed. For the formation of man with special allusion to his animal nature immediately suggests the means by which his physical wants are to be supplied. The order

of time is an open question so far as the mere conjunction of the sentences is concerned. It can only be determined by other considerations.

Here, then, the writer either relates a new creation of trees for the occasion, or reverts to the occurrences of the third day. But though in the previous verses he declares the field to be without timber, yet in the account of the third day the creation of trees is recorded. Now, it is unnecessary, and therefore unreasonable, to assume two creations of trees at so short an interval of time. In the former paragraph the author advanced to the sixth day, in order to lay before his readers without any interruption the means by which the two conditions of vegetative progress were satisfied. This brings man into view, and his appearance gives occasion to speak of the means by which his wants were supplied.

For this purpose the author drops the thread of events following the creation of man, and reverts to the third day. He describes more particularly what was then done. A centre of vegetation was chosen for the trees, from which they were to be propagated by seed over the land. This central spot is called a garden or park. It is situated in a region which is distinguished by its name as a land of delight. It is said, as we understand, to be in the eastern quarter of Eden. For the word מִקֶּדֶם *on the east* is most simply explained by referring to some point indicated in the text. There are two points to which it may here refer, — the place where the man was created, and the country in which the garden was placed. But the man was not created at this time, and, moreover, the place of his creation is not indicated; and hence we must refer to the country in which the garden was placed.

And put there the man whom he had formed. The writer has still the formation of man in thought, and therefore proceeds to state that he was thereupon placed in the garden which had been prepared for his reception, before going on to give a description of the garden. This verse, therefore, forms a transition from the field and its cultivator to the garden and its inhabitants.

Without the previous document concerning the creation, however, it could not have been certainly known that a new line of narrative was taken up in this verse. Neither could we have discovered what was the precise time of the creation of the trees. Hence this verse furnishes a new proof that the present document was composed, not as an independent production, but as a continuation of the former.

9. Having located the newly-formed man of whom he had spoken

in the preceding paragraph, the author now returns to detail the planting and the watering of the garden. *And the Lord God made to grow out of the soil every tree likely for sight and good for food.* We look on while the ornamental trees rise to gratify the sight, and the fruit trees present their mellow fare to the craving appetite. But preëminent among all we contemplate with curious wonder the tree of life in the midst of the garden, and the tree of the knowledge of good and evil. These will come under consideration at a future stage of our narrative.

10. Here is a river the source of which is in Eden. It passes into the garden and waters it. *And thence it was parted and became four heads.* This statement means either that the single stream was divided into four branches, or that there was a division of the river system of the district into four principal streams, whose sources were all to be found in it, though one only passed through the garden. In the latter case the word נָהָר may be understood in its primary sense of a flowing of water in general. This flowing in all the parts of Eden resulted in four particular flowings or streams, which do not require to have been ever united. The subsequent land changes in this district during an interval of five or six thousand years prevent us from determining more precisely the meaning of the text.

11, 12. The Pishon waters in its subsequent course the land of Havilah. This country is noted for the best gold, and for two other products, concerning which interpreters differ. *Bedolach* is, according to the Septuagint, the carbuncle or crystal; according to others, the pearl, or a particular kind of gum. The last is the more probable, if we regard the various Greek and Latin forms of the word: *βδέλλα, βδέλλιον,* Joseph. Ant. iii. 1, 6; *οἱ δὲ μάδελκον, οἱ δὲ βολχὸν καλοῦσι,* Dioscor. i. 71; *alii brochon appellant, alii malacham, alii maldacon,* Plin. H.N. 12, 9. Pliny describes it as black, while the manna, which is compared with it (Num. xi. 7), is white; but עֵין the point of resemblance may refer not to color, but to transparence or some other visible quality. This transparent, aromatic gum is found in Arabia, Babylonia, Bactriana, Media, and India. *Shoham* is variously conjectured to be the beryl, onyx, sardonyx, or emerald. The first, according to Pliny, is found in India and about Pontus. As the name Pishon means the gushing or spouting current, it may have been applied to many a stream by the migratory tribes. The Halys perhaps contains the same root with Havilah; namely, חול (Rawlinson's Her. i., p. 126); and it rises in Armenia (Herod. i. 72). The Chalybes in Pontus, perhaps, contain the same root. The Pishon may have been the Halys or some other stream flowing into the Black Sea.

13, 14. Gihon, the second river, flows by the land of Kush. It is possible that the name Kush remains in Caucasus and in the Caspian. The Gihon is the stream that breaks or bursts forth; a quality common to many rivers. The name is preserved in the Jyhoon, flowing into the sea of Aral. Here it probably designates the leading stream flowing out of Armenia into the Caspian, or in that direction. Hiddekel, the third, goes in front, or on the east of Asshur. The original Asshur embraced northern Mesopotamia, as well as the slopes of the mountain range on the other side of the Tigris. Perath, the fourth, is the well-known Frat or Euphrates.

In endeavoring to determine the situation of Eden, it is evident we can only proceed on probable grounds. The deluge, and even the distance of time, warrant us in presuming great land changes to have taken place since this geographical description applied to the country. Let us see, however, to what result the simple reading of the text will lead us. A river is said to flow out of Eden into the garden. This river is not named, and may, in a primary sense of the term, denote the running water of the district in general. This is then said to be parted into four heads — the upper courses of four great rivers. One of these rivers is known to this day as the Frat or Euphrates. A second is with almost equal unanimity allowed to be the Dijlah or Tigris. The sources of these lie not far asunder, in the mountains of Armenia, and in the neighborhood of the lakes Van and Urumiah. Somewhere in this region must have been the celebrated but unnamed stream. The Hiddekel flowed east of Asshur; the primitive portion of which seems therefore to have been in Mesopotamia. The Gihon may have flowed into the Caspian, on the banks of which was the original Kush. The Pishon may have turned towards the Euxine, and compassed the primitive Havilah, lying to the south and east of that sea.

It may be said that the Kush and Havilah of later times belong to different localities. This, however, is no solid objection, on two grounds, —

1st. Geography affords numerous examples of the transferrence of names from one place to another along the line of migration. Thus Galatia in Asia Minor would be inexplicable or misleading, did not history inform us that tribes from Gallia had settled there and given their name to the province. We may therefore expect names to travel with the tribes that bear them or love them, until they come to their final settlements. Hence Kush may have been among the Caucasian glens and on the Caspian shores. In the progress of his development, whether northward or southward, he may have left his mark in Kossaea and Kissia, while he sent his colonies into southern Arabia Aethiopia and probably India.

2d. Countries agreeing in name may be totally unconnected either in time or place. Thus in the table of nations we meet with two persons called Havilah (Gen. x. 7, 29); the one a Kushite, who settled probably in the south of Arabia, the other a Joctanite, who occupied a more northerly locality in the same peninsula. A primitive Havilah, different from both, may have given his name to the region southeast of the Euxine.

The rivers Pishon and Gihon may have been greatly altered or even effaced by the deluge and other causes. Names similar to these may be found in various places. They cannot prove much more than resemblance in language, and that may be sometimes very remote. There is one other Gihon mentioned in Scripture (1 Kings i. 33), and several like names occur in profane history. At first sight it seems to be stated that the one stream branched into four. If so, this community of origin has disappeared among the other changes of the country. But in the original text the words "and thence" come before the verb "parted." This verb has no subject expressed, and may have its subject implied in itself. The meaning of the sentence will then be, "and thence," after the garden had been watered by the river, "it," the river, or the water system of the country, "was parted into four heads." We cannot tell, and it is not material, which of these interpretations correctly represents the original fact.

According to the above view, the land and garden of Eden lay in Armenia, around the lakes Van and Urumiah, or the district where these lakes now are. The country here is to this day a land of delight, and very well fitted in many respects to be the cradle of the human race. There is only one other locality that has any claim to probability from an examination of Scripture. It is the alluvial ground where the Euphrates and Tigris unite their currents, and then again separate into two branches, by which their waters are discharged into the Persian Gulf. The neck in which they are united is the river that waters the garden. The rivers, before they unite, and the branches, after they separate, are the four rivers. The claim of this position to acceptance rests on the greater contiguity to Kissia or Susiana, a country of the Kushites, on the one side and on the other to Havilah, a district of Arabia, as well as its proximity to Babel, where the confusion of tongues took place. These claims do not constrain our assent. Susiana is nearer the Tigris itself than the present eastern branch after the separation. Havilah is not very near the western branch. If Babel be near, Armenia, where the ark rested, is very far away. Against this position is the forced meaning it puts on the text by its mode of accounting for the four rivers. The garden river in the text rises in Eden, and the whole four have their upper currents in that land. All is different in the case here supposed. Again, the land of Shinar is a great wheat country, and abounds in the date palm. But it is not otherwise distinguished for trees. It is a land of the simoon, the mirage, and the drought, and its summer heat is oppressive and enfeebling. It cannot therefore claim to be a land of delight *(Eden)*, either in point of climate or variety of produce. It is not, consequently, so well suited as the northern position, either to the description in the text or the requirements of primeval man.

It is evident that this geographical description must have been written long after the document in which it is found might have been composed. Mankind must have multiplied to some extent, have spread themselves along these rivers, and become familiar with the countries here designated. All this might have taken place in the lifetime of Adam, and so have been put on record, or handed down by tradition from an eye-witness. But it is remarkable that the three names of countries reappear as proper names among the descendants of Noah after the flood.

Hence arises a question of great interest concerning the composition of the document in which they are originally found. If these names be primeval, the document in its extant form may have been composed in the time of Adam, and therefore before the deluge. In this case Moses has merely authenticated it and handed it down in its proper place in the divine record. And the sons of Noah, from some unexplained association, have adopted the three names and perpetuated them as family names. If, on the other hand, these countries are named after the descendants of Noah, the geographical description of the garden must have been composed after these men had settled in the countries to which they have given their names. At the same time, these territorial designations apply to a time earlier than Moses; hence the whole document may have been composed in the time of Noah, who survived the deluge three hundred and fifty years, and may have witnessed the settlement and the designation of these countries. And, lastly, if not put together in its present form by any previous writer, then the document is directly from the pen of Moses, who composed it out of preëxistent memorials. And as the previous document was solely due to inspiration, we shall in this case be led to ascribe the whole of Genesis to Moses as the immediate human composer.

It must be admitted that any of these ways of accounting for the existing form of this document is within the bounds of possibility. But the question is, Which is the most probable? We are in a fair position for discussing this question in a dispassionate manner, and without any anxiety, inasmuch as on any of the three suppositions Moses, who lived long after the latest event expressed or implied, is the acknowledged voucher for the document before us. It becomes us to speak with great moderation and caution on a point of so remote antiquity. To demonstrate this may be one of the best results of this inquiry.

I. The following are some of the grounds for the theory that the names of countries in the document are original and antediluvian: 1st. It was impossible to present to the postdiluvians in later terms the exact features and conditions of Eden, because many of these were obliterated. The four rivers no longer sprang from one. Two of the rivers remained, indeed, but the others had been so materially altered as to be no longer clearly distinguishable. The Euxine and the Caspian may now cover their former channels. In circumstances like these later names would not answer.

2d. Though the name Asshur represents a country nearly suitable to the original conditions, Havilah and Kush cannot easily have their postdiluvian meanings in the present passage. The presumption that they have has led interpreters into vain and endless conjectures. Supposing Kush to be Aethiopia, many have concluded the Gihon to be the Nile, which in that case must have had the same fountain-head, or at least risen in the same region with the Euphrates. Others, supposing it to be a district of the Tigris, near the Persian Gulf, imagine the Gihon to be one of the mouths of the united Euphrates and Tigris, and thus give a distorted sense to the statement that the four streams issued from one. This supposition, moreover, rests on the precarious hypothesis that the two rivers had always a common neck. The supposition that Havilah was in Arabia or on the Indian Ocean is liable to the same objections. Hence the presumption that these names are postdiluvian embarrasses the meaning of the passage.

3d. If these names be primeval, the present document in its integrity may have been composed in the time of Adam; and this accounts in the most satisfactory manner for the preservation of these traditions of the primitive age.

4th. The existence of antediluvian documents containing these original names would explain in the simplest manner the difference in the localities signified by them before and after the deluge. This difference has tended to invalidate the authenticity of the book in the eyes of some; whereas the existence of antiquated names in a document, though failing to convey to us much historical information, is calculated to impress us with a sense of its antiquity and authenticity. And this is of more importance than a little geographical knowledge in a work whose paramount object is to teach moral and religious truth.

5th. It is the habit of the sacred writers not to neglect the old names of former writers, but to append to them or conjoin with them the later or better known equivalents, when they wish to present a knowledge of the place and its former history. Thus, "Bela, this is Zoar" (Gen. xiv. 2, 8); "Kiriath-Arba, this is Hebron" (Gen. xxiii. 2); "Ephrath, this is Bethlehem" (Gen. xxxv. 19).

6th. These names would be orignally personal; and hence we can see a sufficient reason why the sons of Noah renewed them in their families, as they were naturally disposed to perpetuate the memory of their distinguished ancestors.

II. The second hypothesis, that the present form of the document originated in the time of Noah, after the flood, is supported by the following considerations: 1st. It accounts for the three names of countries in the easiest manner. The three descendants of Noah had by this time given their names to these countries. The supposition of a double origin or application of these names is not necessary.

2d. It accounts for the change in the localities bearing these names. The migrations and dispersions of tribes carried the names to new and various districts in the time intervening between Noah and Moses.

3d. It represents with sufficient exactness the locality of the garden. The deluge may not have greatly altered the general features of the countries. It may not be intended to represent the four rivers as derived from any common head stream; it may only be meant that the water system of the country gathered into four principal rivers. The names of all these are primeval. Two of them have descended to our days, because a permanent body of natives remained on their banks. The other two names have changed with the change of the inhabitants.

4th. It allows for primeval documents, if such existed of so early a date. The surviving document was prepared from such preëxisting writings, or from oral traditions of early days, as yet unalloyed with error in the God-fearing family of Noah.

5th. It is favored by the absence of explanatory proper names, which we might have expected if there had been any change known at the time of composition.

III. The hypothesis that Moses was not merely the authenticator, but the composer of this as well as the preceding and subsequent documents of Genesis, has some very strong grounds. 1st. It explains the local names with the same simplicity as in the preceding case (1). 2d. It allows for primeval and successive documents equally well (4), the rivers Pishon and Gihon and the primary Havilah and Kush being still in the memory of man, though they disappeared from the records of later times. 3d. It notifies with fidelity to the attentive reader the changes in the geographical designations of the past. 4th. It accounts for the occurrence of comparatively late names of localities in an account of primeval times. 5th. It explains the extreme brevity of these ancient notices. If documents had been composed from time to time and inserted in their original state in the book of God, it must have been a very voluminous and unmanageable record at a very early period.

These presumptions might now be summed up and compared, and the balance of probability struck, as is usually done. But we feel bound not to do so. 1st. We have not all the possibilities before us, neither is it in the power of human imagination to enumerate them, and therefore we have not the whole data for a calculation of probabilities. 2d. We have enough to do with facts, without elevating probabilities into the rank of facts, and thereby hopelessly embarrassing the whole premises of our deductive knowledge. Philosophy, and in particular the philosophy of criticism, has suffered long from this cause. Its very first principles have been overlaid with foregone conclusions, and its array of seeming facts has been impaired and enfeebled by the presence of many a sturdy probability or improbability in the solemn guise of a mock fact. 3d. The supposed fact of a set of documents composed by successive authors, duly labelled and handed down to Moses to be merely collected into the book of Genesis, if it was lurking in any mind, stands detected as only a probability or improbability at best. The second document implies facts, which are possibly not recorded till the fifth. 4th. And, *lastly*, there is no impossibility or improbability in Moses being not the compiler but the immediate author of the whole of Genesis, though it be morally certain that he had oral or written memoranda of the past before his mind.

XII. THE COMMAND. — Gen. ii. 15-17.

15. נוּחַ *rest, dwell.* עָבַד *work, till, serve.* שָׁמַר *keep, guard.*

15. And the LORD God took the man, and put him into the garden of Eden to dress it and to keep it. 16. And the LORD God commanded the man, saying, Of every tree of the garden, eat, eat mayest thou. 17. But of the tree of the knowledge of good and evil thou shalt not eat of it; for in the day of thy eating of it, die, die shalt thou.

We have here the education of man summed up in a single sentence. Let us endeavor to unfold the great lessons that are here taught.

15. *The Lord God took the man.* The same omnipotent hand that made him still held him. *And put him into the garden.* The original word is "caused him to rest," or dwell in the garden as an abode of peace and recreation. *To dress it and to keep it.* The plants of nature, left to their own course, may degenerate and become wild through the poverty of the soil on which they alight, or the gradual exhaustion of a once rich soil. The hand of rational man, therefore, has its appropriate sphere in preparing and enriching the soil, and in distributing the seeds and training the shoots in the way most favorable for the full development of the plant, and especially of its seed or fruits. This "dressing" was needed even in the garden. The "keeping" of it may refer to the guarding of it by enclosure from the depredations of the cattle, the wild beasts, or even the smaller animals. It includes also the faithful preservation of it as a trust committed to man by his bounteous Maker. There was now a man to till the soil. The second want of the world of plants was now supplied. Gardening was the first occupation of primeval man.

16, 17. *And the Lord God commanded the man, saying.* This is a pregnant sentence. It involves the first principles of our intellectual and moral philosophy.

I. The command here given in words brings into activity the intellectual nature of man. 1st. The power of understanding language is called forth. The command here addressed to him by his Maker is totally different from the blessings addressed to the animals in the preceding chapter. It was not necessary that these blessings should be understood in order to be carried into effect, inasmuch as He who pronounced them gave the instincts and powers requisite to their accomplishment. But this command addressed to man in words must be understood in order to be obeyed. The capacity for understanding language, then, was originally lodged in the constitution of man, and only required to be called out by the articulate voice of God. Still there is something wonderful here, something beyond the present grasp and promptitude of human apprehension. If we except the blessing, which may not have been heard, or may not have been uttered before this command, these words were absolutely the first that were heard by man. The significance of the sentences they formed must have been at the same time conveyed to man by immediate divine teaching. How the lesson was taught in an instant of time we cannot explain, though we have a distant resemblance of it in an infant learning to understand its mother-tongue. This process, indeed, goes over a space of two years; but still there is an instant in which the first conception of a sign is formed, the first word is apprehended, the first sentence is understood. In that instant the knowledge of language is virtually attained. With man, created at once in his full though undeveloped powers, and still unaffected by any moral taint, this instant came with the first words spoken to his ear and to his soul by his Maker's impressive voice, and the first lesson of language was at once thoroughly taught and learned. Man is now master of the theory of speech; the conception of a sign has been conveyed into his mind. This is the passive lesson of elocution: the practice, the active lesson, will speedily follow.

Not only the secondary part, however, but at the same time the primary and fundamental part of man's intellectual nature is here developed. The understanding of the sign necessarily implies the knowledge of the thing signified. The objective is represented here by the "trees of the garden." The subjective comes before his mind in the pronoun "thou." The physical constitution of man appears in the process of "eating." The moral part of his nature comes out in the significance of the words "mayest" and "shalt not." The distinction of merit in actions and things is expressed in the epithets "good and evil." The notion of reward is conveyed in the terms "life" and "death." And, lastly, the presence and authority of "the Lord God" is implied in the very nature of a command. Here is at least the opening of a wide field of observation for the nascent powers of the mind. He, indeed, must bear the image of God in perceptive powers, who shall scan with heedful eye the loftiest as well as the lowest in these varied scenes of reality. But as with the sign, so with the thing signified, a glance of intelligence instantaneously begins the converse of the susceptible mind with the world of reality around, and the enlargement of the sphere of human knowledge is merely a matter of time without end. How rapidly the process of apprehension would go on in the opening dawn of man's intellectual activity, how many flashes of intelligence would be compressed into a few moments of his first consciousness, we cannot tell. But we can readily believe that he would soon be able to form a just yet an infantile conception of the varied themes which are presented to his mind in this brief command.

Thus the susceptible part of man's intellect is evoked. The conceptive part will speedily follow, and display itself in the many inventions that will be sought out and applied to the objects which are placed at his disposal.

II. 1st. Next, the moral part of man's nature is here called into play. Mark God's mode of teaching. He issues a command. This is required in order to bring forth into consciousness the hitherto latent sensibility to moral obligation which was laid in the original constitution of man's being. A command implies a superior, whose right it is to command, and an inferior, whose duty it is to obey. The only ultimate and absolute ground of supremacy is creating, and of inferiority, being created. The Creator is the only proper and entire owner; and, within legitimate bounds, the owner has the right to do what he will with his own. The laying on of this command, therefore, brings man to the recognition of his dependence for being and for the character of that being on his Maker. From the knowledge of the fundamental relation of the creature to the Creator springs an immediate sense of the obligation he is under to render implicit obedience to the Author of his being. This is, therefore, man's first lesson in morals. It calls up in his breast the sense of duty, of right, of responsibility. These feelings could not have been elicited unless the moral susceptibility had been laid in the soul, and only waited for the first command to awaken it into consciousness. This lesson, however, is only the incidental effect of the command, and not the primary ground of its imposition.

2d. The special mandate here given is not arbitrary in its form, as is sometimes hastily supposed, but absolutely essential to the legal adjustment of things in this new stage of creation. Antecedent to the behest of the Creator, the only indefeasible right to all the creatures lay in himself. These creatures may be related to one another. In the great system of things, through the wonderful wisdom of the grand Designer, the use of some may be needful to the well-being, the development, and perpetuation of others. Nevertheless, no one has a shadow of right in the original nature of things to the use of any other. And when a moral agent comes upon the stage of being, in order to mark out the sphere of his legitimate action, an explicit declaration of the rights over other creatures granted and reserved must be made. The very issue of the command proclaims man's original right of property to be, not inherent, but derived.

As might be expected in these circumstances, the command has two clauses, — a permissive and a prohibitive. "Of every tree of the garden thou mayst freely eat." This displays in conspicuous terms the benignity of the Creator. "But of the tree of the knowledge of good and evil thou shalt not eat." This signalizes the absolute right of the Creator over all the trees, and over man himself. One tree only is withheld, which, whatever were its qualities, was at all events not necessary to the well-being of man. All the others that were likely for sight and good for food, including the tree of life, are made over to him by free grant. In this original provision for the vested rights of man in creation, we cannot but acknowledge with gratitude and humility the generous and considerate bounty of the Creator. This is not more conspicuous in the bestowment of all the other trees than in the withholding of the one, the participation of which was fraught with evil to mankind.

3d. The prohibitory part of this enactment is not a matter of indifference, as is sometimes imagined, but indispensable to the nature of a command, and, in particular, of a permissive act or declaration of granted rights. Every command has a negative part, expressed or implied, without which it would be no command at all. The command, "Go work to-day in my vineyard," implies thou shalt *not* do anything else; otherwise the son who works *not* obeys as well as the son who works. The present address of God to Adam, without the exceptive clause, would be a mere license, and not a command. But with the exceptive clause it is a command, and tantamount in meaning to the following positive injunction: Thou mayest eat of these trees *only*. An edict of license with a restrictive clause is the mildest form of command that could have been imposed for the trial of human obedience. Some may have thought that it would have been better for man if there had been no tree of the knowledge of good and evil. But second thoughts will correct this rash and wrong conclusion. 1st. This tree may have had other purposes to serve in the economy of things of which we are not aware; and, if so, it could not have been absent without detriment to the general good. 2d. But without any supposition at all, the tree was fraught with no evil whatever to man in itself. It was in the first instance the instrument of great good, of the most precious kind, to him. It served the purpose of calling up into view out of the depths of his nature the notion of moral obligation, with all the kindred notions of the inherent authority of the Creator and the innate subordination of himself, the creature, of the aboriginal right of the Creator alone in all the creatures, and the utter absence of any right in himself to any other creature whatsoever. The command concerning this tree thus set his moral convictions agoing, and awakened in him the new and pleasing consciousness that he was a moral being, and not a mere clod of the valley or brute of the field. This is the first thing this tree did for man; and we shall find it would have done a still better thing for him if he had only made a proper use of it. 3d. The absence of this tree would not at all have secured Adam from the possibility or the consequence of disobedience. Any grant to him whatsoever *must* have been made *with the reserve*, implicit or explicit, of the rights of all others. *The thing reserved* must in equity have been made known to him. In the present course of things it must have come in his way, and his trial would have been inevitable, and therefore his fall possible. Now, the forbidden tree is merely the thing reserved. Besides, even if man had been introduced into a sphere of existence where no reserved tree or other thing could ever have come within the range of his observation, and so no outward act of disobedience could have been perpetrated, still, as a being of moral susceptibility, he must come to the acknowledgment, express or implied, of the rights of the heavenly crown, before a mutual good understanding could have been established between him and his Maker. Thus we perceive that even in the impossible Utopia of metaphysical abstraction there is a virtual forbidden tree which forms the test of a man's moral relation to his Creator. Now, if the reserve be necessary, and therefore the test of obedience inevitable, to a moral being, it only remains to inquire whether the test employed be suitable and seasonable.

4th. That which is here made the matter of reserve, and so the test of obedience, is so far from being trivial or out of place, as has been imagined, that it is the proper and the only object immediately available for these purposes. The immediate want of man is food. The kind of food primarily designed for him is the fruit of trees. Grain, the secondary kind of vegetable diet, is the product of the farm rather than of the garden, and therefore does not now come into use. As the law must be laid down before man proceeds to an act of appropriation, the matter of reserve and consequent test of obedience is the fruit of a tree. Only by this can man at present learn the lessons of morality. To devise any other means, not arising from the actual state of things in which man was placed, would have been arbitrary and unreasonable. The immediate sphere of obedience lies in the circumstances in which he actually stands. These afforded no occasion for any other command than that which is given. Adam had no father, or mother, or neighbor, male or female, and therefore the second table of the law could not apply. But he had a relation to his Maker, and legislation on this could not be postponed. The command assumes the kindest, most intelligible, and convenient form for the infantile mind of primeval man.

5th. We are now prepared to understand why this tree is called the tree of the knowledge of good and evil. The prohibition of this tree brings man to the knowledge of good and evil. The products of creative power were all very good (Gen. i. 31). Even this tree itself is good, and productive of unspeakable good in the first instance to man. The discernment of merit comes up in his mind by this tree. Obedience to the command of God not to partake of this tree is a moral good. Disobedience to God by partaking of it is a moral evil. When we have formed an idea of a quality, we have at the same time an idea of its contrary. By the command concerning this tree man became possessed of the conceptions of good and evil, and so, theoretically, acquainted with their nature. This was that first lesson in morals of which we have spoken. It is quite evident that this knowledge could not be any physical effect of the tree, seeing its fruit was forbidden. It is obvious also that evil is as yet known in this fair world only as the negative of good. Hence the tree is the tree of the knowledge of good and evil, because by the command concerning it man comes to this knowledge.

6th. *In the day of thy eating thereof, die surely shalt thou.* The divine command is accompanied with its awful sanction, — death. The man could not at this time have any practical knowledge of the physical dissolution called death. We must, therefore, suppose either that God made him preternaturally acquainted with it, or that he conveyed to him the knowledge of it simply as the negation of life. The latter hypothesis is to be preferred, for several reasons. First, it is the more economical mode of instruction. Such knowledge may be imparted to man without anticipating experience. He was already conscious of life as a pure blessing. He was therefore capable of forming an idea of its loss. And death in the physical sense of the cessation of animal life and the disorganization of the body, he would come to understand in due time by experience. Secondly, death in reference to man is regarded in Scripture much more as the privation of life in the sense of a state of favor with God and consequent happiness than as the mere cessation of animal life (Gen. xxviii. 13; Exod. iii. 6; Matt. xxii. 32). Thirdly, the presence and privilege of the tree of life would enable man to see how easily he could be deprived of life, especially when he began to drink in its life-sustaining juices and feel the flow of vitality rushing through his veins and refreshing his whole physical nature. Take away this tree, and with all the other resources of nature he cannot but eventually droop and die. Fourthly, the man would thus regard his exclusion from the tree of life as the earnest of the sentence which would come to its fulness, when the animal frame would at length sink down under the wear and tear of life like the beasts that perish. Then would ensue to the dead but perpetually existing soul of man the total privation of all the sweets of life, and the experience of all the ills of penal death.

III. Man has here evidently become acquainted with his Maker. On the hearing and understanding of this sentence, at least, if not before, he has arrived at the knowledge of God, as existing, thinking, speaking, permitting, commanding, and thereby exercising all the prerogatives of that absolute authority over men and things which creation alone can give. If we were to draw all this out into distinct propositions, we should find that man was here furnished with a whole system of theology, ethics, and metaphysics, in a brief sentence. It may be said, indeed, that we need not suppose all this conveyed in the sentence before us. But, at all events, all this is implied in the few words here recorded to have been addressed to Adam, and there was not much time between his creation and his location in the garden for conveying any preliminary information. We may suppose the substance of the narrative contained in Gen. i. 2, 3, to have been communicated to him in due time. But it could not be all conveyed yet, as we are only in the sixth day, and the record in question reaches to the end of the seventh. It was not, therefore, composed until after that day had elapsed.

It is to be noticed here that God reserves to himself the administration of the divine law. This was absolutely necessary at the present stage of affairs, as man was but an individual subject, and not yet spread out into a multitude of people. Civil government was not formally constituted till after the deluge.

We can hardly overestimate the benefit, in the rapid development of his mind, which Adam thus derived from the presence and converse of his Maker. If no voice had struck his ear, no articulate sentence had reached his intellect, no authoritative command had penetrated his conscience, no perception of the Eternal Spirit had been presented to his apprehension, he might have been long in the mute, rude, and imperfectly developed state which has sometimes been ascribed to primeval man. But if contact with a highly accomplished master and a highly polished state of society makes all the difference between the savage and the civilized, what instantaneous expansion and elevation of the primitive mind, while yet in its virgin purity and unimpaired power, must have resulted from free converse with the all-perfect mind of the Creator himself! To the clear eye of native genius a starting idea is a whole science. By the insinuation of a few fundamental and germinant notions into his mind, Adam shot up at once into the full height and compass of a master spirit prepared to scan creation and adore the Creator.

XIII. THE NAMING OF THE ANIMALS. — Gen. ii. 18–20.

18. And the LORD God said, It is not good that man should
be alone: I will make a helpmeet for him. 19. And the LORD
God formed out of the soil every beast of the field, and every
fowl of the skies, and brought to the man to see what he
would call them; and whatsoever the man called the living
thing, that was the name thereof. 20. And the man gave
names to all the cattle, and to the fowl of the skies, and to
every beast of the field; and for Adam was not found a helpmeet for him.

Here man's intellectual faculties proceed from the passive and receptive to the active and communicative stage. This advance is made in the review and designation of the various species of animals that frequent the land and skies.

18. A new and final want of man is here stated. The Creator himself, in whose image he was made, had revealed himself to him in language. This, among many other effects, awakened the social affection. This affection was the index of social capacity. The first step towards communication between kindred spirits was accomplished when Adam heard and understood spoken language. Beyond all this God knew what was in the man whom he had formed. And he expresses this in the words, "It is not good for the man to be alone." He is formed to be social, to hold converse, not only with his superior, but also with his equal. As yet he is but a unit, an individual. He needs a mate, with whom he may take sweet counsel. And the benevolent Creator resolves to supply this want. "I will make him a helpmeet for him," — one who may not only reciprocate his feelings, but take an intelligent and appropriate part in his active pursuits.

19. Here, as in several previous instances (Gen. i. 5b, ii. 4, 8, 9), the narrative reverts to the earlier part of the sixth day. This is, therefore, another example of the connection according to thought overruling that according to time. The order of time, however, is restored, when we take in a sufficient portion of the narrative. We refer, therefore, to the fifth verse, which is the regulative sentence of the present passage. The second clause in the verse, however, which in the present case completes the thought in the mind of the writer, brings up the narrative to a point subsequent to that closing the preceding verse. The first two clauses, therefore, are to be combined into one; and when this is done, the order of time is observed.

Man has already become acquainted with his Maker. He has opened his eyes upon the trees of the garden, and learned to distinguish at least two of them by name. He is now to be introduced to the animal kingdom, with which he is connected by his physical nature, and of which he is the constituted lord. Not many hours or minutes before have they been called into existence. They are not yet, therefore, multiplied or scattered over the earth, and so do not require to be gathered for the purpose. The end of this introduction is said to be to see what he would call them. To name is to distinguish the nature of anything and do denote the thing by a sound bearing some analogy to its nature. To name is also the prerogative of the owner, superior, or head. Doubtless the animals instinctively distinguished man as their lord paramount, so far as his person and eye came within their actual observation. God had given man his first lesson in speech, when he caused him to hear and understand the spoken command. He now places him in a condition to put forth his naming power, and thereby go through the second lesson.

With the infant, the acquisition of language must be a gradual process, inasmuch as the vast multitude of words which constitute its vocabulary has to be heard one by one and noted in the memory. The infant is thus the passive recipient of a fully formed and long-established medium of converse. The first man, on the other hand, having received the conception of language, became himself the free and active inventor of the greatest part of its words. He accordingly discerns the kinds of animals, and gives each its appropriate name. The highly excited powers of imagination and analogy break forth into utterance, even before he has any one to hear and understand his words but the Creator himself.

This indicates to us a twofold use of language. First, it serves to register things and events in the apprehension and the memory. Man has a singular power of conferring with himself. This he carries on by means of language, in some form or other. He bears some resemblance to his Maker even in the complexity of his spiritual nature. He is at once speaker and hearer, and yet at the same time he is consciously one. Secondly, it is a medium of intelligent communication between spirits who cannot read another's thoughts by immediate intuition. The first of these uses seems to have preceded the second in the case of Adam, who was the former of the first language. The reflecting reader can tell what varied powers of reason are involved in the use of language, and to what an extent the mind of man was developed, when he proceeded to name the several classes of birds and beasts. He was evidently fitted for the highest enjoyments of social intercourse.

Among the trees in the garden God took the initiative, named the two that were conspicuous and essential to man's well being, and uttered the primeval command. Adam has now made acquaintance with the animal world, and, profiting by the lesson of the garden, proceeds himself to exercise the naming power. The names he gives are thenceforth the permanent designations of the different species of living creatures that appeared before him. These names being derived from some prominent quality, were fitted to be specific, or common to the class, and not peculiar to the individual.

20. We find, however, there was another end served by this review of the animals. "There was not found a helpmeet for the man," — an equal, a companion, a sharer of his thoughts, his observations, his joys, his purposes, his enterprises. It was now evident, from actual survey, that none of these animals, not even the serpent, was possessed of reason, of moral and intellectual ideas, of the faculties of abstracting and naming, of the capacities of rational fellowship or worship. They might be ministers to his purposes, but not helpers meet for him. On the other hand, God was the source of his being and the object of his reverence, but not on a par with himself in wants and resources. It was therefore apparent that man in respect of an equal was alone, and yet needed an associate. Thus in this passage the existence of the want is made out and asserted; in keeping with the mode of composition uniformly pursued by the sacred writer (Gen. i. 2, ii. 5).

XIV. THE WOMAN. — Gen. ii. 21–25.

21. תַּרְדֵּמָה *deep sleep*, ἔκστασις LXX. צֵלָע *rib, side, wing* of a building.

23. פַּעַם *beat, stroke, tread, anvil.* אִישׁ *man*, vir. אשה *be firm*, as a foundation; ישה *be firm* as a substance; אנש *be strong;* אוש *give, help*: hence the strong, the brave, the defender, the nourisher. אִשָּׁה *woman*, fem. of the above; *wife*.

21. And the Lord God caused a deep sleep to fall upon the man, and he slept; and he took one of his ribs, and closed up the flesh instead thereof. 22. And the Lord God built the rib which he had taken from the man into a woman, and brought her unto the man. 23. And the man said, This is now bone of my bones and flesh of my flesh: to her shall be called woman, because she was taken out of a man. 24. Therefore shall a man leave his father and his mother and cleave unto his wife: and they shall be one flesh. 25. And they were both naked, the man and his wife, and they were not ashamed.

The second creative step in the constitution of man as the natural head of a race is now described. This supplies the defect that was drawn forth into consciousness in the preceding passage. Man here passes out of solitude into society, out of unity into multiplicity.

21, 22. Here we find ourselves still in the sixth day. This passage throws a new light on Genesis i. 27. It is there stated that man was first created in the image of God, and then that he was created male and female. From the present passage we learn that these two acts of creation were distinct in point of time. First, we see man was really one in his origin, and contained in this unity the perfection of manhood. It does not appear, however, that man was so constituted by nature as to throw off another of the same kind by his inherent power. In fact, if he had, the other should have been, not a female, but another human being in every respect like himself; and he would thus have resembled those plants that are capable of being propagated by a bud. Besides, he would have been endowed with a power different from his actual posterity; and thus the head would not have corresponded with the members of the race. The narrative, however, is opposed to this view of man's nature. For the change, by which the woman comes into existence, is directly ascribed to the original Maker. A part of the man is taken for the purpose, which can be spared without interfering with the integrity of his nature. It manifestly does not constitute a woman by the mere act of separation, as we are told that the Lord God built it into a woman. It is needless, therefore, to speculate whether the part taken were literally a rib, or some other side piece designedly put there by the provident Creator, for the purpose of becoming the rudiment of a full-grown woman. It is expressly called, not a rib, but one of his ribs; and this evidently implies that he had other similar parts. This binds us, we conceive, to the literal rib of bone and flesh. And thus, in accordance with the account in the foregoing chapter, we have, first, the single man created, the full representative and potential fountain of the race, and then, out of this one, in the way now described, we have the male and the female created.

The original unity of man constitutes the strict unity of the race. The construction of the rib into a woman establishes the individuality of man's person before, as well as after, the removal of the rib. The selection of a rib to form into a woman constitutes her, in an eminent sense, a helpmeet for him, in company with him, on a footing of equality with him. At the same time, the after building of the part into a woman determines the distinct personality and individuality of the woman. Thus we perceive that the entire race, even the very first mother of it, has its essential unit and representative in the first man.

The Almighty has called intelligent beings into existence in two ways. The angels he seems to have created as individuals (Mark xii. 25), constituting an order of beings the unity of which lies in the common Creator. Man he created as the parent of a race about to spring from a single head, and having its unity in that head. A single angel then stands by himself, and for himself; and all his actions belong only to himself, except so far as example, persuasion, or leadership may have involved others in them. But the single man, who is at the same time head of a race, is in quite a different position. He stands for the race, which is virtually contained in him; and his actions belong not only to him as an individual, but, in a certain sense, to the whole race, of which he is at present the sum. An angel counts only for the unit of his order. The first man counts for the whole race as long as he is alone. The one angel is responsible only for himself. The first man is not only an individual, but, as long as he is alone, the sum total of a race; and is therefore so long responsible, not only for himself, but for the race, as the head of which he acts. This deep question of race will meet us again at a future stage of man's history.

As the All-wise Being never does anything without reason, it becomes an interesting question, why the creation of woman was deferred to this precise juncture in human history. *First*, man's original unity is the counterpart of the unity of God. He was to be made in the image of God, and after his likeness. If the male and the female had been created at once, an essential feature of the divine likeness would have been wanting. But, as in the absolute One there is no duality, whether in sex or in any other respect, so is there none in the original form and constitution of man. Hence we learn the absurdity of those who import into their notions of the deity the distinction of sex, and all the alliances which are involved in a race of gods. *Secondly*, the natural unity of the first pair, and of the race descended from them, is established by the primary creation of an individual, from whom is derived, by a second creative process, the first woman. The race of man is thus a perfect unity, flowing from a single centre of human life. *Thirdly*, two remarkable events occur in the experience of man before the formation of the woman, — his instalment in the garden as its owner, keeper, and dresser; and his review of the animals, as their rational superior, to whom they yield an instinctive homage. By the former he is prepared to provide for the sustenance and comfort of his wife;

by the latter, he becomes aware of his power to protect her. Still further, by the interview with his Maker in the garden he came to understand language; and by the inspection of the animals to employ it himself. Speech implies the exercise of the susceptive and conceptive powers of the understanding. Thus Adam was qualified to hold intelligent converse with a being like himself. He was competent to be the instructor of his wife in words and things. Again, he had met with his superior in his Creator, his inferiors in the animals; and he was now to meet his equal in the woman. And, lastly, by the divine command his moral sense had been brought into play, the theory of moral obligation had been revealed to his mind, and he was therefore prepared to deal with a moral being like himself, to understand and respect the rights of another, to do unto another as he would have another do to him. It was especially necessary that the sense of right should grow up in his breast, to keep in due check that might in which he excelled, before the weaker and gentler sex was called into being, and intrusted to his charge. These are some of the obvious reasons for delaying the formation of the woman to the present crisis.

23. Whether the primeval man was conscious of the change in himself, and of the work of the Supreme Being while it was going on, or received supernatural information of the event when he awoke, does not appear. But he is perfectly aware of the nature of her who now for the first time appears before his eyes. This is evinced in his speech on beholding her: "This, *now*,"—in contrast with the whole animal creation *just before* presented to his view, in which he had failed to find a helpmeet for him,—"is bone of my bone, and flesh of my flesh;" whence we perceive that the rib included both bone and flesh. "To this" counterpart of myself "shall be called woman;" the word in the original being a feminine form of *man*, to which we have no exact equivalent, though the word *woman* (womb-man, or wife-man), proves our word *man* to have been originally of the common gender. "Because out of a man was she taken;" being taken out of a man, she is human; and being a perfect individual, she is a female man.

24. These might be the words of the first man. As he thoroughly understood the relation between himself and the woman, there is no new difficulty in conceiving him to become acquainted at the same time with the relationship of son to father and mother, which was in fact only another form of that in which the newly-formed woman stood to himself. The latter is really more intimate and permanent than the

former, and naturally therefore takes its place, especially as the practical of the filial tie, — that of being trained to maturity, — is already accomplished, when the conjugal one begins.

But it seems more probable that this sentence is the reflection of the inspired author on the peculiar mode in which the female was formed from the male. Such remarks of the writer are frequently introduced by the word "therefore" (עַל־כֵּן). It is designed to inculcate on the race that was to spring from them the inviolable sanctity of the conjugal relation. In the primeval wedlock one man was joined to one woman only for life. Hence in the marriage relation the animal is subordinate to the rational. The communication of ideas; the cherishing of the true, the right, the good; the cultivation of the social affections; the spontaneous outflow of mutual good offices; the thousand nameless little thoughts, looks, words, and deeds that cheer the brow and warm the heart; the common care of children, servants, and dependents; the constant and heartfelt worship of the Father of all, constitute the main ends and joys of the married state.

After the exclamation of the man on contemplating the woman, as bone of his bones and flesh of his flesh, and therefore physically, intellectually, and morally qualified to be his mate, we may suppose immediately to follow the blessing of man, and the general endowment of himself and the animals with the fruits of the soil as recorded in the preceding chapter (v. 28–30). The endowment of man embraces every tree in which is the fruit of a tree yielding seed. This general grant was of course understood by man to exclude the tree of the knowledge of good and evil, which was excepted, if not by its specific nature, yet by the previous command given to man. This command we find was given before the formation of the woman, and therefore sometime before the events recorded in the second and third clauses of Gen. i. 27. Hence it preceded the blessing and the endowment. It was not peculiar, however, to the tree of the knowledge of good and evil to be intended for other purposes than the food of man, as there are very many other trees that afford no proper nutriment to man. The endowment, therefore, refers to such trees as were at the same time nutritive and not expressly and previously forbidden.

This chapter is occupied with the "generations, issues or products of the skies and the land," or, in other words, of the things created in the six days. It is the meet preface to the more specific history of man, as it records his constitution, his provision, his moral and intellectual cultivation, and his social perfection. It brings us up to the close of the sixth day. As the Creator pronounced a sentence of approbation on all that he had made at the end of that day, we have reason to believe that no moral derangement had yet taken place in man's nature.

25. This is corroborated by the statement contained in this verse. "They were both naked, and were not ashamed." Of nakedness in our sense of the term they had as yet no conception. On the contrary, they were conscious of being sufficiently clothed in a physical sense by nature's covering, the skin, — and, in a spiritual point of view, they were clad as in a panoply of steel with the consciousness of innocence, or, indeed, the unconsciousness of evil existing anywhere, and the simple ignorance of its nature, except so far as the command of God had awakened in them some speculative conception of it. Hence they were not ashamed. For shame implies a sense of guilt, which they had not, and an exposedness to the searching eye of a condemning judge, from which they were equally free. With the sentence terminates all we know of primeval innocence. May we surmise from it that the first pair spent at least the Sabbath, if not some days, or weeks, or years, in a state of integrity?

From what has been said, it is evident that this sentence was written after the fall; for it speaks in language which was not intelligible till after that event had occurred. Contemplated in this point of view, it is the most melancholy sentence in the book of God. For it is evidently placed here to foreshadow the dark event to be recorded in the next chapter.

Two hallowed institutions have descended to us from the days of primeval innocence, — the wedding and the Sabbath. The former indicates communion of the purest and most perfect kind between equals of the same class. The latter implies communion of the highest and holiest kind between the Creator and the intelligent creature. The two combined import communion with each other in communion with God.

Wedded union is the sum and type of every social tie. It gives rise and scope to all the nameless joys of home. It is the native field for the cultivation of all the social virtues. It provides for the due framing and checking of the overgrowth of interest in self, and for the gentle training and fostering of a growing interest in others. It unfolds the graces and charms of mutual love, and imparts to the susceptible heart all the peace and joy, all the light and fire, all the frankness and life of conscious and constant purity and good-will. Friendship, brotherly-kindness, and love are still hopeful and sacred names among mankind.

Sabbath-keeping lifts the wedded pair, the brethren, the friends, the one-minded, up to communion with God. The joy of achievement is a feeling common to God and man. The commemoration of the auspicious beginning of a holy and happy existence will live in man while memory lasts. The anticipation also of joyful repose after the end of a work well done will gild the future while hope survives. Thus the idea of the Sabbath spans the whole of man's existence. History and prophecy commingle in its peaceful meditations, and both are linked with God. God IS: he is the Author of all being, and the Rewarder of them that diligently seek him. This is the noble lesson of the Sabbath. Each seventh day is well spent in attending to the realization of these great thoughts.

Hence it appears that the social principle lies at the root of a spiritual nature. In the very essence of the spiritual monad is the faculty of self-consciousness. Here is the curious mystery of a soul standing beside itself, cognizing itself, and taking note of its various faculties and acts, and yet perfectly conscious of its unity and identity. And the process does not stop here. We catch ourselves at times debating with ourselves, urging the pros and cons of a case in hand, enjoying the sallies or sorry for the poverty of our wit, nay, solemnly sitting in judgment on ourselves, and pronouncing a sentence of approval or disapproval on the merit or demerit of our actions. Thus, throughout the whole range of our moral and intellectual nature, memory for the past and fancy for the future furnish us with another self, with whom we hold familiar converse. Here there is the social principle living and moving in the very centre of our being. Let the soul only look out through the senses and descry another like itself, and social converse between kindred spirits must begin. The Sabbath and the wedding touch the inner springs of the soul, and bring the social principle into exercise in the two great spheres of our relation to our Maker and to one another.

SECTION III — THE FALL

XV. THE FALL. — Gen. iii. 1–7.

1. נָחָשׁ *serpent;* r. *hiss,* Ges.; *sting,* Mey. עָרוּם *subtle, crafty,* using craft for defence.

7. תָּפַר *sew, stitch, tack* together. חֲגוֹרָה *girdle,* not necessarily *apron.*

III. 1. Now the serpent was more subtle than any beast of the field which the Lord God had made. And he said unto the woman, Then it is so that God hath said, Ye shall not eat of every tree of the garden. 2. Then said the woman to the serpent, Of the fruit of the trees of the garden we may eat. 3. But of the fruit of the tree which is in the midst of the garden hath God said, Ye shall not eat of it, neither touch it, lest ye die. 4. Then said the serpent unto the woman, Not die, die shall ye. 5. For God doth know that in the day ye eat of it, then will your eyes be opened; and ye will be like God, knowing good and evil. 6. And the woman saw that the tree was good for food, and that it was likely to the eyes, and a tree to be desired to make wise; and she took of the fruit thereof and did eat, and gave also unto her husband with her, and he did eat. 7. Then were opened the eyes of them both, and they knew that they were naked; and they sewed the leaves of the fig, and made themselves girdles.

This chapter continues the piece commenced at Gen. ii. 4. The same combination of divine names is found here, except in the dialogue between the serpent and the woman, where God (אֱלֹהִים) alone is used. It is natural for the tempter to use only the more distant and abstract name of God. It narrates in simple terms the fall of man.

1. The serpent is here called a beast of the field; that is, neither a domesticated animal nor one of the smaller sorts. The Lord God had made it, and therefore it was a creature called into being on the same day with Adam. It is not the wisdom, but the wiliness of the serpent which is here noted. This animal is destitute of arms or legs by which to escape danger. It is therefore thrown back upon instinct, aided by a quick and glaring eye, and a rapid dart and recoil, to evade the stroke of violence, and watch and seize the unguarded moment for inflicting the deadly bite. Hence the wily and insidious character of its instinct, which is noticed to account for the mode of attack here chosen, and the style of the conversation. The whole is so deeply designed, that the origin and progress of evil in the breast is as nearly as possible such as it might have been had there been no prompter. No startling proposal of disobedience is made, no advice, no persuasion to partake of the fruit is employed. The suggestion or assertion of the false only is plainly offered; and the bewildered mind is left to draw its own false inferences, and pursue its own misguided course. The tempter addresses the woman as the more susceptible and unguarded of the two creatures he would betray. He ventures upon a half-questioning, half-insinuating remark,—"It is so, then, that God hath said, Ye shall not eat of every tree of the garden." This seems to be a feeler for some weak point, where the fidelity of the woman to her Maker might be shaken. It hints at something strange, if not unjust or unkind, on the part of God. Why was any tree withheld? he would insinuate.

2, 3. The woman gives the natural and distinct answer of unaffected sincerity to this suggestion. The deviations from the strict letter of the law are nothing more than the free and earnest expressions of her feelings. The expression, "neither shall ye touch it," merely implies that they were not to meddle with it, as a forbidden thing.

4, 5. The serpent now makes a strong and bold assertion, denying the deadly efficacy of the tree, or the fatal consequence of partaking of it, and affirming that God was aware that on the eating of it their eyes would be opened, and they would be like himself in knowing good and evil.

Let us remember that this was the first falsehood the woman ever heard. Her mind was also infantile as yet, so far as experience was concerned. The opening mind is naturally inclined to believe the truth of every assertion, until it has learned by experience the falsehood of some. There was also in this falsehood that which gives the power to deceive, a great deal of truth combined with the element of untruth. The tree was not physically fatal to life, and the eating of it really issued in a knowledge of good and evil. Nevertheless, the partaking of that which was forbidden issued in the legal and actual privation of life. And it did not make them know good and evil altogether, as God knows it, but in an experimental sense, as the devil knows it. In point of knowledge, they became like God; in point of morality, like the tempter.

6. *And the woman saw.* She saw the tree, no doubt, and that it was likely to look upon, with the eye of sense. But only with the eye of fancy, highly excited by the hints of the tempter, did she see that it was good for food, and to be desired to make one wise. Appetite, taste, and philosophy, or the love of wisdom, are the great motives in the human breast which fancy assumes this tree will gratify. Other trees please the taste and the sight. But this one has the preëminent charm of administering not only to the sense, but also to the reason.

It would be rash to suppose that we can analyze that lightning process of instinctive thought which then took place in the mind of the woman; and worse than rash, it would be wrong, to imagine that we can show the rationale of that which in its fundamental point was a violation of right reason. But it is evident from this verse that she attached some credit to the bold statement of the serpent, that the eating of the fruit would be attended with the extraordinary result of making them, like God himself, acquainted with good and evil, especially as it did not contradict any assertion of Jehovah, God, and was countenanced by the name, "the tree of the knowledge of good and evil." It was evidently a new thought to her, that the knowledge of good and evil was to result from the eating of it. That God should know this, if a fact, was undeniable. Again, to know good and evil as the effect of partaking of it, implied that the consequence was not a cessation of existence, or of consciousness; for, if so, how could there be any knowledge? And, if death in her conception implied merely exclusion from the favor of God and the tree of life, might she not imagine that the new knowledge acquired, and the elevation to a new resemblance, or even equality to God himself in this respect, would be more than a compensation for such losses; especially as the disinterestedness of the divine motives had been at least called in question by the serpent? Here, no doubt, is a fine web of sophistry, woven by the excited fancy in an instant of time.

It is easy to say the knowledge of good and evil was not a physical effect of eating of the fruit; that the obtaining of this knowledge by partaking of it was an evil, and not a good in itself and in its consequences, as it was the origin of an evil conscience, which is in itself an unspeakable ill, and attended with the forfeiture of the divine favor, and of the tree of life, and with the endurance of all the positive misery which such a condition involves; and that the command of God was founded on the clearest right, — that of creation, — occasioned by the immediate necessity of defining the rights of man, and prompted by disinterested benevolence toward His intelligent creatures, whom He was framing for such intellectual and moral perfection, as was by them attainable. It is easy to cry out, How unreasonable was the conduct of the primeval pair! Let us not forget that any sin is unreasonable, unaccountable, essentially mysterious. In fact, if it were wholly reasonable, it would no longer be sin. Only a moment before, the woman had declared that God had said, "Of the fruit of the tree in the midst of the garden, ye shall not eat." Yet she now sees, and her head is so full of it that she can think of nothing else, that the tree is good for food and pleasant to the eyes, — as if there were no other good and pleasant trees in the garden, and, as she fancies, desirable to make one wise, like God; as if there were no other way to this wisdom but an unlawful one, and no other likeness to God but a stolen likeness, — and therefore takes of the fruit and eats, and gives to her husband, and he eats! The *present desire* is without any necessity gratified by an act known to be wrong, at the risk of all the consequences of disobedience! Such is sin.

7. Certain immediate effects of the act are here stated. *Their eyes were opened.* This cannot mean literally that they were blind up to this moment; for Adam, no doubt, saw the tree in the garden concerning which he received a command, the animals which he named, and the woman whom he recognized as bone of his bones and flesh of his flesh. And of the woman it is affirmed that she saw that the tree possessed certain qualities, one of which at least was conspicuous to the eye.

It must therefore mean that a new aspect was presented by things on the commission of the first offence. As soon as the transgression is actually over, the sense of the wrongfulness of the act rushes on the mind. The displeasure of the great Being whose command has been disobeyed, the irretrievable loss which follows sin, the shame of being looked upon by the bystanders as a guilty thing, crowd upon the view. All nature, every single creature, seems now a witness of their guilt and shame, a condemning judge, an agent of the divine vengeance.

Such is the knowledge of good and evil they have acquired by their fall from obedience, — such is the opening of the eye which has requited their wrong-doing. What a different scene had once presented itself to the eyes of innocence! All had been friendly. All nature had bowed in willing obedience to the lords of the earth. Neither the sense nor the reality of danger had ever disturbed the tranquillity of their pure minds.

They knew that they were naked. This second effect results immediately from the consciousness of guilt. They now take notice that their guilty persons are exposed to view, and they shrink from the glance of every condemning eye. They imagine there is a witness of their guilt in every creature, and they conceive the abhorrence which it must produce in the spectator. In their infantile experience they endeavor to hide their persons, which they feel to be suffused all over with the blush of shame.

Accordingly, *they sewed the leaves of the fig,* which, we may suppose, they wrapped round them, and fastened with the girdles they had formed for this purpose. The leaves of the fig did not constitute the girdles, but the coverings which were fastened on with these. These leaves were intended to conceal their whole persons from observation. Job describes himself sewing sackcloth on his skin (Job xvi. 15), and girding on sackcloth (1 Kings xx. 32; Lam. ii. 10; Joel i. 8) is a familiar phrase in Scripture. The primitive sewing was some sort of tacking together, which is not more particularly described. Every operation of this sort has a rude beginning. The word *girdle* (חֲגוֹרָה) signifies that which girds on the dress.

Here it becomes us to pause for a moment that we may mark what was the precise nature of the first transgression. It was plainly disobedience to an express and well-understood command of the Creator. It matters not what was the nature of the command, since it could not be other than right and pure. The more simple and easy the thing enjoined, the more blameworthy the act of disobedience. But what was the command? Simply to abstain from the fruit of a tree, which was designated the tree of the knowledge of good and evil, upon pain of death. We have seen already that this command arose from the necessity of immediate legislation, and took its shape as the only possible one in the circumstances of the case. The peculiar attraction, however, which the forbidden tree presented, was not its excellence for the appetite or pleasantness to the eyes, since these were common to all the trees, but its supposed power of conferring moral knowledge on those who partook of it, and, according to the serpent's explanation, making them like God in this important respect. Hence the real and obvious motive of the transgressor was the desire of knowledge and likeness to God. Whatever other lusts, therefore, may have afterwards come out in the nature of fallen man, it is plain that the lust after likeness to God in moral discernment was that which originally brought forth sin in man. Sexual desire does not appear here at all. The appetite is excited by other trees as well as this. The desire of knowledge, and the ambition to be, in some sense, divine, are alone peculiar and prevalent as motives. Hence it appears that God proved our first parents, not through any of the animal appetites, but through the higher propensities of their intellectual and moral nature. Though the occasion, therefore, may at first sight appear trivial, yet it becomes awfully momentous when we discover that the rectitude of God is impugned, his prerogative invaded, his command disregarded, his attribute of moral omniscience and all the imaginable advantages attendant thereupon grasped at with an eager and wilful hand. To disobey the command of God, imposed according to the dictates of pure reason, and with the authority of a Creator, from the vain desire of being like him, or independent of him, in knowledge, can never be anything but an offence of the deepest dye.

We are bound, moreover, to acknowledge and maintain, in the most explicit manner, the equity of the divine procedure in permitting the temptation of man. The only new thing here is the intervention of the tempter. It may be imagined that this deciever should have been kept away. But we must not speak with inconsiderate haste on a matter of such import. 1st. We know that God has not used forcible means to prevent the rise of moral evil among his intelligent creatures. We cannot with reason affirm that he should have done so; because, to put force on a voluntary act, and yet leave it voluntary, seems to reason a contradiction in terms, and, therefore, impossible; and unless an act be voluntary, it cannot have any moral character; and without voluntary action, we cannot have a moral agent. 2d. We know that God does not immediately annihilate the evil-doer. Neither can we affirm with reason that he ought to have done so; for, to lay an adequate penalty on sin, and then put the sinner out of existence, so that this penalty can never be exacted, seems to reason a moral inconsistency, and, therefore, impossible in a being of moral perfection. 3d. We know that God does not withdraw the evil-doer from all intercourse with other moral agents. Here, again, reason does not constrain us to pronounce that it is expedient so to do; for the innocent ought, and it is natural that they should, learn a holy abhorrence of sin, and a salutary dread of its penalty, from these waifs of society, rather than follow their pernicious example. The wrong-doers are not less under the control of God than if they were in the most impenetrable dungeon; while they are at the same time constant beacons to warn others from transgression. He leaves them to fill up the measure of their iniquity, while the intelligent world are cognizant of their guilt, that they may acknowledge the justice of their punishment, and comprehend the infinite holiness of the judge of all the earth. 4th. We know that God tries his moral creatures. Abraham, Job, and all his saints have to undergo their trial. He suffered the Lord Jesus Christ, the second Adam, to be tempted. And we must not expect the first Adam to be exempted from the common ordeal. We can only be assured that his justice will not allow his moral creatures to be at any disadvantage in the trial. Accordingly, 1st, God himself in the first instance speaks to Adam, and gives him an explicit command not arbitrary in its conception, but arising out of the necessity of the case. And it is plain that Eve was perfectly aware that he had himself imposed this prohibition. 2d. The tempter is not allowed to appear in his proper person to our first parents. The serpent only is seen or heard by them, — a creature inferior to themselves, and infinitely beneath the God who made them, and condescended to communicate with them with the authority of a father. 3d. The serpent neither threatens nor directly persuades; much less is he permitted to use any means of compulsion: he simply falsifies. As the God of truth had spoken to them before, the false insinuation places them at no disadvantage.

Man has now come to the second step in morals, — the practice. Thereby he has come to the knowledge of good and evil, not merely as an ideal, but as an actual thing. But he has attained this end, not by standing in, but by falling from, his integrity. If he had stood the test of this temptation, as he might have done, he would have come by the knowledge of good and evil equally well, but with a far different result. As he bore the image of God in his higher nature, he would have resembled him, not only in knowledge, thus honorably acquired by resisting temptation, but also in moral good, thus realized in his own act and will. As it is, he has gained some knowledge in an unlawful and disastrous way; but he has also taken in that moral evil, which is the image, not of God, but of the tempter, to whom he has yielded.

This result is rendered still more lamentable when we remember that these transgressors constituted the human race in its primeval source. In them, therefore, the race actually falls. In their sin the race is become morally corrupt. In their guilt the race is involved in guilt. Their character and doom descend to their latest posterity.

We have not yet noticed the circumstance of the serpent's speaking, and of course speaking rationally. This seems to have awakened no attention in the tempted, and, so far as we see, to have exercised no influence on their conduct. In their inexperience, it is probable that they did not yet know what was wonderful, and what not; or, in preciser terms, what was supernatural, and what natural. But even if they had known enough to be surprised at the serpent speaking, it might have told in opposite ways upon their conclusions. On the one hand, Adam had seen and named the serpent, and found in it merely a dumb irrational animal, altogether unfit to be his companion, and therefore he might have been amazed to hear him speak, and, shall we say, led to suspect a prompter. But, on the other hand, we have no reason to suppose that Adam had any knowledge or suspicion of any creature but those which had been already brought before him, among which was the serpent. He could, therefore, have no surmise of any superior creature who might make use of the serpent for its own purposes. We question whether the thought could have struck his mind that the serpent had partaken of the forbidden fruit, and thereby attained to the marvellous elevation from brutality to reason and speech. But, if it had, it would have made a deep impression on his mind of the wonderful potency of the tree. These considerations apply with perhaps still greater force to Eve, who was first deceived.

But to us who have a more extensive experience of the course of nature, the speaking of a serpent cannot be regarded otherwise than as a preternatural occurrence. It indicates the presence of a power above the nature of the serpent, possessed, too, by a being of a malignant nature, and at enmity with God and truth; a spiritual being, who is able and has been permitted to make use of the organs of the serpent in some way for the purposes of temptation. But while for a wise and worthy end this alien from God's home is permitted to test the moral character of man, he is not allowed to make any appearance or show any sign of his own presence to man. The serpent alone is visibly present; the temptation is conducted only through words uttered by bodily organs, and the tempted show no suspicion of any other tempter. Thus in the disposal of a just Providence, man is brought into immediate contact only with an inferior creature, and therefore has a fair field in the season of trial. And if that creature is possessed by a being of superior intelligence, this is only displayed in such a manner as to exert no influence on man but that of suggestive argument and false assertion.

XVI. THE JUDGMENT.—Gen. iii. 8–21.

15. שׁוּף *bruise, wound.* τηρεῖν (= τερεῖν?) ἐκτρίβειν (Job ix. 17), καταπατεῖν (Ps. cxxxix. 11), συντρίβειν (Rom. xvi. 20).
16. תְּשׁוּקָה *desire, inclination.* αποστροφή, ἐπιστροφή (Song vii. 11).
20. חַוָּה *Eve, the living, life, life-place,* or village.

8. And they heard the voice of the Lord God, walking in the garden in the air of the day: and the man and his wife hid themselves from the face of the Lord God amidst the trees of the garden. 9. And the Lord God called to the man and said unto him, Where art thou? 10. And he said, Thy voice I heard in the garden; and I was afraid, because I was naked, and I hid myself. 11. And he said, Who showed thee that thou wast naked? Hast thou eaten of the tree of which I commanded thee not to eat? 12. And the man said, The woman whom thou gavest to be with me, she gave me of the tree and I did eat. 13. Then said the Lord God to the woman, What is this thou hast done? And the woman said, The serpent beguiled me, and I did eat. 14. Then said the Lord God unto the serpent, Because thou hast done this, cursed art thou above all cattle and above every beast of the field: upon thy belly shalt thou go, and dust shalt thou eat all the days of thy life. 15. And enmity will I put between thee and the woman, and between thy seed and her seed; he shall bruise thy head, and thou shalt bruise his heel. § 1.

16. Unto the woman he said, Multiply, multiply will I thy sorrow and thy conception: in sorrow shalt thou bring forth

children; and unto thy husband shall be thy desire, and he shall rule over thee. § 2.

17. And to the man he said, Because thou hast hearkened to the voice of thy wife, and didst eat of the tree of which I commanded thee, saying, Thou shalt not eat of it, cursed is the ground for thy sake; in sorrow shalt thou eat of it all the days of thy life. 18. And thorns and thistles shall it grow to thee; and thou shalt eat the herb of the field. 19. In the sweat of thy face shalt thou eat bread, until thou return to the soil, out of which thou wast taken; for dust thou art, and unto dust shalt thou return.

20. And the man called his wife's name Eve, because she was the mother of all living. 21. And the LORD God made for Adam and for his wife coats of skin, and clothed them. ¶ 8.

This passage contains the examination of the transgressors, 8–13, the sentence pronounced upon each, 14–19, and certain particulars following thereupon, 20, 21.

8, 9. The voice, we conceive, is the thunder of the approach of God and his call to Adam. The hiding is another token of the childlike simplicity of the parents of our race under the shame and fear of guilt. The question, *Where art thou?* implies that the Lord was aware of their endeavor to hide themselves from him.

10–12. Adam confesses that he was afraid of God, because he was naked. There is an instinctive hiding of his thoughts from God in this very speech. The nakedness is mentioned, but not the disobedience from which the sense of it arose. To the direct interrogatory of the Almighty, he confesses who made him acquainted with his nakedness and the fact of his having eaten of the forbidden fruit: "*The woman* gave me of the tree, and *I did eat*."

13. The woman makes a similar confession and a similar indication of the source of her temptation. She has now found out that the serpent *beguiled* her. The result has not corresponded to the benefit she was led to anticipate.

There seems not to be any disingenuousness in either case. Sin does not take full possession of the will all at once. It is a slow poison. It has a growth. It requires time and frequent repetition to sink from a state of purity into a habit of inveterate sin. While it is insensibly gathering strength and subjugating the will, the original integrity of the moral nature manifests a long but fading vitality. The same line of things does not always occupy the attention. When the chain of events linked with the act of sin does not force the attention of the mind, and constrain the will to act a selfish part, another train of things comes before the mind, finds the will unaffected by personal considerations, and therefore ready to take its direction from the reason. Hence the consciousness of a fallen soul has its lucid intervals, in which the conscience gives a verdict and guides the will. But these intervals become less frequent and less decisive as the entanglements of ever-multiplying sinful acts wind round the soul and aggravate its bondage and its blindness.

14, 15. Here begins the judgment. Sentence is pronounced upon the serpent in the presence, no doubt, of the man and woman. The serpent is not examined, *first*, because it is a dumb unreasoning animal in itself, and therefore incapable of judicial examination, and it was the serpent only that was palpable to the senses of our first parents in the temptation; and, *secondly*, because the true tempter was not a new, but an old offender.

This sentence has a literal application to the serpent. The curse (Gen. ix. 25, n.) of the serpent lies in a more grovelling nature than that of the other land animals. This appears in its going on its belly and eating the dust. Other animals have at least feet to elevate them above the dust; the serpent tribe has not even feet. Other animals elevate the head in their natural position above the soil: the serpent lays its head naturally on the sod, and therefore may be said to eat the dust, as the wounded warrior bites the dust in death. The earthworm is probably included in the description here given of the serpent group. It goes upon its belly, and actually does eat the dust. Eating the dust, like feeding upon ashes, is an expression for signal defeat in every aim. The enmity, the mode of its display, and the issue are also singularly characteristic of the literal serpent.

It is the custom of Scripture jurisprudence to visit brute animals with certain judicial consequences of injuries they have been instrumental in doing to man, especially if this has arisen through the design or neglect of the owner, or other responsible agent (Gen. ix. 5; Exod. xxi. 28–36). In the present case the injury done was of a moral, not a physical nature. Hence the penalty consists in a curse; that is, a state of greater degradation below man than the other land animals.

The serpent in the extraordinary event here recorded exercised the powers of human speech and reasoning. And it is natural to suppose that these exhibitions of intelligence were accompanied with an attitude and a gesture above its natural rank in the scale of creation. The effect of the judicial sentence would be to remand it to its original grovelling condition, and give rise to that enmity which was to end in its destruction by man.

But as an evil spirit must have employed the serpent, as the animal whose organs and instincts were most adapted to its purpose, and has accordingly derived its name from it as presenting the animal type most analogous to its own spiritual nature, so the whole of this sentence has its higher application to the real tempter. *Upon thy belly shalt thou go.* This is expressive of the lowest stage of degradation to which a spiritual creature can be sunk. *Dust shalt thou eat.* This is indicative of disappointment in all the aims of being. *I will put enmity.* This is still more strictly applicable to the spiritual enemy of mankind. It intimates a hereditary feud between their respective races, which is to terminate, after some temporary suffering on the part of the woman's seed, in the destruction of the serpent's power against man. The spiritual agent in the temptation of man cannot have literally any seed. But the seed of the serpent is that portion of the human family that continues to be his moral offspring, and follows the first transgression without repentance or refuge in the mercy of God. The seed of the woman, on the other hand, must denote the remnant who are born from above, and hence turn from darkness to light, and from the power of Satan unto God.

Let us now mark the lessons conveyed in the sentence of the serpent to our first parents, who were listening and looking on. 1st. The serpent is styled a mere brute animal. All, then, that seemed to indicate reason as inherent in its nature or acquired by some strange event in its history is thus at once contradicted. 2d. It is declared to be lower than any of the other land animals; as being destitute of any members corresponding to feet or hands. 3d. It is not interrogated as a rational and accountable being, but treated as a mere dumb brute. 4th. It is degraded from the airs and attitudes which may have been assumed, when it was possessed by a serpent-like evil spirit, and falls back without a struggle to that place of debasement in the animal kingdom for which it was designed. 5th. It is fated to be disappointed in its aims at usurpation. It shall bite the dust. 6th. It is doomed to ultimate and utter discomfiture in its hostile assaults on the seed of the woman.

All this must have made a deep impression on our first parents. But two things must have struck them with peculiar force. *First*, it was now evident how vain and hollow were its pretensions to superior wisdom, and how miserably deluded they had been when they listened to its false insinuations. If, indeed, they had possessed maturity of reflection, and taken time to apply it, they would have been strangely bewildered with the whole scene, now that it was past. How the serpent, from the brute instinct it displayed to Adam when he named the animals, suddenly rose to the temporary exercise of reason and speech, and as suddenly relapsed into its former bestiality, is, to the mere observer of nature, an inexplicable phenomenon. But to Adam, who had as yet too limited an experience to distinguish between natural and preternatural events, and too little development of the reflective power to detect the inconsistency in the appearance of things, the sole object of attention was the shameless presumption of the serpent, and the overwhelming retribution which had fallen upon it; and, consequently, the deplorable folly and wickedness of having been misguided by its suggestions.

A *second* thing, however, was still more striking to the mind of man in the sentence of the serpent; namely, the enmity that was to be put between the serpent and the woman. Up to a certain point there had been concord and alliance between these two parties. But, on the very opening of the heavenly court, we learn that the friendly connection had been broken. For the woman said, "The serpent *beguiled me*, and I did eat." This expression indicates that the woman was no longer at one with the serpent. She was now sensible that its part had been that, not of friendship, but of guile, and therefore of the deepest and darkest hostility. When God, therefore, said, "I will put enmity between thee and the woman," this revulsion of feeling on her part, in which Adam no doubt joined, was acknowledged and approved. Enmity with the enemy of God indicated a return to friendship with God, and presupposed incipient feelings of repentance towards him, and reviving confidence in his word. The perpetuation of this enmity is here affirmed, in regard not only to the woman, but to her seed. This prospect of seed, and of a godly seed, at enmity with evil, became a fountain of hope to our first parents, and confirmed every feeling of returning reverence for God which was beginning to spring up in their breast. The word heard from the mouth of God begat faith in their hearts, and we shall find that this faith was not slow to manifest itself in acts.

We cannot pass over this part of the sentence without noticing the expression, "the seed of the woman." Does it not mean, in the first instance, the whole human race? Was not this race at enmity with the serpent? And though that part only of the seed of the woman which eventually shared in her present feelings could be said to be at enmity with the serpent spirit, yet, if all had gone well in Adam's family, might not the whole race have been at enmity with the spirit of disobedience? Was not the avenue to mercy here hinted at as wide as the offer of any other time? And was not this universality of invitation at some time to have a response in the human family? Does not the language of the passage constrain us to look forward to the time when the great mass, or the whole of the human race then alive on the earth, will have actually turned from the power of Satan unto God? This could not be seen by Adam. But was it not the plain import of the language, that, unless there was some new revolt after the present reconciliation, the whole race would, even from this new beginning, be at enmity with the spirit of evil? Such was the dread lesson of experience with which Adam now entered upon the career of life, that it was to be expected he would warn his children against departing from the living God, with a clearness and earnestness which would be both understood and felt.

But, still further, do we not pass from the general to the particular in the sentence, "He shall bruise thy head, and thou shalt bruise his heel?" Is not the seed of the woman here individualized and matched in deadly conflict with the individual tempter? Does not this phraseology point to some preëminent descendant of the woman, who is, with the bruising of his lower nature in the encounter, to gain a signal and final victory over the adversary of man? There is some reason to believe from the expression, "I have gotten a man from the Lord" (Gen. iv. 1), that Eve herself had caught a glimpse of this meaning, though she applied it to the wrong party. The Vulgate also, in what was probably the genuine reading, *ipse* (he himself) points to the same meaning. The reading *ipsa* (she herself) is inconsistent with the gender of the Hebrew verb, and with that of the corresponding pronoun in the second clause (his), and is therefore clearly an error of the transcriber.

Lastly, the retributive character of the divine administration is remarkably illustrated in the phrase. The serpent, in a wily but dastardly spirit, makes the weaker sex the object of his attack. It is the seed of the woman especially that is to bruise his head. It is singular to find that this simple phrase, coming in naturally and incidentally in a sentence uttered four thousand years, and penned at least fifteen hundred years, before the Christian era, describes exactly and literally Him who was made of woman without the intervention of man, that he might destroy the works of the devil. This clause in the sentence of the tempter is the first dawn of hope for the human family after the fall. We cannot tell whether to admire more the simplicity of its terms, the breadth and comprehensiveness of its meaning, or the minuteness of its application to the far-distant event which it mainly contemplates.

The doom here pronounced upon the tempter must be regarded as special and secondary. It refers to the malignant attack upon man, and foretells what will be the issue of this attempt to spread disaffection among the intelligent creation. And it is pronounced without any examination of the offender, or investigation of his motives. If this had been the first offence against the majesty of heaven, we humbly conceive a solemn precognition of the case would have taken place, and a penalty would have been adjudicated adequate to the magnitude of the crime and analagous to the punishment of death in the case of man. The primary act of defiance and apostasy from the Creator must have been perpetrated without a tempter, and was, therefore, incomparably more heinous than the secondary act of yielding to temptation. Whether the presence of the tempter on earth intimates that it was the place of his abode in a state of innocence, or that he visited it because he had heard of the creation of man, or that he was there from some altogether different reason, is a vain and unprofitable inquiry.

16. The sentence of the woman consists of three parts: the former two regard her as a mother, the last as a wife. Sorrow is to be multiplied in her pregnancy, and is also to accompany the bearing of children. This sorrow seems to extend to all the mother's pains and anxieties concerning her offspring. With what solicitude she would long for a manifestation of right feeling toward the merciful God in her children, similar to that which she had experienced in her own breast! What unutterable bitterness of spirit would she feel when the fruits of disobedience would discover themselves in her little ones, and in some of them, perhaps, gather strength from year to year!

The promise of children is implicitly given in these two clauses. It came out also incidentally in the sentence of the serpent. What a wonderful conception is here presented to the minds of the primeval pair! Even to ourselves at this day the subject of race is involved in a great deal of mystery. We have already noticed the unity of the race in its head. But the personality and responsibility of individuals involve great and perplexing difficulties. The descent of a soul from a soul is a secret too deep for our comprehension. The first man was potentially the race, and, so long as he stands alone, actually the whole race for the time. His acts, then, are those not merely of the individual, but of the race. If a single angel fall, he falls alone. If the last of a race were to fall, he would in like manner involve no other in his descent. But if the first of a race fall, before he has any offspring, the race is fallen. The guilt, the depravity, the penalty, all belong to the race. This is a great mystery. But it seems to follow inevitably from the constitution of a race, and it has clear evidences of its truth both in the facts and the doctrines of the Bible.

When we come to view the sin of our first parents in this light, it is seen to entail tremendous consequences to every individual of the race. The single transgression has involved the guilt, the depravity, and the death, not only of Adam, but of that whole race which was in him, and thus has changed the whole character and condition of mankind throughout all time.

In the instructions going before and coming after are found the means of training up these children for God. The woman has learned that God is not only a righteous judge, but a forbearing and merciful Father. This was enough for her at present. It enabled her to enter upon the journey of life with some gleams of hope amidst the sorrows of the family. And in the experience of life it is amazing what a large proportion of the agreeable is mingled with the troubles of our fallen race. The forbearance and goodness of God ought in all reason and conscience to lead us back to a better feeling towards him.

The third part of her sentence refers to her husband,—*Thy desire shall be to thy husband, and he shall rule over thee.* This is evidently a piece of that retributive justice which meets us constantly in the administration of God. The woman had taken the lead in the transgression. In the fallen state, she is to be subject to the will of her husband. "Desire" does not refer to sexual desire in particular. (Gen. iv. 7). It means, in general, *turn*, determination of the will. "The determination of thy will shall be yielded to thy husband, and accordingly he shall rule over thee." The second clause, according to the parallel structure of the sentence, is a climax or emphatic reiteration of the first, and therefore serves to determine its meaning. Under fallen man, woman has been more or less a slave. In fact, under the rule of selfishness, the weaker must serve the stronger. A spiritual resurrection only will restore her to her true place, as the helpmeet for man.

17–19. The key-word in the sentence of the man is the *soil.* The curse (Gen. ix. 25, n.) of the soil is the want of the fruit trees with which the garden was planted, and of that spontaneous growth which would have rendered the toil of man unnecessary. The rank growth of thorns and thistles was also a part of the curse which it occasioned to man when fallen. His sorrow was to arise from the labor and sweat with which he was to draw from the ground the means of subsistence. Instead of the spontaneous fruits of the garden, the herb of the field, which required diligent cultivation, was henceforth to constitute a principal part of his support. And he had the dreary prospect before him of returning at length to the ground whence he was taken. He had an element of dust in him, and this organic frame was eventually to work out its own decay, when apart from the tree of life.

It is to be observed that here is the first allusion to that death which was the essential part of the sentence pronounced on the fallen race. The reasons of this are obvious. The sentence of death on those who should eat of the forbidden fruit had been already pronounced, and was well known to our first parents. Death consisted in the privation of that life which lay in the light of the divine countenance, shining with approving love on an innocent child, and therefore was begun on the first act of disobedience, in the shame and fear of a guilty conscience. The few traits of earthly discomfort which the sentences disclose, are merely the workings of the death here spoken of in the present stage of our existence. And the execution of the sentence, which comes to view in the following passage, is the formal accomplishment of the warning given to the transgressor of the divine will.

In this narrative the language is so simple as to present no critical difficulty. And, on reviewing the passage, the first thing we have to observe is, that the event here recorded is a turning-point of transcendent import in the history of man. It is no less than turning from confidence in God to confidence in his creature when contradicting him, and, moreover, from obedience to his express and well-remembered command to obedience to the dictates of misguided self-interest. It is obvious that, to the moral character of the transaction, it is of no consequence who the third party was who dared to contradict and malign his Maker. The guilt of man consists simply in disobeying the sole command of his beneficent Creator. The only mitigating circumstance is the suggestion of evil by an external party. But the more insignificant the only ostensible source of temptation, the more inexcusable the guilt of man in giving way to it.

This act altered fundamentally the position and character of man. He thereby descended from innocence to guilt in point of law, and at the same time from holiness to sin in point of character. Tremendous was the change, and equally tremendous the consequence. Death is, like most scriptural terms, a pregnant word, and here to be understood in the full compass of its meaning. It is the privation, not of existence, as is often confusedly supposed, but of life, in all its plenitude of meaning. As life includes all the gratifications of which our human susceptibilities are capable, so death is the privation of all the sources of human enjoyment, and among them of the physical life itself, while the craving for ease and the sense of pain retain all their force in the spiritual part of our nature. These poignant emotions reach their highest pitch of intensity when they touch the conscience, the tenderest part of our being, and forebode the meeting of the soul, in its guilty state, with a just and holy God.

This event is real. The narrative expresses in its strongest terms its reality. The event is one of the two alternatives which must follow from the preceding statements concerning the tree of the knowledge of good and evil, and affords an explanation of their nature. It is no less essential to account for that which follows. The problem of the history and condition of man can only be solved by this primeval fact. Conscience still remains an imperishable monument, on the one hand, of his having been formed after a perfect model; and, on the other, of his having fallen from his high estate. And all the facts of his history carry up his fall as far as the traditions of human memory reach.

And the narrative here is a literal record of the details of this great event. So far as regards God and man, the literality has never been questioned by those who acknowledge the event to be real. Some, however, have taken the serpent to be, not a literal, but a figurative serpent; not an animal, but a spiritual being. The great dragon, indeed, is identified with "the ancient serpent called the devil and Satan." And hence we know that a being of a higher nature than the mere animal was present and active on this occasion. And this spiritual being was with great propriety called the serpent, both from its serpentine qualities and from choosing the serpent as the most suitable mask under which to tempt our first parents. But we cannot thence infer that a literal serpent was not employed in the temptation. The serpent is said to be "more subtle than any beast of the field." 1st. The obvious meaning of this is, that it was itself a beast of the field. Thus Joseph, whom Israel loved *more than all his children*, was one of his children (Gen. xxxvii. 8). He that was *higher than any of the people*, was himself one of the people (2 Sam. ix. 2). 2d. If the serpent be here figurative, and denote a spirit, the statement that it was subtle above all the beasts of the field is feeble and inadequate to the occasion. It is not so, that man is distinguished from the other animals. In much more forcible language ought the old serpent to be distinguished from the unreasoning brute. 3d. We have seen a meetness in a being of flesh, and that not superior, or even equal to man, being permitted to be employed as the medium of temptation. Man was thereby put at no disadvantage. His senses were not confounded by a supersensible manifestation. His presence of mind was not disturbed by an unusual appearance. 4th. The actions ascribed to the tempter agree with the literal serpent. Wounding the heel, creeping on the belly, and biting the dust, are suitable to a mere animal, and especially to the serpent. The only exception is the speaking, and, what is implied in this, the reasoning. These, however, do not disprove the presence of the literal serpent when accompanied with a plain statement of its presence. They only indicate, and that to more experienced observers than our first parents, the presence of a lurking spirit, expressing its thoughts by the organs of the serpent.

It may be thought strange that the presence of this higher being is not explicitly noticed by the sacred writer. But it is the manner of Scripture not to distinguish and explain all the realities which it relates, but to describe the obvious phenomena as they present themselves to the senses; especially when the scope of the narrative does not require more, and a future revelation or the exercise of a sanctified experience will in due time bring out their interpretation. Thus the doings of the magicians in Egypt are not distinguished from those of Moses by any disparaging epithet (Ex. vii. 10–12). Only those of Moses are greater, and indicate thereby a higher power. The witch of Endor is consulted, and Samuel appears; but the narrative is not careful to distinguish then and there whether by the means of witchcraft or by the very power of God. It was not necessary for the moral training of our first parents at that early stage of their existence to know who the real tempter was. It would not have altered the essential nature of the temptation, of the sentence pronounced on any of the parties, or of the hopes held out to those who were beguiled.

This brings into view a system of analogy and mutual relation pervading the whole of Scripture as well as nature, according to which the lower order of things is a natural type of the higher, and the nearer of the more remote. This law displays itself in the history of creation, which, in the creative work of the six days, figures to our minds, and, as it were, lays out in the distance those other antecedent processes of creative power that have intervened since the first and absolute creation; in the nature of man, which presents on the surface the animal operations in wonderful harmony with the spiritual functions of his complex being; in the history of man, where the nearer in history, in prophecy, in space, in time, in quality, matter, life, vegetative and animate, shadow forth the more remote. All these examples of the scriptural method of standing on and starting from the near to the far are founded upon the simple fact that nature is a rational system of things, every part of which has its counterpart in every other. Hence the history of one thing is, in a certain form, the history of all things of the same kind.

The serpent is of a crafty instinct, and finds, accordingly, its legitimate place at the lowest step of the animal system. Satan seeks the opportunity of tempting Adam, and, in the fitness of things, turns to the serpent as the ready medium of his assault upon human integrity. He was limited to such a medium. He was not permitted to have any intercourse with man, except through the senses and in the way of speech. He was also necessitated to have recourse to the serpent, as the only creature suited to his purpose.

The place of the serpent in the scale of animals was in keeping with the crookedness of its instinct. It was cursed above all cattle, as it was inferior to them in the want of those limbs which serve for rising, moving, and holding; such as legs and arms. This meaning of *cursed* is familiar to Scripture. "Cursed is the ground for thy seed" (Gen. iii. 17). It needed the toil of man to repress thorns and thistles, and cultivate plants more useful and needful to man. "This people who knoweth not the law are cursed" (John vii. 49). This is a relative use of the word, by which a thing is said to be cursed in respect of its failing to serve a particular end. Hence the serpent's condition was a fit emblem of the spiritual serpent's punishment for its evil doings regarding man.

Through the inscrutable wisdom of the divine providence, however, it was not necessary, or may not have been necessary, to change in the main the state of the natural serpent or the natural earth in order to carry out the ends of justice. The former symbolized in a very striking manner the helplessness and disappointment of the enemy of man. The latter exacted that labor of man which was the just consequence of his disobedience. This consequence would have been avoided if he had continued to be entitled to the tree of life, which could no doubt have been propagated beyond its original bounds. But a change in the moral relation of the heart towards God brings along with it in the unsearchable ways of divine wisdom a change as great in the bearing of the events of time on the destiny of man. While the heart is with God, all things work together for good to us. When the heart is estranged from him, all things as inevitably work together for evil, without any material alteration in the system of nature.

We may even ascend a step higher into the mysteries of providence; for a disobedient heart, that forms the undeserving object of the divine compassion, may be for a time the unconscious slave of a train of circumstances, which is working out its recovery from the curse as well as the power of sin through the teaching of the Divine Spirit. The series of events may be the same in which another is floating down the stream of perdition. But to the former these events are the turning-points of a wondrous moral training, which is to end in reconciliation to God and restoration to his likeness.

A race, in like manner, that has fallen from communion with God, may be the subject of a purpose of mercy, which works out, in the providence of God, the return of some to his home and love, and the wandering of others away further and further into the darkness and misery of enmity with God.

And though this system of things is simple and uniform in the eyes of the only wise God, yet to human view parts of it appear only as special arrangements and retributions, exactly meeting the case of man and serving for his moral education. No doubt they are so. But they are also parts of a constant course of nature, pursued with undeviating regularity, yet ordered with such infallible wisdom as to accomplish at the same time both general and special ends. Hence, without any essential change in the serpent's natural instincts, it serves for a striking monument of the defeat and destruction of the devil and his works. The ground, without any change in its inherent nature, but merely by the removal, it may be, of the tree of life, is cursed to man, as it demands that toil which is the mark of a fallen race.

The question of miracles, or special interpositions of the divine will and power which cross the laws of nature, is not now before us. By the very definition of miracles they transcend the laws of nature; that is, of that system of events which is known to us by observation. But it does not follow that they transcend a higher law of the divine plan, which may, partly by revelation and partly even by a deeper study of ourselves and things around us, be brought to light. By the investigations of geology we seem compelled to acknowledge a succession of creations at great intervals of time, as a law of the divine procedure on our globe. But, thousands of years before geology was conceived, one such creation, subsequent to the great primal act by which the universe was called into existence, was made known to us by divine revelation. And beside periodical miracle, we find recorded in the book of revelation a series of miracles, which were performed in pursuance of the divine purpose of grace toward the fallen race of man. These are certainly above nature, according to the largest view of it which has ever been current among our philosophers. But let us not therefore imagine that they are above reason or grace, — above the resources and determinations of the divine mind and will concerning the development of the universe.

20, 21. These verses record two very significant acts consequent upon the judgment: one on the part of Adam, and another on the part of God.

20. The man here no doubt refers to two expressions in the sentences he had heard pronounced on the serpent and the woman. "He," the seed of the woman, "shall bruise thy head." Here it is the woman who is to bear the seed. And this seed is to bruise the serpent's head; that is, in some way to undo what had been done for the death of man, and so reinvest him with *life*. This life was therefore to come by the woman. Again, in the address of the judge to the woman he had heard the words, "Thou shalt bear children." These children are the seed, among whom is to be the bruiser of the serpent's head, and the author of life. And in an humbler, nearer sense, the woman is to be the mother of children, who are the living, and perpetuate the life of the race amid the ravages which death is daily committing on its individual members. These glimmerings of hope for the future make a deep impression upon the father of mankind. He perceives and believes that through the woman in some way is to come salvation for the race. He gives permanent expression to his hope in the significant name which he gives to his wife. Here we see to our unspeakable

satisfaction the dawn of faith, — a faith indicating a new beginning of spiritual life, and exercising a salutary influence on the will, faintly illuminating the dark bosom of our first parent. The mother of mankind has also come to a better mind. The high and holy Spirit has in mercy withdrawn the cloud of misconception from the minds of both, and faith in the Lord and repentance have sprung up in their new-born souls.

21. As the preceding verse records an instance of humble, apprehending faith in the divine word, so here we have a manifest act of mercy on the part of God, indicating the pardon and acceptance of confessing, believing man, rejoicing in anticipation of that future victory over the serpent which was to be accomplished by the seed of the woman. This act is also suitable to the present circumstances of man, and at the same time strikingly significant of the higher blessings connected with restoration to the divine favor. He had discovered his nakedness, and God provides him with a suitable covering. He was to be exposed to the variations of climate, and here was a durable protection against the weather. But far more than this. He had become morally naked, destitute of that peace of conscience which is an impenetrable shield against the shame of being blamed and the fear of being punished; and the coats of skin were a faithful emblem and a manifest guarantee of those robes of righteousness which were hereafter to be provided for the penitent in default of that original righteousness which he had lost by transgression. And, finally, there is something remarkable in the material out of which the coats were made. They were most likely obtained by the death of animals; and as they do not appear yet to have been slain for food, some have been led to conjecture that they were offered in sacrifice, — slain in prefiguration of that subsequent availing sacrifice which was to take away sin. It is the safer course, however, to leave the origin of sacrifice an open question. Scripture does not intimate that the skins were obtained in consequence of sacrifice; and apart from the presumption derived from these skins, it seems to trace the origin of sacrifice to the act of Habel recorded in the next chapter.

This leads us to a law, which we find frequently exhibited in Sacred Scripture, that some events are recorded without any connection or significance apparent on the surface of the narrative, while at the same time they betoken a greater amount of spiritual knowledge than we are wont to ascribe to the age in which they occurred. The bare fact which the writer states, being looked at with our eyes, may have no significance. But regarded, as it ought to be, with the eyes of the narrator, cognizant of all that he has to record up to his own time, it becomes pregnant with a new meaning, which would not otherwise have been discovered. Even this, however, may not exhaust the import of a passage contained in an inspired writing. To arrive at the full sense it may need to be contemplated with the eyes of the Holy Spirit, conscious of all that is to become matter of revelation to the end of time. It will then stand forth in all the comprehensiveness of meaning which its relation to the whole body of revealed truth imparts, and under the guise of an every-day matter-of-fact will convey some of the sublimest aspects of divine truth. Hence the subsequent scripture, which is the language of the Holy Spirit, may aid us in penetrating the hidden meaning of an earlier part of revelation.

God is the prime mover in this matter. The mercy of God alone is the source of pardon, of the mode in which he may pardon and yet be just, and of the power by which the sinner may be led to accept it with penitence and gratitude. In the brevity of the narrative the results only are noted; namely, the intimation and the earnest of pardon on the side of God, and the feelings and doings of faith and repentance on the side of the parents of mankind. What indications God may have given by the impressive figure of sacrifice or otherwise of the penalty being paid by another for the sinner, as a necessary condition of forgiveness, we are not here informed, simply because those for whom a written record was necessary would learn it more fully at a subsequent stage of the narrative. This suggests two remarks important for interpretation: 1st. This document is written by one who omits many things done and said to primeval man, because they are unnecessary for those for whom he writes, or because the principles they involve will come forward in a more distinct form in a future part of his work. This practice speaks for Moses being not the mere collector, but the composer of the documents contained in Genesis, out of such preëxistent materials as may have come to his hand or his mind. 2d. We are not to import into the narrative a doctrine or institution in all the development it may have received at the latest period of revelation. This would be contrary to the manner in which God was wont to teach man. That concrete form of a great principle, which comported with the infantile state of the early mind, is first presented. The germ planted in the opening, fertile mind, springs forth and grows. The revelations and institutions of God grow with it in compass and grandeur. The germ was truth fitted for babes; the full-grown tree is only the same truth expanded in the advancing development of men and things. They equally err who stretch the past to the measure of the present, and who judge either the past or the future by the standard of the present. Well-meaning but inconsiderate critics have gone to both extremes.

XVII. THE EXECUTION. — Gen. iii. 22-24.

24. כְּרוּב Kerub; כרב in Aram. *carve, plough;* Pers. *grip, grasp.* This word occurs about eighty-seven times in the Hebrew scriptures; in sixty of which it refers to carved or embroidered figures; in twenty-two to the living being in the vision of Ezekiel (Ezek. x); in two figuratively to the king of Tyre (Ezek. xxviii. 14, 16); in two to a being on which the Lord is poetically described as riding (2 Sam. xxii. 11; Ps. xviii. 11); and in the present passage unequivocally to real and well-known beings. The root is not otherwise extant in Hebrew proper. But from the class of actions to which it refers, and from a review of the statements of Scripture concerning these creatures, we are led to the following conclusions:

1st. The cherubim are real creatures, and not mere symbols. In the narrative of the fall they are introduced as real into the scenes of reality. Their existence is assumed as known; for God is said to place or station *the* cherubim at the east of the garden of Eden. The representation of a cherub too in vision, as part of a symbolic figure, implies a corresponding reality (Ezek. x. 14). A symbol itself points to a reality.

2d. They are afterwards described as *living creatures,* especially in the visions of Ezekiel (i. 10). This seems to arise, not from their standing at the highest stage of life, which the term does not denote, but from the members of the various *animals,* which enter into their variously-described figure. Among these appear the faces of the man, the lion, the ox, and the eagle, of which a cherubic form had one, two or four (Ex. xxv. 20; Ezek. xli. 18, i. 10). They had, besides, wings, in number two or four (Ex. xxv. 20; 1 Kings vi. 27; Ezek. i. 6). And they had the hands of a man under their wings on their four sides (Ezek. i. 8, x. 8). Ezekiel also describes their feet as being straight, and having the sole like that of a calf. They sometimes appear too with their bodies, hands, wings, and even accompanying wheels full of eyes (Ezek. i. 18, x. 12). The variety in the figuration of the cherubim is owing to the variety of aspects in which they stand, and of offices or services they have to perform in the varying posture of affairs. This figuration is evidently symbolic. For the real being has not a varying number or order of its constituent parts in the same stage of its existence, though it may be readily represented by a diversity of symbols, according to the diversity of the circumstances in which it appears, and of operations it has to perform. The figuration is merely intended to shadow forth its nature and office in sensible forms to those who have not entered the spiritual world.

3d. The cherubim are intelligent beings. This is indicated by their form, movement, and conduct. In their visible appearance the human form predominates: "They had the likeness of a man" (Ezek. i. 5). The human face is in front, and has therefore the principal place. The "hands of a man" determine the erect posture, and therefore the human form of the body. The parts of other animal forms are only accessory, and serve to mark the possession of qualities which are not prominent in man. The lion indicates the active and destructive powers; the ox, the patient and productive; the eagle denotes rapid motion, with which the wings coincide, and quick sight with which the many eyes accord; and the man signifies reason, which rationalizes all these otherwise physical qualities.

The four faces indicate powers of observation that sweep the whole horizon. The straight feet, with soles like those of a calf, mark an elasticity of step appertaining only to beings unaffected by the force of gravitation. Their motion, "straight forward," combined with the four faces, and the wheel within a wheel going according to its quarters, points to a capacity of moving in any direction without turning by the mere impulse of the will. The intelligence of their conduct will appear from the nature of the duties they have to discharge.

4th. Their special office seems to be *intellectual and potential* rather than moral. They have to do with the physical more than the moral aspect of being. Hence they stand related, on the one side, to God, as אֱלֹהִים *the Everlasting*, the God of omnipotence; and, on the other, to the universe of created things, in its material, animal, and intellectual departments, and to the general administration of the divine will in this comprehensive sphere. The radical meanings of the terms *carve, plough, grasp*, point to the potential. The hand symbolizes intelligent agency. The multiplicity of eyes denotes many-sided intelligence. The number four is evidently normal and characteristic. It marks their relation to the cosmos — universe or system of created things.

5th. Their place of ministry is about the throne, and in the presence of the Almighty. Accordingly, where he manifests himself in a stated place, and with all the solemnity of a court, there they generally appear.

6th. Their special functions correspond with these indications of their nature and place. They are stationed at the east of the garden of Eden, where God had condescended to walk with man before his fall, and where he still lingers on earth to hold communion with man, for the purpose of mercy, and their business is to keep the way of the tree of life. They are figured in the most holy place, which was appropriated to the divine presence, and constructed after the pattern seen in the mount. They stand on the mercy-seat, where God sits to rule his people, and they look down with intelligent wonder on the mysteries of redemption. In the vision of the likeness of the glory of God vouchsafed to Ezekiel, they appear under the expanse on which rests the throne of God, and beside the wheels which move as they move. And when God is represented as in movement for the execution of his judgments, the physical elements and the spiritual essences are alike described as the vehicles of his irresistible progress (Ps. xviii. 11). All these movements are mysteries to us, while we are in a world of sense. We cannot comprehend the relation of the spiritual and the physical. But of this we may be assured, that material things are at bottom centres of multiform forces, or fixed springs of power, to which the Everlasting Potentate has given a local habitation and a name, and therefore cognate with spiritual beings of free power, and consequently manageable by them.

7th. The cherubim seem to be officially distinct from angels or messengers who go upon special errands to a distance from the presence-chamber of the Almighty. It is possible that they are also to be distinguished in function from the seraphim and the living beings of the Apocalypse, who like them appear among the attendants in the court of heaven.

22. And the Lord God said, Behold, the man is become as one of us to know good and evil: and now lest he put forth his hand, and take also of the tree of life, and eat, and live for ever. 23. Then the Lord God sent him forth from the garden of Eden, to till the soil from which he was taken. 24. So he drove out the man; and he placed at the east of the garden

of Eden the cherubim and the flaming sword which turned around, to keep the way of the tree of life. § 3.

Here we enter upon the record of the steps taken to carry into effect the forfeiture of life by man, consequent upon his wilful transgression of the divine command.

22. *As one of us.* This is another indication of the plurality in unity which is evidently inherent in the Eternal Spirit. It is still more significant than the expression of concert in the creation of man, as it cannot be explained by anything short of a personal distinction.

Behold, the man is become as one of us to know good and evil. We are now prepared to understand the nature of the two trees which were in the midst of the garden. The tree of the knowledge of good and evil effected a change, not in the physical constitution of man, but in his mental experience, — in his knowledge of good and evil. There do not appear to have been any seeds of death, — any poisonous or malignant power in the tree. "The woman saw that the tree was *good for food*, and likely to the eyes," as well as a tree to be desired to make one wise. Neither does it appear that the virtue of making wise on the particular point of moral distinctions lay in the digestion of its fruit when received into the stomach. The natural effect of food is on the body, not on the understanding. The moral effect lay rather in the conduct of man in regard to the tree, as a thing prohibited. The result of his conduct, whether in the way of obedience or disobedience to the divine command, was to be the knowledge of good and evil. If man had obeyed, he would have come to this knowledge in a legitimate way. For he would have perceived that distrust of God and disobedience to his will, as they were externally presented to his view in the suggestions of the tempter, were evil; and that confidence and obedience, internally experienced in himself in defiance of such suggestions, were good. And this was the germ of the knowledge of good and evil. But, by disregarding the express injunction of his Maker with respect to this tree, he attained to the knowledge of good and evil in an unlawful and fatal way. He learned immediately that he himself was the guilty party, whereas, before, he was free from guilt; and thus became aware, in his own person and to his own condemnation, of good and evil, as distinct and opposite qualities.

This view of the tree is in accordance with all the intimations of Scripture. 1st. The terms in which it is prohibited are, "Of the tree of the knowledge of good and evil thou shalt not eat; for in the day thou eatest of it, die surely shalt thou." Here it is important to mark the consequence which is pointed out as flowing from the eating of it. It is not, Thou shalt know good and evil by any physical virtue of the tree, a process by which knowledge comes not at all; but, "Thou shalt surely die." Now, this is not any physical result of the fruit being received into the system, since man did not die for centuries after, but a penal result, in fact, the awful sanction of that divine command by which man's probation was to be accomplished. 2d. The points brought out by the serpent are to the same effect. He suggests that God had not given permission to eat of every tree of the garden. There was some reserve. This reserve is an injury to man, which he makes out by denying that death is the consequence of eating of the tree reserved, and asserting that special benefits, such as the opening of the eyes, and being as God in knowing good and evil, would follow. In both of these statements there is equivocation. Death is not indeed the natural, but it is the legal consequence of disobedience. The eyes of them both were opened, and they became like God in knowing good and evil; but, in both instances, to their own shame and confusion, instead of their glory and honor. They *saw* that they were "naked," and they were "ashamed" and "afraid." They *knew* good and evil; but they knew the evil to be present with them, and the good to have departed from them. 3d. The interview of God with the culprits is also in keeping with the same view. The question to the man is, "Who told thee that thou wast naked? Hast thou eaten of the tree of which I commanded thee not to eat?" Mark the tenor of this question. It is not, Hast thou eaten of the tree of the knowledge of good and evil? but, "of which I commanded thee not to eat;" by which it is indicated that, not the physical character of the tree, but the moral character of the action, is the point of the interrogatory.

The tree, then, was the ordained occasion of man's becoming as God in knowing good and evil. He had now reached the second, or experimental lesson in morals. When God gave him the theoretical lesson in the command, he expected that the practical one would follow. He now says, "Behold the man is become as one of us, to know good and evil." In the style of his word he notes the result, without marking the disobedience of man as the means. This is understood from the circumstances. Man is therefore guilty, and the law must be vindicated.

Hence, it is added, *Lest he put forth his hand and take also of the tree of life, and eat and live for ever.* This sentence is completed by an act, not a word, as we shall see in the next verse. Measures must be taken to prevent his access to this tree, now that he has incurred the penalty of death.

From this sentence it follows that the tree of life must have had some virtue by which the human frame was to be kept free from the decrepitude of age, or the decay that terminates in death. Its name, the tree *of life*, accords with this conclusion. Only on such a ground could exclusion from it be made the penalty of disobedience, and the occasion of death. Thus also may we meet and answer all the difficulties which physiology presents to the immortality of unfallen man. We have it on record that there was an herbal virtue in paradise capable of counteracting the effects of the wear and tear of the animal frame. This confirms our account of the tree of the knowledge of good and evil. Death, which, it is to be remembered, is, to a moral and responsible being, in a comprehensive sense, exclusion from the *blessings* of conscious existence, and preëminently from that of the divine complacence, was not the physical effect of its fruit being eaten, but the penal consequence of a forbidden act. And this consequence is brought about by a special judicial process, recorded in the next verse.

The two trees stand related to one another in a way that touches the very centre of man's moral being. "Do this and live" is the fundamental dictum of the moral law. Its implied counterpart is, "If thou do it not, thou shalt die." The act of disobedience is evidently decisive for the whole conduct, character, and relation to God. It therefore necessarily forfeits that life which consists in the favor of God and all consequent blessings. The two trees correspond with the condition and the benefit in this essential covenant of law. The one is the test of man's obedience, or disobedience; the other, the benefit which is retained by obedience and lost by disobedience. Man fails in obedience, and loses the blessing. Henceforth both the legal and the beneficial parts of the covenant must come from a higher source to all that are saved. Christ bestows both the one and the other by his obedience and by his Spirit. In the old form of the covenant of grace, the passover typifies the one, and circumcision the other; in the new, the Lord's Supper and baptism have a similar import. These all, from first to last, betoken the two essential parts of salvation, redemption, and regeneration. This is a clear example of the unity and constancy which prevail in the works of God.

It is evident that the *idea* of immortality is familiar to the early chapters of Genesis. The primeval command itself implies it. Mortality, moreover, applies to the נֶפֶשׁ, the organic living body; not to the particles of matter in that body, nor to the נִשְׁמַת חַיִּים, breath of life which came from God. It means not annihilation, but dissolution. Still further, the first part of death is exclusion from the tree of life, which takes place on the very day of disobedience. This indicates its nature. It is not annihilation of the spiritual essence, which does not in fact take place, but the withdrawal from it of the blessings and enjoyments in communion with God of which it is capable. And, lastly, the whole tenor of the narrative is, that death is a penalty for transgression; whereas annihilation is not a penalty, but a release from the doom of perdition. Accordingly, the tempter is not annihilated, but left to bear his doom; and so man's existence is perpetuated under partial privation, — the emblem and earnest of that death which consists in the total privation of life. Death is, no doubt, in its primary meaning, the dissolution of the living body. But even in the execution of the primeval sentence it begins to expand into that compass of meaning which all the great primitives of the scriptural language sooner or later express. Earth, sky, good, evil, life, and death are striking specimens of this elasticity of signification. Hence we perceive that the germs of the doctrine of the immortality of the soul lie even in these primeval documents. And more we could not expect, unless we were to concentrate the whole fulness of revelation on this subject into its opening pages.

23. In consequence of man's disobedience the tree of life is withdrawn from the reach of man as a forfeited boon, and the dissolution of the present life allowed to take place according to the laws of nature, still remaining in force in regard to other animated beings; aided, indeed, and accelerated in their operation, by the sinful abuse of human passions. And thus the expression, "in the day thou eatest thereof thou shalt die," receives its simple application. It is a conditional sentence, pronounced antecedently as a warning to the responsible party. On the very day of transgression it becomes legally valid against him, and the first step towards its regular execution in the ordinary course of things is taken. This step is his exclusion from the tree of life. This is effected by sending man out of the garden into the common, to till the soil whence he was taken.

24. *So he drove out the man.* This expresses the banishment of man from the garden as a judicial act. While he is left to the fruits

of his labor for the means of subsistence until his return to the dust, his access to the source of perpetual life and vigor is effectually barred by a guard stationed east of the garden, where was no doubt its only entrance, consisting of the cherubim and the flame of a sword waving in all directions. The flaming sword is the visible form of the sword of justice, repelling the transgressors from the seat and source of happiness and life. The cherubim, who are here mentioned as well-known objects, whose figure does not require description, are the ministers of the divine presence and judgment, — of his presence which was not entirely withdrawn from man; and of his judgment, by which he was excluded from the garden of delight.

There is unspeakable mercy here in every respect for the erring race. This present life in the flesh was now tainted with sin, and impregnated with the seeds of the curse, about to spring forth into an awful growth of moral and physical evil. It is not worth preserving for itself. It is not in any way desirable that such a dark confusion of life and death in one nature should be perpetuated. Hence there is mercy as well as judgment in the exclusion of man from that tree which could have only continued the carnal, earthly, sensual and even devilish state of his being. Let it remain for a season, until it be seen whether the seed of spiritual life will come to birth and growth, and then let death come and put a final end to the old man.

But, still further, God does not annihilate the garden or its tree of life. Annihilation does not seem to be his way. It is not the way of that omniscient One who sees the end from the beginning, of that infinite Wisdom that can devise and create a self-working, self-adjusting universe of things and events. On the other hand, he sets his cherubim to keep the way of the tree of life. This paradise, then, and its tree of life are in safe keeping. They are in reserve for those who will become entitled to them after an intervening period of trial and victory, and they will reappear in all their pristine glory and in all their beautiful adaptedness to the high-born and new-born perfection of man. The slough of that serpent nature which has been infused into man will fall off, at least from the chosen number who take refuge in the mercy of God; and in all the freshness and freedom of a heaven-born nature will they enter into all the originally congenial enjoyments that were shadowed forth in their pristine bloom in that first scene of human bliss.

We have now gone over the prelude to the history of man. It consists of three distinct events: the absolute creation of the heavens and the earth, contained in one verse; the last creation, in which man himself came into being, embracing the remainder of the first chapter; and the history of the first pair to the fall, recorded in the second and third chapters. The first two fall into one, and reveal the invisible everlasting Elohim coming forth out of the depths of his inscrutable eternity, and manifesting himself to man in the new character of Jehovah, the author and perpetuator of a universe of being, and preëminently of man, a type and specimen of the rational order of beings. Whenever moral agents come into existence, and wherever they come into contact, there must be law, covenant, or compact. Hence the command is laid upon man as the essential prerequisite to his moral deportment; and Jehovah appears further as the vindicator of law, the keeper of covenant, the performer of promise. Man, being instructed by him in the fundamental principle of all law, namely, the right of the Creator over the creature, and the independence of each creature in relation to every other, takes the first step in moral conduct. But it is a false one, violating this first law of nature and of God in both its parts. "Thus by one man sin entered into the world, and death by sin." Hence the prospect of man's future history is clouded, and it cannot be darker than it afterwards turns out to be. But still it is tinged even in its early dawn with some rays of heavenly hope. The Lord God has held out signals of mercy to the tempted and fallen pair. The woman and the man have not been slow to acknowledge this, and to show symptoms of returning faith and repentance. And though they have been shut out of the garden, yet that region of bliss and its tree of life are not swept out of existence, but, in the boundless mercy of God, reserved in safe keeping for those who shall become heirs of glory, honor, and immortality.

Let it be observed that we here stand on the broad ground of our common humanity. From this wide circumference Scripture never recedes. Even when it recounts the fortunes of a single individual, family, or nation, its eye and its interest extend to the whole race; and it only dwells on the narrower circle of men and things as the potential spring of nascent, growing, and eternal life and blessing to the whole race. Let us endeavor to do justice to this ancient record, in the calm and constant grandeur and catholicity of its revelations concerning the ways of God with man.

SECTION IV.—THE FAMILY OF ADAM.

XVIII. CAIN AND ABEL.—Gen. iv. 1-16.

1. קַיִן Qain, *spear-shaft*, and קָנָה *set up*, *establish*, *gain*, *buy*, contain the biliteral root קן *set up*, *erect*, *gain*. The relations of root-words are not confined to the narrow rules of our common etymology, but really extend to such instinctive usages as the unlettered speaker will invent or employ. A full examination of the Hebrew tongue leads to the conclusion that a biliteral root lies at the base of many of those triliterals that consist of two firm consonants and a third weaker one varying in itself and its position. Thus יָטַב and טוֹב. So קַיִן and קָנָה grow from one root.

2. הֶבֶל Habel, *breath*, *vapor*.

3. מִנְחָה *gift*, *offering*, *tribute*. In contrast with זֶבַח, it means a bloodless offering.

7. חַטָּאת *sin*, *sin-penalty*, *sin-offering*. רָבַץ *lie*, *couch* as an animal.

16. נוֹד Nod, *flight*, *exile*; r. *flee*.

IV. 1. And the man knew Eve his wife; and she conceived and bare Cain, and said, I have gotten a man from the Lord. 2. And she added to bear his brother Habel: and Habel became a keeper of sheep, and Cain a tiller of the soil. 3. And it came to pass at the end of days that Cain brought of the fruit of the soil an offering unto the Lord. 4. And Habel brought he also of the firstlings of his flock, and of the fat thereof: and the Lord had respect unto Habel and to his offering. 5. But unto Cain and to his offering he had not respect: and Cain was very wroth, and his countenance fell. 6. And the Lord said unto Cain, Why art thou wroth? and why is thy countenance fallen? 7. If thou do well, shalt thou not be accepted? and if thou do not well, at the door is sin lying:

and unto thee shall be his desire, and thou shalt rule over him.
8. And Cain talked with Habel his brother: and it came to pass, when they were in the field, that Cain rose up against Habel his brother, and slew him.
9. And the LORD said unto Cain, Where is Habel, thy brother? And he said, I know not: am I my brother's keeper?
10. And he said, What hast thou done? The voice of thy brother's blood crieth unto me from the soil.
11. And now cursed art thou from the soil which hath opened its mouth to receive thy brother's blood from thy hand.
12. When thou tillest the soil, it shall not add to yield its strength to thee: a vagabond and a fugitive shalt thou be in the land.
13. And Cain said unto the LORD, Great is my iniquity above bearing.
14. Behold, thou hast driven me out this day from the face of the soil, and from thy face shall I be hid: and I shall be a vagabond and a fugitive in the land, and it shall be that any one that findeth me shall slay me.
15. And the LORD said unto him, Therefore on any one slaying Cain, he shall be avenged seven-fold. And the LORD gave Cain a sign, that no one finding him should smite him.
16. And Cain went out from the face of the LORD, and dwelt in the land of Nod, on the east of Eden.

This chapter is a continuation of the second document. Yet it is distinguished from the previous part of it by the use of the name Jehovah alone, and, in one instance, Elohim alone, to designate the Supreme Being. This is sufficient to show that distinct pieces of composition are included within these documents. In the creation week and in the judgment, God has proved himself an originator of being and a keeper of his word, and, therefore, the significant personal name Jehovah is ready on the lips of Eve and from the pen of the writer. The history of fallen man now proceeds. The first family comes under our notice.

1. Here the first husband and wife become father and mother. This new relation must be deeply interesting to both, but at first peculiarly so to the mother. Now was begun the fulfilment of all the intimations she had received concerning her seed. She was to have conception

and sorrow multiplied. But she was to be the mother of all living. And her seed was to bruise the serpent's head. All these recollections added much to the intrinsic interest of becoming a mother. Her feelings are manifested in the name given to her son and the reason assigned for it. She "bare Cain and said, I have gained a man from Jehovah." Cain occurs only once as a common noun, and is rendered by the Seventy δόρυ, *spear-shaft*. The primitive meaning of the root is to set up, or to erect, as a cane, a word which comes from the root; then it means to create, make one's own, and is applied to the Creator (Gen. xiv. 19) or the parent (Deut. xxxii. 6). Hence the word here seems to denote a thing gained or achieved, a figurative expression for a child born. The gaining or bearing of the child is therefore evidently the prominent thought in Eve's mind, as she takes the child's name from this. This serves to explain the sentence assigning the reason for the name. If the meaning had been, "I have gained a man, namely, Jehovah," then the child would have been called Jehovah. If Jehovah had even been the emphatic word, the name would have been a compound of Jehovah, and either אִישׁ *man*, or קָנָה *qain*, such as Ishiah or Coniah. But the name Cain proves קָנִיתִי *I have gained* to be the emphatic word, and therefore the sentence is to be rendered "I have gained (borne) a man (with the assistance) of Jehovah."

The word "man" probably intimates that Eve fully expected her son to grow to the stature and maturity of her husband. If she had daughters before, and saw them growing up to maturity, this would explain her expectation, and at the same time give a new significance and emphasis to her exclamation, "I have gained *a man* (heretofore only women) from Jehovah." It would heighten her ecstasy still more if she expected this to be the very seed that should bruise the serpent's head.

Eve is under the influence of pious feelings. She has faith in God, and acknowledges him to be the author of the precious gift she has received. Prompted by her grateful emotion, she confesses her faith. She also employs a new and near name to designate her maker. In the dialogue with the tempter she had used the word God (אֱלֹהִים). But now she adopts Jehovah. In this one word she hides a treasure of comfort. "He is true to his promise. He has not forgotten me. He is with me now again. He will never leave me nor forsake me. He will give me the victory." And who can blame her if she verily expected that this would be the promised deliverer who should bruise the serpent's head?

2. *His brother Habel.* Habel means *breath, vanity.* Does a sense of the vanity of earthly things grow in the minds of our first parents? Has the mother found her sorrow multiplied? Has she had many daughters between these sons? Is there something delicate and fragile in the appearance of Habel? Has Cain disappointed a mother's hopes? Some of all these thoughts may have prompted the name. There is something remarkable in the phrase "*his brother* Habel." It evidently points with touching simplicity to the coming outrage that was to destroy the peace and purity of the first home.

The two primitive employments of men were the agricultural and the pastoral. Here is the second allusion to some use which was made of animals soon after the fall. Coats of skin were provided for the first pair; and now we have Habel keeping sheep. In the garden of Eden, where the tree of life was accessible, an exclusively vegetable diet was designed for man. Whether this continued after the fall, we are not informed. It is certain that man had dominion over the whole animal kingdom. It can scarcely be doubted that the outer coverings of animals were used for clothing. Animals are presently to be employed for sacrifice. It is not beyond the bounds of probability that animal food may have been used before the flood, as a partial compensation for the want of the tree of life, which may have been fitted to supply all the defects of vegetable and even animal fare in sustaining the human frame in its primeval vigor.

Man in his primitive state, then, was not a mere gatherer of acorns, a hunter, or a nomad. He began with horticulture, the highest form of rural life. After the fall he descended to the culture of the field and the tending of cattle; but still he had a home, and a settled mode of living. It is only by a third step that he degenerates to the wandering and barbarous state of existence. And only by the predominance of might over right, the selfish lust of power, and the clever combinations of rampant ambition, comes that form of society in which the highest state of barbaric civilization and the lowest depth of bondage and misery meet.

3. *At the end of days.* This may denote the end of the week, of the year, or of some longer period. The season of the year was probably the ingathering, when the fruits of the earth and the firstlings of the flock would come in, and when it was not unnatural for the first family to celebrate with a subdued thankfulness the anniversary of their creation. And the present occasion seems to have been the time when Cain and Habel, have arrived at the years of discretion and self-

dependence, solemnly come forward with their first voluntary offerings to the Lord. Hitherto they may have come under their parents, who were then the actual offerers. Now they come on their own account.

Here, accordingly, we ascend from the secular to the eternal. We find a church in the primeval family. If Cain and Habel offer to God, we may imagine it was the habit of their parents, and has descended to them with all the sanction of parental example. But we may not venture to affirm this in all its extent. Parental example they no doubt had, in some respects; but whether Adam and Eve had yet ascended so far from the valley of repentance and humiliation as to make bold to offer anything to the Lord, admits of question. Right feeling in the first offenders would make the confidence of faith very slow of growth. It is even more natural for their children, being one remove from the actual transgressors, to make the first essay to approach God with an offering.

Cain brings of the fruits of the soil. We cannot say this was the mere utterance of nature giving thanks to the Creator for his benefits, and acknowledging that all comes from him, and all is due to him. History, parental instruction, and possibly example, were also here to give significance to the act. The offering is also made to Jehovah, the author of nature, of revelation, and now, in man's fallen state, of grace. There is no intimation in this verse of the state of Cain's feelings towards God. And there is only a possible hint, in the "coats of skin," in regard to the outward form of offering that would be acceptable. We must not anticipate the result.

4, 5. *And Habel brought.* Habel's offering differs from that of his brother in outward form. It consists of the firstlings of his flock. These were slain; for their fat is offered. Blood was therefore shed, and life taken away. To us who are accustomed to partake of animal food, there may appear nothing strange here. We may suppose that each brother offered that which came to hand out of the produce of his own industry. But let us ascend to that primeval time when the fruit tree and the herb bearing seed were alone assigned to man for food, and we must feel that there is something new here. Still let us wait for the result.

And the Lord had respect unto Habel and his offering, but not unto Cain. We have now the simple facts before us. Let us hear the inspired comment: "Πίστει, *by faith* Abel offered unto God πλείονα θυσίαν *a more excellent sacrifice* than Cain" (Heb. xi. 4). There was, then, clearly an internal moral distinction in the intention or disposition of the offerers. Habel had faith, — that confiding in God which is not bare and cold, but is accompanied with confession of sin, and a sense of gratitude for his mercy, and followed by obedience to his will. Cain had not this faith. He may have had a faith in the existence, power, and bounty of God; but it wanted that penitent returning to God, that humble acceptance of his mercy, and submission to his will, which constitute true faith. It must be admitted the faith of the offerer is essential to the acceptableness of the offering, even though other things were equal.

But, in this case, there is a difference in the things offered. The one is a vegetable offering, the other an animal; the one a presentation of things without life, the other a sacrifice of life. Hence the latter is called πλείων θυσία; there is *more in it* than in the former. The two offerings are therefore expressive of the different kinds of faith in the offerers. They are the excogitation and exhibition in outward symbol of the faith of each. The fruit of the soil offered to God is an acknowledgment that the means of this earthly life are due to him. This expresses the barren faith of Cain, but not the living faith of Habel. The latter has entered deeply into the thought that life itself is forfeited to God by transgression, and that only by an act of mercy can the Author of life restore it to the penitent, trusting, submissive, loving heart. He has pondered on the intimations of relenting mercy and love that have come from the Lord to the fallen race, and cast himself upon them without reserve. He slays the animal of which he is the lawful owner, as a victim, thereby acknowledging that his life is due for sin; he offers the life of the animal, not as though it were of equal value with his own, but in token that another life, equivalent to his own, is due to justice if he is to go free by the as yet inscrutable mercy of God.

Such a thought as this is fairly deducible from the facts on the surface of our record. It seems necessary in order to account for the first slaying of an animal under an economy where vegetable diet was alone permitted. We may go further. It is hard to suppose the slaying of an animal *acceptable*, if not previously allowed. The coats of skin seem to involve a practical allowance of the killing of animals for certain purposes. Thus we arrive at the conclusion that there was *more* in the animal than in the vegetable offering, and *that more* essential to the full expression of a right faith in the mercy of God, without borrowing the light of future revelation. Hence the nature of Habel's sacrifice was the index of the genuineness of his faith. And the Lord had respect unto him *and* his offering; thereby intimating that his heart was right, and his offering suitable to the expression of his feelings. This finding is also in keeping with the manner of Scripture, which takes the outward act as the simple and spontaneous exponent of the inward feeling. The mode of testifying his respect to Habel was by consuming his offering with fire, or some other way equally open to observation.

And Cain was very wroth, and his countenance fell. A feeling of resentment, and a sense of disgrace and condemnation take possession of Cain's breast. There is no spirit of inquiry, self-examination, prayer to God for light, or pardon. This shows that Cain was far from being in a right frame of mind.

6, 7. *Why art thou wroth? and why is thy countenance fallen?* The Lord does not yet give up Cain. In great mercy he expostulates with him. He puts a question which implies that there is no just cause for his present feelings. Neither anger at his brother, because his offering has been accepted, nor vexation in himself, because his own has not, is a right feeling in the presence of the just and merciful God, who searches the heart. Submission, self-examination, and amendment of what has been wrong in his approach to God, alone benefit the occasion. To this, accordingly, the Lord directs his attention in the next sentence.

If thou do well, shalt thou not be accepted? To do well is to retrace his steps, to consider his ways, and find out wherein he has been wrong, and to amend his offering and his intention accordingly. He has not duly considered the relation in which he stands to God as a guilty sinner, whose life is forfeited, and to whom the hand of mercy is held out; and accordingly he has not felt this in offering, or given expression to it in the nature of his offering. Yet the Lord does not immediately reject him, but with longsuffering patience directs his attention to this, that it may be amended. And on making such amendment, he holds out to him the clear and certain hope of acceptance still. But he does more than this. As Cain seems to have been of a particularly hard and unheedful disposition, he completes his expostulation, and deepens its awful solemnity, by stating the other alternative, both in its condition and consequence,—

And if thou do not well, at the door is sin lying. Sin past, in its unrequited and unacknowledged guilt; sin present, in its dark and stubborn passion and despair; but, above all, sin future, as the growing habit of a soul that persists in an evil temper, and therefore must add iniquity unto iniquity, is awaiting thee at the door, as a crouching slave the bidding of his master. As one lie borrows an endless train of others to keep up a vain appearance of consistency, so one sin if not repented of and forsaken involves the dire necessity of plunging deeper and deeper into the gulf of depravity and retribution. This dread warning to Cain, expressed in the mildest and plainest terms, is a standing lesson written for the learning of all mankind. Let him who is in the wrong retract at once, and return to God with humble acknowledgment of his own guilt, and unreserved submission to the mercy of his Maker; for to him who perseveres in sin there can be no hope or help. Another sentence is added to give intensity to the warning, —

"*And unto thee shall be his desire, and thou shalt rule over him.*" This sentence has all the pithiness and familiarity of a proverb. It has been employed before, to describe part of the tribulation the woman brought upon herself by disobedience, namely, the forced subjection of her will to that of her husband in the fallen state of humanity (Gen. iii. 16). It is accordingly expressive of the condition of a slave under the hard bondage and arbitrary caprice of a master and a tyrant. Cain is evidently the master. The question is, Who is the slave? To whom do the pronouns "his" and "him" refer? Manifestly, either to sin or to Habel. If to sin, then the meaning of the sentence is, the desire, the entire submission and service of sin will be yielded to thee, and thou wilt in fact make thyself master of it. Thy case will be no longer a heedless ignorance, and consequent dereliction of duty, but a wilful overmastering of all that comes by sin, and an unavoidable going on from sin to sin, from inward to outward sin, or, in specific terms, from wrath to murder, and from disappointment to defiance, and so from unrighteousness to ungodliness. This is an awful picture of his fatal end, if he do not instantly retreat. But it is necessary to deal plainly with this dogged, vindictive spirit, if by any means he may be brought to a right mind.

If the pronouns be referred to Habel, the meaning will come to much the same thing. The desire, the forced compliance, of thy brother will be yielded unto thee, and thou wilt rule over him with a rigor and a violence that will terminate in his murder. In violating the image of God by shedding the blood of thy brother, thou wilt be defying thy Maker, and fiercely rushing on to thy own perdition. Thus, in either case, the dark doom of sin unforsaken and unremitted looms fearfully in the distance.

The general reference to sin, however, seems to be the milder and more soothing form of expostulation. The special reference to Habel might only exasperate. It appears, moreover, to be far-fetched, as there is no allusion to his brother in the previous part of the address. The boldness of the figure by which Cain is represented as making himself master of sin, when he with reckless hand grasps at all that comes by sin, is not unfamiliar to Scripture. Thus the doer of wickedness is described as the master of it (Eccl viii. 8). On these grounds we prefer the reference to sin, and the interpretation founded on it.

There are two other expositions of this difficult sentence which deserve to be noticed. 1st. "And as to thy brother, unto thee shall be his desire, and thou shalt rule over him *with all the right of the first born*." But (1) the reference to his brother is remote; (2) the rights of primogeniture are perhaps not yet established; (3) the words do not express a right, but an exercise of might against right arising in a fallen state (Gen. iii. 16); (4) the Judge of all the earth is not wont to guarantee the prerogatives of birth to one who is in positive rebellion against him, but, on the other hand, he withdraws them from the unworthy to confer them on whom he will. For these reasons we conceive this exposition is to be rejected. 2d. "And unto thee shall be *sin's* desire; *but* thou shalt overcome it." But (1) the parallelism between the two members of the sentence is here neglected; (2) a different meaning is assigned to the words here and in Gen. iii. 16, (3) the connection between the sentence thus explained and what goes before is not clear; (4) the lesson taught is not obvious; and (5) the assurance given is not fulfilled. On these grounds we cannot adopt this explanation.

The above address of the Lord to Cain, expressed here perhaps only in its substance, is fraught with the most powerful motives that can bear on the mind of man. It holds out acceptance to the wrong-doer, if he will come with a broken heart and a corresponding expression of repentance before God, in the full faith that he can and will secure the ends of justice so that he can have mercy on the penitent. At the same time it points out, with all clearness and faithfulness to a soul yet unpractised in the depths of iniquity, the insidious nature of sin, the proneness of a selfish heart to sin with a high hand, the tendency of one sinful temper, if persisted in, to engender a growing habit of aggravated crime which ends in the everlasting destruction of the soul. Nothing more than this can be done by argument or reason for the warning of a wrong-doer. From the mouth of the Almighty these words must have come with all the evidence and force they were capable of receiving.

8. *And Cain talked with Habel his brother.* Cain did not act on the divine counsel. He did not amend his offering to God, either in point of internal feeling or external form. Though one speak to him from heaven he will not hear. He conversed with Habel his brother, The topic is not stated. The Septuagint supplies the words, "Let us go into the field." If in walking side by side with his brother he touched upon the divine communication, the conference did not lead to any better results. If the divine expostulation failed, much more the human. Perhaps it only increased his irritation. When they were in the field, and therefore out of view, he rose up against his brother and slew him. The deed is done that cannot be recalled. The motives to it were various. Selfishness, wounded pride, jealousy, and a guilty conscience were all at work (1 John iii. 12). Here, then, is sin following upon sin, proving the truth of the warning given in the merciful forbearance of God.

9. *Where is Habel thy brother?* The interrogatory here reminds us of the question put to the hiding Adam, "Where art thou?" It is calculated to strike the conscience. The reply is different from that of Adam. The sin has now advanced from hasty, incautious yielding to the tempter, to reiterated and deliberate disobedience. Such a sinner *must* take different ground. Cain, therefore, attempts to parry the question, apparently on the vain supposition that no eye, not even that of the All-seeing, was present to witness the deed. "I know not." In the madness of his confusion he goes further. He disputes the right of the Almighty to make the demand. "Am I my brother's keeper?" There is, as usual, an atom of truth mingled with the amazing falsehood of this surly response. No man is the absolute keeper of his brother, so as to be responsible for his safety when he is not present. This is what Cain means to insinuate. But every man is his brother's keeper so far that he is not himself to lay the hand of violence on him, nor suffer another to do so if he can hinder it. This sort of keeping the Almighty has a right to demand of every one, — the first part of it on the ground of mere justice, the second on that of love. But Cain's reply betrays a desperate resort to falsehood, a total estrangement of feeling, a quenching of brotherly love, a predominence of that selfishness which freezes affection and kindles hatred. This is the way of Cain (Jude 11).

10. *What hast thou done?* The Lord now charges him with his guilt: "The voice of thy brother's blood crieth unto me from the soil." In the providence of God blood has a voice crying to him to which he cannot but give heed. It is vain, then, to attempt concealment.

11, 12. The curse (Gen. ix. 25, n.) which now fell on Cain was in some sense retributive, as it sprang from the soil which had received his brother's blood. The particulars of it are the withdrawal of the full strength or fruitfulness of the soil from him, and the degradation from the state of a settled dweller in the presence of God to that of a vagabond in the earth. He was to be banished to a less productive part of the earth, removed from the presence of God and the society of his father and mother, and abandoned to a life of wandering and uncertainty. The sentence of death had been already pronounced upon man.

13, 14. *My iniquity is more than I can bear.* To bear iniquity is in Hebrew phrase to undergo the punishment of it. And the prospect of this, as it presents itself to the eyes of Cain, is so appalling that he shrinks from it as intolerable. To be driven from the face of the soil, inhabited by the other surviving members of the human family, to an unknown and therefore terrible region; to be hidden from the face of God, who manifested himself still to the race of Adam in their present abode; to be a vagabond and a fugitive in the earth, far away from the land of his birth; and to be liable to be slain in just revenge by any one who should find him,— such is the hard fate he sees before him. It is dark enough in itself, and no doubt darker still in the exaggeration which an accusing conscience conjures up to his imagination. The phrase, *every one finding me*, implies that the family of Adam had now become numerous. Not only sons and daughters, but their children and grandchildren may have been growing up when Cain was sent into exile. But in his present terror even an excited fancy suggested an enemy at every turn.

15. The reply of the Lord is fitted to quell the troubled breast of Cain. *Therefore.* Because thy fears of what thou deservest go beyond what it is my purpose to permit, I give thee assurance of freedom from personal violence. To be *avenged seven-fold* is to be avenged fully. Cain will no doubt receive even-handed justice from the Almighty. The assurance given to Cain is a sign, the nature of which is not further specified.

This passage unfolds to us a mode of dealing with the first murderer which is at first sight somewhat difficult to be understood. But we are to bear in mind that the sentence of death had been already pronounced upon man, and therefore stood over Adam and all his posterity, Cain among the rest. To pronounce the same sentence therefore upon him for a new crime, would have been weak and unmeaning. Besides, the great crime of crimes was disobedience to the divine will; and any particular form of crime added to that was comparatively unimportant. Wrong done to a creature, even of the deepest dye, was not to be compared in point of guilt with wrong done to the Creator. The grave element in the criminality of every social wrong is its practical disregard of the authority of the Most High. Moreover, every other sin to the end of time is but the development of that first act of disobedience to the mandate of heaven by which man fell; and accordingly every penalty is summed up in that death which is the judicial consequence of the first act of rebellion against heaven.

We are also to bear in mind that God still held the sword of justice in his own immediate hands, and had not delegated his authority to any human tribunal. No man was therefore clothed with any right from heaven to call Cain to account for the crime he had committed. To fall upon him with the high hand in a wilful act of private revenge, would be taking the law into one's own hands, and therefore a misdemeanor against the majesty of heaven, which the Judge of all could not allow to pass unpunished. It is plain that no man has an inherent right to inflict the sanction of a broken law on the transgressor. This right originally belongs to the Creator, and derivatively only to those whom he has intrusted with the dispensation of civil government according to established laws.

Cain's offences were great and aggravated. But let us not exaggerate them. He was first of all defective in the character of his faith and the form of his sacrifice. His carnal mind came out still more in the wrath and vexation he felt when his defective offering was not accepted. Though the Almighty condescends now to plead with him and warn him against persisting in impenitent silence and discontent, lest he should thereby only become more deeply involved in sin, he does not retreat, but, on the contrary, proceeds to slay his brother, in a fit of jealousy; and, lastly, he rudely and falsely denies all knowledge of him, and all obligation to be his protector. Notwithstanding all this, it is still to be remembered that the sentence of death from heaven already hung over him. This was in the merciful order of things comparatively slow of execution in its full extent, but at the same time absolutely certain in the end. The aggravation of the first crime of man by the sins of self-will, sullenness, envy, fratricide, and defiant falsehood, was but the natural fruit of that beginning of disobedience. It is accordingly visited by additional tokens of the divine displeasure, which manifest themselves in this life, and are mercifully calculated to warn Cain still further to repent.

Cain's guilt seems now to have been brought home in some measure to his conscience; and he not only stands aghast at the sentence of banishment from the divine presence, but instinctively trembles, lest, upon the principle of retributive justice, whoever meets him may smite him to the death, as he had done his brother. The longsuffering of God, however, interferes to prevent such a catastrophe, and even takes steps to relieve the trembling culprit from the apprehension of a violent death. This leads us to understand that God, having formed a purpose of mercy toward the human family, was sedulously bent upon exercising it even towards the murderer of a brother. Hence he does not punish his repeated crimes by *immediate death*, which would have defeated his design of giving him a long day of grace and opportunity to reflect, repent, return to God, and even yet offer in faith a typical atonement by blood for his sin. Thus the prohibition to slay him is sanctioned by a seven-fold, that is, an ample and complete vengeance, and a sign of protection mercifully vouchsafed to him. The whole dealing of the Almighty was calculated to have a softening, conscience-awakening, and hope-inspiring effect on the murderer's heart.

16. *The presence of the Lord* seems to have been at the entrance of the garden where the cherubim were stationed. There, probably, the children of men still lingered in faith and hope before the Lord, whom they still regarded as their Maker and merciful Saviour. They acknowledged his undeserved goodness in the form of sacrifice. The retreat of Cain from the scene of parental affection, of home associations, and of divine manifestation, must have been accompanied with many a deep, unuttered pang of regret and remorse. But he has deeply and repeatedly transgressed, and he must bear the consequence. Such is sin. Many a similar deed of cruelty and bloodshed might the sacred writer have recorded in the after-history of man. But it is the manner of Scripture to note the first example, and then to pass over in silence its subsequent repetitions, unless when a particular transaction has an important bearing on the ways of God with man.

XIX. THE LINE OF CAIN. — Gen. iv. 17–24.

17. חֲנוֹךְ Chanok, *initiation*, *instruction*.

18. עִירָד 'Irad, *fleet* as the wild ass, citizen. מְחוּיָאֵל Mechujael, *smitten of El*, or *life of El*. מְתוּשָׁאֵל Methushael, *man of El*, *or man asked*. לֶמֶךְ Lemek, *man of prayer*, *youth*.

19. עָדָה 'Adah, *beauty*. צִלָּה Tsillah, *shade* or *tinkling*.

20. יָבָל Jabal, *stream*, *leader* of cattle, *produce*, *the walker* or *wanderer*. אֹהֶל pl. אֹהָלִים for אֳהָלִים *tent*, *awning*, *covering* of goats' hair over the poles or timbers which constituted the original booth, סֻכָּה.

21. יוּבָל Jubal, *player* on an instrument?

22. תּוּבַל־קַיִן Tubal-qain, *brass-smith?* The scion or son of the lance. נַעֲמָה Na'amah, *pleasant*, *lovely*.

17. And Cain knew his wife: and she conceived and bare Henok: and he was building a city, and called the name of the city after the name of his son Henok. 18. And unto Henok was born Irad; and Irad begat Mehujael; and Mehujael begat Methushael; and Methushael begat Lamek. 19 And Lamek took unto him two wives: the name of the one was Adah, and the name of the second Zillah. 20. And Adah bare Jabal; he was the father of such as dwell in tents and have cattle. 21. And the name of his brother was Jubal; he was the father of all that handle harp and pipe. 22. And Zillah, she also bare Tubal-cain, a forger of every tool of brass and iron. And the sister of Tubal-cain was Naamah. 23. And Lamek said unto his wives:

Adah and Zillah, hear my voice,
Wives of Lamek, hearken to my speech:
For a man have I slain for my wound,
And a youth for my hurt.
24. If seven-fold avenged be Cain,
Then Lamek seventy and seven.

Mankind is now formally divided into two branches, — those who still abide in the presence of God, and those who have fled to a distance from him. Distinguishing names will soon be given to these according to their outward profession and practice (Gen. vi. 1). The awful distinction according to the inward state of the feelings has been already given in the terms, *the seed of the woman* and *the seed of the serpent.*

17. Cain is not unaccompanied in his banishment. A wife, at least, is the partner of his exile. And soon a son is born to him. He was building a city at the time of this birth. The city is a keep or fort, enclosed with a wall for the defence of all who dwell within. The building of the city is the erection of this wall or barricade. Here we find the motive of fear and self-defence still ruling Cain. His hand has been imbrued in a brother's blood, and he expects every man's hand will be against him.

He calls his son Henok, and his city after the name of his son. The same word is employed as a name in the lines of Seth (Gen. v. 18), of Midian (Gen. xxv. 4), and of Reuben (Gen. xlvi. 9). It signifies dedication or initiation, and, in the present case, seems to indicate a new beginning of social existence, or a consciousness of initiative or inventive power, which necessity and self-reliance called forth particularly in himself and his family. It appears, from the flocks kept by Habel, the fear of persons meeting and slaying the murderer, the marriage and family of Cain, and the beginning of a city, that a considerble time had elapsed since the fall. The wife of Cain was of necessity his sister, though this was forbidden in after times, for wise and holy reasons, when the necessity no longer existed.

18. The names in this verse seem to denote, respectively, fleet as a wild ass, stricken by God, man of prayer, and youth. They indicate a mingling of thoughts and motives in men's minds, in which the word אֵל *mighty* as a name of God occurs. This name is a common noun, signifying hero or potentate, and also power or might, and is transferred to God as *the* Potentate, or Almighty One. It is distinguished from אֱלֹהִים *God,* since they are put in apposition (Jos. xxii. 22); and seems to be properly an epithet applied to God by way of preëminence. The denomination, "stricken of the Mighty," is a recognition of the divine power. "The man of prayer," or "asking," may also have reference to an act of worship. Among these higher thoughts we also find a value put upon youth and physical superiority, as the fleetness of the wild ass. This is all we can learn from these imperfectly understood names.

19. This is the first record and probably the first instance of polyg-

amy. The names of the two wives, Adah, *beauty*, and Zillah, *shade* or *tinkling*, seem to refer to the charms which attracted Lamek. Superabundance of wealth and power perhaps led Lamek to multiply wives.

20. Here is the first notice of the tent and of cattle. The tent was the thin shining and shading canvas of goats' hair, which was placed over the poles or timbers that constituted the original booth. In process of time it would supplant the branches and foliage of the booth as a covering from the sun or the wind. The cattle are designated by a word denoting property, as being chattels personal, and consisting chiefly of sheep and oxen. The idea of property had now been practically realized. The Cainites were now prosperous and numerous, and therefore released from that suspicious fear which originated the fortified keep of their progenitor. The sons of Jabal rove over the common with their tents and cattle, undismayed by imaginary terrors.

21. Here is the invention of musical instruments in their two leading varieties, the harp and the pipe. This implies the previous taste for music and song. It seems not unlikely that Zillah, the mother of Jubal, was a daughter of song. The fine arts follow in the train of the useful. All this indicates the easy circumstances in which the Cainites now found themselves.

22. The three names Jabal, Jubal, and Tubal are formed from a root signifying to *flow*, *run*, *go forth*, perhaps *blow*, from which comes יוֹבֵל, the *blast* or trumpet-note of joy and release. Accordingly all sorts of going forth, that were suitable to the life of a nomad, seem to have distinguished this family. The addition of Cain to the name of Tubal may have been a memorial of his ancestor, or an indication of his pursuit. Tubal of the spear or lance may have been his familiar designation. The making of tents implies some skill in carpentry, and also in spinning and weaving. The working in brass and iron furnishes implements for war, hunting, or husbandry. The construction of musical instruments shows considerable refinement in carving and moulding wood. Naamah, the lovely, seems to be mentioned on account of her personal charms.

23, 24. In this fragment of ancient song, we have Lamek, under the strong excitement of having slain a man in self-defence, reciting to his wives the deed, and at the same time comforting them and himself with the assurance that if Cain the murderer would be avenegd sevenfold, he the manslayer in self-defence would be avenged seventy and seven fold. This short ode has all the characteristics of the most perfect Hebrew poetry. Every pair of lines is a specimen of the Hebrew parallelism or rhythm of sentiment and style. They all belong to the synthetic, synonymous, or cognate parallel, the second member reiterating with emphasis the first. Here we observe that Lamek was a poet; one of his wives was probably a songstress, and the other had a taste for ornament. One daughter was the lovely, and three sons were the inventors of most of the arts which sustain and embellish life. This completes the picture of this remarkable family.

It has been noticed that the inventive powers were more largely developed in the line of Cain than in that of Sheth. And it has been suggested that the worldly character of the Cainites accounts for this. The Shethites contemplated the higher things of God, and therefore paid less attention to the practical arts of life. The Cainites, on the other hand, had not God in their thoughts, and therefore gave the more heed to the requisites and comforts of the present life.

But besides this the Cainites, penetrating into the unknown tracts of this vast common, were compelled by circumstances to turn their thoughts to the invention of the arts by which the hardships of their condition might be abated. And as soon as they had conquered the chief difficulties of their new situation, the habits of industry and mental activity which they had acquired were turned to the embellishments of life.

We have no grounds, however, for concluding that the descendants of Cain were as yet entirely and exclusively ungodly on the one hand, or on the other that the descendants of Sheth were altogether destitute of inventive genius or inattentive to its cultivation. With the exception of the assault that seemed to have provoked the homicidal act of Lamek, and the bigamy of Lamek himself, we find not much to condemn in the recorded conduct of the race of Cain; and in the names of some of them we discover the remembrance and recognition of God. Habel had a keeper of cattle before Jabal. The Cainites were also an older race than the Shethites. And when Noah was commissioned to build the ark, we have no reason to doubt that he was qualified in some measure by natural ability and previous training for such a task.

The line of Cain is traced no further than the seventh generation from Adam. We cannot tell whether there were any more in that line before the flood. The design of tracing it thus far, is to point out the origin of the arts of life, and the first instances of bigamy and homicide in self-defence.

XX. SHETH. — Gen. iv. 25. 26.

25. שֵׁת Sheth, *placed, put.*

26. אֱנוֹשׁ Enosh, *man, sickly.* קְרֹא בְשֵׁם means, 1st, to call an object by its name (Is. xl. 26, xliii. 1, xlv. 3, 4); 2d, to call an object by the name of another, who is the parent, leader, husband, owner (Num. xxxii. 42; Judg. xviii. 29; Ps. xlix. 12; Is. xliii. 7, xliv. 5, xlviii. 1; lxv. 1); 3d, to proclaim the name of (Ex. xxxiii. 19, xxxv. 5, 6); 4th, to call upon the name of God, to address him by his proper name with an audible voice in the form of prayer. This is the most common meaning of the phrase. In this sense it is followed by Jehovah as the proper name of the true God among the Hebrews. It is not to be forgotten that names were still significant, at this early period.

25. And Adam knew again his wife; and she bare a son, and called his name Sheth. For God hath given me another seed instead of Habel, whom Cain slew. 26. And to Sheth himself also was born a son; and he called his name Enosh. Then was it begun to call upon the name of the Lord. § 4.

This passage completes the account of Adam's family. Henceforth we generally meet with two parallel lines of narrative, as the human family is divided into two great branches, with opposing interests and tendencies. The main line refers to the remnant of the race that are on terms of open reconciliation with God; while a collateral line notes as far as necessary the state of those who have departed from the knowledge and love of the true God.

25. The narrative here reverts to a point subsequent to the death of Habel, when another son is born to Adam, whom his mother Eve regards as a substitute for Habel, and names Sheth in allusion to that circumstance. She is in a sadder, humbler frame than when she named her first-born, and therefore does not employ the personal name of the Lord. Yet her heart is not so much downcast as when she called her second son a *breath.* Her faith in God is sedate and pensive, and hence she uses the more distant and general term Elohim, God.

Yet there is a peculiar significance in the form of expression she employs. *For God* hath given me another seed instead of Habel. He is to be instead of Habel, and God-fearing like Habel. Far above this consideration, God hath given him. This son is from God. She regards him as God's son. She receives this gift from God, and in faith expects him to be the seed of God, the parent of a godly race. Her faith was not disappointed. His descendants earn the name of the sons of God. As the ungodly are called the seed of the serpent, because they are of his spirit, so the godly are designated the seed of God, because they are of God's Spirit. The Spirit of God strives and rules in them, and so they are, in the graphic language of Scripture, the sons of God (Gen. vi. 1).

26. A son is born to Sheth also, whom he calls Enosh. In this name there is probably an allusion to the meaning of sickliness and dependence which belongs to the root. These qualities were now found to be characteristic of man in his present state.

The closing sentence signalizes a remarkable event, which took place at the birth of Enosh, about two hundred and forty years after the creation of Adam. *Then was it begun to call upon the name of the Lord.* The solemn invocation of God by his proper name in audible and social prayer and praise is the most usual meaning of the phrase now before us, and is to be adopted unless there be something in the context or the circumstances demanding another meaning. This involves also the first of the meanings given above, as we call God by his name in oral worship. It includes the third in one of its forms, as in praise we proclaim the name of our God. And it leads to the second, as those who call on the name of the Lord are themselves called the children of God.

Some change is here intimated in the mode of approaching God in worship. The gist of the sentence, however, does not lie in the name *Jehovah.* For this term was not then new in itself, as it was used by Eve at the birth of Cain; nor was it new in this connection, as the phrase now appears for the first time, and Jehovah is the ordinary term employed in it ever afterwards to denote the true God. As a proper name, Jehovah is the fit and customary word to enter into a solemn invocation. It is, as we have seen, highly significant. It speaks of the Self-existent, the Author of all existing things, and in particular of man; the Self-manifest, who has shown himself merciful and gracious to the returning penitent, and with him keeps promise and covenant. Hence it is the custom itself of calling on the name of Jehovah, of addressing God by his proper name, which is here said to have been commenced.

At first sight, with our habits and associations, it seems a very strange thing that calling upon the name of the Lord should only begin two hundred and forty years after the creation of man. But let us endeavor to divest ourselves of these limitations, and rise to the primeval simplicity of man's thoughts in regard to God. We read of God speaking to man in paradise, but not of man speaking to God. In the examination that preceded the sentence passed upon the transgressors, we hear Adam and Eve replying to the questions of God, but not venturing to open a conversation with the Most High. If the feeling of reverence and solemn awe did not permit such a liberty before the fall, much more would the superadded sense of guilt after that event restrain man from making any advances toward the infinitely holy Being whom he had so wantonly offended. The rebuking examination, the judicial sentence, and the necessary execution of this sentence in its preliminary form, were so prominent and impressive as to throw into the background any intimations of the divine mercy with which they were accompanied. The latter, however, were not unnoticed, or without a salutary effect on the primeval pair. Adam *believed* the indications of mercy, whether in word or deed, which God gave him. Faith was prompt and natural in that early stage of comparative nearness to God, to his manifest presence and his conspicuous wonders of creative power. It was also a native tendency of the human breast, and would be so still, had we not become so sophisticated by education that doubt has come to be the prominent attitude of our minds. This faith of the first pair led to confession; not directly, however, to God, but indirectly in the names Adam gave his wife, and Eve her first-born son. Here humble, distant, self-condemning faith soliloquizes, or, at most, the penitent pair converse in humble hope about the mercy of the Most High.

The bringing of an offering to God was a step in advance of this penitent, humble, submissive, self-accusing faith. It was the exact counterpart and representation by a well-devised symbol of the nature of the offerer's faith. It was therefore a confession of faith and certain accompanying feelings towards God by a symbolic act. It was quite natural that this mute sign should precede the actual address. The consequences, however, of the approach of Cain and Habel were calculated to deepen again the feeling of dread, and to strike the onlooker dumb in the presence of the High and Holy One. Still would this be so in that infantile state of man when one thought would take full possession of the soul, until another was plainly and directly brought before the attention. In this simple, unsophisticated state of the penitent, we can conceive him to resign himself passively to the merciful will of that Maker whom he has grievously offended, without venturing to breathe a wish or even to lift up a note of thanksgiving. Such mute acquiescence in the divine will for two hundred and forty years was well-befitting the humble penitents of that infantile age, standing in solemn awe under a sense of their own demerit and of the infinite holiness of the Majesty on high. There were even an eloquent pathos and power in that tacit reverence fitted to move the heart of the All-searching Spirit more than ten thousand voices less deeply penetrated with a sense of the guilt of sin and the beauty of holiness.

At length, however, Sheth was given to Eve, and accepted by her as a substitute for Habel. Enosh, the child of sorrow, was born to him. Collateral with this line of descent, and all the anxieties and wants which it involved, was the growth of a class of men who were of the spirit of Cain, and receded further and further from God. In these circumstances of growing iniquity on the one hand, and growing faith on the other, believing reason comes to conceive the full import of the mercy of God, freely and fully accepts of pardon, and realizes the peace and privilege which it bestows. Growing man now comprehends all that is implied in the proper name of God, *Jehovah*, the author of being, of promise, and of performance. He finds a tongue, and ventures to express the desires and feelings that have been long pent up in his breast, and are now bursting for utterance. These petitions and confessions are now made in an audible voice, and with a holy urgency and courage rising above the depressing sense of self-abasement to the confidence of peace and gratitude. These adorations are also presented in a social capacity, and thereby acquire a public notoriety. The father, the elder of the house, is the master of words, and he becomes the spokesman of the brotherhood in this new relationship into which they have spontaneously entered with their Father in heaven. The spirit of adoption has prompted the confiding and endearing terms, *Abba*, *Father*, and now the winged words ascend to heaven, conveying the adorations and aspirations of the assembled saints. The new form of worship attracts the attention of the early world, and the record is made, "Then began they to call upon the name of the Lord," that keepeth covenant and mercy.

Here we perceive that the holy race has passed beyond its infancy. It has learned to speak with God in the language of faith, of conscious acceptance, of freedom, of hope, of love. This is a far nobler attainment than the invention of all the arts of life. It is the return from that revulsive dread with which the conscious sinner shrank back from the felt holiness of God. It is the drawing of the divine mercy and love let into the penitent soul, by which it has come to itself, and taken courage to return to the merciful Jehovah, and speak to him the language of penitence, of confession, of gratitude. These believing penitents, chiefly it is to be supposed in the line of Sheth, of which this paragraph speaks, began to be distinguished as the followers of the Lord; whereas others at the same time had forgotten the Lord, and renounced even the form of reverence for him. The seed of the woman was now distinguished from the seed of the serpent. The latter are in a spiritual sense called *the seed of the serpent*, because they cling to the principles of the tempter; and the former may in the same sense be designated *the seed* or *sons of God*, because they follow after him as the God of mercy and truth. Thus the lamentable fact obtrudes itself upon our view that a portion of the human family have persisted in the primeval apostasy, and are no longer associated with their fellows in acknowledging their common Maker.

The progress of moral evil in the antediluvian world was manifested in fratricide, in going out from the presence of the Lord, in personal violence, and in polygamy. The first is the normal character of all murder; the second gave scope for the third, the daring and presumptuous violence of the strong; and the fourth ultimately led to an almost total corruption of manners. It is curious to observe that ungodliness, in the form of disobedience and departure from God and therefore of the practical breach of the first commandment, and unrighteousness in the form of murder, the crime of masterful passion and violence, which is the transgression of the first commandment concerning our neighbor, are the starting-points of sin in the world. They do not seem to have yet reached idolatry and adultery. This appears to point out that the prohibitions into which the law is developed in the ten commandments are arranged in the order of time as well as of nature.

The preceding chapters, if written in substance by Adam, formed the primeval Bible of mankind. But, whether written at that time or not, they contain the leading facts which occurred in the early history of man in relation to his Maker. These facts were well known to the antediluvian world, and formed the rule by which it was to be guided in approaching to God, presenting to him an acceptable offering, calling upon his name, and so walking with him in peace and love. Here we have all the needful germs of a gospel for the infantile race. If we ask why they were not effectual, the answer is at hand. They were effectual with a few, and are thereby proved sufficient to recover man from sin, and vindicate the mercy of God. But the All-wise Being, who made man a moral agent, must thoroughly guard his freedom, even in the dealings of mercy. And in the folly and madness of their self-will, some will revolt more and more. The history was written for our learning. Let its lessons be pondered. Let the accumulated experience of bygone wanderings recorded in the book of God be our warning, to return at length with our whole heart to our merciful Father.

SECTION V — THE LINE TO NOAH

XXI. THE LINE OF SHETH. — Gen. v.

1. סֵפֶר *writing, a writing, a book.*
9. קֵינָן Qenan, *possessor*, or *spearsman.*
12. מַהֲלַלְאֵל Mahalalel, *praise of El.*
15. יֶרֶד Jered, *going down.*
21. מְתוּשֶׁלַח Methushelach, *man of the missile.*
29. נֹחַ Noach, *rest,* נִחַם *sigh; repent; pity; comfort oneself; be revenged.*
32. שֵׁם Shem, *name, fame;* r. *be high.* חָם Cham, *hot.* יֶפֶת Japheth, *spreading;* r. *spread out.*

V. 1. This is the book of the generations of man. In the
day that God created man, in the likeness of God made he
him. 2. Male and female created he them; and blessed them,
and called their name man, in the day of their being created.
3. And Adam lived thirty and a hundred years, and begat (a
son) in his likeness, after his image; and he called his name
Sheth. 4. And the days of Adam, after he begat Sheth, were
eight hundred years; and he begat sons and daughters. 5.
And all the days of Adam that he lived were nine hundred and
thirty years; and he died.

6. And Sheth lived five and a hundred years, and begat
Enosh. 7. And Sheth lived, after he begat Enosh, seven and
eight hundred years, and begat sons and daughters. 8. And
all the days of Sheth were twelve and nine hundred years; and
he died. § 6.

9. And Enosh lived ninety years, and begat Kenan. 10.
And Enosh lived, after he begat Kenan, fifteen and eight hun-

dred years, and begat sons and daughters. 11. And all the days of Enosh were five and nine hundred years; and he died.

§ 7.

12. And Kenan lived seventy years, and begat Mahalalel. 13. And Kenan lived, after he begat Mahalalel, forty and eight hundred years, and begat sons and daughters. 14. And all the days of Kenan were ten and nine hundred years; and he died.

§ 8.

15. And Mahalalel lived five and sixty years and begat Jared. 16. And Mahalalel lived, after he begat Jared, thirty and eight hundred years, and begat sons and daughters. 17. And all the days of Mahalalel were five and ninety and eight hundred years; and he died.

§ 9.

18. And Jared lived two and sixty and a hundred years, and begat Henok. 19. And Jared lived, after he begat Henok, eight hundred years, and begat sons and daughters. 20. And all the days of Jared were two and sixty and nine hundred years; and he died.

§ 10.

21. And Henok lived five and sixty years, and begat Methushelah. 22. And Henok walked with the God, after he begat Methushelah, three hundred years, and begat sons and daughters. 23. And all the days of Henok were five and sixty and three hundred years. 24. And Henok walked with the God; and he was not, for God took him.

§ 11.

25. And Methushelah lived seven and eighty and a hundred years, and begat Lamek. 26. And Methushelah lived, after he begat Lamek, two and eighty and seven hundred years, and begat sons and daughters. 27. And all the days of Methushelah were nine and sixty and nine hundred years; and he died.

§ 12.

28. And Lamek lived two and eighty and a hundred years, and begat a son. 29. And he called his name Noah; saying: This shall comfort us in our work and the toil of our hands, from the soil which the Lord hath cursed. 30. And Lamek

lived, after he begat Noah, five and ninety and five hundred years, and begat sons and daughters. 31. And all the days of Lamek were seven and seventy and seven hundred years; and he died. § 13.

32. And Noah was the son of five hundred years; and Noah begat Shem, Ham, and Japheth.

We now enter upon the third of the larger documents contained in Genesis. The first is a diary, the second is a history, the third a genealogy. The first employs the name Elohim exclusively; the second uses Jehovah Elohim in the second and third chapters, and Jehovah usually in the fourth; the third has Elohim in the first part, and Jehovah in the second part. The name Elohim is employed in the beginning of the chapter with a manifest reference to the first document, which is here quoted and abridged.

This chapter contains the line from Adam to Noah, in which are stated some common particulars concerning all, and certain special details concerning three of them. The genealogy is traced to the tenth in descent from Adam, and terminates with the flood. The scope of the chapter is to mark out the line of faith and hope and holiness from Adam, the first head of the human race, to Noah, who became eventually the second natural head of it.

1, 2. These verses are a recapitulation of the creation of man. The first sentence is the superscription of the new piece of composition now before us. The heading of the second document was more comprehensive. It embraced the generations, evolutions, or outworkings of the skies and the land, as soon as they were called into existence, and was accordingly dated from the third day. The present document confines itself to the generations of man, and commences, therefore, with the sixth day. The generations here are literal for the most part, though a few particulars of the individuals mentioned are recorded. But taken in a large sense this superscription will cover the whole of the history in the Old and New Testaments. It is only in the prophetic parts of these books that we reach again in the end of things to the wider compass of the heavens and the earth (Isa. lxv. 17; 2 Pet. iii. 13; Rev. xxi. 1). Then only does the sphere of history enlarge itself to the pristine dimensions in the proper and blessed sense, when the second Adam appears on earth, and re-connects heaven and earth in a new, holy, and everlasting covenant.

The present superscription differs from the former one in the introduction of the word סֵפֶר *book*. There is here some ground in the text for supposing the insertion by Moses of an authentic document, handed down from the olden time, in the great work which he was directed to compose. The chapter before us could not have been completed, indeed, till after the birth of Shem, Ham, and Japheth. But if we except the last verse, there is no impossibility or improbability in its being composed before the deluge.

The invention of writing at that early period is favored by some other circumstances connected with these records. We cannot say that it is impossible for oral tradition to preserve the memory of minute transactions, — sayings, songs, names, and numbers of years up to a thousand, — especially in a period when men's lives exceeded nine hundred years. But we can easily see that these details could be much more easily handed down if there was any method of notation for the help of the memory. The minute records of this kind, therefore, which we find in these early chapters, though not very numerous, afford a certain presumption in favor of a very early knowledge of the art of writing.

2. *And called their name man.* This name seems to connect man (אָדָם) with the soil from which he was taken (אֲדָמָה Gen. ii. 7). It is evidently a generic or collective term, denoting the species. God, as the maker, names the race, and thereby marks its character and purpose.

3–5. In the compass of these three verses the course of Adam's life is completed. And after the same model the lines of all his lineal descendants in this chapter are drawn up. The certain particulars stated are the years he lived before the birth of a certain son, the number of years he afterwards lived during which sons and daughters were born to him, and his death. Two sons, and most probably several daughters, were born to Adam before the birth of Sheth. But these sons have been already noticed, and the line of Noah is here given. It is obvious, therefore, that the following individuals in the genealogy may, or may not, have been first-born sons. The stated formula, *and he died*, at the close of each life except that of Henok, is a standing demonstration of the effect of disobedience.

The writer, according to custom, completes the life of one patriarch before he commences that of the next; and so the first event of the following biography is long antecedent to the last event of the preceding one. This simply and clearly illustrates the law of Hebrew narrative.

The only peculiarity in the life of Adam is the statement that his son was *in his likeness, after his image.* This is no doubt intended to include that depravity which had become the characteristic of fallen man. It is contrasted with the preceding notice that Adam was originally created in the image of God. If it had been intended merely to indicate that the offspring was of the same species with the parent, the phrase, *after his kind* (לְמִינֵהוּ), would have been employed, as in the first chapter. This is one of the mysteries of the race, when the head of it is a moral being, and has fallen. His moral depravity, affecting the essential difference of his nature, descends to his offspring.

As this document alludes to the first in the words, *in the day of God's creating man, in the likeness of God made he him,* quotes its very words in the sentence, *male and female created he them,* refers to the second in the words, *and called their name man* (Gen. ii. 7), and also needs this second for the explication of the statement that the offspring of man bore his likeness, it presupposes the existence and knowledge of these documents at the time when it was written. If it had been intended for an independent work, it would have been more full and explanatory on these important topics.

21–24. The history of the Shethite Henok is distinguished in two respects: *First,* after the birth of Methushelah, he *walked with the God.* Here for the first time we have God (אֱלֹהִים) with the definite article, with which it occurs more than four hundred times. By this he is emphatically distinguished as *the* God, now made known by his acts and manifestations, in opposition to atheism, the sole God in opposition to polytheism, and the true God in opposition to all false gods or notions of God. It is possible that in the time of Henok some had forsaken the true God, and fallen into various misconceptions concerning the Supreme Being. His walking with *the God* is a hint that others were walking without this God.

The phrase "walked with God" is rendered in the Septuagint εὐηρέστησε τῷ θεῷ, *pleased God,* and is adduced in the Epistle to the Hebrews (ii. 5, 6) as an evidence of Henok's faith. Walking with God implies community with him in thought, word, and deed, and is opposed in Scripture to walking contrary to him. We are not at liberty to infer that Henok was the only one in this line who feared God. But we are sure that he presented an eminent example of that faith which purifies the heart and pleases God.

He made a striking advance upon the attainment of the times of his ancestor Sheth. In those days they began to call upon the name of the Lord. Now the fellowship of the saints with God reaches its highest form,—that of walking with him, doing his will and enjoying his presence in all the business of life. Hence this remarkable servant of God is accounted a prophet, and foretells the coming of the Lord to judgment (Jude 14, 15). It is further to be observed that this most eminent saint of God did not withdraw from the domestic circle, or the ordinary duties of social life. It is related of him as of the others, that during the three hundred years of his walking with God he begat sons and daughters.

Secondly, The second peculiarity of Henok was his translation. This is related in the simple language of the times. *And he was not, for God took him*; or, in the version of the Septuagint, "and he was not found, for God translated him." Hence in the New Testament it is said, Heb. xi. 5, "By faith Enoch was translated, that he should not see death." This passage is important for the interpretation of the phrase וְאֵינֶנּוּ *καὶ οὐχ εὑρίσκετο, and he was not* (*found*). It means, we perceive, not absolutely, he was not, but relatively, he was not extant in the sphere of sense. If this phrase do not denote annihilation, much less does the phrase "and he died." The one denotes absence from the world of sense, and the other indicates the ordinary way in which the soul departs from this world. Here, then, we have another hint that points plainly to the immortality of the soul (see on Gen. iii. 22).

This glimpse into primeval life furnishes a new lesson to the men of early times and of all succeeding generations. An atonement was shadowed forth in the offering of Habel. A voice was given to the devout feelings of the heart in the times of Sheth. And now a walk becoming one reconciled to God, calling upon his name, and animated by the spirit of adoption, is exhibited. Faith has now returned to God, confessed his name, and learned to walk with him. At this point God appears and gives to the antediluvian race a new and conclusive token of the riches and power of mercy in counteracting the effects of sin in the case of the returning penitent. Henok does not die, but lives; and not only lives, but is advanced to a new stage of life, in which all the power and pain of sin are at an end forever. This crowns and signalizes the power of grace, and represents in brief the grand finale of a life of faith. This renewed man is received up into glory without going through the intermediate steps of death and resurrection. If we omit the violent end of Habel, the only death on record that precedes the translation of Henok is that of Adam. It would have been incon gruous that he who brought sin and death into the world should not have died. But a little more than half a century after his death, Henok is wafted to heaven without leaving the body. This translation took place in the presence of a sufficient number of witnesses, and furnished a manifest proof of the presence and reality of the invisible powers. Thus were life and immortality as fully brought to light as was necessary or possible at that early stage of the world's history. Thus was it demonstrated that the grace of God was triumphant in accomplishing the final and full salvation of all who returned to God. The process might be slow and gradual, but the end was now shown to be sure and satisfactory.

25–27. Methushelah is the oldest man on record. He lived to be within thirty-one years of a thousand, and died in the year of the flood.

28–31. In the biography of Lamek the name of his son is not only given, but the reason of it is assigned. The parents were cumbered with the toil of cultivating the ground. They looked forward with hope to the aid or relief which their son would give them in bearing the burden of life, and they express this hope in his name. In stating the reason of the name, they employ a word which is connected with it only by a second remove. נוּחַ and נָחַם are stems not immediately connected; but they both point back to a common root נח signifying to sigh, breathe, rest, lie down.

This is only another recorded instance of the habit of giving names indicative of the thoughts of the parents at the time of the child's birth. All names were originally significant, and have still to this day an import. Some were given at birth, others at later periods, from some remarkable circumstance in the individual's life. Hence many characters of ancient times were distinguished by several names conferred at different times and for different reasons. The reason of the present name is put on record simply on account of the extraordinary destiny which awaited the bearer of it.

Which the Lord hath cursed. Here is another incidental allusion to the second document, without which it would not be intelligible. If the present document had been intended to stand alone, this remark would have had its explanation in some previous part of the narrative.

32. *And Noah was the son of five hundred years.* A man is the son of a certain year, in and up to the close of that year, but not beyond it. Thus Noah was in his six hundredth year when he was the son of six hundred years (Gen. vii. 11, 6), and a child was circumcised on

the eighth day, being then the son of eight days (Lev. xii. 3; Gen. xvii. 12).

When the phrase indicates a point of time, as in Lev. xxvii., it is the terminating point of the period in question. The first part only of the biography of Noah is given in this verse, and the remainder will be furnished in due time and place. Meanwhile Noah is connected with the general history of the race, which is now to be taken up. His three sons are mentioned, because they are the ancestors of the postdiluvian race. This verse, therefore, prepares for a continuation of the narrative, and therefore implies a continuator or compiler who lived after the flood.

From the numbers in this chapter it appears that the length of human life in the period before the deluge was ten times its present average. This has seemed incredible to some, and hence they have imagined that the years must have consisted of one month, or at least of a smaller number than twelve. But the text will not admit of such amendment or interpretation. In the account of the deluge the tenth month is mentioned, and sixty-one days are afterwards indicated before the beginning of the next year, whence we infer that the primeval year consisted of twelve lunar months at least. But the seemingly incredible in this statement concerning the longevity of the men before the flood, will be turned into the credible if we reflect that man was made to be immortal. His constitution was fitted for a perpetuity of life, if only supplied with the proper nutriment. This nutriment was provided in the tree of life. But man abused his liberty, and forfeited the source of perpetual life. Nevertheless, the primeval vigor of an unimpaired constitution held out for a comparatively long period. After the deluge, however, through the deterioration of the climate and the soil, and perhaps much more the degeneracy of man's moral and physical being, arising from the abuse of his natural propensities, the average length of human life gradually dwindled down to its present limits. Human physiology, founded upon the present data of man's constitution, may pronounce upon the duration of his life so long as the data are the same; but it cannot fairly affirm that the data were never different from what they are at present. Meanwhile, the Bible narrative is in perfect keeping with its own data, and is therefore not to be disturbed by those who still accept these without challenge.

The following table presents the age of each member of this genealogy, when his son and successor was born, and when he himself died, as they stand in the Hebrew text, the Samaritan Pentateuch, the Septuagint, and Josephus:

	HEBREW.		SAM. PENT.		SEPTUAGINT.		JOSEPHUS.		DATE.	
	Son's Birth.	Own Death.	Son's Birth.	Own Death.	Son's Birth.	Own Death.	Son's Birth.	Own Death.	Of Birth.	Of Death.
1. Adam . . .	130	930	130	930	230	930	230	930	0	930
2. Sheth . . .	105	912	105	912	205	912	205	912	130	1042
3. Enosh	90	905	90	905	190	905	190	905	235	1140
4. Kenan . . .	70	910	70	910	170	910	170	910	325	1235
5. Mahalalel.	65	895	65	895	165	895	165	895	395	1290
6. Jared . . .	162	962	62	847	162	962	162	962	460	1422
7. Henok . .	65	365	65	365	165	365	165	365	622	987
8. Methuselah	187	969	67	720	187	969	187	969	687	1656
9. Lamek . .	182	777	53	653	188	753	182	777	874	1651
10. Noah . . .	500	950	500	950	500	950	500	950	1056	2006
	100		100		100		100			
Deluge . .	1656		1307		2262		2256			

On comparing the series of numbers in the Hebrew with those in the Samaritan, the Septuagint, and Josephus, it is remarkable that we have the main body of the original figures in all. In the total ages of the first five and the seventh, and in that of Noah at the flood, they all agree. In those of the sixth and eighth, the Hebrew, Septuagint, and Josephus agree. In that of the ninth, the Hebrew and Josephus agree, while the Samaritan and Septuagint differ from them and from each other. On examining the figures of the Samaritan, it appears that the sixth, eighth, and ninth total ages would have reached beyond the flood, if the numbers found in the other authorities had been retained. And they are so shortened as to terminate all in the year of the flood. This alteration betrays design. The totals in the Hebrew, then, have by far the preponderating authority.

Of the numbers before the birth of a successor, which are chiefly important for the chronology, the units agree in all but Lamek, in regard to whom the Hebrew and Josephus agree, while the Samaritan and the Septuagint differ from them and from each other. The tens agree in all but two, Methushelah and Lamek, where the Hebrew, the Septuagint, at least in the Codex Alex., and Josephus agree, while the Samaritan differs from them all. In the hundreds a systematic and designed variation occurs. Still they agree in Noah. In Jared, Methushelah, and Lamek, the Hebrew, Septuagint, and Josephus agree in a number greater by a hundred than the Samaritan. In the remaining six the Hebrew and Samaritan agree; while the Septuagint and Josephus agree in having a number greater by a hundred. On the whole, then, it is evident that the balance of probability is decidedly in favor of the Hebrew. To this advantage of concurring testimonies are to be added those of being the original, and of having been guarded with great care. These grounds of textual superiority may be supported by several considerations of less weight. The Samaritan and the Septuagint follow a uniform plan; the Hebrew does not, and therefore has the mark of originality. Josephus gives the sum total to the deluge as two thousand six hundred and fifty-six years, agreeing with the total of the Hebrew in three figures, with that of the Septuagint only in two, and with that of the Samaritan in none. Some MSS. even give one thousand six hundred and fifty-six, which is the exact sum of the Hebrew numbers. Both these readings, moreover, differ from the sum of his own numbers, which itself agrees with the Hebrew in two figures and with the Septuagint in the other two. This looks like a studied conformation of the figures to those of the Septuagint, in which the operator forgot to alter the sum total. We do not at present enter into the external arguments for or against the Hebrew text. Suffice it to observe, that the internal evidence is at present clearly in its favor, so far as the antediluvian figures go.

XXII. THE GROWTH OF SIN. — Gen. vi. 1-8.

3. דּוֹן *be down, strive, subdue, judge.* בְּשַׁגָּם *inasmuch, as also.* The rendering *in their error* requires the pointing בְּשַׁגָּם, and the plural form of the following pronoun. It is also unknown to the Septuagint.

4. נְפִּלִים *assailants, fellers, men of violence, tyrants.*

VI. 1. And it came to pass, when man began to multiply on the face of the soil, that daughters were born to them. 2. And the sons of God saw the daughters of man that they were goodly, and they took to them wives of all whom they chose.

3. And the LORD said, My Spirit shall not strive with man forever, inasmuch as he is also flesh; and his days shall be a hundred and twenty years. 4. The giants were in the earth in those days; and also after that, when the sons of God went in unto the daughters of man and they bare to them, these were the heroes, who were of old men of renown. ¶ 10.

5. And the LORD saw that the evil of man was great in the earth, and every imagination of the thoughts of his heart was only evil every day. 6. And it repented the LORD that he had made man on the earth, and he was grieved at his heart. 7. And the LORD said, I will wipe away man whom I have created from off the face of the soil; from man to cattle to creeper and to the fowl of the sky; for it repenteth me that I have made them. 8. And Noah found grace in the eyes of the LORD. 2 ¶¶ 11.

Having traced the line of descent from Adam through Sheth, the seed of God, to Noah, the author proceeds to describe the general spread and growth of moral evil in the race of man, and the determination of the Lord to wipe it away from the face of the earth.

1–4. There are two stages of evil set forth in this passage, — the one contained in the present four verses, and the other in the following. The former refers to the apostasy of the descendants of Sheth, and the cause and consequences of it. When man began to multiply, the separate families of Cain and Sheth would come into contact. The daughters of the stirring Cainites, distinguished by the graces of nature, the embellishments of art, and the charms of music and song, even though destitute of the loftier qualities of likemindedness with God, would attract attention and prompt to unholy alliances. The phrase *sons of God*, means an order of intelligent beings who *retain the purity of moral character* originally communicated, or subsequently restored, by their Creator. They are called the sons of God, because they have his spirit or disposition. The sons of God mentioned in Job xxxviii. 7, are an order of rational beings existing before the creation of man, and joining in the symphony of the universe, when the earth and all things were called into being. Then all were holy, for all are styled the sons of God. Such, however, are not meant in the present passage. For they were not created as a race, have no distinction of sex, and therefore no sexual desire; they "neither marry nor are given in marriage" (Mat. xxii. 30). It is contrary to the law of nature for different species even on earth to cohabit in a carnal way; much more for those in the body, and those who have not a body of flesh. Moreover, we are here in the region of humanity, and not in the sphere of superhuman spirits; and the historian has not given the slightest intimation of the existence of spiritual beings different from man.

The sons of God, therefore, are those who are on the Lord's side, who approach him with duly significant offerings, who call upon him by his proper name, and who walk with God in their daily conversation. The figurative use of the word *son* to denote a variety of relations incidental, and moral as well as natural, was not unfamiliar to the early speaker. Thus Noah is called *the son of five hundred years* (Gen. v. 32). Abraham calls Eliezer בֶּן־בֵּיתִי *son of my house* (Gen. xv. 3). The dying Rachel names her son Ben-oni, *son of my sorrow*, while his father called him Benjamin, *son of thy right hand* (Gen. xxxv. 18). An obvious parallel to the moral application is presented in the phrases *the seed of the woman* and *the seed of the serpent*. The word *generations* (תּוֹלְדוֹת v. 1) exhibits a similar freedom and elasticity of meaning, being applied to the whole doings of a rational being, and even to the physical changes of the material world (Gen. ii. 4). The occasion for the present designation is furnished in the remark of Eve on the birth of Sheth. God hath given me another seed instead of Habel. Her son Sheth she therefore regarded as the son of God. Accordingly, about the birth of his son Enosh, was begun the custom of calling upon the name of the Lord, no doubt in the family-circle of Adam, with whom Sheth continued to dwell. And Enok, the seventh from Adam in the same line, exhibited the first striking example of a true believer walking with God in all the intercourse of life. These descendants of Sheth, among whom were also Lamek who spoke of the Lord, and Noah who walked with God, are therefore by a natural transition called the sons of God, the godlike in a moral sense, being born of the Spirit, and walking not after the flesh, but after the Spirit (Ps. lxxxii. 6; Hos. ii. 1).

Some take *the daughters of man* to be the daughters of the Cainites only. But it is sufficient to understand by this phrase, the daughters of man in general, without any distinction of a moral or spiritual kind, and therefore including both Cainite and Shethite females. *And they took them wives of all whom they chose.* The evil here described is that of promiscuous intermarriage, without regard to spiritual character.

The godly took them wives of all; that is, of the ungodly as well as the godly families, without any discrimination. "Whom they chose," not for the godliness of their lives, but for the goodliness of their looks. Ungodly mothers will not train up children in the way they should go; and husbands who have taken the wrong step of marrying ungodly wives cannot prove to be very exemplary or authoritative fathers. Up to this time they may have been consistent as the sons of God in their outward conduct. But a laxity of choice proves a corresponding laxity of principle. The first inlet of sin prepares the way for the flood-gates of iniquity. It is easy to see that now the degeneracy of the whole race will go on at a rapid pace.

3. *My Spirit*, in contradistinction to the spirit of disobedience which, by the fall, obtained entrance into the soul of man. *Shall not strive with man forever.* To strive (דון) is to keep down, rule, judge, or strive with a man by moral force. From this passage we learn that the Lord by his Spirit strives with man up to a certain point. In this little negative sentence streams out the bright light of God's free and tender mercy to the apostate race of man. He sends his Spirit to irradiate the darkened mind, to expostulate with the conscience, to prompt and strengthen holy resolve, and to bring back the heart, the confidence, the affection to God. He effects the blessed result of repentance towards God in some, who are thus proved to be born of God. But it is a solemn thought that with others he will not strive perpetually. There is a certain point beyond which he will not go, for sufficient reasons known fully to himself, partly to us. Two of these we are to notice for our instruction: *First*, he will not touch the free agency of his rational creatures. He can put no *force* on the volitions of men. An involuntary or compulsory faith, hope, love, obedience, is a contradiction in terms; and anything that could bear the name can have no moral validity whatsoever. *Secondly*, after giving ample warning, instruction, and invitation, he will, as a just judgment on the unbelieving and the impenitent, withdraw his Spirit and let them alone. The antediluvian world was fast approaching to this point of final perversity and abandonment.

Inasmuch as he is also flesh, in contradistinction to spirit, the breath of life which the Almighty breathed into his nostrils. These two parts of man's complex being were originally in true and happy adjustment, the corporeal being the fit organ and complement of the spiritual as it is in him. But now by the fall the flesh has gained the upper hand, and the spirit is in the bondage of corruption. The fact that he is flesh also as well as spirit, has therefore come out into sad prominence. The doctrine of the carnal mind in the Epistle to the Romans (viii.) is merely the outgrowth of the thought expressed in this passage.

His days shall be an hundred and twenty years. "His days" are the days of *man*, not the individual, but the race, with whom the Lord still strives. Hence they refer to the duration, not of the life of an individual, but of the existence of the race. From this we learn that the narrative here reverts to a point of time before the birth of Shem, Ham, and Japheth, recorded in the close of the preceding passage, as there were only a hundred years from their birth to the deluge. This is according to the now well-known method of Scripture, when it has two lines of events to carry on. The former narrative refers to the godly portion of mankind; this to the ungodly remnant.

Not forever will the Lord strive with man; but his longsuffering will still continue for one hundred and twenty years. Meanwhile he does not leave himself or his clemency without a witness. He sent Noah with the message of warning, who preached by his voice, by his walking with God, and also by his long labor and perseverance in the building of the ark. The doomed race, however, filled up the measure of their iniquity, and when the set number of years was accomplished, the overwhelming flood came.

4. Two classes of men, with strong hand and strong will, are here described. *The giants*, the well-known men of great stature, physical force, and violent will, who were enabled by these qualities to claim and secure the supremacy over their fellow-men. *Had been in the land in those days.* In the days when those intermarriages were beginning to take place, the warriors were asserting the claim of might. Violence and rapine were becoming rampant in the land. *And after that.* The progeny of the mixed marriages were the second and subsequent class of leading men. *The sons of God* are here contradistinguished from the *nephilim*, or giants, who appear therefore to have belonged to the Cainites. The offspring of these unhallowed unions were the heroes, the gallants, the mighty men, the men of renown. They were probably more refined in manners and exalted in thought than their predecessors of pure Cainite descent. "Men of name," whose names are often in men's mouths, because they either deserved or required to be named frequently on account of their influential or representative character. Being distinguished from the common herd by prominent qualities or memorable exploits, thev were also frequently

marked out by a special name or surname, derived from such trait of character or deed of notoriety. "Of old" (מֵעוֹלָם). This has been sometimes explained *of the world*, in the sense of αἰὼν; but the meaning is too late for the present passage. The phrase uniformly means *of old*, covering a more or less extensive length of time. This note of time implies a writer probably after the deluge, who could speak of antediluvian affairs, as happening of old.

It is remarkable that we have no hint of any kind of government in the antediluvian world. It is open to us to suppose that the patriarchal polity would make its appearance, as it is an order based upon natural relations. But it is possible that God himself, being still present and manifest, was recognized as the governor. To him offerings were brought, and he deals with Cain on his first and second transgression. In that case the lawless violence of the strong and wilful is to be regarded as rebellion, not only against the patriarchal rule, but the divine supremacy. A notice of civil law and government would not of course affect the authority of the book. But the absence of such notice is in favor of its divine origin. It is obvious that higher things than these have the attention of the sacred writer.

5–8. In these verses we are to conceive the hundred and twenty years of respite to be at an end. The iniquity of the race is now full, and the determination of the Lord is therefore announced, with a statement of the grounds on which it rests, and a glance at the individual to be excepted from the general destruction.

5. *And God saw.* The course of the primeval world was a great experiment going on before the eye of God, and of all intelligent observers, and manifesting the thorough depravity and full-grown degeneracy of the fallen race, when left to the bent of its perverted inclinations. *Every imagination* (יֵצֶר). Here the object of thought is distinguished from the thought itself. This is a distinction not generally or constantly recognized by the mental philosopher, though of essential importance in the theory of the mind. The thought itself is a real phase or attitude of mind; the form, idea, species, object of thought may have matter, real content, or it may not. *Only evil every day.* This is an unlimited condemnation of the state and process of the carnal man. The reason is obvious. Homage to God, to truth, to right, to love, does not reign in his heart; and the imaginations or purposes that are not regulated by this, however excellent and praiseworthy in other respects, are destitute of the first, the essential principle of moral good. This is now made palpable to the eye of

observation by the almost universal predominance of the ungodly spirit. This accordingly forms the ground of the divine procedure.

6. *And it repented the Lord* that he had made man. The Scripture is frank and unreserved; some men would say, imprudent or regardless of misconstruction, in its statements of truth. Repentance ascribed to the Lord seems to imply wavering or change of purpose in the Eternal Self-existent. But the sublime dictate of the inspired word is, "God is not a man, that he should lie; neither the son of man, that he should repent: hath he said and shall he not do it? or hath he spoken and shall he not make it good?" (Num. xxiii. 19.) In sooth, every act here recorded — the observation, the resolve, the exception — seems equally with the repentance to jar with the unchangeableness of God. To go to the root of the matter, every act of the divine will, of creative power, or of interference with the order of nature, seems at variance with inflexibility of purpose. But, in the first place, man has a finite mind and a limited sphere of observation, and therefore is not able to conceive or express thoughts or acts exactly as they are in God, but only as they are in himself. Secondly, God is a spirit, and therefore has the attributes of personality, freedom, and holiness; and the passage before us is designed to set forth these in all the reality of their action, and thereby to distinguish the freedom of the eternal mind from the fatalism of inert matter. Hence, thirdly, these statements represent real processes of the Divine Spirit, analogous at least to those of the human. And, lastly, to verify this representation, it is not necessary that we should be able to comprehend or construe to ourselves in all its practical detail that sublime harmony which subsists between the liberty and the immutability of God. That change of state which is essential to will, liberty, and activity, may be, for aught we know, and from what we know must be, in profound unison with the eternity of the divine purpose.

7. *I will wipe away man from the face of the soil.* The resolve is made to sweep away the existing race of man. Heretofore, individuals had departed this life. Adam himself had long since paid the debt of nature. These solemn testimonies to the universal doom had not made any salutary or lasting impression on the survivors. But now a general and violent destruction is to overtake the whole race, — a standing monument of the divine wrath against sin, to all future generations of the only family saved.

From man to cattle, creeper and fowl of the sky. These classes of animated nature being mingled up with man are involved in the same ruin with him. This is of a piece with the curse laid upon the serpent, which was the unconscious organ of the tempter. It is an instance of a law which runs through the whole course of nature, as we observe that it is the method of the divine government to allow for the time the suffering inflicted on an inferior animal, or even on a fellow-creature, by selfish passion. It has an appearance to some minds of harshness and unfairness. But we must remembeı that these animated creatures are not moral, and, therefore, the violent termination of their organic life is not a punishment; that the pain incidental to this, being apart from guilt, is in itself a beneficial provision for the conservation of life; and that it was not intended that the life of animals should be perpetual. The return of the land to a state of desolation by the destruction of animal and vegetable life, however, has its lesson for man, for whom ultimately all of this beauty and fertility were designed, and from whom it is now withdrawn, along with all the glories it foreshadows, as part of the punishment of his guilt. The tenant has become unworthy of the tabernacle, and accordingly he is dispossessed, and it is taken down and removed.

8. *And Noah found grace in the eyes of the Lord.* Noah and his family are the only exceptions to this sweeping destruction. Hitherto we have met with distant and indirect intimations of the divine favor, and significant deeds of regard and acceptance. Now for the first time *grace* itself finds a tongue to express its name. Grace has its fountain in the divine breast. The stream has been flowing forth to Adam, Eve, Habel, Henok, and others, we hope, unknown to fame. By the time it reaches Noah it has found a name, by which it is recognized among men to this day. It is opposed to works as a source of blessing. Whither grace comes there merit cannot be. Hence we learn even from the case of Noah that original sin asserts its presence in the whole race of Adam. This completes the circle of saving doctrine in regard to God that comes down from the antediluvian times. He intimates that the seed of the woman, an individual preëminently so called, will bruise the serpent's head. He clothes our first parents with coats of skin — an earnest and an emblem of the better, the moral clothing of the soul. He regards Habel and his offering. He *accepts* him that in faith does well. He translates Enok, who walked with him. His Spirit, we learn, has been striving with antediluvian man. Here are the Spirit of God and the seed of the woman. Here are clothing, regarding, accepting, translating. Here, then, is salvation provided and applied, begun, continued, and completed. And last,

though not least, grace comes out to view, the eternal fountain of the whole. On the part of man, also, we have repenting, believing, confessing, offering, calling on the name of the Lord, and walking with God.

The two parts of the document which is now closed are as distinct from each other as it is from the following one. They combine, in fact, to form the needful preliminary to the fourth document. The genealogy brings us to the leading agent in the succeeding narrative; the description of the corruption of the human race furnishes the occasion for his agency. The third is therefore the prologue, as the fifth is the epilogue, to the fourth document, in which the main action lies.

SECTION VI — THE DELUGE

XXIII. THE ARK. — Gen. vi. 9–22.

9. הוֹר *age*, time from birth to death, applied either to an individual or the whole contemporary race, running parallel with some leading individual. Hence the *race* or *generation* living during that time.

14. תֵּבָה *chest, ark.* It is used only of this vessel of Noah's construction, and of the little vessel in which Moses was put (Ex. ii. 3, 5). The root, according to Fürst, means *to be hollow.* אֵבֶה a cognate word, signifies *a reed*; κιβωτὸς, LXX. גֹּפֶר α. λ., perhaps *fir, cypress,* resinous wood. קֵן *nest, room;* r. *prepare, rear up.*

16. צֹהַר *shining, light;* not the same as the חַלּוֹן (Gen. viii. 6), or the aperture through which Noah let out the raven.

18. בְּרִית *covenant;* r. *cut, eat, choose, decide.*

9. These are the generations of Noah. Noah was a just man; perfect had he been in his ages; with the God walked Noah. 10. And Noah begat three sons, — Shem, Ham, and Japeth. 11. And the land was corrupt before God, and the land was filled with violence. 12. And God saw the land, and, behold, it was corrupt; for all flesh had corrupted its way upon the land. § 15.

13. And God said unto Noah, The end of all flesh is come before me; for the land is filled with violence through them; and, behold, I will destroy them with the land. 14. Make thee an ark of gopher wood: rooms shalt thou make in the ark, and shalt pitch it within and without with pitch. 15. And this is the way that thou shalt make it: three hundred cubits the length of the ark, fifty cubits the breadth of it, and thirty cubits the height of it. 16. Lighting shalt thou make for the

ark, and to a cubit shalt thou finish it above; and the door of the ark shalt thou set in the side thereof: with lower, second, and third stories shalt thou make it. 17. And I, behold, I do bring the flood of water upon the land, to destroy all flesh, wherein is the breath of life, from under the skies: all that is in the land shall expire. 18. And I will establish my covenant with thee; and thou shalt go into the ark, thou and thy sons, and thy wife, and thy sons' wives with thee. 19. And of all the living of all flesh two of each shalt thou bring into the ark to keep alive with thee: male and female shall they be. 20. Of the fowl after its kind, and of the cattle after its kind, of every creeper of the soil after its kind; two of each shall come unto thee to keep alive. 21. And thou take unto thee of all food that may be eaten, and gather it for thee: and it shall be to thee and to them for food. 22. And Noah did so: according to all that God commanded him, so he did.

The close of the preceding document introduces the opening topic of this one. The same rule applies to all that have gone before. The generations of the skies and the land (Gen. ii. 4) are introduced by the finishing of the skies and the land (ii. 1); the generations of man in the line of Sheth (v. 1), by the birth of Sheth (iv. 25); and now the generations of Noah, by the notice that Noah found grace in the eyes of the Lord. The narrative here also, as usual, reverts to a point of time before the stage of affairs described in the close of the preceding passage. Yet there is nothing here that seems to indicate a new author. The previous paragraph is historical, and closely connected with the end of the fourth chapter; and it suitably prepares for the proceedings of Noah, under the divine direction, on the eve of the deluge. We have now a recapitulation of the agent and the occasion, and then the divine commission and its execution.

9–12. Here are the man and the occasion. 9, 10. *The generations of Noah.* In the third document we had the generations of man; now we are limited to Noah, because he is himself at peace with God, and is now the head and representative of those who are in the same blessed relation. The narrative, therefore, for the first time, formally confines itself to the portion of the human family in communion with God.

Noah is here characterized by two new and important epithets, —*just* and *perfect*. It is to be remembered that he had already found grace in the eyes of the Lord. Adam was created good; but by disobedience he became guilty, and all his race, Noah among the rest, became involved in that guilt. To be just is to be right in point of law, and thereby entitled to all the blessings of the acquitted and justified. When applied to the guilty, this epithet implies pardon of sin among other benefits of grace. It also presupposes that spiritual change by which the soul returns from estrangement to reconciliation with God. Hence Noah is not only just, but perfect. This attribute of character imports not only the turning from darkness to light, from error to truth, from wrong to right, but the stability of moral determination which arises from the struggle, the trial, the victory of good over evil, therein involved. The just is the right in law; the perfect is the tested in holiness. *In his ages;* among the men of his age. This phrase indicates the contrast between Noah and the men of his day. It is probable, moreover, that he was of pure descent, and in that respect also distinguished from his contemporaries who were the offspring of promiscuous intermarriage between the godly and the ungodly. *Noah walked with God*, like Henok. This is the native consequence of his victory over sin, and his acceptance with God. His sons are mentioned, as they are essentially connected with the following events.

11, 12. *And the land was corrupt.* In contrast with Noah, the rest of the race were corrupt, — entirely depraved by sin. It was *filled with violence*, — with the outward exhibition of inward carnality. *And God saw this.* It was patent to the eye of Heaven. This is the ground of the following commission.

13–21. The directions concerning the ark embrace the purpose to destroy the race of man (13), the plan and specification of the ark (14–16), the announcement of the deluge (17), the arrangements for the preservation of Noah and his family, and certain kinds of animals (18–21).

13. *The end of all flesh.* The end may mean either the point to which it tends, or the extermination of the race. The latter is the simpler. *All* flesh is to be understood of the *whole* race, while yet it does not preclude the exception of Noah and his family. This teaches us to beware of applying an inflexible literality to such terms as *all*, when used in the sense of ordinary conversation. *Is come before me*, is in the contemplation of my mind as an event soon to be realized. *For the land is filled with violence.* The reason. *I will destroy them.*

The resolve. There is retribution here, for the words *corrupt* and *destroy* are the same in the original.

14–16. The ark. Reckoning the cubit at 1.8 feet, we find the length to be about 540, the breadth 90, and the height 54 feet. The construction of such a vessel implies great skill in carpentry. The lighting apparatus is not described so particularly that we can form any conception of it. It was probably in the roof. The roof may have been flat. *And to a cubit shalt thou finish it above.* The cubit is possibly the height of the parapet round the lighting and ventilating aperture. The opening occupied, it may be, a considerable portion of the roof, and was covered during the rain with an awning (מִכְסֶה Gen. viii. 13). If, however, it was in the sides of the ark, the cubit was merely its height. It was then finished with a strong railing, which went round the whole ark, and over which the covering, above mentioned, hung down on every side. The door was in the side, and the stories were three. In each were of course many "nests" or chambers, for animals and stores. It may be curious to a mechanical mind to frame the details of this structure from the general hints here given; but it could not serve any practical end. Only the animals necessary to man, or peculiar to the region covered by the deluge, required to be included in the ark. It seems likely that wild animals in general were not included. It is obvious, therefore, that we cannot calculate the number of animals preserved in the ark, or compare the space they would require with its recorded dimensions. We may rest assured that there was accommodation for all that needed to be there.

17. The method of destruction is now specified. A water flood shall cover the land, in which all flesh shall perish. *I, behold, I.* This catastrophe is due to the interposition of the Creator. It does not come according to the ordinary laws of physics, but according to the higher law of ethics.

18–21. The covenant with Noah. Here is the first appearance of a covenant between God and man on the face of Scripture. A covenant is a solemn compact, tacit or express, between two parties, in which each is bound to perform his part. Hence a covenant implies the moral faculty; and wherever the moral faculty exists, there must needs be a covenant. Consequently, between God and man there was of necessity a covenant from the very beginning, though the name do not appear. At first it was a covenant of works, in regard to man; but now that works have failed, it can only be a covenant of grace to the penitent sinner. *My covenant.* The word *my* points to its original establishment with Adam. My primeval covenant, which I am resolved not to abandon. *Will I establish.* Though Adam has failed, yet will I find means of maintaining my covenant of life with the seed of the woman. *With thee.* Though all flesh be to perish through breach of my covenant, yet will I uphold it with thee. *Go into the ark.* This is the means of safety. Some may say in their hearts, this is a clumsy way to save Noah. But if he is to be saved, there must be *some* way. And it is not a sign of wisdom to prescribe the way to the All-wise. Rather let us reflect that the erection of this ark was a daily warning to a wicked race, a deepening lesson of reliance on God to Noah and his household, and a most salutary occupation for the progenitors of the future race of mankind. *And thy sons*, etc. Noah's household share in the covenant.

19, 20. *And of all the living.* For the sake of Noah, the animal species also shall be preserved, *two of each, male and female.* They are to come in pairs for propagation. 20. The fowl, the cattle, the creeping thing or smaller animals, are to come. From this it appears that the wild animals are not included among the inmates of the ark. (See Gen. vii. 2, 3, 8.) The word *all* is not to be pressed beyond the specification of the writer. As the deluge was universal only in respect to the human race, it was not necessary to include any animals but those that were near man, and within the range of the overwhelming waters. 21. Fodder and other provisions for a year have to be laid in.

22. The obedience of Noah and the accomplishment of his task are here recorded. The building of so enormous a fabric must have occupied many years.

XXIV. THE ARK ENTERED. — Gen. vii. 1-9.

2. טָהוֹר *clean*, fit for food or sacrifice.

4. יְקוּם *standing thing;* that which grows up, whether animal or plant. Comp. קָמָה *stalk*, or *standing corn.*

VII. 1. And the Lord said unto Noah, go thou and all thy house into the ark: for thee have I seen righteous before me in this age. 2. Of all clean cattle thou shalt take to thee seven each, he and his mate; and of cattle that are not clean two, he and his mate. 3. Also of the fowl of the skies seven each, male and female: to keep alive seed upon the face of all the land. 4. For in yet seven days will I cause it to rain upon the land forty days and forty nights: and I will wipe out every standing thing that I have made from the face of the soil.

5. And Noah did according to all that the LORD commanded him. 6. And Noah was the son of six hundred years, when the flood of waters came upon the land. 7. And Noah went in, and his sons, and his wife, and his sons' wives with him, into the ark, from before the waters of the flood. 8. Of the clean cattle and of the cattle that are not clean, and of the fowl and all that creepeth upon the soil, 9. Two each went they unto Noah into the ark, male and female; as God commanded Noah.

1–4. The command to enter the ark. The general direction in the preceding chapter was given many years ago, before the ark was commenced. Now, when it is completed, a more specific command is issued. *For thee have I seen righteous before me.* Noah has accepted the mercy of God, is therefore set right in point of law, and walks aright in point of practice. The Lord recognizes this indication of an adopted and renewed son. *In this age* he and his were the solitary family so characterized.

2, 3. *Of all clean cattle.* Here the distinction of clean and unclean animals meets us without any previous notice. How it became known to Noah we are not informed. From the former direction it appears that the animals were to enter by pairs. Now it is further arranged that there are to be seven pairs of the clean cattle and fowl, and only one pair of the unclean.

4. Seven days after the issue of the command the rain is to commence, and continue for forty days and nights without ceasing. *Every standing thing* means every plant and animal on the land.

5–9. The execution of the command is recorded and fully particularized with the additional circumstance of the age of Noah. 6. *The son of six hundred years,* in his six hundredth year. 9. *Went they unto Noah.* They seem to have come under the influence of a special instinct, so that Noah did not require to gather them. Seven days were employed in receiving them, and storing provisions for them.

XXV. THE FLOOD.—Gen. vii. 10-24.

10. And it came to pass in seven days that the waters of the flood were upon the land. 11. In the six hundredth year of Noah's life, in the second month, in the seventeenth day of the month, in this day were broken up all the fountains of the great deep, and the windows of the skies were opened. 12. And the shower was upon the land forty days and forty nights. 13. In the self-same day were gone Noah and Shem and Ham and Japheth, the sons of Noah, and Noah's wife, and the three wives of his sons with them, into the ark. 14. They and every living thing after its kind, and all cattle after their kind, and every creeper that creepeth on the land after its kind, and every fowl after its kind, every bird of every wing. 15. And they went in unto Noah into the ark, two each of all flesh wherein was the breath of life. 16. And they that went in, male and female of all flesh went they in, as God had com manded him: and the Lord shut him in.

17. And the flood was forty days upon the land; and the waters increased and bare up the ark, and it rose from upon the land. 18. And the waters prevailed and increased greatly upon the land; and the ark went upon the face of the waters. 19. And the waters had prevailed exceedingly on the land; and all the high hills that were under the whole skies were covered. 20. Fifteen cubits upward had the waters prevailed, and the hills were covered. 21. Then expired all flesh that creepeth upon the land, in the fowl and in the cattle, and in the living thing, and in every crawler that crawleth upon the land, and every man. 22. All in whose nostrils was the breath of the spirit of life, of all that was in the dry *land* died. 23.

Then was wiped away every standing thing which was upon the face of the soil, from man to cattle, to creeper and to fowl of the skies, and they were wiped away from the land; and there remained only Noah and they that were with him in the ark. 24. And the waters prevailed upon the land fifty and a hundred days.

10–16. The date is here given, at which the flood commenced and the entrance into the ark was completed. 10. *In seven days.* On the seventh day from the command. 11. *In the second month.* The primeval year commenced about the autumnal equinox; we may say, on the nearest new moon. The rains began about a month or six weeks after the equinox, and, consequently, not far from the seventeenth of the second month. *All the fountains of the great deep, and the windows of the skies.* It appears that the deluge was produced by a gradual commotion of nature on a grand scale. The gathering clouds were dissolved into incessant showers. But this was not sufficient of itself to effect the overwhelming desolation that followed. The beautiful figure of the windows of the skies being opened is preceded by the equally striking one of the fountains of the great deep being broken up. This was the chief source of the flood. A change in the level of the land was accomplished. That which had emerged from the waters on the third day of the last creation was now again submerged. The waters of the great deep now broke their bounds, flowed in on the sunken surface, and drowned the world of man, with all its inhabitants. 12. The accompanying heavy rain of forty days and nights was, in reality, only a subsidiary instrument in the deluging of the land. We may imagine the sinking of the land to have been so gradual as to occupy the whole of these forty days of rain. There is an awful magnificence in this constant uplifting of the billows over the yielding land.

13–16. There is a simple grandeur in the threefold description of the entrance of Noah and his retinue into the ark, first in the command, next in the actual process during the seven days, and, lastly, in the completed act on the seventh day. *Every living thing after its kind* is here unaccompanied with the epithet רָעָה *evil*, or the qualifying term of the land or of the field, and therefore may, we conceive, be taken in the extent of Gen. vi. 20, vii. 2, 3, 6. At all events the whole of the wild animals did not need to be included in the ark, as their range was greater than that of antediluvian man or of the flood. *And the Lord shut him in.* This is a fitting close to the scene. The whole work was manifestly the Lord's doing, from first to last. The personal name of God is appropriately introduced here. For the Everlasting now shows himself to be the causer or effecter of the covenant blessing promised to Noah. In what way the Lord shut him in is an idle question, altogether unworthy of the grandeur of the occasion. We can tell nothing more than what is written. We are certain that it would be accomplished in a manner worthy of him.

17–24. The prevalence of the waters. The forty days are now completed. And at the end of this period the ark had been afloat for a long time. It was drifted on the waters in the direction in which they were flowing, and towards what was formerly the higher ground.

19. *Upon the land.* The land is to be understood of the portion of the earth's surface known to man. This, with an unknown margin beyond it, was covered with the waters. But this is all that Scripture warrants us to assert. Concerning the distant parts of Europe, the continents of Africa, America, or Australia, we can say nothing. *All the high hills were covered.* Not a hill was above water within the horizon of the spectator or of man. There were ten generations from Adam to Noah inclusive. We cannot tell what the rate of increase was. But, supposing each couple to have ten children, and therefore the common ratio to be five, the whole number of births would be about five millions, and the population in the time of Noah less than four millions. It is probable that they did not scatter further than the necessities and conveniences of life demanded. In a fertile region, an area equal to that of the British Isles would be amply sufficient for four millions of men, women, and children. Let us suppose, then, a circle of five hundred miles in diameter inhabited by man. Let this occupy the central region of a concentric circle of eight hundred miles in diameter. With a centre a little southwest of Mosul, this larger circle would reach fifty miles into the Mediterranean, the Euxine, and the Caspian, and would probably have touched the Persian Gulf at the time of the deluge. If this region were covered with water, it is obvious that no land or mountain would be visible to a spectator within the inner circle of five hundred miles in diameter. 20. *Fifteen cubits upward.* This was half the depth of the ark. It may have taken this draught of water to float it. If so, its grounding on a hill under water would indicate the depth of water on its summit. The gradual rise of the waters was accomplished by the depression of the land, aided,

possibly, by a simultaneous elevation of the bed of the ocean. The water, by the mere necessity of finding its level, overflowed the former dry land. The extent of this oscillation of the solid crust of the earth is paralleled by the changes of level which geology indicates, the last of which took place at the time of the six days' creation. It is possible that most of the land that was then raised was now again temporarily submerged in the returning waters; while distant continents may have all along existed, which never came within the ken of antediluvian man. The sobriety and historical veracity of the narrative are strikingly exhibited in the moderate height to which the waters are said to have risen above the ancient hills.

21–23. *There expired all flesh.* The resulting death of all by drowning is here recounted. *All in whose nostrils was the breath of the spirit of life died.* This statement refers solely to man, whose higher life is exclusively expressed by the phrase נִשְׁמַת חַיִּים *breath of life* (Gen. ii. 7). It affirms the death of the whole of mankind. 23. The sum-total of animal and vegetable life, with the exception of those in the ark, is here declared to be extinguished.

24. *Fifty and a hundred days.* These, and the forty days of rain, make one hundred and ninety days: about six lunar months and thirteen days. If to this we add the month and seventeen days before the commencement of the rain, we have eight months completed, and are therefore brought to the first day of the ninth month. The waters may be said to prevail as long as the ark had its full draught of water. It is probable they were still rising during the first half of the hundred and fifty days, and then gradually sinking during the other half.

XXVI. THE LAND DRIED. — Gen. viii. 1–14.

1. שׁכך *stoop, assuage.*

3. חָסֵר *want, fail, be abated.*

4. אֲרָרָט *Ararat*, a land forming part of Armenia. It is mentioned in 2 Kings xix. 37, and Isa. xxxvii. 38, as the retreat of Adrammelek and Sharezer after the murder of their father; and in Jer. li. 27 as a kingdom.

8. קלל *be light, lightened, lightly esteemed, swift.*

10. חוּל *twist, turn, dance, writhe, tremble, be strong, wait.* יָחַל *remain, wait, hope.*

13. חָרַב *be drained, desolated, amazed.*

VIII. 1. And God remembered Noah, and every living
thing, and all the cattle that was with him in the ark; and
God made a wind to pass over the land, and the waters as-
suaged. 2. And the fountains of the deep and the windows
of the skies were shut; and the shower from the skies was re-
strained. 3. And the waters returned gradually from upon
the land; and the waters decreased from the end of fifty and
a hundred days.

4. And the ark rested in the seventh month, on the seven-
teenth day of the month, upon the hills of Ararat. 5. And
the waters decreased continually until the tenth month; in
the tenth, on the first of the month, the tops of the hills were
seen.

6. And it was at the end of forty days that Noah opened
the windows of the ark which he had made. 7. And sent out
the raven, and it went forth to and fro, until the waters were
dried up from upon the land. 8. And he sent the dove from
with him, to see if the waters were abated from upon the
face of the soil. 9. And the dove found no rest for the sole
of her foot, and she returned to him into the ark, for there
was water on the face of all the land; and he put forth his
hand and took her, and brought her to him into the ark. 10.
And he stayed yet other seven days, and again sent forth the
dove from the ark. 11. And the dove came in to him in the
evening; and, lo, an olive leaf plucked off, in her mouth; and
Noah knew that the waters were abated from upon the land.
12. And he stayed yet other seven days, and sent forth the
dove, and she returned not again to him.

13. And it was in the one and six hundredth year, on the
first of the first month, that the waters were drained from upon
the land; and Noah removed the covering of the ark, and saw,
and, behold, the face of the soil was drained. 14. And in the
second month, on the seven and twentieth day of the month,
was the land dried.

1–3. The waters commence their retreat. *And God remembered Noah.* He is said to remember him when he takes any step to deliver him from the waters. The several steps to this end are enumerated. *A wind.* This would promote evaporation, and otherwise aid the retreat of the waters. *The fountains of the deep and the windows of the skies were shut.* The incessant and violent showers had continued for six weeks. It is probable the weather remained turbid and moist for some time longer. In the sixth month, however, the rain probably ceased altogether. Some time before this, the depressing of the ground had reached its lowest point, and the upheaving had set in. This is the main cause of the reflux of the waters. All this is described, as we perceive, according to appearance. It is probable that the former configuration of the surface was not exactly restored. At all events it is not necessary, as the ark may have drifted a considerable space in a hundred and fifty days. Some of the old ground on which primeval man had trodden may have become a permanent water bed, and a like amount of new land may have risen to the light in another place. Hence it is vain to seek for a spot retaining the precise conditions of the primitive Eden. The Euphrates and Tigris may substantially remain, but the Pishon and Gihon may have considerably changed. The Black Sea, the Caspian, the lakes Van and Urumiah may cover portions of the Adamic land. At the end of the hundred and fifty days the prevalence of the waters begins to turn into a positive retreat.

4, 5. *The ark rested.* It is stranded on some hill in Ararat. This country forms part of Armenia. As the drying wind most probably came from the east or north, it is likely that the ark was drifted towards Asia Minor, and caught land on some hill in the reaches of the Euphrates. It cannot be supposed that it rested on either of the peaks now called Ararat, as Ararat was a country, not a mountain, and these peaks do not seem suitable for the purpose. The seventh month began usually with the new moon nearest the vernal equinox, or the 21st of March. *The tenth month.* The waters ceased to prevail on the first of the ninth month. The ark, though grounded six weeks before, was still deep in the waters. The tops of the hills began to appear a month after. The subsiding of the waters seems to have been very slow.

6–12. The raven and the dove are sent out to bring tidings of the external world. *Forty days.* Before Noah made any experiment he seems to have allowed the lapse of forty days to undo the remaining effect of the forty days' rain. *The window.* He seems to have been unable to take any definite observations through the aperture here called a window. The raven found carrion in abundance, floated probably on the waters, and did not need to return. This was such a token of the state of things as Noah might expect from such a messenger. He next sends the dove, who returns to him. *Yet other seven days.* This intimates that he stayed seven days also after the raven was sent out. The olive leaf plucked off was a sign of returning safety to the land. It is said by Theophrastus (Hist. Plant. 4, 7) and Pliny (H. N. 13, 50) that the olive strikes leaves even under water. From this event, the olive branch became the symbol of peace, and the dove the emblem of the Comforter, the messenger of peace. After seven other days, the dove being despatched, returns no more. The number seven figures very conspicuously in this narrative. Seven days before the showers commence the command to enter the ark is given ; and at intervals of seven days the winged messengers are sent out. These intervals point evidently to the period of seven days, determined by the six days of creation and the seventh day of rest. The clean beasts also and the birds are admitted into the ark by seven pairs. This points to the sacredness associated with the number arising from the hallowed character of the seventh day. The number forty also, the product of four, the number of the world or universe, and ten the number of completeness, begins here to be employed for a complete period in which a process will have run its course.

13, 14. Noah delays apparently another month, and, on the first day of the new year, ventures to remove the covering of the ark and look around. The date of the complete drying of the land is then given. The interval from the entrance to the exit consists of the following periods:

Rain continued	40	days.
Waters prevailed	150	"
Waters subside	29	"
Noah delays	40	"
Sending of raven and dove	20	"
Another month	29	"
Interval till 27th of second month	57	"
Sum-total of days	365	

Hence it appears that the interval was a lunar year of three hundred and fifty-six days nearly, and ten days; that is, as nearly as possible, a solar year. This passage is important on account of the divisions of time which it brings out at this early epoch. The week of seven days is plainly intimated. The lunar month and year are evidently known. It is remarkable that the ten additional days bring up the lunar year in whole numbers to the solar. It seems a tacit agreement with the real order of nature. According to the Hebrew text, the deluge commenced in the 1656th year of the race of man. According to all texts it occurred in the time of Noah, the ninth in descent from Adam.

XXVII. THE ARK LEFT. — Gen. viii. 15-22.

19. מִשְׁפָּחָה *kind, clan, family.* שִׁפְחָה *maid-servant ;* r. *spread.*
20. מִזְבֵּחַ *altar ;* r. *slay animals, sacrifice.*
21. עֹלָה *whole burnt-offering.* That which goes up. *Step ;* r. *go up.*

15. And God spake unto Noah, saying, 16. Come forth
from the ark, thou, and thy wife, and thy sons, and thy sons'
wives with thee. 17. Every living thing that is with thee, of
all flesh, the fowl and the cattle, and every creeper that creepeth upon the land, bring forth with thee; and let them breed in
the land and be fruitful, and multiply upon the land. 18. And
Noah came forth, and his sons, and his wife, and his sons'
wives with him. 19. Every living thing, every creeper, and
every fowl, all that creepeth upon the land, after their families,
came forth out of the ark.

20. And Noah builded an altar unto the Lord, and took of
all clean cattle, and of every clean fowl, and offered burnt-offerings on the altar. 21. And the Lord smelled the sweet
savor ; and the Lord said in his heart, I will not again curse
the soil any more on account of man, because the imagination
of man's heart is evil from his youth ; neither will I again
smite any more all living as I have done. 22. Henceforth all
the days of the earth, sowing and reaping, and cold and heat,
and summer and winter, and day and night shall not cease.

15-19. The command to leave the ark is given and obeyed. As Noah did not enter, so neither does he leave the ark, without divine direction. *The fowl, the cattle, and the creeper.* Here, again, these three classes are specified under the general head of every living thing. They are again to multiply on the earth. 19. *Every living thing.* This evidently takes the place of the cattle mentioned before. *After their families.* This word denotes their tribes. It is usually applied to families or clans.

20-22. The offering of Noah accepted. The return to the dry land, through the special mercy of God to Noah and his house, is celebrated by an offering of thanksgiving and faith. *Builded an altar.* This is the first mention of the altar, or structure for the purpose of sacrifice. The Lord is now on high, having swept away the garden, and withdrawn his visible presence at the same time from the earth. The altar is therefore erected to point towards his dwelling-place on high. *Unto the Lord.* The personal name of God is peculiarly appropriate here, as he has proved himself a covenant keeper and a deliverer to Noah. *Of all clean cattle, and every clean fowl.* The mention of clean birds renders it probable that these only were taken into the ark by seven pairs (Gen. vii. 3). *Every* fit animal is included in this sacrifice, as it is expressive of thanksgiving for a complete deliverance. We have also here the first mention of the burnt-offering (עֹלָה); the whole victim, except the skin, being burned on the altar. Sacrifice is an act in which the transgressor slays an animal and offers it in whole, or in part as representative of the whole, to God. In this act he acknowledges his guilt, the claim of the offended law upon his life, and the mercy of the Lord in accepting a substitute to satisfy this claim for the returning penitent. He at the same time actually accepts the mercy of the Most High, and comes forward to plead it in the appointed way of reconciliation. The burnt-offering is the most perfect symbol of this substitution, and most befitting the present occasion, when life has been granted to the inmates of the ark amidst the universal death.

21. The effect of this plea is here described. The Lord smelled the sweet savor. He accepted the typical substitute, and, on account of the sacrifice, the offerers, the surviving ancestors of the post-diluvian race. Thus the reëntrance of the remnant of mankind upon the joys and tasks of life is inaugurated by an articulate confession of sin, a well-understood foreshadowing of the coming victim for human guilt, and a gracious acceptance of this act of faith. *The Lord said*

in his heart. It is the inward resolve of his will. The purpose of mercy is then expressed in a definite form, suited to the present circumstances of the delivered family. *I will not again curse the soil any more on account of man.* This seems at first sight to imply a mitigation of the hardship and toil which man was to experience in cultivating the ground (Gen. iii. 17). At all events, this very toil is turned into a blessing to him who returns from his sin and guilt, to accept the mercy, and live to the glory of his Maker and Saviour. But the main reference of the passage is doubtless to the curse of a deluge such as that which was now past. This will not be renewed. *Because the imagination of his heart is evil from his youth.* This is the reason for the past judgment, the curse upon the soil: not for the present promise of a respite for the future. Accordingly, it is to be taken in close connection with the cursing of the soil, of which it assigns the judicial cause. It is explanatory of the preceding phrase, *on account of man.* The reason for the promise of escape from the fear of a deluge for the future is the sacrifice of Noah, the priest and representative of the race, with which the Lord is well pleased. The closing sentence of this verse is a reiteration in a more explicit form of the same promise. *Neither will I again smite all living as I have done.* There will be no repetition of the deluge that had just overswept the land and destroyed the inhabitants.

22. *Henceforth all the days of the earth.* After these negative assurances come the positive blessings to be permanently enjoyed while the present constitution of the earth continues. These are summed up in the following terms:

HEAT.	Sowing, beginning in October. Reaping, ending in June.
COLD.	Early fruit, in July. Fruit harvest, ending in September.

The cold properly occupies the interval between sowing and reaping, or the months of January and February. From July to September is the period of heat. In Palestine, the seedtime began in October or November, when the wheat was sown. Barley was not generally sown till January. The grain harvest began early in May, and continued in June. The early fruits, such as grapes and figs, made their appearance in July and August; the full ingathering, in September and October. But the passage before us is not limited to the seasons of any particular country. Besides the seasons, it guarantees the continuance of the agreeable vicissitudes of day and night. It is probable that even these could not be distinguished during part of the deluge of waters. At all events, they did not present any sensible change when darkness reigned over the primeval abyss.

The term of this continuance is here defined. It is to last as long as the order of things introduced by the six days' creation endures. This order is not to be sempiternal. When the race of man has been filled up, it is here hinted that the present system of nature on the earth may be expected to give place to another and a higher order of things.

Here it is proper to observe the mode of Scripture in the promise of blessing. In the infancy of mankind, when the eye gazed on the present, and did not penetrate into the future, the Lord promised the immediate and the sensible blessings of life, because these alone are as yet intelligible to the childlike race, and they are, at the same time, the immediate earnest of endless blessings. As the mind developes, and the observable universe becomes more fully comprehended, these present and sensible sources of creature happiness correspondingly expand, and higher and more ethereal blessings begin to dawn upon the mind. When the prospect of death opens to the believer a new and hitherto unknown world of reality, then the temporal and corporeal give way to the eternal and spiritual. And as with the individual, so is it with the race. The present boon is the earnest in hand, fully satisfying the existing aspirations of the infantile desire. But it is soon found that the present is always the bud of the future; and as the volume of promise is unrolled, piece by piece, before the eye of the growing race, while the present and the sensible lose nothing of their intrinsic value, the opening glories of intellectual and spiritual enjoyment add an indescribable zest to the blessedness of a perpetuated life. Let not us, then, who flow in the full tide of the latter day, despise the rudiment of blessing in the first form in which it was conferred on Noah and his descendants; but rather remember that is not the whole content of the divine good-will, but only the present shape of an ever-expanding felicity, which is limited neither by time nor sense.

XXVIII. THE BLESSING OF NOAH.—Gen. ix. 1-7.

2. מוֹרָא *fear, reverence, awful deed.* חַת *dread,* breaking of the courage.

IX. 1. And God blessed Noah and his sons; and he said unto them, Be fruitful, and multiply, and replenish the earth.
2. And the fear of you and the dread of you shall be upon every beast of the land, and upon every fowl of the skies: with all that creepeth on the soil, and with all the fishes of the sea, into your hand are they given. 3. Every creeper that is alive shall be food for you: as the green herb have I given you all. 4. Only flesh with its life, its blood, shall ye not eat. 5. And also your blood of your lives will I require, from the hand of every beast will I require it; and from the hand of man, from the hand each of his brother, will I require the life of man.
6. Whoso sheddeth man's blood, by man shall his blood be shed; for in the image of God hath he made man. 7. And you, be fruitful and multiply; abound in the earth, and multiply therein. § 16.

Noah is saved from the deluge. His life is twice given to him by God. He had found grace in the sight of the Lord, and now he and his family have been graciously accepted when they approached the Lord with burnt-offerings. In him, therefore, the race of man is to be begun anew. Accordingly, as at the beginning, the Lord proceeds to bless him. 1st. The grant of increase is the same as at first, but expressed in ampler terms. 2d. Dominion over the other animals is renewed. But some reluctance on their part to yield obedience is intimated. *The fear and dread of you.* These terms give token of a master whose power is dreaded, rather than of a superior whose friendly protection is sought. *Into your hand are they given.* They are placed entirely at the disposal of man.

3. The grant of sustenance is no longer confined to the vegetable, but extended to the animal kinds, with two solemn restrictions. This explains how fully the animals are handed over to the will of man

They were slain for sacrifice from the earliest times. Whether they were used for food before this time we are not informed. But now *every creeper that is alive* is granted for food. *Every creeper* is every thing that moves with the body prone to the earth, and therefore in a creeping posture. This seems to describe the inferior animals in contradistinction to man, who walks erect. The phrase *that is alive* seems to exclude animals that have died a natural death from being used as food.

4. The first restriction on the grant of animal food is thus expressed: *Flesh with its life, its blood, shall ye not eat.* The animal must be slain before any part of it is used for food. And as it lives so long as the blood flows in its veins, the life-blood must be drawn before its flesh may be eaten. The design of this restriction is to prevent the horrid cruelty of mutilating or cooking an animal while yet alive and capable of suffering pain. The draining of the blood from the body is an obvious occasion of death, and therefore the prohibition to eat the flesh with the blood of life is a needful restraint from savage cruelty. It is also intended, perhaps, to teach that the life of the animal, which is in the blood, belongs not to man, but to God himself, who gave it. He makes account of it for atonement in sacrifice; otherwise it is to be poured on the ground and covered with dust (Lev. xvii. 11-13).

5, 6. The second restriction guards human life. The shedding of human blood is sternly prohibited. *Your blood of your lives.* The blood which belongs to your lives, which constitutes the very life of your corporeal nature. *Will I require.* I, the Lord, will find the murderer out, and exact the penalty of his crime. The very beast that causes the death of man shall be slain. The suicide and the homicide are alike accountable to God for the shedding of man's blood. 6. The penalty of murder is here proclaimed, — death for death. It is an instance of the law of retaliation. This is an axiom of moral equity. He that deprives another of any property is bound to make it good or to suffer the like loss.

The first law promulgated in Scripture was that between Creator and creature. If the creature refuse to the Creator the obedience due, he forfeits all the Creator has given him, and, therefore, his life. Hence, when Cain murdered his brother, he only displayed a new development of that sin which was in him, and, being already condemned to the extreme penalty under the first transgression, had only a minor punishment annexed to his personal crime. And so it continued to be in the antediluvian world. No civil law is on record for the restriction of crime. Cain, indeed, feared the natural vengeance which his conscience told him his sin deserved. But it was not competent in equity for the private individual to undertake the enforcement of the penalties of natural law. So long as the law was between Creator and creature, God himself was not only the sole legislator, but the sole administrator of law.

The second law is that between creature and creature, which is here introduced on the occasion of giving permission to partake of animal food, as the first was published on that of granting the use of vegetable diet. In the former case, God is the administrator of the law, as he is the immediate and sovereign party in the legal compact. In the latter case, man is, by the express appointment of the Lord of all, constituted the executive agent. *By man shall his blood be shed.* Here, then, is the formal institution of civil government. Here the civil sword is committed to the charge of man. The judgment of death by the executioner is solemnly delegated to man in vindication of human life. This trust is conveyed in the most general terms. *By man.* The divine legislator does not name the sovereign, define his powers, or determine the law of succession. All these practical conditions of a stable government are left open questions. The emphasis is laid solely on *man.* On man is impressively laid the obligation of instituting a civil constitution suited to his present fallen condition. On the nation as a body it is an incumbent duty to select the sovereign, to form the civil compact between prince and people, to settle the prerogative of the sovereign and the rights of the subjects, to fix the order of succession, to constitute the legislative, judicial, and administrative bodies, and to render due submission to the constituted authorities. And all these arrangements are to be made according to the principles of Scripture and the light of nature.

The reason why retribution is exacted in the case of man is here also given. *For in the image of God has he made man.* This points on the one hand to the function of the magistrate, and on the other to the claims of the violated law; and in both respects illustrates the meaning of being created in the image of God. Man resembles God in this, that he is a moral being, judging of right and wrong, endowed with reason and will, and capable of holding and exercising rights. Hence he is in the first place competent to rule, and on his creation authorized to exercise a mild and moral sway over the inferior creatures. His capacity to govern even among his fellow-men is now recognized. The function of self-government in civil things is now conferred upon man. When duly called to the office, he is declared to be at liberty to discharge the part of a ruler among his fellow-men, and is entitled on the ground of this divine arrangement to claim the obedience of those who are under his sway. He must rule in the Lord, and they must obey in the Lord.

But, in the next place, man is capable of, and has been actually endowed with, rights of property in himself, his children, his industrial products, his purchases, his receipts in the way of gift, and his claims by covenant or promise. He can also recognize such rights in another. When, therefore, he is deprived of anything belonging to him, he is sensible of being wronged, and feels that the wrongdoer is bound to make reparation by giving back that which he has taken away, or an equivalent in its place. This is the law of requital, which is the universal principle of justice between the wrongdoer and the wrong-sufferer. Hence the blood of him who sheds blood is to be shed. And, in setting up a system of human government, the most natural and obvious case is given, according to the manner of Scripture, as a sample of the law by which punishment is to be inflicted on the transgressor in proportion to his crime. The case in point accordingly arises necessarily out of the permission to use animal food, which requires to be guarded on the one hand by a provision against cruelty to animals, and, on the other, by an enactment forbidding the taking away of human life, on the pain of death, by order of the civil magistrate. This case, then, turns out to be the most heinous crime which man can commit against his fellow-man, and strikingly exemplifies the great common principle of retributive justice.

The brute is not a moral being, and has, therefore, no proper rights in itself. Its blood may therefore be shed with impunity. Nevertheless, man, because he is a moral being, owes a certain negative duty to the brute animal, because it is capable of pain. He is not to inflict gratuitous or unnecessary suffering on a being susceptible of such torture. Hence the propriety of the blood being shed before the flesh is used for food. Life, and therefore the sense of pain, is extinguished when the blood is withdrawn from the veins.

XXIX. THE COVENANT WITH NOAH.—Gen. ix. 8-17.

13. קֶשֶׁת *bow;* r. *be bent.*
14. עָנַן *cover, cast over;* n. *cloud.*

8. And God said unto Noah, and to his sons with him, saying, 9. And I, behold, I establish my covenant with you, and with your seed after you, 10. And with every breathing living thing that is with you, in the fowl, in the cattle, and in every beast of the land with you, from all that come out of the ark to every beast of the land. 11. And I have established my covenant with you; and all flesh shall not be cut off any more by the waters of a flood, neither shall there be any more a flood to destroy the land.

12. And God said, This is the token of the covenant which I give between me and you and every breathing living thing that is with you for perpetual ages: 13. My bow have I given in the cloud, and it shall be a token of a covenant between me and the land. 14. And it shall come to pass, when I bring a cloud over the land, that the bow shall be seen in the cloud. 15. And I will remember my covenant, which is between me and you and every breathing living thing of all flesh; and the water shall no more be a flood to destroy all flesh. 16. And the bow shall be in the cloud, and I will look upon it, to remember the perpetual covenant between God and every breathing living thing of all flesh that is upon the land.

17. And God said unto Noah, This is the token of the covenant, which I have established between me and all flesh that is upon the land. ¶ 12.

The covenant made with Noah (Gen. vi. 18) is now formally confirmed. The purpose conceived in the heart (Gen. viii. 21) now receives significant expression. Not only a new blessing is bestowed, but also a new covenant is formed with Noah. For he that has offered an acceptable sacrifice is not only at peace with God, but renewed in mind after the image of God. He is therefore a fit subject for entering into a covenant.

8-11. *Unto Noah and to his sons.* God addresses the sons of Noah as the progenitors of the future race. 9. *I establish.* He not merely makes (כָּרַת), but ratifies, his covenant with them. *My covenant.* The covenant which was before mentioned to Noah in the directions concerning the making of the ark, and which was really, though tacitly, formed with Adam in the garden.

9, 10. The party with whom God now enters into covenant is here fully described. *You and your seed after you, and every breathing living thing;* the latter merely *on account of the former.* The animals are specially mentioned because they partake in the special benefit of preservation from a flood, which is guaranteed in this covenant. There is a remarkable expression employed here,— *From all that come out of the ark, to every beast of the land.* It seems to imply that the beast of the land, or the wild beast, was not among those that came out of the ark, and, therefore, not among those that went in. This coincides with the view we have given of the inmates of the ark.

11. The benefits conferred by this form of God's covenant are here specified. First, all flesh shall no more be cut off by a flood; secondly, the land shall no more be destroyed by this means. The Lord has been true to his promise in saving Noah and his family from the flood of waters. He now perpetuates his promise by assuring him that the land would not again be overwhelmed with water. This is the new and present blessing of the covenant. Its former blessings are not abrogated, but only confirmed and augmented by the present. Other and higher benefits will flow out of this to those who rightly receive it, even throughout the ages of eternity. The present benefit is shared by the whole race descended from Noah.

12-16. The token of the covenant is now pointed out. *For perpetual ages.* This stability of sea and land is to last during the remainder of the human period. What is to happen when the race of man is completed, is not the question at present. 13. *My bow.* As God's covenant is the well-known and still remembered compact formed with man when the command was issued in the Garden of Eden, so God's bow is the primeval arch, coexistent with the rays of light and the drops of rain. It is caused by the rays of the sun reflected from the falling raindrops at a particular angle to the eye of the spectator. A beautiful arch of reflected and refracted light is in this way formed for every eye. The rainbow is thus an index that the sky is not wholly overcast, since the sun is shining through the shower, and thereby demonstrating its partial extent. There could not, therefore, be a more beautiful or fitting token that there shall be no more a flood to sweep away all flesh and destroy the land. It comes with its mild radiance only when the cloud condenses into a shower. It consists of heavenly light, variegated in hue, and mellowed in lustre, filling the beholder with an involuntary pleasure. It forms a perfect arch, extends as far as the shower extends, connects heaven and earth, and spans the horizon. In these respects it is a beautiful emblem of mercy rejoicing against judgment, of light from heaven irradiating and beatifying the soul, of grace always sufficient for the need of the reunion of earth and heaven, and of the universality of the offer of salvation. *Have I given.* The rainbow existed as long as the present laws of light and air. But it is now mentioned for the first time, because it now becomes the fitting sign of security from another universal deluge, which is the peculiar blessing of the covenant in its present form. *In the cloud.* When a shower-cloud is spread over the sky, the bow appears, if the sun, the cloud, and the spectator are in the proper relation to one another. 16. *And I will look upon it to remember.* The Scripture is most unhesitating and frank in ascribing to God all the attributes and exercises of personal freedom. While man looks on the bow to recall the promise of God, God himself looks on it to remember and perform this promise. Here freedom and immutability of purpose meet.

The covenant here ostensibly refers to the one point of the absence, for all time to come, of any danger to the human race from a deluge. But it presupposes and supplements the covenant with man subsisting from the very beginning. It is clearly of grace; for the Lord in the very terms affirms the fact that the imagination of man's heart is evil from his youth, while at the same time the original transgression belonged to the whole race. The condition by which any man becomes interested in it is not expressed, but easily understood from the nature of a covenant, a promise, and a sign, all of which require of us consenting faith in the party who covenants, promises, and gives the sign. The meritorious condition of the covenant of grace is dimly shadowed forth in the burnt-offerings which Noah presented on coming out of the ark. One thing, however, was surely and clearly revealed to the early saints; namely, the mercy of God. Assured of this, they were prepared humbly to believe that all would redound to the glory of his holiness, justice, and truth, as well as of his mercy, grace, and love, though they might not yet fully understand how this would be accomplished.

17. God seems here to direct Noah's attention to a rainbow actually existing at the time in the sky, and presenting to the patriarch the assurance of the promise, with all the impressiveness of reality.

XXX. THE PROPHECY OF NOAH.—Gen. ix. 18–29.

18. כְּנַעַן Kena'an, *bowed down.*
19. נָפַץ *break, scatter, spread.* פּוּץ *break, scatter, flow.*
20. כֶּרֶם *orchard, vineyard.*
21. יַיִן *wine ;* r. *ferment.*

18. And the sons of Noah that came forth from the ark, were Shem and Ham and Japheth ; and Ham was the father of Kenaan.
19. These three were the sons of Noah ; and of them was the whole land overspread.

20. And Noah began to be a man of the soil ; and he planted a vineyard.
21. And he drank of the wine, and was drunken ; and he was uncovered in the midst of his tent.
22. And Ham, the father of Kenaan, saw the nakedness of his father ; and he told his two brethren without.
23. And Shem and Japheth took the garment and laid it on the shoulder of them both, and went backward, and covered the nakedness of their father ; and their faces were backward, and they saw not their father's nakedness.
24. And Noah awoke from his wine, and knew what his youngest son had done unto him.
25. And he said,

Cursed be Kenaan.
A servant of servants shall he be unto his brethren.

26. And he said,

Blessed be the Lord, the God of Shem ;
And Kenaan shall be servant unto them.

27. God shall enlarge Japheth,
And he shall dwell in the tents of Shem;
And Kenaan shall be servant unto them.

28. And Noah lived after the flood three hundred and fifty years. 29. And all the days of Noah were nine hundred and fifty years, and he died. ¶ 13.

After the blessing on the new heads of the human race has been pronounced, and the covenant with them renewed, we are prepared for a new development of human action. This appears, however, in the form of an event which is itself a meet preliminary to the subsequent stage of affairs. The prophecy of Noah, delivered in the shape of a solemn paternal doom, pronounced upon his three sons, sketches in a few striking traits the future history of the separate families of mankind.

18, 19. The two verses form a connecting link between the preceding and the following passage. After the recital of the covenant, comes naturally the statement, that by the three sons of Noah, duly enumerated, was the whole land overspread. This forms a fit conclusion to the previous paragraph. But the penman of these sentences had evidently the following paragraph in view. For he mentions that Ham was the father of Kenaan; which is plainly the preface to the following narrative.

20–27. Then comes the prediction, which has a peculiar interest, as the first prophetic utterance of man recorded in the Old Testament. The occasion of it is first stated. Noah becomes *a man of the soil.* If he was before a mechanic, it is evident he must now attend to the cultivation of the soil, that he may draw from it the means of subsistence. *He planted a vineyard.* God was the first planter (Gen. ii. 8); and since that time we hear nothing of the cultivation of trees till Noah becomes a planter. The cultivation of the vine and the manufacture of wine might have been in practice before this time, as the mention of them is merely incidental to the present narrative. But it seems likely from what follows, that, though grapes may have been in use, wine had not been extracted from them. *And was drunken.* We are not in a position to estimate the amount of Noah's guilt in this case, as we do not know how far he was acquainted with the properties of wine. But we should take warning by the consequences, and beware of the abuse of any of God's gifts. 22. *Ham the father of Kenaan.*

It is natural to suppose, as some have done, that Kenaan had something to do with the guilt of this act. But there is no clear indication of this in the text, and Kenaan's relationship to Ham may be again mentioned simply in anticipation of the subsequent prophecy. Ham is punished in his youngest son, who was perhaps a favorite. 23. The intention of this act is eminently pure and befitting dutiful sons. *The garment.* The loose mantle or shawl which was used for wrapping round the body when going to sleep. 24. The actions of the sons in this unpleasant occurrence, especially that of Ham, give occasion to the following prophetic sentence: *His youngest son.* This seems plainly the meaning of the phrase בְּנוֹ הַקָּטָן *his son the little.* He must be regarded here as contrasted with the other two, and therefore distinguished as the youngest.

The manner of Scripture here is worthy of particular remark. First, the prediction takes its rise from a characteristic incident. The conduct of the brothers was of comparatively slight importance in itself, but in the disposition which it betrayed it was highly significant. Secondly, the prediction refers in terms to the near future and to the outward condition of the parties concerned. Thirdly, it foreshadows under these familiar phrases the distant future, and the inward, as well as the outward, state of the family of man. Fourthly, it lays out the destiny of the whole race from its very starting-point. These simple laws will be found to characterize the main body of the predictions of Scripture.

25–27. The prophecy consists of two parts, — a malediction and a benediction. 25. *Cursed be Kenaan.* A curse (Gen. iii. 14, 17, iv. 11) is any privation, inferiority, or other ill, expressed in the form of a doom, and bearing, not always upon the object directly expressed, but upon the party who is in the transgression. Thus the soil is cursed on account of Adam the transgressor (Gen. iii. 17). It is apparent that in the present case the prime mover was Ham, who is therefore punished in the prospect of a curse resting on his posterity, and especially on a particular line of it. Let us not imagine, however, that the ways of the Lord are not equal in this matter; for Kenaan and his descendants no doubt abundantly deserved this special visitation. And as the other descendants of Ham are not otherwise mentioned in the prophecy, we may presume that they shared in the curse pronounced upon Kenaan. At all events, they are not expressly included in the blessing pronounced on the other two divisions of the human family. It is proper to observe, also, that this prediction does not affirm an absolute perpetuity in the doom of Ham or Kenaan. It only delineates their relative condition until the whole race is again brought within the scope of prophecy.

A servant of servants shall he be unto his brethren. The curse here consists in servitude, which is in itself an inferiority, and, among the children of self-will, tends more and more to all the horrid ills of slavery. Slavery originated in war and conquest. The mere warrior put the captives to death, the cannibal devoured them, the economist fed them for their labor. Accordingly, slavery soon made its appearance in all countries which were trodden by the conqueror. A system of slavery, imposed without consent and for no crime, is a dire evil. Besides the direct injustice of robbing a fellow-man of his personal liberty, it dissolves wedlock, breaks the family tie, and disregards the conscience. It trades, therefore, in the souls as well as the bodies of men. It is a historical fact that the degradation of slavery has fallen especially upon the race of Ham. A portion of the Kenaanites became bondsmen among the Israelites, who were of the race of Shem. The early Babylonians, the Phœnicians, the Carthaginians, and Egyptians, who all belonged to the race of Ham, were subjugated by the Assyrians, who were Shemites, the Persians, the Macedonians, and the Romans, who were all Japhethites. And in modern times it is well known that most of the nations of Europe traded in African slaves. *A servant of servants* means a slave of the most abject kind. *Unto his brethren.* If the doom of slavery be referred to the race of Ham, then his brethren are the descendants of Japheth and Shem, who have held many of the Hamites in bondage. If we limit the sentence to Kenaan, then his brethren may include the other descendants of Ham. It is said that the servile tribe is also the most tyrannical; and it is the fact that the Africans have lent themselves to the forcible seizing and selling into slavery in distant lands of their own kinsmen and fellow-countrymen.

26, 27. *And he said.* The prediction concerning the other two brothers is a distinct utterance of Noah. *Blessed be Jehovah, the God of Shem.* The characteristic boon of Shem is that Jehovah, the one true, living, known God, is his God. The knowledge and worship of the Creator is preserved in the family of Shem, when it is lost or fatally obscured among the other descendants of Noah. The prophet is so conscious of the unspeakable blessing of knowing and loving the true God, that he breaks out into thanksgiving in the very act of announcing the transcendent privilege of Shem. There is a dark side, however, to this prophetic thought, as it implies that the two other families of mankind, at least for part of the period under the prophet's view, were estranged from the true and living God. History corroborates both aspects of this prophetic sentence for the space of two thousand four hundred years. During the most part of this long period the Holy Jehovah Omnipotent was unknown to the great mass of the Japhethites, Hamites, and even Shemites. And it was only by the special election and consecration of an individual Shemite to be the head of a peculiar people, and the father of the faithful, that he did not cease to be the God of even a remnant of Shem.

Then follows the refrain, *And Kenaan shall be servant unto them.* The phrase *unto them* proves that Shem here comprehends the race descended from him, and consisting of many individuals. Scripture sees the race in the father, traces up its unity to him, discerns in him the leading traits of character that often mark his remotest posterity, and identifies with him in destiny all those of his race who continue to take after him. Thus Adam denotes the whole race, Shem, Ham, and Japheth, its three great branches. Attention to this law of the unity, continuity, and identity of a race, will aid us much in understanding the dealings of Providence with the several branches of the human family. We learn also from the same phrase that this solemn sentence is no mere ebullition of the personal feelings of Noah. He is not speaking of Shem and Kenaan merely, but of the future races that are to spring from them. This appears still more plainly from the fact that Japheth, as well as Ham, is described as long estranged from the true God. And now that we are on spiritual ground, it ought to be observed that Kenaan's curse is not exclusion, either present or prospective, from the mercy of God. That is an evil he brings on himself by a voluntary departure from the living God. The curse merely affects the body,—the personal liberty. It is a mere degradation from some of the natural rights of our common humanity; and does not of itself cut him off from any offer of mercy, or benefit of repentant faith.

God shall enlarge Japheth. God is here spoken of by his generic name. This intimates, or at least coincides, with the fact that Japheth did not continue that nearness of approach to him which is implied in the use of the personal name. There is in the original a play upon the word *Japheth,* which itself signifies enlargement. This enlargement is the most striking point in the history of Japheth, who is the progenitor of the inhabitants of Europe, Asia, and America, except the region between the Persian Gulf, the Red Sea, the Mediterranean, the Euxine, the Caspian, and the mountains beyond the Tigris, which was the main seat of the Shemites. This expansive power refers not only to the territory and the multitude of the Japhethites, but also to their intellectual and active faculties. The metaphysics of the Hindoos, the philosophy of the Greeks, the military prowess of the Romans, and the modern science and civilization of the world, are due to the race of Japheth. And though the moral and the spiritual were first developed among the Shemites, yet the Japhethites have proved themselves capable of rising to the heights of these lofty themes, and have elaborated that noble form of human speech, which was adopted, in the providence of God, as best fitted to convey to mankind that further development of Old Testament truth which is furnished in the New.

And he shall dwell in the tents of Shem. We regard Japheth as the subject of this sentence; because, if God were its subject, the meaning would be substantially the same as the blessing of Shem, already given, and because this would intermingle the blessing of Shem with that of Japheth, without any important addition to our information. Whereas, when Japheth is the subject of the sentence, we learn that he shall dwell in the tents of Shem — an altogether new proposition. This form of expression does not indicate a direct invasion and conquest of the land of Shem, which would not be in keeping with the blessing pronounced on him in the previous sentence: it rather implies that this dwelling together would be a benefit to Japheth, and no injury to Shem. Accordingly, we find that when the Persians conquered the Babylonian empire, they restored the Jews to their native land; when Alexander the Great conquered the Persians, he gave protection to the Jews; and when the Romans subdued the Greek monarchy, they befriended the chosen nation, and allowed them a large measure of self-government. In their time came the Messiah, and instituted that new form of the church of the Old Testament which not only retained the best part of the ancient people of God, but extended itself over the whole of Europe, the chief seat of Japheth; went with him wherever he went; and is at this day, through the blessing of God on his political and moral influence, penetrating into the moral darkness of Ham, as well as the remainder of Shem and Japheth himself. Thus, in the highest of all senses, Japheth is dwelling in the tents of Shem.

Again comes the refrain, *And Keenan shall be servant unto them.*

A portion of Japheth still holds a portion of Ham in bondage. But this very bondage has been the means of bringing some of the sons of Ham to dwell in the tents of Shem; and the day is not far distant when Japheth will relinquish altogether the compulsory hold upon his brother, and consecrate his entire moral influence over him to the revival in his race of the knowledge and love of God our Father, and our Lord Jesus Christ.

Thus it appears that the destiny of these three great branches of the Noachic family, during the time of their separation on the high question of their relation to God, is traced out with great fidelity in this remarkable prediction. Ham is aptly represented by Kenaan, the slave, who is seized, enslaved, and sold even by his kinsmen to one another, and to the descendants of Shem and Japheth. Shem includes within his posterity the select family who know God as the Lord, the God of promise, of mercy, of salvation. Japheth is enlarged by God, and at length becomes acquainted with him whom he once ignorantly worshipped. The historian recognizes these as salient points in the experience of the three races, so long as they continue apart. The time is approaching when this strange intermediate development will come to a happy issue, in the reunion of all the members of the human family, according to clearer and further-reaching prophecies yet to be delivered.

28, 29. The history of Noah is now closed, in the customary form of the fifth chapter. This marks a connection between the third and fourth documents, and points to one hand as the composer, or at least compiler, of both. The document now closed could not have had the last paragraph appended to it till after the death of Noah. But, with the exception of these two verses, it might have been composed hundreds of years before. This strongly favors the notion of a constant continuator, or, at all events, continuation of the sacred history. Every new prophet and inspired writer whom God raised up added the necessary portion and made the necessary insertions in the sacred record. And hence the Word of God had a progressive growth and adaptation to the successive ages of the church.

The present document stands between the old world and the new. Hence it has a double character, being the close of the antediluvian history, and the introduction to that of the postdiluvian race. It records a great event, pregnant with warning to all future generations of men. And it notes the delegation, by God to man, of authority to punish the murderer by death, and therefore to enforce all the minor sanctions of law for breaches of the civil compact. It therefore points out the institution of civil government as coming from God, and clearly exhibits the accountability of all governments to God for all the powers they hold, and for the mode in which they are exercised. This also is a great historical lesson for all ages.

SECTION VIII — THE NATIONS

XXXI. JAPHETH. — Gen. x. 1–5.

2. גֹּמֶר Gomer, *completion*; r. *complete*; Κιμμέριοι. מָגוֹג Magog, Caucasian, Skyth. מָדַי Madai, *middle*: Mede. יָוָן Javan; Ἰάων; Sanscr., Javana; Old Pers., Juna. תֻּבַל Tubal; Τιβαρηνοὶ. מֶשֶׁךְ Meshek, *drawing possession, valor*; Μόσχοι. תִּירָס Tiras; Θρᾷξ.

3. אַשְׁכְּנַז Ashkenaz, Ἀσκάνιος. רִיפַת Riphath, ὄρη Ῥίπαια. תֹּגַרְמָה Togarmah, Thorgom, ancestor of the Armenians.

4. אֱלִישָׁה Elishah; Ἦλις Ἑλλὰς, Αἰολεῖς. תַּרְשִׁישׁ Tarshish, *breaking, fastness*: Tartessus, Tarsus, Tyrseni. כִּתִּים Kittim, *smiters*; Citienses; Κᾶρες; דֹּדָנִים Dodanim, Dodona, Dardani.

5. אִי *meadow, land reached by water, island*; r. *be marked off* or *bounded* (by a water line). גּוֹי *nation*; r. *be born*; γεγάασι.

X. 1. And these are the generations of the sons of Noah: Shem, Ham, and Japheth; and unto them were born sons after the flood. 2. The sons of Japheth: Gomer and Magog and Madai and Javan and Tubal and Meshek and Tiras. 3. And the sons of Gomer: Ashkenaz and Riphath and Togarmah. 4. And the sons of Javan: Elishah and Tarshish Kittim and Dodanim. 5. From these were divided the isles of the nations in their lands, every one after his tongue, after their families, in their nations.

The fifth document relates to the generations of the sons of Noah. It presents first a genealogy of the nations, and then an account of the distribution of mankind into nations, and their dispersion over the earth. This is the last section which treats historically of the whole human race. Only in incidental, didactic, or prophetic passages do we again meet with mankind as a whole in the Old Testament.

The present chapter signalizes a new step in the development of the human race. They pass from the one family to the seventy nations. This great process covers the space of time from Noah to Abraham. During this period the race was rapidly increasing under the covenant made with Noah. From Shem to Abraham were ten generations inclusive; and, therefore, if we suppose the same rate of increase after as we have supposed before, there would be about fifteen millions of inhabitants when Abraham was thirty years of age. If, however, we take eight as the average of a family, and suppose eleven generations after Shem at the hundredth year of Abraham's life, we have about thirty millions of people on the earth. The average of the three sons of Noah is higher than this; for they had sixteen sons, and we may suppose as many daughters, making in all thirty-two, and, therefore, giving ten children to each household. The present chapter does not touch on the religious aspect of human affairs: it merely presents a table of the primary nations, from which all subsequent nationalities have been derived.

1–2. *The sons of Japheth.* Japheth is placed first, because he was, most probably, the eldest brother (Gen. ix. 24; x. 21), and his descendants were the most numerous and most widely spread from the birthplace of mankind. The general description of their territory is "the isles of the nations." These were evidently maritime countries, or such as were reached by sea. These coast-lands were preëminently, but not exclusively, the countries bordering on the north side of the Mediterranean and its connected waters. They are said to belong to the nations, because the national form of association was more early and fully developed among them than among the other branches of the race. There is, probably, a relic of Japheth in the Ιαπετὸς, Japetus of the Greeks, said to be the son of Uranus (heaven), and Gaea (earth), and father of Prometheus, and thus in some way connected with the origin or preservation of the human race.

Fourteen of the primitive nations spring from Japheth. Seven of these are of immediate descent. (1) GOMER is mentioned again, in Ezekiel (xxxviii. 6), as the ally of Gog, by which the known existence of the nation at that period is indicated. Traces of this name are perhaps found in the Κιμμέριοι (Hom. Odys. xi. 14; Herod. i. 15; iv. 12), who lay in the dark north, in the Krimea, the Kimbri who dwelt in north Germany, the Kymry, Cambri, and Cumbri who occupied Britain. These all belong to the race now called Keltic, the first wave of population that reached the Atlantic. Thus the Γομαρεῖς of

Josephus (Ant. i. 6. 1) may even be identified with the Galatae. This nation seems to have lain to the north of the Euxine, and to have spread out along the southern coasts of the Baltic into France, Spain, and the British Isles.

(2) Magog is mentioned, by Ezekiel (xxxviii. 6), as the people of which Gog was the prince. It is introduced in the Apocalypse (xx. 8), as a designation of the remote nations who had penetrated to the ends or corners of the earth. This indicates a continually progressing people, occupying the north of Europe and Asia, and crossing, it may be, over into America. They seem to have been settled north of the Caspian, and to have wandered north and east from that point. They are accordingly identified by Josephus (Ant. i. 6. 1) with the Skyths, and include the Mongols among other Skythic tribes.

(3) Madai has given name to the Medes, who occupied the southern shore of the Caspian. From this region they penetrated southward to Hindostan.

(4) Javan is traced in the Ἰάονες, *Iones*, who settled in the coasts of the Aegean, in Peloponnesus, Attica, and subsequently on the coast of Asia Minor, and accordingly denotes the Greeks in the language of the Old Testament (Isa. lxvi. 19; Ezek. xxvii. 13; Dan. viii. 21). The name Yunau is found in the cuneiform inscriptions of the times of Sargon, referring to a western people.

(5) Tubal and (6) Meshek are generally associated. Ezekiel (xxvii. 13, xxxviii. xxxix.) connects them, on the one hand, with Magog, and on the other, with Javan. Josephus (Ant. i. 6. 1) finds Tubal in Iberia, and Meshek in Cappadocia, tracing the name in Mazaca. Their names are seemingly detected in the Tibareni and Moschi, and their seat was probably between the Euxine and the Caspian, whence they spread themselves northward and westward. The names of the rivers Tobal and Mosqua bear a strong resemblance to these patriarchal names.

(7) Tiras is referred by Josephus to Thrace. The name is perhaps discernible in the Tyras or Dniester. The seat of the nation was east of the Euxine, whence it spread to the north. Thus we have the original starting-points of these seven nations about the Caspian, the Euxine, and the Aegean Seas.

3. Gomer has three sons, who are the founders of as many nations. (8) *Ashkenaz* is supposed to have lain south of the Euxine, and to be traceable in its original name ἄξενος, and in the Ascanius and Ascania of Bithynia, perhaps in Scandinavia. Part of the nation may have

migrated to Germany, which is called Ashkenaz by the Jews, and where the word Sachsen (Saxon) occurs. It perhaps contains the root of the name Asia. (9) *Riphath* seems to have travelled north, and left his name in the Rhipaean mountains. Josephus, however, places him in Paphlagonia, where the name Tobata occurs (Diphath) (1 Chr. i. 6). (10) *Togarmah* is said to have been settled in Armenia. By a tradition in Moses Chorenensis, Haik, the ancestor of the Armenians, is the son of Thorgom, the son of Gomer. At all events, the Black Sea might convey colonies from Gomer to Asia Minor and Armenia.

4. Javan has four sons, who are the heads of nations. (11) *Elishah* is noted by Ezekiel (xxvii. 7) as a nation whose maritime country produced purple, which agrees with the coast of Laconia or the Corinthian Gulf. The name has been variously sought in Elis, Hellas, and Aeolis. The last is due to Josephus. It is possible that Elea or Velia, in the south of Italy, may contain some reference to the name. (12) *Tarshish* is conjectured by Josephus to be the people of Cilicia; which, he affirms, was anciently called Tharsus, and the capital of which was Tarsus. But whether this be the primitive seat of Tarshish or not, it is almost certain that Spain retains the name, if not in Tarraco, at least in Tartessus. (13) *Kittim* is discovered, by Josephus, in Cyprus, where we meet with the town of Citium (Κίτιον). He adds, however, that all the islands and the greater part of the seacoasts are called Χεδίμ by the Hebrews. We may therefore presume that the Kittim spread into northern Greece, where we have a Κίτιον in Macedonia, and ultimately into Italy, which is designated as "the isles of Kittim" (Num. xxiv. 24; Isa. xxiii. 1; Jer. ii. 10; Ezek. xxvii. 6; Dan. xi. 30.) (14) *Dodanim* leaves a trace, perhaps, in Dodona, an ancient site of the Hellenes in Epirus, and perhaps in Dardania, a district of Illyricum.

5. Thus we have discovered the ancient seats of Japheth (Ἰαπετὸς) around the Caspian, the Euxine, the Aegean, and the north of the Mediterranean. From these coast-lands they seem to have spread over Europe, northern, western, and southern Asia, and, both by Behring's Straits and the Atlantic, they at length poured into America. So true is it that Japheth was enlarged, and that by them were "the isles of the nations divided."

In their nations. We here note the characteristics of a nation. 1st. It is descended from one head. Others may be occasionally grafted on the original stock by intermarriage. But there is a vital union subsisting between all the members and the head, in consequence of which the name of the head is applied to the whole body of the nation. In the case of Kittim and Dodanim we seem to have the national name thrown back upon the patriarchs, who may have themselves been called Keth and Dodan. Similar instances occur in the subsequent parts of the genealogy. 2d. A nation has a country or "land" which it calls its own. In the necessary migrations of ancient tribes, the new territories appropriated by the tribe, or any part of it, were naturally called by the old name, or some name belonging to the old country. This is well illustrated by the name of Gomer, which seems to reappear in the Cimmerii, the Cimbri, the Cymri, the Cambri, and the Cumbri. 3d. A nation has its own "tongue." This constitutes at once its unity in itself and its separation from others. Many of the nations in the table may have spoken cognate tongues, or even originally the same tougue. Thus the Kenaanite, Phœnician, and Punic nations had the same stock of languages with the Shemites. But it is a uniform law, that one nation has only one speech within itself. 4th. A nation is composed of many "families," clans, or tribes. These branch off from the nation in the same manner as it did from the parent stock of the race.

XXXII. HAM. — Gen. x. 6–20.

6. מִצְרַיִם Mitsraim. מֵצֶר *straitness, limit, pressure.* מָצוֹר *distress, siege, mound, bulwark;* Egypt. מִצְרַיִם perhaps double Egypt, lower and upper. פּוּט Put, *troubled.*

7. סְבָא Seba, *drinking* (*man,* Ethiop.). סַבְתָּה Sabtah. רַעְמָה Ra'mah, *shaking, trembling.* סַבְתְּכָא Sabtekha. שְׁבָא Sheba, *captive?* דְּדָן Dedan, *going slowly?*

8. נִמְרֹד Nimrod, *strong, rebel.*

10. בָּבֶל Babel; r. *pour, mingle, confound.* אֶרֶךְ Erek, *length.* אַכַּד Akkad, *fortress.* כַּלְנֵה Kalneh. שִׁנְעָר Shin'ar.

11. נִינְוֵה Nineveh, *dwelling?* רְחֹבֹת עִיר Rechoboth 'ir, *streets of a city.* כֶּלַח Kelach, *completion, end, age.*

12. רֶסֶן Resen, *bridle, bit.*

13. לוּדִים Ludim, *born?* עֲנָמִים 'Anamim, *possession, sheep.* לְהָבִים Lehabim, *fiery, flaming?* נַפְתֻּחִים Naphtuchim, *opening.*

14. פַּתְרֻסִים Pathrusim. כַּסְלֻחִים Kasluchim. פְּלִשְׁתִּים Pelishtim, Αλλόφυλοι; r. *break, scatter;* Aeth. *migrate.* כַּפְתֹּרִים Kaphtorim; r. *crown, capital.*

15. צִידוֹן Tsidon, *hunting.* חֵת Cheth, *breaking, affrighting.*

16. יְבוּסִי Jebusi; r. *tread.* אֱמֹרִי Emori; r. *Say, be high.* גִּרְגָּשִׁי Girgashi; r. *clay, clod.*

17. חִוִּי Chivvi; r. *live.* עַרְקִי ʿArqi; r. *gnaw, sting.* סִינִי Sini; r. *mud, clay.*

18. אַרְוָדִי Arvadi; r. *roam, ramble.* צְמָרִי Tsemari; n. *wool;* v. *cover.* חֲמָתִי Chamathi; n. *fastness;* v. *guard.*

19. גְּרָר Gerar; r. *draw, saw, abide.* עַזָּה ʿAzzah, *strong.* סְדֹם Sodom; r. *shut, stop.* עֲמֹרָה ʿAmorah; n. *sheaf;* v. *bind.* אַדְמָה Admah; a. *red;* n. *soil.* צְבֹיִם Tseboim, *gazelles;* v. *go forth, shine.* לֶשַׁע Leshaʿ; v. *pierce, cleave.*

6. And the sons of Ham: Kush and Mizraim and Put and
Kenaan. 7. And the sons of Kush: Seba and Havilah and
Sabtah and Ramah and Sabteka; and the sons of Ramah:
Sheba and Dedan. 8. And Kush begat Nimrod: he began
to be mighty in the land. 9. He was mighty in hunting,
before the LORD: wherefore it is said, As Nimrod, mighty in
hunting, before the LORD. 10. And the beginning of his king-
dom was Babel and Erek and Akkad and Kalneh, in the
land of Shinar. 11. Out of that land came he forth to
Asshur, and builded Nineveh and Rehoboth-ir and Kelah,
12. And Resen between Nineveh and Kelah; that is, the great
city. 13. And Mizraim begat Ludim and Anamim and
Lehabim and Naphtuhim, 14. And Pathrusim and Kasluhim,
whence came Philistim and Kaphtorim. § 17.

15. And Kenaan begat Zidon, his first-born, and Heth, 16.
And the Jebusite and the Amorite and the Girgashite, 17.
And the Hivite and the Arkite and the Sinite, 18. And the
Arvadite and the Zemarite and the Hamathite; and after-
ward were spread abroad the families of the Kenaanite. 19.
And the border of the Kenaanite was from Zidon, as thou
goest to Gerar, unto Azzah; as thou goest to Sodom and
Amorah and Admah and Zeboim, unto Lesha. 20. These
are the sons of Ham, after their families, after their tongues,
in their lands, in their nations. § 18.

6. *And the sons of Ham.* Ham the youngest of the three brothers (Gen. ix. 24), is placed here because he agrees with Japheth in becoming estranged from the true God, and because the last place as the more important is reserved for Shem. As the name of Japheth is preserved in the Ιαπετος of the Greeks, so Cham is supposed to appear in Chemi of the Koptic, χημία of Plutarch, Chme of the Rosetta Stone, an old name of Egypt. This country is also called the land of Ham in Scripture (Ps. lxxviii. 51, cv. 23, 27, cvi. 22). But this term was of more comprehensive import, as we find some ancient inhabitants of a region in the south of Judah, said to have come from Ham (1 Chro. iv. 40). Thirty primitive nations sprang from Ham. Of these, only four were immediate descendants.

(15) Kush has left traces of his name perhaps in the Caucasus, the Caspian, and the Cossaei of Khusistan. There is an allusion in Amos (ix. 7) to his migration to the land south of Egypt which bears his name. This name is preserved in Gheez, the name of the ancient language of the people, and some say even in Habesh. It is possible, that some of the Kushites went towards India. To Ethiopia, however, the name generally refers in Scripture. The Ethiopians were called by Homer (Odyss. I. 23), ἔσχατοι ἀνδρῶν, *remotest of men.*

(16) Mizraim is the ordinary name for Egypt in the Hebrew scriptures. The singular form, Mazor, is found in later books (2 Kings xix. 24; Is. xix. 6, xxxv. 25).

(17) Put has with one consent been placed beyond Egypt, in the north of the continent of Africa. He is mentioned along with Lubim as the helper of Nineveh (Nah. iii. 9), and with Kush, as forming part of the army of Neko (Jer. xlvi. 9). His descendants penetrated far westward. A river bearing the name of Phutes has been mentioned in Mauretania, and an inland country is designated by the name of Futa. The name may be preserved also in Buto, the capital of lower Egypt, on the Sebennytic mouth of the Nile.

(18) Kenaan settled in the country called after his name. There are some grounds for believing that this land was previously inhabited by Shemites, as the land was Shemitic. If so, the Kenaanites came in as intruders, and followed the language of their predecessors. But of this hereafter.

7. Kush had five sons and two grandsons, who were reckoned among the founders of nations. (19) *Seba* is associated with Kush (Is. xliii. 3, xlv. 14). Josephus (Ant. I. 6. 2, II. 10. 2) places him in Meroe, a country almost insulated by the Nile and its branches, the Astapus

(Blue Nile) and Astaboras (Atbarah). (20) *Havilah* occurs as the name of a country in the antediluvian times. The present Havilah may refer to a tribe in Africa, called Avalitae, lying south of Bab-el-mandeb, which corresponds very well with the situation of Kush and Seba. This nation, however, may also have a representative in the Χαυλοταῖοι of Strabo (xvi. 728), situated on the Persian Gulf, where some other Kushites were to be found. The fragments of this nation may have separated by migration, and left its name in both localities. (21) *Sabtah*, Josephus finds in the Astaborans of Ethiopia, others in Sabota, a town in southwest Arabia. (22) *Ramah* is traced in Rhegma on the southeast of Arabia. (23) *Sabteka* is the third name, beginning with the same syllable. Such names are frequent from the Persian Gulf to the coast of Africa. Some find this place on the coast of Abyssinia, others in Samydake on the east side of the Persian Gulf. From Ramah are two tribes descended, — (24) *Sheba*, and (25) Dedan, lying in the south of Arabia or on the Persian Gulf. Daden, an island in the gulf, now Barhein, may represent the latter.

8–12. In this episode the author turns aside from the table of nations to notice the origin of the first great empires that were established on the earth. *And Kush begat Nimrod.* The author had before enumerated the sons of Kush, who were heads of nations. Here he singles out one of his sons or descendants, who became the first potentate of whom we have any record. He notices his qualities for rising to this position among men. *He began to be a mighty one in the land. He was mighty in hunting, before the Lord.* Hunting is a comprehensive term, indicating the taking of any species of animal, whether of the air, the sea, or the land. Nimrod's distinction in this respect was so great as to become proverbial. The expression, "before the Lord," intimates, not merely that the Lord was cognizant of his proceedings, for he knoweth all things, but that Nimrod himself made no secret of his designs, pursued them with a bold front and a high hand, and at the same time was aware of the name and will of Jehovah. This defiant air gives a new character to his hunting, which seems to have extended even to man, as the term is sometimes so applied (1 Sam. xxiv. 12 [11], Jer. xvi. 16). His name, which literally means *we shall rebel*, is in keeping with the practice of an arbitrary and violent control over men's persons and property.

10. The beginning or first seat and the extent of his kingdom among men are then described. It consists of four towns, — *Babel and Erek and Akkad and Kalneh, in the land of Shinar.* The number four is

characteristic of Nimrod's kingdom. It is the mark of the four quarters of the earth, of universality in point of extent, and therefore of ambition. The site of Babel (Babylon) has been discovered in certain ruins near Hillah, chiefly on the opposite or eastern bank of the Euphrates, where there is a square mound called Babil by the natives. Erek has been traced also on the east bank of the Euphrates, about one hundred miles southeast of Babil, or half way between the city and the confluence of the rivers. It is the Orchoe of the Greeks, and the ruins now bear the name of Urka, or Warka. This name appears as Huruk on the cuneiform inscriptions of the place. Akkad, in the Sept. Archad, Col. Taylor finds in Akkerkoof, north of Babel, and about nine miles west of the Tigris, where it approaches the Euphrates. Here there is a hill or mound of ruins called Tel Nimrud. Rawlinson finds the name Akkad frequent in the inscriptions, and mentions Kingi Akkad as part of the kingdom of Urukh, but without identifying the site. Kalneh, Kalno, Isa. x. 9; Kanneh, Ezek. xxvii. 23, is regarded by Jerome, and the Targum of Jonathan, as the same with Ktesiphon on the Tigris, in the district of Chalonitis. Its ruins are near Takti Kesra. Rawlinson identifies it with Niffer, but without assigning satisfactory grounds. The sites of these towns fix that of Shinar, which is evidently the lower part of Mesopotamia, or, more precisely, the country west of the Tigris, and south of Is, or Hit, on the Euphrates, and Samara on the Tigris. It is otherwise called Babylonia and Chaldæa.

11, 12. *Out of that land came he forth to Asshur.* This may be otherwise rendered, "out of that land came forth Asshur." The probabilities in favor of the former translations are the following: 1st. The discourse relates to Nimrod. 2d. The words admit of it. 3d. The word Asshur has occurred hitherto only as the name of a country. 4th. Asshur, the person, was considerably older than Nimrod, and had probably given name to Asshur before Nimrod's projects began. 5th. Asshur would have been as great a man as Nimrod, if he had founded Nineveh and its contiguous towns; which does not appear from the text. 6th. *The beginning of his kingdom* implies the addition to it contained in these verses. 7th. And the phrases *in the land of Shinar, out of that land*, and the need of some definite locality for the second four cities, are in favor of the former rendering.

Asshur was a country intersected by the Tigris. It included the part of Mesopotamia north of Shinar, and the region between the Tigris and Mount Zagros. Its extension westward is undefined by any natural boundary, and seems to have varied at different times. *Nineveh* was a well-known city of antiquity, situated opposite Mosul on the Tigris. The country in which it was placed is called by Strabo Aturia, a variation seemingly of Asshur. Its remains are now marked by the names Nebbi-yunus and Koyunjik. *Rehoboth-ir*, the city broadway or market, has not been identified. Kelah is said to be now marked by the ruin called Nimrud. This lies on the left bank of the Tigris, near its confluence with the greater Zab. Its name seems to be preserved in the Calachene of Strabo. It was about twenty miles south of Nineveh. It is possible, however, so far as we can conjecture from conflicting authorities, that Kelah may be Kileh Sherghat, about fifty miles south of Mosul, on the right bank of the Tigris. Resen is placed by the text between Nineveh and Kelah, and is therefore probably represented by Selamiyeh, a village about half way between Koyunjik and Nimrud. If Kelah, however, be Kileh Sherghat, Resen will coincide with Nimrud. *That is the great city.* This refers most readily to Resen, and will suit very well if it be Nimrud, which was evidently extensive. It may, however, refer to Nineveh. This completion of Nimrod's kingdom, we see, contains also four cities. The Babylonian and Assyrian monarchies were akin in origin, and allied in their history and in their fall. They were too near each other to be independent, and their mutual jealousies at length brought about the ruin of the northern capital. A Kushite, and therefore a Hamite, founded this first world-monarchy or tyranny. Another Hamite power arose simultaneously in Egypt. A branch of the Kushites seem to have gone eastward, and spread over India. But another branch spread through the South of Arabia, and, crossing into Africa, came into contact, sometimes into alliance, and sometimes into collision with the Egyptian monarchy. The eastern empire is noticed particularly, because it intruded into Shemitic ground, and aimed continually at extending its sway over the nations descended from Shem.

13, 14. Mizraim has seven sons, from whom are derived eight nations. (26) The *Ludim* are probably mentioned in Isa. lxvi. 19, in connection with Tarshish and Put; in Jer. xlvi. 9, in connection with Kush and Put; and in Ezek. xxvii. 10, xxx. 5, in connection with Put. In all these instances the name is in the singular, but in our text in the plural, expressly denoting the nation of which Lud was the progenitor. The Ludim were distinguished for the use of the bow. They were, doubtless, an African tribe, related to the Egyptians, and well known to the prophets, though their country cannot now be pointed out. Josephus intimates that they were destroyed, as well as other tribes descended from Mizraim, in the Ethiopic war of the time of Moses; but they still existed in the times of Ezekiel. Movers finds them in the Lewatah, a tribe of Berbers. Others place them in Mauretania. Pliny mentions a river Laud in Tingitana.

(27) The *Anamim* are not elsewhere mentioned. (28) The *Lehabim* are generally identified with the Lubim (2 Chr. xii. 3, xvi. 8; Dan. ii. 43; Nah. iii. 9), who are introduced in connection with the Kushim. They are probably the Libyans, who lay to the west of Egypt, and, extending from the Mediterranean indefinitely to the south, came into contact with the Kushites of Abyssinia. (29) The Naphtuhim Bochart places in Nephthys, near Pelusium on the Lake Sirbonis. Others find a trace of them in Napata, a town of Meroe. This agrees with the indications of Josephus and the Targum of Jonathan.

(30) The *Pathrusim* have their place in Pathros, a name of upper Egypt or the Thebais. It is arranged by Isaiah (ii. 11) between Egypt and Kush. (31) The *Kasluhim* are supposed by some to be represented by the Colchians, whom Herodotus (ii. 104) traces to Egypt. It is possible the Colchians may have been a colony from them. But their original seat must have been somewhere on the coast of the Red Sea. *Out of whom came* (32) *Philistim.* The Philistines dwelt on the coast of the Mediterranean, from the border of Egypt to Joppa. They had five principal cities, — Gaza, Ashdod, Ashkelon, Gath, and Ekron. They gave the name פְּלֶשֶׁת *Pelesheth* to the whole of Kenaan, from which is derived the Greek name Παλαιστὶνη, Palaestina. They are stated by the text to be a colony or offshoot of the Kasluhim. (33) *Kaphtorim.* From Jer. xlvii. 4, it appears that Kaphtor was a coast-land. From Amos xi. 7, we learn that the Philistines came from this land. Hence we conclude that the Kaphtorim dwelt on the coast of the Red Sea, adjacent to the Kasluchim, and left their name, perhaps, in Koptos and Αἴγυπτος. Cappadocia, Crete, and Cyprus only slightly resemble the name, and have no other recommendation. The Kasluhim may have been their southern neighbors, and thus the Philistines may have occupied a part of Kaphtor, before their settlement on the coast of the Great Sea, within the borders of Kenaan, where they would, of course, be another tribe (ἀλλόφυλοι). This account of these descendants of Mizraim agrees best with the hint of Josephus, that many of them bordered on the Ethiopians; and perished, or perhaps were forced to migrate, in the Ethiopic or other wars (i. 6. 3). Thus it appears that the descendants of Mizraim were settled in Africa, with the exception of the

Philistines, who migrated into the country to which they gave their name.

15–19. From Kenaan are descended eleven nations. (34) *Zidon* is styled his first-born. The name is retained in the well-known town on the coast of Phœnicia, which is accordingly of the highest antiquity among the cities of that region. The Sidonians were reckoned coextensive with the Phœnicians, and are mentioned by Homer (Il. xxiii. 743; Od. iv. 618). (35) *Heth.* This tribe dwelt about Hebron and in the mountains around, and perhaps still further north in the districts extending towards the Euphrates (Gen. xxiii. 3; Num. xiii. 29; Jos. i. 4). Esau took wives from the Hittites (Gen. xxvi. 34, 35), and some part of the nation existed even after the captivity (Ezr. ix. 1).

(36) The *Jebusite* has his chief seat in and around Jerusalem, which was called Jebus, from his chief; and the citadel of which was wrested from him only in the time of David (2 Sam. v. 7). (37) The *Amorite* was one of the most important and extensive tribes of Kenaan. Five kings of this nation dwelt in the mountains afterwards occupied by Judah (Gen. xiv. 7, 13; Nu. xiii. 29; Jos. x. 5), and two on the east of the Jordon, in Heshbon and Bashan, north of Moab (Nu. xxi. 13; Deut. iv. 47). The eastern Amorites were conquered under Moses, the western under Joshua. A remnant of them were made bondsmen by Solomon (1 Ki. ix. 20). They survived the captivity (Ezr. ix. 1). (38) The *Girgashite* seems to have lain on the west of the Jordan, and the name may be preserved in the reading Γεργεσηνῶν, of Matt. viii. 28. The town of the Gergesenes is supposed to have been at the southeast of the lake of Gennesaret (Gen. xv. 21; Deut. vii. 1; Jos. xxiv. 11).

(39) The *Hivite* was found at Shalem, Gibeon, and also at the foot of Hermon and Antilibanus (Gen. xxxiv. 2; Jos. ix. 7, xi. 3; Judg. iii. 3). The former were also classed under the Amorites (Gen. xlviii. 22; 2 Sam. xxi. 2). With the exception of four cities of the Gibeonites, they were conquered by Joshua (ix. 17; xi. 3, 19). (40) The *Arkite* probably dwelt near a town called Arke or Caesarea Libani, lying some miles north of Tripolis, at the foot of Lebanon. Its ruins are still extant at Tel Arka. (41) The *Sinite* is supposed to have dwelt in Sinna, a town mentioned by Strabo, called Sine by Jerome, and Syn in the fifteenth century (Strab. xvi. 2, 18; Hieron. Quaest. in Gen., Breitenbach, Travels, p. 47), not far from Arke.

(42) The *Arvadite* dwelt in Arvad, Aradus, now Ruad, a Phœnician town on an island of the same name. (43) The *Zemarite* has

been traced in the town Σίμυρα, the ruins of which were found by Shaw at the western foot of Lebanon, under the name of Sumra. (44) The *Hamathite* was the inhabitant of Hamath, called Hamath Rabbah (the great), by the Greeks Epiphaneia, and at present Hamah. It is situated on the Orontes, and held an important place in the history of Israel. The land of Hamath was of great extent, including the town of Riblah (2 Kings xxv. 21) and reaching even to Antioch. The entrance of Hamath בּוֹא חֲמָת, the northern part of the valley between Lebanon and Antilibanus, formed the utmost boundary of Palestine to the north (Num. xiii. 21 ; Jos. xiii. 5 ; 1 Kings viii. 65). Its king was in alliance with David (2 Sam. viii. 10).

And afterwards were the families of the Kenaanites spread abroad. After the confusion of tongues were these nations formed ; and after the formation of these Kenaanic tribes occurred the dispersion spoken of in the text. We do not know what was the original seat of the Kenaanites ; or whether the dispersion here mentioned was violent or not. Its primary result, however, seems to have been their settlement in the country of which the boundaries are next described. It is not improbable that this land was allotted to a portion of the Shemites, and occupied by them when the Kenaanites entered and established themselves among them (Gen. xl. 15). The Kenaanites probably had the same grasping tendency which displayed itself in Nimrod, their kinsman ; and therefore seized upon the country with a high hand, and called it after their name. Their expulsion, on the conquest of the land by the Israelites, and their commercial activity, led to a still further dispersion ; as colonies were sent out by them to the distant shores of the Mediterranean, to Asia Minor, Greece, Africa, Spain, and even the British Isles. But it can scarcely be supposed that reference is here made to these subsequent events in their history.

19. The border of Kenaan, as here described, extends along the coast from Zidon in the direction of (as thou goest unto) Gerar, which lay between Kadesh and Shur (Gen. xx. 1), and has its name preserved in the Wady el-Jerur, which is nearly in a line connecting Ain el-Weibeh and Suez. It turns at Azzah (Gaza), and passes to the cities of the plain, of which the after-history is so memorable. Its terminating point is Lesha, which is generally supposed to be Callirrhoë, to the northeast of the Dead Sea, so called from the hot springs which form a stream flowing into the lake. It is possible, however, that Lesha is only another variation of Laish and Leshem, a

city belonging to the Sidonians, and situated near the sources of the Jordan. Thus we have the western, southern, and eastern border briefly given in this verse. It is manifest, however, that they did not confine themselves to these limits, but "afterward spread abroad" into the adjacent regions. The Hittite went to the northeast; the Amorite crossed the Jordan, and occupied a great part of Peraea; the Hivite, the Arkite, the Sinite, the Arvadite, the Zemarite, and the Hamathite stretched far north of the boundary.

20. The list of the Hamites is here summed up in the usual form. It appears that Ham occupied Africa and a certain portion of Asia along the eastern coast of the Mediterranean, in the south of Arabia, about the lower valley of the Frat and Diljah, and perhaps along the south of Asia. In extent of territory, Japheth ultimately far exceeded, as he occupied most of Asia and almost all of Europe and the New World. Ham is next to him, as he inherited Africa and a portion of Asia. Some of his descendants have also been forcibly transplanted to the New Hemisphere. But in point of political intercourse with Shem, Japheth, in early times, sinks comparatively into the shade, and Ham assumes the prominent place. Babylon, Kush, Egypt, and Kenaan are the powers which come into contact with Shem, in that central line of human history which is traced in the Bible. Hence it is that in the table of nations special attention is directed to Kush, Nimrod, Mizraim, and to the tribes and borders of Kenaan.

XXXIII. SHEM.— Gen. x. 21–32

21. עֵבֶר 'Eber, *yonder side;* v. *pass, cross.*

22. עֵילָם 'Elam. עוּל *suckle.* עָלַם *hide; be mature.* אַרְפַּכְשַׁד Arpakshad. אַרְךְּ כֶּשֶׂד *boundary of Kesed,* or (von-Bohlen) Arjapakshatâ, *beside Aria.* אֲרָם Aram, *high;* v. *be high.*

23. עוּץ 'Uts; v. *counsel; be firm, solid.* חוּל Chul; v. *rub, twist, writhe, be strong, await.* גֶּתֶר Gether, *bridge?* מַשׁ Mash; r. *feel, touch.*

24. שֶׁלַח Shelach, *missile, shoot.*

25. פֶּלֶג Peleg; n. *brook, canal;* v. *divide.* יָקְטָן Joctan, *small.*

26. אַלְמוֹדָד Almodad. לָמַד *learn.* מָדַד *measure.* שֶׁלֶף Sheleph; v. *draw out* or *off.* חֲצַרְמָוֶת Chatsarmaveth, *court of death.* יֶרַח Jerach, *moon, month.*

27. הֲדוֹרָם Hadoram, *majesty, beauty;* v. *swell, honor.* אוּזָל Uzal; v. *go out* or *away.* דִּקְלָה Diclah, *palm.*

28. עוֹבָל 'Obal, *bare, bald.* אֲבִימָאֵל Abimael, *father of Mael* (*circumcision*).

29. אוֹפִיר Ophir; v. *break, veil.* יוֹבָב Jobab; v. *cry, call.*

30. מֵשָׁא Mesha, שָׁאָה = שׁוֹא *roar, crash.* סְפָר Sephar, *counting, writing.*

21. And to Shem was born issue, even to him, the father of all the sons of Heber, the elder brother of Japheth. 22. The sons of Shem: Elam and Asshur and Arpakshad and Lud and Aram. 23. And the sons of Aram: Uz and Hul and Gether and Mash. 24. And Arpakshad begat Shelah; and Shelah begat Heber. 25. And to Heber were born two sons: the name of the one was Peleg, for in his days was the land divided; and his brother's name was Joctan. 26. And Joctan begat Almodad and Sheleph and Hazarmaveth and Jerah, 27. And Hadoram and Uzal and Diclah, 28. And Obal and Abimael and Sheba, 29. And Ophir and Havilah and Jobab: all these were the sons of Joctan. 30. And their dwelling was from Mesha as thou goest unto Sephar, a mount of the east. 31. These are the sons of Shem after their families, after their tongues, in their lands, after their nations. 32. These are the families of the sons of Noah, after their generations, in their nations: and by these were the nations divided in the land after the flood. ¶ 14.

From Japheth, who penetrated into the remotest regions, the writer proceeds to Ham, who came into close contact with Shem. From Ham he passes to Shem, in whom the line of history is to be continued.

21. Shem is here distinguished by two characteristics — the former referring to a subsequent, the latter to an antecedent event. He is *the father of all the sons of Heber.* It is evident from this that the sons of Heber cast lustre on the family of Shem, and therefore on the whole human race. It is unnecessary to anticipate the narrative, except so far as to note that the sons of Heber include most of the Arabians, a

portion of those who mingled with the race and inhabited the land of Aram, and, most probably, the original element of the population in the land of Kenaan. This characteristic of Ṣhem shows that the table in which it is found was composed after the Hebrews had become conspicuous among the descendants of Shem.

Shem is next distinguished as the *elder brother of Japheth;* that is, older than Ham. This interpretation of the words is most agreeable to the Hebrew idiom, and is the only one which affords an important sense. That Shem was the second son appears from the facts that Ham was the youngest (Gen. ix. 24), that Shem was born in the five hundred and third year of Noah (Gen. xi. 10), and, therefore, Japheth must have been the one born when Noah was in his five hundredth year (Gen. v. 32). The reason for inserting this statement is to prevent the order in which the brothers are introduced in the pedigree from being taken as that of their age, instead of that of the historical relationship subsisting among the nations descended from them.

22. Twenty-six of the primitive nations are descended from Shem, of which five are immediate. (45) ELAM was settled in a part of the modern Persia, to which he gave name. This name seems to be preserved in Elymais, a province of that country bordering on the Dijlah, and now included in Khusistan. It was early governed by its own kings (Gen. xiv. 1), and continued to occupy a distinct place among the nations in the time of the later prophets (Isa. xxii. 6; Jer. xlix. 34; Eze. xxxii. 24). Its capital was Shushan or Susa (Dan. viii. 2), now Shuster.

(46) ASSHUR seems to have originally occupied a district of Mesopotamia, which was bounded on the east by the Tigris (Gen. ii. 14). The inviting plains and slopes on the east of the Tigris would soon occasion a migration of part of the nation across that river. It is possible there may have been an ancient Asshur occupying the same region even before the flood (Gen. ii. 14).

(47) ARPAKSHAD is traced in Ἀῤῥαπαχῖτις, Arrhapachitis, a region in the north of Assyria. V. Bohlen and Benfey identify it with Ariapakshata, denoting a country beside Aria. Gesenius renders it border or stronghold of the Kasdim; but the components of the word are uncertain. The nations descended from Arpakshad are noted at the close on account of their late origin, as well as their import for the subsequent narrative.

(48) LUD is usually identified with the Lydians, Λυδοὶ, who by migration at length reached and gave their name to a part of the west coast of Asia Minor.

(49) Aram gave name to the upper parts of Mesopotamia and the parts of Syria north of Palestine. Hence we read of Aram Naharaim (of the two rivers), Aram Dammesek (of Damascus), Aram Maakah on the southwest border of Damascus, about the sources of the Jordan, Aram Beth Rechob in the same neighborhood, and Aram Zoba to the north of Damascus. The name is perhaps varied in the Ἄριμοι of Homer (Il. ii. 783) and Strabo (xiii. 4. 6). From Aram are descended four later nations.

23. (50) *Uz* (Ἀυσῖτις, LXX.) is the chief of a people having their seat in the north of Arabia Deserta, between Palestine and the Euphrates. From this Uz it is possible that the sons of Nahor and of Seir (Gen. xxii. 21; xxxvi. 28) obtained their name. Job dwelt in this land. (51) *Hul* is supposed to have his settlement about the sources of the Jordan in Huleh. Others trace this nation in the Hylatae (Plin. v. 19) near Emesa. (52) *Gether* is of uncertain position, probably in Arabia. (53) *Mash* may have left a trace of his name in Mons Masius, Karajah Dagh, south of Diarbekir, and perhaps also in the Mysians and Mœsians, who may have wandered westward from under this mountain.

24. Arpakshad begat (54) *Shelah*. We know nothing of the nation of which he was the founder. He begat (55) *Heber*. He is the progenitor of the Hebrews, the race to which Abraham belonged. He is marked out very prominently for reasons partly unknown to us at this distance of time, but partly no doubt because he was the ancestor of the chosen race who immediately preceded the confusion of tongues, and to whom belonged that generic Hebrew tongue, which afterwards branched into several dialects, of which the Hebrew, now strictly so called, was one. It is probable that most of the diversified modes of speech retained the substance of the primeval speech of mankind. And it is not improbable, for various reasons, that this Hebrew tongue, taken in its largest sense, deviated less from the original standard than any other. The Shemites, and especially the Hebrews, departed less from the knowledge of the true God than the other families of man, and, therefore, may be presumed to have suffered less from the concussion given to the living speech of the race. The knowledge previously accumulated of the true God, and of his will and way, would have been lost, if the terms and other modes of expressing divine things had been entirely obliterated. It is consonant with reason, then, to suppose that some one language was so little shaken from its primary structure as to preserve this knowledge. We know as a fact, that, while other nations retained some faint traces of the primeval history, the

Hebrews have handed down certain and tangible information concerning former things in a consecutive order from the very first. This is a proof positive that they had the distinct outline and material substance of the primeval tongue in which these things were originally expressed. In keeping with this line of reasoning, while distinct from it, is the fact that the names of persons and things are given and explained in the Hebrew tongue, and most of them in that branch of it in which the Old Testament is composed. We do not enter further into the peculiar nature of the Hebrew family of languages, or the relationship in which they are found to stand with the other forms of human speech than to intimate that such investigations tend to confirm the conclusions here enunciated.

25. This nation was very extensive, and accordingly branched out into several, of which the immediate ones are Peleg and Joctan. (56) *Peleg* is remarkable on account of the origin assigned to his name. *In his days was the land divided.* Here two questions occur. What is the meaning of the earth being divided, and what is the time denoted by *his days?* The verb *divide* (פָּלַג) occurs only three times elsewhere in the Hebrew scriptures (1 Chron. i. 19; Job xxxviii. 25; Ps. lv. 10). The connection in which this rare word is used in the Psalm, "divide their tongues," seems to determine its reference in the present passage to the confusion of tongues and consequent dispersion of mankind recorded in the following chapter. This affords a probable answer to our first question. The land was in his days divided among the representative heads of the various nations. But to what point of time are we directed by the phrase *in his days?* Was the land divided at his birth, or some subsequent period of his life? The latter is possible, as Jacob and Gideon received new names, and Joshua an altered name, in after-life. The phrase *in his days* seems to look the same way. And the short interval from the deluge to his birth appears scarcely to suffice for such an increase of the human family as to allow of a separation into nations. Yet, on the other hand, it is hard to find any event in after-life which connected this individual more than any other with the dispersion of man. It is customary to give the name at birth. The phrase *in his days* may, without any straining, refer to this period. And if we suppose, at a time when there were only a few families on the earth, an average increase of ten children in each in four generations, we shall have a thousand, or twelve hundred full-grown persons, and, therefore, may have five hundred families at the birth of Peleg. We cannot suppose more than fifty-five nations distin-

guished from one another at the dispersion, as Heber is the fifty-fifth name, and all the others are descended from him. And if three families were sufficient to propagate the race after the flood, nine or ten were enough to constitute a primeval tribe or nation. We see some reason, therefore, to take the birth of Peleg as the occasion on which he received his name, and no stringent reason for fixing upon any later date. At all events the question seems to be of no chronological importance, as in any case only four generations preceded Peleg, and these might have been of comparatively longer or shorter duration without materially affecting the number of mankind at the time of his birth. Peleg is also remarkable as the head of that nation out of which, at an after period, the peculiar people of God sprang. Of the Palgites, as a whole, we hear little or nothing further in history.

(57) *Joctan*, if little or insignificant as an individual or a nation, is the progenitor of a large group of tribes, finding their place among the wandering races included afterwards under the name Arab. Cachtan, as the Arabs designate him in their traditions, may have given name to Cachtan, a town and province mentioned by Niebuhr.

26–29. The thirteen tribes of the Joctanites or primitive Arabs are here enumerated. (58) *Almodad* is usually referred to Yemen. The first syllable may be the Arabic article. Mudad is the name of one celebrated in Arab story as the stepfather of Ishmael and chief of the Jurhum tribe of Joctanites. The Ἀλλουμαιῶται of Ptolemy belonged to the interior of Arabia Felix. (59) *Sheleph* is traced in the Σαλαπηνοὶ of Ptolemy (6. 7), belonging to the interior. (60) *Hazarmaveth* gives name to a district on the Indian Ocean, abounding in spices, now called Hadramaut. This tribe is the Chatramitae of Greek writers. (61) *Jerah* occupied a district where are the coast and mountain of the moon, near Hadramaut. (62) *Hadoram* is preserved in the tribe called Ἀδραμῖται Atramitae, placed by Pliny (6. 28) between the Homerites and the Sachalites on the south coast of Arabia. (63) *Uzal* perhaps gave the ancient name of Azal to Sana, the capital of Yemen, a place still celebrated for the manufacture of beautiful stuffs. (64) *Diclah* settled possibly in the palm-bearing region of the Minaei in Hejaz. (65) *Obal* is otherwise unknown. (66) *Abimael* is equally obscure. Bochart supposes there is a trace of the name in Μάλι, a place in Arabia Aromatifera. (67) *Sheba* is the progenitor of the Sabaei in Arabia Felix, celebrated for spices, gold, and precious stones, and noted for the prosperity arising from traffic in these commodities. A queen of Sheba visited Solomon. The dominant family among the Sabæans was that of Himjar, from whom the Himjarites (Homeritæ) of a later period descended.

(68) *Ophir* gave name to a country celebrated for gold, precious stones, and almug wood, which seems to have lain on the south side of Arabia, where these products may be found. What kind of tree the almug is has not been clearly ascertained. Some suppose it to be the sandal wood which grows in Persia and India; others, a species of pine. If this wood was not native, it may have been imported from more distant countries to Ophir, which was evidently a great emporium. Others, however, have supposed Ophir to be in India, or Eastern Africa. The chief argument for a more distant locality arises from the supposed three years' voyage to it from Ezion-geber, and the products obtained in the country so reached. But the three years' voyage (1 Kings x. 22; 2 Chron. ix. 21) seems to be in reality to Tarshish, a very different region.

(69) *Havilah* here is the founder of a Joctanite tribe of Arabs, and therefore his territory must be sought somewhere in the extensive country which was occupied by these wandering tribes. A trace of the name is probably preserved in Khawlan, a district lying in the northwest of Yemen, between Sana and Mecca, though the tribe may have originally settled or extended further north. (70) *Jobab* has been compared with the Ἰωβαρῖται of Ptolemy (6. 7). Bochart finds the name in the Arabic *yobab*, a desert.

29. The situation of Mesha is uncertain. But it is obviously the western boundary of the settlement, and may have been in the neighborhood of Mecca and Medina. Sephar is perhaps the Arabic Zaphari, called by the natives Isfor, a town on the south coast near Mirbat. It seems, however, to be, in the present passage, the "mount of the east" itself, a thuriferous range of hills, adjacent, it may be, to the seaport so-called. Gesenius and others fix upon Mesene, an island at the head of the Persian Gulf, as the Mesha of the text. But this island may have had no existence at the time of the Joctanite settlement. These boundaries include the greater part of the west and south coast of the peninsula, and are therefore sufficient to embrace the provinces of Hejaz (in part), Yemen, and Hadramaut, and afford space for the settlements of the thirteen sons of Joctan. The limits thus marked out determine that all these settlers, Ophir among the rest, were at first to be found in Arabia, how far soever they may have wandered from it afterwards.

31, 32. The first of these verses contains the usual closing formula for the pedigree of the Shemite tribes ; and the second, the corresponding form for the whole table of nations.

From a review of these lands it is evident that Shem occupied a much smaller extent of territory than either of his brothers. The mountains beyond the Tigris, the Persian Gulf, the Red Sea, the Levant, the Archipelago, and the Black Sea, bound the countries that were in part peopled by Shem. Arabia, Syria, and Assyria contained the great bulk of the Shemites, intermingled with some of the Hamites. The Kushites, Kenaanites, and Philistines trench upon their ground. The rest of the Hamites peopled Africa, and such countries as were supplied from it. The Japhethites spread over all the rest of the world.

In this table there are seventy names, exclusive of Nimrod, of heads of families, tribes, or nations descended from the three sons of Noah, —fourteen from Japheth, thirty from Ham, and twenty-six from Shem. Among the heads of tribes descended from Japheth are seven grandsons. Among those from Ham are twenty-three grandsons and three great-grandsons. Among those of Shem are five grandsons, one great-grandson, two of the fourth generation, and thirteen of the fifth. Whence it appears that the subdivisions are traced further in Ham and much further in Shem than in Japheth, and that they are pursued only in those lines which are of importance for the coming events in the history of Shem.

It is to be observed, also, that, though the different races are distinguished by the diversity of tongues, yet the different languages are much less numerous than the tribes. The eleven tribes of Kenaanites, and the thirteen tribes of Joctanites, making allowance for some tribal peculiarities, most probably spoke at first only two dialects of one family of languages, which we have designated the Hebrew, itself a branch of, if not identical with, what is commonly called the Shemitic. Hence some Hamites spoke the language of Shem. A similar community of language may have occurred in some other instances of diversity of descent.

XXXIV. THE CONFUSION OF TONGUES.—Gen. xi. 1-9.

1. נָסַע *pluck out, break up, journey.* מִקֶּדֶם *eastward,* or on the east side, as in Gen. ii. 14, xiii. 11; Isaiah ix. 11 (12).

6. הַחִלָּם *their beginning,* for הֵחִלָּם the regular form of this infinitive with a suffix. יָזְמוּ as if from יָזַם = זָמַם.

7. נָבְלָה usually said to be for נָבֹלָּה from בָּלַל; but evidently designed by the punctuator to be the thrid sing. fem. perf. of נָבַל *to be confounded,* having for its subject שָׂפָה, "and there let their lip be confounded." The two verbs have the same root.

9. בָּבֶל Babel, *confusion,* derived from בל the common root of בָּלַל and נָבַל, by doubling the first radical.

XI. 1. And the whole land was of one lip, and one stock
of words. 2. And it came to pass, as they journeyed eastward,
that they found a plain in the land of Shinar; and they dwelt
there. 3. And they said one to another, Go to, let us make
brick, and burn them thoroughly. And they had brick for
stone, and asphalt had they for mortar. 4. And they said, Go
to, let us build us a city, and a tower whose top may be in
the sky, and let us make us a name; lest we be scattered
abroad upon the face of the whole land. 5. And the LORD
came down to see the city and the tower, which the sons of
man had builded. 6. And the LORD said, Behold, the people
is one, and they have all one lip, and this they have begun to
do; and now nothing will be restrained from them, which
they have imagined to do. 7. Go to, let us go down, and there
confound their lip, that they may not understand one another's lip. 8. And the LORD scattered them abroad thence
upon the face of all the land; and they left off to build the
city. 9. Therefore was the name of it called Babel, because
the LORD had there confounded the lip of all the land; and
thence had the LORD scattered them abroad upon the face of
all the land. ¶ 15.

Having completed the table of nations, the sacred writer, according to his wont, goes back to record an event of great moment, both for the explanation of this table and for the future history of the human race. The point to which he reverts is the birth of Peleg. The present singular passage explains the nature of that unprecedented change by which mankind passed from one family with a mutually intelligible speech, into many nations of diverse tongues and lands.

1. The previous state of human language is here briefly described. *The whole land* evidently means the whole then known world with all its human inhabitants. The universality of application is clearly and constantly maintained throughout the whole passage. "Behold, *the people* is one." And the close is on this point in keeping with the commencement. "Therefore was the name of it called Babel, because the Lord had there confounded the lip *of all the land*."

Of one lip, and one stock of words. In the table of nations the term "tongue" was used to signify what is here expressed by two terms. This is not undesigned. The two terms are not synonymous or parallel, as they form the parts of one compound predicate. "One stock of words," then, we conceive, naturally indicates the matter, the substance, or material of language. This was one and the same to the whole race. The term "lip," which is properly one of the organs of articulation, is, on the other hand, used to denote the form, that is, the manner, of speaking; the mode of using and connecting the matter of speech; the system of laws by which the inflections and derivations of a language are conducted. This also was one throughout the human family. Thus the sacred writer has expressed the unity of language among mankind, not by a single term as before, but, with a view to his present purpose, by a combination of terms expressing the two elements which go to constitute every organic reality.

2–4. The occasion of the lingual change about to be described is here narrated. *As they journeyed eastward.* The word "they" refers to the whole land of the previous verse, which is put by a common figure for the whole race of man. "Eastward" is proved to be the meaning of the phrase מִקֶּדֶם by Gen. xiii. 11, where Lot is said to journey (מִקֶּדֶם) from Bethel to the plain of the Jordan, which is to the east. The human race, consisting it might be of five hundred families, journeys eastward, with a few points of deflection to the south, along the Euphrates valley, and comes to a plain of surpassing fertility in the land of Shinar (Herod. i. 178, 193). A determination to make a permanent abode in this productive spot is immediately formed.

3, 4. A building is to be erected of brick and asphalt. The Babylonian soil is still celebrated for these architectural materials. There is here a fine clay, mingled with sand, forming the very best material for brick, while stones are not to be found at a convenient distance. Asphalt is found boiling up from the soil in the neighborhood of Babylon and of the Dead Sea, which is hence called the *lacus Asphaltites.* The asphalt springs of Is or Hit on the Euphrates are celebrated by many writers. *Burn them thoroughly.* Sun-dried bricks are very much used in the East for building purposes. These, however, were to be burned, and thereby rendered more durable. *Brick for stone.* This indicates a writer belonging to a country and an age in which stone buildings were familiar, and therefore not to Babylonia. Brick-making was well-known to Moses in Egypt; but this country also abounds in quarries and splendid erections of stone, and the Sinaitic peninsula is a mass of granitic hills. The Shemites mostly inhabited countries abounding in stone. *Asphalt for mortar.* Asphalt is a mineral pitch. The word rendered *mortar* means at first clay, and then any kind of cement.

4. The purpose of their hearts is now more fully expressed. *Let us build us a city, and a tower whose top may be in the skies.* A city is a fortified enclosure or keep for defence against the violence of the brute creation. A tower whose top may be in the skies for escape from the possibility of a periodical deluge. This is the language of pride in man, who wishes to know nothing above himself, and to rise beyond the reach of an over-ruling Providence. *And let us make us a name.* A name indicates distinction and preëminence. To make us a name, then, is not so much the cry of the multitude as of the few, with Nimrod at their head, who alone could expect that which is not common, but distinctive. It is here artfully inserted, however, in the popular exclamation, as the people are prone to imagine the glory even of the despot to be reflected on themselves. This gives the character of a lurking desire for empire and self-aggrandizement to the design of the leaders, — a new form of the same selfish spirit which animated the antediluvian men of name (Gen. vi. 4). But despotism for the few or the one, implies slavery and all its unnumbered ills for the many. *Lest we be scattered abroad upon the face of the whole land.* The varied instincts of their common nature here speak forth. The social bond, the tie of kinsmanship, the wish for personal safety, the desire to be independent, perhaps even of God, the thirst for absolute power, all plead for union; but it is union for selfish ends.

5–7. These verses describe the nature of that change by which this form of human selfishness is to be checked. 5. *The Lord came down.* The interposing providence of God is here set forth in a sublime simplicity, suited to the early mind of man. Still there is something here characteristic of the times after the deluge. The presence of the Lord seems not to have been withdrawn from the earth before that event. He walked in the garden when Adam and Eve were there. He placed the ministers and symbols of his presence before it when they were expelled. He expostulated with Cain before and after his awful crime. He said, "My Spirit shall not always strive with man." He *saw* the wickedness of man; and the land was corrupt *before him.* He communicated with Noah in various ways, and finally established his covenant with him. In all this he seems to have been present with man on earth. He lingered in the garden as long as his forbearance could be expected to influence man for good. He at length appointed the limit of a hundred and twenty years. And after watching over Noah during the deluge, he seems to have withdrawn his visible and gracious presence from the earth. Hence the propriety of the phrase, "the Lord came down." He still deals in mercy with a remnant of the human race, and has visited the earth and manifested his presence in a wondrous way. But he has not yet taken up his abode among men as he did in the garden, and as he intimates that he will sometime do on the renovated earth.

6. In like simplicity is depicted the self-willed, god-defying spirit of combination and ambition which had now budded in the imagination of man. *The people is one,* — one race, with one purpose. *And they have all one lip.* They understand one another's mind. No misunderstanding has arisen from diversity of language. *This is their beginning.* The beginning of sin, like that of strife, is as when one letteth out water. The Lord sees in this commencement the seed of growing evil. All sin is dim and small in its first rise; but it swells by insensible degrees to the most glaring and gigantic proportions. *And now nothing will be restrained from them, which they have imagined to do.* Now that they have made this notable beginning of concentration, ambition, and renown, there is nothing in this way which they will not imagine or attempt.

7. Here is announced the means by which the defiant spirit of concentration is to be defeated. From this and the previous verse we learn that the lip, and not the stock of words, is the part of language which is to be affected, and hence perceive the propriety of distin-

guishing these two in the introductory statement. To confound, is to introduce several kinds, where before there was only one; and so in the present case to introduce several varieties of form, whereas language was before of one form. Hence it appears that the one primitive tongue was made manifold by diversifying the law of structure, without interfering with the material of which it was composed. The bases or roots of words are furnished by instinctive and evanescent analogies between sounds and things, on which the etymological law then plays its part, and so vocables come into existence. Thus from the root *fer*, we get *fer*, *ferre*, *ferens*, *fert*, *ferebat*, *feret*, *ferat*, *ferret*; φέρε, φέρειν, φέρων, φέρει, ἔφερε, φέρῃ, φέροι, etc.; פָּרָה, פֹּרֶה, פָּרֹה פְּרֵה, יִפְרֶה, etc., according to the formative law of each language. It is evident that some roots may become obsolete and so die out, while others, according to the exigencies of communication and the abilities of the speaker, may be called into existence in great abundance. But whatever new words come into the stock, are made to comply with the formative law which regulates the language of the speaker. This law has been fixed as the habitude of his mind, from which he only deviates on learning and imitating some of the formative processes of another tongue. In the absence of any other language, it is not conceivable that he should on any account alter this law. To do so would be to rebel against habit without reason, and to put himself out of relation with the other speakers of the only known tongue.

The sacred writer does not care to distinguish the ordinary from the extraordinary in the procedure of Divine Providence, inasmuch as he ascribes all events to the one creating, superintending, and administering power of God. Yet there is something beyond nature here. We can understand and observe the introduction of new words into the vocabulary of man as often as the necessity of designating a new object or process calls the naming faculty into exercise. But the new word, whether a root or not, if engrafted into the language, invariably obeys the formative law of the speech into which it is admitted. A nation adds new words to its vocabulary, but does not of itself, without external influence, alter the principle on which they are formed. Here, then, the divine interference was necessary, if the uniform was ever to become multiform. And accordingly this is the very point in which the historian marks the interposition of the Almighty.

Philologists have distinguished three or four great types or families of languages. The first of these was the Shemitic or Hebrew family. It is probable that most of the Shemites spoke dialects of this well-defined type of human speech. Aram (the Syrians), Arpakshad, (the Hebrews and Arabs), and Asshur (the Assyrians), certainly did so. Elam (Elymais), succumbed first to the Kushite race (Κίσσιοι, Κοσσαῖοι) and afterwards to the Persian, and so lost its language and its individuality among the nations. Lud (the Lydians) was also overrun by other nationalities. But this type of language was extended beyond the Shemites to the Kenaanites and perhaps some other Hamites. It includes the language of the Old Testament.

The second family of languages has been variously designated Japhetic, Indo-Germanic, Indo-European and Arian. It is spoken by the great bulk of the descendants of Japheth, and embraces a series of cognate modes of communication, extending from India to the various European colonies of America. It includes Greek, the tongue of the New Testament.

A third class, including the Kushite (Babylonian), Egyptian, and other African languages, has been termed Hamitic. Some of its stocks have affinities both with the Shemitic and Japhetic families.

It is probable that the congeries of unclassed languages (Allophylian, Sporadic, Turanian), including even the Chinese tongues, have relations more or less intimate with one or other of these three tolerably definite families. But the science of comparative philology is only approaching the solution of its final problem, the historical or natural relationship of all the languages of the world. It is evident, however, that the principle of classification is not so much the amount of roots in common, as the absence or presence of a given form. The diversity in the matter may be brought about by assignable natural causes; but the diversity in the form can only arise from a preternatural impulse. Forms may wear off; but they do not pass from one constituent law to another without foreign influence. The speech of a strong and numerous race may gradually overbear and annihilate that of a weak one; and in doing so may adopt many of its words, but by no means its form. So long as a national speech retains any of its forms, they continue to be part of that special type by which it is characterized.

Hence we perceive that the interposition of Providence in confounding the lip of mankind, is the historical solution of the enigma of philology; the existence of diversity of language at the same time with the natural persistency of form and the historical unity of the human race. The data of philology, indicating that the form is the side of language needing to be touched in order to produce diversity, coincide also with the facts here narrated. The preternatural diversification of the form, moreover, marks the order amid variety which prevailed in this great revolution of mental habitude. It is not necessary to suppose that seventy languages were produced from one at the very crisis of this remarkable change, but only the few generic forms that sufficed to effect the divine purpose, and by their interaction to give origin to all subsequent varieties of language or dialect. Nor are we to imagine that the variant principles of formation went into practical development all at once, but only that they started a process which, in combination with other operative causes, issued in all the diversities of speech which are now exhibited in the human race.

That they may not understand one another's lip. This is the immediate result of diversifying the formative law of human speech, even though the material elements were to remain much the same as before. Further results will soon appear.

8, 9. The effect of the divine interposition is here noted. *And the Lord scattered them abroad.* Not understanding one another's mode of speech, they feel themselves practically separated from one another. Unity of counsel and of action becomes impossible. Misunderstanding naturally follows, and begets mistrust. Diversity of interest grows up, and separation ensues. Those who have a common speech retreat from the centre of union to a sequestered spot, where they may form a separate community among themselves. The want of pasture for their flocks and provision for themselves leads to a progressive migration. Thus the divine purpose, that they should be fruitful and multiply and replenish the land (Gen. ix. 1) is fulfilled. The dispersion of mankind at the same time put an end to the ambitious projects of the few. *They left off to build the city.* It is probable that the people began to see through the plausible veil which the leaders had cast over their selfish ends. The city would henceforth be abandoned to the immediate party of Nimrod. This would interrupt for a time the building of the city. Its dwellings would probably be even too numerous for its remaining inhabitants. The city received the name of Babel (confusion), from the remarkable event which had interrupted its progress for a time.

This passage, then, explains the table of nations, in which they are said to be distinguished, not merely by birth and land, but "every one after his tongue." It is therefore attached to the table as a needful appendix, and thus completes the history of the nations so far as it is carried on by the Bible. At this point the line of history leaves the universal, and by a rapid contraction narrows itself into the individual, in the person of him who is to be ultimately the parent of a chosen seed, in which the knowledge of God and of his truth is to be preserved, amidst the degeneracy of the nations into the ignorance and error which are the natural offspring of sin.

Here, accordingly, ends the appendix to the second Bible, or the second volume of the revelation of God to man. As the first may have been due to Adam, the second may be ascribed in point of matter to Noah, with Shem as his continuator. The two joined together belong not to a peculiar people, but to the universal race. If they had ever appeared in a written form before Moses, they might have descended to the Gentiles as well as to the Israelites. But the want of interest in holy things would account for their disappearance among the former. The speakers of the primitive language, however, would alone retain the knowledge of such a book if extant. Some of its contents might be preserved in the memory, and handed down to the posterity of the founders of the primeval nations. Accordingly we find more or less distinct traces of the true God, the creation, the fall and the deluge, in the traditions of all nations that have an ancient history.

But even if this two-volumed Bible were not possessed by the nations in a written form, its presence here, at the head of the writings of divine truth, marks the catholic design of the Old Testament, and intimates the comprehension of the whole family of man within the merciful purposes of the Almighty. In the issues of Providence the nations appear now to be abandoned to their own devices. Such a judicial forsaking of a race, who had a second time heard the proclamation of his mercy, and a second time forsaken the God of their fathers, was naturally to be expected. But it is never to be forgotten that God twice revealed his mercy *to the whole human race* before they were left to their own ways. And even when they were given over to their own wilful unrighteousness and ungodliness, it was only to institute and develop the mystery by which they might be again fully and effectually brought back to reconciliation with God.

The new developments of sin during this period are chiefly three, — drunkenness, dishonoring of a parent, and the ambitious attempt to be independent of God's power, and to thwart his purpose of peopling the land. These forms of human selfishness still linger about the primary commands of the two tables. Insubordination to the supreme authority of God is accompanied with disrespect to parental authority. Drunkenness itself is an abuse of the free grant of the fruit of the trees originally made to man. These manifestations of sin do not advance to the grosser or more subtle depths of iniquity afterwards explicitly forbidden in the ten commandments. They indicate a people still comparatively unsophisticated in their habits.

The additional motives brought to bear on the race of man during the interval from Noah to Abraham, are the preaching of Noah, the perdition of the unbelieving antediluvians, the preservation of Noah and his family, the distinction of clean and unclean animals, the permission to partake of animal food, the special prohibition of the shedding of man's blood, the institution thereupon of civil government, and the covenant with Noah and his seed that there should not be another deluge.

The preaching of Noah consisted in pressing the invitations and warnings of divine mercy on a wicked race. But it bore with new power on the succeeding generations, when it was verified by the drowning of the impenitent race and the saving of the godly household. This was an awful demonstration at the same time of the divine vengeance on those who persisted in sin, and of the divine mercy to the humble and the penitent. The distinction of the clean and the unclean was a special warning against that conformity with the world by which the sons of God had died out of the human race. The permission to partake of animal food was in harmony with the physical constitution of man, and seems to have been delayed till this epoch for moral as well as physical reasons. In the garden, and afterwards in Eden, the vegetable products of the soil were adequate to the healthy sustenance of man. But in the universal diffusion of the human race, animal food becomes necessary. In some regions where man has settled, this alone is available for a great portion of the year, if not for the whole. And a salutary dread of death, as the express penalty of disobedience, was a needful lesson in the infancy of the human race. But the overwhelming destruction of the doomed race was sufficient to impress this lesson indelibly on the minds of the survivors. Hence the permission of animal food might now be safely given, especially when accompanied with the express prohibition of manslaying, under the penalty of death by the hands of the executioner. This prohibition was directly intended to counteract the bad example of Cain and Lamek, and to deter those who slew animals from slaying men; and provision was made for the enforcement of its penalty by the institution of civil government. The covenant with Noah was a recognition of the race being reconciled to God in its new head, and therefore fitted to be treated as a party at peace with God, and to enter on terms of communion with him. Its promise of security from destruction by a flood was a pledge of all greater and after blessings which naturally flow from amity with God.

Thus we perceive that the revelation of God to the antediluvian world was confirmed in many respects, and enlarged in others, by that made to the postdiluvians. The stupendous events of the deluge were a marvellous confirmation of the justice and mercy of God revealed to Adam. The preaching of Noah was a new mode of urging the truths of God on the minds of men, now somewhat exercised in reflective thought. The distinction of clean and unclean enforced the distinction that really exists between the godly and the ungodly. The prohibition of shedding human blood is the growth of a specific law out of the great principle of moral rectitude in the conscience, apace with the development of evil in the conduct of men. The covenant with Noah is the evolution into articulate utterance of that federal relation which was virtually formed with believing and repentant Adam. Adam himself was long silent in the depth of his self-abasement for the disobedience he had exhibited. In Noah the spirit of adoption had attained to liberty of speech, and accordingly, God, on the momentous occasion of his coming out of the ark and presenting his propitiatory and eucharistic offering, enters into a covenant of peace with him, assuring him of certain blessings.

There is something specially interesting in this covenant with Noah, as it embraces the whole human race, and is in force to this day. It is as truly a covenant of grace as that with Abraham. It is virtually the same covenant, only in an earlier and less developed form. Being made with Noah, who had found grace in the eyes of the Lord, and added to the former expression of the divine favor to man, it explicitly mentions a benefit which is merely the first and most palpable of the series of benefits, temporal and eternal, flowing from the grace of God, all of which are in due time made over to the heirs of salvation. We cannot tell how many of the Gentiles explicitly or implicitly consented to this general covenant and partook of its blessings. But it is only just to the God of Noah to be thankful that there was and is an offer of mercy to the whole family of man, all who accept of which are partakers of his grace, and that all subsequent covenants only help to the ultimate and universal acceptance of that fundamental covenant which, though violated by Adam and all his ordinary descendants, was yet in the fulness of time to be implemented by him who became the seed of the woman and the second Adam.

SECTION IX — LINE TO ABRAM

XXXV. THE LINE OF ABRAM. — Gen. xi. 10-26.

18. רְעוּ Re'u, *friend ; v. feed, delight in, enjoy.*
20. שְׂרוּג Serug, *vine-shoot.*
22. נָחוֹר Nachor, *snorting.*
24. תֶּרַח Terach, *delay?* Ch.
26. אַבְרָם Abram, *high father.* הָרָן Haran, *mountaineer.*

10. These are the generations of Shem: Shem was the son of a hundred years, and begat Arpakshad two years after the flood. 11. And Shem lived after he begat Arpakshad five hundred years, and begat sons and daughters. § 19.

12. And Arpakshad lived five and thirty years, and begat Shelah. 13. And Arpakshad lived after he begat Shelah three and four hundred years, and begat sons and daughters. § 20.

14. And Shelah lived thirty years, and begat Heber. 15. And Shelah lived after he begat Heber three and four hundred years, and begat sons and daughters. § 21.

16. And Heber lived four and thirty years, and begat Peleg. 17. And Heber lived after he begat Peleg thirty and four hundred years, and begat sons and daughters. § 22.

18. And Peleg lived thirty years and begat Reu. 19. And Peleg lived after he begat Reu nine and two hundred years, and begat sons and daughters. § 23.

20. And Reu lived two and thirty years, and begat Serug. 21. And Reu lived after he begat Serug seven and two hundred years, and begat sons and daughters. § 24.

22. And Serug lived thirty years, and begat Nahor. 23.

And Serug lived after he begat Nahor two hundred years, and begat sons and daughters. § 25.

24. And Nahor lived nine and twenty years, and begat Terah. 25. And Nahor lived after he begat Terah nineteen and a hundred years, and begat sons and daughters. § 26.

26. And Terah lived seventy years, and begat Abram, Nahor, and Haran.

The usual phrase, *These are the generations,* marks the beginning of the fifth document. Accordingly, we now enter upon a new phase of human development. The nations have gradually departed from the living God. They have not, however, stopped at this negative stage of ungodliness. They have fallen into polytheism and idolatry. And the knowledge of the one true God, the Maker, Possessor, and Upholder of heaven and earth, is on the verge of being entirely lost. Nevertheless the promises, first to the race of Adam, that the seed of the woman should bruise the serpent's head, and next to the family of Noah, that the Lord should be the God of Shem, were still in force. It is obvious, from the latter promise, that the seed of the woman is to be expected in the line of Shem.

The present passage contains the pedigree of Abram from Shem. From this it appears that the sacred writer here reverts to the second year after the flood,— a point of time long before the close of the preceding narrative. *Shem was the son of a hundred years,* or in his hundredth year, two years after the flood, and therefore in the six hundred and third year of Noah, and consequently three years after Japheth. Abram was the twentieth, inclusive, from Adam, the tenth from Shem, and the seventh from Heber. A second Kenan is inserted after Arpakshad in the Septuagint, and in the Gospel according to Luke. But this name does not occur even in the Septuagint in 1 Chron. i. 24, where the genealogy of Abram is given. It is not found in the Samaritan Pentateuch, the Targums, or the ancient versions. It does not appear in Josephus or Philo. Neither is it found in the Codex Bezae in the Gospel of Luke. It must therefore be regarded as an interpolation.

The following table is a continuation of that given at the fifth chapter, and will serve for the comparison of the different forms in which the numbers are presented:

	HEBREW.		SAM. PENT.		SEPTUAGINT.		JOSEPHUS.		DATE.	
	Son's Birth.	Own Death.	Son's Birth.	Own Death.	Son's Birth.	Own Death.	Son's Birth.	Own Death.	Of Birth.	Of Death.
11. Shem . . .	(97) 2	600	(97) 2	600	(97) 2	600	(97)12		1559	2159
12. Arpakshad	35	438	135	438	135	535	135		1658	2096
(Καινᾶν)					130	460				
13. Shelah . .	30	433	130	433	130	460	130		1693	2126
14. Heber . . .	34	464	134	404	134	404	134		1723	2187
15 Peleg . . .	30	239	130	239	130	339	130		1757	1996
16 Reu	32	239	132	239	132	339	130		1787	2026
17. Serug . . .	30	230	130	230	130	330	132		1819	2049
18. Nahor . . .	29	148	79	148	175	304	120		1849	1997
19. Terah . . .	{ 70	205	70	145	70	205	70	205	1878	2083
(Haran)	{ 60		60		60		{ 292			
20. Abram ed.	70		70		70		{ 130		2008	2078
Enters Ken.		75		75		75		75		
Sum	422		1072		1302		422			
D. of Flood	1656		1307		2262		2256			
Date of call	2078		2379		3564		2678			

From this table it appears that in the total years of life the Hebrew, Samaritan, and Septuagint agree in Shem; the Hebrew and Septuagint in Terah; the Samaritan and Septuagint in Heber; and the Hebrew and Samaritan in all the rest. In regard, however, to the years of paternity, the Hebrew stands alone, against the Samaritan and Septuagint agreeing, except in Terah, where they all agree. The difference is not in units or tens, but in the addition to the Hebrew numbers of a hundred years, except in the case of Nahor, where the addition is fifty years, or a hundred and fifty according to the *Codex Vaticanus* of the Septuagint. Here, again, it is remarkable that Josephus while agreeing with the Samaritan and Septuagint in most of the separate numbers before paternity, agrees with the Hebrew in the sum of years from the flood to the 70th year of Terah (292 years, Jos. I. 6. 5). In Reu and Serug the numbers are transposed, seemingly by a mistake arising from the inverted order in which he gives the numbers. In Nahor he, or his transcriber, seems to have added a hundred years according to the uniform law, and neglected the nine. To make up for this omission, the inexact round number 10 has been apparently added to the number of years after the flood, when Arpakshad was born. We have already noticed that some MSS. of Josephus gave 1656 as the sum-total of years from the creation to the flood, in which case the sums of Josephus and the Hebrew exactly agree. We find him also stating (viii. 3. 1) that the world was created 3102 years before Solomon began to build the temple, and that the deluge took place 1440 before the same point of time. Hence we obtain 1662 years between the creation and the deluge; and this, if we only deduct from it the six years added to Lamek, agrees with the Hebrew. In the same passage he states that the entrance of Abram into Kenaan was 1020 years before the building of the temple. Hence we infer that 420 years elapsed from the flood to the call of Abram, which, if we count from the birth of Arpakshad, allow sixty years to elapse between the births of Haran and Abram, and date the call of Abram at 70, will exactly tally with the Hebrew. These sums cannot in any probable way be reconciled with the details in his own text, or in the Septuagint, or Samaritan. Again, Josephus calculates (x. 8. 5) that the temple was burnt 3513 years from the creation, and 1957 from the flood. Hence the interval from the creation to the deluge would be 1556 years, differing from the Hebrew by 100 years, and reconcilable with it, if we suppose the 500th year of Noah to be the terminating date. He also concludes that the burning of the temple took place 1062 years after the exodus, thus making the interval from the flood to the exodus 895 years, while the Hebrew makes it 852. If we reckon the 100 years from the 500th year of Noah to the flood, the 292 which Josephus gives from the flood to the birth of Abraham, the 75 years to the call of Abraham, and the 430 from that to the exodus, we have 897 years, which will be reduced to Josephus's number by omitting the 2 years from the flood to the birth of Arpakshad; and to the Hebrew number by omitting the 100 years before the flood, adding the 60 between Haran and Abram, which Josephus here neglects, and dating the call of Abram at 70 years. But by no process that we are aware of can these calculated numbers of Josephus be reconciled with the details of his own text, or the Samaritan, or Septuagint. It seems perfectly clear that the Hebrew numbers lie at the basis of these calculations of our author.

The age of paternity in the Samaritan from Peleg down is beyond the middle age of life, which is contrary to all experience. The editor of the Septuagint seems to have observed this anomaly, and added 100 years to three of these lives, and 156 to that of Nahor, against the joint testimony of the Hebrew and Samaritan. If the year of paternity in the Vatican be the correct reading, a much greater number should have been here added. The Samaritan deducts 60 years from the age of Terah, against the joint testimony of the Hebrew, Samaritan, and Josephus, seemingly because the editor conceived that Abram was born in his seventieth year.

From the Targum of Onkelos and the Peshito it is evident that the Hebrew text was the same as now up to the Christian era. Before that time there was no conceivable reason for shortening the chronology, while national vanity and emulation might easily prompt men to lengthen it. It is acknowledged that the text of the Septuagint is inferior to that of the Hebrew.

The age of puberty in the Hebrew affords more scope for the increase of population than that in the other texts. For if a man begin to have a family at thirty, it is likely to be larger than if he began a hundred years later and only lived the same number of years altogether. Now the Hebrew and Samaritan agree generally, against the Septuagint, in the total years of life; and in two instances, Heber and Terah, the Samaritan has even a less number than the Hebrew. It is to be remembered, also, that the number of generations is the same in every case. Hence in all human probability the Hebrew age of paternity will give the greater number of inhabitants to the world in the age of Abram. If we take the moderate average of five pairs for each family, we shall have for the estimated population 4×5^9 pairs, or 15,625,000 souls. This number is amply sufficient for all the kingdoms that were in existence in the time of Abram. If we defer the time of becoming a father for a whole century, we shall certainly diminish, rather than increase, the chance of his having so large a family, and thereby the probability of such a population on the earth in the tenth generation from Noah.

In these circumstances we are disposed to abide by the Hebrew text, that has descended to us in an original form, at least until we see some more cogent reasons for abandoning any of its numbers than chronologers have yet been able to produce. And we content ourselves, meanwhile, with the fact that the same system of numbers manifestly lay at the basis of all our present texts, though it may be difficult in some cases to determine to the satisfaction of all what was the original figure. The determination of the chronology of ancient history is neither a question of vital importance, nor, to us now, a part of the primary or direct design of the Hebrew records.

SECTION X — ABRAHAM

XXXVI. FATHER OF ABRAM. — Gen. xi. 27-32.

27. לוֹט Lot, *veil ;* v. *cover.*

28. אוּר Ur, *light, flame.* כַּשְׂדִּים Kasdim, Cardi, Kurds, Χαλδαῖοι. כֶּסֶד *gain?* Arab. Ur Kasdim has been identified with Hur, now called Mugheir (the bitumened), a heap of ruins lying south of the Euphrates, nearly opposite its junction with the Shat el-Hie. Others place it at Edessa, now Orfa, a short way north of Carrhae.

29. שָׂרַי Sarai, *strife ;* שָׂרָה *strive, rule.* מִלְכָּה Milkah, *counsel, queen ;* v. *counsel, reign.* יִסְכָּה Jiskah, *one who spies, looks out.*

31. חָרָן Charan, *burnt place.* Χαῤῥάν, Κάῤῥαι, a town on the Bilichus (Bililk), a tributary of the Frat, still called Harran. This has been identified by some with Harae, on the other side of the Frat, not far from Tadmor or Palmyra.

27. And these are the generations of Terah: Terah begat Abram, Nahor, and Haran; and Haran begat Lot. 28. And Haran died before Terah his father, in the land of his birth, in Ur of the Kasdim. 29. And Abram and Nahor took them wives; the name of Abram's wife was Sarai; and the name of Nahor's wife Milkah, the daughter of Haran, the father of Milkah and the father of Iskah. 30. And Sarai was barren; she had no child. 31. And Terah took Abram his son, and Lot the son of Haran his son's son, and Sarai his daughter-in-law, wife of Abram his son; and they went forth with them from Ur of the Kasdim, to go into the land of Kenaan; and they went into Haran, and dwelt there. 32. And the days of Terah were five and two hundred years; and Terah died in Haran.

27–32. This passage forms the commencement of the sixth document, as is indicated by the customary phrase, *These are the generations.* The sense also clearly accords with this distinction; and it accounts for the repetition of the statement, "Terah begat Abram, Nahor, and Haran." Yet the scribe who finally arranged the text makes no account of this division; as he inserts neither a פ nor even a ס at its commencement, while he places the threefold פ, marking the end of a Sabbath lesson, at its close. We learn from this that the Jewish rabbis did not regard the opening phrase as a decided mark of a new beginning, or any indication of a new author. Nevertheless, this passage and the preceding one form the meet prelude to the history of Abram, — the one tracing his genealogy from Shem and Heber, and the other detailing his relations with the family out of which he was called.

God has not forsaken the fallen race. On the contrary, he has once and again held out to them a general invitation to return, with a promise of pardon and acceptance. Many of the descendants of Noah have already forsaken him, and he foresees that all, if left to themselves, will sink into ungodliness. Notwithstanding all this, he calmly and resolutely proceeds with his purpose of mercy. In the accomplishment of this eternal purpose he moves with all the solemn grandeur of long-suffering patience. One day is with him as a thousand years, and a thousand years as one day. Out of Adam's three sons he selects one to be the progenitor of the seed of the woman; out of Noah's three sons he again selects one; and now out of Terah's three is one to be selected. Among the children of this one he will choose a second one, and among his a third one before he reaches the holy family. Doubtless this gradual mode of proceeding is in keeping with the hereditary training of the holy nation, and the due adjustment of all the divine measures for at length bringing the fulness of the Gentiles into the covenant of everlasting peace.

The history here given of the postdiluvians has a striking resemblance in structure to that of the antediluvians. The preservation of Noah from the waters of the flood, is the counterpart of the creation of Adam after the land had risen out of the roaring deep. The intoxication of Noah by the fruit of a tree corresponds with the fall of Adam by eating the fruit of a forbidden tree. The worldly policy of Nimrod and his builders is parallel with the city-building and many inventions of the Cainites. The pedigree of Abram the tenth from Shem, stands over against the pedigree of Noah the tenth from Adam; and the paragraph now before us bears some resemblance to that which precedes the personal history of Noah. All this tends to strengthen the impression made by some other phenomena, already noticed, that the book of Genesis is the work of one author, and not a mere file of documents by different writers.

The present paragraph is of special interest for the coming history. Its opening word *and* intimates its close connection with the preceding document; and accordingly we observe that the one is merely introductory to the other. The various characters brought forward are all of moment. Terah is the patriarch and leader of the migration for part of the way. Abram is the subject of the following narrative. Nahor is the grandfather of Rebekah. Haran is the father of Lot the companion of Abram, of Milcah the wife of Nahor and grandmother of Rebekah, and of Iskah. Iskah alone seems to have no connection with the subsequent narrative. Josephus says Sarai and Milkah were the daughters of Haran, taking no notice of Iskah. He seems, therefore, to identify Sarai and Iskah. Jerome, after his Jewish teachers, does the same. Abram says of Sarai, "She is the daughter of my father, but not the daughter of my mother" (Gen. xx. 12). In Hebrew phrase the granddaughter is termed a daughter; and therefore this statement might be satisfied by her being the daughter of Haran. Lot is called the brother's son and the brother of Abram (Gen. xiv. 12, 16). If Sarai be Haran's daughter, Lot is Abram's brother-in-law. This identification would also explain the introduction of Iskah into the present passage. Still it must be admitted, on the other hand, that persons are sometimes incidentally introduced in a history of facts, without any express connection with the course of the narrative, as Naamah in the history of the Cainites. The studied silence of the sacred writer in regard to the parentage of Sarai, in the present connection, tells rather in favor of her being the actual daughter of Terah by another wife, and so strictly the half-sister of Abram. For the Mosaic law afterwards expressly prohibited marriage with "the daughter of a father" (Lev. xviii. 9). And, lastly, the text does not state of Iskah, "This is Sarai," which would accord with the manner of the sacred writer, and is actually done in the Targum of Pseudo-Jonathan.

28. *And Haran died in the presence of his father Terah.* There is reason to believe that Haran was the eldest son of Terah. Though mentioned in the third place, like Japheth the eldest son of Noah, yet, like Japheth, also, his descendants are recounted first. He is the father of Lot, Milkah, and Iskah. His brother Nahor marries his

daughter Milkah. If Iskah be the same as Sarai, Haran her father must have been some years older than Abram, as Abram was only ten years older than Sarai; and hence her father, if younger than Abram, must have been only eight or nine when she was born, which is impossible. Hence, those who take Iskah to be Sarai, must regard Abram as younger than Haran.

In the land of his birth. The migration of Terah, therefore, did not take place till after the death of Haran. At all events, his three grandchildren, Lot, Milkah, and Iskah, were born before he commenced his journey. Still further, Milkah was married to Nahor for some time before that event. Hence, allowing thirty years for a generation, we have a period of sixty years and upwards from the birth of Haran to the marriage of his daughter. But if we take seventy years for a generation, which is far below the average of the Samaritan or the Septuagint, we have one hundred and forty years, which will carry us beyond the death of Terah, whether we reckon his age at one hundred and forty-five with the Samaritan, or at two hundred and five with the other texts. This gives another presumption in favor of the Hebrew average for a generation.

In Ur of the Kasdim. The Kasdim, Cardi, Kurds, or Chaldees are not to be found in the table of nations. They have been generally supposed to be Shemites. This is favored by the residence of Abram among them, by the name Kesed, being a family name among his kindred (Gen. xxii. 22), and by the language commonly called Chaldee, which is a species of Aramaic. But among the settlers of the country, the descendants of Ham probably prevailed in early times. Nimrod, the founder of the Babylonian Empire, was a Kushite. The ancient Babylonish language, Rawlinson (Chaldaea) finds to be a peculiar dialect, having affinities with the Shemitic, Arian, Turanian, and Hamitic tongues. The Chaldees were spread over a great extent of surface; but their most celebrated seat was Chaldaea proper, or the land of Shinar. The inhabitants of this country seem to have been of mixed descent, being bound together by political rather than family ties. Nimrod, their centre of union, was a despot rather than a patriarch. The tongue of the Kaldees, whether pure or mixed, and whether Shemitic or not, is possibly distinct from the Aramaic, in which they addressed Nebuchadnezzar in the time of Daniel (i. 4, ii. 4). The Kaldin at length lost their nationality, and merged into the caste or class of learned men or astrologers, into which a man might be admitted, not merely by being a Kaldai by birth, but by acquiring the language and learning of the Kasdim (Daniel i. 4, v. 11). The seats of Chaldee learning were Borsippa (Birs Nimrud), Ur, Babylon, and Sepharvaim (Sippara, Mosaib). Ur or Hur has been found by antiquarian research (see Rawlinson's Ancient Monarchies) in the heap of ruins called Mugheir, "the bitumened." This site lies now on the right side of the Frat; but the territory to which it belongs is mainly on the left. And Abram coming from it would naturally cross into Mesopotamia on his way to Haran. Orfa, the other supposed site of Ur, seems to be too near Haran. It is not above twenty or twenty-five miles distant, which would not be more than one day's journey.

29, 30. *But Sarai was barren.* From this statement it is evident that Abram had been married for some time before the migration took place. It is also probable that Milkah had begun to have a family; a circumstance which would render the barrenness of Sarai the more remarkable.

31, 32. *And Terah took Abram.* Terah takes the lead in this emigration, as the patriarch of the family. In the Samaritan Pentateuch Milkah is mentioned among the emigrants; and it is not improbable that Nahor and his family accompanied Terah, as we find them afterwards at Haran, or the city of Nahor (Gen. xxiv. 10). *And they went forth with them.* Terah and Abram went forth with Lot and the other companions of their journey. *To go into the land of Kenaan.* It was the design of Terah himself to settle in the land of Kenaan. The boundaries of this land are given in the table of nations (Gen. x. 19). The Kenaanites were therefore in possession of it when the table of nations was drawn up. It is certain, however, that there were other inhabitants, some of them Shemites probably, anterior to Kenaan, and subjected by his invading race. The prime motive to this change of abode was the call to Abram recorded in the next chapter. Moved by the call of God, Abram "obeyed; and he went out not knowing whither he went" (Heb. xi. 8). But Terah was influenced by other motives to put himself at the head of this movement. The death of Haran, his eldest son, loosened his attachment to the land of his birth. Besides, Abram and Sarai were no doubt peculiarly dear to him, and he did not wish to lose their society. The inhabitants also of Ur had fallen into polytheism, or, if we may so speak, allotheism, the worship of other gods. Terah had himself been betrayed into compliance with this form of impiety. It is probable that the revelation Abram had received from heaven was the means of removing this cloud from his mind, and restoring in him the knowledge and worship of the true God. Hence his desire to keep up his connection with Abram, who was called of God. Prayerful intercourse with the true and living God, also, while it was fast waning in the land of the Kasdim, seems to have been still maintained in its ancient purity in some parts of the land of Kenaan and the adjacent countries. In the land of Uz, a Shemite, perhaps even at a later period, lived Job; and in the neighboring districts of Arabia were his several friends, all of whom acknowledged the true God. And in the land of Kenaan was Melkizedec, the king of Salem, and the priest of the Most High God. A priest implies a considerable body of true worshippers scattered over the country. Accordingly, the name of the true God was known and revered, at least in outward form, wherever Abram went, throughout the land. The report of this comparatively favorable state of things in the land of Kenaan would be an additional incentive to the newly enlightened family of Terah to accompany Abram in obedience to the divine call.

Terah set out on his journey, no doubt, as soon after the call of Abram as the preparatory arrangements could be made. Now the promise to Abram was four hundred and thirty years before the exodus of the children of Israel out of Egypt (Ex. xii. 40). Of this long period his seed was to be a stranger in a land that was not theirs for four hundred years (Gen. xv. 13). Hence it follows that Isaac, his seed, was born thirty years after the call of Abram. Now Abram was one hundred years old when Isaac was born, and consequently the call was given when he was seventy years of age, — about five years before he entered the land of Kenaan (Gen. xii. 4). This whole calculation exactly agrees with the incidental statement of Paul to the Galatians (Gal. iii. 17) that the law was four hundred and thirty years after the covenant of promise. Terah was accordingly two hundred years old when he undertook the long journey to the land of Kenaan; for he died at two hundred and five, when Abram was seventy-five. Though proceeding by easy stages, the aged patriarch seems to have been exhausted by the length and the difficulty of the way. *They came to Haran and dwelt there.* Broken down with fatigue, he halts for a season at Haran to recruit his wasted powers. Filial piety, no doubt, kept Abram watching over the last days of his venerable parents, who probably still cling to the fond hope of reaching the land of his adoption. Hence they all abode in Haran for the remainder of the five years from the date of Abram's call to leave his native land. *And*

Terah died in Haran. This intimates that he would have proceeded with the others to the land of Kenaan if his life had been prolonged, and likewise that they did not leave Haran until his death.

We have already seen that Abram was seventy-five years of age at the death of Terah. It follows that he was born when Terah was one hundred and thirty years old, and consequently sixty years after Haran. This is the reason why we have placed one hundred and thirty (seventy and sixty), in the genealogical table opposite Terah, because the line of descent is not traced through Haran, who was born when he was seventy, but through Abram, who by plain inference was born when he was one hundred and thirty years old. It will be observed, also, that we have set down seventy opposite Abram as the date of his call, from which is counted the definite period of four hundred and thirty years to the exodus. And as all our texts agree in the numbers here involved, it is obvious that the same adjustment of years has in this case to be made, whatever system of chronology is adopted. Hence Abram is placed first in the list of Terah's sons, simply on account of his personal preëminence as the father of the faithful and the ancestor of the promised seed; he and his brother Nahor are both much younger than Haran, are married only after his death, and one of them to his grown-up daughter Milkah; and he and his nephew Lot are meet companions in age as well as in spirit. Hence also Abram lingers in Haran, waiting to take his father with him to the land of promise, if he should revive so far as to be fit for the journey. But it was not the lot of Terah to enter the land, where he would only have been a stranger. He is removed to the better country, and by his departure contributes no doubt to deepen the faith of his son Abram, of his grandson Lot, and of his daughter-in-law Sarai. This explanation of the order of events is confirmed by the statement of Stephen: "The God of glory appeared unto our father Abraham when he was in Mesopotamia, *before he dwelt in Charran.* Then came he out of the land of the Chaldeans and dwelt in Charran; and from thence, *when his father was dead,* he removed him into this land, wherein ye now dwell" (Acts vii. 2-4).

XXXVII. THE CALL OF ABRAM. — Gen. xii. 1-9.

6. שְׁכֶם Shekem, *the upper part of the back.* Here it is the name of a person, the owner of this place, where afterwards is built the town called at first Shekem, then Flavia Neapolis, and now Nablous. אֵלוֹן *the oak;* r. *be lasting, strong.* מוֹרֶה In Onk. *plain;* Moreh, *archer, early rain, teacher.* Here the name of a man who owned the oak that marked the spot. In the Septuagint it is rendered *ὑψηγήν.*

8. בֵּית־אֵל Bethel, *house of God.* יָם *sea, great river, west.* עַי Ai, *heap.*

9. נֶגֶב *south.*

XII. 1. And the Lord said unto Abram, Get thee out of thy land, and from thy kindred, and from thy father's house, unto the land that I will show thee. 2. And I will make of thee a great nation, and bless thee, and make thy name great; and thou shalt be a blessing. 3. And I will bless them that bless thee, and curse him that curseth thee; and blessed in thee shall be all the families of the ground. 4. And Abram went as the Lord had spoken to him, and with him went Lot; and Abram was the son of five and seventy years when he came out of Haran. 5. And Abram took Sarai his wife, and Lot his brother's son, and all their gaining that they had gained, and the souls that they had gotten in Haran; and they came forth to go into the land of Kenaan, and they went into the land of Kenaan. 6. And Abram passed through the land into the place of Shekem, unto the oak of Moreh; and the Kenaanite was then in the land. 7. And the Lord appeared unto Abram, and said, Unto thy seed will I give this land. And he builded there an altar unto the Lord, who appeared unto him. 8. And he removed thence to the mountain on the east of Bethel, and pitched his tent, having Bethel on the west and Ai on the east; and he builded there an altar to the Lord, and called upon the name of the Lord. 9. And Abram journeyed, going on still towards the south. ¶ 17.

The narrative now takes leave of the rest of the Shemites, as well as the other branches of the human family, and confines itself to Abram. It is no part of the design of Scripture to trace the development of worldliness. It marks its source, and indicates the law of its downward tendency; but then it turns away from the dark detail, to devote its attention to the way by which light from heaven may again pierce the gloom of the fallen heart. Here, then, we have the starting of a new spring of spiritual life in the human race.

1–3. Having brought the affairs of Terah's family to a fit resting point, the sacred writer now reverts to the call of Abram. This, we have seen, took place when he was seventy years of age, and therefore five years before the death of Terah. *The Lord said unto Abram.* Four hundred and twenty-two years on the lowest calculation after the last recorded communication with Noah, the Lord again opens his mouth, to Abram. Noah, Shem, or Heber, must have been in communication with heaven, indeed, at the time of the confusion of tongues, and hence we have an account of that miraculous interposition. The call of Abram consists of a command and a promise. The command is to leave the place of all his old and fond associations, for a land which he had not yet seen, and therefore did not know. Three ties are to be severed in complying with this command, — his country, in the widest range of his affections; his place of birth and kindred comes closer to his heart; his father's house is the inmost circle of all his tender emotions. All these are to be resigned; not, however, without reason. The reason may not be entirely obvious to the mind of Abram. But he has entire faith in the reasonableness of what God proposes. So with reason and faith he is willing to go to the unknown land. It is enough that God will show him the land to which he is now sent.

2, 3. The promise corresponds to the command. If he is to lose much by his exile, he will also gain in the end. The promise contains a lower and a higher blessing. The lower blessing has three parts: First, *I will make of thee a great nation.* This will compensate for the loss of his country. The nation to which he had hitherto belonged was fast sinking into polytheism and idolatry. To escape from it and its defiling influence was itself a benefit; but to be made himself the head of a chosen nation was a double blessing. Secondly, *And bless thee.* The place of his birth and kindred was the scene of all his past earthly joys. But the Lord will make up the loss to him in a purer and safer scene of temporal prosperity. Thirdly, *And make thy name great.* This was to compensate him for his father's house. He was to be the patriarch of a new house, on account of which he would be known and venerated all over the world.

The higher blessing is expressed in these remarkable terms: *And be thou a blessing.* He is to be not merely a subject of blessing, but a medium of blessing to others. It is more blessed to give than to receive. And the Lord here confers on Abram the delightful prerogative of dispensing good to others. The next verse expands this higher element of the divine promise. *I will bless them that bless thee, and curse him that curseth thee.* Here the Lord identifies the cause of Abram with his own, and declares him to be essentially connected with the weal or woe of all who come into contact with him. *And blessed in thee shall be all the families of the ground.* The ground was cursed for the sake of Adam, who fell by transgression. But now shall the ground again participate in the blessing. *In thee.* In Abram is this blessing laid up as a treasure hid in a field to be realized in due time. *All the families* of mankind shall ultimately enter into the enjoyment of this unbounded blessing. Thus, when the Lord saw fit to select a man to preserve vital piety on the earth and be the head of a race fitted to be the depository of a revelation of mercy, he at the same time designed that this step should be the means of effectually recalling the sin-enthralled world to the knowledge and love of himself. The race was twice already since the fall put upon its probation, — once under the promise of victory to the seed of the woman, and again under the covenant with Noah. In each of these cases, notwithstanding the growing light of revelation and accumulating evidence of the divine forbearance, the race had apostatised from the God of mercy, with lamentably few known exceptions. Yet, undeterred by the gathering tokens of this second apostasy, and after reiterated practical demonstration to all men of the debasing, demoralizing effect of sin, the Lord, with calm determination of purpose, sets about another step in the great process of removing the curse of sin, dispensing the blessing of pardon, and eventually drawing all the nations to accept of his mercy. The special call of Abram contemplates the calling of the Gentiles as its final issue, and is therefore to be regarded as one link in a series of wonderful events by which the legal obstacles to the divine mercy are to be taken out of the way, and the Spirit of the Lord is to prevail with still more and more of men to return to God.

It is sometimes inadvertently said that the Old Testament is narrow and exclusive, while the New Testament is broad and catholic in its spirit. This is a mistake. The Old and New Testaments are of one mind on this matter. Many are called, and few chosen. This is the common doctrine of the New as well as of the Old. They are both equally catholic in proclaiming the gospel to all. The covenant with Adam and with Noah is still valid and sure to all who return to God; and the call of Abram is expressly said to be a means of extending blessing to all the families of man. The New Testament does not aim at anything more than this; it merely hails the approaching accomplishment of the same gracious end. They both concur also in limiting salvation to the few who repent and believe the gospel. Even when Abram was called there were a few who still trusted in the God of mercy. According to the chronology of the Masoretic text, Heber was still alive, Melkizedec was contemporary with Abram, Job was probably later, and many other now unknown witnesses for God were doubtless to be found, down to the time of the exodus, outside the chosen family. God marks the first symptoms of decaying piety. He does not wait till it has died out before he calls Abram. He proceeds in a leisurely, deliberate manner with his eternal purpose of mercy, and hence a single heir of promise suffices for three generations, until the set time comes for the chosen family and the chosen nation. Universalism, then, in the sense of the offer of mercy to man, is the rule of the Old and the New Testament. Particularism in the acceptance of it is the accident of the time. The call of Abram is a special expedient for providing a salvation that may be offered to all the families of the earth.

In all God's teachings the near and the sensible come before the far and the conceivable, the present and the earthly before the eternal and the heavenly. Thus Abram's immediate acts of self-denial are leaving his country, his birthplace, his home. The promise to him is to be made a great nation, be blessed, and have a great name in the new land which the Lord would show him. This is unspeakably enhanced by his being made a blessing to all nations. God pursues this mode of teaching for several important reasons. First, the sensible and the present are intelligible to those who are taught. The Great Teacher begins with the known, and leads the mind forward to the unknown. If he had begun with things too high, too deep, or too far for the range of Abram's mental vision, he would not have come into relation with Abram's mind. It is superfluous to say that he might have enlarged Abram's view in proportion to the grandeur of the conceptions to be revealed. On the same principle he might have made Abram cognizant of all present and all developed truth. On the same principle he might have developed all things in an instant of time, and so have had done with creation and providence at once. Secondly, the present and the sensible are the types of the future and the conceivable; the land is the type of the better land; the nation of the spiritual nation; the temporal blessing of the eternal blessing; the earthly greatness of the name of the heavenly. And let us not suppose that we are arrived at the end of all knowledge. We pique ourselves on our advance in spiritual knowledge beyond the age of Abram. But even we may be in the very infancy of mental development. There may be a land, a nation, a blessing, a great name, of which our present realizations or conceptions are but the types. Any other supposition would be a large abatement from the sweetness of hope's overflowing cup. Thirdly, these things which God now promises are the immediate form of his bounty, the very gifts he begins at the moment to bestow. God has his gift to Abram ready in his hand in a tangible form. He points to it and says, This is what thou presently needest; this I give thee, with my blessing and favor. But, fourthly, these are the earnest and the germ of all temporal and eternal blessing. Man is a growing thing, whether as an individual or a race. God graduates his benefits according to the condition and capacity of the recipients. In the first boon of his good-will is the earnest of what he will continue to bestow on those who continue to walk in his ways. And as the present is the womb of the future, so is the external the symbol of the internal, the material the shadow of the spiritual, in the order of the divine blessing. And as events unfold themselves in the history of man and conceptions in his soul within, so are doctrines gradually opened up in the Word of God, and progressively revealed to the soul by the Spirit of God.

4, 5. Abram obeys the call. He had set out from Ur under the revered guardianship of his aged father, Terah, with other companions, *as the Lord had spoken unto him.* Lot is now mentioned as his companion. Terah's death has been already recorded. Sarai is with him, of course, and therefore it is unnecessary to repeat the fact. But Lot is associated with him as an incidental companion for some time longer. The age of Abram at the second stage of his journey is now mentioned. This enables us to determine, as we have seen, that he departed from Ur five years before.

5. This is the record of what is presumed in the close of the previous verse; namely, the second setting out for Kenaan. *Abram took.* He is now the leader of the little colony, as Terah was before his death.

Sarai, as well as Lot, is now named. *The gaining they had gained* during the five years of their residence in Haran. If Jacob became comparatively rich in six years (Gen. xxx. 43), so might Abram, with the divine blessing, in five. *The souls they had gotten,* — the bondservants they had acquired. Where there is a large stock of cattle, there must be a corresponding number of servants to attend to them. Abram and Lot enter the land as men of substance. They are in a position of independence. The Lord is realizing to Abram the blessing promised. They start for the land of Kenaan, and at length arrive there. This event is made as important as it ought to be in our minds by the mode in which it is stated.

6–9. Abram does not enter into immediate possession, but only travels through the land which the Lord had promised to *show* him (v. 1). He arrives at *the place of Shekem.* The town was probably not yet in existence. It lay between Mount Gerizzim and Mount Ebal. It possesses a special interest as the spot where the Lord first appeared to Abram in the land of promise. It was afterwards dedicated to the Lord by being made a Levitical town, and a city of refuge. At this place Joshua convened an assembly of all Israel to hear his farewell address. "So Joshua made a covenant with the people that day, and set them a statute and an ordinance in Shekem" (Jos. xxiv. 1–25). The particular point in the place of Shekem where Abram halted is the oak of Moreh; so called, probably, from its planter or owner. The oak attains to great antiquity, and a single tree, well grown, becomes conspicuous for its grandeur and beauty, and was often chosen in ancient times as a meeting-place for religious rites.

And the Kenaanite was then in the land. This simply implies that the land was not open for Abram to enter upon immediate possession of it without challenge. Another was in possession. The sons of Kenaan had already arrived and preoccupied the country. It also intimates, or admits, of the supposition that there had been previous inhabitants who may have been subjugated by the invading Kenaanites. Thus אָז *then* alludes to the past, as in Gen. iv. 26. Some of these former inhabitants will meet us in the course of the narrative. It admits also of the supposition that the Kenaanites afterwards ceased to be its inhabitants. Hence some have inferred that this could not have been penned by Moses, as they were expelled after his death. If this supposition were the necessary or the only one implied in the form of expression, we should acquiesce in the conclusion that this sentence came from one of the prophets to whom the conservation, revision, and continuation of the living oracles were committed. But we have seen that two other presuppositions may be made that satisfy the import of the passage. Moreover, the first of the three accounts for the fact that Abram does not instantly enter on possession, as there was an occupying tenant. And, finally, the third supposition may fairly be, not that the Kenaanites afterwards ceased, but that they should afterwards cease to be in the land. This, then, as well as the others, admits of Moses being the writer of this interesting sentence.

We are inclined to think, however, that the term Kenaanite here means, not the whole race of Kenaan, but the special tribe so called. If the former were meant, the statement would be in a manner superfluous, after calling the country the land of Kenaan. If the proper tribe be intended, then we have evidence here that they once possessed this part of the land which was afterwards occupied by the Hivite and the Amorite (Gen. xxxiv. 2; Jos. xi. 3); for, at the time of the conquest by Abram's descendants, the mountainous land in the centre, including the place of Shekem, was occupied by the Amorites and other tribes, while the coast of the Mediterranean and the west bank of the Jordan was held by the Kenaanites proper (Jos. v. 1, xi. 3). This change of occupants had taken place before the time of Moses.

7. *And the Lord appeared unto Abram.* Here, for the first time, this remarkable phrase occurs. It indicates that the Lord presents himself to the consciousness of man in any way suitable to his nature. It is not confined to the sight, but may refer to the hearing (1 Sam. iii. 15). The possibility of God appearing to man is antecedently undeniable. The fact of his having done so proves the possibility. On the mode of his doing this it is vain for us to speculate. The Lord said unto him, *Unto thy seed will I give this land.* "Unto thy seed," not unto thee. To Abram himself "he gave none inheritance in it, no, not so much as to set his foot on" (Acts vii. 5). "This land" which the Lord had now shown him, though at present occupied by the Kenaanite invader. *An altar.* This altar is erected on the spot which is hallowed by the appearance of the Lord to Abram. The place of Shekem might have been supposed to have received its name from Shekem, a son of Gilead (Num. xxvi. 31), did we not meet with Shekem, the son of Hamor, in this very place in the time of Jacob (Gen. xxxiv. 2). We learn from this the precariousness of the inference that the name of a place is of later origin because a person of that name lived there at a later period. The place of Shekem was doubt-

less called after a Shekem antecedent to Abram. Shekem and Moreh may have preceded even the Kenaanites, for anything we know.

8, 9. From the oak of Moreh Abram now moves to the hill east of Bethel, and pitches his tent, with *Bethel on the west and Ai on the east.* These localities are still recognized—the former as Beiten, and the latter as Tell er-Rijmeh (the mount of the heap). Bethel was *a place*, adjacent to which was the town called *Luz at the first* (Gen. xxviii. 19). Jacob gave this name to the place twice (Gen. xxviii. 19, xxxv. 15). The name, then, was not *first* given at the second nomination by him. It follows that it may not have been first given at his first nomination. Accordingly we meet with it as an existing name in Abram's time, without being constrained to account for it by supposing the present narrative to have been composed in its present form after the time of Jacob's visit. On the other hand, we may regard it as an interesting trace of early piety having been present in the land even before the arrival of Abram. We shall meet with other corroborating proofs. Bethel continued afterwards to be a place hallowed by the presence of God, to which the people resorted for counsel in the war with Benjamin (Judg. xx. 18, 26, 31, xxi. 2), and in which Jeroboam set up one of the golden calves (1 Kings xii. 29).

On the hill east of this sacred ground Abram built another altar, and called upon the name of the Lord. Here we have the reappearance of an ancient custom, instituted in the family of Adam after the birth of Enok (Gen. iv. 26). Abram addresses God by his proper name, Jehovah, with an audible voice, in his assembled household. This, then, is a continuation of the worship of Adam, with additional light according to the progressive development of the moral nature of man. But Abram has not yet any settled abode in the land. He is only surveying its several regions, and feeding his flocks as he finds an opening. Hence he continues his journey southward.

XXXVIII. ABRAM IN EGYPT.—Gen. xii. 10-20.

15. פַּרְעֹה Par'oh, *ouro.* Koptic for *king*, with the masculine article *pi.* or *p.* P-ouro, *the king.* If we separate the article p. from the Hebrew form, we have רְעֹה for *king*, which may be compared with רֹעֶה *pastor*, *leader*, and the Latin *rex*, king. This is the common

title of the Egyptian sovereigns, to which we have the personal name occasionally added, as Pharoh Neko, Pharoh Hophrah.

10. And there was a famine in the land: and Abram went down into Mizraim to sojourn there; for grievous was the famine in the land. 11. And it came to pass, when he was come near to enter into Mizraim, that he said unto Sarai his wife, Behold, now, I know that thou art a woman fair to look upon. 12. And it shall come to pass that the Mizrites shall see thee and say, This is his wife; and they will kill me, but they will save thee alive. 13. Say now, thou art my sister; that it may be well with me for thy sake, and my soul may live because of thee. 14. And it came to pass, when Abram was gone into Mizraim, that the Mizrites beheld the woman that she was very fair. 15. And the princes of Pharoh saw her, and commended her to Pharoh; and the woman was taken into Pharoh's house. 16. And he treated Abram well for her sake; and he had sheep and oxen and he-asses and men-servants and maid-servants and she-asses and camels. 17. And the Lord plagued Pharoh and his house with great plagues, on account of Sarai, Abram's wife. 18. And Pharoh called Abram and said, What is this thou hast done unto me? Why didst thou not tell me that she was thy wife? 19. Why saidst thou, She is my sister, and I took her to me to wife? And now behold thy wife, take her and go thy way. 20. And Pharoh commanded men concerning him; and they sent him away, and his wife, and all that he had.

10. This first visit of Abram to Mizraim, or Egypt, is occasioned by the famine in the land of promise. This land is watered by periodical rains. A season of drought arrests the progress of vegetation, and brings on a famine. But in Egypt, the fertility of the loamy soil depends not on local showers, but on the annual rise of the Nile, which is fed by the rains of a far-distant mountain range. Hence, when the land of Kenaan was wasted by drought and consequent famine, Egypt was

generally so productive as to be the granary of the neighboring countries. As Kenaan was the brother of Mizraim, the intercourse between the two countries in which they dwelt was natural and frequent. Dry seasons and dearth of provisions seem to have been of frequent occurrence in the land of Kenaan (Gen. xxvi. 1, xli. 56, 57). Even Egypt itself was not exempt from such calamitous visitations. Famine is one of God's rods for the punishment of the wicked and the correction of the penitent (2 Sam. xxiv. 13). It visits Abram even in the land of promise. Doubtless the wickedness of the inhabitants was great even in his day. Abram himself was not out of the need of that tribulation that worketh patience, experience, and hope. He may have been left to himself under this trial, that he might find out by experience his own weakness, and at the same time the faithfulness and omnipotence of Jehovah the promiser. In the moment of his perplexity he flees for refuge to Egypt, and the Lord having a lesson for him, there permits him to enter that land of plenty.

11–13. It is not without misgivings, however, that Abram approaches Egypt. All the way from Ur to Haran, from Haran to the land of Kenaan, and from north to south of the land in which he was a stranger, we hear not a word of apprehension. But now he betakes himself to an expedient which had been preconcerted between him and Sarai before they set out on their earthly pilgrimage (Gen. xx. 13). There are some obvious reasons for the change from composure to anxiety he now betrays. Abram was hitherto obeying the voice of the Lord, and walking in the path of duty, and therefore he was full of unhesitating confidence in the divine protection. Now he may be pursuing his own course, and, without waiting patiently for the divine counsel, venturing to cross the boundary of the land of promise. He may therefore be without the fortifying assurance of the divine approval. There is often a whisper of this kind heard in the soul, even when it is not fully conscious of the delinquency which occasions it. Again, the countries through which he had already passed were inhabited by nomadic tribes, each kept in check by all the others, all unsettled in their habits, and many of them not more potent than himself. The Kenaanites spoke the same language with himself, and were probably only a dominant race among others whose language they spoke, if they did not adopt. But in Egypt all was different. Mizraim had seven sons, and, on the average, the daughters are as numerous as the sons. In eight or nine generations there might be from half a million to a million of inhabitants in Egypt, if we allow five daughters as the average of a family. The definite area of the arable ground on the two sides of the Nile, its fertilization by a natural cause without much human labor, the periodical regularity of the inundation, and the extraordinary abundance of the grain crops, combined both to multiply the population with great rapidity, and to accelerate amazingly the rise and growth of fixed institutions and a stable government. Here there were a settled country with a foreign tongue, a prosperous people, and a powerful sovereign. All this rendered it more perilous to enter Egypt than Kenaan.

If Abram is about to enter Egypt of his own accord, without any divine intimation, it is easy to understand why he resorts to a device of his own to escape the peril of assassination. In an arbitrary government, where the will of the sovereign is law, and the passions are uncontrolled, public or private resolve is sudden, and execution summary. The East still retains its character in this respect. In these circumstances, Abram proposes to Sarai to conceal their marriage, and state that she was his sister; which was perfectly true, as she was the daughter of his father, though not of his mother. At a distance of three or four thousand years, with all the development of mind which a completed Bible and an advanced philosophy can bestow, it is easy to pronounce, with dispassionate coolness, the course of conduct here proposed to be immoral and imprudent. It is not incumbent on us, indeed, to defend it; but neither does it become us to be harsh or excessive in our censure. In the state of manners and customs which then prevailed in Egypt, Abram and Sarai were not certainly bound to disclose *all* their private concerns to every impertinent inquirer. The seeming simplicity and experience which Abram betrays in seeking to secure his personal safety by an expedient which exposed to risk his wife's chastity and his own honor, are not to be pressed too far. The very uncertainty concerning the relation of the strangers to each other tended to abate that momentary caprice in the treatment of individuals which is the result of a despotic government. And the prime fault and folly of Abram consisted in not waiting for the divine direction in leaving the land of promise, and in not committing himself wholly to the divine protection when he did take that step.

It may seem strange that the Scripture contains no express disapprobation of the conduct of Abram. But its manner is to affirm the great principles of moral truth, on suitable occasions, with great clearness and decision; and in ordinary circumstances simply to record the actions of its characters with faithfulness, leaving it to the reader's intelligence to mark their moral quality. And God's mode of teaching the individual is to implant a moral principle in the heart, which, after many struggles with temptation, will eventually root out all lingering aberrations.

Sarai was sixty-five years of age (Gen. xvii. 17) at the time when Abram describes her as a woman fair to look upon. But we are to remember that beauty does not vanish with middle age; that Sarai's age corresponds with twenty-five or thirty years in modern times, as she was at this time not half the age to which men were then wont to live; that she had no family or other hardship to bring on premature decay; and that the women of Egypt were far from being distinguished for regularity of feature or freshness of complexion.

14–16. The inadequacy of Abram's expedient appears in the issue, which is different from what he expected. Sarai is admired for her beauty, and, being professedly single, is selected as a wife for Pharoh; while Abram, as her brother, is munificently entertained and rewarded. His property seems to be enumerated according to the time of acquirement, or the quantity, and not the quality of each kind. Sheep and oxen and he-asses he probably brought with him from Kenaan; men-servants and maid-servants were no doubt augmented in Egypt. For she-asses the Septuagint has mules. These, and the camels, may have been received in Egypt. The camel is the carrier of the desert. Abram had now become involved in perplexities, from which he had neither the wisdom nor the power to extricate himself. With what bitterness of spirit he must have kept silence, received these accessions to his wealth which he dared not to refuse, and allowed Sarai to be removed from his temporary abode! His cunning device had saved his own person for the time; but his beautiful and beloved wife is torn from his bosom.

17. The Lord, who had chosen him, unworthy though he was, yet not more unworthy than others, to be the agent of his gracious purpose, now interposes to effect his deliverance. *And the Lord plagued Pharoh.* The mode of the divine interference is suited to have the desired effect on the parties concerned. As Pharoh is punished, we conclude he was guilty in the eye of heaven in this matter. He committed a breach of hospitality by invading the private abode of the stranger. He further infringed the law of equity between man and man in the most tender point, by abstracting, if not with violence, at least with a show of arbitrary power which could not be resisted, a female, whether sister or wife, from the home of her natural guardian without the con-

sent of either. A deed of ruthless self-will, also, is often rendered more heinous by a blamable inattention to the character or position of him who is wronged. So it was with Pharoh. Abram was a man of blameless life and inoffensive manners. He was, moreover, the chosen and special servant of the Most High God. Pharoh, however, does not condescend to inquire who the stranger is whom he is about to wrong; and is thus unwittingly involved in an aggravated crime. But the hand of the Almighty brings even tyrants to their senses. *And his house.* The princes of Pharoh were accomplices in his crime (v. 15), and his domestics were concurring with him in carrying it into effect. But even apart from any positive consent or connivance in a particular act, men, otherwise culpable, are brought into trouble in this world by the faults of those with whom they are associated. *On account of Sarai.* Pharoh was made aware of the cause of the plagues or strokes with which he was now visited.

18–20. Pharoh upbraids Abram for his deception, and doubtless not without reason. He then commands his men to dismiss him and his, unharmed, from the country. These men were probably an escort for his safe conduct out of Egypt. Abram was thus reproved through the mouth of Pharoh, and will be less hasty in abandoning the land of promise, and betaking himself to carnal resources.

XXXIX. ABRAM AND LOT SEPARATE.—Gen. xiii.

7. פְּרִזִּי Perizzi, descendant of Paraz. פָּרָז *leader*, or inhabitant of the plain or open country.

10. כִּכָּר *circle*, *border*, *vale*, *cake*, *talent*; r. *bow*, *bend*, *go round*, *dance*. יַרְדֵּן Jardan, *descending*. Usually with the article in prose. צֹעַר Tso'ar, *smallness*.

18. מַמְרֵא Mamre, *fat*, *strong*, *ruler*. חֶבְרוֹן Chebron, *conjunction*, *confederacy*.

XIII. 1. And Abram went up out of Mizraim, he and his wife, and all that he had, and Lot with him, into the south. 2. And Abram was very rich in cattle, in silver, and in gold. 3. And he went on his journeys from the south, even to Bethel, unto the place where his tent had been at the beginning, between Bethel and Ai. 4. Unto the place of the altar which he had made there at the first; and there Abram called on the name of the LORD.

5. And Lot also, who went with Abram, had flocks and herds and tents. 6. And the land did not bear them to dwell together; for their gaining was great, and they could not dwell together. 7. And there was a strife between the herdmen of Abram's cattle and the herdmen of Lot's cattle; and the Kenaanite and Perizzite were then dwelling in the land. 8. And Abram said unto Lot, Let there be now no striving between me and thee, and between my herdmen and thy herdmen; for we are brethren. 9. Is not the whole land before thee? Separate thyself now from me: if to the left hand, then I will go to the right; or if to the right hand, then I will go to the left. 10. And Lot lifted up his eyes, and beheld all the vale of the Jordan that it was well-watered; before the LORD destroyed Sodom and Amorah, like the garden of the LORD, like the land of Mizraim as thou goest unto Zoar. 11. Then Lot chose him all the vale of the Jordan, and Lot journeyed east; and they separated themselves the one from the other. 12. And Abram dwelled in the land of Kenaan; and Lot dwelled in the cities of the vale, and moved his tent towards Sodom. 13. And the men of Sodom were wicked, and sinners before the LORD exceedingly.

14. And the LORD said unto Abram, after that Lot was separated from him, Lift up now thine eyes, and look from the place where thou art, northward and southward and eastward and westward. 15. For all the land which thou seest, to thee will I give it, and to thy seed forever. 16. And I will make thy seed as the dust of the earth; so that if a man can number the dust of the earth, then may thy seed be numbered. 17. Arise, walk through the land, in the length of it and in the breadth of it; for to thee will I give it. 18. Then Abram moved his tent, and went and dwelled by the oaks of Mamre,

which are in Hebron, and there he built an altar unto the LORD.

¶ 18.

Lot has been hitherto kept in association with Abram by the ties of kinmanship. But it becomes gradually manifest that he has an independent interest, and is no longer disposed to follow the fortunes of the chosen of God. In the natural course of things this under-feeling comes to the surface. Their serfs come into collision; and as Abram makes no claim of authority over Lot, he offers him the choice of a dwelling-place in the land. This issues in a peaceable separation, in which Abram appears to great advantage. The chosen of the Lord is now in the course of providence isolated from all associations of kindred. He stands alone, in a strange land. He again obeys the summons to survey the land promised to him and his seed in perpetuity.

1–4. *Went up out of Mizraim.* Egypt is a low-lying valley, out of which the traveller ascends into Arabia Petraea and the hill-country of Kenaan. Abram returns, a wiser and a better man. When called to leave his native land, he had forthwith obeyed. Such obedience evinced the existence of the new power of godliness in his breast. But he gets beyond the land of promise into a land of carnality, and out of the way of truth into a way of deceit. Such a course betrays the struggle between moral good and evil which has begun within him. This discovery humbles and vexes him. Self-condemnation and repentance are at work within him. We do not know that all these feelings rise into consciousness, but we have no doubt that their result, in a subdued, sobered, chastened spirit, is here, and will soon manifest itself.

And Lot with him. Lot accompanied him into Egypt, for he comes with him out of it. The south is so called in respect, not to Egypt, but to the land of promise. It acquired this title before the times of the patriarch, among the Hebrew-speaking tribes inhabiting it. The great riches of Abram consist in cattle and the precious metals. The former is the chief form of wealth in the East. Abram's flocks are mentioned in preparation for the following occurrence. He advances north to the place between Bethel and Ai, and perhaps still further, according to verse 4, to the place of Shekem, where he built the first altar in the land. He now calls on the name of the Lord. The process of contrition in a new heart, has come to its right issue in confession and supplication. The sense of acceptance with God, which he had before experienced in these places of meeting with God, he has now recovered. The spirit of adoption, therefore, speaks within him.

5–7. The collision. Lot now also abounded in the wealth of the East. The two opulent sheiks (elders, heads of houses) cannot dwell together any more. Their serfs come to strife. The carnal temper comes out among their dependents. Such disputes were unavoidable in the circumstances. Neither party had any title to the land. Landed property was not yet clearly defined or secured by law. The land therefore was a common, where everybody availed himself of the best spot for grazing he could find unoccupied. We can easily understand what facilities and temptations this would offer for the strong to overbear the weak. We meet with many incidental notices of such oppression (Gen. xxi. 25, xxvi. 15–22; Ex. ii. 16–19). The folly and impropriety of quarrelling among kinsmen about pasture grounds on the present occasion is enhanced by the circumstance that Abram and Lot are mere strangers among the Kenaanites and the Perizzites, the settled occupants of the country. Custom had no doubt already given the possessor a prior claim. Abram and Lot were there merely on sufferance, because the country was thinly peopled, and many fertile spots were still unoccupied. The Perizzite is generally associated with, and invariably distinguished from, the Kenaanite (Gen. xv. 20, xxxiv. 30; Ex. iii. 8, 17). This tribe is not found among the descendants of Kenaan in the table of nations. They stand side by side with them, and seem therefore not to be a subject, but an independent race. They may have been a Shemite clan, roaming over the land before the arrival of the Hamites. They seem to have been by name and custom rather wanderers or nomads than dwellers in the plain or in the villages. They dwelt in the mountains of Judah and Ephraim (Judges i. 4; Jos. xvii. 15). They are noticed even so late as in the time of Ezra (ix. 1). The presence of two powerful tribes, independent of each other, was favorable to the quiet and peaceful residence of Abram and Lot, but not certainly to their living at feud with each other.

8, 9. The strife among the underlings does not alienate their masters. Abram appeals to the obligations of brotherhood. He proposes to obviate any further difference by yielding to Lot the choice of all the land. The heavenly principle of forbearance evidently holds the supremacy in Abram's breast. He walks in the moral atmosphere of the sermon on the mount (Matt. vi. 28–42).

10–13. Lot accepts the offer of his noble-hearted kinsman. He cannot do otherwise, as he is the companion, while his uncle is the principal. He willingly concedes to Abram his present position, and, after a lingering attendance on his kinsman, retires to take the ground of self-dependence. Outward and earthly motives prevail with him in the selection of his new abode. He is charmed by the well-watered lowlands bordering on the Jordan and its affluents. He is here less liable to a periodical famine, and he roams with his serfs and herds in the direction of Sodom. This town and Amorah (Gomorrah), were still flourishing at the time of Lot's arrival. The country in which they stood was of extraordinary beauty and fertility. The river Jordan, one of the sources of which is at Panium, after flowing through the waters of Merom, or the lake Semechonitis (Huleh), falls into the Sea of Galilee or Kinnereth, which is six hundred and fifty-three feet below the level of the Mediterranean, and thence descends into the basin of the Salt Sea, which is now thirteen hundred and sixteen feet beneath the same level, by a winding course of about two hundred miles, over twenty-seven threatening rapids. This river may well be called the Descender. We do not know on what part of the border of Jordan Lot looked down from the heights about Shekem or Ai, as the country underwent a great change at a later period. But its appearance was then so attractive as to bear comparison with the garden of the Lord and the land of Egypt. The garden of Eden still dwelt in the recollections of men. The fertility of Egypt had been lately witnessed by the two kinsmen. It was a valley fertilized by the overflowing of the Nile, as this vale was by the Jordan and its tributary streams. *As thou goest unto Zoar.* The origin of this name is given in Gen. xix. 20–22. It lay probably to the south of the Salt Sea, in the wady Kerak. 11. *And Lot journeyed east* (מִקֶּדֶם). From the hill-country of Shekem or Ai the Jordan lay to the east.

12. *The men of Sodom were wicked.* The higher blessing of good society, then, was wanting in the choice of Lot. It is probable he was a single man when he parted from Abram, and therefore that he married a woman of Sodom. He has in that case fallen into the snare of matching, or, at all events, mingling with the ungodly. This was the damning sin of the antediluvians (Gen. vi. 1–7). *Sinners before the Lord exceedingly.* Their country was as the garden of the Lord. But the beauty of the landscape and the superabundance of the luxuries it afforded, did not abate the sinful disposition of the inhabitants. Their moral corruption only broke forth into greater vileness of lust, and more daring defiance of heaven. They sinned *exceedingly* and *before the Lord.* Lot has fallen into the very vortex of vice and blasphemy.

14–18. The man chosen of God now stands alone. He has evinced an humble and self-renouncing spirit. This presents a suitable occasion for the Lord to draw nigh and speak to his servant. His works are reassuring. The Lord has not yet done with showing him the land. He therefore calls upon him to look northward and southward and eastward and westward. He *then* promises again to give all the land which he saw, as far as his eye could reach, to him and to his seed forever. Abram is here regarded as the head of a chosen seed, and hence the bestowment of this fair territory on the race is an actual grant of it to the head of the race. The term "forever," for a perpetual possession, means as long as the order of things to which it belongs lasts. The holder of a promise has his duties to perform, and the neglect of these really cancels the obligation to perpetuate the covenant. This is a plain point of equity between parties to a covenant, and regulates all that depends on the personal acts of the covenanter. He, *thirdly*, announces that he will make his seed *as the dust of the earth*. This multitude of seed, even when we take the ordinary sense which the form of expression bears in popular use, far transcends the productive powers of the promised land in its utmost extent. Yet to Abram, who was accustomed to the petty tribes that then roved over the pastures of Mesopotamia and Palestine, this disproportion would not be apparent. A people who should fill the land of Canaan, would seem to him innumerable. But we see that the promise begins already to enlarge itself beyond the bounds of the natural seed of Abram. 17. He is again enjoined to walk over his inheritance, and contemplate it in all its length and breadth, with the reiterated assurance that it will be his.

18. Abram obeys the voice of heaven. He moves his tent from the northern station, where he had parted with Lot, and encamps by the oaks of Mamre, an Amorite sheik. He loves the open country, as he is a stranger, and deals in flocks and herds. The oaks, otherwise rendered by Onk. and the Vulg. *plains of Mamre*, are said to be in Hebron, a place and town about twenty miles south of Jerusalem, on the way to Beersheba. It is a town of great antiquity, having been built seven years before Zoan (Tanis) in Egypt (Num. xiii. 22). It was sometimes called Mamre in Abram's time, from his confederate of that name. It was also named Kiriath Arba, the city of Arba, a great man among the Anakim (Jos. xv. 13, 14). But on being taken by Kaleb it recovered the name of Hebron. It is now el-Khulil (the friend, that is, of God; a designation of Abram). The variety of

name indicates variety of masters; first, a Shemite it may be, then the Amorites, then the Hittites (Gen. xxiii.), then the Anakim, then Judah, and lastly the Mahometans.

A third altar is here built by Abram. His wandering course requires a varying place of worship. It is the Omnipresent whom he adores. The previous visits of the Lord had completed the restoration of his inward peace, security, and liberty of access to God, which had been disturbed by his descent to Egypt, and the temptation that had overcome him there. He feels himself again at peace with God, and his fortitude is renewed. He grows in spiritual knowledge and practice under the great Teacher.

XL. ABRAM RESCUES LOT. — Gen. xiv.

1. אַמְרָפֶל Amraphel; r. unknown. אַרְיוֹךְ Ariok, *leonine?* r. אֲרִי *a lion:* a name reappearing in the time of Daniel (ii. 14). אֶלָּסָר Ellasar (r. un.) is identified with Larsa or Larancha, the *Λάρισσα* or *Λαράχων* of the Greeks, now Senkereh, a town of lower Babylonia, between Mugheir (Ur) and Warka (Erek) on the left bank of the Frat. כְּדָרְלָעֹמֶר Kedorla'omer, was compared by Col. Rawlinson with *Kudur-mapula* or *mabuk*, whose name is found on the bricks of Chaldæa, and whose title is *Apda martu*, ravager of the west. He translates it "servant of Lagamer," one of the national divinities of Susiana. It is also compared with Kedar el-Ahmar, "Kedar the Red," a hero in Arabian story. תִּדְעָל Tid'al, *terror.* גּוֹיִם Goim, *nations.*

2. בֶּרַע Bera', *gift?* בִּרְשַׁע Birsha, *long and thick?* Arab. שִׁנְאָב Shinab, *coolness?* אַדְמָה Admah, *red soil.* שֶׁמְאֵבֶר Shemeber, *high-soaring?* צְבֹיִים Tseboim, *gazelles.* בֶּלַע Bela, *devouring.*

3. שִׂדִּים Siddim, *plains, fields.*

5. רְפָאִים Rephaim, *the still, the shades, the giants.* עַשְׁתְּרֹת קַרְנַיִם 'Ashteroth Qurnaim, *ewes of the two horns*; according to Gesen., *stars* of the two horns. The first word may be singular, ewe, or star. The latter meaning is gained by connecting the word with the Pers. sitareh and the Greek *ἀστήρ, star.* Ashteroth is the moon or the planet Venus, whence Astarte. זוּזִים Zuzim; r. *glance, gush.* הָם Ham, *rush, sound, crowd.* אֵימִים Emim, *terrible.* שָׁוֵה Shaveh, plain. קִרְיָתַיִם Qiriathaim, *two cities;* r. *meet.*

6. חֹרִי Chori, *troglodyte;* v. *bore;* n. *cave.* שֵׂעִיר Se'ir, *rough,*

shaggy. אֵיל Eil, *tree, oak, terebinth, palm.* פָּארָן Paran, *bushy*, or *cavernous.*

7. עֵין מִשְׁפָּט 'En-mishpat, *well of judgment.* קָדֵשׁ Qadesh, *consecrated.* עֲמָלֵקִי 'Amaleki, a people that licks up. חַצְצֹן תָּמָר Chatsatson-tamar, *cutting* of the palm.

13. עִבְרִי 'Ibri, a descendant of Eber. אֶשְׁכֹּל, Eshkol, *cluster of grapes.* עָנֵר 'Aner ; r. un.

14. דָּן Dan, *ruler, judge.*

15. חוֹבָה Chobah, *hidden.* דַּמֶּשֶׂק Dammeseq. quad. ; r. *hasty, active, alert.*

18. מַלְכִּי־צֶדֶק Malkitsedeq, *king of righteousness.* שָׁלֵם Shalem. *peace.* אֵל El, *lasting, strong ; strength.*

20. מִגֵּן, *give, deliver ;* r. *mag, may.*

XIV. 1. And it came to pass in the days of Amraphel, king of Shinar ; Ariok, king of Ellasar ; Kedorlaomer, king of Elam ; and Tidal, king of Goim, 2. That they made war with Bera, king of Sodom ; and with Birsha, king of Amorah ; Shinab, king of Admah ; and Shemeber, king of Zeboim ; and the king of Bela, that is, Zoar. 3. All these joined together in the dale of Siddim, which is the Salt Sea. 4. Twelve years had they served Kedorlaomer, and the thirteenth year they rebelled. 5. And in the fourteenth year came Kedorlaomer and the kings that were with him, and smote the Rephaim in Ashteroth-carnaim, and the Zuzim in Ham, and the Emim in the plain of Kiriathaim. 6. And the Horite in their mount Seir, unto el-Paran, which is by the wilderness. 7. And they returned and came to En-mishpat, that is, Kadesh, and smote all the field of the Amalekite, and also the Amorite, that dwelt in Hazazon-tamar. 8. Then came out the king of Sodom, and the king of Amorah, and the king of Admah, and the king of Zeboim, and the king of Bela, that is, Zoar ; and they joined battle with them in the dale of Siddim. 9. With Kedorlaomer, king of Elam ; and Tidal, king of Goim ; and Amraphel, king of Shinar ; and Ariok, king of Ellasar : four kings with five. 10. And the dale of Siddim was full of pits of asphalt, and the kings of Sodom and Amorah fled and fell in there; and they that remained fled to the mountain. 11. And they took all the goods of Sodom and Amorah, and all their victuals, and went away. 12. And they took Lot and his goods, brother's son of Abram, and went away; for he was dwelling in Sodom.

13. Then came a fugitive, and told Abram the Hebrew; and he was abiding by the oaks of Mamre the Amorite, brother of Eshkol and brother of Aner; and these were confederate with Abram. 14. And Abram heard that his brother was taken captive, and drew out his trained men, born in his house, eighteen and three hundred, and pursued unto Dan. 15. And he divided himself against them by night, he and his servants, and smote them; and pursued them unto Hobah, which is on the left hand of Damascus. 16. And he brought back all the goods, and also Lot, his brother, and his goods brought he back, and also the women and the people.

17. And the king of Sodom came out to meet him on his return from smiting Kedorlaomer, and the kings that were with him, at the dale of Shaveh, which is the King's dale. 18. And Melkizedec, king of Shalem, brought forth bread and wine; and he was priest to the most high God. 19. And he blessed him, and said, Blessed be Abram of the most high God, Founder of heaven and earth. 20. And blessed be the most high God, who hath delivered thy foes into thy hand. And he gave him a tithe of all. 21. And the king of Sodom said unto Abram, Give me the persons, and take the goods to thyself. 22. And Abram said to the king of Sodom, I have lifted up my hand to the Lord, the most high God, Founder of heaven and earth, 23. That from a thread even to a shoe-latchet I will not take of all that is thine; and thou shalt not say, I made Abram rich: 24. Save only that which the young men have eaten, and the portion of the men who went with me, Aner, Eshkol, and Mamre; let them take their portion.

§ 27.

The community of feeling and of faith was not yet wholly broken up between Abram and Lot, or between them and the nations out of whom Abram had been called. An interesting glimpse is at the same time presented of the daring and doing of fierce ambition in those early times. A confederacy of potentates enter upon an extensive raid or foray, in which Lot is taken captive. This rouses the clannish or family affection of Abram, who pursues, overtakes, and defeats the retreating enemy, and recovers his friend, as well as all the prisoners, and property that had been taken. On his return he receives refreshment and blessing from a native prince who is priest to the most high God.

1–12. The raid is here minutely described. The dominant confederacy consists of four kings. Many generations back the first world-power, consisting of *four* cities, was established by Nimrod in the land of Shinar (Gen. x. 8–10). This has now given way to a world-confederacy, consisting of *four* kings. From the vicinity of the places in which they reigned it is evident that they were petty princes of domains varying from a town and its suburbs to a comparatively extensive territory. The first, Amraphel, is king of Shinar. He is therefore the successor of Nimrod, and the sovereign of the most ancient kingdom, and on these grounds occupies the first place in the list. But this kingdom is no longer the sole or even the supreme power. Amraphel is probably the descendant of Nimrod, and a Kushite. The second, Ariok, is king of Ellasar. If this town be the same as Larsa, lying between the Frat and the Shat el-Hie, the land of Shinar has been divided between two sovereigns, and no longer belongs entirely to the successor of Nimrod. Lower Shinar includes also Ur of the Kasdim; and hence Ariok probably represents that race. The third, Kedorlaomer, is king of Elam, or Elymais, a country east of the lower Tigris, and separated by it from Shinar. He is probably a Shemite, as the country over which he ruled received its name from a son of Shem (Gen. x. 22). He is the lord paramount of the others, and commander-in-chief of the united forces. Hence the Hamite seems to have already succumbed to the Shemite. The fourth, Tidel, is designated "king of Goim." Goim means nations; and it is doubtful whether it denotes here a special nation or a congeries of tribes. The Gentiles, specially so called, seem to have been Japhethites (Gen. x. 5). It is obvious that four nationalities are here leagued together, corresponding probably to the *Kiprat arbat*, four nations or tongues mentioned by Rawlinson (Anc. Mon. I. p. 69). But Kedorlaomer, king of Elam, is clearly not a Kushite. The only question seems to be whether he is a Shemite or a Japhethite, or

Arian, in which race the Shemite was ultimately absorbed. If the former alternative be adopted, we may have two Shemite languages among the four. If the latter be accepted, Kedorlaomer is an Arian; Tidal, a Turanian; Amraphel, a Hamite; and Ariok, a Shemite. In either case the Kushite has become subordinate, and a Japhethite or a Shemite has attained the predominance.

2, 3. *They made war.* Shinar was the central region from which the different branches of the human family dispersed after the confusion of tongues. It is possible that the mother country claimed some supremacy over the colonies. Shinar was also a great centre of commerce, and the cities of the dale of Siddim formed another, of secondary importance. Intercourse between the two countries was therefore frequent. Abram himself had come from Ur Kasdim. The spirit of despotism had descended from Nimrod to the present potentates of the East, and prompted them to aim at universal empire. The five kings are the petty sovereigns, each of a single town and its neighborhood. The area in which these towns lay was very circumscribed. With the exception of the territory of Bela it was afterwards submerged and formed part of the basin of the Salt Sea. Hence Siddim is said to be the Salt Sea. The dale is the deep valley or glen in which these kings dwelt on the banks of the Jordan, or the salt lake into which it flowed. Of the five cities, Sodom was the chief in power, luxury, and wickedness; whence it is mentioned first. Bela is also called Zoar, *the little*, and hence is placed last; even the name of its king is not given. *All these joined together.* They formed a league in self-defence, and marched out to meet the enemy in the dale of Siddim.

4–7. The narrative here reverts to the previous circumstances which gave occasion to the present raid. *Twelve years had they served Kedorlaomer.* These years date probably from the commencement of his reign. They may have been previously dependent on the dominant power in Shinar, and connected with it by national descent. If Kedorlaomer had wrested the supremacy from the king of Shinar, and so was regarded as an alien by the princes of Siddim, their coolness might gradually ripen into disaffection. In the thirteenth year they rebelled, and in the fourteenth Kedorlaomer came to quell the revolt. This military expedition embraced far loftier objects than the mere subjugation of the Pentapolis in the dale of Siddim. In passing from Shinar the invaders must have marched in a northwesterly direction along the Frat, touching upon Tadmor and Damascus. We are not informed whether they held any sway or made any conquest in these intervening regions. But they overran the country that stretches along the whole east side of the Jordan, and the parts south and west of the Salt Sea.

The Rephaim lay in Peraea. Some of them also were once found on the west side of the Jordan (Gen. xv. 20), where they gave name to the valley of Rephaim (Wady el-Werd), southwest of Jerusalem, on the way to Bethlehem (Jos. xv. 8), occupied part of Mount Ephraim (Jos. xvii. 15), and lingered for a long time among the Philistines (2 Sam. xxi. 16, ff.). They were a tall or gigantic race. They were not Kenaanites, but seem to have entered the country before them. They were conquered in Peraea by the Amorites, a branch of the Kenaanite family; and by the descendants of Lot, the Ammonites and Moabites. A remnant of them only lingered in the country when the Israelites arrived (Deut. ii. 20, iii. 11, 13). They may have been Shemites or Japhethites. The site of Ashteroth Carnaim has not been ascertained. Ritter finds it in Tell Ash'areh. Porter suggests 'Afineh, eight miles from Busrah, as the Samaritan version has 'Aphinit for 'Ashtaroth.

The Zuzim dwelt between the Jabbok and the Arnon. They are supposed to be the same as the Zamzummin, who were dispossessed by the Ammonites. If so, they were a branch of the Rephaim (Deut. ii. 20). Their town, Ham, is of unknown site.

The Emim were also accounted Rephaim. They lay on the east of the Salt Sea, and were afterwards conquered by the Moabites, who gave them this name (Deut. ii. 10, 11). Of Shaveh Kiriathaim, the plain of the two cities, the name probably remains in el-Kureiyât, a site near Jebel Attarus in Moab.

The Horites were perhaps a Shemite tribe, the aboriginal inhabitants of Mount Seir, where they dwelt in caves; such as are still to be seen in Petra and other places around. They were afterwards absorbed into the Edomites. Mount Seir stretches between the Salt Sea and the Elanitic Gulf. El-Paran, terebinth of Paran, is perhaps the same as Elath, at the head of the gulf of Aelana or Akaba. Paran lay west of Mount Seir and south of Palestine, and stretched into the peninsula of Sinai, where the name may yet be preserved in Wady Feiran. El-Paran would thus be *by* the wilderness of that name, now et-Tih.

7. This was the extreme point of their march southward. They now turned back by another route. Enmishpat, which is Kadesh, lay between Mount Hor and the Salt Sea, at a site now called Ain el-Weibeh. *The field of the Amalekite* was some part of the country

lying between Palestine and Egypt, which was afterwards occupied by the Amalekites. Instead of *field*, the Septuagint has *ἄρχοντας*, *rulers* of Amalek; but this reading is not supported. The tribe is descended from Amalek, the son of Eliphaz and grandson of Esau (Gen. xxxvi. 12). Traces of them are found as far north as Ephraim (Judg. v. 14, xii. 15). Balaam calls Amalek the beginning of the nations (Num. xxiv. 20); but this cannot be understood absolutely, as the name does not even occur in the table of nations. It is therefore well explained to mean that Amalek was the first that attacked Israel on coming out of Egypt. The invading host advance still further, to Hazazon-tamar, cutting of the palm, which is En-gedi (well of the kid, 2 Chron. xx. 2), situated on the western shore of the Salt Sea, and now called Ain Jidy. This was a settlement of the Amorites.

8–12. We have now arrived again at the point we had reached in v. 3. The five kings came out and joined battle with the four in the dale of Siddim. This dale abounded in pits of mineral pitch, or asphalt. The kings of Sodom and Amorah fled toward these pits, and seem to have fallen into them and perished. The others betook themselves to the mountain — probably the heights on the east of the dale.

11. The provisions and other movable property of the vanquished are carried away from Sodom and Amorah. For רְכֻשׁ *goods*, the Septuagint has here and in the 21st verse *τὴν ἵππον*, *the cavalry*. This implies the reading רֶכֶב, which is not supported by other authorities, nor suitable to the context. Among the prisoners is Lot, the son of Abram's brother. This designation prepares us for what is to follow. It is added that he was *dwelling in Sodom*, to explain why he was among the captives. *They went away.* The invaders were now laden with booty. Their first concern was to transfer this to their native country, and deposit it in a place of safety. It was not prudent to delay while they were encumbered with so much valuable property. The terms on which the conquered tribes were to "serve" them could be settled by negotiation. If these terms were not accepted, they would be quite ready for another predatory incursion.

This great foray is only incidentally introduced into our narrative, on account of the capture of Lot. It was not the first visit probably of these marauders to the same lands. It is interesting to the historian, as a sample of the mode in which conquest was made. It opens up to the view one of the ancient scenes of human activity. It teaches us that the wave of war often flowed over the lands of the ancient world, and left more or less lasting marks of its disturbing power. Tribes were not unfrequently moved from place to place, intermingled with one another, and enslaved by other tribes. The actual state of things in the land of Abram's pilgrimage is suddenly presented to us under a new light. The Rephaim, including the Zuzim and the Emim, occupy the east of the Jordan, and had once a place on the west. The Perizzites also dwell side by side with the Kenaanites in the western district. The Horites are found in Mount Seir. As none of these were Kenaan's descendants, we have the undeniable traces of a Shemitic population before and along with the Kenaanites. The language of Heber, therefore, was in the country before the latter arrived.

13–16. Abram rescues Lot. הַפָּלִיט "the fugitive" party, as "the Kenaanite" for the whole nation. The escaped party inform Abram when one of their number does so. *The Hebrew.* This designation is given to Abram plainly for the purpose of connecting him with Lot. The Septuagint translates the word by περάτης, one who passes. This has been explained by *transfluvialis*, one who has come across the river; namely, the Frat. This no doubt applies to Lot as well as Abram; but it also applies to every other tribe in the country, inasmuch as all had originally migrated across the Euphrates. Besides, the word is nowhere else used in this sense, but always as a patronymic. And moreover Abram is here distinguished as the Hebrew, just as his confederate Mamre is distinguished as the Amorite. The object of these designations is to mark, not only their relation to each other, but also their connection with those who were carried off as prisoners of war. The term *Hebrew* does not come into the narrative by hap-hazard. "The sons of Heber" are distinctly mentioned in the table of nations among the descendants of Shem. Its introduction here intimates that there were other descendants of Heber besides Abram already in the land. They could not but be a widespread race. One branch of them, the Joctanites, were the first stock of Arabia's inhabitants, and the Palgites may have been the earliest settlers in the adjacent Palestine. How many of the non-Kenaanites belong to them we cannot tell; but we learn from the statement now before us that the Hebrew was at this time a known patronymic. The way between Mesopotamia and Palestine has been often trodden.

Abram was dwelling by the oaks of Mamre, near Hebron, and therefore not far from the scene of war. He was also in league with Mamre and his brothers Eshkol and Aner. This league was, it is evident from the result, for mutual defence.

14. *His brother.* This is a customary extension of the term, whether

we regard Lot as his brother's son, or at the same time his brother-in-law. *His trained men.* Abram had now a company of three hundred and eighteen trained men, born in his own house; which implies a following of more than one thousand men, women, and children. His flocks and herds must have corresponded in extent to such an establishment. *Unto Dan.* This name is found in the Hebrew, Samaritan, Septuagint, and Onkelos. It might naturally be supposed that the sacred reviser of the text had inserted it here, had we not grounds for a contrary supposition. The custom of the reviser was to add the other name without altering the original; of which we have several examples in this very chapter (v. 2, 3, 7, 8, 17). We are, therefore, led to regard Dan as in use at the time of Abram. Held at that remote period perhaps by some Hebrew, it fell at length into the hands of the Sidonians (Judg. xviii.), who named it Laish (lion) and Leshem (ligure). Names of places in that eastern land vary, from a slight resemblance in sound (paronomasia), a resemblance in sense (synonyms), a change of masters, or some other cause. Laish and Leshem are significant names, partly alike in sound, and applied to the same town. They took the place of Dan when the town changed masters. The recollection of its ancient name and story may have attracted the Danites to the place, who burned Laish and built a new city which they again called Dan. This town was situated at the source of the lesser Jordan, with which some have connected its name. Its site is now occupied by Tell el-Kady, the hill of *the judge.* This is a case of resemblance in sense between varying names. Others, however, distinguish the present Dan from the Laish Dan, and identify it with Danjaan or jaar, "Dan in the wood" (2 Sam. xxiv 6). The former is not on the road to Damascus, while the latter was north of Gilead, and may have been near the route either by the south of the sea of Kinnereth, or of the waters of Merom. This is possible, and deserves consideration. But there may have been a third way to Damascus, passing Tell el-Kady; this place itself is on the east side of the main stream of the Jordan, and the expression דָּנָה יַּעַן is confessedly obscure.

15, 16. Abram and his confederates found the enemy secure and at their ease, not expecting pursuit. They attack them on two quarters; Abram, probably, on the one, and his allies on the other, by night, discomfit and pursue them unto Hobah. *On the left hand of Damascus.* Hobah was on the north of Damascus. An Eastern, in fixing the points of the heavens, faces the rising sun, in which position the east is before him, the west behind, the south at the right hand, and the north at the left. Hobah is referred by the Jews to Jobar, a place northeast of Damascus. J. L. Porter suggests a place due north, called Burzeh, where there is a Moslem wely or saint's tomb, called Makam Ibrahim, the sanctuary of Abraham (Handb. p. 492). This route, by the north of Damascus, illustrates the necessity of advancing far north to get round the desert intervening between Shinar and the cities of the plain.

Damascus, Dimishk, esh-Sham, is a very ancient city of Aram. The choice of the site was probably determined by the Abana (Barada) and Pharpar (Awaj), flowing, the one from Anti-Libanus, and the other from Mount Hermon, and fertilizing a circuit of thirty miles. Within this area arose a city which, amidst all the changes of dynasty that have come over it, has maintained its prosperity to the present day, when it has one hundred and fifty thousand inhabitants. It was originally occupied by the descendants of Aram, and may have been built, as Josephus informs us, by Uz his son.

Abram, with his allies, succeeded in defeating the enemy and recovering the property, with the prisoners, male and female, that had been carried away, and, among the rest, Lot, the object of his generous and gallant adventure.

17–24. Abram's reception on his return. *The king of Sodom.* This is either Bera, if he survived the defeat, or, if not, his successor. *The dale of Shaveh, which is the King's dale.* The word עֵמֶק is here rendered uniformly by the familiar term *dale.* The dale of Shaveh is here explained by the *King's dale.* This phrase occurs at a period long subsequent as the name of the valley in which Absalom reared his pillar (2 Sam. xviii. 18). There is nothing to hinder the identity of the place, which must, according to the latter passage, have been not far from Jerusalem. Josephus makes the distance two stadia, which accords with the situation of Absalom's tomb, though the building now so-called, in the valley of Jehoshaphat, seems to be of later origin. The identity of the King's dale with the valley east of Jerusalem, through which the Kedron flows, corresponds very well with the present passage.

18–20. An incident of the deepest interest here takes us by surprise. The connecting link in the narrative is obviously the place where the king of Sodom meets with Abram. The King's dale is plainly adjacent to the royal residence of Melkizedec, who therefore comes forth to greet and entertain the returning victor. This prince is the king of Shalem. This is apparently an ancient name of Jerusalem, which is so designated in Ps. lxxvi. 8. The other Shalem, which lay in the vicinity of Shekem (Gen. xxxiii. 18, if this be a proper name) is far away from the King's dale and the town of Sodom. Jerusalem is convenient to these localities, and contains the element Shalem in its composition, as the name signifies the foundation of peace (Shalem).

The king of Shalem, by name king of righteousness, and by office king of peace, *brought forth bread and wine.* These are the standing elements of a simple repast for the refreshment of the body. In after times they were by divine appointment placed on the table of the presence in the tabernacle (Ex. xxv. 29, 30). They were the accompaniments of the Paschal lamb (Matt. xxvi. 26, 27), and they were adopted by the Messiah as the sacred symbols of that heavenly fare, of which, if a man partake, he shall live forever (John vi. 48–58). The Author of revelation has made all nature intrinsically good and pure. He has realized therein a harmony of the laws of intelligence and design; everything meets and matches all that comes into contact with it; and all together form a cosmos, a system of things, a unity of types and antitypes. His word cannot but correspond to his work. Bread and wine are common things, familiar to the eye, the touch, and the taste of men. The great Teacher takes them up out of the hands of man as emblems of grace, mercy, and peace, through an accepted ransom, of the lowliest as well as the loftiest boon of an everlasting salvation, and they have never lost their significance or appropriateness.

And he was priest to the most high God. From this we are assured that the bread and wine refreshed not only the body, but the soul of Abram. In close connection with the preceding sentence, it seems to intimate that the bringing forth of bread and wine was a priestly act, and, accordingly, the crowning part of a sacred feast. The kohen, or priest, who is here mentioned for the first time in Scripture, was one who acted in sacred things on the part of others. He was a mediator between God and man, representing God holding out the hand of mercy, and man reaching forth the hand of faith. The necessity of such an office grew out of the distance between God and man produced by sin. The business of the priest was to offer sacrifice and to intercede; in the former making amends to the law, in the latter appealing to the mercy of God. We do not learn by express statement what was the mode of intervention on the part of Melkizedec. But we know that sacrifice was as early as Habel, and that calling on the name of the Lord was commenced in the time of Enosh. These were early forms of approach to God. The offices of king and priest were combined in Melkizedec — a condition of things often exemplified in after times.

The most high God. Here we meet with a new name of God, *El*, the Lasting, the Mighty, cognate with Elohim, and previously occurring in the compound proper names Mehujael, Mahalalel, and Bethel. We have also an epithet of God, *Elion the most high*, now appearing for the first time. Hence we perceive that the unity, the omnipotence, and the absolute preëminence of God were still living in the memory and conscience of a section at least of the inhabitants of this land. Still more, the worship of God was not a mere domestic custom, in which the father or head of the family officiated, but a public ordinance conducted by a stated functionary. And, lastly, the mode of worship was of such a nature as to represent the doctrine and acknowledge the necessity of an atonement, since it was performed by means of a priest.

18. *And he blessed him.* Here it comes out clearly that Melkizedec acts not only in a civil but in a sacred capacity. He blesses Abram. In the form of benediction employed we have two parts: the former of which is strictly a blessing or asking of good things for the person in question. *Blessed be Abram.* It is the part of the father to bless the child, of the patriarch or superior to bless the subject or inferior, and of the priest to bless the people (Heb. vii. 7). Here, accordingly, Melkizedec assumes and Abram concedes to him the superiority. The most high God is here further designated as the Founder of heaven and earth, the great Architect or Builder, and, therefore, Possessor of all things. There is here no indistinct allusion to the creation of "heaven and earth," mentioned in the opening of the Book of God. This is a manifest identification of the God of Melkizedec with the one Creator and Upholder of all things. We have here no mere local or national deity, with limited power and province, but the sole and supreme God of the universe and of man.

20. The second part of this benedictory prayer is a thanksgiving to the common God of Melkizedec and Abram for the victory which had been vouchsafed to the latter. *Thy foes.* Here Abram is personally addressed. Melkizedec as a priest first appeals to God on behalf of Abram, and then addresses Abram on behalf of God. He thus performs the part of a mediator.

And he gave him a tithe of all. This is a very significant act. In presenting the tenth of all the spoils of victory, Abram makes a practical acknowledgment of the absolute and exclusive supremacy of the God whom Melkizedec worshipped, and of the authority and validity of the priesthood which he exercised. We have here all the indications of a stated order of sacred rites, in which a costly service, with a fixed official, is maintained at the public expense, according to a definite rate of contribution. The gift in the present case is the tenth of the spoils of war. This act of Abram, though recorded last, may have taken place at the commencement of the interview. At all events, it renders it extremely probable that a sacrifice had been offered to God, through the intervention of Melkizedec, before he brought forth the bread and wine of the accepted feast.

It is obvious that here we stand on broader ground than the special promise made to Abram. Melkizedec was not a partner in the call of Abram, and yet the latter acknowledges him as a priest of the most high God. Hence we must fall back on the covenant made with Noah, — the representative of the whole race after the deluge, — as the broad basis of authority on which Melkizedec acted. That covenant, then, was not a dead letter. It still lived in the heart and will of a part of the nations. Its hallowing and exalting truths had produced at least one centre of pure and spiritual worship on the earth. Even Abram, the called of God, acknowledges its constituted head. And the most high God, Founder and Upholder of heaven and earth, thereby guarantees its validity for all who in every place call on his name in sincerity and truth. And his special call to Abram is given with a view to the final removal of all obstacles to the acceptance and application of this his everlasting covenant. We are thankful for this glimpse into the comprehensive grandeur of the divine purpose concerning man, which is for some time forward cast into the shade, until it begins to break forth again in the anticipations of the prophets, and at length shines forth with imperishable splendor in the revelations of the New Testament.

The genealogy of Melkizedec seems designedly veiled in impenetrable obscurity. To lift this veil entirely is therefore hopeless. Yet we may venture to hint the possibility that here we have another Shemite chieftain in the land of Kenaan. The indefinite statement of Josephus, that he was a potentate of the Kenaanites, is no proof to the contrary, even if it were of much value. The address of Ezekiel to Jerusalem: "Thy origin and thy birth are of the land of Kenaan; thy father was an Amorite, and thy mother a Hittite" (xvi. 3), may refer to the period immediately before the entrance of Israel into the land. At and after that time the Amorite and the Jebusite seem to have been in possession of the city (Jos. x. 5; Judg. i. 21). But in the time of Abram, more than four hundred years before, it may have been different. We have discovered other tribes in this land that were not of the race of Kenaan. It is not likely that Kenaan would furnish a priest of the most high God. It is evident that Melkizedec was not in the confederacy of the Pentapolis with the king of Sodom. He comes out separately and suddenly to meet Abram, who was one of "the children of Heber," of whom Shem was the father. And he is the acknowledged head of the worshippers of the most high God, who is "the Lord, the God of Shem." But be this as it may, it is only a secondary question here. The matter of primary importance, as has been already noted, is the existence of a community of pure worshippers of the true God in the land of Kenaan, antecedent to Abram. If this community be descendants of Kenaan, it only renders the discovery the more striking and impressive. The knowledge of the true God, the confession of the one everlasting supreme Creator of heaven and earth, the existence of a stated form of worship by means of a priest and a ritual attested by Abram the elect of God, in a community belonging to the Gentiles, form at once a remarkable vindication of the justice and mercy of God in having made known to all mankind the mode of acceptable approach to himself, and a singular evidence that such a revelation had been made to Noah, from whom alone it could have descended to the whole race, and consequently to this particular branch of it. We have reason to believe that this was not the sole line in which this precious tradition was still preserved in comparative purity and power. Job and his companions belong to one other known line in which the knowledge of the one God was still vital. The fundamental principles of divine truth planted in the human breast by this and antecedent revelations were never afterwards wholly eradicated; and from the hereditary germs of a primitive theology, cherished by intercourse with the Sidonians and other Phœnicians, were Homer, Socrates, Plato, Aristotle, and other sages of the East and West, enabled to rise to the exalted conceptions which they occasionally formed of the unity, purity, spirituality, and supremacy of the Divine Being. The idea of God, conveyed into a soul of any power and freedom, is wonderfully prolific. It bursts the bonds of the animal nature, and expands and elevates the rational to some shadowy semblance of its primeval glory. Where it has become altogether extinct, the human has sunk down under the debasing bondage of the brutal. During the four centuries that elapsed from the arrival of Abram to the conquest of the country by his descendants, this interesting relic of a pure Gentile worship seems to have disappeared. But the traces of such a purifying and elevating knowledge of God were not even then effaced from the memories, the customs, and the phrases of the people.

21–24. The king of Sodom concedes to Abram, according to custom, the spoils of conquest as his right, and claims for himself only his subjects who had been rescued from the foe. Abram however declines any personal advantage from the enterprise, or material recompense for his services. To this he was led partly by the present disposition of his mind, in which the spiritual prevailed over the carnal, and partly by the character of him with whom he had to deal; as the Sodomites were notorious for their wickedness. On other occasions he accepted unmerited gifts (Gen. xii. 16, xx. 14, 16). On the present occasion he no doubt felt himself amply rewarded by the recovery of his kinsman, and the blessing of Melkizedec. Disinterestedness has had another victory in Abram. And accordingly the minister of God meets him on the field of a common humanity, and pronounces on him a blessing. The unselfish, unsectarian heart of the heir of special promise, bows in acknowledgment of the representative of the universal and anterior covenant of God with Noah.

22. *I have lifted up my hand.* This is a serious matter with Abram. Either before, or then and there, he made an oath or solemn asseveration before God, with uplifted hand, that he would not touch the property of Sodom. He must have felt there was danger of moral contamination in coming into any political relationship with the cities of the vale. *The* LORD, *the most high God, the Founder of heaven and earth.* In this conjunction of names Abram solemnly and expressly identifies the God of himself and of Melkizedec in the presence of the king of Sodom. The most high God of Melkizedec is the God of the first chapter of Genesis, and the Jehovah of Adam, Noah, and Abram.

24. While Abram refrains from accepting any part of the spoils beyond what had been consumed in supplying the necessities of his followers in the expedition, he expressly excepts the portion to which his confederates, Aner, Eshcol, and Mamre, became entitled by their share in the recovery of the property. This is sufficient to prove that the transaction regarding the spoil was not an offer of generosity on the part of the king of Sodom, but an act of disinterestedness on the part of Abram.

XLI. THE FAITH OF ABRAM. — Gen. xv.

1. דָּבָר *a word, a thing;* the word being the sign of the thing.

2. אֲדֹנָי Adonai, *the Lord;* r. *bring down, lay down.* This is the name usually read in place of Jehovah; but when as in the present case Jehovah and Adonai are in apposition, Elohim is read instead of the former. The Jews from a feeling of reverence avoided the utterance of this sacred name except on the most solemn occasions. This is said to have arisen from a stringent interpretation of Lev. xxiv. 16. According to some, this name was pronounced only once a year by the high priest, on the day of atonement, in the Holy of Holies, and according to others only in the solemn benedictions pronounced by the priests. At an earlier period, however, the name must have been freely used by the people, as it enters into the composition of proper names. Adon in the singular and plural is used as a common name. מֶשֶׁק *possession,* בֶּן־מֶשֶׁק *possessor.* This forms a paronomasia with דַּמֶּשֶׂק, which is for דַּמְשֶׂק. אֱלִיעֶזֶר Eliezer, *God of help,* or *mighty to help.*

19. קֵינִי Kenite, patronymic of קַיִן Kain. קְנִזִּי Kenizzite, patr. of קְנַז Kenaz, *hunter.* קַדְמֹנִי Kadmonite, *eastern, old.*

XV. 1. After these things came the word of the Lord unto
Abram in a vision; saying, Fear not, Abram: I am thy shield,
thy exceeding great reward. 2. And Abram said, Lord Jeho-
vah, what wilt thou give me, seeing I go childless, and the
possessor of my house is Eliezer of Damascus? 3. And Abram
said, Behold, to me thou hast given no seed; and, behold, a
son of my house is mine heir. 4. And, behold, the word of
the Lord came unto him, saying, This shall not be thine heir;
but he that shall come out of thine own bowels shall be thine
heir. 5. And he brought him forth abroad and said, Look
now towards heaven, and tell the stars, if thou be able to tell
them. And he said unto him, So shall thy seed be. 6. And
he believed in the Lord; and he counted to him for righteous-
ness.

7. And he said unto him, I am the Lord, that brought thee
out of Ur of the Kasdim, to give thee this land to possess it.

8. And he said, Lord JEHOVAH, whereby shall I know that I shall possess it? 9. And he said unto him, Take me a heifer three years old, and a she-goat three years old, and a ram three years old, and a turtle dove, and a young pigeon. 10. And he took him all these, and divided them in the midst, and laid each piece one against another; but the birds divided he not. 11. And the birds of prey came down upon the carcasses, and Abram drove them away. 12. And the sun was about to set, and a trance fell upon Abram; and, lo, a horror, a great darkness, fell upon him. 13. And he said unto Abram, Know, know thou, that thy seed shall be strangers in a land that is not theirs, and shall serve them, and they shall afflict them four hundred years. 14. And also the nation whom they shall serve will I judge; and afterward shall they come out with great wealth. 15. And thou shalt go to thy fathers in peace; thou shalt be buried in a happy old age. 16. And in the fourth age shall they return hither; for the iniquity of the Amorite is not yet full. 17. And the sun went down, and deep darkness was come on, and, behold, a smoking oven and a burning lamp that passed between those pieces.

18. In that day the LORD made a covenant with Abram, saying, Unto thy seed have I given this land, from the river of Mizraim unto the great river, the river Phrat: 19. The Kenite and Kenizzite and the Kadmonite, 20. And the Hittite and the Perizzite and the Rephaim, 21. And the Amorite and the Kenaanite and the Girgashite and the Jebusite.

§ 28.

The events recorded in the preceding chapter manifest the sway of the new nature in Abram, and meet the approval of the Lord. This approval is exhibited in a heavenly visit to the patriarch, in which the Lord solemnly reiterates the promise of the seed and the land. Abram believes in the Lord, who thereupon enters into covenant with him.

1–6. *After these things,* — the victory, the blessing, and the self-denial recorded in the previous chapter. *The word of the Lord,* manifesting himself by speech to his servant. *In the vision* the intelligent observer passes from the merely sensible to the supersensible sphere of reality. *Fear not, Abram.* The patriarch had some reason to fear. The formidable allies had indeed been discomfited, and the fruits of their marauding enterprise wrested from them. But they might resume their purpose, and return with an overwhelming force. And Abram was still a stranger in a foreign land, preoccupied by tribes of another race, who would combine against him as soon as they suspected him of being an intruder. But the Lord had stood by him and given him the victory, and now speaks to him in the language of encouragement. *I am thy shield, thy exceeding great reward.* The word *I* is separately expressed, and, therefore, emphatic in the original. I, JEHOVAH, the Self-existent, the Author of existence, the Performer of promise, the Manifester of myself to man, and not any creature however exalted. This was something beyond a seed, or a land, or any temporal thing. The Creator infinitely transcends the creature. The mind of Abram is here lifted up to the spiritual and the eternal. 1. Thy shield. 2. Thy exceeding great reward. Abram has two fears, — the presence of evil, and the absence of good. Experience and conscience had begun to teach him that both of these were justly his doom. But Jehovah has chosen him, and here engages himself to stand between him and all harm, and himself to be to him all good. With such a shield from all evil, and such a source of all good, he need not be afraid. The Lord, we see, begins, as usual, with the immediate and the tangible; but he propounds a principle that reaches to the eternal and the spiritual. We have here the opening germ of the great doctrine of "the Lord our righteousness," redeeming us on the one hand from the sentence of death, and on the other to a title to eternal life.

2, 3. Notwithstanding the unbounded grandeur and preciousness of the promise, or rather assurance, now given, Abram is still childless and landless; and the Lord has made as yet no sign of action in regard to these objects of special promise. *Lord* JEHOVAH. The name Adonai is here for the first time used in the divine records. It denotes one who has authority; and, therefore, when applied to God, the Supreme Lord. Abram hereby acknowledges Jehovah as Supreme Judge and Governor, and therefore entitled to dispose of all matters concerning his present or prospective welfare. *What wilt thou give me?* Of what use will *land* or wealth be to me, the immediate *reward* specified by the promise? Eliezer of Damascus is master of my house. *To me thou hast given no seed.* This was the present shield mentioned also in former words of promise. There is something strikingly human in all this. Abram is no enthusiast or fanatic. He fastens on the substantive blessings which the Lord had expressly named.

4, 5. The Lord reiterates the promise concerning the *seed.* As he had commanded him to view the land, and see in its dust the emblem of the multitude that would spring from him, so now, with a sublime simplicity of practical illustration, he brings him forth to contemplate the stars, and challenges him to tell their number, if he can; adding, *So shall thy seed be.* He that made all these out of nothing, by the word of his power, is able to fulfil his promise, and multiply the seed of Abram and Sarai. Here, we perceive, the vision does not interfere with the notice of the sensible world, so far as is necessary (Dan. x. 7; John xii. 29).

6. *And Abram believed in the Lord.* Thus, at length, after many throes of labor, has come to the birth in the breast of Abram *faith in Jehovah*, on his simple promise in the absence of all present performance, and in the face of all sensible hinderance. The command to go to the land which the Lord would show him, accompanied with the promise to make of him a great nation, had awakened in him a certain expectation; which, however, waited for some performance to ripen it into faith. But waiting in a state of suspense is not faith, but doubt; and faith after performance is not faith, but sight. The second and third renewal of the promise, while performance was still unseen in the distance, was calculated to slay the expectancy that still paused for realization, to give it the vitality of a settled consent and acquiescence in the faithfulness of God, and mature it into conviction and confession.

What was there now, then, to call forth Abram's faith more than at the first promise? There was the reiteration of the promise. There was the withholding of the performance, leaving room for the exercise of pure faith. There was time to train the mind to this unwonted idea and determination. And, lastly, there was the sublime assurance conveyed in the sentence, "*I* am thy shield, thy exceeding great reward," transcending all the limits of time and place, comprehending alike the present and the eternal, the earthly and the heavenly. This, coupled with all the recorded and unrecorded dealings of the Lord, leads him to conceive the nobler feeling of faith in the Promiser, antecedent to any part of the execution, any unfolding of the plan, or any removal of the obvious difficulty. The moment of deliverance draws nigh, when Abram at length ventures to open his mouth and lay bare, in articulate utterance, the utmost questionings of his soul before the Lord. And then, in due time, is effected the birth of faith; not by commencing the accomplishment of the promise, but by the explicit reassertion of its several parts, in the light of that grand assurance which covers it in its narrowest and in its most expanded forms. Thus faith springs solely from the seed of promise. And from that moment there stands up and grows within the breast of man the right frame of mind towards the God of mercy, — the germ of a mutual good understanding between God and man which will spread its roots and branches through the whole soul, to the exclusion of every noxious plant, and blossom forth unto the blessed fruit of all holy feelings and doings.

And he counted it to him for righteousness. 1st. From this confessedly weighty sentence we learn, implicitly, that Abram had no righteousness. And if he had not, no man had. We have seen enough of Abram to know this on other grounds. And here the universal fact of man's depravity comes out into incidental notice, as a thing usually taken for granted, in the words of God. 2d. Righteousness is here imputed to Abram. Hence mercy and grace are extended to him; mercy taking effect in the pardon of his sin, and grace in bestowing the rewards of righteousness. 3d. That in him which is counted for righteousness is faith in Jehovah promising mercy. In the absence of righteousness, this is the only thing in the sinner that can be counted for righteousness. First, it is not of the nature of righteousness. If it were actual righteousness, it could not be counted as such. But believing God, who promises blessing to the undeserving, is essentially different from obeying God, who guarantees blessing to the deserving. Hence it has a negative fitness to be counted for what it is not. Secondly, it is trust in him who engages to bless in a holy and lawful way. Hence it is that in the sinner which brings him into conformity with the law through another who undertakes to satisfy its demands and secure its rewards for him. Thus it is the only thing in the sinner which, while it is not righteousness, has yet a claim to be counted for such, because it brings him into union with one who is just and having salvation.

It is not material what the Almighty and All-gracious promises in the first instance to him that believes in him, whether it be a land, or a seed, or any other blessing. All other blessing, temporal or eternal, will flow out of that express one, in a perpetual course of development, as the believer advances in experience, in compass of intellect, and capacity of enjoyment. Hence it is that a land involves a better land, a seed a nobler seed, a temporal an eternal good. The patriarchs were children to us in the comprehension of the love of God: we are children to those who will hereafter experience still grander manifestations of what God has prepared for them that love him. The shield and exceeding great reward await a yet inconceivable enlargement of meaning.

7–21. The Lord next confirms and explains the promise of the *land* to Abram. When God announces himself as Jehovah, who purposed to give him the land, Abram asks, Whereby *shall I know that I shall possess it?* He appears to expect some intimation as to the time and mode of entering upon possession. 9, 10. The Lord now directs him to make ready the things requisite for entering into a formal covenant regarding the land. These include all the kinds of animals afterwards used in sacrifice. The number *three* is sacred, and denotes the perfection of the victim in point of maturity. The division of the animals refers to the covenant between two parties, who participate in the rights which it guarantees. The birds are two without being divided. 11. *Abram drove them away.* As the animals slain and divided represent the only mean and way through which the two parties can meet in a covenant of peace, they must be preserved pure and unmutilated for the end they have to serve.

12–17. *And the sun was about to set.* This visit of the Lord to Abram continues for two nights, with the intervening day. In the former night he led him forth to view the stars (v. 5). The second night sets in with the consummation of the covenant (v. 17). The revelation comes to Abram in a trance of deep sleep. The Lord releases the mind from attention to the communications of sense in order to engage it with higher things. And he who makes the loftier revelation can enable the recipient to distinguish the voice of heaven from the play of fancy.

13–15. *Know, know thou.* Know certainly. This responds to Abram's question, Whereby shall I know? (v. 8). Four hundred years are to elapse before the seed of Abram shall actually proceed to take possession of the land. This interval can only commence when the seed is born; that is, at the birth of Isaac, when Abram was a hundred years of age, and therefore thirty years after the call. During this interval they are to be, *first, strangers in a land not theirs* for one hundred and ninety years; and then for the remaining two hundred and ten years in Egypt: at first, *servants*, with considerable privilege

and position ; and at last, *afflicted* serfs, under a hard and cruel b
14. At the end of this period Pharoh and his nation were visit
a succession of tremendous *judgments*, and Israel went out fre
bondage *with great wealth* (Ex. xii.–xiv.). 15. *Go to thy fathers.* This implies that the fathers, though dead, still exist. To *go* from one place to another implies, not annihilation, but the continuance of existence. The doctrine of the soul's perpetual existence is here intimated. Abram died in *peace* and *happiness*, one hundred and fifteen years before the descent into Egypt.

16. *In the fourth age.* An age here means the average period from the birth to the death of one man. This use of the word is proved by Numb. xxxii. 13,—"He made them wander in the wilderness forty years, until all the *generation* that had done evil in the sight of the Lord was consumed." This age or generation ran parallel with the life of Moses, and therefore consisted of one hundred and twenty years. Joseph lived one hundred and ten years. Four such generations amount to four hundred and eighty or four hundred and forty years. From the birth of Isaac to the return to the land of promise was an interval of four hundred and forty years. Isaac, Levi, Amram, and Eleazar may represent the four ages.

For the iniquity of the Amorite is not yet full. From this simple sentence we have much to learn. 1st. The Lord foreknows the moral character of men. 2d. In his providence he administers the affairs of nations on the principle of moral rectitude. 3d. Nations are spared until their iniquity is full. 4th. They are then cut off in retributive justice. 5th. The Amorite was to be the chief nation extirpated for its iniquity on the return of the seed of Abram. Accordingly we find the Amorites occupying by conquest the country east of the Jordan, from the Arnon to Mount Hermon, under their two kings, Sihon and Og (Num. xxi. 21–35). On the west of Jordan we have already met them at En-gedi and Hebron, and they dwelt in the mountains of Judah and Ephraim (Num. xiii. 29), whence they seem to have crossed the Jordan for conquest (Num. xxi. 26). Thus had they of all the tribes that overspread the land by far the largest extent of territory. And they seem to have been extinguished as a nation by the invasion of Israel, as we hear no more of them in the subsequent history of the country.

17. *And the sun went down.* The light of day is gone. The covenant is now formally concluded. Abram had risen to the height of faith in the God of promise. He is come into the position of the

father of the faithful. He is therefore qualified for entering into this solemn compact. This covenant has a peculiarity which distinguishes it from that with Noah. It refers to a patriarch and his seed chosen out of a coexisting race. It is not, however, subversive of the ancient and general covenant, but only a special measure for overcoming the legal and moral difficulties in the way, and ultimately bringing its comprehensive provisions into effect. It refers to the land of promise, which is not only a reality, but a type and an earnest of all analogous blessings.

The oven of smoke and lamp of flame symbolize the smoke of destruction and the light of salvation. Their passing through the pieces of the victims and probably consuming them as an accepted sacrifice are the ratification of the covenant on the part of God, as the dividing and presenting of them were on the part of Abram. The propitiatory foundation of the covenant here comes into view, and connects Abram with Habel and Noah, the primeval confessors of the necessity of an atonement.

18–21. In that instant the covenant was solemnly completed. Its primary form of benefit is the grant of the promised land with the extensive boundaries of the river of Egypt and the Euphrates. The former seems to be the Nile with its banks which constitute Egypt, as the Phrat with its banks describes the land of the East, with which countries the promised land was conterminous.

19–21. The ten principal nations inhabiting this area are here enumerated. Of these five are Kenaanite, and the other five probably not. The first three are new to us, and seem to occupy the extremities of the region here defined. The *Kenite* dwelt in the country bordering on Egypt and south of Palestine, in which the Amalekites also are found (Num. xxiv. 20–22; 1 Sam. xv. 6). They dwelt among the Midianites, as Hobab was both a Midianite and a Kenite (Num. x. 29; Judg. i. 16, iv. 11). They were friendly to the Israelites, and hence some of them followed their fortunes and settled in their land (1 Chr. ii. 55). The *Kenizzite* dwelt apparently in the same region, having affinity with the Horites, and subsequently with Edom and Israel (Gen. xxxvi. 11, 20–23; Jos. xv. 17; 1 Chr. ii. 50–52). The *Kadmonite* seems to be the Eastern, and, therefore, to hold the other extreme boundary of the promised land, towards Tadmor and the Phrat. These three tribes were probably related to Abram, and, therefore, descendants of Shem. The other seven tribes have already come under our notice.

XLII. THE BIRTH OF ISHMAEL. — Gen. xvi.

1. הָגָר Hagar, *flight.* Hejrah, the flight of Mahomet.

7. מַלְאָךְ *messenger, angel.* A deputy commissioned to discharge a certain duty for the principal whom he represents. As the most usual task is that of bearing messages, commands, or tidings, he is commonly called a *messenger* (ἄγγελος). The word is therefore a term of office, and does not further distinguish the office-bearer than as an intelligent being. Hence a mal'ak may be a man deputed by a man (Gen. xxxii. 3 ; Job i. 14), or by God (Hag. i. 13 ; Mal. iii. 1), or a superhuman being delegated in this case only by God. The English term *angel* is now specially appropriated to the latter class of messengers.

1st. The nature of angels is spiritual (Heb. i. 14). This characteristic ranges over the whole chain of spiritual being from man up to God himself. The extreme links, however, are excluded : man, because he is a special class of intelligent creatures; and God, because he is supreme. Other classes of spiritual beings may be excluded, — as the cherubim, the seraphim, — because they have not the same office, though the word *angelic* is sometimes used by us as synonymous with heavenly or spiritual. They were all of course originally good; but some of them have fallen from holiness, and become evil spirits or devils (Matt. xxv. 31, 41 ; Jude vi. ; Rev. xii. 7). The latter are circumscribed in their sphere of action, as if confined within the walls of their prison, in consequence of their fallen state and malignant disposition (Gen. iii. ; Job i. 2 ; 1 Peter ii. 4 ; Rev. xx. 2). Being spiritual, they are not only moral, but intelligent. They also excel in strength (Ps. ciii. 20). The holy angels have the full range of action for which their qualities are adapted. They can assume a real form, expressive of their present functions, and affecting the senses of sight, hearing, and touch, or the roots of those senses in the soul. They may even perform innocent functions of a human body, such as eating (Gen. xviii. 8, xix. 3). Being spirits, they can resolve the material food into its original elements in a way which we need not attempt to conceive or describe. But this case of eating stands altogether alone. Angels have no distinction of sex (Matt. xxii. 30). They do not grow old or die. They are not a race, and have not a body in the ordinary sense of the term.

2d. Their office is expressed by their name. In common with other intelligent creatures, they take part in the worship of God (Rev. vii. 11) ; but their special office is to execute the commands of God in the natural world (Ps. ciii. 20), and especially to minister to the heirs of salvation (Heb. i. 14; Matt. xviii. 10; Luke xv. 10, xvi. 22). It is not needful here to enter into the peculiarities of their ministry.

3d. *The angel of* JEHOVAH. This phrase is specially employed to denote the Lord himself in that form in which he condescends to make himself manifest to man; for the Lord God says of this angel, "Beware of him, and obey his voice; provoke him not, for he will not pardon your transgressions; for my name is in his inmost" (Ex. xxiii. 21); that is, my nature is in his essence. Accordingly, he who is called the angel of the Lord in one place is otherwise denominated the Lord or God in the immediate context (Gen. xvi. 7, 13, xxii. 11, 12, xxxi. 11, 13, xlviii. 15, 16; Ex. iii. 2–15, xxiii. 20–23 with xxxiii. 14, 15). It is remarkable, at the same time, that the Lord is spoken of in these cases as a distinct person from the angel of the Lord, who is also called the Lord. The phraseology intimates to us a certain inherent plurality within the essence of the one only God, of which we have had previous indications (Gen. i. 26, iii. 22). The phrase *angel of the Lord,* however, indicates a more distant manifestation to man than the term Lord itself. It brings the medium of communication into greater prominence. It seems to denote some person of the Godhead in angelic form. שׁוּר Shur, *wall.* A city or place probably near the head of the gulf of Suez. The desert of Shur is now Jofar.

11. יִשְׁמָעֵאל Jishm'ael, *the Mighty will hear.*

13. אֵל רֳאִי *God of vision* or *seeing.*

14. בְּאֵר לַחַי רֹאִי Beer-lachai-roi, *well of vision to the living.* בֶּרֶד Bered, *hail.* The site is not known.

XVI. 1. And Sarai, Abram's wife, bare not to him; and she had a Mizrite handmaid, whose name was Hagar. 2. And Sarai said to Abram, Behold now the LORD hath restrained me from bearing: go in now unto my maid; mayhap I shall be builded by her. And Abram hearkened to the voice of Sarai. 3. And Sarai, Abram's wife, took Hagar the Mizrite, her maid, after Abram had dwelt ten years in the land of Kenaan, and gave her to Abram, her husband, to be his wife. 4. And he went in unto Hagar, and she conceived; and she saw that she had conceived, and her mistress was despised in her eyes. 5. And Sarai said unto Abram, My wrong be upon thee; I myself gave my maid into thy bosom, and she saw that she had conceived, and I was despised in her eyes; the LORD judge between me and thee. 6. And Abram said unto Sarai, Behold, thy maid is in thy hand: do to her that which is good in thine eyes. And Sarai humbled her, and she fled from her face.

7. And the angel of the LORD found her by a spring of water in the wilderness, by the spring in the way to Shur. 8. And he said, Hagar, Sarai's maid, whence art thou come, and whither goest thou? And she said, From the face of Sarai, Sarai my mistress, am I fleeing. 9. And the angel of the LORD said unto her, Return to thy mistress, and humble thyself under her hands. 10. And the angel of the LORD said unto her, Multiply, multiply will I thy seed, and it shall not be numbered for multitude. 11. And the angel of the LORD said unto her, Behold, thou art with child, and shalt bear a son; and thou shalt call his name Ishmael, because the LORD hath heard thy humiliation. 12. And he will be a wild man, his hand against every man, and every man's hand against him; and in the presence of all his brethren shall he dwell.

13. And she called the name of the LORD that spake unto her, Thou art the God of my vision; for she said, Have I even still seen, after my vision? 14. Wherefore the well is called Beer-lahai-roi: behold, it is between Kadesh and Bered. 15. And Hagar bare Abram a son; and Abram called the name of his son, whom Hagar bare, Ishmael. 16. And Abram was the son of eighty and six years when Hagar bare Ishmael to Abram.

§ 29.

Sarah has been barren probably much more than twenty years. She appears to have at length reluctantly arrived at the conclusion that she would never be a mother. Nature and history prompted the union of one man to one wife in marriage, and it might have been presumed that God would honor his own institution. But the history of the creation of man was forgotten or unheeded, and the custom of the East prompted Sarai to resort to the expedient of giving her maid to her husband for a second wife, that she might have children by her.

1–6. *A Mizrite handmaid.* Hagar was probably obtained, ten years before, during their sojourn in Egypt. 2. *The Lord hath restrained me.* It was natural to the ancient mind to recognize the power and will of God in all things. *I shall be builded by her,* אִבָּנֶה, built as the foundation of a house, by the addition of sons or daughters (בָּנִים or בָּנוֹת). She thought she had or wished to have a share in the promise, if not by herself personally, yet through her maid. The faith of Sarah had not yet come fully to the birth. Abram yields to the suggestion of his wife, and complies with the custom of the country. 3. Ten years had elapsed since they had entered the land they were to inherit. Impatience at the long delay leads to an invention of their own for obtaining an heir. 4–6. The contempt of her maid was unjustifiable. But it was the natural consequence of Sarai's own improper and imprudent step, in giving her to her husband as a concubine. Unwilling, however, to see in herself the occasion of her maid's insolence, she transfers the blame to her husband, who empowers or reminds her of her power still to deal with her as it pleased her. Hagar, unable to bear the yoke of humiliation, flees from her mistress.

7–12. The angel of the Lord either represents the Lord, or presents the Lord in angelic form. The Lord manifests himself to Hagar seemingly on account of her relationship to Abram, but in the more distant form of angelic visitation. She herself appears to be a believer in God. The spring of water is a place of refreshment on her journey. She is on the way to Shur, which was before Mizraim as thou goest towards Asshur (Gen. xxv. 18), and therefore fleeing to Egypt, her native land. 8, 9. The angel of the Lord interrogates her, and requires her to return to her mistress, and humble herself under her hands.

10. *I will multiply.* This language is proper only to the Lord himself; for it claims a divine prerogative. The Lord is, therefore, in this angel. He promises to Hagar a numerous offspring. 11, 12. *Ishmael. El,* the Mighty, will hear; but *Jehovah,* the Lord, heard her humiliation. Jehovah, therefore, is the same God as El. He describes Ishmael and his progeny in him as resembling the wild ass. This animal is a fit symbol of the wild, free, untamable Bedawin of the desert. He is to live in contention, and yet to dwell independently, among all his brethren. His brethren are the descendants of Heber, the Joctanites, composing the thirteen original tribes of the Arabs, and the Palgites to whom the descendants of Abram belonged. The Ishmaelites constituted the second element of the great Arab nation, and shared in their nomadic character and independence. The character here given of them is true even to the present day.

13–16. *God of my vision* (El-roi). Here we have the same divine name as in Ishmael. *Have I even still seen* — continued to live and see the sun after having seen God? Beer-lahai-roi, the well of vision (of God) to the living. To see God and live was an issue contrary to expectation (Ex. xxxiii. 20). The well is between Kadesh and Bered. The site of the latter has not been ascertained. R. Jonathan gives חֲלוּצָא the Ἔλουσα of Ptolemy, now el-Khulasa, about twelve miles south of Beersheba. Rowland finds the well at Moyle or Muweilah, still further south in the same direction. 15, 16. The birth of Ishmael is in the sixteenth year after Abram's call, and the eleventh after his arrival in Kenaan.

XLIII. THE SEALING OF THE COVENANT. — Gen. xvii.

1. שַׁדַּי Shaddai, *Irresistible, able to destroy, and by inference to make, Almighty.* שָׁדַד *be strong, destroy.* This name is found six times in Genesis, and thirty-one times in Job.

5. אַבְרָהָם Abraham, from אַבְרָם *high-father*, and הָם the radical part of הָמוֹן *a multitude*, is obtained by a euphonic abbreviation אַבְרָהָם *high-father of a multitude.* The root רהם is a variation of רום; affording, however, a link of connection in sound and sense with the root הָמָה *hum, be tumultuous*, from which comes הָמוֹן *a multitude.* The confluence of the biliterals רם and הם yields the triliteral רהם occurring in Arabic, though not elsewhere in our written Hebrew. The law of formation here noticed is interesting and real, though רהם may not have been an actual result of it.

11. נִמַלְתֶּם formed from נָמַל *circumcised.* מוּל *cut, circumcise.*

15. שָׂרָה Sarah, *princess.*

19. יִצְחָק Jitschaq, *laughing.*

XVII. 1. And Abram was the son of ninety and nine years, and the Lord appeared to Abram and said unto him, I am God Almighty: walk before me, and be perfect. 2. And I will grant my covenant between me and thee, and multiply thee exceedingly. 3. And Abram fell on his face; and God talked with him, saying, 4. As for me, behold, my covenant is with thee; and thou shalt be father of many nations. 5. And thy name shall no more be called Abram; but thy name shall be Abraham; for a father of many nations have I made thee. 6. And I will make thee exceeding fruitful, and make nations of thee; and kings shall come out of thee. 7. And I will establish my covenant between me and thee, and thy seed after thee, in their generations, for a perpetual covenant, to be a God unto thee, and to thy seed after thee. 8. And I will give unto thee, and to thy seed after thee, the land of thy sojournings, all the land of Kenaan, for a perpetual possession; and I will be their God.

9. And God said to Abraham, And thou my covenant shalt keep, thou and thy seed after thee in their generations. 10. This is my covenant, which ye shall keep, between me and you and the seed after thee: that every male of you be circumcised. 11. And ye shall circumcise the flesh of your foreskin; and it shall be a token of the covenant betwixt me and you. 12. And the son of eight days shall be circumcised for you, every male in your generations; born in the house, and bought with money, of every stranger who is not of thy seed. 13. Circumcised shall he be that is born in thy house and bought with thy money; and my covenant shall be in your flesh for a perpetual covenant. 14. And the uncircumcised male, the flesh of whose foreskin is not circumcised, that soul shall be cut off from his people: my covenant hath he broken.

§ 30.

15. And God said unto Abraham, As for Sarai thy wife, thou shalt not call her name Sarai; but Sarah shall be her name. 16. And I will bless her, and give thee a son also of her: and I will bless her, and she shall become nations; kings of peoples shall be of her. 17. And Abraham fell on his face, and laughed, and said in his heart, Shall a child be born to the son of a hundred years? or Sarah — shall the daughter of ninety years bear? 18. And Abraham said unto God, Oh that Ishmael might live before thee! 19. And God said, Certainly Sarah

thy wife shall bear thee a son, and thou shalt call his name Isaac: and I will establish my covenant with him for a perpetual covenant for his seed after him. 20. And for Ishmael I have heard thee: behold, I have blessed him, and made him fruitful, and multiplied him exceedingly: twelve princes shall he beget, and I will make him a great nation. 21. But my covenant will I establish with Isaac, whom Sarah shall bear unto thee at this season in the next year. 22. And he left off talking with him; and God went up from Abraham.

23. And Abraham took Ishmael his son, and all that were born in his house, and all that were bought with his money, every male among the men of Abraham's house, and circumcised the flesh of their foreskin in the self-same day, as God had spoken with him. 24. And Abraham was the son of ninety and nine years when he was circumcised in the flesh of his foreskin. 25. And Ishmael his son was the son of thirteen years when he was circumcised in the flesh of his foreskin. 26. In the self-same day was Abraham circumcised and Ishmael his son. 27. And all the men of his house, born in the house, and bought with money of the stranger, were circumcised with him. 4 ¶¶¶ 19.

The present form of the covenant is not identical with the former. That referred chiefly to the land; this chiefly to the seed. That dwelt much on temporal things; this rises to spiritual things. That specifies only Abram; this mentions both Abram and Sarai. At the former period God formally entered into covenant with Abram (כָּרַת בְּרִית Gen. xv. 18); at present he takes the first step in the fufilment of the covenant (נָתַן בְּרִית), seals it with a token and a perpetual ordinance, and gives Abram and Sarai new names in token of a new nature. There was an interval of fourteen years at least between the ratification of the covenant and the preparation for the fulfilment of its conditions, during which Abraham's faith had time to unfold.

1–8. The covenant in its spiritual aspect. *The Lord*, the Author of existence and performance. *God Almighty*, El Shaddai. *El*, the Lasting, Eternal, Absolute. *Shaddai*, the Irresistible, Unchangeable,

Destructive (Isa. xiii. 6; Joel i. 15). This term indicates on the one hand his judicial, punitive power, and points to his holiness; and on the other hand, his alterative, reconstructive power, and points to his providence. The complex name, therefore, describes God as the Holy Spirit, who works in the development of things, especially in the punishment and eradication of sin and its works, and in the regeneration and defence of holiness. It refers to potence, and potence combined with promise affords ground for faith.

Walk before me and be perfect. In the institution of the covenant we had "fear not,"—an encouragement to the daunted or the doubting. In its confirmation we have a command, a rule of life, prescribed. This is in keeping with the circumstances of Abraham. For, first, he has now faith in the Lord, which is the fruit of the new man in him prevailing over the old, and is therefore competent to obey; and, next, the Lord in whom he believes is God Almighty, the all-efficient Spirit, who worketh both to will and to do in the destroying of sin and building up of holiness. *Walk,*—act in the most comprehensive sense of the term; *before me,* and not behind, as one conscious of doing what is, not displeasing, but pleasing to me; *and be perfect,* not sincere merely, unless in the primitive sense of duty, but complete, upright, holy, not only in walk, which is provided for in the previous clause, but in heart, the spring of action.

2. *My covenant,* which I have already purposed and formally closed. *I will grant,* carry into effect, the provisions of it. *Multiply thee.* The seed is here identified with the head or parent seat of life. The seed now comes forward as the prominent benefit of the covenant.

3–6. *Abram fell on his face.* This is the lowliest form of reverence, in which the worshipper leans on his knees and elbows, and his forehead approaches the ground. Prostration is still customary in the East. Abram has attained to loftier notions of God. *God talked with him.* Jehovah, El Shaddai, is here called God. The Supreme appears as the Author of existence, the Irresistible and Everlasting, in this stage of the covenant relation.

4. *As for me.* The one party to the covenant is here made prominent, as in verse 9 the other party is brought out with like emphasis. The exalted Being who has entered into it imparts a grandeur, solemnity, and excellence to the covenant. *Father of many nations.* The promise of seed is here expanded and particularized. A multitude of nations and kings are to trace their descent from Abram. This is true in a literal sense. The twelve tribes of Israel and many Arab tribes,

the twelve princes of Ishmael, Keturah's descendants, and the dukes of Edom sprang from him. But it is to be more magnificently realized in a spiritual sense. *Nations* is a term usually applied, not to the chosen people, but to the other great branches of the human race. This points to the original promise, that in him should all the families of the earth be blessed. *Abraham.* The father of many nations is to be called by a new name, as he has come to have a new nature, and been elevated to a new dignity. The high father has become the father of the multitude of the faithful.

7. Next, the spiritual part of the covenant comes into view. *To be a God unto thee, and to thy seed after thee.* Here we find God, in the progress of human development, for the third time laying the foundations of a covenant of grace with man. He dealt with Adam and with Noah, and now he deals with Abraham. *A perpetual covenant.* This covenant will not fail, since God has originated it, notwithstanding the moral instability of man. Though we cannot as yet see the possibility of fulfilling the condition on man's side, yet we may be assured that what God purposes will somehow be accomplished. The seed of Abraham will eventually embrace the whole human family in fellowship with God.

8. Thirdly, the temporal and the spiritual are brought together. The land of promise is made sure to the heir of promise, *for a perpetual possession,* and God engages to *be their God.* The phrase *perpetual possession* has here two elements of meaning,—first, that the possession, in its coming form of a certain land, shall last as long as the coexisting relations of things are continued; and, secondly, that the said possession in all the variety of its ever grander phases will last absolutely forever. Each form will be perfectly adequate to each stage of a progressive humanity. But in all its forms and at every stage it will be their chief glory that God is their God.

9–14. The sign of the covenant. *And thou.* The other party to the covenant now learns his obligation. *Every male of you shall be circumcised.* Circumcision, as the rainbow, might have been in existence before it was adopted as the token of a covenant. The sign of the covenant with Noah was a purely natural phenomenon, and therefore entirely independent of man. That of the Abrahamic covenant was an artificial process, and therefore, though prescribed by God, was dependent on the voluntary agency of man. The former marked the sovereignty of God in ratifying the covenant and insuring its fulfilment, notwithstanding the mutability of man; the latter indicates the responsibility of man, the trust he places in the word of promise, and the assent he gives to the terms of the divine mercy. As the former covenant conveys a common natural blessing to all mankind and contemplates a common spiritual blessing, so the latter conveys a special spiritual blessing and contemplates its universal acceptance. The rainbow was the appropriate natural emblem of preservation from a flood; and the removal of the foreskin was the fit symbol of that removal of the old man and renewal of nature, which qualified Abraham to be the parent of a holy seed. And as the former sign foreshadows an incorruptible inheritance, so the latter prepares the way for a holy seed, by which the holiness and the heritage will at length be universally extended.

It is worthy of remark that in circumcision, after Abraham himself, the parent is the voluntary imponent, and the child merely the passive recipient of the sign of the covenant. Hereby is taught the lesson of parental responsibility and parental hope. This is the first formal step in a godly education, in which the parent acknowledges his obligation to perform all the rest. It is also, on the command of God, the formal admission of the believing parents' offspring into the privileges of the covenant, and therefore cheers the heart of the parent in entering upon the parental task. This admission cannot be reversed but by the deliberate rebellion of the child.

Still further, the sign of the covenant is to be applied to every male in the household of Abraham. This indicates that the servant or serf stands in the relation of a child to his master or owner, who is therefore accountable for the soul of his serf, as for that of his son. It points out the applicability of the covenant to others, as well as the children of Abraham, and therefore its capability of universal extension when the fulness of time should come. It also intimates the very plain but very often forgotten truth, that our obligation to obey God is not cancelled by our unwillingness. The serf is bound to have his child circumcised as long as God requires it, though he may be unwilling to comply with the divine commandments.

12–14. The time of circumcision is the eighth day. Seven is the number of perfection. Seven days are therefore regarded as a type of perfect age and individuality. At this stage, accordingly, the sign of sanctification is made on the child, betokening the consecration of the heart to God, when its rational powers have come into noticeable activity. To be *cut off from his people* is to be excluded from any part in the covenant, and treated simply as a Gentile or alien, some of whom seem to have dwelt among the Israelites. It was sometimes accompanied with the sentence of death (Ex. xxxi. 14); and this shows that it did not of itself imply such a doom. Excommunication, however, for the omission of circumcision, would be extremely rare, as no parent would intentionally neglect the sacred interest of his child. Yet the omission of this rite has not been unprecedented, as the children of Israel did not generally circumcise their children in the wilderness (Jos. v. 5).

15–22. Sarai is now formally taken into the covenant, as she is to be the mother of the promised seed. Her name is therefore changed to Sarah, princess. Aptly is she so named, for she is to bear the child of promise, to become nations, and be the mother of kings. 17. *Abraham fell upon his face and laughed.* From the reverential attitude assumed by Abraham we infer that his laughter sprang from joyful and grateful surprise. *Said in his heart.* The following questions of wonder are not addressed to God; they merely agitate the breast of the astonished patriarch. Hence his irrepressible smile arises not from any doubt of the fulfilment of the promise, but from surprise at the unexpected mode in which it is to be fulfilled. Laughing in Scripture expresses joy in the countenance, as dancing does in the whole body.

18–20. Abraham seems up to this time to have regarded Ishmael as the promised seed. Hence a feeling of anxiety instantly penetrates his breast. It finds utterance in the prayer, *Oh that Ishmael might live before thee.* He asks *life* for his beloved son, — that is, a share in the divine favor; and that *before God,* — that is, a life of holiness and communion with God. But God asseverates his purpose of giving him a son by Sarah. This son is to be called Isaac, — he that laughs or he shall laugh, in reference to the various emotions of surprise and delight with which his parents regarded his birth. Abram's prayer for Ishmael, however, is not unanswered. He is to be fruitful, beget twelve princes, and become a great nation. 21, 22. But Isaac is to be the heir of promise. At the present season next year he is to be born. The communication being completed, *God went* up from Abram.

23–27. *In the self-same day.* In this passage we have the prompt and punctual fulfilment of the command concerning circumcision detailed with all the minuteness due to its importance. Ishmael was thirteen years of age when he was circumcised. Josephus relates that the Arabs accordingly delay circumcision till the thirteenth year (Ant. I. 12. 2).

XLIV. VISIT OF THE LORD TO ABRAHAM.—Gen. xviii.

2. הִשְׁתַּחֲוָה *bow*, or bend the body in token of respect to God or man. The attitude varies from a slight inclination of the body to entire prostration with the forehead touching the ground.

6. סְאָה a *seah*, about an English peck, the third part of an ephah. The ephah contained ten omers. The omer held about five pints.

XVIII. 1. And the LORD appeared unto him by the oaks
of Mamre, and he sat at the tent door in the heat of the day.
2. And he lift up his eyes and looked, and, lo, three men stood
before him; and he saw and ran to meet them from the tent
door, and bowed himself to the earth; 3. And said, O LORD,
if now I have found favor in thine eyes, pass not away now
from thy servant. 4. Let a little water now be fetched, and
wash your feet, and rest yourselves under the tree; 5. And
I will fetch a morsel of bread, and comfort ye your hearts:
afterwards ye shall pass on; for therefore are ye come to your
servant. And they said, So do, as thou hast spoken. 6. And
Abraham hastened into the tent unto Sarah, and said, Hasten
with three seahs of fine meal, knead it, and make hearth-cakes.
7. And Abraham ran unto the herd, and fetched a calf, tender
and good, and gave it to the lad, and he hasted to dress it.
8. And he fetched butter and milk and the calf which he had
dressed, and set before them, and he stood by them under the
tree, and they did eat.

9. And they said unto him, Where is Sarah, thy wife?
And he said, Behold, in the tent. 10. And he said, I will
surely return unto thee at the time of life, and lo, Sarah, thy
wife, shall have a son. And Sarah heard in the tent door
which was behind him. 11. Now Abraham and Sarah were
old, far gone in days: it ceased to be with Sarah after the
manner of women. 12. And Sarah laughed within herself,
saying, After I am faded is pleasure come to me, and my lord
is old? 13. And the LORD said unto Abraham, Why hath

Sarah laughed, saying, Shall I indeed bear when I am old? 14. Is anything too hard for the Lord? At the set time will I return unto thee about the time of life, and Sarah shall have a son. 15. Then Sarah denied, saying, I laughed not; for she was afraid. And he said, Nay, but thou didst laugh.

16. And the men rose up thence and looked toward Sodom; and Abraham went with them to convoy them. 17. And the Lord said, Shall I hide from Abraham that which I do? 18. And Abraham shall surely become a nation, great and mighty, and blessed in him shall be all the nations of the earth. 19. For I have known him, that he may command his children and his house after him, and they shall keep the way of the Lord, to do justice and judgment; that the Lord may bring upon Abraham that which he hath spoken of him. 20. And the Lord said, Because the cry of Sodom and Amorah is great, and their sin is very grievous, 21. Let me go down now, and see if they have done altogether according to the cry of it which is come unto me; and if not, let me know. 22. And the men turned their faces thence, and went toward Sodom; and Abraham was yet standing before the Lord.

23. And Abraham drew near and said, Wilt thou also destroy the righteous with the wicked? 24. Mayhap there be fifty righteous within the city: wilt thou also destroy and not spare the place for the fifty righteous that are therein? 25. Far be it from thee to do after this manner, to slay the righteous with the wicked, that the righteous be as the wicked: far be it from thee. Shall not the judge of all the earth do right? 26. And the Lord said, If I find in Sodom fifty righteous within the city, then I will spare all the place for their sake. 27. And Abraham answered and said, Behold now I have taken upon me to speak unto the Lord, who am but dust and ashes. 28. Mayhap the fifty righteous lack five: wilt thou destroy for the five all the city? And he said I will not destroy it, if I find there forty and five. 29. And he spake unto him yet again and said, Mayhap there be forty found

there? And he said, I will not do it for the forty's sake. 30. And he said, Let not the LORD now be angry, and I will speak: mayhap there be thirty found there? And he said, I will not do it if I find thirty there. 31. And he said, Behold now, I have taken upon me to speak unto the LORD: mayhap there be twenty found there? And he said, I will not destroy it for the twenty's sake. 32. And he said, let not the LORD be angry, and I will speak but this once: mayhap there be ten found there? And he said, I will not destroy it for the ten's sake. 33. And the LORD went his way, as soon as he had left speaking with Abraham; and Abraham returned to his place.

This chapter describes Abraham's fellowship with God. On the gracious assurance of the Redeemer and Vindicator, "Fear not, I am thy shield and thy exceeding great reward," he ceased to fear, and believed. On the solemn announcement of the Conqueror of evil and the Quickener of the dead, "I am God Almighty; walk before me and be perfect," he began anew to walk with God in holiness and truth. The next step is, that God enters into communion with him as a man with his friend (Isa. xli. 8; John. xiv. 23). Hitherto he has appeared to him as God offering grace and inclining the will to receive it. Now, as God who has bestowed grace, he appears to him who has accepted it and is admitted into a covenant of peace. He visits him for the twofold purpose of drawing out and completing the faith of Sarah, and of communing with Abraham concerning the destruction of Sodom.

1–15. The Lord visits Abraham and assures Sarah of the birth of a son. Abraham is sitting in the tent door in the heat of the day, reposing. *Three men stood before him.* Whenever visitants from the celestial world appear to men, they have the form of man. This is the only form of a rational being known to us. It is not the design of God in revealing his mercy to us to make us acquainted with the whole of the nature of things. The science of things visible or invisible he leaves to our natural faculties to explore, as far as occasion allows. Hence we conclude that the celestial visitant is a real being, and that the form is a real form. But we are not entitled to infer that the human is the only or the proper form of such beings, or that they have any ordinary or constant form open to sense. We only discern that they are intelligent beings like ourselves, and, in order to manifest themselves to us as such, put on that form of intelligent creatures with which we are familiar, and in which they can intelligibly confer with us. For the same reason they speak the language of the party addressed, though, for ought we know, spiritual beings use none of the many languages of humanity, and have quite a different mode of communicating with one another. Other human acts follow on the occasion. They accept the hospitality of Abraham and partake of human food. This, also, was a real act. It does not imply, however, that food is necessary to spiritual beings. The whole is a typical act representing communion between God and Abraham. The giving and receiving of a meal was the ground of a perpetual or inviolable friendship.

He ran to meet him. This indicates the genuine warmth of unsophisticated nature. *Bowed himself to the earth.* This indicates a low bow, in which the body becomes horizontal, and the head droops. This gesture is employed both in worship and doing obeisance.

3–5. *O Lord.* Abraham uses the word אדני denoting one having authority, whether divine or not. This the Masorites mark as sacred, and apply the vowel points proper to the word when it signifies God. These men in some way represent God; for the Lord on this occasion appeared unto Abraham (v. 1). The number is in this respect notable. Abraham addresses himself first to one person (v. 3), then to more than one (v. 4, 5). It is stated that "*they* said, So do (v. 5), *they* did eat (v. 8), *they* said unto him, Where is Sarah thy wife" (v. 9). Then the singular number is resumed in the phrase *and he said* (v. 10), and at length, "The Lord said unto Abraham" (v. 13), and then, "and he said" (v. 15). Then we are told "*the men* rose up, and Abraham went with them" (v. 16). Then we have "The Lord said" twice (v. 17, 20). And lastly, it is said (v. 22) "*the men* turned their faces and went toward Sodom, and Abraham was yet standing before the Lord." From this it appears that of the three men one, at all events, was the Lord, who, when the other two went towards Sodom, remained with Abraham while he made his intercession for Sodom, and afterwards he also went his way. The other two will come before us again in the next chapter. Meanwhile we have here the first explicit instance of the Lord appearing as man to man, and holding familiar intercourse with him.

The narrative affords a pleasing instance of the primitive manners of the East. The hospitality of the pastoral tribes was spontaneous and unreserved. The washing of the feet, which were partly at least uncovered in walking, the reclining under the tree, and the offer of refreshment, are indicative of an unchanging rural simplicity. The phrases *a little water, a morsel of bread,* flow from a thoughtful courtesy. *Therefore are ye come.* In the course of events it has so fallen out, in order that you might be refreshed. The brief reply is a frank and unaffected acceptance of the hospitable invitation.

6–8. *Abraham hastened.* The unvarying customs of Eastern pastoral life here come up before us. There is plenty of flour and of live cattle. But the cakes have to be kneaded and baked on the hearth, and the calf has to be killed and dressed. Abraham personally gives directions, Sarah personally attends to the baking, and the boy or lad — that is, the domestic servant whose business it is — kills and dresses the meat. Abraham himself attends upon his guests. *Three seahs.* About three pecks, and therefore a superabundant supply for three guests. An omer, or three tenths of a seah, was considered sufficient for one man for a day (Ex. xvi. 16). But Abraham had a numerous household, and plentifulness was the character of primitive hospitality. *Hearth cakes,* baked among the coals. *Butter,* — seemingly any preparation of milk, cream, curds, or butter, all of which are used in the East.

9–15. The promise to Sarah. The men now enter upon the business of their visit. *Where is Sarah thy wife?* The jealousy and seclusion of later times had not yet rendered such an inquiry uncourteous. Sarah is within hearing of the conversation. *I will certainly return unto thee.* This is the language of self-determination, and therefore suitable to the sovereign, not to the ambassador. *At the time of life;* literally the living time, seemingly the time of birth, when the child comes to manifest life. *Sarah thy wife shall have a son.* Sarah hears this with incredulous surprise, and laughs with mingled doubt and delight. She knows that in the nature of things she is past child-bearing. 14. *Is anything too hard for the Lord?* Sarah laughed within herself, within the tent and behind the speaker; yet to her surprise her internal feelings are known to him. She finds there is One present who rises above the sphere of nature. In her confusion and terror she denies that she laughed. But he who sees what is within, insists that she did laugh, at least in the thought of her heart. There is a beautiful simplicity in the whole scene. Sarah now doubtless received faith and strength to conceive.

16–33. The conference concerning Sodom. The human manner of

the interview is carried out to the end. Abraham convoys his departing guests. The Lord then speaks, apparently debating with himself whether he shall reveal his intentions to Abraham. The reasons for doing so are assigned. 1st. Abraham shall surely become a nation great and mighty, and therefore has the interest of humanity in this act of retribution on Sodom. All that concerns man concerns him. 2d. Blessed in him shall be all the nations of the earth. Hence he is personally and directly concerned with all the dealings of mercy and judgment among the inhabitants of the earth. 3d. *I have known him.* The Lord has made himself known to him, has manifested his love to him, has renewed him after his own image; and hence this judgment upon Sodom is to be explained to him, that he may train his household to avoid the sins of this doomed city, to *keep the way of the Lord, to do justice and judgment;* and all this to the further intent that the *Lord may bring upon Abraham that which he hath spoken of him.* The awful judgments of the Lord on Sodom, as before on the antediluvian world, are a warning example to all who are spared or hear of them. And those who, notwithstanding these monuments of the divine vengeance, will cease to do justice and judgment, may be certain that they will not continue to enjoy the benefits of the covenant of grace. For all these reasons it is meet that the secret of Lord be with him (Ps. xxv. 11).

20–22. The Lord now proceeds to unfold his design. There is justice in every step of the divine procedure. He comes down to inquire and act according to the merits of the case. The men now depart on their errand; but Abraham still stands before the Lord.

23–33. Abraham intercedes for Sodom. His spiritual character is unfolded and exalted more and more. He employs the language of a free-born son with his heavenly Father. He puts forward the plea of justice to the righteous in behalf of the city. He ventures to repeat his intervention six times, every time diminishing the number of the righteous whom he supposes to be in it. The patience of the Lord is no less remarkable than the perseverance of Abraham. In every case he grants his petition. 27. *Dust and ashes.* This may refer to the custom of burning the dead, as then coexistent with that of burying them. Abraham intimates by a homely figure the comparative insignificance of the petitioner. He is dust at first, and ashes at last.

This completes the full and free intercourse of God with Abraham. He accepts his hospitable entertainment, renews his promise of a son by Sarah, communicates to him his counsel, and grants all his requests.

It is evident that Abraham has now fully entered upon all the privileges of the sons of God. He has become the friend of God (James ii. 23).

XLV. DESTRUCTION OF SODOM AND AMORAH.—Gen. xix.

9. גֶּשׁ־הָלְאָה *approach to a distant point*, stand back.
11. סַנְוֵרִים *blindness*, affecting the mental more than the ocular vision.
37. מוֹאָב Moab, מֵאָב from a father. בֶּן־עַמִּי Ben-ʻammi, *son of my people.* עַמּוֹן ʻAmmon, *of the people.*

XIX.
1. And the two angels came to Sodom at even, and Lot sat in the gate of Sodom: and Lot saw and rose up to meet them, and bowed with his face to the earth.
2. And he said, Behold, now, my lords, turn aside now to your servant's house, and lodge, and wash your feet; and ye shall rise up early, and go on your way. And they said, Nay, but in the street will we lodge.
3. And he pressed upon them greatly; and they turned aside to him, and went into his house: and he made them a feast, and baked unleavened cakes, and they did eat.

4. They lay not yet down, and the men of the city, the men of Sodom, compassed the house, both young and old, all the people from every quarter.
5. And they called unto Lot, and said unto him, Where are the men who went in to thee to-night? Bring them out unto us, and we shall know them.
6. And Lot came out to them at the door, and shut the door after him.
7. And said, Do not now, my brethren, so wickedly.
8. Behold, now, I have two daughters, who have not known man; let me now bring them out unto you, and do ye to them as is good in your eyes: only unto these men do nothing; for therefore came they under the shadow of my roof.
9. And they said, Stand back. And they said, This one is come in to sojourn, and he will needs be a judge; now will we deal worse with thee than with them. And they pressed sore upon the man, even Lot, and drew near to break the door.

10. And the men put forth their hand, and pulled Lot to them
into the house, and shut the door. 11. And the men that were
at the door of the house they smote with blindness, both small
and great: and they wearied themselves to find the door.

12. And the men said unto Lot, Whom else hast thou here?
Son-in-law, and thy sons, and thy daughters, and all that thou
hast in the city, bring out of this place. 13. For destroy will
we this place, because the cry of them is waxen great before
the LORD, and the LORD sent us to destroy it. 14. And Lot
went out, and spake unto his sons-in-law, who married his
daughters, and said, Up, get ye out of this place, for the LORD
will destroy this city. But he was as a mocker in the eyes of
his sons-in-law. 15. And when the dawn arose, then the an-
gels urged Lot, saying, Arise, take thy wife and thy two daugh-
ters, who are here, lest thou be consumed in the iniquity of
the city. 16. And he lingered, and the men laid hold on his
hand, and on the hand of his wife, and on the hand of his
two daughters, in the mercy of the LORD unto him: and they
brought him forth, and set him without the city. 17. And it
came to pass, when they had brought them forth abroad, that
he said, Escape for thy life; look not behind thee, and stay
not in all the vale; escape to the mountain, lest thou be con-
sumed. 18. And Lot said unto them, Not so now, O LORD.
19. Behold now, thy servant hath found grace in thine eyes,
and thou didst magnify thy mercy, which thou hast showed
unto me in saving my life; and I, I cannot escape to the moun-
tain, lest evil overtake me, and I die. 20. Behold, now, this
city is near to flee unto, and it is a small place: let me now
escape thither; is it not a small place? and my soul shall live.
21. And he said unto him, Lo, I have accepted thee also con-
cerning this thing, not to overthrow the city for which thou
hast spoken. 22. Haste thee, escape thither; for I cannot do
anything till thou go thither. Therefore was the name of the
city called Zoar. 23. The sun was come forth upon the earth,
when Lot entered Zoar.

24. Then the LORD rained upon Sodom and Amorah brim stone and fire from the LORD from the skies. 25. And he overthrew those cities, and all the vale, and all the inhabitants of the cities, and that which grew upon the soil. 26. And his wife looked from behind him, and she became a pillar of salt.

27. And Abraham gat up early in the morning to the place where he stood before the Lord. 28. And looked out upon Sodom and Amorah, and upon all the land of the vale, and beheld, and lo, the smoke of the land went up as the smoke of a furnace. 29. And it came to pass when God destroyed the cities of the vale, that God remembered Abraham, and sent Lot out of the midst of the overthrow when he overthrew the cities in which Lot dwelt.

30. And Lot went up out of Zoar, and dwelt in the mountain, and his two daughters with him; for he feared to dwell in Zoar: and he dwelt in a cave, he and his two daughters. 31. And the first-born said unto the younger, Our father is old, and there is not a man in the land to come in unto us after the manner of all the land. 32. Come, let us make our father drink wine, and we will lie with him, that we preserve seed of our father. 33. And they made their father drink wine that night: and the first-born went in and lay with her father; and he knew not of her lying down or of her rising up. 34. And it came to pass on the morrow that the first-born said unto the younger, Behold, I lay yesternight with my father: let us make him drink wine this night also, and go lie with him, that we may preserve seed of our father. 35. And they made their father drink wine that night also: and the younger arose and lay with him; and he knew not of her lying down or of her rising up. 36. And the two daughters of Lot were with child by their father. 37. And the first-born bare a son, and called his name Moab: the same is the father of Moab unto this day. 38. And the younger, she also bare a son, and called his name Ben-ammi: the same is the father of the children of Ammon unto this day. § 31.

This chapter is the continuation and conclusion of the former. It records a part of God's strange work, — strange, because it consists in punishment, and because it is foreign to the covenant of grace. Yet it is closely connected with Abraham's history, inasmuch as it is a signal chastisement of wickedness in his neighborhood, a memorial of the righteous judgment of God to all his posterity, and at the same time a remarkable answer to the spirit, if not to the letter, of his intercessory prayer. His kinsman Lot, the only righteous man in Sodom, with his wife and two daughters, is delivered from destruction in accordance with his earnest appeal on behalf of the righteous.

1–3. *The two angels.* These are the two men who left Abraham standing before the Lord (Gen. xviii. 22). *Lot sat in the gate*, the place of public resort for news and for business. He courteously rises to meet them, does obeisance to them, and invites them to spend the night in his house. *Nay, but in the street will we lodge.* This is the disposition of those who come to inquire, and, it may be, to condemn and to punish. They are twice in this chapter called angels, being sent to perform a delegated duty. This term, however, defines their office, not their nature. Lot, in the first instance, calls them "my lords," which is a term of respect that may be addressed to men (Gen. xxxi. 35). He afterwards styled one of them Adonai, with the peculiar vowel pointing which limits it to the Supreme Being. He at the same time calls himself his servant, appeals to his grace and mercy, and ascribes to him his deliverance. The person thus addressed replies, in a tone of independence and authority, "I have accepted thee." "I will not overthrow this city for which thou hast spoken." "I cannot do anything till thou go thither." All these circumstances point to a divine personage, and are not so easily explained of a mere delegate. He is preëminently the Saviour, as he who communed with Abraham was the hearer of prayer. And he who hears prayer and saves life, appears also as the executor of his purpose in the overthrow of Sodom and the other cities of the vale. It is remarkable that only two of the three who appeared to Abraham are called angels. Of the persons in the divine essence two might be the angels or deputies of the primary in the discharge of the divine purpose. These three men, then, either immediately represent, or, if created angels, mediately shadow forth persons in the Godhead. Their number indicates that the persons in the divine unity are three.

Lot seems to have recognized something extraordinary in their appearance, for he made a lowly obeisance to them. The Sodomites heed not the strangers. Lot's invitation, at first declined, is at length accepted, because Lot is approved of God as righteous, and excepted from the doom of the city.

4–11. The wicked violence of the citizens displays itself. 4, 5. They compass the house, and demand the men for the vilest ends. 6–8. How familiar Lot had become with vice, when any necessity whatever could induce him to offer his daughters to the lust of these Sodomites! We may suppose it was spoken rashly, in the heat of the moment, and with the expectation that he would not be taken at his word. So it turned out. 9. *Stand back.* This seems to be a menace to frighten Lot out of the way of their perverse will. It is probable, indeed, that he and his family would not have been so long safe in this wicked place, had he not been the occasion of a great deliverance to the whole city when they were carried away by the four kings. The threat is followed by a taunt, when the sorely vexed host hesitated to give up the strangers. *He will needs be a judge.* It is evident Lot had been in the habit of remonstrating with them. From threats and taunts they soon proceed to violence. 10, 11. His guests now interfere. They rescue Lot, and smite the rioters with blindness, or a wandering of the senses, so that they cannot find the door. This ebullition of the vilest passion seals the doom of the city.

12–23. The visitors now take steps for the deliverance of Lot and his kindred before the destruction of the cities. 12–14. All that are related to him are included in the offer of deliverance. There is a blessing in being connected with the righteous, if men will but avail themselves of it. 15, 16. Lot seems bewildered by the contemptuous refusal of his connections to leave the place. His early choice and his growing habits have attached him to the place, notwithstanding its temptations. His married daughters, or at least the intended husbands of the two who were at home ("who are here"), are to be left behind. But though these thoughts make him linger, the mercy of the Lord prevails. The angels use a little violence to hasten their escape. 17. *The mountain* was preserved by its elevation from the flood of rain, sulphur, and fire which descended on the low ground on which the cities were built. 18–22. Lot begs for a small town to which he may retreat, as he shrinks from the perils of a mountain dwelling, and his request is mercifully granted.

24–26. Then follows the overthrow of the cities. *The Lord rained brimstone and fire from the Lord from the skies.* Here the Lord is represented as present in the skies, whence the storm of desolation comes, and on the earth where it falls. The dale of Siddim, in which the cities were, appears to have abounded in asphalt and other combustible materials (Gen. xiv. 10). The district was liable to earthquakes and volcanic eruptions from the earliest to the latest times. We read of an earthquake in the days of king Uzziah (Am. i. 1). An earthquake in 1759 destroyed many thousands of persons in the valley of Baalbec. Josephus (*De Bell. Jud.* iii. 10, 7) reports that the Salt Sea sends up in many places black masses of asphalt, which are not unlike headless bulls in shape and size. After an earthquake in 1834, masses of asphalt were thrown up from the bottom, and in 1837 a similar cause was attended with similar effects. The lake lies in the lowest part of the valley of the Jordan, and its surface is about thirteen hundred feet below the level of the sea. In such a hollow, exposed to the burning rays of an unclouded sun, its waters evaporate as much as it receives by the influx of the Jordan. Its present area is about forty-five miles by eight. A peninsula pushes into it from the east called the Lisan, or tongue, the north point of which is about twenty miles from the south end of the lake. North of this point the depth is from forty to two hundred and eighteen fathoms. This southern part of the lake seems to have been the original dale of Siddim, in which were the cities of the vale. The remarkable salt hills lying on the south of the lake are still called Khashm Usdum (Sodom). A tremendous storm, accompanied with flashes of lightning, and torrents of rain, impregnated with sulphur, descended upon the doomed cities. From the injunction to Lot to *flee to the mountain*, as well as from the nature of the soil, we may infer that at the same time with the awful conflagration there was a subsidence of the ground, so that the waters of the upper and original lake flowed in upon the former fertile and populous dale, and formed the shallow southern part of the present Salt Sea. In this pool of melting asphalt and sweltering, seething waters, the cities seem to have sunk forever, and left behind them no vestiges of their existence. Lot's wife lingering behind her husband, and looking back, contrary to the express command of the Lord, is caught in the sweeping tempest, and becomes a pillar of salt: so narrow was the escape of Lot. The dashing spray of the salt sulphurous rain seems to have suffocated her, and then encrusted her whole body. She may have burned to a cinder in the furious conflagration. She is a memorable example of the indignation and wrath that overtakes the halting and the backsliding.

27–29. Abraham rises early on the following morning, to see what had become of the city for which he had interceded so earnestly, and views from afar the scene of smoking desolation. Remembering Abraham, who was Lot's uncle, and had him probably in mind in his importunate pleading, God delivered Lot from this awful overthrow. The Eternal is here designated by the name Elohim, the Everlasting, because in the war of elements in which the cities were overwhelmed, the eternal potencies of his nature were signally displayed.

30–38. The descendants of Lot. Bewildered by the narrowness of his escape, and the awful death of his wife, Lot seems to have left Zoar, and taken to the mountain west of the Salt Sea, in terror of impending ruin. It is not improbable that all the inhabitants of Zoar, panic-struck, may have fled from the region of danger, and dispersed themselves for a time through the adjacent mountains. He was now far from the habitations of men, with his two daughters as his only companions. 32–36. The manners of Sodom here obtrude themselves upon our view. Lot's daughters might seem to have been led to this unnatural project, first, because they thought the human race extinct with the exception of themselves, in which case their conduct may have seemed a work of justifiable necessity; and next, because the degrees of kindred within which it was unlawful to marry had not been determined by an express law. But they must have seen some of the inhabitants of Zoar after the destruction of the cities; and carnal intercourse between parent and offspring must have been always repugnant to nature. 37, 38. *Unto this day.* This phrase indicates a variable period, from a few years to a few centuries: a few years, not more than seven, as Jos. xxii. 3; part of a lifetime, as Num. xxii. 39, Jas. vi. 25, Gen. xlviii. 15; and some centuries, as Exod. x. 6. This passage may therefore have been written by one much earlier than Moses. Moab afterwards occupied the district south of the Arnon, and east of the Salt Sea. Ammon dwelt to the northeast of Moab, where they had a capital called Rabbah. They both ultimately merged into the more general class of the Arabs, as a second Palgite element.

XLVI. ABRAHAM IN GERAR. — Gen. xx.

2. אֲבִימֶלֶךְ Abimelekh, *father of the king.*

7. נָבִיא *prophet*, he who speaks by God, of God, and to God, who declares to men not merely things future, but also things past and

present, that are not obvious to the sense or the reason; r. *flow, go forth.*

13. הִתְעוּ is plural in punctuation, agreeing grammatically with אֱלֹהִים. Vau, however, may be regarded as the third radical, and the verb may thus really be singular.

16. נֹכַחַת an unusual form, either for נֹכַחַתְּ 2d s. f. perfect or נֹכְחָה 3d s. f. perf., from a verb signifying in hiphil, *make straight, right.*

17. אָמָה *hand-maid,* free or bond. שִׁפְחָה *bond-maid* (1 Sam. xxv. 41).

XX. 1. And Abraham journeyed thence to the land of the south, and dwelled between Kadesh and Shur, and he sojourned in Gerar. 2. And Abraham said of Sarah his wife, She is my sister: and Abimelek king of Gerar sent and took Sarah. 3. And God came to Abimelek in a dream by night, and said to him, Behold, thou wilt die on account of the woman whom thou hast taken; for she is a man's wife. 4. And Abimelek had not come near her: and he said, Lord, wilt thou slay a righteous nation also? 5. Said he not unto me, She is my sister? And she, even herself, said, He is my brother. In the integrity of my heart and innocency of my hands have I done this. 6. And the God said unto him in the dream, I also know that in the integrity of thy heart thou hast done this; I also, I withheld thee from sinning against me: therefore suffered I thee not to touch her. 7. And now restore the man's wife; for he is a prophet, and he shall pray for thee, and thou shalt live: but if thou restore her not, know that die, die shalt thou, thou, and all that are thine.

8. And Abimelek rose early in the morning, and called all his servants, and spake all these words in their ears: and the men were sore afraid. 9. Then Abimelek called Abraham, and said unto him, What hast thou done unto us? And how have I sinned against thee, that thou hast brought on me and on my kingdom a great sin? Deeds that ought not to be done hast thou done unto me. 10. And Abimelek said unto Abraham, What sawest thou, that thou hast done this thing? 11. And Abraham said, Because I said, Surely the fear of God

is not in this place: and they will slay me on account of my wife. 12. And yet in truth she is my sister, the daughter of my father, but not the daughter of my mother; and she became my wife. 13. And it came to pass, when God caused me to wander from my father's house, that I said unto her, This is thy kindness which thou shalt do unto me; at every place whither we shall go, say of me, He is my brother.

14. And Abimelek took sheep and oxen and men-servants and maid-servants and gave unto Abraham; and restored him Sarah his wife. 15. And Abimelek said, Behold, my land is before thee; dwell where it is good in thine eyes. 16. And unto Sarah he said, Behold, I have given a thousand silver pieces to thy brother; behold, this is for thee a covering of the eyes unto all that are with thee; and all this that thou mayest be righted. 17. Then Abraham prayed to God: and God healed Abimelek and his wife and his handmaids; and they bare. 18. For the LORD had fast closed up every womb in the house of Abimelek, on account of Sarah, Abraham's wife. § 32.

The concealment of his relation to Sarah calls to our mind a similar act of Abraham recorded not many pages back. We are to remember, however, that an interval of twenty-four years has elapsed since that event. From the present passage we learn that this was an old agreement between him and his wife, while they were wandering among strangers. It appears that Abraham was not yet conscious of anything wrong or even imprudent in this piece of policy. He therefore practises it without any hesitation. On this occasion he appears for the first time as a prophet. He is the first of this order introduced to our notice in the Old Testament, though Henok had prophesied at an earlier period (Jude 14), and Noah's benediction was, at the same time, a prediction.

1–7. Abimelek takes Sarah. 1. Abraham had been dwelling near Hebron. But the total separation between him and Lot, and the awful overthrow of Sodom and Amorah in the vicinity, may have loosened his tie to Hebron, and rendered it for the present not an agreeable place of residence. He therefore travels southward and takes up his abode at Gerar (see on Gen. x. 19). 2. Sarah, though now eighty-nine years of age, was as youthful in look as a person of forty would now be. She had, moreover, had no family, was remarkable for her good looks, and was at present, no doubt, renewed in health and vigor (Gen. xii. 11–16).

3–7. The Supreme Being here appears as God (Elohim), and therefore in his eternal power and independence, as he was antecedent to the creation of man. He communicates with Abimelek in a dream. This prince addresses him as Adonai, Lord. We have already seen that the knowledge of the true God had not yet disappeared from the Gentile world, who were under the Noachic covenant. 3. *Thou wilt die.* Thou art dying or at the point of death if thou persist. A deadly plague was already in the body of Abimelek, on account of Sarah. 4. *Wilt thou slay a righteous nation also?* Abimelek associates his nation with himself, and expects that the fatal stroke will not be confined to his own person. 5–7. He pleads his integrity in the matter, which the Lord acknowledges. Gentiles sometimes act according to the dictates of conscience, which still lives in them, though it be obscured by sin. Abimelek was innocent in regard to the "great sin" of seizing another man's wife, of which God acquitted him. He was wrong in appropriating a woman to himself by mere stretch of power, and in adding wife to wife. But these were common customs of the time, for which his conscience did not upbraid him in his pleading with God. *And the God.* The presence of the definite article seems to intimate a contrast of the true God with the false gods to which the Gentiles were fast turning. Abimelek was at least in the doubtful ground on the borders of polytheism.

7. Abraham is here designated by the Lord a prophet. This constituted at once the gravity of Abimelek's offence (Ps. cv. 15), and the ground of his hope of pardon. It is at the same time a step in advance of all the previous spiritual attainments of Abraham. A prophet is God's spokesman, who utters with authority certain of the things of God (Ex. vii. 1, iv. 15). This implies two things: first, the things of God are known only to him, and therefore must be communicated by him; secondly, the prophet must be enabled of God to announce in correct terms the things made known to him. These things refer not only to the future, but in general to all such matters as fall within the purpose and procedure of God. They may even include things otherwise known or knowable by man, so far as these are necessary to the exposition of the divine will. Now Abraham

has heretofore received many communications from God. But this did not constitute him a prophet. It is the divinely authorized utterance of new truth which raises him to this rank. And Abraham's first exercise in prophecy is not in speaking to men of God, but to God for men. *He shall pray for thee.* The prophetic and the priestly offices go together in the father of the faithful. These dignities belong to him, not from any absolute merit, for this he has not, but from his call to be the holder of the promise, and the father of that seed to whom the promises were made.

8–13. Abimelek retraces his steps, and rectifies his conduct. He makes known his dream to his assembled court, who are filled with astonishment and apprehension. He then calls Abraham, and in bold and manly style remonstrates with him for leading him into error and sin. 10. Abraham is apparently silent from confusion and self-condemnation. Abimelek, after a pause, demands of him his reason for so doing. 11–13. Abraham now replies with great simplicity and candor. He had said within himself, "The fear of God is not in this place." This is another indication that polytheism was setting in. He concluded that his life would be in danger on account of his wife, and resorted to his wonted expedient for safety. He had learned to trust in the Lord in all things; but he did not think this inconsistent with using all lawful means for personal security, and he was not yet fully alive to the unlawfulness of his usual pretence. He pleads also in extenuation that she is in reality his sister (see Gen. ii. 29, 30). 13. *Caused me to wander.* The verb here is not necessarily plural. But if it be, it is only an instance of the literal meaning of Elohim, the Eternal Supernatural Powers, coming into view. *Thy kindness.* The old compact of Abraham with Sarah tended to palliate his conduct in the eyes of Abimelek, as he would see that it had no special reference to himself.

14–18. Abimelek seems to have accepted his apology, as he probably felt that there was truth in the character Abraham gave of his people, and was precluded from resenting it by the salutary impression of his dream; while at the same time Abraham's mode of avoiding danger appeared warrantable according to his own and the common code of morals. He therefore hastens to make honorable amends for his conduct. He makes Abraham a valuable present, restores his wife, and makes him free to dwell in any part of his dominions. 16. He then accosts Sarah in respectful terms, informing her that he had presented her brother with one thousand silver pieces, probably shekels, on her account. He does not offer this directly to herself, that it may be distinctly understood that her honor was unstained. *This* may refer either to Abraham or to the sum of money. The latter is more natural, as the sentence then affords a reason for addressing Sarah, and mentioning this particular gift. *A covering of the eyes* does not mean a veil, the proper word for which is צָעִיף, but is a figurative phrase for a recompense or pacificatory offering, in consideration of which an offence is overlooked. *Unto all that are with thee.* All her family were concerned in this public vindication of her character. *And all this that thou mayest be righted.* The original of this is most naturally taken as a part of Abimelek's speech, and then it is to be translated as above. All this has been done or given that the injury to Sarah may be redressed. If the original be regarded as a part of the narrative, it must be rendered, "And all this (was done) that she might be righted." The sense is the same in substance. In the former case the verb is in the second person, in the latter in the third.

17, 18. These verses record the fact of Abraham's intercession for Abimelek, and explain in what sense he was on the point of dying (v. 3). *They bare* means that they were again rendered capable of procreating children, and in the natural course of things did so. The verb is in the masculine form, because both males and females were involved in this judicial malady. The name Jehovah is employed at the end of the chapter, because the relation of the Creator and Preserver to Sarah is there prominent.

XLVII. BIRTH OF ISAAC. — Gen. xxi.

7. מִלֵּל *speak*, an ancient and therefore solemn and poetical word.

14. חֵמֶת *bottle*, akin to חָמָה *surround, enclose*, and חוּם *black*. בְּאֵר שֶׁבַע Beer-sheba', *well of seven.*

22. פִּיכֹל Pikhol, *mouth or spokesman of all.*

23. נִין *offspring, kin;* r. *sprout, flourish.* נֶכֶד *progeny*, perhaps *acquaintance*, cognate with נגד *be before* (the eyes) and נכד *mark.*

33. אֵשֶׁל *grove; ἄρουρα*, LXX.; אִילָבָה *a tree*, Onk.

XXI. 1. And the Lord had visited Sarah as he had said. And the Lord did unto Sarah as he had spoken. 2. And

Sarah conceived, and bare Abraham a son in his old age, at the set time of which God had spoken to him. 3. And Abraham called the name of his son that was born unto him, whom Sarah bare to him, Isaac. 4. And Abraham circumcised Isaac his son, being the son of eight days, as God had commanded him. 5. And Abraham was the son of a hundred years, when Isaac his son was born unto him. 6. And Sarah said, God hath made me to laugh; all that hear will laugh with me. 7. And she said, Who had said unto Abraham, Sarah hath suckled children? for I have borne him a son in his old age. 8. And the child grew, and was weaned; and Abraham made a great feast in the day that Isaac was weaned.

9. And Sarah saw the son of Hagar the Mizrite, whom she had borne unto Abraham, laughing. 10. And she said unto Abraham, Cast out this handmaid and her son: for the son of this handmaid shall not be heir with my son, with Isaac. 11. And the word was very grievous in Abraham's eyes, on account of his son. 12. And God said unto Abraham, Let it not be grievous in thine eyes because of the lad, and because of thy handmaid: in all that Sarah saith unto thee, hearken unto her voice; for in Isaac shall thy seed be called. 13. And also the son of the handmaid will I make a nation, because he is thy seed. 14. And Abraham rose up early in the morning, and took bread, and a bottle of water, and gave unto Hagar, putting it on her shoulder, and the lad, and sent her away: and she went and wandered in the wilderness of Beer-sheba. 15. And the water was spent in the bottle, and she laid the lad under one of the shrubs. 16. And she went and sat by herself apart, as far as they shoot the bow: for she said, Let me not see the death of the lad. And she sat apart, and lifted up her voice and wept.

17. And God heard the voice of the lad, and an angel of God called to Hagar out of heaven, and said unto her, What aileth thee, Hagar? fear not: for God hath heard the voice of the lad where he is. 18. Arise, lift up the lad, and hold

thy hand upon him: for I will make him a great nation. 19.
And God opened her eyes, and she saw a well of water; and
she went and filled the bottle with water, and gave the lad
drink. 20. And God was with the lad, and he grew; and he
dwelt in the wilderness, and became an archer. 21. And he
dwelt in the wilderness of Paran; and his mother took him a
wife out of the land of Mizraim. ¶ 20.

22. And it came to pass at that time that Abimelek and Phi-
kol, the captain of his host, said unto Abraham, saying, God
is with thee in all that thou doest. 23. And now swear unto
me by God here, that thou wilt not deal falsely with me, nor
with my kin and kith: according to the kindness that I have
done unto thee, shalt thou do unto me, and to the land where-
in thou hast sojourned. 24. And Abraham said, I will swear.
25. And Abraham reproved Abimelek on account of the well
of water which Abimelek's servants had seized. 26. And
Abimelek said, I wot not who hath done this thing: and thou
also hadst not told me, and I also had not heard of it but to-
day. 27. And Abraham took sheep and oxen, and gave unto
Abimelek: and both of them made a covenant. 28. And
Abraham set seven ewe-lambs of the flock by themselves.
29. And Abimelek said unto Abraham, What are these seven
ewe-lambs which thou hast set by themselves? 30. And he
said, For the seven ewe-lambs shalt thou take of my hand,
that it may be a witness to me that I have digged this well.
31. Wherefore he called that place Beer-sheba, because there
they sware both of them. 32. And they made a covenant at
Beer-sheba: then rose up Abimelek and Phikol the captain
of his host, and returned into the land of the Philistines.
33. And he planted a grove in Beer-sheba, and called there
on the name of the LORD, the God of eternity. 34. And
Abraham sojourned in the land of the Philistines many
days. ¶ 21.

This chapter records the birth of Isaac with other concomitant circumstances. This is the beginning of the fulfilment of the second part of the covenant with Abraham — that concerning the seed. This precedes, we observe, his possession of even a foot-breadth of the soil, and is long antecedent to the entrance of his descendants as conquerors into the land of promise.

1–8. Isaac is born according to promise, and grows to be weaned. 1. *The Lord had visited Sarah.* It is possible that this event may have occurred before the patriarchal pair arrived in Gerar. To visit, is to draw near to a person for the purpose of either chastising or conferring a favor. The Lord had been faithful to his gracious promise to Sarah. *He did as he had spoken.* The object of the visit was accomplished. 2–5. In due time she bears a son, whom Abraham, in accordance with the divine command, calls Isaac, and circumcises on the eighth day. Abraham was now a hundred years old, and therefore Isaac was born thirty years after the call. 6, 7. Sarah expressed her grateful wonder in two somewhat poetic strains. The first, consisting of two sentences, turns on the word *laugh.* This is no longer the laugh of delight mingled with doubt, but that of wonder and joy at the power of the Lord overcoming the impotence of the aged mother. The second strain of three sentences turns upon the object of this admiring joy. The event that nobody ever expected to hear announced to Abraham, has nevertheless taken place ; *for I have borne him a son in his old age.* 8. The time of weaning, the second step of the child to individual existence, at length arrives, and the household of Abraham make merry, as was wont, on the festive occasion. The infant was usually weaned in the second or third year (1 Sam. i. 22–24; 2 Chron. xxxi. 16). The child seems to have remained for the first five years under the special care of the mother (Lev. xxvii. 6). The son then came under the management of the father.

9–21. The dismissal of Hagar and Ishmael. *The son of Hagar . . . laughing.* The birth of Isaac has made a great change in the position of Ishmael, now at the age of at least fifteen years. He was not now, as formerly, the chief object of attention, and some bitterness of feeling may have arisen on this account. His laugh was therefore the laugh of derision. Rightly was the child of promise named Isaac, the one at whom all laugh with various feelings of incredulity, wonder, gladness, and scorn. Sarah cannot brook the insolence of Ishmael, and demands his dismissal. 11–13. This was painful to Abraham. Nevertheless, God enjoins it as reasonable, on the ground that in Isaac was his seed to be called. This means not only that Isaac was to be called his seed, but in Isaac as the progenitor was included the seed of Abraham in the highest and utmost sense of the phrase. From him the holy seed was to spring that was to be the agent in eventually bringing the whole race again under the covenant of Noah, in that higher form which it assumes in the New Testament. Abraham is comforted in this separation with a renewal of the promise concerning Ishmael (Gen. xvii. 20). 14. He proceeds with all singleness of heart and denial of self to dismiss the mother and the son. This separation from the family of Abraham was, no doubt, distressing to the feelings of the parties concerned. But it involved no material hardship to those who departed, and conferred certain real advantages. Hagar obtained her freedom. Ishmael, though called a lad, was at an age when it is not unusual in the East to marry and provide for one's self. And their departure did not imply their exclusion from the privileges of communion with God, as they might still be under the covenant with Abraham, since Ishmael had been circumcised, and, at all events, were under the broader covenant of Noah. It was only their own voluntary rejection of God and his mercy, whether before or after their departure, that could cut them off from the promise of eternal life. It seems likely that Hagar and Ishmael had so behaved as to deserve their dismissal from the sacred home. *A bottle of water.* This was probably a kid-skin bottle, as Hagar could not have carried a goat-skin. Its contents were precious in the wilderness, but soon exhausted. *And the lad.* He *took* the lad and *gave* him to Hagar. The bread and water-skin were on her shoulder; the lad she held by the hand. *In the wilderness of Beer-sheba.* It is possible that the departure of Hagar occurred after the league with Abimelek and the naming of Beer-sheba, though coming in here naturally as the sequel of the birth and weaning of Isaac. The wilderness in Scripture is simply the land not profitable for cultivation, though fit for pasture to a greater or less extent. The wilderness of Beer-sheba is that part of the wilderness which was adjacent to Beer-sheba, where probably at this time Abraham was residing. 15, 16. *Laid the lad.* Ishmael was now, no doubt, thoroughly humbled as well as wearied, and therefore passive under his mother's guidance. She led him to a sheltering bush, and caused him to lie down in its shade, resigning herself to despair. The artless description here is deeply affecting.

17–21. The fortunes of Ishmael. God cares for the wanderers. He hears the voice of the lad, whose sufferings from thirst are greater than those of the mother. An angel is sent, who addresses Hagar in the simple words of encouragement and direction. *Hold thy hand upon him.* Lay thy hand firmly upon him. The former promise (Gen. xvi. 10) is renewed to her. God also opened her eyes that she saw a well of water, from which the bottle is replenished, and she and the lad are recruited for their further journey. It is unnecessary to determine how far this opening of the eyes was miraculous. It may refer to the cheering of her mind and the sharpening of her attention. In Scripture the natural and supernatural are not always set over against each other as with us. All events are alike ascribed to an ever-watchful Providence, whether they flow from the ordinary laws of nature or some higher law of the divine will. 20. *God was with the lad.* Ishmael may have been cured of his childish spleen. It is possible also his father did not forget him, but sent him a stock of cattle with which to begin the pastoral life on his account. *He became an archer.* He grew an archer, or multiplied into a tribe of archers. 21. Paran (Gen. xiv. 6) lay south of Palestine, and therefore on the way to Egypt, out of which his mother took him a wife. The Ishmaelites, therefore, both root and branch, were descended on the mother's side from the Egyptians.

22–34. According to the common law of Hebrew narrative, this event took place before some of the circumstances recorded in the previous passage; probably not long after the birth of Isaac. Abimelek, accompanied by Phikol, his commander-in-chief, proposes to form a league with Abraham. The reason assigned for this is that God was with him in all that he did. Various circumstances concurred to produce this conviction in Abimelek. The never-to-be-forgotten appearance of God to himself in a dream interposing on behalf of Abraham, the birth of Isaac, and the consequent certainty of his having an heir, and the growing retinue and affluence of one who, some ten years before, could lead out a trained band of three hundred and eighteen men-at-arms, were amply sufficient to prove that God was the source of his strength. Such a man is formidable as a foe, but serviceable as an ally. It is the part of sound policy, therefore, to approach him and endeavor to prevail upon him to swear by God not to deal falsely with him or his. *Kin and kith.* We have adopted these words to represent the conversational alliterative phrase of the original. They correspond tolerably well with the σπέρμα and ὄνομα, *seed* and *name*, of the Septuagint. Abraham frankly consents to this oath. This is evidently a personal covenant, referring to existing circumstances. A similar confederacy had been already formed with Aner, Eshkol, and

Mamre. Abraham was disposed to such alliances, as they contributed to peaceful neighborhood. He was not in a condition to make a national covenant, though it is a fact that the Philistines were scarcely ever wholly subjugated by his descendants.

25, 26. Abraham takes occasion to remonstrate with Abimelek about a well which his people had seized. Wells were extremely valuable in Palestine, on account of the long absence of rain between the latter or vernal rain ending in March, and the early or autumnal rain beginning in November. The digging of a well was therefore a matter of the greatest moment, and often gave a certain title to the adjacent fields. Hence the many disputes about wells, as the neighboring Emirs or chieftains were jealous of rights so acquired, and often sought to enter by the strong hand on the labors of patient industry. 27–31. Hence Abraham lays more stress on a public attestation that he has dug, and is therefore the owner of this well, than on all the rest of the treaty. Seven is the number of sanctity, and therefore of obligation. This number is accordingly figured in some part of the form of confederation; in the present case, in the seven ewe-lambs which Abraham tenders, and Abimelek, in token of consent, accepts at his hand. The name of the well is remarkable as an instance of the various meanings attached to nearly the same sound. Even in Hebrew it means *the well of seven*, or *the well of the oath*, as the roots of seven, and of the verb meaning to swear, have the same radical letters. Bir es-Seba means *the well of seven* or *of the lion.*

32–34. *Returned unto the land of the Philistines.* Beer-sheba was on the borders of the land of the Philistines. Going therefore to Gerar, they returned into that land. In the transactions with Hagar and with Abimelek, the name God is employed, because the relation of the Supreme Being with these parties is more general or less intimate than with the heir of promise. The same name, however, is used in reference to Abraham and Sarah, who stand in a twofold relation to him as the Eternal Potentate, aud the Author of being and blessing. Hence the chapter begins and ends with Jehovah, the proper name of God in communion with man. 33, 34. Eshel is *a field under tillage* in the Septuagint, and *a tree* in Onkelos. It is therefore well translated *a grove* in the A. V., though it is rendered *the tamarisk* by many. The planting of a grove implies that Abraham now felt he had a resting-place in the land, in consequence of his treaty with Abimelek. He calls upon the name of the Lord with the significant surname of the God of perpetuity, the eternal, unchangeable God. This marks him as the *sure and able* performer of his promise, as the everlasting vindicator of the faith of treaties, and as the infallible source of the believer's rest and peace. Accordingly, Abraham sojourned in the land of the Philistines many days.

XLVIII. ABRAHAM PROVED.—Gen. xxii.

2. מֹרִיָּה Moriah; Samaritan, מוראה; Septuagint, ὑψηλή; Onkelos, *worship*. Some take the word to be a simple derivative, as the Sept. and Onk., meaning *vision*, *high*, *worship*. It might mean *rebellious*. Others regard it as a compound of יָה Jah, a name of God, and מֻרְאָה *shown*, מוֹרֶה *teacher*, or מוֹרָא *fear*.

14. יִרְאֶה Jireh, *will provide*.

16. נְאֻם ῥῆμα, dictum, *oracle;* r. *speak low*.

21. בּוּז Buz, *scoffing*. קְמוּאֵל Qemuel, *gathered of God*.

22. חֲזוֹ Chazo, *vision*. פִּלְדָּשׁ Pildash, *steelman? wanderer?* יִדְלָף Jidlaph; r. *trickle, weep*. בְּתוּאֵל Bethuel, *dwelling of God*.

23. רִבְקָה Ribqah, *noose*.

24. רְאוּמָה Reumah, *exalted*. טֶבַח Tebach, *slaughter*. גַּחַם Gacham, *brand*. תַּחַשׁ Tachash, *badger* or *seal*. מַעֲכָה Ma'akah; r. *press, crush*.

XXII. 1. And it came to pass after these things, that the God tempted Abraham, and said unto him, Abraham. And he said, Here I am. 2. And he said, Take now thy son, thine only one, whom thou lovest, Isaac, and get thee into the land of Moriah; and offer him there a burnt-offering upon one of the hills of which I will tell thee. 3. And Abraham rose up early in the morning, and saddled his ass, and took two of his lads with him, and Isaac his son; and clave the wood for a burnt-offering, and rose up, and went unto the place of which the God had told him.

4. On the third day then Abraham lifted up his eyes, and saw the place afar off. 5. And Abraham said unto his lads, Abide ye here with the ass, and I and the lad will go yonder; and we will worship and return unto you. 6. And Abraham

took the wood of the burnt-offering, and laid upon Isaac his son; and he took in his hand the fire and the knife: and they went both of them together. 7. And Isaac said unto Abraham his father, and he said, My father. And he said, Here am I, my son. And he said, Behold the fire and the wood; and where is the sheep for a burnt-offering. 8. And Abraham said, God will provide himself the sheep for a burnt-offering, my son: so they went both of them together. 9. And they came to the place of which the God had told him; and Abraham built there an altar, and put on the wood; and he bound Isaac his son, and laid him on the altar upon the wood. 10. And Abraham stretched forth his hand, and took the knife to slay his son.

11. And the angel of the LORD called unto him out of heaven, and said, Abraham, Abraham. And he said, Here am I. 12. And he said, Lay not thy hand upon the lad, neither do anything unto him: for now I know that thou fearest God, and hast not withheld thy son, thine only one, from me. 13. And Abraham lifted up his eyes and looked, and, lo, a ram behind, caught in the thicket by his horns; and Abraham went and took the ram, and offered him for a burnt-offering instead of his son. 14. And Abraham called the name of that place Jehovah-jireh: as it is said to-day, In the mount of the LORD he is seen.

15. And the angel of the LORD called unto Abraham a second time out of heaven, 16. And said, By myself have I sworn, saith the LORD, because thou hast done this thing, and hast not withheld thy son, thine only one; 17. That bless, bless thee will I, and multiply, multiply will I thy seed, as the stars of heaven, and as the sand which is upon the seashore; and thy seed shall possess the gate of his enemies. 18. And blessed in thy seed shall be all the nations of the earth; because thou hast obeyed my voice. 19. So Abraham returned unto his lads; and they rose up and went together to Beer-sheba; and Abraham dwelt at Beer-sheba. ¶ 22.

20. And it came to pass after these things, that it was told Abraham, saying, Behold Milkah, she also hath borne children unto Nahor thy brother. 21. Uz his first-born, and Buz his brother, and Kemuel the father of Aram. 22. And Kesed and Hazo and Pildash and Jidlaph and Bethuel. 23. And Bethuel begat Rebekah: these eight bare Milkah to Nahor, Abraham's brother. 24. And his concubine, whose name was Reumah, she also bare Tebah and Gaham and Tahash and Maakah. 5 ¶¶¶ 23.

The grand crisis, the crowning event in the history of Abraham, now takes place. Every needful preparation has been made for it. He has been called to a high and singular destiny. With expectant acquiescence he has obeyed the call. By the delay in the fulfilment of the promise, he has been taught to believe in the Lord on his simple word. Hence, as one born again, he has been taken into covenant with God. He has been commanded to walk in holiness, and circumcised in token of his possessing the faith which purifieth the heart. He has become the intercessor and the prophet. And he has at length become the parent of the child of promise. He has now something of unspeakable worth, by which his spiritual character may be thoroughly tested. Since the hour in which he believed in the Lord, the features of his resemblance to God have been shining more and more through the darkness of his fallen nature — freedom of resolve, holiness of walk, interposing benevolence, and paternal affection. The last prepares the way for the highest point of moral likeness.

1–19. God tests Abraham's unreserved obedience to his will. *The God.* The true, eternal, and only God, not any tempter to evil, such as the serpent or his own thoughts. *Tempted Abraham.* To tempt is originally to try, prove, put to the test. It belongs to the dignity of a moral being to be put to a moral probation. Such assaying of the will and conscience is worthy both of God the assayer, and of man the assayed. 2. *Thine only one.* The only one born of Sarah, and heir of the promise. *Whom thou lovest.* An only child gathers round it all the affections of the parent's heart. *The land of Moriah.* This term, though applied in 2 Chron. iii. 1 to the mount on which the temple of Solomon was built, is here the name of a country, containing, it may be, a range of mountains or other notable place to which it was specially appropriated. Its formation and meaning are very doubtful, and there is nothing in the context to lend us any aid in its explanation. It was evidently known to Abraham before he set out on his present journey. It is not to be identified with Moreh in Gen. xii. 6, as the two names occur in the same document, and, being different in form, they naturally denote different things. Moreh is probably the name of a man. Moriah probably refers to some event that had occurred in the land, or some characteristic of its inhabitants. If a derivative, like פֹּרִיָּה *poriah,* fruitful, it may mean the land of the rebellious, a name not inapposite to any district inhabited by the Kenaanites, who were disposed to rebellion themselves (Gen. xiv. 4), or met with rebellion from the previous inhabitants. If a compound of the divine name, Jah, whatever be the other element, it affords an interesting trace of the manifestation and worship of the true God under the name of Jah at some antecedent period. The land of Moriah comprehended within its range the population to which Melkizedec ministered as priest.

And offer him for a burnt-offering. Abraham must have felt the outward inconsistency between the sacrifice of his son, and the promise that in him should his seed be called. But in the triumph of faith he accounted that God was able to raise him up, even from the dead. On no other principle can the prompt, mute, unquestioning obedience of Abraham be explained. Human sacrifice may have been not unknown; but this in no way met the special difficulty of the promise. The existence of such a custom might seem to have smoothed away the difficulty of a parent offering the sacrifice of a son. But the moral difficulty of human sacrifice is not so removed. The only solution of this, is that which the case itself actually presents; namely, the divine command. It is evident that the absolute Creator has by right entire control over his creatures. He is no doubt bound by his eternal rectitude to do no wrong to his moral creatures. But the creature in the present case has forfeited the life that was given, by sin. And, moreover, we cannot deny that the Almighty may, for a fit moral purpose, direct the sacrifice of a holy being, who should eventually receive a due recompense for such a degree of voluntary obedience. This takes away the moral difficulty, either as to God who commands, or Abraham who obeys. Without the divine command, it is needless to say that it was not lawful for Abraham to slay his son.

Upon one of the hills of which I will tell thee. This form of expression clearly shows that Moriah was not at that time the name of the particular hill on which the sacrifice was to be offered. It was the general designation of the country in which was the range of hills on one of which the solemn transaction was to take place. 3. *And Abraham rose up early in the morning.* There is no hesitation or lingering in the patriarch. If this has to be done, let it be done at once.

4–10. The story is now told with exquisite simplicity. *On the third day.* From Beer-sheba to the Shalem of Melkizedec, near which this hill is supposed to have been, is about forty-five miles. If they proceeded fifteen miles on the first broken day, twenty on the second, and ten on the third, they would come within sight of the place early on the third day. *Lifted up his eyes.* It is scarcely necessary to remind the reader of the Bible that this phrase does not imply that the place was above his point of view. Lot lifted up his eyes and beheld all the vale of Jordan (Gen. xiii. 10), which was considerably below the position of the observer. 5. *And return unto you.* The intimation that he and the lad would return, may seem to have rested on a dim presentiment that God would restore Isaac to him even if sacrificed. But it is more in keeping with the earnestness of the whole transaction to regard it as a mere concealment of his purpose from his servants. 9. *And he bound Isaac his son.* There is a wonderful pathos in the words *his son*, *his father*, introduced in the sacred style in this and similar narratives. Isaac, when the trying moment came, seems to have made no resistance to his father's will. The binding was merely a sacrificial custom. He must have concluded that his father was in all this obeying the will of God, though he gave him only a distant hint that it was so. 8. Abraham is thoroughly in earnest in the whole procedure.

11–14. At this critical moment the angel of the Lord interposes to prevent the actual sacrifice. 12. *Lay not thy hand upon the lad.* Here we have the evidence of a voice from heaven that God does not accept of human victims. Man is morally unclean, and therefore unfit for a sacrifice. He is, moreover, not in any sense a victim, but a doomed culprit, for whom the victim has to be provided. And for a typical sacrifice that cannot take away, but only shadow forth, the efficacious sacrifice, man is neither fit nor necessary. The lamb without blemish, that has no penal or protracted suffering, is sufficient for a symbol of the real atonement. The intention, therefore, in this case was enough, and that was now seen to be real. *Now I know that thou fearest God.* This was known to God antecedent to the event that demonstrated it. But the original *I have known* denotes an eventual knowing, a discovering by actual experiment; and this observable probation of Abraham was necessary for the judicial eye of God, who is to govern the world, and for the conscience of man, who is to be instructed by practice as well as principle. *Thou hast not withheld thy son from me.* This voluntary surrender of all that was dear to him, of all that he could in any sense call his own, forms the keystone of Abraham's spiritual experience. He is henceforth a tried man.

13, 14. *A ram behind.* For "behind" we have "one" in the Samaritan, the Septuagint, Onkelos, and some MSS. But neither a "single ram" nor a "certain ram" adds anything suitable to the sense. We therefore retain the received reading. The voice from heaven was heard from behind Abraham, who, on turning back and lifting up his eyes, saw the ram. This Abraham took and offered as a substitute for Isaac. Both in the intention and in the act he rises to a higher resemblance to God. He withholds not his only son in intent, and yet in fact he offers a substitute for his son. 14. *Jehovah-jireh*, the Lord will provide, is a deeply significant name. He who provided the ram caught in the thicket will provide the really atoning victim of which the ram was the type. In this event we can imagine Abraham seeing the day of that preëminent seed who should in the fulness of time actually take away sin by the sacrifice of himself. *In the mount of the Lord he will be seen.* This proverb remained as a monument of this transaction in the time of the sacred writer. The mount of the Lord here means the very height of the trial into which he brings his saints. There he will certainly appear in due time for their deliverance.

15–19. Abraham has arrived at the moral elevation of self-denial and resignation to the will of God, and that in its highest form. The angel of the Lord now confirms all his special promises to him with an oath, in their amplest terms. An oath with God is a solemn pledging of himself in all the unchangeableness of his faithfulness and truth, to the fulfilment of his promise. The multitude of his seed has a double parallel in the stars of heaven and the sands of the ocean. They are to possess the gate of their enemies; that is, to be masters and rulers of their cities and territories. The great promise, *and blessed in thy seed shall be all the nations of the earth*, was first given absolutely without reference to his character. Now it is confirmed to him as the man of proof, who is not only accepted as righteous, but proved to be actually righteous after the inward man; *because thou hast obeyed my voice* (Gen. xxvi. 5). The reflexive form of the verb signifying to bless is here employed, not to denote emphasis, but to intimate that the nations, in being blessed of God, are made willing to be so, and therefore bless themselves in Abraham's seed. In hearing this transcendent blessing repeated on this momentous occasion, Abraham truly saw the day of the seed of the woman, the seed of Abraham, the Son of man. We contemplate him now with wonder as the man of God, manifested by the self-denying obedience of a regenerate nature, intrusted with the dignity of the patriarchate over a holy seed, and competent to the worthy discharge of all its spiritual functions.

With the nineteenth verse of this chapter may be said to close the main revelation of the third Bible given to mankind, to which the remainder of this book is only a needful appendix. It includes the two former Bibles or revelations, — that of Adam and that of Noah; and it adds the special revelation of Abraham. The two former applied directly to the whole race; the latter directly to Abraham and his seed as the medium of an ultimate blessing to the whole race. The former revealed the mercy of God offered to all, which was the truth immediately necessary to be known; the latter reveals more definitely the seed through whom the blessings of mercy are to be conveyed to all, and delineates the leading stage in the spiritual life of a man of God. In the person of Abraham is unfolded that spiritual process by which the soul is drawn to God. He hears the call of God and comes to the decisive act of trusting in the revealed God of mercy and truth; on the ground of which act he is accounted as righteous. He then rises to the successive acts of walking with God, covenanting with him, communing and interceding with him, and at length withholding nothing that he has or holds dear from him. In all this we discern certain primary and essential characteristics of the man who is saved through acceptance of the mercy of God proclaimed to him in a primeval gospel. Faith in God (ch. xv.), repentance towards him (ch. xvi.), and fellowship with him (ch. xviii.), are the three great turning-points of the soul's returning life. They are built upon the effectual call of God (ch. xii.), and culminate in unreserved resignation to him (ch. xxii.). With wonderful facility has the sacred record descended in this pattern of spiritual biography from the rational and accountable race to the individual and immortal soul, and traced the footsteps of its path to God.

The seed that was threatened to bruise the serpent's head is here the seed that is promised to bless all the families of the earth. The threefold individuality in the essence of the one eternal Spirit, is adumbrated in the three men who visited the patriarch, and their personal and practical interest in the salvation of man is manifested, though the part appropriated to each in the work of grace be not yet apparent.

Meanwhile, contemporaneous with Abraham are to be seen men (Melkizedec, Abimelek) who live under the covenant of Noah, which was not abrogated by that of Abraham, but only helped forward by the specialities of the latter over the legal and moral difficulties in the way to its final and full accomplishment. That covenant, which was simply the expansion and continuation of the Adamic covenant, is still in force, and contains within its bosom the Abrahamic covenant in its culminating grandeur, as the soul that gives life and motion to its otherwise inanimate body.

20–24. This family notice is inserted as a piece of contemporaneous history, to explain and prepare the way for the marriage of Isaac. *Milkah, she also*, in allusion to Sarah, who has borne Isaac. So far as we know, they may have been sisters, but they were at all events sisters-in-law. The only new persons belonging to our histoy are Bethuel and Rebekah. Uz, Aram, and Kesed are interesting, as they show that we are in the region of the Shemites, among whom these are ancestral names (Gen. x. 23, xi. 28). Buz may have been the ancestor of Elihu (Jer. xxv. 23; Job xxxii. 2). Maakah may have given rise to the tribes and land of Maakah (Deut. iii. 14; 2 Sam. x. 6). The other names do not again occur. *And his concubine.* A concubine was a secondary wife, whose position was not considered disreputable in the East. Nahor, like Ishmael, had twelve sons, — eight by his wife, and four by his concubine.

XLIX. DEATH OF SARAH. — Gen. xxiii.

2. קִרְיַת אַרְבַּע, Qirjath-arba', *city of Arba.* אַרְבַּע, Arba', *four.*
8. עֶפְרוֹן 'Ephron, *of the dust*, or resembling a calf. צֹחַר, Tsochar, *whiteness.*
9. מַכְפֵּלָה, Makpelah, *doubled.*

XXIII. 1. And the life of Sarah was a hundred and twenty and seven years, the years of the life of Sarah. 2. And Sarah died in Kirjath-arba, this is Hebron, in the land of Kenaan: and Abraham went to mourn for Sarah, and to weep for her.

3. And Abraham rose up from before his dead, and spake unto the sons of Heth, saying, 4. A stranger and a sojourner am I with you: give me a possession of a burying-place with you, and let me bury my dead out of my sight. 5. And the sons of Heth answered Abraham, saying unto him, 6. Hear us, my lord: a prince of God art thou among us: in the choice of our sepulchres bury thy dead; none of us shall withhold his sepulchre from thee to bury thy dead. 7. And Abraham stood up, and bowed himself to the people of the land, to the sons of Heth. 8. And he spake with them, saying, If it be your mind that I should bury my dead out of my sight, hear me, and treat for me with Ephron the son of Zohar. 9. And he shall give me the cave of Makpelah, which he hath, which is in the end of his field: for the full silver shall he give it me among you, for a possession of a burying-place. 10. And Ephron was sitting among the sons of Heth; and Ephron the Hittite answered Abraham in the ears of the sons of Heth, before all that went in at the gate of his city, saying, 11. Nay, my lord, hear me; the field give I thee, and the cave that is therein, to thee I give it; in the sight of the sons of my people give I it thee: bury thy dead. 12. And Abraham bowed himself before the people of the land. 13. And he spake unto Ephron in the ears of the people of the land, saying, But if thou wilt, hear me: I give silver for the field; take it of me, and let me bury my dead there. 14. And Ephron answered Abraham, saying unto him, 15. My lord, hear me: the land is four hundred shekels of silver; between me and thee what is that? bury, then, thy dead. 16. And Abraham hearkened unto Ephron; and Abraham weighed the silver, which he had named in the ears of the sons of Heth, four hundred shekels of silver current with the merchant.

17. Then was made sure the field of Ephron, which was in Makpelah, which was before Mamre, the field and the cave

which was therein, and all the trees which were in the field, that were in all its border round about, 18. Unto Abraham for a possession in the sight of the sons of Heth, among all that went in at the gate of his city. 19. And after this Abraham buried Sarah his wife in the cave of the field of Makpelah, before Mamre, this is Hebron, in the land of Kenaan. 20. Then was made sure the field, and the cave that is therein, unto Abraham for a possession of a burying-place, from the sons of Heth. § 33.

The death and burial of Sarah are here recorded. This occasions the purchase of the field of Makpelah, in the cave of which is her sepulchre.

1, 2. Sarah is the only woman whose age is recorded in Scripture. She meets with this distinction as the wife of Abraham and the mother of the promised seed. *A hundred and twenty and seven years*, and therefore thirty-seven years after the birth of her son. *In Kiriath-arba.* Arba is called the father of Anak (Jos. xv. 13, xxi. 11); that is, of the Anakim or Bene Anak, a tall or gigantic tribe (Num. xiii. 22, xxviii. 33), who were subsequently dispossessed by Kaleb. The Anakim were probably Hittites. Abraham had been absent from Hebron, which is also called Mamre in this very chapter (v. 17, 19), not far from forty years, though he appears to have still kept up a connection with it, and had at present a residence in it. During this interval the sway of Arba may have commenced. *In the land of Kenaan*, in contradistinction to Beer-sheba in the land of the Philistines, where we last left Abraham. *Abraham went to mourn for Sarah*, either from Beer-sheba or some out-field where he had cattle pasturing.

3–16. Abraham purchases a burying-ground in the land. *The sons of Heth.* These are the lords of the soil. 4. *A stranger and a sojourner.* He is a stranger, not a Hittite; a sojourner, a dweller in the land, not a mere visitor or traveller. The former explains why he has no burial-ground; the latter, why he asks to purchase one. *Bury my dead out of my sight.* The bodies of those most dear to us decay, and must be removed from our sight. Abraham makes his request in the most general terms. 5, 6. In the somewhat exaggerated style of Eastern courtesy, the sons of Heth reply, *Hear us, my lord.* One speaks for all; hence the change of number. "My lord" is simply equivalent to our *Sir*, or the German *mein Herr*. *A prince of God* in those times of simple faith was a chief notably favored of God, as Abraham had been in his call, his deliverance in Egypt, his victory over the kings, his intercession for the cities of the vale, and his protection in the court of Abimelek. Some of these events were well known to the Hittites, as they had occurred while he was residing among them.

7–9. Abraham now makes a specific offer to purchase the field of Makpelah from Ephron the son of Zohar. *Treat for me*, — deal, use your influence with him. Abraham approaches in the most cautious manner to the individual with whom he wishes to treat. *The cave of Makpelah*. The burial of the dead in caves, natural and artificial, was customary in this Eastern land. The field seems to have been called Makpelah (doubled) from the double form of the cave, or the two caves perhaps communicating with each other, which it contained. *For the full silver*. Silver seems to have been the current medium of commerce at this time. God was known, and mentioned at an earlier period (Gen. ii. 11; xiii. 2). *A possession of a burying-ground*. We learn from this passage that property in land had been established at this time. Much of the country, however, must have been a common, or unappropriated pasture ground.

10–16. The transaction now comes to be between Abraham and Ephron. *Was sitting*. The sons of Heth were seated in council, and Ephron among them. Abraham seems to have been seated also; for he stood up to make his obeisance and request (v. 7). *Before all that went in at the gate of his city*. The conference was public. The place of session for judicial and other public business was the gate of the city, which was common ground, and where men were constantly going in and out. *His city*. This implies not that he was the king or chief, but simply that he was a respectable citizen. If Hebron was the city of the Hittites here intended, its chief at the time seems to have been Arba. 11. *The field give I thee*. Literally, have I given thee, — what was resolved upon was regarded as done. *In the sight of the sons of my people*. This was a public declaration or deed before many witnesses. He offers the field as a gift, with the Eastern understanding that the receiver would make an ample recompense. This mode of dealing had its origin in a genuine good-will, that was prepared to gratify the wish of another as soon as it was made known, and as far as it was reasonable or practicable. The feeling seems to have been still somewhat fresh and unaffected in the time of Abraham, though it has degenerated into a mere form of courtesy.

13. *If thou wilt, hear me.* The language is abrupt, being spoken in the haste of excitement. *I give silver.* "I have given" in the original; that is, I have determined to pay the full price. If the Eastern giver was liberal, the receiver was penetrated with an equal sense of the obligation conferred, and a like determination to make an equivalent return. 15. *The land is four hundred shekels.* This is the familiar style for "the land is worth so much." The shekel is here mentioned for the first time. It was originally a weight, not a coin. The weight at least was in common use before Abraham. If the shekel be nine pennyweights and three grains, the price of the field was about forty-five pounds sterling. 16. *And Abraham weighed.* It appears that the money was uncoined silver, as it was weighed. *Current with the merchant.* The Kenaanites, of whom the Hittites were a tribe, were among the earliest traders in the world. The merchant, as the original imports, is the traveller who brings the wares to the purchasers in their own dwellings or towns. To him a fixed weight and measure were necessary.

17–20. The completion of the sale is stated with great formality in two verses. No mention is made of any written deed of sale. Yet Abraham, Isaac, and Jacob remained in undisturbed possession of this burial-ground. Undisputed tenure seems to have been acknowledged as a title. 19. The burial of Sarah is then simply noted. 20. The validity of Abraham's title is practically evinced by the actual burial of Sarah, and is recited again on account of the importance of the fact.

This chapter is interesting as containing the first record of mourning for the dead, of burial, of property in land, of purchase of land, of silver as a medium of purchase, and of a standard of weight. Mourning for the dead was, no doubt, natural on the first death. Burial was a matter of necessity, in order, as Abraham says, to remove the body out of sight, as soon as it was learned by experience that it would be devoured by beasts of prey, or become offensive by putrefaction. To bury or cover it with earth was a more easy and natural process than burning, and was therefore earlier and more general. Property in land was introduced where tribes became settled, formed towns, and began to practise tillage. Barter was the early mode of accommodating each party with the articles he needed or valued. This led gradually to the use of the precious metals as a "current" medium of exchange — first by weight, and then by coins of a fixed weight and known stamp.

The burial of Sarah is noted because she was the wife of Abraham and the mother of the promised seed. The purchase of the field is worthy of note, as it is the first property of the chosen race in the promised land. Hence these two events are interwoven with the sacred narrative of the ways of God with man.

L. MARRIAGE OF ISAAC.—Gen. xxiv.

26. קָדַד *bow the head.* הִשְׁתַּחֲוָה *bow the body.*
29. לָבָן Laban, *white.*

XXIV. 1. And Abraham was an old man, far gone in
days: and the LORD had blessed Abraham in all things. 2.
And Abraham said unto his servant, the elder of his house,
that ruled over all that he had, Put now thy hand under my
thigh, 3. And I will make thee swear by the LORD God of
heaven, and God of the earth, that thou shalt not take a wife
unto my son of the daughters of the Kenaanite, among whom
I dwell. 4. But unto my land and to my kindred shalt thou
go, and take a wife unto my son Isaac. 5. And the servant
said unto him, Mayhap the woman will not wish to come after
me to this land: must I needs bring back thy son unto the
land whence thou camest. 6. And Abraham said unto him,
Beware thou, that thou bring not back my son thither. 7.
The LORD God of heaven, who took me from my father's house,
and from the land of my kindred, and who spake unto me,
and who sware unto me, saying, Unto thy seed will I give this
land, he shall send his angel before thee, and thou shalt take
a wife for my son thence. 8. And if the woman do not wish
to come after thee, then thou shalt be clear from this my oath:
only my son bring not back thither. 9. And the servant put
his hand under the thigh of Abraham his master, and sware
to him concerning this matter.

10. And the servant took ten camels of the camels of his

master, and went, and all the best belonging to his master in his hand; and he arose and went to Aram of the two rivers, to the city of Nahor. 11. And he made the camels kneel down without the city by a well of water, at the time of evening, the time when the maidens that draw water come out. 12. And he said, O LORD, God of my master Abraham, open the way before me to-day, and show kindness unto my master Abraham. 13. Here am I standing by the well of water; and the daughters of the men of the city are coming out to draw water. 14. And let it come to pass, that the damsel to whom I shall say, Let down now thy pitcher that I may drink, and she shall say, Drink, and also to thy camels will I give drink, the same hast thou adjudged to thy servant Isaac; and thereby shall I know that thou hast shown kindness unto my master.

15. And it came to pass that he had not yet done speaking, and, lo, Rebekah came forth, who was born to Bethuel, son of Milkah, the wife of Nahor, Abraham's brother, and her pitcher upon her shoulder. 16. And the damsel was very fair to look upon, a virgin, and no man had known her; and she went down to the well and filled her pitcher and came up. 17. And the servant ran to meet her, and said, Let me now drink a little water out of thy pitcher. 18. And she said, Drink, my lord; and she hasted, and let down her pitcher upon her hand and gave him drink. 19. And she had done giving him drink; and she said, Also for thy camels will I draw until they have done drinking. 20. And she hasted, and emptied her pitcher into the trough, and ran again unto the well to draw, and drew for all his camels. 21. And the man wondered at her, holding his peace, to wit, whether the LORD had prospered his way or not.

22. And it came to pass, as the camels had done drinking, that the man took a ring of gold, a beka in weight, and two bracelets for her hands, ten of gold in weight, 23. And said, whose daughter art thou? tell me now: is there in thy father's

house room for us to lodge in? 24. And she said unto him, I am the daughter of Bethuel, the son of Milkah, whom she bare unto Nahor. 25. And she said unto him, Both straw and provender enough we have, and room to lodge in. 26. And the man bowed his head, and worshipped the LORD. 27. And he said, Blessed be the LORD, God of my master Abraham, who hath not withdrawn his mercy and his truth from my master: when I was in the way, the LORD led me to the house of my master's brethren. 28. And the damsel ran, and told her mother's house according to all these words.

29. And Rebekah had a brother, and his name was Laban: and Laban ran to the man without, unto the well. 30. And it came to pass, when he saw the ring and the bracelets on his sister's hands, and when he heard the words of Rebekah his sister, saying, Thus spake the man unto me, that he went unto the man, and, lo, he was standing by the camels at the well. 31. And he said, Come in, thou blessed of the LORD; wherefore standest thou without? and I have prepared the house and a place for the camels. 32. And the man went into the house; and he ungirded the camels, and gave straw and provender to the camels, and water to wash his feet, and the men's feet that were with him. 33. And he set before him to eat: and he said, I will not eat till I have told mine errand. And he said, Speak on.

34. And he said, I am Abraham's servant. 35. And the LORD hath blessed my master much, and he has become great: and he gave him flocks and herds, and silver and gold, and men-servants and maid-servants, and camels and asses. 36. And Sarah, my master's wife, bare a son to my master after her old age; and he hath given unto him all that he hath. 37. And my master made me swear, saying, Thou shalt not take a wife to my son of the daughters of the Kenaanite, in whose land I dwell. 38. But unto my father's house shalt thou go and to my kindred, and take a wife for my son. 39. And I said unto my master, Mayhap the woman will not come

after me. 40. And he said unto me, The LORD before whom I walk, will send his angel with thee, and prosper thy way; and thou shalt take a wife for my son from my family, and from my father's house. 41. Then shalt thou be clear from my oath, when thou goest to my family; and if they give thee not, thou shalt be clear from my oath. 42. And I came this day unto the well, and said, O LORD, God of my master Abraham, if now thou do prosper my way which I go, 43. Lo, I stand at the well of water, and let it come to pass, that the maiden coming forth to draw to whom I say, Let me drink now a little water out of thy pitcher, 44. And she says to me, Both thou drink, and for thy camels I will draw, the same be the woman whom the LORD hath adjudged to my master's son. 45. I had not yet done speaking in my heart, and, lo, Rebekah came forth, and her pitcher on her shoulder; and she went down unto the well and drew; and I said unto her, Let me now drink. 46. And she hasted, and let down her pitcher from upon her, and said, Drink, and also to thy camels will I give drink; and I drank, and she made the camels drink also. 47. And I asked her, and said, whose daughter art thou? And she said, the daughter of Bethuel, Nahor's son, whom Milkah bare unto him: and I put the ring upon her face, and the bracelets upon her hands. 48. And I bowed my head, and worshipped the LORD, and blessed the LORD, God of my master Abraham, who had led me in the way of truth to take the daughter of my master's brother for his son. 49. And now, if ye will do kindness and truth to my master, tell me; and I will turn to the right hand or to the left. 50. And Laban and Bethuel answered and said, The thing proceedeth from the LORD; we cannot speak unto thee bad or good. 51. Behold, Rebekah is before thee; take her and go, and let her be wife to thy master's son, as the LORD hath spoken. 52. And it came to pass, when Abraham's servant heard their words, he bowed to the earth to the LORD. 53. And the servant brought forth jewels of silver, and jewels of gold, and raiment,

and gave to Rebekah; and precious things gave he to her
brother and to her mother. 54. And they ate and drank, he
and the men that were with him, and tarried all night; and
they rose up in the morning, and he said, Send me away unto
my master. 55. And her brother and her mother said, Let
the damsel abide with us a few days, at the least ten; after
that she shall go. 56. And he said unto them, Hinder me
not, seeing the LORD hath prospered my way; send me away,
that I may go to my master. 57. And they said, We will call
the damsel and inquire at her mouth. 58. And they called
Rebekah, and said unto her, Wilt thou go with this man?
And she said, I will go. 59. And they sent away Rebekah
their sister, and her nurse, and Abraham's servant and his
men. 60. And they blessed Rebekah, and said unto her, Our
sister, be thou mother to thousands of myriads, and let thy
seed possess the gate of those that hate them. 61. And Re-
bekah arose, and her damsels, and they rode upon the camels,
and went after the man: and the servant took Rebekah and
went his way.

62. And Isaac went from the way to Beer-lahai-roi; for he
was dwelling in the land of the south. 63. And Isaac came
out to meditate in the field at eventide: and he lifted up his
eyes and saw, and behold the camels were coming. 64. And
Rebekah lifted up her eyes and saw Isaac, and she lighted off
the camel. 65. And she said unto the servant, Who is this
man that walketh in the field to meet us? And the servant
said, This is my master. And she took the veil and covered
herself. 66. And the servant told Isaac all things that he had
done. 67. And Isaac brought her unto Sarah his mother's
tent, and took Rebekah and she became his wife, and he loved
her; and Isaac was comforted after his mother.

In this circumstantial account of the marriage of Isaac, we have a beautiful picture of ancient manners in the East, the living original of which the present customs of that cradle of mankind are a striking copy.

1–9. Abraham binds the chief servant of his house to seek a wife for his son Isaac among his kindred. 1. The first movement in this matrimonial arrangement is on the part of the father, who does not consult his son, but the chief manager of his household affairs. Abraham is now a hundred and forty years of age, and Sarah has been three years dead. Isaac seems to have been of an easy, sedate turn of mind, and was not in circumstances to choose a partner for life such as his father would approve. The promise of a numerous offspring by the son of Sarah is before the mind of the patriarch. All these considerations impel him to look out for a suitable wife for his son, and the blessing of the Lord encourages him to proceed. 2. The person whom Abraham intrusted with this delicate task has a threefold designation. First, he is *his servant* or minister. Secondly, he is the old man, ancient, or elder of his house. Here the term *elder* approaches its official signification. In early times age was taken into account, along with good conduct and aptitude, as the qualification for services of trust. Thirdly, he *ruled over all that he had.* He was therefore a master as well as a minister. If this be Eliezer of Damascus (Gen. xv. 2), he was the steward of Abraham before the birth of Ishmael fifty-four years ago. *Under my thigh.* The thigh was the seat of generative power, and the region of sacramental consecration, and to put the hand under the thigh was to acknowledge and pledge obedience to him who requires the oath.

3, 4. The appeal is to God as *Jehovah, God of heaven and God of the earth.* Jehovah is the personal name of God, which is properly used by those who are in fellowship with him. He is the Author of all being, and therefore of heaven and earth; and hence the arbiter of the destiny of the oath-taker, both in spiritual and material things, both in this life and in that which is to come. *Not of the daughters of the Kenaanite,* a race sinking fast into ungodliness and unrighteousness, doomed to extirpation, to whom the promised seed is to succeed. The kindred of Abraham were Shemites, Hebrews, and still retained some knowledge of the true God, and some reverence for him and his will. 5–8. The experienced elder of Abraham's house does not wish to bind himself by an oath to that which it may be impossible to fulfil. He makes the supposition of the unwillingness of the bride whom he may select, and obtains a quittance from his oath in that case. The patriarch, however, charges him not to bring his son back to the land of his fathers, and expresses his confidence in the God of promise, that he will direct his servant to the suitable wife for his son. *His angel* (Gen xvi. 7). This is the Lord in the function of an angel or messenger opening the way for the servant of Abraham. He does not make any appearance to the servant, though a superintending Providence is strikingly displayed in the whole affair. 9. The faithful elder now understands and takes the required oath.

10–14. He proceeds on his journey. *Took ten camels.* These are designed for conducting the bride and her companions home to his master. *All the best belonging to his master in his hand.* This refers to the presents for the bride and her friends, and to the accommodations for her comfort on the journey. *Aram-Naharaim.* Aram was an extensive area, embracing not only the country west of the Frat and north of Palestine, but the northern part of Mesopotamia, or the country between the Frat and the Dijlah. The latter region is for the sake of distinction called Aram of the two rivers. It did not include the southern part of Mesopotamia, which was called Shinar (Gen. xi. 2), and probably extended only to the Chaboras, Khabour. The part of it in which Haran was situated was called Padan-aram (Gen. xxviii. 2). *The city of Nahor.* It is probable that Nahor accompanied his father, Terah, to Haran (Gen. xi. 31). If not, he must have followed him very soon.

11. *Made the camels kneel,* for repose. *The time when the maidens that draw water come out.* The evening was the cool part of the day. The simple maidens of primitive days attended personally to domestic affairs. The experienced steward might therefore naturally expect to see the high-born damsels of the land at the public well, which had probably given rise to the neighboring town. 12–14. The prayer of the aged servant is conceived in a spirit of earnest, childlike faith. The matter in hand is of extraordinary importance. A wife is to be found for the heir of promise. This was a special concern of God, and so the single-hearted follower of Abraham makes it. He takes upon himself the choice of a maiden among those that come to draw, to whom he will make the request of a particular act of kindness to a stranger, and he prays God that the intended bride may be known by a ready compliance with his request. The three qualifications, then, in the mind of the venerable domestic for a bride for his master's son, are a pleasing exterior, a kindly disposition, and the approval of God.

15–21. The answer is immediate and direct. *He had not yet done speaking,* when the answer came. A damsel *very fair to look upon,* satisfying the taste of the old man, appears. He thereupon prefers his request, with which she promptly complies. The old man waits in wonder and silence to see if the Lord's approval will follow.

22–28. Rebekah makes herself known in reply to his inquiries. *A ring of gold.* The single ring was worn in the nose, the side cartilage of which was pierced for the purpose. This is a custom of the East. *A beka* was half a shekel, somewhat less than a quarter of an ounce. *Ten of gold in weight.* Ten bekas would be about two ounces and a quarter. If shekels, however, be understood, the weight will be double. These were merely a reward for her kindness and courtesy to a stranger. Two questions are now asked by the stranger, — the one relating to her kindred, and the other to the means and the inclination they had to entertain a stranger, when inns were not yet in existence. She announces herself to be the daughter of his master's nephew, and assures him of the requisite accommodation.

26, 27. *Bowed his head and worshipped.* The bowing of the head and of the body are here combined to indicate the aged servant's deep thankfulness for the guidance of the Lord. 27. The utterance of the mouth accompanies the external gesture of reverence. 28. *Her mother's house;* those who were in the department of the females. We may imagine with what excitement and alacrity Rebekah would communicate the extraordinary intelligence.

29–33. The reception of Abraham's servant. Laban now comes on the scene. He is ready to run with his sister to find the man, and invite him, as a matter of course, to his father's house. 30. *When he saw the ring.* The presents to his sister assure him that this is the envoy of some man of wealth and position. 31. *Thou blessed of the Lord.* The name of Jehovah was evidently not unfamiliar to Laban's ears. He calls this stranger "blessed of Jehovah," on account of his language, demeanor, and manifest prosperity. The knowledge and worship of the living God, the God of truth and mercy, was still retained in the family of Nahor. 32, 33. Being warmly invited, the man enters the house. *And he ungirded the camels.* Laban is the actor here, and in the following duties of hospitality. *The men's feet that were with him.* It comes out here, incidentally, as it was reasonable to infer from the number of camels, that Abraham's steward had a retinue of servants with him. The crowning act of an Eastern reception is the presenting of food. But the faithful servant must deliver his message before partaking of the friendly meal.

34–49. The servant's errand told. He explains his business in a singularly artless and pleasing manner. He then leaves the matter in the hands of the family. 36. *Given unto him all that he hath.* His children by Hagar and Keturah were dismissed with portions during his life, and the main bulk of his property was conveyed to Isaac.

50–61. The servant's return with Rebekah. 50, 51. So plain an interposition of Providence admits of no refusal on the part of those who revere the Lord. Bethuel now appears as a concurring party. Laban, as the full brother of Rebekah, has a voice in the disposal of her hand; but the father only has the power to ratify the contract. 52, 53. The patriarch's servant first bows in acknowledgment to the Lord, who had now manifested his approval of the choice he had made, and then proceeds to distribute costly gifts to the bride, and to her brother and mother. 54. Now at length the thankful guest partakes of the fare set before him along with his entertainers, and after the night's repose requests to be dismissed. 55. *A few days;* perhaps a week or ten days. The mother and brother naturally plead for a little time to prepare for parting with Rebekah. They could not expect the servant, however, to stay months. 57, 58. *Inquire at her mouth.* This is the only free choice in the matter that seems to be given to Rebekah. Her consent may have been modestly indicated, before her family ratified the contract. It is plain, however, that it was thought proper that the parents should receive and decide upon a proposal of marriage. The extent to which the maiden's inclinations would be consulted would depend very much on the custom of the country, and the intelligence and good feeling of the parents. In later times the custom became very arbitrary. Rebekah's decision shows that she concurred in the consent of her relatives. 59–61. *And her nurse.* Her name, we learn afterwards (Gen. xxxv. 8), was Deborah. The nurse accompanied the bride as her confidential adviser and faithful attendant, and died in her service; a beautiful trait of ancient manners. The blessing consists in a boundless offspring, and the upper hand over their enemies. These are indicative of a thin population, and a comparatively rude state of society. *And her damsels.* We here learn, again, incidentally, that Rebekah had more female attendants than her nurse.

62–67. Isaac receives his bride. He had been at Beer-lahai-roi, the scene of the interview of Hagar with the angel of the Lord, — a spot calculated to awaken thoughts of an overruling Providence. *To meditate.* This is a characteristic of Isaac's retiring, contemplative mood. Abraham was the active, authoritative father; Isaac was the passive, submissive son. To meditate was to hold converse with his own thoughts, to ponder on the import of that never-to-be-forgotten scene when he was laid on the altar by a father's hand, and a ram caught in the thicket became his substitute, and to pour out his soul unto the God of his salvation. In this hour of his grave reflection comes his destined bride with her faithful escort upon his view. 64–67. Rebekah lights off the camel. Doubtless the conversation by the way with the elder of Abraham's house had made her aware of their approach to the residence of her future husband. She concludes at once that this must be he, and, alighting, asks if it be. On being informed by the servant that this is his young master, she puts on the veil, which covers the head, and hangs down gracefully both behind and before. The aged servant reports the success of his mission, and presents Rebekah. Isaac brings his cousin's daughter into the apartments formerly occupied by his mother, and accepts her as his wife. The formalities of the interview, and of her presentation to Abraham as his daughter-in-law, are all untold. *And he loved her.* This is the first mention of the social affections. It comes in probably because Isaac had not before seen his bride, and now felt his heart drawn towards her, when she was presented to his view. All things were evidently done in the fear of God, as became those who were to be the progenitors of the seed of promise. We have here a description of the primeval marriage. It is a simple taking of a woman for a wife before all witnesses, and with suitable feelings and expression of reverence towards God, and of desire for his blessing. It is a pure and holy relation, reaching back into the realms of innocence, and fit to be the emblem of the humble, confiding, affectionate union between the Lord and his people.

LI. THE DEATH OF ABRAHAM.—Gen. xxv. 1-11.

1. קְטוּרָה Qeturah, *incense.*

2. זִמְרָן Zimran, *celebrated in song.* יָקְשָׁן Joqshan, *fowler.* מְדָן Medan, *judge.* מִדְיָן Midian, *one who measures.* יִשְׁבָּק Jishbaq, *he who leaves.* שׁוּחַ Shuach, *pit.*

3. לְטוּשִׁם Letushim, *hammered, sharpened.* לְאֻמִּים Leummim, *peoples.*

4. עֵיפָה, 'Ephah, *darkness.* עֵפֶר 'Epher, *dust.* אֲבִידָע 'Abida, *father of knowledge.* אֶלְדָּעָה Elda'ah, *knowing?*

XXV. 1. And Abraham added and took a wife, and her name was Keturah. 2. And she bare him Zimran and Jokshan and Medan and Midian and Ishbak and Shuah. 3. And Jokshan begat Sheba and Dedan. And the sons of Dedan were Asshurim and Letushim and Leummim. 4. And the sons of Midian, Ephah and Epher and Henok and Abida and Eldaah. All these were the children of Keturah. 5. And Abraham gave all that he had unto Isaac. 6. And unto the sons of the concubines, which Abraham had, gave Abraham gifts, and sent them away from Isaac his son, while he yet lived eastward; unto the land of the East.

7. And these are the days of the years of Abraham's life, which he lived, a hundred and seventy and five years. 8. And Abraham expired, and died in a happy old age, old and full; and was gathered to his peoples. 9. And Isaac and Ishmael, his sons, buried him in the cave of Makpelah, in the field of Ephron, the son of Zohar the Hittite, which is before Mamre. 10. The field which Abraham purchased of the sons of Heth, there was buried Abraham, and Sarah his wife. 11. And it came to pass after the death of Abraham, that God blessed his son Isaac: and Isaac dwelt at Beer-lahai-roi. ¶ 25.

Another family is born to Abraham by Keturah, and portioned off, after which he dies and is buried.

1–6. *Added and took a wife.* According to the laws of Hebrew composition, this event may have taken place before that recorded in the close of the previous chapter. Of this law we have several examples in this very chapter. And there is nothing contrary to the customs of that period in adding wife to wife. We cannot say that Abraham was hindered from taking Keturah in the lifetime of Sarah by any moral feeling which would not also have hindered him from taking Hagar. It has been also noticed that Keturah is called a concubine, which is thought to imply that the proper wife was still living; and that Abraham was a very old man at the death of Sarah. But, on the other hand, it is to be remembered that these sons were in any case born after the birth of Isaac, and therefore after Abraham was renewed in vital powers. If this renewal of vigor remained after the birth of Isaac, it may have continued some time after the death of Sarah, whom he survived thirty-eight years. His abstinence from any concubine until Sarah gave him Hagar is against his taking any other during Sarah's lifetime. His loneliness on the death of Sarah may have prompted him to seek a companion of his old age. And if this step was delayed till Isaac was married, and therefore separated from him, an additional motive would impel him in the same direction. He was not bound to raise this wife to the full rights of a proper wife, even though Sarah were dead. And six sons might be born to him twenty-five years before his death. And if Hagar and Ishmael were dismissed when he was about fifteen years old, so might Keturah when her youngest was twenty or twenty-five. We are not warranted, then, still less compelled, to place Abraham's second marriage before the death of Sarah, or even the marriage of Isaac. It seems to appear in the narrative in the order of time.

2. The endeavors to ascertain the tribes that descended from these six sons of Keturah have not been very successful. Zimran has been compared with *Ζαβράμ* (Ptol. vi. 7. 5), situated west of Mecca on the Red Sea. Jokshan with the *Κασσανῖται* (Ptol. vi. 7. 6), and with the tribe Jakish among the Himyarites in South Arabia. Medan with *Μοδιάνα* on the east coast of the Aelanitic Gulf. Midian is found in two localities west of the Aelanitic Gulf and east of the Salt Sea. Among the former, Moses afterwards found refuge. The latter are probably east of Abraham's residence. Ishbak is compared with Shobek, a place in Idumaea. Shuah probably belongs to the same region. He may be the ancestor of Bildad the Shuhite (Job ii. 11). Of these, Midian alone appears to be ascertained. The others may have been absorbed in that congeries of tribes, the Arabs.

3, 4. Sheba, Dedan, and Asshurim are recurring names (Gen. x. 7, 22, 28), describing other tribes of Arabs equally unknown. The three sons of Dedan may be traced in the tribe Asir of the south of Hejaz, the Beni Leits of Hejaz, and the Beni Lam of the borders of Mesopotamia. 4. Of the sons of Midian, Epha is mentioned in Is. lx. 6 along with Midian. Epher is compared with Beni Ghifar in Hejaz, Henok with Hanakye north of Medinah, Abida with the Abide, and Eldaah with the Wadaa. These conjectures of Burckhardt are chiefly useful in showing that similar names are still existing in the country. There are here six sons of Abraham, seven grandsons, and three great-grandsons, making sixteen descendants by Keturah. If there were any daughters, they are not noticed. It is not customary to mention females, unless they are connected with leading historical characters These descendants of Abraham and Keturah are the third contribution of Palgites to the Joktanites, who constituted the original element of the Arabs, the descendants of Lot and Ishmael having preceded them. All these branches of the Arab nation are descended from Heber.

5, 6. Abraham makes Isaac his heir (Gen. xxiv. 36). He gives portions to the sons of the concubines during his lifetime, and sends them away to the East. Ishmael had been portioned off long before (Gen. xxi. 14). The East is a general name for Arabia, which stretched away to the southeast and east of the point where Abraham resided in the south of Palestine. The northern part of Arabia, which lay due east of Palestine, was formerly more fertile and populous than now. The sons of Keturah were probably dismissed before they had any children. Their notable descendants, according to custom, are added here before they are dismissed from the main line of the narrative.

7–11. The death of Abraham. His years were a hundred and seventy-five. He survived Sarah thirty-eight years, and Isaac's marriage thirty-five. His grandfather lived a hundred and forty-eight years, his father two hundred and five, his son Isaac a hundred and eighty, and his grandson Jacob a hundred and forty-seven ; so that his years were the full average of that period. 8. *Expired* — breathed his last. *In a happy old age*, in external and internal blessedness (Gen. xv. 15). *Old and full* — having attained to the standard length of life in his days, and being satisfied with this life, so that he was ready and willing to depart. *Gathered to his peoples* (Gen. xv. 15). To be gathered is not to cease to exist, but to continue existing in another sphere. His peoples, the departed families, from whom he is descended, are still in being in another not less real world. This, and the like expression in the passage quoted, give the first fact in the history of the soul after death, as the burial is the first step in that of the body.

9, 10. *Isaac and Ishmael*, in brotherly coöperation. Ishmael was the eldest son, dwelt in the presence of all his brethren, and had a special blessing. The sons of Keturah were far away in the East, very young, and had no particular blessing. Ishmael is therefore properly associated with Isaac in paying the last offices to their deceased father. The burying-place had been prepared before. Its purchase is here rehearsed with great precision as a testimony of the fact. This burial-ground is an earnest of the promised possession.

11. This verse is an appendix to the history of Abraham, stating

that the blessing of God, which he had enjoyed till his death, now descended upon his son Isaac, who abode at Beer-lahai-roi. The general name God is here employed, because the blessing of God denotes the material and temporal prosperity which had attended Abraham, in comparison with other men of his day. Of the spiritual and eternal blessings connected with Jehovah, the proper name of the Author of being and blessing, we shall hear in due time.

The section now completed contains the seventh of the documents commencing with the formula, "these are the generations." It begins in the eleventh chapter and ends in the twenty-fifth, and therefore contains a greater number of chapters and amount of matter than the whole of the preceding narrative. This is as it should be in a record of the ways of God with man. In the former sections, things anterior and external to man come out into the foreground; they lie at the basis of his being, his mental and moral birth. In the present section, things internal to man and flowing from him are brought into view. These are coincident with the growth of his spiritual nature. The latter are no less momentous than the former for the true and full development of his faculties and capacities.

In the former sections the absolute being of God is assumed; the beginning of the heavens and the earth asserted. The reconstruction of skies and land and the creation of a new series of plants and animals are recorded. This new creation is completed by the creating of man in the image of God and after his likeness. The placing of man in a garden of fruit trees prepared for his sustenance and gratification; the primeval command, with its first lessons in language, physics, ethics, and theology; the second lesson in speaking when the animals are named; and the separation of man into the male and the female, are followed by the institutions of wedlock and the Sabbath, the fountain-heads of sociality with man and God, the foreshadows of the second and first tables of the law. The fall of man in the second lesson of ethics; the sentence of the Judge, containing in its very bosom the intimation of mercy; the act of fratricide, followed by the general corruption of the whole race; the notices of Sheth, of calling on the name of Jehovah begun at the birth of Enosh, of Henok who walked with God, and of Noah who found grace in his sight; the flood sweeping away the corruption of man while saving righteous Noah; and the confusion of tongues, defeating the ambition of man, while preparing for the replenishing of the earth and the liberties of men — these complete the chain of prominent facts that are to be seen standing in the background of man's history. These are all moments, potent elements in the memory of man, foundation-stones of his history and philosophy. They cannot be surmounted or ignored without absurdity or criminality.

In the section now completed the sacred writer descends from the general to the special, from the distant to the near, from the class to the individual. He dissects the soul of a man, and discloses to our view the whole process of the spiritual life from the new-born babe to the perfect man. Out of the womb of that restless selfish race, from whom nothing is willingly restrained which they have imagined to do, comes forth Abram, with all the lineaments of their moral image upon him. The Lord calls him to himself, his mercy, his blessing, and his service. He obeys the call. That is the moment of his new birth. The acceptance of the divine call is the tangible fact that evinces a new nature. Henceforth he is a disciple, having yet much to learn before he becomes a master, in the school of heaven. From this time forward the spiritual predominates in Abram; very little of the carnal appears. Two sides of his mental character present themselves in alternate passages, which may be called the physical and the metaphysical, or the things of the body and the things of the soul. In the former only the carnal or old corrupt nature sometimes appears; in the latter, the new nature advances from stage to stage of spiritual growth unto perfection. His entrance into the land of promise is followed by his descent into Egypt, his generous forbearance in parting with Lot, his valorous conduct in rescuing him, and his dignified demeanor towards Melkizedec and the king of Sodom. The second stage of its spiritual development now presents itself to our view; on receiving the promise, Fear not, Abram: I am thy shield, thy exceeding great reward, he believes in the Lord, who counts it to him for righteousness, and enters into covenant with him. This is the first fruit of the new birth, and it is followed by the birth of Ishmael. On hearing the authoritative announcement, I am God Almighty; walk before me and be perfect, he performs the first act of that obedience which is the keystone of repentance, by receiving the sign of covenant, and proceeds to the high functions of holding communion and making intercession with God. These spiritual acts are followed by the destruction of the cities of the Jordan vale, with the preservation of Lot, the sojourning in Gerar, the birth of Isaac, and the league with Abimelek. The last great act of the spiritual life of Abraham is the surrender of his only son to the will of God, and this again is followed by the death and burial of Sarah, the marriage of Isaac, and the second marriage of Abraham.

It is manifest that every movement in the physical and ethical history of Abraham is fraught with instruction of the deepest interest for the heirs of immortality. The leading points in spiritual experience are here laid before us. The susceptibilities and activities of a soul born of the Spirit are unfolded to our view. These are lessons for eternity. Every descendant of Abraham, every collateral branch of his family, every contemporary eye or ear-witness, might have profited in the things of eternity by all this precious treasury of spiritual knowledge. Many of the Gentiles still had, and all might have had, a knowledge of the covenant with Noah, and a share in its promised blessings. This would not have precluded, but only promoted, the mission of Abraham to be the father of the seed in whom all the families of man should effectually be blessed. And in the meantime it would have caused to be circulated to the ends of the earth that new revelation of spiritual experience which was displayed in the life of Abraham for the perfecting of the saints.

SECTION XI. — ISAAC.

LII. HISTORY OF ISHMAEL. — Gen. xxv. 12–18.

13. נְבָיֹת Nebajoth, *heights.* קֵדָר Qedar, *black.* אַדְבְּאֵל Adbeel, *miracle of God?* מִבְשָׂם Mibsam, *sweet odor.*

14. מִשְׁמָע Mishma', *hearing.* דּוּמָה Dumah, *silence.* מַשָּׂא Massa, *burden.*

15. חֲדַר Chadar, *chamber;* or חֲדַד Chadad, *sharpness*; תֵּימָא Tema. יְטוּר Jetur, *enclosure,* akin to טוּר *a wall,* and טִירָה *a wall.* נָפִישׁ Naphish, *breathing.* קֵדְמָה Qedemah, *before, eastward*

16. חָצֵר *court, village, town.*

12. And these are the generations of Ishmael, Abraham's son, whom Hagar the Mizrite, Sarah's handmaid, bare unto Abraham. 13. And these are the names of the sons of Ishmael, by their names, after their generations: the firstborn of Ishmael, Nebaioth, and Kedar and Abdeel and Mibsam, 14. And Mishma and Dumah and Massa, 15. Hadar and Tema, Itur, Naphish, and Kedemah. 16. These are the sons of Ishmael, and these their names, in their towns, and in their castles: twelve princes after their nations. 17. And these are the years of the life of Ishmael, a hundred and thirty and seven years: and he expired, and died, and was gathered unto his peoples. 18. And they dwelt from Havilah unto Shur, that is before Mizraim, as thou goest to Asshur: in the presence of all his brethren he had fallen. 6 ¶¶¶ 26.

According to custom, before the history of the principal line is taken up, that of the collateral branch is briefly given. Thus Cain's history is closed before Sheth's is commenced; Japheth and Ham are before

Shem; Haran and Nahor before Abram. And so the sons of Keturah are first dismissed from the pages of history, and then Ishmael.

12. The present passage begins with the formula, "and these are the generations," and forms the eighth document so commencing. The appearance of a document consisting of seven verses is clearly against the supposition that each of these documents is due to a different author. The phrase points to a change of subject, not of author.

13–16. *Nebaioth* (Is. lx. 7) is preserved in the Nabataei inhabiting Arabia Petraea, and extending far toward the East. *Kedar* (Is. xxi. 17) appears in the Cedrei of Pliny (H. N. 5. 12) who dwell east of Petraea. *Adbeel Mibsam*, and *Mishma* are otherwise unknown. The last is connected with the Μαισαιμενεῖς of Ptol. (v. 7. 21). *Dumah* (Is. xxi. 11) is probably Δούμεθα (Ptol. vi. 19. 7) and Domata (Plin. H. N. 6. 32) and Dumat el-Jendel in Nejd and the Syrian desert. *Massa* may be preserved in the Μασανοὶ of Ptolemy (v. 19. 2), northeast of Duma. *Hadar* is Hadad in 1 Chron. i. 30, the Sam., Onk., perhaps the Sept., and many cod. It is supposed to be Χαττηνία (Polyb.), Attene, and to lie between Oman and Bahrein. *Tema* (Job vi. 19; Is. xxi. 14; Jer. xxv. 23) lay on the borders of Nejd and the Syrian desert. *Jetur* remains in Ituraea, Jedur, northeast of the sea of Galilee. Some suppose the Druses descended from him. *Naphish* (1 Chron. vi. 19, 22) lay in the same quarter. *Kedemah* is otherwise unknown. 16. *In their towns and in their castles.* The former are unwalled collections of houses or perhaps tents; the latter, fortified keeps or encampments. *Twelve princes*, one for each tribe, descended from his twelve sons.

17, 18. Ishmael dies at the age of a hundred and thirty-seven. *From Havilah*, on the borders of Arabia Petraea and Felix. *Unto Shur*, on the borders of Arabia and Egypt. This was the original seat of the Ishmaelites, from which they wandered far into Arabia. *In the presence of all his brethren* — the descendants of Abraham by Sarah and Keturah, those of Lot, and the Egyptians who were his brethren or near kindred by his mother and wife. *He had fallen* into the lot of his inheritance. Thus was fulfilled the prediction uttered before his birth (Gen. xvi. 12).

LIII. BIRTH OF ESAU AND JACOB. — Gen. xxv. 19-34.

20. פַּדָּן Paddan, *ploughed field;* r. *cut, plough.*

25. עֵשָׂו Esav, *hairy*, or *made.*

26. יַעֲקֹב Ja'aqob, *he shall take the heel.*

27. תָּם *perfect, peaceful, plain.* The epithet refers to disposition, and contrasts the comparatively civilized character of Jacob with the rude temper of Esau.

30. אֱדוֹם Edom, *red.*

19. And these are the generations of Isaac, Abraham's son: Abraham begat Isaac. 20. And Isaac was the son of forty years when he took Rebekah, daughter of Bethuel the Aramite of Paddan-aram, sister of Laban the Aramite, to wife. 21. And Isaac entreated the Lord in regard to his wife; for she was barren: and the Lord was entreated of him, and Rebekah his wife conceived. 22. And the children struggled together within her: and she said, If it be so, why am I thus? And she went to inquire of the Lord. 23. And the Lord said unto her, Two nations are in thy womb, and two folks shall be separated from thy bowels; and folk shall be stronger than folk, and the elder shall serve the younger. 24. And her days to be delivered were fulfilled: and, lo, twins were in her womb. 25. And the first came out red, all of him like a hair mantle; and they called his name Esau. 26. And after that came out his brother, and his hand holding Esau's heel; and he called his name Jacob: and Isaac was the son of sixty years when she bare them.

27. And the boys grew: and Esau was a man cunning in the chase, a man of the field; and Jacob was a plain man, dwelling in tents. 28. And Isaac loved Esau, because his venison was in his mouth; and Rebekah loved Jacob. 29. And Jacob sod pottage: and Esau went in from the field, and he was faint. 30. And Esau said to Jacob, Let me feed now on that red, red; for I am faint. Therefore was his name called

Edom. 31. And Jacob said, Sell me this day thy birthright.
32. And Esau said, Behold, I am going to die: and for what
is this birthright to me? 33. And Jacob said, Swear to me
this day; and he sware unto him; and he sold his birthright
unto Jacob. 34. And Jacob gave Esau bread and pottage of
lentiles; and he ate and drank, and rose up and went his way;
and Esau despised his birthright. ¶ 27.

The ninth document here begins with the usual phrase, and continues to the end of the thirty-fifth chapter. It contains the history of the second of the three patriarchs, or rather, indeed, as the opening phrase intimates, of the generations of Isaac; that is, of his son Jacob. Isaac himself makes little figure in the sacred history. Born when his mother was ninety, and his father a hundred years of age, he is of a sedate, contemplative, and yielding disposition. Consenting to be laid on the altar as a sacrifice to God, he had the stamp of submission early and deeply impressed on his soul. His life corresponds with these antecedents. Hence, in the spiritual aspect of his character he was the man of patience, of acquiescence, of susceptibility, of obedience. His qualities were those of the son, as Abraham's were those of the father. He carried out, but did not initiate; he followed, but did not lead; he continued, but did not commence. Accordingly, the docile and patient side of the saintly character is now to be presented to our view.

19–26. The birth of Esau and Jacob. 20. *The son of forty years.* Hence we learn that Isaac was married the third year after his mother's death, when Abraham was in his hundred and fortieth year. *Bethuel the Aramaean.* As Bethuel was a descendant of Arpakshad, not of Aram, he is here designated, not by his descent, but by his adopted country Aram. By descent he was a Kasdi or Kaldee. 21. Sarah was barren for at least thirty years; Rebekah for nineteen. This drew forth the prayer of Isaac in regard to his wife. The heir of promise was to be a child of prayer, and accordingly when the prayer ascended the fruit of the womb was given. 22, 23. Rebekah had unwonted sensations connected with her pregnancy. She said to herself, *If it be so*, if I have conceived seed, *why am I thus*, why this strange struggle within me? In the artlessness of her faith she goes to the Lord for an explanation. We are not informed in what way she consulted God, or how he replied. The expression, *she went to inquire of the Lord,* implies that there was some place of worship and communion with God by prayer. We are not to suppose that she went to Abraham, or any other prophet, if such were then at hand, when we have no intimation of this in the text. Her communication with the Lord seems to have been direct. This passage conveys to us the intimation that there was now a fixed mode and perhaps place of inquiring at the Lord. The Lord answers the mother of the promised seed. Two children are in her womb, the parents of two nations, differing in their dispositions and destinies. The one is to be stronger than the other. The order of nature is to be reversed in them; for the elder will serve the younger. Their struggles in the womb are a prelude to their future history.

24–26. The twins are in due time born. The difference is manifest in the outward appearance. The first is red and hairy. These qualities indicate a passionate and precocious nature. He is called *Esau the hairy*, or *the made up*, the prematurely developed. His brother is like other children. An act takes place in the very birth foreshadowing their future history. The second has a hold of his brother's heel, as if he would trip him up from his very birth. Hence he is called *Jacob the wrestler*, who takes hold by the heel.

27–34. The brothers prove to be different in disposition and habit. The rough fiery Esau takes to the field, and becomes skilled in all modes of catching game. Jacob is of a homely, peaceful, orderly turn, dwelling in tents and gathering round him the means and appliances of a quiet social life. The children please their parents according as they supply what is wanting in themselves. Isaac, himself so sedate, loves the wild, wandering hunter, because he supplies him with pleasures which his own quiet habits do not reach. Rebekah becomes attached to the gentle, industrious shepherd, who satisfies those social and spiritual tendencies in which she is more dependent than Isaac. Esau is destructive of game; Jacob is constructive of cattle.

29–34. A characteristic incident in their early life is attended with very important consequences. *Jacob sod pottage.* He has become a sage in the practical comforts of life. Esau leaves the field for the tent, exhausted with fatigue. The sight and smell of Jacob's savory dish of lentile soup are very tempting to a hungry man. *Let me feed now on that red, red broth.* He does not know how to name it. The lentile is common in the country, and forms a cheap and palatable dish of a reddish brown color, with which bread seems to have been eaten. The two brothers were not congenial. They would therefore act each independently of the other, and provide each for himself. Esau was no doubt occasionally rude and hasty. Hence a selfish habit would grow up and gather strength. He was probably wont to supply himself with such fare as suited his palate, and might have done so on this occasion without any delay. But the fine flavor and high color of the mess, which Jacob was preparing for himself, takes his fancy, and nothing will do but the red red. Jacob obviously regarded this as a rude and selfish intrusion on his privacy and property, in keeping with similar encounters that may have taken place between the brothers.

It is here added, *therefore was his name called Edom*, that is, Red. The origin of surnames, or second names for the same person or place, is a matter of some moment in the fair interpretation of an ancient document. It is sometimes hastily assumed that the same name can only owe its application to one occasion; and hence a record of a second occasion on which it was applied is regarded as a discrepancy. But the error lies in the interpreter, not in the author. The propriety of a particular name may be marked by two or more totally different circumstances, and its application renewed on each of these occasions. Even an imaginary cause may be assigned for a name, and may serve to originate or renew its application. The two brothers now before us afford very striking illustrations of the general principle. It is pretty certain that Esau would receive the secondary name of Edom, which ultimately became primary in point of use, from the red complexion of skin, even from his birth. But the exclamation "that red red," uttered on the occasion of a very important crisis in his history, renewed the name, and perhaps tended to make it take the place of Esau in the history of his race. Jacob, too, the holder of the heel, received this name from a circumstance occurring at his birth. But the buying of the birthright and the gaining of the blessing, were two occasions in his subsequent life on which he merited the title of the supplanter or the holder by the heel (Gen. xxvii. 36). These instances prepare us to expect other examples of the same name being applied to the same object, for different reasons on different occasions.

31. *Sell me this day thy birthright.* This brings to light a new cause of variance between the brothers. Jacob was no doubt aware of the prediction communicated to his mother, that the elder should serve the younger. A quiet man like him would not otherwise have thought of reversing the order of nature and custom. In after times the right of primogeniture consisted in a double portion of the father's goods (Deut. xxi. 17), and a certain rank as the patriarch and priest

of the house on the death of the father. But in the case of Isaac there was the far higher dignity of chief of the chosen family and heir of the promised blessing, with all the immediate and ultimate temporal and eternal benefits therein included. Knowing all this, Jacob is willing to purchase the birthright, as the most peaceful way of bringing about that supremacy which was destined for him. He is therefore cautious and prudent, even conciliating in his proposal. He availed himself of a weak moment to accomplish by consent what was to come. Yet he lays no necessity on Esau, but leaves him to his own free choice. We must therefore beware of blaming him for endeavoring to win his brother's concurrence in a thing that was already settled in the purpose of God. His chief error lay in attempting to anticipate the arrangements of Providence. 32. Esau is strangely ready to dispose of his birthright for a trivial present gratification. He might have obtained other means of recruiting nature equally suitable, but he will sacrifice anything for the desire of the moment. Any higher import of the right he was prepared to sell so cheap seems to have escaped his view, if it had ever occurred to his mind. 33. Jacob, however, is deeply in earnest. He will bring this matter within the range of heavenly influence. He will have God solemnly invoked as a witness of the transfer. Even this does not startle Esau. There is not a word about the price. It is plain that Esau's thoughts were altogether on "the morsel of meat." He swears unto Jacob. 34. He then ate and drank, and rose up and went his way, as the sacred writer graphically describes his reckless course. Most truly did he despise his birthright. His mind did not rise to higher or further things. Such was the boyhood of these wondrous twins.

LIV. EVENTS OF ISAAC'S LIFE. — Gen. xxvi.

5. מִשְׁמֶרֶת *charge, ordinance.* מִצְוָה *command,* special order. חֹק *decree, statute,* engraven on stone or metal. תּוֹרָה *law,* doctrine, system of moral truth.

10. עֵשֶׂק 'Eseq, *strife.*

21. שִׂטְנָה Sitnah, *opposition.*

22. רְחֹבוֹת Rechoboth, *room.*

26. אֲחֻזַּת Achuzzath, *possession.*

33. שִׁבְעָה Shib'ah, *seven ; oath.*

34. יְהוּדִית Jehudith, *praised.* בְּאֵרִי Beeri, *of a well.* בָּשְׂמַת Basemath, *sweet smell.* אֵילֹן Elon, *oak.*

XXVI. 1. And there was a famine in the land, beside the
first famine that was in the days of Abraham: and Isaac went
unto Abimelek, king of the Philistines, unto Gerar. 2. And
the LORD appeared unto him, and said, Go not down into
Mizraim: dwell in the land of which I shall tell thee. 3. So-
journ in this land, and I will be with thee and bless thee; for
unto thee and unto thy seed will I give all these lands, and I
will establish the oath which I sware unto Abraham thy father.
4. And I will multiply thy seed as the stars of heaven, and give
unto thy seed all these lands; and blessed in thy seed shall be
all the nations of the earth: 5. Because Abraham hearkened
to my voice, and kept my charge, my commandments, my stat-
utes, and my laws.

6. And Isaac dwelt in Gerar. 7. And the men of the place
asked about his wife, and he said, She is my sister: for he
feared to say, My wife, lest the men of the place kill me for
Rebekah: because she was fair to look upon. 8. And it came
to pass, that he was there a long time, and Abimelek, king of
the Philistines, looked through the window, and saw, and be-
hold Isaac sporting with Rebekah his wife. 9. And Abimelek
called Isaac, and said, Behold, surely she is thy wife; and how
saidst thou, She is my sister? And Isaac said unto him, Be-
cause I said, Lest I die for her. 10. And Abimelek said, What
is this thou hast done to us? Lightly might one of the people
have lain with thy wife, and thou shouldest have brought
guiltiness upon us. 11. And Abimelek commanded all the
people, saying, He that toucheth this man or his wife shall
surely die.

12. And Isaac sowed in that land, and received in the same
year a hundred-fold: and the LORD blessed him. 13. And
the man grew, and went on, and grew until he became very
great. 14. And he had possession of flocks, and possession

of herds, and great store of servants: and the Philistines envied him. 15. And all the wells which his father's servants had digged in the days of Abraham his father, the Philistines had stopped them and filled them with dust. And Abimelek said unto Isaac, Go from us, for thou art much mightier than we.

17. And Isaac went thence, and pitched in the valley of Gerar, and dwelt there. 18. And Isaac again digged the wells of water, which they had digged in the days of Abraham his father, and the Philistines stopped them after the death of Abraham: and he called them names after the names which his father had called them. 19. And Isaac's servants digged in the valley, and found there a well of spring water. 20. And the herdmen of Gerar strove with Isaac's herdmen, saying, The water is ours: and he called the name of the well Esek, because they strove with him. 21. And they digged another well; and strove not for that also; and he called the name of it Sitnah. 22. And he removed thence, and digged another well; and they strove not for it; and he called the name of it Rehoboth, and said, For now the Lord hath made room for us, and we shall be fruitful in the land.

23. And he went up thence to Beer-sheba. 24. And the Lord appeared to him in that night, and said, I am the God of Abraham thy father: fear not, for I am with thee, and will bless thee, and multiply thy seed for the sake of Abraham my servant. 25. And he builded there an altar, and called on the name of the Lord, and pitched there his tent; and there Isaac's servants digged a well.

26. And Abimelek went to him from Gerar, and Ahuzzath his friend, and Phikol the captain of his host. 27. And Isaac said unto them, Why are ye come to me, and ye hated me, and sent me away from you? 28. And they said, We saw certainly that the Lord was with thee: and we said, Let there be now an oath betwixt us, between us and thee, and let us make a covenant with thee. 29. That thou wilt do us no hurt, as we have not touched thee, and as we have done unto

thee only good, and sent thee away in peace; thou art now blessed of the LORD. 30. And he made them a feast, and they ate and drank. 31. And they rose up early in the morning, and sware one to another: and Isaac sent them away, and they went from him in peace. 32. And it came to pass in that day, that Isaac's servants came and told him concerning the well which they had digged; and they said unto him, We have found water. 33. And he called it Sheba. Therefore the name of the city is Beer-sheba unto this day. § 34.

34. And Esau was the son of forty years, and he took a wife, Judith, daughter of Beeri the Hittite, and Basemath, daughter of Elon the Hittite; 35. And they were a grief of mind to Isaac and to Rebekah. § 35.

This chapter presents the leading events in the quiet life of Isaac. It is probable that Abraham was now dead. In that case, Esau and Jacob would be at least fifteen years of age when the following event occurred.

1–5. Renewal of the promise to Isaac. *A famine in the land.* We left Isaac, after the death of Abraham, at Beer-lahai-roi (Gen. xxv. 11). The preceding events have only brought us up to the same point of time. This well was in the land of the south (xxiv. 62). The present famine is distinguished from that which occurred in the time of Abraham (xii. 10). The interval between them is at least a hundred years. The author of this, the ninth document, is, we find, acquainted with the seventh document; and the famine to which he refers is among the earliest events recorded in it. There is no reason to doubt, then, that he has the whole history of Abraham before his mind. *Unto Abimelek unto Gerar.* The Abimelek with whom Abraham had intercourse about eighty years before may have been the father of the present sovereign. Both Abimelek and Phikol seem to have been official names. Gerar (x. 19) was apparently on the brook of Mizraim (Numb. xxxiv. 5), the Wady el-Arish, or the Wady el-Khubarah, a northern affluent of the former, or in the interval between them. It is on the way to Egypt, and is the southern city of the Philistines, who probably came from Egypt (x. 14). Isaac was drawing towards Egypt, when he came to Gerar.

2–5. Isaac is now the heir, and therefore the holder, of the promise. Hence the Lord enters into communication with him. *First*, the present difficulty is met. *Go not down into Mizraim*, the land of corn, even when other lands were barren. *Dwell in the land of which I shall tell thee.* This reminds us of the message to Abraham (xii. 1). The land here spoken of refers to "all these lands" mentioned in the following verses. *Sojourn in this land:* turn aside for the present, and take up thy temporary abode here. *Next*, the promise to Abraham is renewed with some variety of expression. *I will be with thee* (xxi. 22), a notable and comprehensive promise, afterwards embodied in the name Immanuel, *God with us*. *Unto thee and unto thy seed.* This was fulfilled to his seed in due time. *All these lands*, now parcelled out among several tribes. *And blessed in thy seed* (xii. 3, xxii. 18). This is the great, universal promise to the whole human race through the seed of Abraham, twice explicitly announced to that patriarch. *All the nations.* In constancy of purpose the Lord contemplates, even in the special covenant with Abraham, the gathering in of the nations under the covenant with Noah and with Adam (Gen. ix. 9; Hos. vi. 7). *Because Abraham hearkened to my voice*, in all the great moments of his life, especially in the last act of proceeding on the divine command to offer Isaac himself. Abraham, by the faith which flows from the new birth, was united with the Lord, his shield and exceeding great reward (xv. 1), with God Almighty, who quickened and strengthened him to walk before him and be perfect (xvii. 1). The Lord his righteousness worketh in him, and his merit is reflected and reproduced in him (xxii. 16, 18). Hence the Lord reminds Isaac of the oath which he had heard at least fifty years before confirming the promise, and of the declaration then made that this oath of confirmation was sworn *because* Abraham had obeyed the voice of God. How deeply these words would penetrate into the soul of Isaac, the intended victim of that solemn day! But Abraham's obedience was displayed in all the acts of his new life. He kept the *charge* of God, the special commission he had given him; his *commandments*, his express or occasional orders; his *statutes*, his stated prescriptions, graven on stone; his *laws*, the great doctrines of moral obligation. This is that unreserved obedience which flows from a living faith, and withstands the temptations of the flesh.

6–11. Rebekah preserved from dishonor in Gerar. Gerar was probably a commercial town trading with Egypt, and therefore Isaac's wants during the famine are here supplied. "The men of the place" were struck with the appearance of Rebekah, "because she was fair." Isaac, in answer to their inquiries, pretends that she is his sister, feeling that his life was in peril, if she was known to be his wife. Rebekah was at this time not less than thirty-five years married, and had two sons upwards of fifteen years old. She was still however in the prime of life, and her sons were probably engaged in pastoral and other field pursuits. From the compact between Abraham and Sarah (xx. 13), and from this case of Isaac about eighty years after, it appears that this was a ready pretence with married people among strangers in those times of social insecurity. 8–11. Abimelek observes Isaac sporting with Rebekah as only husband and wife should, constrains him to confess that she is his wife, charges him with the impropriety of his conduct, and commands his people to refrain from harming either of them on pain of death. We see how insecure a female's honor was in those days, if she was in a strange land, and had not a band of men to keep back the hand of violence. We perceive also that God mercifully protects his chosen ones from the perils which they bring upon themselves by the vain self-reliance and wicked policy of the old corrupt nature. This remnant of the old man we find in the believers of old, as in those of the present time, though it be different and far less excusable in its recent manifestations.

12–16. The growing prosperity of Isaac. *And Isaac sowed in that land.* This does not imply a fixed property in the soil, but only an annual tenancy. *A hundred-fold.* The rates of increase vary from thirty to a hundred. Sixty-fold is very good, and was not unusual in Palestine. A hundred-fold was rare, and only in spots of extraordinary fertility. Babylonia, however, yielded two hundred and even three hundred-fold, according to Herodotus (I. 193). Thus the Lord began to "bless him." 13, 14. The amazing growth of the stranger's wealth in flocks and herds and servants awakens the envy of the inhabitants. 15. The digging of the well was an enterprise of great interest in rural affairs. It conferred a sort of ownership on the digger, especially in a country where water was precious. And in a primeval state of society the well was the scene of youthful maidens drawing water for domestic use, and of young men and sometimes maidens watering the bleating flocks and lowing herds, and therefore the gathering centre of settled life. Hence the envious Philistines were afraid that from a sojourner he would go on to be a settler, and acquire rights of property. They accordingly took the most effectual means of making his abiding place uncomfortable, when they stopped up the wells. 16. At length the sovereign advised a separation, if he did not enjoin the departure of Isaac.

17–22. Isaac retires, and sets about the digging of wells. He retreats from Gerar and its suburbs, and takes up his abode in the valley, or wady of Gerar. These wadys are the hollows in which brooks flow, and therefore the well-watered and fertile parts of the country. 18. He digs again the old wells, and calls them by the old names. 19–22. He commences the digging of new ones. For the first the herdmen of Gerar strive, claiming the water as their property. Isaac yields. He digs another; they strive, and he again yields. He now removes apparently into a distinct region, and digs a third well, for which there is no contest. This he calls Rehoboth, *room,* — a name which appears to be preserved in Wady er-Ruhaibeh, near which is Wady esh-Shutein, corresponding to Sitnah. *For now the Lord hath made room for us.* Isaac's homely realizing faith in a present and presiding Lord here comes out.

23–25. Isaac now proceeds to Beer-sheba. *Went up.* It was an ascent from Wady er-Ruhaibeh to Beer-sheba; which was near the watershed between the Mediterranean and the Salt Sea. *In that night,* — the night after his arrival, in a dream or vision. *I am the God of Abraham thy father.* Isaac is again and again reminded of the relation in which his father stood to God. That relation still subsists; for Abraham still lives with God, and is far nearer to him than he could be on earth. "The God of Abraham" is another name for Jehovah. *Fear not,* as he had said to Abraham after his victory over the four kings (xv. 1). Then follow the reasons for courage: *I,* with thee, blessing thee, multiplying thy seed; a reassurance of three parts of the promise involving all the rest. Then comes the instructive reason for this assurance, — *for the sake of Abraham my servant.* 25. *An altar,* — the first on record erected by Isaac. *Called on the name of the Lord,* — engaged in the solemn and public invocation of Jehovah (iv. 26, xii. 8). *His tent there.* It was hallowed ground to his father (xxi. 33), and now to himself. *Digged a well,* and thereby took possession of the soil at least for a time. We hear of this well again in the next passage.

26–33. The treaty with Abimelek. This is an interview similar to that which Abraham had with the king of Gerar; and its object is a renewal of the former league between the parties. Besides Phikol, the commander-in-chief, he is now accompanied by Ahuzzath, his privy counsellor. 27–29. Isaac upbraids him with his unkindness in sending him away, and his inconsistency in again seeking a conference with him. *We clearly saw.* His prosperity was such as to be a manifest token of the Lord's favor. Hence they desired the security of a treaty with him by an oath of execration on the transgressor. *Do us no hurt.* The covenant is one-sided, as expressed by Abimelek. *As we have not touched thee.* This implies the other side of the covenant. *Thou art now blessed of Jehovah.* This explains the one-sidedness of the covenant. Isaac needed no guarantee from them, as the Lord was with him. Abimelek is familiar with the use of the name Jehovah. 30, 31. Isaac hospitably entertains and lodges the royal party, and on the morrow, after having sworn to the treaty, parts with them in peace. 32, 33. On the same day Isaac's servants report concerning the well they had digged (v. 25) that they had found water. This well he calls Sheba, *an oath,* and hence the town is called Beer-sheba, *the well of the oath.* Now the writer was aware that this place had received the same name on a former occasion (xxi. 31). But a second well has now been dug in like circumstances in the same locality. This gives occasion for a new application of the name in the memories of the people. This is another illustration of the principle explained at xxv. 30. Two wells still exist at this place to attest the correctness of the record.

34, 35. Esau at forty years of age forms matrimonial connections with the Hittites. Heth was the second son of Kenaan, and had settled in the hills about Hebron. Esau had got acquainted with this tribe in his hunting expeditions. From their names we learn that they spoke the same language with himself. They belonged to a family far gone in transgression and apostasy from God. The two wives chosen from such a stock were a source of great grief to the parents of Esau. The choice manifested his tolerance at least of the carnal, and his indifference to the spiritual.

LV. ISAAC BLESSING HIS SONS.—Gen. xxvii.

XXVII. 1. And it came to pass that Isaac was old, and his eyes were dim in seeing; and he called Esau his elder son, and said unto him, My son. And he said unto him, Here am I. 2. And he said, Behold now, I am old; I know not the day of my death. 3. And now take now thy weapons, thy quiver and thy bow, and go out to the field and hunt for me venison. 4. And make me savory meat, such as I love, and bring to me, and let me eat, that my soul may bless thee before I die.

5. And Rebekah was listening when Isaac spake to Esau his son: and Esau went to the field to hunt for venison to bring. 6. And Rebekah said unto Jacob her son, saying, Behold, I heard thy father speaking to Esau thy brother, saying, 7. Bring me venison, and make me savory meat, and let me eat; and I shall bless thee before the LORD before I die. 8. And now, my son, hearken to my voice, according to that which I command thee. 9. Go now to the flock, and fetch me thence two good kids of the goats; and I will make them savory meat for thy father, such as he loveth. 10. And thou shalt bring it to thy father, and he shall eat, that he may bless thee before he die. 11. And Jacob said to Rebekah his mother, Behold, Esau my brother is a hairy man, and I a smooth man. 12. Mayhap my father will feel me, and I shall be in his eyes as a deceiver; and I shall bring upon me a curse and not a blessing. 13. And his mother said unto him, Upon me be thy curse, my son; only hearken to my voice, and go fetch me.

14. And he went and fetched and brought to his mother; and his mother made savory meat, such as his father loved. 15. And Rebekah took goodly garments of Esau her elder son, which were with her in the house, and put them upon Jacob her younger son. 16. And the skins of the kids of the goats put she upon his hands, and upon the smooth of his neck. 17. And she gave the savory meat and the bread which she had made into the hand of Jacob her son. 18. And he went unto his father and said, My father. And he said, Here am I; who art thou, my son? 19. And Jacob said unto his father, I am Esau, thy first-born: I have done as thou spakest to me; arise, now, sit and eat of my venison, that thy soul may bless me. 20. And Isaac said unto his son, How is this thou hast hastened to find, my son? And he said, Because the LORD thy

God prospered me. 21. And Isaac said unto Jacob, Come near now, and let me feel thee, my son, whether thou be my very son Esau or not. 22. And Jacob went near unto Isaac his father, and he felt him: and he said, The voice is the voice of Jacob, and the hands are the hands of Esau. 23. And he discerned him not, because his hands were hairy as Esau his brother's hands: and he blessed him. 24. And he said, Art thou my very son Esau? And he said, I am. 25. And he said, Bring near to me and let me eat of my son's venison, that my soul may bless thee: and he brought near to him, and he ate: and he brought him wine, and he drank. 26. And Isaac his father said unto him, Come near now, and kiss me, my son. 27. And he came near, and kissed him; and he smelled the smell of his raiment, and blessed him, and said, See, the smell of my son is as the smell of a field which the LORD hath blessed. 28. And the God give thee of the dew of heaven, and of the fatness of the earth, and plenty of corn and wine. 29. Let peoples serve thee, and nations bow down to thee; be lord of thy brethren, and let thy mother's sons bow down to thee; he that curseth thee be cursed, and he that blesseth thee be blessed.

30. And it came to pass when Isaac had ended the blessing of Jacob, and Jacob was in the act of coming out from the presence of Isaac his father, that Esau his brother was come in from his hunting. 31. And he also made savory meat, and brought to his father; and he said unto his father, Let my father arise and eat of his son's venison, that thy soul may bless me. 32. And Isaac his father said unto him, Who art thou? And he said, I am thy son, thy first-born, Esau. 33. And Isaac trembled with an exceeding great trembling, and said, Who, then, is he that hath hunted venison, and brought me, and I ate of all before thou camest, and blessed him? Yea, blessed he shall be. 34. When Esau heard the words of his father, then he cried with an exceeding great and bitter cry; and he said unto his father, Bless me, me also, my father.

35. And he said, Thy brother hath come with deceit and taken thy blessing. 36. And he said, Is it that his name is called Jacob, and he supplanted me these two times? my birthright he had taken, and, behold, now he hath taken my blessing. And he said, Hast thou not in reserve for me a blessing? 37. And Isaac answered and said unto Esau, Behold, thy lord I have made him, and all his brethren have I given him for servants; and with corn and wine have I sustained him: and to thee now what shall I do, my son? 38. And Esau said unto his father, Hast thou but one blessing, my father? Bless me, also me, my father. And Esau lifted up his voice and wept. 39. And Isaac his father answered and said unto him, Behold, away from the fatness of the earth shall be thy dwelling, and from the dew of heaven from above. 40. And on thy sword shalt thou live, and thy brother shalt thou serve: and it shall come to pass when thou prevailest, that thou shalt break his yoke from thy neck. 41. And Esau hated Jacob because of the blessing wherewith his father blessed him: and Esau said in his heart, The days of mourning for my father draw nigh, and I will slay Jacob, my brother.

42. And the words of Esau, her elder son, were told to Rebekah: and she sent and called Jacob, her younger son, and said unto him, Behold, Esau thy brother comforteth himself concerning thee, purposing to slay thee. 43. And now, my son, hearken to my voice: and arise, flee thou to Laban my brother to Haran. 44. And tarry with him a few days, until thy brother's fury turn away; 45. Until thy brother's anger turn from thee, and he forget that which thou hast done to him: then will I send and fetch thee hence: why should I be bereaved even of you both in one day? 46. And Rebekah said to Isaac, I am weary of my life on account of the daughters of Heth: if Jacob take a wife of the daughters of Heth, such as these of the daughters of the land, what good is life to me?

The life of Isaac falls into three periods. During the first seventy-five years he is contemporary with his father. For sixty-one years more his son Jacob remains under the paternal roof. The remaining forty-four years are passed in the retirement of old age. The chapter before us narrates the last solemn acts of the middle period of his life.

1–4. *Isaac was old.* Joseph was in his thirtieth year when he stood before Pharaoh, and therefore thirty-nine when Jacob came down to Egypt at the age of one hundred and thirty. When Joseph was born, therefore, Jacob was ninety-one, and he had sojourned fourteen years in Padan-aram. Hence Jacob's flight to Laban took place when he was seventy-seven, and therefore in the one hundred and thirty-sixth year of Isaac. *His eyes were dim.* Weakness and even loss of sight is more frequent in Palestine than with us. *His elder son.* Isaac had not yet come to the conclusion that Jacob was heir of the promise. The communication from the Lord to Rebekah concerning her yet unborn sons in the form in which it is handed down to us merely determines that the elder shall serve the younger. This fact Isaac seems to have thought might not imply the transferrence of the birthright; and if he was aware of the transaction between Esau and Jacob, he may not have regarded it as valid. Hence he makes arrangements for bestowing the paternal benediction on Esau, his elder son, whom he also loves. *I am old.* At the age of one hundred and thirty-six, and with failing sight, he felt that life was uncertain. 3, 4. In the calmness of determination he directs Esau to prepare savory meat, such as he loved, that he may have his vigor renewed and his spirits revived for the solemn business of bestowing that blessing, which he held to be fraught with more than ordinary benefits.

5–13. Rebekah forms a plan for diverting the blessing from Esau to Jacob. 5–7. She was within hearing when the infirm Isaac gave his orders, and communicates the news to Jacob. 8–10. Rebekah has no scruples about primogeniture. Her feelings prompt her to take measures, without waiting to consider whether they are justifiable or not, for securing to Jacob that blessing which she has settled in her own mind to be destined for him. She thinks it necessary to interfere that this end may not fail of being accomplished. 11–13. Jacob views the matter more coolly, and starts a difficulty. He may be found out to be a deceiver, and bring his father's curse upon him. Rebekah, anticipating no such issue, undertakes to bear the curse that she conceived would never come. Only let him obey.

14–29. The plan is successful. 14–17. Jacob now, without further objection, obeys his mother. She clothes him in Esau's raiment, and puts the skins of the kids on his hands and his neck. The camel-goat affords a hair which bears a great resemblance to that of natural growth, and is used as a substitute for it. 18–20. Now begins the strange interview between the father and the son. *Who art thou, my son?* The voice of Jacob was somewhat constrained. He goes, however, deliberately through the process of deceiving his father. *Arise, now, sit and eat.* Isaac was reclining on his couch, in the feebleness of advancing years. Sitting was the posture convenient for eating. *The Lord thy God prospered me.* This is the bold reply to Isaac's expression of surprise at the haste with which the dainty fare had been prepared. 21–23. The bewildered father now puts Jacob to a severer test. He feels him, but discerns him not. The ear notes a difference, but the hand feels the hairy skin resembling Esau's; the eyes give no testimony. After this the result is summarily stated in a single sentence, though the particulars are yet to be given. 24, 25. *Art thou my very son Esau?* A lurking doubt puts the definite question, and receives a decisive answer. Isaac then calls for the repast and partakes.

26–29. He gives the kiss of paternal affection, and pronounces the benediction. It contains, first, a fertile soil. *Of the dew of heaven.* An abundant measure of this was especially precious in a country where the rain is confined to two seasons of the year. *Of the fatness of the earth;* a proportion of this to match and render available the dew of heaven. *Corn and wine,* the substantial products, implying all the rest. *Second,* a numerous and powerful offspring. *Let peoples serve thee,* — preëminence among the nations. *Be lord of thy brethren,* — preëminence among his kindred. Isaac does not seem to have grasped the full meaning of the prediction, "The elder shall serve the younger." *Third,* Prosperity, temporal and spiritual. He that curseth thee be cursed, and he that blesseth thee be blessed. This is the only part of the blessing that directly comprises spiritual things; and even this is of a peculiar form. It is to be recollected that it was Isaac's intention to bless Esau, and he may have felt that Esau, after all, was not to be the progenitor of the holy seed. Hence the form of expression is vague enough to apply to temporal things, and yet sufficiently comprehensive to embrace the infliction of the ban of sin, and the diffusion of the blessing of salvation by means of the holy seed.

30–41. Esau's blessing. Esau comes in, but it is too late. 31–33. *Who then?* The whole illusion is dispelled from the mind of Isaac.

Yea, blessed he shall be. Jacob had no doubt perpetrated a fraud, at the instigation of his mother; and if Esau had been worthy in other respects, and above all if the blessing had been designed for him, its bestowment on another would have been either prevented or regarded as null and void. But Isaac now felt that, whatever was the misconduct of Jacob in interfering, and especially in employing unworthy means to accomplish his end, he himself was culpable in allowing carnal considerations to draw his preference to Esau, who was otherwise unworthy. He knew too that the paternal benediction flowed not from the bias of the parent, but from the Spirit of God guiding his will, and therefore when so pronounced could not be revoked. Hence he was now convinced that it was the design of Providence that the spiritual blessing should fall on the line of Jacob. 34–38. The grief of Esau is distressing to witness, especially as he had been comparatively blameless in this particular instance. But still it is to be remembered that his heart had not been open to the paramount importance of spiritual things. Isaac now perceives that Jacob has gained the blessing by deceit. Esau marks the propriety of his name, the wrestler who trips up the heel, and pleads pathetically for at least some blessing. His father enumerates what he has done for Jacob, and asks what more he can do for Esau; who then exclaims, *Hast thou but one blessing?*

39–41. At length, in reply to the weeping suppliant, he bestows upon him a characteristic blessing. *Away from the fatness.* The preposition (מִ־) is the same as in the blessing of Jacob. But there, after a verb of giving, it had a partitive sense; here, after a noun of place, it denotes distance or separation; for example, Prov. xx. 3 The pastoral life has been distasteful to Esau, and so it shall be with his race. The land of Edom was accordingly a comparative wilderness (Mal. i. 3). *On thy sword.* By preying upon others. *And thy brother shalt thou serve.* Edom was long independent; but at length Saul was victorious over them (1 Sam. xiv. 47), and David conquered them (2 Sam. viii. 14). Then followed a long struggle, until John Hyrcanus, 129 B. C., compelled them to be circumcised and incorporated into Judaism. *Break his yoke.* The history of Edom was a perpetual struggle against the supremacy of Israel. Conquered by Saul, subdued by David, repressed by Solomon, restrained after a revolt by Amaziah, they recovered their independence in the time of Ahab. They were incorporated into the Jewish state, and furnished it with the dynasty of princes beginning with Antipater. Esau was now exasperated against his brother, and could only compose his mind by resolving to slay him during the days of mourning after his father's death.

42–46. Rebekah hearing this, advises Jacob to flee to Laban her brother, and await the abatement of his brother's anger. *That which thou hast done to him.* Rebekah seems not to have been aware that she herself was the cause of much of the evil and of the misery that flowed from it. All the parties to this transaction are pursued by a retributive chastisement. Rebekah, especially, parts with her favorite son to meet him only after an absence of twenty years, if ever in this life. She is moreover grievously vexed with the connection which Esau formed with the daughters of Heth. She dreads a similar matrimonial alliance on the part of Jacob.

LVI. JACOB'S JOURNEY TO HARAN. — Gen. xxviii.

3. קָהָל *congregation.*
9. מַחֲלַת Machalath, *sickness,* or *a harp.*
19. לוּז Luz, *almond.*

XXVIII. 1. And Isaac called Jacob, and blessed him, and commanded him, and said unto him, Thou shalt not take a wife of the daughters of Kenaan. 2. Arise, go to Padan-aram, to the house of Bethuel, thy mother's father, and take thee thence a wife of the daughters of Laban, thy mother's brother. 3. And God Almighty bless thee, and make thee fruitful, and multiply thee, that thou mayest be a congregation of peoples. 4. And give thee the blessing of Abraham, to thee and to thy seed with thee: that thou mayest possess the land of thy sojournings, which God gave unto Abraham. 5. And Isaac sent away Jacob; and he went unto Padan-aram, to Laban, son of Bethuel the Aramite, brother of Rebekah, mother of Jacob and Esau.

6. And Esau saw that Isaac had blessed Jacob, and sent him to Padan-aram to take him thence a wife; and as he blessed

him, he commanded him, saying, Thou shalt not take a wife of the daughters of Kenaan. 7. And Jacob hearkened to his father and his mother, and went to Padan-aram. 8. And Esau saw that the daughters of Kenaan were evil in the eyes of Isaac his father. 9. And Esau went unto Ishmael, and took Mahalath, daughter of Ishmael, Abraham's son, sister of Nebaioth, unto his wives, to be his wife. 7 §§§ 36.

10. And Jacob came forth from Beer-sheba, and went to Haran. 11. And he lighted on a place, and lodged there, because the sun was set: and he took of the stones of the place and put for his pillow; and he lay down in that place. 12. And he dreamed, and, behold, a ladder set up on the earth, and the top of it reaching to heaven; and, behold, the angels of God ascending and descending on it. 13. And, behold, the LORD stood above it, and said, I am the LORD, God of Abraham thy father, and God of Isaac: the land whereon thou liest, to thee will I give it, and to thy seed. 14. And thy seed shall be as the dust of the earth, and thou shalt break forth to the west and to the east and to the north and to the south; and blessed in thee shall be all the families of the earth, and in thy seed. 15. And, behold, I am with thee, and will keep thee in all the way that thou goest, and will bring thee back into this soil; for I will not leave thee until I have done that which I have spoken to thee. 16. And Jacob awoke out of his sleep, and said, Surely the LORD is in this place, and I knew it not. 17. And he was afraid, and said, How dreadful is this place! This is none other but the house of God, and this is the gate of heaven. 18. And Jacob rose up early in the morning, and took the stone that he had put for his pillow and set it up for a pillar; and he poured oil upon the top of it. 19. And he called the name of that place Bethel: but Luz was the name of the city at the first. 20. And Jacob vowed a vow, saying, If God will be with me, and keep me in the way that I go, and give me bread to eat and raiment to put on, 21. And I return in peace to my father's

house, then shall the LORD be my God: 22. And this stone, which I have set up for a pillar, shall be God's house; and of all that thou shalt give me, a tenth will I surely give unto thee.

The blessing of his sons was the last passage in the active life of Isaac, after which he retires from the scene. Jacob now becomes the leading figure in the sacred history. His spiritual character has not yet come out to view. But even now we can discern the general distinction in the lives of the three patriarchs. Abraham's is a life of authority and decision; Isaac's, of submission and acquiescence; and Jacob's, of trial and struggle.

1–5. Isaac has now become alive to the real destiny of Jacob. He therefore calls for him to bless him, and give him a command. The command is to take a wife, not from Kenaan, but from the kindred of his parents. The blessing comes from *God Almighty* (xvii. 1). It is that belonging to the chosen seed, *the blessing of Abraham.* It embraces a numerous offspring, the land of promise, and all else that is included in the blessing of Abraham. *A congregation of peoples.* This is the word *congregation* (קָהָל Qahal) which is afterwards applied to the assembled people of God, and to which the Greek *ἐκκλησία, ecclesia,* answers. Jacob complies with his mother's advice and his father's command, and, at the same time, reaps the bitter fruit of his fraud against his brother in the hardship and treachery of an exile of twenty years. The aged Isaac is not without his share in the unpleasant consequences of endeavoring to go against the will of God.

6–9. Esau is induced, by the charge of his parents to Jacob, the compliance of the latter with their wishes, and by their obvious dislike to the daughters of Kenaan, to take Mahalath, a daughter of Ishmael, in addition to his former wives. *Went unto Ishmael;* that is, to the family or tribe of Ishmael, as Ishmael himself was now thirteen years dead. Esau's hunting and roving career had brought him into contact with this family, and we shall presently find him settled in a neighboring territory.

10–22. Jacob's dream and vow. Setting out on the way to Haran, he was overtaken by night, and slept in the field. He was far from any dwelling, or he did not wish to enter the house of a stranger. 12–15. He dreams. A ladder or stair is seen reaching from earth to heaven, on which angels ascend and descend. This is a medium of communication between heaven and earth, by which messengers pass to and fro on errands of mercy. Heaven and earth have been separated by sin. But this ladder has re-established the intercourse. It is therefore a beautiful emblem of that which mediates and reconciles (John i. 51). It here serves to bring Jacob into communication with God, and teaches him the emphatic lesson that he is accepted through a mediator. *The Lord stood above it*, and Jacob, the object of his mercy, beneath. 1st. He reveals himself to the sleeper as *the Lord* (ii. 4), *the God of Abraham thy father, and of Isaac.* It is remarkable that Abraham is styled his father, that is, his actual grandfather, and covenant father. 2d. He renews the promise of the land, of the seed, and of the blessing in that seed for the whole race of man. Westward, eastward, northward, and southward are they to break forth. This expression points to the world-wide universality of the kingdom of the seed of Abraham, when it shall become the fifth monarchy, that shall subdue all that went before, and endure forever. This transcends the destiny of the natural seed of Abraham. 3d. He then promises to Jacob personally to be with him, protect him, and bring him back in safety. This is the third announcement of the seed that blesses to the third in the line of descent (xii. 2, 3, xxii. 18, xxvi. 4).

16–19. Jacob awakes, and exclaims, *Surely the Lord is in this place, and I knew it not.* He knew his omnipresence; but he did not expect a special manifestation of the Lord in this place, far from the sanctuaries of his father. He is filled with solemn awe, when he finds himself in the house of God and at the gate of heaven. 18, 19. The pillar is the monument of the event. The pouring of oil upon it is an act of consecration to God who has there appeared to him (Num. vii. 1). He calls the name of the place Bethel, *the house of God.* This is not the first time it received the name. Abraham also worshipped God here, and met with the name already existing (see on xii. 8, xiii. 3, xxv. 30.

20–22. Jacob's vow. A vow is a solemn engagement to perform a certain duty, the obligation of which is felt at the time to be specially binding. It partakes, therefore, of the nature of a promise or a covenant. It involves in its obligation, however, only one party, and is the spontaneous act of that party. Here, then, Jacob appears to take a step in advance of his predecessors. Hitherto God had taken the initiative in every promise, and the everlasting covenant rests solely on his eternal purpose. Abraham had responded to the call of God, believed in the Lord, walked before him, entered into communion with him, made intercession with him, and given up his only son to him at his demand. In all this there is an acceptance on the part of the creature of the supremacy of the merciful Creator. But now the spirit of adoption prompts Jacob to a spontaneous movement towards God. This is no ordinary vow, referring to some special or occasional resolve. It is the grand and solemn expression of the soul's free, full, and perpetual acceptance of the Lord to be its own God. This is the most frank and open utterance of new-born spiritual liberty from the heart of man that has yet appeared in the divine record. *If God will be with me.* This is not the condition on which Jacob will accept God in a mercenary spirit. It is merely the echo and the thankful acknowledgment of the divine assurance, "I am with thee," which was given immediately before. It is the response of the son to the assurance of the father: "Wilt thou indeed be with me? Thou shalt be my God." *This stone shall be God's house,* a monument of the presence of God among his people, and a symbol of the indwelling of his Spirit in their hearts. As it comes in here it signalizes the grateful and loving welcome and entertainment which God receives from his saints. *A tenth will I surely give unto thee.* The honored guest is treated as one of the family. Ten is the whole: a tenth is a share of the whole. The Lord of all receives one share as an acknowledgment of his sovereign right to all. Here it is represented as the full share given to the king who condescends to dwell with his subjects. Thus Jacob opens his heart, his home, and his treasure to God. These are the simple elements of a theocracy, a national establishment of the true religion. The spirit of power, and of love, and of a sound mind, has begun to reign in Jacob. As the Father is prominently manifested in regenerate Abraham, and the Son in Isaac, so also the Spirit in Jacob.

LVII. JACOB'S MARRIAGE.—Gen. xxix.

6. רָחֵל Rachel, *a ewe.*

16. לֵאָה Leah, *wearied.*

24. זִלְפָּה Zilpah, *drop?*

29. בִּלְהָה Bilhah, *timidity.*

32. רְאוּבֵן Reuben, *behold a son.* A paronomasia in allusion to the phrase רָאָה בְּעָנְיִי. Derivatives and compounds, being formed by the common speaker, are sometimes founded upon resemblance in sound,

and not always on precise forms of the original sentence which prompted them.

33. שִׁמְעוֹן Shim'on, *hearing, answer.*

34. לֵוִי Levi, *junction, union.*

35. יְהוּדָה Jehudah, *praised.*

XXIX. 1. And Jacob lifted up his feet, and went to the land of the sons of the east. 2. And he saw, and behold, a well in the field, and behold there three flocks of sheep lying by it; for out of that well they watered the flocks: and the stone was great upon the well's mouth. 3. And thither are all the flocks gathered, and they roll the stone from the well's mouth, and water the sheep, and put the stone again upon the well's mouth in its place. 4. And Jacob said unto them, My brethren, whence are ye? And he said, Of Haran are we. 5. And he said unto them, Know ye Laban, son of Nahor? And they said, We know him. 6. And he said unto them, Is he well? And they said, Well; and behold Rachel his daughter coming with the sheep. 7. And he said, Lo, yet the day is great; it is not time for the cattle to be gathered: water ye the sheep, and go feed them. 8. And they said, We cannot, until all the flocks are gathered, and they roll the stone from the well's mouth, and we water the sheep.

9. He was yet speaking with them, and Rachel came with her father's sheep; for she kept them. 10. And it came to pass when Jacob saw Rachel, daughter of Laban his mother's brother, and the sheep of Laban his mother's brother, that Jacob drew near, and rolled the stone from the well's mouth, and watered the sheep of Laban his mother's brother. 11. And Jacob kissed Rachel, and lifted up his voice and wept. 12. And Jacob told Rachel that he was her father's brother, and that he was Rebekah's son: and she ran and told her father. 13. And it came to pass, when Laban heard the tidings of Jacob his sister's son, that he ran to meet him, and embraced him, and kissed him, and brought him to his house:

and he told Laban all these things. 14. And Laban said to him, Surely my bone and my flesh art thou. And he abode with him a month of days.

15. And Laban said unto Jacob, Because thou art my brother, shouldst thou serve me for naught? Tell me what shall thy wages be? 16. And Laban had two daughters: the name of the elder Leah, and the name of the younger Rachel. 17. And Leah's eyes were tender: and Rachel was beautiful in form and in look. 18. And Jacob loved Rachel: and he said, I will serve thee seven years for Rachel thy younger daughter. 19. And Laban said, It is better that I give her to thee than that I give her to another man: abide with me. 20. And Jacob served for Rachel seven years; and they were in his eyes like a few days, for the love he had to her.

21. And Jacob said unto Laban, Give my wife, for my days are fulfilled, that I may go in unto her. 22. And Laban gathered all the men of the place, and made a feast. 23. And it came to pass in the evening, that he took Leah his daughter, and brought her to him; and he went in unto her. 24. And Laban gave her Zilpah his maid, for a handmaid to Leah his daughter. 25. And it came to pass in the morning, that behold it was Leah: and he said to Laban, What is this that thou hast done unto me? Have I not served with thee for Rachel? And why hast thou beguiled me? 26. And Laban said, It must not be so done in our country, to give the younger before the firstborn. 27. Fulfil the week of this, and we will give thee this also, for the service which thou shalt serve with me yet other seven years. 28. And Jacob did so, and fulfilled her week; and he gave him Rachel his daughter to be his wife. 29. And Laban gave to Rachel his daughter Bilhah his maid, to be her handmaid. 30. And he went in also unto Rachel, and loved also Rachel more than Leah: and he served with him yet other seven years.

31. And the Lord saw that Leah was hated, and he opened her womb; and Rachel was barren. 32. And Leah conceived,

and bare a son, and called his name Reuben: for she said, For the LORD hath looked on my affliction; for now will my husband love me. 33. And she conceived again, and bare a son, and said, For the LORD hath heard that I was hated, and gave me also this. And she called his name Simon. 34. And she conceived again, and bare a son, and said, Now this time will my husband be joined unto me: for I have him three sons. Therefore was his name called Levi. 35. And she conceived again, and bare a son, and said, This time will I praise the LORD. Therefore she called his name Judah, and she stayed from bearing.

In this chapter and the following Jacob grows from a solitary fugitive with a staff in his hand (xxxii. 10) to be the father of a large family and the owner of great wealth. He proves himself to be a man of patience and perseverance, and the Lord according to promise is with him.

1–8. Jacob arrives at the well of Haran. *The land of the sons of the east.* The points of the heavens were defined by the usage of practical life, and not by the standard of a science yet unknown. Hence the east means any quarter toward the sunrising. Haran was about four degrees east of Beer-sheba, and five and a half degrees north. The distance was about four hundred and fifty miles, and therefore it would take Jacob fifteen days to perform the journey at thirty miles a day. If he reached Bethel the first night, he must have travelled about fifty miles the first day. After this he proceeds on his journey without any memorable incident. 2, 3. In the neighborhood of Haran he comes upon a well, by which lay three flocks. This is not the well near Haran where Abraham's servant met Rebekah. It is in the pasture grounds at some distance from the town. On its mouth was a large stone, indicating that water was precious, and that the well was the common property of the surrounding natives. The custom was to gather the flocks, roll away the stone, which was too great to be moved by a boy or a female, water the flocks, and replace the stone. 4–6. Jacob, on making inquiry, learns that Haran is at hand, that Laban is well, and that Rachel is drawing nigh with her father's flocks. Laban is called by Jacob the son of Nahor, that is, his grandson, with the usual latitude of relative names in Scripture (xxviii. 13). 7, 8. *The day is great.* A great part of it yet remains. It is not yet the time to shut up the cattle for the night; "water the sheep and go feed them." Jacob may have wished to meet with Rachel without presence of the shepherds. *We cannot.* There was a rule or custom that the flocks must be all assembled before the stone was rolled away for the purpose of watering the cattle. This may have been required to insure a fair distribution of the water to all parties, and especially to those who were too weak to roll away the stone.

9–14. Jacob's interview with Rachel, and hospitable reception by Laban. Rachel's approach awakens all Jacob's warmth of feeling. He rolls away the stone, waters the sheep, kisses Rachel, and bursts into tears. The remembrance of home and of the relationship of his mother to Rachel overpowers him. 12–14. He informs Rachel who he is, and she runs to acquaint her father. Laban hastens to welcome his relative to his house. *Surely my bone and my flesh art thou.* This is a description of kinsmanship probably derived from the formation of the woman out of the man (ii. 23). A month here means the period from new moon to new moon, and consists of twenty-nine or thirty days.

15. Jacob serves seven years for Rachel. *What shall thy wages be?* An active, industrious man like Jacob was of great value to Laban. 16. *Two daughters.* Daughters in those countries and times were also objects of value, for which their parents were wont to receive considerable presents (xxiv. 53). Jacob at present, however, is merely worth his labor. He has apparently nothing else to offer. 18–20. As he loves Rachel, he offers to serve seven years for her, and is accepted. Isaac loved Rebekah after she was sought and won as a bride for him. Jacob loves Rachel before he makes a proposal of marriage. His attachment is pure and constant, and hence the years of his service seem but days to him. The pleasure of her society both in the business and leisure of life makes the hours pass unnoticed. It is obvious that in those early days the intercourse of the sexes before marriage was more unrestrained than it afterwards became.

21–30. Jacob is betrayed into marrying Leah, and on consenting to serve other seven years obtains Rachel also. He claims his expected reward when due. 22–24. *Made a feast.* The feast in the house of the bride's father seems to have lasted seven days, at the close of which the marriage was completed. But the custom seems to have varied according to the circumstances of the bridegroom. Jacob had no house of his own to which to conduct the bride. *In the evening:* when it was dark. The bride was also closely veiled, so that it was easy for Laban to practise this piece of deceit. *A handmaid.* It was customary to give the bride a handmaid, who became her confidential servant (xxiv. 59, 61). 25–27. In the morning Jacob discovers that Laban had overreached him. This is the first retribution Jacob experiences for the deceitful practices of his former days. He expostulates with Laban, who pleads the custom of the country. It is still the custom not to give the younger in marriage before the older, unless the latter be deformed or in some way defective. It is also not unusual to practise the very same trick that Laban now employed, if the suitor is so simple as to be off his guard. Jacob, however, did not expect this at his relative's hands, though he had himself taken part in proceedings equally questionable. *Fulfil the week of this.* If this was the second day of the feast celebrating the nuptials of Leah, Laban requests him to complete the week, and then he will give him Rachel also. If, however, Leah was fraudulently put upon him at the close of the week of feasting, then Laban in these words proposes to give Rachel to Jacob on fulfilling another week of nuptial rejoicing. The latter is in the present instance more likely. In either case the marriage of Rachel is only a week after that of Leah. 28–30. Rather than lose Rachel altogether, Jacob consents to comply with Laban's terms. Rachel was the wife of Jacob's affections and intentions. The taking of a second wife in the lifetime of the first was contrary to the law of nature, which designed one man for one woman (ii. 21–25). But the marrying of a sister-in-law was not yet incestuous, because no law had yet been made on the subject. Laban gives a handmaid to each of his daughters. To Rebekah his sister had been given more than one (xxiv. 61). Bond-slaves had been in existence long before Laban's time (xvi. 1). *And loved also Rachel more than Leah.* This proves that even Leah was not unloved. At the time of his marriage Jacob was eighty-four years of age; which corresponds to half that age according to the present average of human life.

31–35. Leah bears four sons to Jacob. *The Lord saw.* The eye of the Lord is upon the sufferer. It is remarkable that both the narrator and Leah employ the proper name of God, which makes the performance of promise a prominent feature of his character. This is appropriate in the mouth of Leah, who is the mother of the promised seed. *That Leah was hated,* — less loved than Rachel. He therefore recompenses her for the want of her husband's affections by giving her children, while Rachel was barren. *Reuben,* — behold a son. *The Lord hath looked on my affliction.* Leah had qualities of heart, if not of outward appearance, which commanded esteem. She had learned to acknowledge the Lord in all her ways. *Simon*, — answer. She had prayed to the Lord, and this was her answer. *Levi*, — union, the reconciler. Her husband could not, according to the prevailing sentiments of those days, fail to be attached to the mother of three sons. *Judah*, — praised. Well may she praise the Lord ; for this is the ancestor of the promised seed. It is remarkable that the wife of priority, but not of preference, is the mother of the seed in whom all nations are to be blessed. Levi the reconciler is the father of the priestly tribe. Simon is attached to Judah. Reuben retires into the background.

Reuben may have been born when Jacob was still only eighty-four, and consequently Judah when he was eighty-seven.

LVIII. JACOB'S FAMILY AND WEALTH. — Gen. xxx.

6. דָּן Dan, *judge, lord.*

8. נַפְתָּלִי Naphtali, *wrestling.*

11. גָּד Gad, *overcoming, victory.* בְּגָד *in victory* or = בָּא גָד *victory cometh.* גּוּד *press down.* גְּדוּד *troop.*

13. אָשֵׁר Asher, *prosperity, happiness.*

18. יִשָּׂשכָר Jissakar, *reward.* The second ש seems to have been merely a full mode of writing the word, instead of the abbreviated form יִשָּׂכָר.

20. זְבֻלוּן Zebulun, *dwelling.* There is here a play upon the two words זָבַד *to endow* and זָבַל *to dwell*, the latter of which, however, prevails in the name. They occur only here as verbs.

21. דִּינָה Dinah, *judgment.*

14. יֹסֵף Joseph, *he shall add.* There is, however, an obvious allusion to the thought. " God hath taken away (אָסַף) my reproach." Double references, we find, are usual in the giving of names (see xxv. 30).

XXX. 1. And Rachel saw that she bare not to Jacob, and Rachel envied her sister ; and said unto Jacob, Give me children, or else I do. 2. And Jacob's anger was kindled against Rachel ; and he said, Am I instead of God. Who hath withheld from thee the fruit of the womb ? 3. And she said, Behold, my maid Billhah, go in unto her ; and she shall bear upon my knees, and I also shall be built up from her. 4. And she gave him Bilhah her maid to wife, and Jacob went in unto her. 5. And Bilhah conceived and bare Jacob a son. 6. And Rachel said, God hath judged me, and also heard my voice, and given me a son. Therefore called she his name Dan. 7. And Bilhah, Rachel's maid, conceived again, and bare a second son to Jacob. 8. And Rachel said, Wrestlings of God have I wrestled with my sister, and have prevailed. And she called his name Naphtali.

9. And Leah saw that she had stayed from bearing: and she took Zilpah her maid, and gave her to Jacob to wife. 10. And Zilpah, Leah's maid, bare Jacob a son. 11. And Leah said, Victory cometh. And she called his name Gad. 12. And Zilpah, Leah's maid, bare a second son to Jacob. 13. And Leah said, Happy am I; for the daughters will call me happy. And she called his name Asher.

14. And Reuben went in the days of wheat harvest, and found mandrakes in the field, and brought them unto Leah his mother. And Rachel said to Leah, Give me now of thy son's mandrakes. 15. And she said unto her, Is it a small matter to take my husband, and wouldest thou take also my son's mandrakes? And Rachel said, Therefore he shall lie with thee to-night for thy son's mandrakes. 16. And Jacob came out of the field in the evening, and Leah came out to meet him, and said, Thou art to come in unto me; for surely I have hired thee with my son's mandrakes. And he lay with her that night. 17. And God hearkened unto Leah, and she conceived, and bare Jacob a fifth son. 18. And Leah said, God hath given my hire, because I gave my maiden to my husband. And she called his name Issakar. 19. And Leah conceived again, and bare a sixth son to Jacob. 20. And Leah said, God hath endowed me with a good dowry: this time will my husband dwell with me, for I have borne him six sons. And she called his name Zebulun. 21. And afterwards she bare a daughter, and called her name Dinah.

22. And God remembered Rachel: and God hearkened to her, and opened her womb. 23. And she conceived and bare a son: and she said, God hath taken away my reproach. 24. And she called his name Joseph, saying, the LORD shall add to me another son.

25. And it came to pass when Rachel had borne Joseph, that Jacob said unto Laban, Send me away, and let me go to my place and to my land. 26. Give my wives and my children for whom I have served thee, and let me go: for thou knowest my service which I have done thee. 27. And Laban said unto him, Let me now find favor in thine eyes: I have divined, and the LORD blessed me for thy sake. 28. And he said, Appoint thy hire upon me, and I will give it. 29. And he said unto him, Thou knowest how I have served thee, and how thy cattle was with me. 30. For it was little which thou hadst before I came, and it brake forth into abundance, and the LORD blessed thee at my foot: and now, when shall I do for my own house? 31. And he said, What shall I give thee? And Jacob said, Thou shalt not give me anything: if thou wilt do for me this thing, I will again feed and keep thy flock. 32. I will pass through all thy flock to-day: remove thou thence every speckled and spotted sheep, and every brown sheep among the lambs, and the spotted and speckled among the goats: and such shall be my hire. 33. And my righteousness shall answer for me in time to come, when thou shalt go over my hire before thee; any that is not speckled or spotted among the goats, or brown among the sheep, is stolen with me. 34. And Laban said, Behold, may it be according to thy word. 35. And he removed that day all the straked and spotted he-goats, and all the speckled and spotted she-goats, all in which was any white, and all the brown among the sheep, and gave them into the hand of his sons. 36. And he set three days' journey between himself and Jacob; and Jacob fed the rest of Laban's flock.

37. And Jacob took him fresh rods of poplar and hazel and

plane; and pilled them in white strakes, stripping the white that was in the rods. 38. And he set the rods, which he had pilled, in the troughs in the vessels of water, whither the flock went to drink, before the flock, and they conceived when going to drink. 39. And the flock conceived before the rods; and the flock bare straked, speckled, and spotted. 40. And Jacob separated the lambs, and set the faces of the flock to the straked and all the brown in the flock of Laban; and he put his own folds by themselves, and put them not unto Laban's flock. 41. And it came to pass when the strong cattle conceived, that Jacob set the rods before the flock in the troughs, that they might conceive at the rods. 42. And when the sheep were weak he set them not; and the feeble were Laban's, and the strong Jacob's. 43. And the man brake forth exceedingly; and he had much cattle, and maid-servants and men-servants, and camels and asses.

This chapter is the continuation of the former, and completes the history of Jacob in Haran. The event immediately following probably took place after Leah had borne two of her sons, though not admitted into the narrative till she had paused for a short time (see page 79).

1–8. Bilhah, Rachel's maid, bears two sons. 1–4. Rachel becomes impatient of her barrenness and jealous of her sister, and unjustly reproaches her husband, who indignantly rebukes her. God, not he, has withheld children from her. She does what Sarah had done before her (xvi. 2, 3), gives her handmaid to her husband. No express law yet forbade this course, though nature and Scripture by implication did (ii. 23–25). 5, 6. *Dan. God hath judged me.* In this passage Jacob and Rachel use the common noun, God, the Everlasting, and therefore Almighty, who rules in the physical relations of things, — a name suitable to the occasion. He had judged her, dealt with her according to his sovereign justice in withholding the fruit of the womb, when she was self-complacent and forgetful of her dependence on a higher power; and also in hearing her voice when she approached him in humble supplication. 7, 8. *Naphtali. Wrestlings of God,* with God, in prayer, on the part of both sisters, so that they wrestled with one another in the self-same act. Rachel, though looking first to Jacob and then to her maid, had at length learned to look to her God, and then had prevailed.

9–13. Leah having stayed from bearing, resorts to the same expedient. Her fourth son was seemingly born in the fourth year of Jacob's marriage. Bearing her first four sons so rapidly, she would the sooner observe the temporary cessation. After the interval of a year she may have given Zilpah to Jacob. 10, 11. *Gad. Victory cometh.* She too claims a victory. 12, 13. *Asher.* Daughters will pronounce her happy who is so rich in sons. Leah is seemingly conscious that she is here pursuing a device of her own heart; and hence there is no explicit reference to the divine name or influence in the naming of the two sons of her maid.

14–21. *Reuben* was at this time four or five years of age, as it is probable that Leah began to bear again before Zilpah had her second son. *Mandrakes,* — the fruit of the *mandragora vernalis,* which is to this day supposed to promote fruitfulness of the womb. Rachel therefore desires to partake of them, and obtains them by a compact with Leah. 16–18. Leah betakes herself to prayer, and bears a fifth son. She calls him *Issakar,* with a double allusion. She had hired her husband with the mandrakes, and had received this son as her hire for giving her maid to her husband; which she regards as an act of generosity or self-denial. 19, 20. *Zebulun.* Here Leah confesses, "God hath endowed me with a good dowry." She speaks now like Rachel of the God of nature. The cherished thought that her husband will dwell with her who is the mother of six sons takes form in the name. 21. *Dinah* is the only daughter of Jacob mentioned (xlvi. 7), and that on account of her subsequent connection with the history of Jacob (xxxiv). Issakar appears to have been born in the sixth year after Jacob's marriage, Zebulun in the seventh, and Dinah in the eighth.

22–24. *God remembered Rachel,* in the best time for her, after he had taught her the lessons of dependence and patience. *Joseph.* There is a remote allusion to her gratitude for the reproach of barrenness taken away. But there is also hope in the name. The selfish feeling also has died away, and the thankful Rachel rises from Elohim, the invisible Eternal, to Jehovah, the manifest Self-existent. The birth of Joseph was after the fourteen years of service were completed. He and Dinah appear to have been born in the same year.

25–36. Jacob enters into a new contract of service with Laban. 25, 26. *When Rachel had borne Joseph.* Jacob cannot ask his dismissal till the twice seven years of service were completed. Hence the birth of Joseph, which is the date of his request, took place at the earliest in the fifteenth year of his sojourn with Laban. Jacob now wishes to return home, from which he had been detained so long by serving for Rachel. He no doubt expects of Laban the means at least of accomplishing his journey. 27, 28. Laban is loath to part with him. *I have divined,* — I have been an attentive observer. The result of his observation is expressed in the following words. *Appoint.* Laban offers to leave the fixing of the hire to Jacob. *Thy hire upon me,* which I will take upon me as binding. 29, 30. Jacob touches upon the value of his services, perhaps with the tacit feeling that Laban in equity owed him at least the means of returning to his home. *Brake forth,* — increased. *At my foot,* — under my guidance and tending of thy flocks. *Do,* — provide. 31–33. *Thou shalt not give me anything.* This shows that Jacob had no stock from Laban to begin with. "I will pass through all thy flock to-day" with thee. "Remove thou thence every speckled and spotted sheep, and every brown sheep among the lambs, and the spotted and speckled among the goats." These were the rare colors, as in the East the sheep are usually white, and the goats black or dark brown. *And such shall be my hire* Such as these uncommon party-colored cattle, when they shall appear among the flock already cleared of them; and not those of this description that are now removed. For in this case Laban would have given Jacob something; whereas Jacob was resolved to be entirely dependent on the divine providence for his hire. *And my righteousness will answer for me.* The color will determine at once whose the animal is. 34–36. Laban willingly consents to so favorable a proposal, removes the party-colored animals from the flock, gives them into the hands of his sons, and puts an interval of three days' journey between them and the pure stock which remains in Jacob's hands. Jacob is now to begin with nothing, and have for his hire any party-colored lambs or kids that appear in those flocks, from which every specimen of this rare class has been carefully removed.

37–43. Jacob devises means to provide himself with a flock in these unfavorable circumstances. 37–40. His first device is to place party-colored rods before the eyes of the cattle at the rutting season, that they might drop lambs and kids varied with speckles, patches, or streaks of white. He had learned from experience that there is a congruence between the colors of the objects contemplated by the dams at that season and those of their young. At all events they bare many straked, speckled, and spotted lambs and kids. He now separated the lambs, and set the faces of the flock toward the young of the rare colors, doubtless to affect them in the same way as the pilled rods. *Put his own folds by themselves.* These are the party-colored cattle that from time to time appeared in the flock of Laban. 41, 42. In order to secure the stronger cattle, Jacob added the second device of employing the party-colored rods only when the strong cattle conceived. The sheep in the East lamb twice a year, and it is supposed that the lambs dropped in autumn are stronger than those dropped in the spring. On this supposition Jacob used his artifice in the spring, and not in the autumn. It is probable, however, that he made his experiments on the healthy and vigorous cattle, without reference to the season of the year. 43. The result is here stated. *The man brake forth exceedingly,* — became rapidly rich in hands and cattle.

It is obvious that the preceding and present chapters form one continuous piece of composition; as otherwise we have no account of the whole family of Jacob from one author. But the names Elohim and Jehovah are both employed in the piece, and hence their presence and interchange cannot indicate diversity of authorship.

LIX. JACOB'S FLIGHT FROM HARAN. — Gen. xxxi.

19. תְּרָפִים Teraphim. This word occurs fifteen times in the Old Testament. It appears three times in this chapter, and nowhere else in the Pentateuch. It is always in the plural number. The root does not appear in Biblical Hebrew. It perhaps means *to live well,* intransitively (Gesen., Roedig.), *to nourish,* transitively (Fürst). The teraphim were symbols or representatives of the Deity, as Laban calls them his gods. They seem to have been busts (προτομαί, Aquila) of the human form, sometimes as large as life (1 Sam. xix. 13). Those of full size were probably of wood; the smaller ones may have been of metal. In two passages (Jud. xvii. xviii.; Hos. iii. 4) they are six times associated with the ephod. This intimates either that they were worn on the ephod, like the Urim and Thummim, or more probably that the ephod was worn on them; in accordance with which they were employed for the purposes of divination (xxx. 27; Zeph. x. 2.) The employment of them in the worship of God, which Laban seems to have inherited from his fathers (Josh. xxiv. 2), is denounced as

idolatry (1 Sam. xv. 23); and hence they are classed with the idols and other abominations put away by Josiah (2 Kings xxiii. 24).

47. יְגַר שָׂהֲדוּתָא Jegar-sahadutha, *cairn of witness*, in the Aramaic dialect of the old Hebrew, or Shemite speech. גַּלְעֵד and גִּלְעָד Gal'ed and Gil'ad, *cairn of witness*, in Hebrew specially so called (see xi. 1–9).

49. מִצְפָּה Mizpah, *watch-tower*.

XXXI. 1. And he heard the words of Laban's sons, saying Jacob hath taken all that was our father's; and of that which was our father's hath he made all this glory. 2. And Jacob saw the face of Laban; and, behold, it was not with him as heretofore. 3. And the Lord said unto Jacob, Return unto the land of thy fathers, and to thy kindred; and I will be with thee. 4. And Jacob sent and called Rachel and Leah to the field unto his flock. 5. And said unto them, I see your father's face that it is not towards me as heretofore; and the God of my father hath been with me. 6. And ye know that with all my might I served your father. 7. And your father hath deceived me, and changed my wages ten times: and God suffered him not to hurt me. 8. If he said thus, The speckled shall be thy hire, then all the cattle bare speckled: and if he said thus, The straked shall be thy hire, then all the cattle bare straked. 9. And God took away the cattle of your father, and gave them to me. 10. And it came to pass at the time that the cattle conceived, that I lifted up mine eyes and saw in a dream, and beheld the bucks that leaped upon the flock were straked, speckled, and grisled. 11. And the angel of God said to me in a dream, Jacob; and I said, Here am I. 12. And he said, Lift up now thine eyes and see, all the bucks that leap upon the flock are straked, speckled, and grisled; for I have seen all that Laban doeth unto thee. 13. I am the God of Bethel, where thou anointedst a pillar, when thou vowedst to me a vow: now arise, come out of this land, and return unto the land of thy kindred.

14. And Rachel and Leah answered and said unto him, Is there yet to us any portion or inheritance in our father's house? 15. Are we not counted of him strangers? For he hath sold us; and he quite devoured also our silver. 16. For all the riches which God hath taken from our father, belongs to us and our children; and now all that God hath said unto thee, do. 17. And Jacob rose up, and set his sons and his wives upon camels. 18. And he carried away all his cattle, and all his gain which he had gained, the cattle of his getting, which he had gained in Padan-aram, to go to Isaac his father, to the land of Kenaan. 19. And Laban went to shear his sheep: and Rachel stole the teraphim which were her father's.

20. And Jacob stole the heart of Laban the Aramite, in that he told him not that he fled. 21. And he fled and all that he had; and he rose up and passed over the river: and he set his face toward Mount Gilead. 22. And it was told Laban on the third day, that Jacob was fled. 23. And he took his brethren with him, and pursued after him seven days' journey: and overtook him in Mount Gilead. 24. And God came to Laban the Aramite in a dream of the night: and said unto him, Take heed that thou speak not with Jacob from good to bad.

25. And Laban overtook Jacob: and Jacob had pitched his tent in the mount; and Laban pitched with his brethren in Mount Gilead. 26. And Laban said to Jacob, What hast thou done? and stolest my heart, and carriedst away my daughters as captives of the sword. 27. Why hast thou fled away secretly, and stolen away from me: and hast not told me, that I might send thee away with gladness and with songs, and with tabret and with harp? 28. And hast not suffered me to kiss my sons and my daughters. Now hast thou done foolishly. 29. It is in the power of my hand to do you hurt: and the God of your father yesternight said to me, saying, Take heed that thou speak not with Jacob from good to bad. 30. And now thou hast indeed gone, because thou sorely longedst after thy fa-

ther's house; wherefore hast thou stolen my gods? 31. And
Jacob answered and said to Laban, Because I was afraid; for
I said, Lest thou snatch thy daughters from me. 32. With
whomsoever thou findest thy gods, let him not live; before our
brethren discern what is thine with me, and take it to thee.
For Jacob knew not that Rachel had stolen them.

33. And Laban went into Jacob's tent, and into Leah's tent,
and into the two handmaids' tents, and found *them* not: and
he came from Leah's tent, and went into Rachel's tent. 34.
And Rachel had taken the teraphim and put them into the
camel's saddle, and sat upon them: and Laban felt all the
tent, and found *them* not. 35. And she said to her father, Let
it not displease my lord that I cannot rise up before thee, for
the custom of women is upon me. And he searched and found
not the teraphim. 36. And Jacob was wroth, and chode with
Laban: and Jacob answered and said to Laban, What is my
trespass, and what my sin, that thou hast pursued after me?
37. When thou hast felt all my stuff, what hast thou found of
all thy household stuff? Set *it* here before my brethren and
thy brethren, and let them judge between us both. 38. These
twenty years have I been with thee: thy ewes and thy she-
goats have not cast their young, and the rams of thy flock
have I not eaten. 39. That which was torn brought I not unto
thee: I myself bare the loss of it; of my hand didst thou re-
quire it, stolen by day or stolen by night. 40. Thus I was:
by day the drought consumed me, and the frost by night; and
my sleep fled from mine eyes. 41. Thus was I twenty years
in thy house; I served thee fourteen years for thy two daugh-
ters, and six years for thy cattle: and thou changedst my
wages ten times. 42. Unless the God of my father, the God
of Abraham, and the fear of Isaac, had been with me, thou
hadst now sent me away empty: my affliction and the labor
of my hands God hath seen, and judged yesternight.

43. And Laban answered and said unto Jacob, The daugh-
ters are my daughters, the sons my sons, and the cattle my

cattle, and all that thou seest is mine: and what can I do this day unto these my daughters, or unto their children which they have borne? 44. And now come, make we a covenant, I and thou, and let it be a witness between me and thee. 45. And Jacob took a stone, and set it up for a pillar. 46. And Jacob said unto his brethren, Gather stones. And they took stones and made a heap, and they ate there upon the heap. 47. And Laban called it Jegar-sahadutha: and Jacob called it Galeed.

48. And Laban said, This heap is witness between me and thee this day; therefore was its name called Galeed; 49. And Mizpah, for he said, The LORD watch between me and thee, when we are absent one from another. 50. If thou shalt afflict my daughters, or if thou take other wives beside my daughters, no man is with us; see, God is witness between me and thee. 51. And Laban said to Jacob, Behold this heap, and behold the pillar, which I have cast between me and thee. 52. Witness be this heap, and witness the pillar, that I will not pass over this heap to thee, and that thou shalt not pass over this heap and this pillar to me, for harm. 53. The God of Abraham, and the God of Nahor, the God of their father, judge between us. And Jacob sware by the fear of his father Isaac. 54. And Jacob offered sacrifice upon the mount, and called his brethren to eat bread; and they ate bread, and lodged in the mount.

Jacob had now been twenty years in Laban's service, and was therefore ninety-six years of age. It has now become manifest that he cannot obtain leave of Laban to return home. He must, therefore, either come off by the high hand, or by secret flight. Jacob has many reasons for preferring the latter course.

1–13. Circumstances at length induce Jacob to propose flight to his wives. 1, 2. His prosperity provokes the envy and slander of Laban's sons, and Laban himself becomes estranged. 3. The Lord now commands Jacob to return, and promises him his presence to protect him. 4–13. Jacob now opens his mind fully to Rachel and Leah. Rachel, we observe, is put first. Several new facts come out in his discourse to them. *Ye know* — Jacob appeals to his wives on this point — *that with all my might I served your father.* He means, of course, to the extent of his engagement. During the last six years he was to provide for his own house, as the Lord permitted him, with the full knowledge and concurrence of Laban. Beyond this, which is a fair and acknowledged exception, he has been faithful in keeping the cattle of Laban. *Your father deceived me, and changed my wages ten times;* that is, as often as he could. If, at the end of the first year, he found that Jacob had gained considerably, though he began with nothing, he might change his wages every following half-year, and so actually change them ten times in five years. In this case, the preceding chapter only records his original expedients, and then states the final result. *God suffered him not to hurt me.* Jacob, we are to remember, left his hire to the providence of God. He thought himself bound at the same time to use all legitimate means for the attainment of the desired end. His expedients may have been perfectly legitimate in the circumstances, but they were evidently of no avail without the divine blessing. And they would become wholly ineffectual when his wages were changed. Hence he says, God took the cattle and gave them to me. 10–13. Jacob seems here to record two dreams, the former of which is dated at the rutting season. The dream indicates the result by a symbolic representation, which ascribes it rather to the God of nature than to the man of art. The second dream makes allusion to the former as a process still going on up to the present time. This appears to be an encouragement to Jacob now to commit himself to the Lord on his way home. The angel of the Lord, we observe, announces himself as the God of Bethel, and recalls to Jacob the pillar and the vow. The angel, then, is Jehovah manifesting himself to human apprehension.

14–19. His wives entirely accord with his view of their father's selfishness in dealing with his son-in-law, and approve of his intended departure. Jacob makes all the needful preparations for a hasty and secret flight. He avails himself of the occasion when Laban is at a distance probably of three or more days' journey, shearing his sheep. *Rachel stole the teraphim.* It is not the business of Scripture to acquaint us with the kinds and characteristics of false worship. Hence we know little of the teraphim, except that they were employed by those who professed to worship the true God. Rachel had a lingering attachment to these objects of her family's superstitious reverence, and secretly carried them away as relics of a home she was to visit no more, and as sources of safety to herself against the perils of her flight.

20–24. Laban hears of his flight, pursues, and overtakes him. *Stole the heart*, *κλέπτειν νοῦν*. The heart is the seat of the understanding in Scripture. To steal the heart of any one is to act without his knowledge. *The river.* The Frat, near which, we may conclude, Jacob was tending his flocks. Haran was about seventy miles from the river, and therefore Laban's flocks were on the other side of Haran. *Toward mount Gilead;* about three hundred miles from the Frat. *On the third day.* This shows that Laban's flocks kept by his sons were still three days' journey apart from Jacob's. *His brethren,* — his kindred and dependents. *Seven days' journey.* On the third day after the arrival of the messenger, Laban might return to the spot whence Jacob had taken his flight. In this case, Jacob would have at least five days of a start; which, added to the seven days of pursuit, would give him twelve days to travel three hundred English miles. To those accustomed to the pastoral life this was a possible achievement. God appears to Laban on behalf of Jacob, and warns him not to harm him. *Not to speak from good to bad*, is merely to abstain from language expressing and prefacing violence.

25–32. Laban's expostulation and Jacob's reply. *What hast thou done?* Laban intimates that he would have dismissed him honorably and affectionately, and therefore that his flight was needless and unkind; and finally charges him with stealing his gods. Jacob gives him to understand that he did not expect fair treatment at his hands, and gives him leave to search for his gods, not knowing that Rachel had taken them.

33–42. After the search for the teraphim has proved vain, Jacob warmly upbraids Laban. *The camel's saddle.* This was a pack-saddle, in the recesses of which articles might be deposited, and on which was a seat or couch for the rider. Rachel pleads the custom of women as an excuse for keeping her seat; which is admitted by Laban, not perhaps from the fear of ceremonial defilement (Lev. xv. 19–27), as this law was not yet in force, but from respect to his daughter and the conviction that in such circumstances she would not sit upon the teraphim. *My brethren and thy brethren,* — their common kindred. Jacob recapitulates his services in feeling terms. *By day the drought;* caused by the heat, which is extreme during the day, while the cold is not less severe in Palestine during the night. *The fear of Isaac,* — the

God whom Isaac fears. 42. *Judged,* — requited by restraining thee from wrong-doing.

43–47. Laban, now pacified, if not conscience-stricken, proposes a covenant between them. Jacob erects a memorial pillar, around which the clan gather a cairn of stones, which serves by its name for a witness of their compact. *Jegar-sahadutha.* Here is the first decided specimen of Aramaic, as contradistinguished from Hebrew. Its incidental appearance indicates a fully formed dialect known to Jacob, and distinct from his own. *Gilead* or Galeed remains to this day in Jebel Jel'ad, though the original spot was further north.

48–54. The covenant is then completed. 49, 50. *And Mizpah.* This refers to some prominent cliff from which, as a watch-tower, an extensive view might be obtained. It was in the northern half of Gilead (Deut. iii. 12, 13), and is noticed in Judges xi. 29. It is not to be confounded with other places called by the same name. The reference of this name to the present occurrence is explained in these two verses. The names Gilead and Mizpah may have arisen from this transaction, or received a new turn in consequence of its occurrence. 51–53. The terms of the covenant are now formally stated. *I have cast.* The erection of the pillar was a joint act of the two parties; in which Laban proposes, Jacob performs, and all take part. *The God of Abraham, Nahor, and Terah.* This is an interesting acknowledgment that their common ancestor Terah and his descendants down to Laban still acknowledged the true God even in their idolatry. Jacob swears by the fear of Isaac, perhaps to rid himself of any error that had crept into Laban's notions of God and his worship. 54. The common sacrifice and the common meal ratify the covenant of reconciliation.

LX. JACOB WRESTLES IN PRAYER. — Gen. xxxii.

3. מַחֲנַיִם Machanaim, *two camps.*
22. יַבֹּק Jabboq; r. בָּקַק *gush* or *gurgle out,* or אָבַק in niph. *wrestle.* Now Wady Zurka.
29. יִשְׂרָאֵל Jisrael, *prince of God.*
31. פְּנִיאֵל = פְּנוּאֵל Peniel, Penuel, *face of God.*

XXXII. 1. And Laban rose early in the morning, and kissed his sons and his daughters, and blessed them: and Laban went and returned unto his place. 2. And Jacob went on his way, and the angels of God met him. 3. And Jacob said, when he saw them, This is God's camp: and he called the name of the place Mahanaim. 8 ¶¶¶ 28

4. And Jacob sent messengers before him to Esau his brother, unto the land of Seir, the field of Edom. 5. And he commanded them, saying, Thus shall ye say unto my lord Esau: Thus saith thy servant Jacob, With Laban have I sojourned and tarried until now. 6. And I have oxen and asses, flocks, and men-servants and maid-servants: and I sent to tell my lord, to find grace in thine eyes. 7. And the messengers returned to Jacob, saying, We have gone to thy brother Esau, and also he cometh to meet thee, and four hundred men with him. 8. And Jacob was greatly afraid and distressed, and he divided the people that was with him, and the flocks, and the herds, and the camels, into two camps. 9. And he said, If Esau go to the one camp, and smite it, then the camp that is left shall escape.

10. And Jacob said, O God of my father Abraham, and God of my father Isaac, thou LORD who saidst unto me, Return unto thy land, and to thy kindred, and I will deal well with thee, 11. I am less than all the mercies and all the truth which thou hast done unto thy servant; for with my staff I passed over this Jordan, and now I am become two camps. 12. Deliver me now from the hand of my brother, from the hand of Esau: for I fear him, lest he come and smite me, the mother with the children. 13. And thou saidst, I will surely deal well with thee, and make thy seed as the sand of the sea, which cannot be numbered for multitude.

14. And he lodged there that night; and took of that which was come into his hand a present for Esau his brother: 15. She-goats two hundred, and he-goats twenty, ewes two hundred, and rams twenty. 16. Milch camels and their colts thirty, kine forty, and bulls ten, she-asses twenty, and foals ten. 17. And he delivered into the hand of his servants every drove by

itself; and said unto his servants, Pass over before me, and put a space between drove and drove. 18. And he commanded the foremost, saying, When Esau my brother meeteth thee, and asketh thee, saying, Whose art thou? and whither goest thou? and whose are these before thee? 19. Then shalt thou say, Thy servant Jacob's: this is a present sent unto my lord Esau: and behold, also, he is behind us. 20. And he commanded also the second and the third, and all that went after the droves, saying, On this manner shall ye speak unto Esau, when ye find him. 21. And ye shall say also, Behold, thy servant Jacob is behind us. For he said, I will appease him with the present that goeth before me, and afterwards I will see his face: mayhap he will lift up my face. 22. And the present passed over before him; and he himself lodged that night in the camp.

23. And he rose up that night, and took his two wives, and his two handmaids, and his eleven sons, and passed over the ford of Jabbok. 24. And he took them and sent them over the brook, and sent over that he had. 25. And Jacob was left alone; and a man wrestled with him until the dawn arose. 26. And he saw that he prevailed not over him, and he touched the socket of his thigh, and the socket of Jacob's thigh was wrenched in his wrestling with him. 27. And he said, Let me go, for the dawn ariseth. And he said, I will not let thee go, except thou bless me. 28. And he said unto him, What is thy name? And he said, Jacob. 29. And he said, No more Jacob shall thy name be called, but Israel; for thou hast striven to be prince with God and with men, and didst prevail. 30. And Jacob asked and said, Tell now thy name. And he said, Why is this that thou askest for my name? And he blessed him there. 31. And Jacob called the name of the place Peniel: for I have seen God face to face, and my life is preserved. 32. And the sun rose upon him as he passed over Penuel, and he halted upon his thigh. 33. Therefore the children of Israel eat not the sinew that shrank, which is upon the socket

of the thigh, unto this day; because he touched the socket of Jacob's thigh in the sinew that shrank.

After twenty years spent in Aram, Jacob now returns to Kenaan. As his departure was marked by a great moment in his spiritual life, so he is now approaching to a crisis in his life of no less significance

1–3. Jacob has a vision of the heavenly host. 1. This passage, recording Laban's farewell and departure, closes the connection of Jacob with Haran and all its toils of servitude, and is hence annexed to the previous chapter in the English version. In the distribution of the original text, it is regarded as the counterpart of the two following verses, in which Jacob's onward progress is mentioned, and so placed with them at the beginning of a new chapter. 2, 3. *The angels of God met him.* Twenty years ago Jacob saw the mystical ladder connecting heaven and earth, and the angels of God thereupon ascending and descending from the one to the other. Now, in circumstances of danger, he sees the angels of God on earth, encamped beside or around his own camp (Ps. xxxiv. 8). He recognizes them as God's camp, and names the place Mahanaim, from the double encampment. This vision is not dwelt upon, as it is the mere sequel of the former scene at Bethel. Mahanaim has been identified with Mahneh, about eight miles from the cairn of Laban and Jacob.

4–9. Jacob now sends a message to Esau apprising him of his arrival. *Unto the land of Seir.* Arabia Petraea, with which Esau became connected by his marriage with a daughter of Ishmael. He was now married fifty-six years to his first two wives, and twenty to his last, and therefore had a separate and extensive establishment of children and grandchildren. Jacob endeavors to make amends for the past by an humble and respectful approach to his elder brother, in which he styles himself, "thy servant," and Esau, "my lord." He informs him of his wealth, to intimate that he did not expect anything from him. *Four hundred men with him.* This was a formidable force. Esau had begun to live by the sword (xxvii. 40), and had surrounded himself with a numerous body of followers. Associated by marriage with the Hittites and the Ishmaelites, he had rapidly risen to the rank of a powerful chieftain. It is vain to conjecture with what intent Esau advanced at the head of so large a retinue. It is probable that he was accustomed to a strong escort, that he wished to make an imposing appearance before his brother, and that his mind was in that wavering state, when the slightest incident might soothe him into good-will, or arouse him to vengeance. 8, 9. Jacob, remembering his own former dealings with him, has good cause for alarm. He betakes himself to the means of deliverance. He disposes of his horde into two camps, that if one were attacked and captured, the other might meanwhile escape. He never neglects to take all the precautions in his power.

10–13. Next he betakes himself to prayer. He appeals to the God of Abraham and Isaac, to Jehovah the God of promise and performance. *I am less than;* unworthy of all the mercy and truth of God. *With my staff.* Jacob seems to have left his home without escort and without means. It was evidently intended that he should return in a short time; but unforeseen circumstances lengthened the period. *Me, the mother with the children.* *Me* is here used in that pregnant sense which is familiar in Scripture, to include his whole clan; as Ishmael, Israel, Edom, often stand for their respective races. He then pleads the express promise of God (xxviii. 13–15, xxxi. 3).

14–22. Jacob sends forward a present to Esau. *He lodged there that night.* Mahanaim may have been about twenty-five miles from the Jabbok. At some point in the interval he awaited the return of his messengers. Abiding during the night in the camp, not far from the ford of the Jabbok, he selects and sends forward to Esau his valuable present of five hundred and fifty head of cattle. *That which was come into his hand,* into his possession. The cattle are selected according to the proportions of male and female which were adopted from experience among the ancients (Varro, *de re rust.* II. 3). *Every drove by itself,* with a space between, that Esau might have time to estimate the great value of the gift. The repetition of the announcement of the gift, and of Jacob himself being at hand, was calculated to appease Esau, and persuade him that Jacob was approaching him in all brotherly confidence and affection. *Appease him.* Jacob designs this gift to be the means of propitiating his brother before he appears in his presence. *Lift up my face,* accept me. *Lodged that night in the camp;* after sending this present over the Jabbok. This seems the same night referred to in v. 14.

23–33. Jacob wrestles with a man. 23, 24. *Passed over the ford of Jabbok.* The Jabbok rose near Rabbath Ammon, and flowed into the Jordan, separating North Gilead from South, or the kingdom of Og from that of Sihon. 25. *Jacob was left alone,* on the north side, after all had passed over. *A man wrestled with him.* When God has a new thing of a spiritual nature to bring into the experience of man, he begins with the senses. He takes man on the ground on which he finds him, and leads him through the senses to the higher things of reason, conscience, and communion with God.

Jacob seems to have gone through the principles or foundations of faith in God and repentance towards him, which gave a character to the history of his grandfather and father, and to have entered upon the stage of spontaneous action. He had that inward feeling of spiritual power which prompted the apostle to say, "I can do all things." Hence we find him dealing with Esau for the birthright, plotting with his mother for the blessing, erecting a pillar and vowing a vow at Bethel, overcoming Laban with his own weapons, and even now taking the most prudent measures for securing a welcome from Esau on his return. He relied indeed on God, as was demonstrated in many of his words and deeds; but the prominent feature of his character was a strong and firm reliance on himself. But this practical self-reliance, though naturally springing up in the new man and highly commendable in itself, was not yet in Jacob duly subordinated to that absolute reliance which ought to be placed in the Author of our being and our salvation. Hence he had been betrayed into intrusive, dubious, and even sinister courses, which in the retributive providence of God had brought, and were yet to bring him, into many troubles and perplexities. The hazard of his present situation arose chiefly from his former unjustifiable practices towards his brother. He is now to learn the lesson of unreserved reliance on God.

A man appeared to him in his loneliness; one having the bodily form and substance of a man. *Wrestled with him,* — encountered him in the very point in which he was strong. He had been a taker by the heel from his very birth (25, 26), and his subsequent life had been a constant and successful struggle with adversaries. *And when he,* the stranger, *saw that he prevailed not over him.* Jacob, true to his character, struggles while life remains, with this new combatant. *He touched the socket of his thigh,* so that it was wrenched out of joint. The thigh is the pillar of a man's strength, and its joint with the hip the seat of physical force for the wrestler. Let the thigh bone be thrown out of joint, and the man is utterly disabled. Jacob now finds that this mysterious wrestler has wrested from him, by one touch, all his might, and he can no longer stand alone. Without any support whatever from himself, he hangs upon the conqueror, and in that condition learns by experience the practice of sole reliance on one mightier than himself. This is the turning-point in this strange drama. Henceforth Jacob now feels himself strong, not in himself, but in the Lord, and in the power of his might. What follows is merely the explication and the consequence of this bodily conflict.

And he, the Mighty Stranger, *said, Let me go, for the dawn ariseth.* The time for other avocations is come: let me go. He does not shake off the clinging grasp of the now disabled Jacob, but only calls upon him to relax his grasp. *And he*, Jacob, *said, I will not let thee go except thou bless me.* Despairing now of his own strength, he is Jacob still: he declares his determination to cling on until his conqueror bless him. He now knows he is in the hand of a higher power, who can disable and again enable, who can curse and also bless. He knows himself also to be now utterly helpless without the healing, quickening, protecting power of his victor, and, though he die in the effort, he will not let him go without receiving this blessing. Jacob's sense of his total debility and utter defeat is now the secret of his power with his friendly vanquisher. He can overthrow all the prowess of the self-reliant, but he cannot resist the earnest entreaty of the helpless.

28–30. *What is thy name?* He reminds him of his former self, Jacob, the supplanter, the self-reliant, self-seeking. But now he is disabled, dependent on another, and seeking a blessing from another, and for all others as well as himself. No more Jacob shall thy name be called, but Israel, — a prince of God, in God, with God. In a personal conflict, depending on thyself, thou wert no match for God. But in prayer, depending on another, thou hast prevailed with God and with men. The new name is indicative of the new nature which has now come to its perfection of development in Jacob. Unlike Abraham, who received his new name once for all, and was never afterwards called by the former one, Jacob will hence be called now by the one and now by the other, as the occasion may serve. For he was called from the womb (xxv. 23), and both names have a spiritual significance for two different aspects of the child of God, according to the apostle's paradox, "Work out your own salvation with fear and trembling, for it is God that worketh in you both to will and to do of his good pleasure" (Phil. ii. 12, 13). *Tell now thy name.* Disclose to me thy nature. This mysterious Being intimates by his reply that Jacob was to learn his nature, so far as he yet required to know it, from the event that had just occurred; and he was well acquainted with his name. *And he blessed him there.* He had the power of disabling the self-sufficient creature, of upholding that creature when unable to stand, of answering prayer, of conferring a new name, with a new phase of spiritual life, and of blessing with a bodily renovation, and with spiritual capacity for being a blessing to mankind. After all this, Jacob could not any longer doubt who he was. There are, then, three acts in this dramatic scene: *first,* Jacob wrestling with the Omnipresent in the form of a man, in which he is signally defeated; *second,* Jacob importunately supplicating Jehovah, in which he prevails as a prince of God; *third,* Jacob receiving the blessing of a new name, a new development of spiritual life, and a new capacity for bodily action.

31–33. *Peniel,* — the face of God. The reason of this name is assigned in the sentence, *I have seen God face to face.* He is at first called a man. Hosea terms him *the angel* (xii. 4, 5 (3, 4). And here Jacob names him God. Hence some men, deeply penetrated with the ineffable grandeur of the divine nature, are disposed to resolve the first act at least into an impression on the imagination. We do not pretend to define with undue nicety the mode of this wrestling. And we are far from saying that every sentence of Scripture is to be understood in a literal sense. But until some cogent reason be assigned, we do not feel at liberty to depart from the literal sense in this instance. The whole theory of a revelation from God to man is founded upon the principle that God can adapt himself to the apprehension of the being whom he has made in his own image. This principle we accept, and we dare not limit its application *further than the demonstrative laws of reason and conscience demand.* If God walk in the garden with Adam, expostulate with Cain, give a specification of the ark to Noah, partake of the hospitality of Abraham, take Lot by the hand to deliver him from Sodom, we cannot affirm that he may not, for a worthy end, enter into a bodily conflict with Jacob. These various manifestations of God to man differ only in degree. If we admit any one, we are bound by parity of reason to accept all the others.

We have also already noted the divine method of dealing with man. He proceeds from the known to the unknown, from the simple to the complex, from the material to the spiritual, from the sensible to the super-sensible. So must he do, until he have to deal with a world of philosophers. And even then, and only then, will his method of teaching and dealing with men be clearly and fully understood. The more we advance in the philosophy of spiritual things, the more delight will we feel in discerning the marvellous analogy and intimate nearness of the outward to the inward, and the material to the spiritual world. We have only to bear in mind that in man there is a spirit as well as a body; and in this outward wrestling of man with man we have a token of the inward wrestling of spirit with spirit, and therefore an experimental instance of that great conflict of the Infinite Being with the finite self, which grace has introduced into our fallen world, recorded here for the spiritual edification of the church on earth.

My life is preserved. The feeling of conscience is, that no sinner can see the infinitely holy God and live. *And he halted upon his thigh.* The wrenching of the tendons and muscles was mercifully healed, yet so as to leave a permanent monument, in Jacob's halting gait, that God had overcome his self-will.

LXI. JACOB AND ESAU MEET. — Gen. xxxiii.

17. סֻכֹּת Sukkoth, *booths,* consisting of poles forming a roof covered with branches, leaves, or grass.

19. חֲמוֹר Chamor, *ass, red, heap.* קְשִׂיטָה Qesitah, weighed or measured. Ἀμνὸς, LXX. and Onk.

XXXIII. 1. And Jacob lifted up his eyes, and looked, and behold, Esau came, and with him four hundred men. And he divided the children unto Leah, and unto Rachel, and unto the two handmaids. 2. And he put the handmaids and their children foremost, and Leah and her children after, and Rachel and Joseph hindmost. 3. And he passed over before them, and bowed to the earth seven times, until he came near to his brother. 4. And Esau ran to meet him, and embraced him, and fell on his neck and kissed him: and they wept. 5. And he lifted up his eyes and saw the women and the children, and he said, Who are these of thine? And he said, The children whom God hath granted to thy servant. 6. And the handmaids came near, they and their children, and they bowed. 7. And Leah also came near and her children, and they bowed; and after came near Joseph and Rachel, and they bowed. 8. And he said, What is all this horde of thine which I met? And he said, To find grace in the eyes of my lord. 9. And Esau said, I have enough, my brother; be that to thee that is thine. 10. And Jacob said, Nay, now, if now I have found grace in thine eyes, then receive my present from my hand; for therefore have I seen thy face, as if I had seen the face of God, and thou wast pleased with me. 11. Take now my blessing that is brought to thee, because God has favored me and I have all. And he urged him, and he took it. 12. And he said, Let us set out and go, and I will go with thee. 13. And he said unto him, My lord knoweth that the children are tender, and the flocks and herds are suckling with me, and they will overdrive them one day and all the flock will die. 14. Let my lord now pass over before his servant, and I will lead on softly, at the pace of the cattle that are before me, and at the pace of the children, until I come unto my lord unto Seir. 15. And Esau said, Let me now leave with thee of the men that are with me. And he said, Wherefore this? Let me find grace in the eyes of my lord. 16. And Esau returned that day on his way to Seir.

17. And Jacob journeyed to Sukkoth, and built him a house: and for his cattle he made booths; therefore he called the name of the place Sukkoth. § 37.

18. And Jacob went in peace to the city of Shekem, which is in the land of Kenaan, where he went from Padan-aram: and he pitched before the city. 19. And he bought a parcel of the field where he had spread his tent, at the hand of the sons of Hamor, the father of Shekem, for a hundred kesitahs. 20. And he set up there an altar, and called it El-Elohe-Israel. § 38.

Jacob has a friendly interview with Esau, and reënters Kenaan.

1–3. Jacob, on seeing Esau approach with his four hundred men, advances with circumspection and lowly obeisance. He divided his family, arranged them according to their preciousness in his eyes, and walks himself in front. In drawing near, he bows seven times, in token of complete submission to his elder brother. 4–7. Esau, the wild hunter, is completely softened, and manifests the warmest affection, which is reciprocated by Jacob. The *puncta extraordinaria* over וַיִּשָּׁקֵהוּ (and kissed him), seemingly intimating a doubt of the reading or of the sincerity of Esau, are wholly unwarranted. Esau then observes the women and children, and inquires who they are. Jacob replies that God had granted, graciously bestowed on him, these children. They approach in succession, and do obeisance. 8–11. Esau now inquires of the caravan or horde he had already met. He had heard the announcement of the servants; but he awaited the confirmation of the master. *To find grace in the eyes of my lord.* Jacob values highly the good-will of his brother. The acceptance of this present is the security for that good-will, and for all the safety and protection which it involved. Esau at first declines the gift, but on being urged by Jacob accepts it, and thereby relieves Jacob of all his anxiety. His brother is now his friend indeed. *Therefore have I seen thy face*, that I might give thee this token of my affection. *As if I had seen the face of God.* The unexpected kindness with which his brother had received him was a type and proof of the kindness of the All-provident, by whom it had been added to all his other mercies. *My blessing;* my gift which embodies my good wishes. *I have all;* not only enough, but all that I can wish.

12–16. They now part for the present. *I will go with thee;* as an escort or vanguard. Jacob explains that this would be inconvenient for both parties, as his tender children and suckling cattle could not keep pace with Esau's men, who were used to the road. *At the pace of the cattle;* as fast as the business (מְלָאכָה) of travelling with cattle will permit. *Unto Seir.* Jacob is travelling to the land of Kenaan, and to the residence of his father. But, on arriving there, it will be his first duty to return the fraternal visit of Esau. The very circumstance that he sent messengers to apprise his brother of his arrival, implies that he was prepared to cultivate friendly relations with him. Jacob also declines the offer of some of the men that Esau had with him. He had, doubtless, enough of hands to manage his remaining flock, and he now relied more than ever on the protection of that God who had ever proved himself a faithful and effectual guardian.

17. *Sukkoth* was south of the Jabbok, and east of the Jordan, as we learn from Judges viii. 4–9. From the same passage it appears to have been nearer the Jordan than Penuel, which was at the ford of Jabbok. Sukkoth cannot therefore be identified with Sakut, which Robinson finds on the other side of the Jordan, about ten miles north of the mouth of the Jabbok. *And built him a house.* This indicates a permanent residence. *Booths,* or folds, composed of upright stakes wattled together, and sheltered with leafy branches. The closed space

in the text is properly introduced here, to indicate the pause in the narrative, while Jacob sojourned in this place. Dinah, who is not noticed on the journey, was now not more than six years of age. Six or seven years more, therefore, must have elapsed before the melancholy events of the next chapter took place. In the interval, Jacob may have visited his father, and even returned the visit of Esau.

18–20. Jacob at length crosses the Jordan, and enters again the land of Kenaan. *In peace.* The original word (שָׁלֵם *safe, in peace*) is rendered Shalem, the name of the town at which Jacob arrived, by the Septuagint. The rendering *safe*, or *in peace*, is here adopted, because (1) the word is to be taken as a common noun or adjective, unless there be a clear necessity for a proper name; (2) the *place* was called Shekem in the time of Abraham (xii. 6), and the *town* is so designated in the thirty-fifth chapter (v. 4); and (3) the statement that Jacob arrived in safety accounts for the additional clauses, " which is in the land of Kenaan," and " when he went from Padan-aram," and is in accordance with the promise (xxviii. 21) that he would return *in peace.* If, however, the Salim found by Robinson to the west of Nablous be the present town, it must be called the city of Shekem, because it belonged to the Shekem mentioned in the following verse and chapter. *Pitched before the city.* Jacob did not enter into the city, because his flocks and herds could not find accommodation there, and he did not want to come into close contact with the inhabitants. *He bought a parcel of the field.* He is anxious to have a place he may call his own, where he may have a permanent resting-place. *For a hundred kesitahs.* The kesitah may have been a piece of silver or gold, of a certain weight, equal in value to a lamb (see Gesenius). *El-Elohe-Israel.* Jacob consecrates his ground by the erection of an altar. He calls it the altar of the Mighty One, the God of Israel, in which he signalizes the omnipotence of him who had brought him in safety to the land of promise through many perils, the new name by which he himself had been lately designated, and the blessed communion which now existed between the Almighty and himself. This was the very spot where Abraham, about one hundred and eighty-five years ago, built the first altar he erected in the promised land (xii. 6, 7). It is now consecrated anew to the God of promise.

LXII. DINAH'S DISHONOR.—Gen. xxxiv.

XXXIV. 1. Then went out Dinah, the daughter of Leah, whom she bare unto Jacob, to see the daughters of the land. 2. And Shekem, son of Hamor the Hivite, prince of the land, saw her; and he took her, and lay with her, and humbled her. 3. And his soul clave unto Dinah, daughter of Jacob; and he loved the damsel, and spake to the heart of the damsel. 4. And Shekem said unto Hamor his father, saying, Get me this damsel to wife. 5. And Jacob heard that he had defiled Dinah his daughter: and his sons were with his cattle in the field: and Jacob held his peace until they were come.

6. And Hamor, the father of Shekem, came out unto Jacob to speak with him. 7. And the sons of Jacob came from the field when they heard it: and the men were grieved, and were very wroth, because he had wrought folly in Israel, to lie with the daughter of Jacob; which ought not to be done. 8. And Hamor spake with them, saying, Shekem, my son, his soul clingeth to your daughter; give her now to him to wife. 9. And intermarry ye with us; your daughters give unto us, and our daughters take unto you. 10. And ye shall dwell with us: and the land shall be before you; dwell and trade therein, and get possessions therein. 11. And Shekem said unto her father and unto her brethren, Let me find grace in your eyes, and what ye shall say unto me I will give. 12. Multiply upon me much dowry and gift, and I will give according as ye shall say unto me: and give me the damsel to wife. 13. And the sons of Jacob answered Shekem and Hamor his father with deceit, and spake: because he had defiled Dinah their sister. 14. And they said unto them, We cannot do this thing, to give our sister to a man that hath a foreskin; for that were a reproach unto us. 15. Only in this will we consent unto you, if ye will be as we, to be circumcised every male of you. 16. Then will we give our daughters unto you,

and we will take your daughters to us; and we will dwell with you, and become one people. 17. And if ye will not hearken unto us to be circumcised, then will we take our daughter and be gone.

18. And their words were good in the eyes of Hamor, and of Shekem, Hamor's son. 19. And the young man delayed not to do the thing, because he delighted in the daughter of Jacob: and he was more honorable than all the house of his father. 20. Then went Hamor and Shekem his son unto the gate of their city, and spake to the men of their city, saying, 21. These men are peaceable with us: and let them dwell in the land, and trade therein; and the land, behold, is wide enough before them: their daughters let us take to us for wives, and our daughters let us give to them. 22. Only herein will the men consent to us to dwell with us, to become one people, if every male of us be circumcised, as they are circumcised. 23. Their flocks, their property, all their cattle, shall they not be ours? Only let us consent unto them, and they will dwell with us. 24. Then hearkened unto Hamor and unto Shekem his son all that came out of the gate of his city: and every male was circumcised; all that came out of the gate of his city.

25. And it came to pass on the third day, when they were sore, that two of Jacob's sons, Simon and Levi, Dinah's brethren, took each man his sword, and went unto the city boldly, and slew every male. 26. And Hamor and Shekem his son they slew with the edge of the sword, and took Dinah out of Shekem's house, and came out. 27. The sons of Jacob went upon the slain, and spoiled the city, because they had defiled their sister. 28. Their sheep and their oxen and their asses and that which was in the city and that which was in the field they took. 29. And all their wealth and all their little ones and their wives took they captive and spoiled, and all that was in the house. 30. And Jacob said to Simon and to Levi, Ye have troubled me, to make me stink to the inhabitant of

the land, the Kenaanite and the Perizzite: and I am a few men, and they will gather against me and smite me, and I shall be destroyed, I and my house. 31. And they said, Should he deal with our sister as with a harlot? ¶ 29.

This chapter records the rape of Dinah and the revenge of her brothers.

1–5. Dinah went out to see the daughters of the land. The Jewish doctors of a later period fix the marriageable age of a female at twelve years and a day. It is probable that Dinah was in her thirteenth year when she went out to visit the daughters of the land. Six or seven years, therefore, must have been spent by Jacob between Sukkoth, where he abode some time, and the neighborhood of Shekem, where he had purchased a piece of ground. If we suppose Dinah to have been born in the same year with Joseph, who was in his seventeenth year at the time of his being sold as a bondslave (xxxvii. 2), the events of this chapter must have occurred in the interval between the completion of her twelfth and that of her sixteenth year. *Shekem.* This name is hereditary in the family, and had taken hold in the locality before the time of Abraham. The *Hivite* was a descendant of Kenaan. We find this tribe now occupying the district where the Kenaanite was in possession at a former period (xii. 6). 3. *Spake to the heart of the damsel.* After having robbed her of her honor, he promises to recognize her as his wife, provided he can gain the consent of her relatives. *Shekem spake unto his father Hamor.* He is in earnest about this matter. *Jacob held his peace.* He was a stranger in the land, and surrounded by a flourishing tribe, who were evidently unscrupulous in their conduct.

6–17. A conference takes place between the parties. Hamor and Jacob, the parents on both sides, are the principals in the negotiation. 7. The sons of Jacob, being brothers of the injured damsel, are present, according to custom. *Wrought fully in Israel;* a standing phrase from this time forward for any deed that was contrary to the sanctity which ought to characterize God's holy people. Israel is here used to designate the descendants of Israel, the peculiar people. 8–10. Hamor makes his proposal. *Shekem, my son.* These words are a nominative pendent, for which "his soul" is substituted. He proposes a political alliance or amalgamation of the two tribes, to be sealed and actually effected by intermarriage. He offers to make them joint-possessors of the soil, and of the rights of dwelling, trading, and acquiring property.

11, 12. Shekem now speaks with becoming deference and earnestness. He offers any amount of dowry, or bridal presents, and of gift to the mother and brothers of the bride. It must be acknowledged that the father and the son were disposed to make whatever amends they could for the grievous offence that had been committed. 13–17. The sons of Jacob answer with deceit. They are burning with resentment of the wrong that " ought not to have been done," and that cannot now be fully repaired. Yet they are in presence of a superior force, and therefore resort to deceit. *And spake.* This goes along with the previous verb "answered," and is meant to have the same qualification " with deceit." The last clause of the verse then assigns the cause of this deceitful dealing. 14–17. Their speech, for the matter of it, is reasonable. They cannot intermarry with the uncircumcised. Only on condition that every male be circumcised will they consent. On these terms they promise to " become one people " with them. Otherwise they take their daughter, and depart. *Our daughter.* They here speak as a family or race, and therefore call Dinah their daughter, though her brothers are the speakers.

18–24. Hamor and Shekem accept the terms, and forthwith proceed to carry them into effect. It is testified of Shekem, that he delayed not to do the thing, and that he was more honorable than all his house. 20–23. They bring the matter before their fellow-citizens, and urge them to adopt the rite of circumcision, on the ground that the men are peaceable, well-conducted, and they and their cattle and goods would be a valuable addition to the common wealth of their tribe. Hence it appears that the population was still thin, that the neighboring territory was sufficient for a much larger number than its present occupants, and that a tribe found a real benefit in an accession to his numbers. 24. The people were persuaded to comply with the terms proposed. There is nothing said here of the religious import of the rite, or of any diversity of worship that may have existed between the two parties. But it is not improbable that the Shekemites were prepared for mutual toleration, or even for the adoption of the religion of Israel in its external forms, though not perhaps to the exclusion of their own hereditary customs. It is also possible that the formal acknowledgment of the one true God was not yet extinct. Circumcision has been in use among the Egyptians, Colchians (Herod. ii. 104), and other eastern nations; but when and how introduced we are not informed. The present narrative points out one way in which it may have spread from nation to nation.

25–31. Simon and Levi, at the head no doubt of all their father's men, now fall upon the Shekemites, when feverish with the circumcision, and put them to the sword. Simon and Levi were the sons of Leah, and therefore full brothers of Dinah. If Dinah was of the same year as Joseph, they would be respectively seven and six years older than she was. If she was in her thirteenth year, they would therefore be respectively in their twentieth and nineteenth years, and therefore fitted by age and passion for such an enterprise. 27–29. All the sons of Jacob joined in the sacking of the city. They seized all their cattle and goods, and made captives of their wives and little ones. 30. Jacob is greatly distressed by this outrage, which is equally contrary to his policy and his humanity. He sets before his sons, in this expostulation, the danger attendant upon such a proceeding. The *Kenaanite and the Perizzite*, whom Abraham found in the land on his return from Egypt (xiii. 7). *I am a few men*, — men of number that might easily be counted. *I* here denotes the family or tribe with all its dependents. When expanded, therefore, it is, "I and my house." 31. Simon and Levi have their reply. It justifies the retribution which has fallen on the Shekemites for this and all their other crimes. But it does not justify the executioners for taking the law into their own hands, or proceeding by fraud and indiscriminate slaughter. The employment of circumcision, too, which was the sign of the covenant of grace, as a means of deception, was a heinous aggravation of their offence.

LXIII. DEATH OF ISAAC. — Gen. xxxv.

8. דְּבֹרָה Deborah, *bee.* אַלּוֹן בָּכוּת Allon-bakuth, *oak of weeping.*

16. כִּבְרָה *length, stretch.* A certain but unknown distance, a stadium or furlong (Jos.) a hippodrome (Sept.) which was somewhat longer, a mile (Kimchi). אֶפְרַת Ephrath, *fruitful* or *ashy.*

18. בֶּן־אוֹנִי Ben-oni, *son of my pain.* בִּנְיָמִין Binjamin, *son of the right hand.*

19. בֵּית לֶחֶם Beth-lechem, *house of bread.*

21. עֵדֶר 'Eder, *flock, fold.*

XXXV. 1. And God said unto Jacob, Arise, go up to Bethel, and dwell there: and make there an altar to the God

that appeared unto thee when thou fleddest from the face of
Esau thy brother. 2. Then said Jacob unto his house, and to
all that were with him, Put away the strange gods that are
among you, and be clean, and change your garments. 3. And
let us arise and go up to Bethel; and I will there make an
altar to the God who answered me in the day of my distress,
and was with me in the way that I went. 4. And they gave
unto Jacob all the strange gods that were in their hand, and
the rings that were in their ears; and Jacob hid them under
the oak which was by Shekem. 5. And they set out: and the
terror of God was upon the cities that were round about them,
and they did not pursue after the sons of Jacob. 6. And Jacob
went to Luz, which is in the land of Kenaan, that is, Bethel,
he and all the people that were with him. 7. And he built
there an altar, and called the place El-beth-el; because there
God revealed himself unto him, when he fled from the face of
his brother. 8. And Deborah, Rebekah's nurse, died, and was
buried beneath Bethel, under the oak; and the name of it was
called Allon-bakuth. ¶ 30.

9. And God appeared unto Jacob again, when he went out
of Padan-aram, and blessed him. 10. And God said unto
him, Thy name is Jacob: thy name shall not be called any
more Jacob, but Israel shall be thy name. And he called his
name Israel. 11. And God said unto him, I am God Almighty;
be fruitful and multiply; a nation and a congregation of nations shall be of thee, and kings shall come out of thy loins.
12. And the land which I gave Abraham and Isaac, to thee
will I give it; and to thy seed after thee will I give the land.
13. And God went up from him, in the place where he talked
with him. 14. And Jacob set up a pillar in the place where
he talked with him, a pillar of stone: and he poured thereon
a drink offering, and poured thereon oil. 15. And Jacob called
the name of the place where God spake with him, Beth-el.

16. And they set out from Beth-el; and there was yet a
stretch of the land to go into Ephrath; and Rachel travailed

and had hard labor. 17. And it came to pass, when she was in hard labor, that the midwife said unto her, Fear not, for this is also to thee a son. 18. And it came to pass, as her soul was departing when she died, that she called his name Ben-oni; and his father called him Benjamin. 19. And Rachel died, and was buried in the way to Ephrath, which is Beth-lehem. 20. And Jacob set a pillar upon her grave; that is the pillar of Rachel's grave unto this day. 21. And Israel set out and spread his tent beyond the tower of Eder. 22. And it came to pass, when Israel dwelt in the land, that Reuben went and lay with Bilhah his father's concubine: and Israel heard it. ¶ 31.

And the sons of Jacob were twelve. 23. The sons of Leah: Jacob's first-born, Reuben, and Simon and Levi and Judah and Issakar and Zebulun. 24. The sons of Rachel: Joseph and Benjamin. 25. And the sons of Bilhah, Rachel's handmaid: Dan and Naphtali. 26. And the sons of Zilpah, Leah's handmaid: Gad and Asher: these are the sons of Jacob, who were born to him in Padan-aram. 27. And Jacob went unto Isaac his father to Mamre, the city of Arba, which is Hebron, where Abraham and Isaac sojourned. 28. And the days of Isaac were a hundred and eighty years. 29. And Isaac expired, and died, and was gathered unto his peoples, old and full of days: and Esau and Jacob his sons buried him. ¶ 32.

This chapter contains the return of Jacob to his father's house, and then appends the death of Isaac.

1–8. Jacob returns to Bethel. *And God said unto Jacob.* He receives the direction from God. He had now been six years lingering in Sukkoth and Shekem. There may have been some intercourse between him and his father's house during this interval. The presence of Deborah, Rebekah's nurse, in his family, is a plain intimation of this. But Jacob seems to have turned aside to Shekem, either to visit the spot where Abraham first erected an altar to the Lord, or to seek pasture for his numerous flocks. *Arise, go up to Bethel, and dwell there.* In his perplexity and terror the Lord comes to his aid. He reminds him of his former appearance to him at that place, and directs him to erect an altar there. This was Abraham's second resting-place in the land. He who had there appeared to Jacob as the Jehovah, the God of Abraham and Isaac, is now described as El, the Mighty One, probably in allusion to Bethel (house of El), which contains this name, and was at that time applied by Jacob himself to the place. 2, 3. *His house;* his wives and children. *All that were with him;* his men-servants and maid-servants. *The strange gods,* belonging to the stranger or the strange land. These include the teraphim, which Rachel had secreted, and the rings which were worn as amulets or charms. *Be clean;* cleanse the body, in token of the cleaning of your souls. *Change your garments;* put on your best attire, befitting the holy occasion. *The God,* in contradistinction to the strange gods already mentioned. 4. *Hid them;* buried them. *The oak which was by Shekem.* This may have been the oak of Moreh, under which Abraham pitched his tent (xii. 6). 5–7. *The terror of God;* a dread awakened in their breast by some indication of the divine presence being with Jacob. The patriarch seems to have retained possession of the land he had purchased and gained by conquest, in this place. His flocks are found there very shortly after this time (xxxvii. 12), he alludes to it, and disposes of it in his interview with Joseph and his sons (xlviii. 22), and his well is there to this day. *Luz, which is in the land of Kenaan.* This seems at first sight to intimate that there was a Luz elsewhere, and to have been added by the revising prophet to determine the place here intended. Luz means an almond tree, and may have designated many a place. But the reader of Genesis could have needed no such intimation, as Jacob is clearly in the land of Kenaan, going from Shekem to Hebron. It seems rather to call attention again (xxxiii. 18) to the fact that Jacob has returned from Padan-aram to the land of promise. The name Luz still recurs, as the almond tree may still be flourishing. *And he built there an altar, and called the place El-beth-el.* Thus has Jacob obeyed the command of God, and begun the payment of the vow he made twenty-six years before at this place (xxviii. 20–22). *There God revealed himself unto him.* The verb here נִגְלוּ is plural in the Masoretic Hebrew, and so it was in the copy of Onkelos. The Sam. and the Sept. have the singular. The reading is therefore various. The original was probably singular, and may have been so even with its present letters. If not, this is one of the few instances in which Elohim is construed grammatically with a plural verb. 8. Deborah dies in the family in which she began life. She is buried under "the well-known oak" at Bethel. Jacob drops a natural tear of sorrow over the grave of this faithful servant, and hence the oak is called *the oak of weeping.* It is probable that Rebekah was already dead, since otherwise we should not expect to find Deborah transferred to Jacob's household. She may not have lived to see her favorite son on his return.

9–15. God appears to Jacob again at Bethel, and renews the promise made to him there (xxviii. 13, 14). *Again.* The writer here refers to the former meeting of God with Jacob at Bethel, and thereby proves himself cognizant of the fact, and of the record already made of it. *When he went out of Padan-aram.* This corroborates the explanation of the clause, v. 6, "which is in the land of Kenaan." Bethel was the last point in this land that was noticed in his flight from Esau. His arrival at the same point indicates that he has now returned *from Padan-aram* to the land of Kenaan. *He called his name Israel.* At Bethel he renews the change of name, to indicate that the meetings here were of equal moment in Jacob's spiritual life with that at Penuel. It implies also that this life had been declining in the interval between Penuel and Bethel, and had now been revived by the call of God to go to Bethel, and by the interview. The renewal of the naming aptly expresses this renewal of spiritual life. 11, 12. *I am God Almighty.* So he proclaimed himself before to Abraham (xvii. 1). *Be fruitful, and multiply.* Abraham and Isaac had each only one son of promise. But now the time of increase is come. Jacob has been blessed with eleven sons, and at least one daughter. And now he receives the long-promised blessing, "be fruitful and multiply." From this time forth the multiplication of Israel is rapid. In twenty-six years after this time he goes down into Egypt with seventy souls, besides the wives of his married descendants, and two hundred and ten years after that Israel goes out of Egypt numbering about one million eight hundred thousand. *A nation and a congregation of nations,* such as were then known in the world, had at the last date come of him, and "kings" were to follow in due time. The land, as well as the seed, is again promised. 13–15. Jacob now, according to his wont, perpetuates the scene of divine manifestation with a monumental stone. *God went up;* as he went up from Abraham (xvii. 22) after a similar conference with him. He had now spoken to Jacob face to face, as he communed with Abraham. *A pillar* in the place where he talked with him, a consecrated monument of this second interview, not in a dream as before, but in a waking vision. On this he pours a drink-offering of wine, and then anoints it with oil. Here, for the first time, we meet with the libation. It is possible there was such an offering when Melkizedec brought forth bread and wine, though it is not recorded. The drink-offering is the complement of the meat-offering, and both are accompaniments of the sacrifice which is offered on the altar. They are in themselves expressive of gratitude and devotion. Wine and oil are used to denote the quickening and sanctifying power of the Spirit of God. *Bethel.* We are now familiar with the repetition of the naming of persons and places. This place was already called Bethel by Jacob himself; it is most likely that Abraham applied this name to it: and for aught we know, some servant of the true God, under the Noachic covenant, may have originated the name.

16–22a. On the journey, Rachel dies at the birth of her second son. *A stretch.* It was probably a few furlongs. 17. *Fear not.* The cause for encouragement was that the child was born, and that it was a son. Rachel's desire and hope expressed at the birth of Joseph were therefore fulfilled (xxx. 24). 18. *When her soul was departing.* This phrase expresses not annihilation, but merely change of place. It presupposes the perpetual existence of the soul. *Ben-oni*, son of my pain, is the natural expression of the departing Rachel. *Benjamin.* The right hand is the seat of power. The son of the right hand is therefore the child of power. He gave power to his father, as he was his twelfth son, and so completed the number of the holy family. 19, 20. *Ephrath* and *Beth-lehem* are names the origin of which is not recorded. *The pillar of Rachel's grave.* Jacob loves the monumental stone. *Unto this day.* This might have been written ten or twenty years after the event, and therefore before Jacob left Kenaan (see on xix. 37). The grave of Rachel was well known in the time of Samuel (1 Sam. x. 2), and the Kubbet Rahil, dome or tomb of Rachel, stands perhaps on the identical spot, about an English mile north of Bethlehem.

21, 22. *Eder.* The tower of the flock was probably a watch-tower where shepherds guarded their flocks by night. It was a mile (Jerome) or more south of Bethlehem. Here Reuben was guilty of the shameful deed which came to the knowledge of his father, and occasions the allusion in xlix. 4. He was by this act degraded from his position in the holy family. The division of the open parashah in the text here is more in accordance with the sense than that of the verse.

22b–31. Jacob's return and his father's death. The family of Jacob is now enumerated, because it has been completed by the birth of Benjamin. *In Padan-aram.* This applies to all of them but Benjamin; an exception which the reader of the context can make for himself.

27. Jacob at length arrives with his whole establishment at Hebron, the third notable station occupied by Abraham in the land (xiii. 18). Here also his father sojourns. 28, 29. The life of Isaac is now closed. Joseph must have been, at the time of Jacob's return, in his thirteenth year, and therefore his father in his hundred and fourth. Isaac was consequently in his hundred and sixty-third year. He survived the return of Jacob to Hebron about seventeen years, and the sale of Joseph his grandson about thirteen. *Esau and Jacob his sons buried him.* Hence we learn that Esau and Jacob continued to be on brotherly terms from the day of their meeting at the ford of Jabbok.

This chapter closes the ninth of the pieces or documents marked off by the phrase " these are the generations." Its opening event was the birth of Isaac (xxv. 19), which took place in the hundreth year of Abraham, and therefore seventy-five years before his death recorded in the seventh document. As the seventh purports to be the generations of Terah (xi. 27) and relates to Abraham who was his offspring, so the present document, containing the generations of Isaac, refers chiefly to the sons of Isaac, and especially to Jacob, as the heir of promise. Isaac as a son learned obedience to his father in that great typical event of his life, in which he was laid on the altar, and figuratively sacrificed in the ram which was his substitute. This was the great significant passage in his life, after which he retires into comparative tranquillity.

SECTION XII — JACOB

LXIV. HISTORY OF ESAU. — Gen. xxxvi.

2. אָהֳלִיבָמָה Oholibamah, *tent of the high place.* עֲנָה ʿAnah, *answering.* צִבְעוֹן Tsibʿon, *dyer, colored.*

4. אֱלִיפַז Eliphaz, *God of strength.* רְעוּאֵל Reʿuel, *friend of God.*

5. יְעוּשׁ Jeʿush, *haste.* יַעְלָם Jaʿlam, *hiding.* קֹרַח Qorach, *ice.*

11. תֵּימָן Teman, *right-hand man.* אוֹמָר Omar, *eloquent.* צְפוֹ Tsepho, *watch.* גַּעְתָּם Gaʿtam, *touch.* קְנַז Qenaz, *hunting.*

12. תִּמְנַע Timnaʿ, *restraint.* עֲמָלֵק ʿAmaleq, *licking up, laboring.*

13. נַחַת Nachath, *going down, rest.* זֶרַח Zerach, *rising* (of light). שַׁמָּה Shammah, *wasting.* מִזָּה Mizzah, *fear, sprinkling.*

20. לוֹטָן Lotan, *covering, veiled.* שׁוֹבָל Shobal, *flowing, a shoot.*

21. דִּשׁוֹן Dishon, *a kind of gazelle, fat.* אֵצֶר Etser, *store.* דִּישָׁן Dishan, *threshing.*

22. חֹרִי Chori, *troglodyte.* הֵימָם Hemam, *noise, commotion.*

23. עַלְוָן ʿAlvan, *lofty.* מָנַחַת Manachath, *rest.* עֵיבָל ʿEbal, *stripped of leaves.* שְׁפוֹ Shepho, *bare.* אוֹנָם Onam, *strong.*

24. אַיָּה Ajjah, *cry, hawk.* יֵמִם *hot springs.* Not mules (פְּרָדִים) nor giants (אֵימִים).

26. חֶמְדָּן Chemdan, *pleasant.* אֶשְׁבָּן Eshban, *thought?* יִתְרָן Jithran, *gain.* כְּרָן Keran, *harp?*

27 בִּלְהָן Bilhan, *timid.* זַעֲוָן Zaʿavan, *troubled?* עֲקָן ʿAqan, *twisting.*

28. אֲרָן Aran, *wild-goat?*

32. בֶּלַע Belaʿ *devouring.* בְּעוֹר Beʿor, *torch.* דִּנְהָבָה Dinhabah.

33. יוֹבָב Jobab, *shout.* בָּצְרָה Botsrah, *fold, fort.*

34. חֻשָׁם Chusham, *haste.*

35. הֲדַד Hadad, *breaking, shout.* בְּדַד Bedad, *separation.* עֲוִית Avith, *twisting.*

36. שַׂמְלָה Samlah, *garment.* מַשְׂרֵקָה Maśreqah, *vineyard.*

37. שָׁאוּל Shaul, *asked.*

38. בַּעַל חָנָן Baal-chanan, *lord of grace.* עַכְבּוֹר ʿAkbor, *mouse.*

39. הֲדַר Hadar, *honor.* פָּעוּ Pa'u, *bleeting.* מְהֵיטַבְאֵל Mehetab'el, *God benefiting.* מַטְרֵד Matred, *push.* מֵי זָהָב Me-zahab, *water of gold.*

40. יְתֵת Jetheth, *a nail?*

41. אֵלָה Elah, *terebinth.* פִּינֹן Pinon, *dark?*

42. מִבְצָר Mibtsar, *fortress.*

43. מַגְדִּיאֵל Magdiel, *prince of God.* עִירָם 'Iram, *civic* or *naked.*

XXXVI. 1. And these are the generations of Esau, who is Edom. 2. Esau took his wives of the daughters of Kenaan: Adah, daughter of Elon the Hittite; and Oholibamah, daughter of Anah, daughter of Zibon the Hivite; 3. And Basemath, Ishmael's daughter, sister of Nebaioth. 4. And Adah bare to Esau Eliphaz: and Basemath bare Reuel. 5. And Oholibamah bare Jeush and Jalam and Corah. These are the sons of Esau, who were born unto him in the land of Kenaan. 6. And Esau took his wives and his sons and his daughters, and all the souls of his house, and his cattle and all his beasts, and all his property which he had gained in the land of Kenaan, and went unto a land apart from Jacob his brother. 7 For their gaining was more than that they might dwell together; and the land of their sojournings could not bear them on account of their cattle. 8. Then dwelt Esau in mount Seir. Esau is Edom.

9. And these are the generations of Esau, father of Edom, in mount Seir. 10. These are the names of Esau's sons: Eliphaz, son of Adah, wife of Esau; Reuel, son of Basemath, wife of Esau. 11. And the sons of Eliphaz were Teman, Omar, Zepho, and Gatam and Kenaz. 12. And Timna was concubine to Eliphaz, Esau's son: and she bare to Eliphaz Amalek: these were the sons of Adah, Esau's wife. 13. And these are the sons of Reuel: Nahath and Zerah, Shammah and Mizzah: these were the sons of Basemath, Esau's wife. 14. And these are the sons of Oholibamah, daughter of Anah, daughter of Zibon, Esau's wife; and she bare to Esau, Jeush and Jalam and Corah.

15. These were dukes of the sons of Esau; the sons of Eliphaz, first-born of Esau, duke Teman, duke Omar, duke Zepho, duke Kenaz, 16. Duke Corah, duke Gatam, duke Amalek; these were dukes of Eliphaz in the land of Edom: these are the sons of Adah. 17. And these are the sons of Reuel, Esau's son: duke Nahath, duke Zerah, duke Shammah, duke Mizzah; these were dukes of Reuel in the land of Edom: these are the sons of Basemath, Esau's wife. 18. And these are the sons of Oholibamah, Esau's wife: duke Jeush, duke Jalam, duke Corah: these were dukes of Oholibamah, daughter of Anah, Esau's wife. 19. These are the sons of Esau, who is Edom; and these their dukes. § 39.

20. These are the sons of Seir the Horite, who dwelt in the land: Lotan and Shobal and Zibon and Anah, 21. And Dishon and Ezer and Dishan: these are dukes of the Horite, sons of Seir in the land of Edom. 22. And the sons of Lotan were Hori and Hemam: and Lotan's sister was Timna. 23. And these are the sons of Shobal: Alvan and Manahath and Ebal, Shepho and Onam. 24. And these are the sons of Zibon, both Ajah and Anah: this is Anah who found the hot springs in the wilderness, as he fed the asses of Zibon his father. 25. And these are the sons of Anah, Dishon: and Oholibamah was the daughter of Anah. 26. And these are the sons of Dishon: Hemdan and Eshban and Ithran and Keran. 27. And these are the sons of Ezer: Bilhan and Zaavan and Acan. 28. These are the sons of Dishan: Uz and Aran. 29. These were dukes of the Horite: duke Lotan, duke Shobal, duke Zibon, duke Anah. 30. Duke Dishon, duke Ezer, duke Dishan: these were dukes of the Horite, according to their dukes, in the land of Seir. ¶ 33.

31. And these are the kings that reigned in the land of Edom, before a king reigned over the children of Israel. 32. And Bela, son of Beor, reigned in Edom: and the name of his city was Dinhabah. 33. And Bela died, and in his stead reigned Jobab, son of Zerah of Bozrah. 34. And Jobab died,

and in his stead reigned Husham, of the land of the Temanite. 35. And Husham died, and in his stead reigned Hadad, son of Bedad, who smote Midian in the field of Moab; and the name of his city was Avith. 36. And Hadad died, and in his stead reigned Samlah of Masrecah. 37. And Samlah died, and in his stead reigned Saul of Rehoboth by the river. 38. And Saul died, and in his stead reigned Baal-hanan, son of Akbor. 39. And Baal-hanan, son of Akbor, died, and in his stead reigned Hadar, and the name of his city was Pau; and his wife's name Mehetabel, daughter of Matred, daughter of Mezahab.

40. And these are the names of the dukes of Esau after their families, after their places, by their names: duke Timna, duke Alvah, duke Jetheth, 41. Duke Oholibamah, duke Elah, duke Pinon, 42. Duke Kenaz, duke Teman, duke Mibzah, 43. Duke Magdiel, duke Iram: these are the dukes of Edom, according to their habitations, in the land of their possessions: this is Esau, father of Edom. 9 ¶¶ 34.

The two documents that now remain run parallel to one another in point of time. They relate to the two sons of Isaac; and, as usual, the record of the one, who, though first born, falls into the ranks of heathenism, is first given briefly, and thus dismissed, in order to make way for the more elaborate history of the chosen seed. The latter document does not terminate with the book of Genesis. We do not again meet with the phrase, "and these are the generations," until we come to the third chapter of Numbers, and even then it is only applied in a subordinate sense to the family of Aaron and Moses, and the priesthood connected with them. Hence the latter document may be regarded as extending through the remaining books of the Pentateuch. The former may therefore be of like extent in regard to time. The last of the eight kings, of whom it is not said that he died, seems to have been the contemporary of Moses, who made application to him for leave to pass through his land. If this be so, it follows that the remainder of Genesis comes immediately from the hand of Moses; a result which is in accordance with other indications that have presented themselves in the previous part of this book. This interesting monument of antiquity, from its extreme brevity, leaves many questions which it suggests to our minds unanswered, and in the absence of all other information, we must rest contented with the meagre notices of the race of Edom which it has furnished. And where we cannot ascertain the actual connection of the events and individuals mentioned, we must be satisfied with any possible relation in which they may be placed. The notice, notwithstanding its brevity, we shall find to be arranged with admirable precision.

1–8. This passage is introductory, and records the settlement of Esau with his family in Mount Seir. 1. *Esau, who is Edom.* This is a fact of which we were informed in the previous history (xxv. 25, 30). It is mentioned here because the latter name gave origin to the national designation; namely, the Edomites or Idumæans. The occurrence of this explanatory or definitive clause here and in other parts of this chapter throws light on the manner in which this work was composed. Such parenthetical explanations are sometimes ascribed to the reviser or redactor of the original text. And to this there is no theoretic objection, provided the reviser be allowed to be of equal authority with the original author, and the explanatory addition be necessary for the reader of a later period, and could not have been furnished by the original author. Otherwise, such a mode of accounting for these simple clauses is unnecessary, and therefore unwarrantable. The present case the writer has already explained, and the latest reader requires the clause no more than the earliest, as he is aware from the previous notices that Esau is Edom. We are thus led to regard these explanatory clauses as marks of an early or artless simplicity of style, and not as any clear or certain traces of revision.

2–5. *Esau took his wives.* From the word *his* we conclude that this sentence does not refer to his marrying these wives, but to his taking them with him when he removed from Kenaan. Hence the sentence, after being interrupted by the intervening particulars, is resumed and completed in the sixth verse. The date of this event is therefore some time after Jacob's flight to Padan-aram, and before his return. The daughter of Ishmael he only married after Jacob's departure, and by her he had one son who was born in Kenaan. We may therefore suppose that, about eighteen years after Jacob's flight, Isaac had assigned to Esau a sufficient stock of cattle and goods for a separate establishment, the extent of Esau's portion and of that which Isaac had reserved for Jacob had become so great as to demand pasture grounds widely removed from one another, and Esau's former habits and his last matrimonial alliances had drawn him towards Mount Seir. He married his first wives when he was forty years of age (xxvi. 34), and as Jacob was seventy-seven when he left his home, at eighteen years after that date, Esau had been fifty-five years married to his first two wives, and somewhat less than eighteen to Ishmael's daughter.

Of the daughters of Kenaan. This refers to the two following wives mentioned in this verse, and distinguishes them from the third, mentioned in the following verse, who is of the family of Ishmael. *Adah, daughter of Elon the Hittite.* On comparing the account of his two wives whom he married at forty with the present, the first, namely, Judith, daughter of Beeri the Hittite, no longer appears either by her own name, that of her father, or that of her tribe. Hence we presume that in the course of the past forty-seven years she has died without male issue. This presumption is favored by the circumstance that the daughter of Elon the Hittite is now advanced into the first place. If it seems to any one undesirable to make any presumption of this kind, we have only to say that in the absence of the connecting links in a historical statement like this, we must make some supposition to show the possibility of the events related. The presumption we have made seems easier and therefore more likely than that the names of the individual, the father and the tribe, should be all different, and the order of the two wives reversed, and yet that the same person should be intended; and hence we have adopted it as a possible arrangement, leaving to others the preference of any other possibility that may be suggested. For after all it should be remembered that testimony only could determine what were the actual circumstances. She who was formerly called Basemath appears here with the name of Adah. At a time when proper names were still significant, the application of more than one name to the same individual was not unusual.

Oholibamah, daughter of Anah, daughter of Zibon the Hivite. This may have been the fourth wife of Esau in the order of time, though she is here classed with the daughter of Elon, because she was of the daughters of Kenaan. "Daughter of Zibon" means his granddaughter, by the mother's side. *The Hivite* (x. 17). Zibon is thus distinguished from the Horite of the same name (v. 20). The Hivite race we have already met with at Shekem (xxxiv. 2). They also held four cities a short way north of Jerusalem, of which Gihon was the chief (Jos. ix. 3, 7, 17). It was easy, therefore, for Anah the Horite to marry the daughter of Zibon the Hivite. *Basemath,* previously called Mahalath.

4, 5. Five sons were born to Esau in Kenaan, of whom Adah and Basemath bare each one. As Oholibamah bare him three sons before leaving Kenaan, she must have been married to him four or five years before that event, perhaps on the death of his first wife, and in consequence of his connection with the south.

6–8. The sentence that was left incomplete in v. 2 is now resumed and completed. His departure from Kenaan is ascribed to the abounding wealth of himself and his brother. What remained in the hands of Isaac was virtually Jacob's, though he had not yet entered into formal possession of it. Mount Seir is the range of hills extending from the Elanitic Gulf to the Salt Sea; the northern part of which is called Jebal (Γεβαλήνη), and the southern part esh-Sherah, and parallel to which on the west lies Wady Arabah. In this range is situated the celebrated rock city, Sela or Petra, adjacent to Mount Hor.

9–14. After the removal to Mount Seir the race of Esau is traced further. It is remarkable that the phrase, "And these are the generations of Esau," is now repeated. This is sufficient to show us that it does not necessarily indicate diversity of authorship, or is a very distinct piece of composition. Here it merely distinguishes the history of Esau's descent in Mount Seir from that in Kenaan. *Father of Edom.* Edom here denotes the nation sprung from him. Eliphaz has five sons by his wife, and by a concubine a sixth, named Amalek, most probably the father of the Amalekites (xiv. 7). *Timna* was probably a very young sister of Lotan (v. 22), perhaps not older than her niece Oholibamah (v. 25). Eliphaz was at least forty-one years younger than Esau. Yet it is curious that the father takes the niece to wife, and the son the aunt. *Teman* is the father of the Temanites, among whom we find Eliphaz the Temanite mentioned in Job (ii. 11). The name Kenaz may indicate some affinity of Edom with the Kenizzites (xv. 19), though these were an older tribe. The other tribes are not of any note in history. Zepho is Zephi in Chronicles, by the change of a feeble letter. Such variations are not unusual in Hebrew speech, and so make their appearance in writing. Thus in Genesis itself we have met with Mehujael and Mehijael, Peniel and Penuel (iv. 18, xxxii. 30, 31). The sons of Esau by Oholibamah are younger than the other two, and hence these sons are not enumerated along with those of the latter.

15–19. The first dukes of Edom. The Alluph or duke is the head of the tribe among the Edomites, like the Nasi or prince among the Israelites. The ten grandsons of Esau by Adah and Basemath take rank with his three sons by Oholibamah. This favors the presumption that she was his fourth and latest wife. 16. *Duke Corah.* This appears to be inserted by a slip of the pen, though it occurs in the Sept. and Onk. It is wanting, however, in the Sam. It would make twelve dukes, whereas it appears from the closing verses of the chapter that there were only eleven. It is possible, however, that there may have been a Corah descended from Eliphaz who attained to a dukedom; and that Amalek separated himself from the rest of the Edomites and asserted his independence. In the absence of explanatory testimony we must leave this point undecided as we find it.

20–30. This notice of the Horites is in matter more distinct from that which precedes, than the second is from the first paragraph in the chapter. *Seir the Horite.* The Horite (xiv. 6,) was the cave-dweller, and probably got his name from the cave hewn out of the solid rock in which he was wont to dwell. Sela was a city of such excavated dwellings. If Seir here mentioned be the original Seir, then he is the remote father of the seven Horite dukes who belonged to the time of Esau. If he be their immediate parent, then he is named after that earlier Seir who gave name to the mountain range. *Who dwelt in the land.* The sons of Seir dwelt in this land before the coming of the Edomites. 22–28. Here follow the descendants of the then living dukes of the Horim. *Hori,* Lotan's son, bears the name of the nation. *Hemam,* in Chronicles Homam, by a change of letter. *Timna,* the concubine of Eliphaz (v. 12). *Alvan* and *Shepho,* in Chronicles Aljan and Shephi, by a reverse change of the same letters (see v. 11). *Zibon.* This we suppose to be different from Zibon the Hivite (v. 2, 14). *Anah* is of course different from his uncle Anah the brother of Zibon the Horite. *The hot springs in the wilderness.* There were various hot springs in the vicinity, as Kallirrhoe in Wady Zurka Main, those in Wady Hemad between Kerak and the Salt Sea, and those in Wady el-Ahsy. 25. *Sons of Anah.* The plural, sons, here is used according to the general formula, though only one son is mentioned. Oholibamah, being the daughter of Anah, and wife of Esau, while Eliphaz is married to her aunt Timna, is not likely to be the granddaughter by the mother's side of her uncle Zibon. This is in favor of Zibon the Hivite and Zibon the Horite being different individuals (v. 2). *Anah* is here the brother of Zibon. The nephew Anah (v. 24), bears the name of his uncle (v. 20). *Dishon* is an example of the same community of name (v. 21). 26, 27. All Dishon's and Ezer's sons have names ending in *an*. *Acan* יַעֲקָן (Jaacan) in 1 Chron. i. 41 is a graphic error for וַעֲקָן (and Acan). 28. *Uz;* see x. 23, xxii. 21. In

v. 29, 30, the dukes are formally enumerated. *According to their dukes;* the seven officials of preëminent authority among the Horites. The official is here distinguished from the personal. This is a distinction familiar to Scripture.

31–39. The series of eight kings here enumerated are plainly elective, as not one succeeds his father. The king coexists with the dukes, who are again enumerated at the close of the list, and are mentioned in the song of Moses (Ex. xv. 15). These dukes are no doubt the electors of the common sovereign, who is designed to give unity and strength to the nation. It is natural to suppose that no sovereign was elected till after the death of Esau, and, therefore, if he lived as long as Jacob, after the children of Israel had been seventeen years in Egypt. As we calculate that they were two hundred and ten years in that country, and forty years afterwards in the wilderness, this would allow two hundred and thirty-three (250—17) years for seven reigns, and a part of the eighth, during which Moses and his host marched along the borders of Edom. Allowing some interval before the first election, we have an average of thirty-three years for each reign. 31. *Before a king reigned over the children of Israel.* This simply means before there was a monarchy established in Israel. It does not imply that monarchy began in Israel immediately after these kings; as Lot's beholding the vale of Jordan to be well-watered *before* the Lord destroyed Sodom and Amorah, does not imply that the cities were destroyed immediately after Lot beheld this sight (xiii. 10). Nor does it imply that monarchy in Israel had begun in the time of the writer; as Isaac's saying, "That my soul may bless thee before I die" (xxvii. 4) does not imply that he was dead at the time of his saying so. It merely implies that Israel was expected to have kings (xxxv. 11), as Isaac was expected to die. 32. Of the several sovereigns here mentioned we have no other historical notice. *Beor* is also the name of Balaam's father (Num. xxii. 5). This indicates affinity of language between their respective tribes. The site of *Dinhabah*, the capital of Bela, though the name is applied to many towns, has not been ascertained. 33. *Bozrah* is el-Busaireh, about twenty-one miles nearly south of the Salt Sea. 34. *The land of the Temanite* has its name from Teman, son of Eliphaz. His town was, according to Jerome, five miles from Petra. 35. *Hadad* is a name of frequent recurrence among the Aramaeans. *Who smote Midian in the field of Moab.* This records an event not otherwise known, and indicates external conquest on the part of the Idumæan state. *Avith* or Ajuth (1 Chron. i. 46, probably a graphic error) is not otherwise known. 36. *Masrecah* is likewise unknown. 37. *Rehoboth by the river.* If the river be the Phrat (Onk.), Rehoboth may be er-Rahabah, not far from the mouth of the Khabur. Otherwise it may be er-Ruhaibeh on a wady joining the Sihor or el-Arish (xxvi. 22), or the Robotha of Eusebius and Jerome, the site of which is not known. 39. *Hadar* is probably a colloquial variation of Hadad (v. 35) which is found in Chron. Pau or Pai is unknown. Matred is the father of his wife. Mezahab her mother's father. The death of all these sovereigns is recorded except the last, who is therefore supposed to have been contemporary with Moses.

40–43. The hereditary dukes who were contemporaneous with this sovereign, and formed no doubt his council, are now enumerated. Timna, once the name of a female, now appears as a male, unless we allow a duchess in her own right to have occurred among them. The same applies to Oholibamah. Alva or Aljah is near akin to Alvan or Alian (v. 23). Jetheth, Elah, Pinon, Mibzar, Magdiel, Iram, are new names. Four of the old names reappear. One is only slightly different. The number of dukes is eleven. It is probable that Amalek separated from the family confederacy; and the number of tribes may have been originally twelve. The seven Horite dukedoms probably merged into the Idumæan eleven.

LXV. JOSEPH SOLD INTO EGYPT. — Gen. xxxvii.

17. דֹּתַיִן Dothain, *two wells?* (Ges.)

25. נְכֹאת *tragacanth* or goat's-thorn gum, yielded by the *astragalus gummifer*, a native of Mount Lebanon. צֳרִי. *opobalsamum*, the resin of the balsam tree, growing in Gilead, and having healing qualities. לֹט λῆδον, *ledum*, *ladanum*, in the Septuagint *στακτή*. The former is a gum produced from the cistus rose. The latter is a gum resembling liquid myrrh.

36. פּוֹטִיפַר Potiphar, *belonging to the sun.*

XXXVII. 1. And Jacob dwelt in the land of his father's sojournings, in the land of Kenaan. 2. These are the generations of Jacob. Joseph, the son of seventeen years, was with his brethren feeding the flock, and he a lad with the sons of

Bilhah, and with the sons of Zilpah, his father's wives; and Joseph brought an evil report of them unto their father. 3. And Israel loved Joseph above all his sons, because he was the son of his old age: and he made him a coat of many colors. 4. And his brethren saw that their father loved him above all his brethren, and they hated him, and could not bid peace to him.

5. And Joseph dreamed a dream and told his brethren: and they hated him yet the more. 6. And he said unto them, Hear now this dream which I have dreamed. 7. And, behold, we were binding sheaves in the field, and- lo, my sheaf arose, and also stood upright; and, lo, your sheaves stood around, and bowed down to my sheaf. 8. And his brethren said unto him, Shalt thou reign indeed over us? Shalt thou have the rule over us? And they hated him yet the more for his dreams and for his words. 9. And he dreamed yet another dream, and told it his brethren, and said, Behold, I have dreamed a dream more; and lo, the sun and the moon and eleven stars bowed down to me. 10. And he told his father and his brethren: and his father rebuked him, and said unto him, What is this dream thou hast dreamed? Shall I and thy mother and thy brethren come indeed to bow down to thee to the earth? 11. And his brethren envied him, and his father observed the saying.

12. And his brethren went to feed their father's flock in Shekem. 13. And Israel said unto Joseph, Are not thy brethren herding in Shekem? Come, and I will send thee unto them. And he said to him, Here am I. 14. And he said to him, Go, now, see that it is well with thy brethren and well with the flock; and bring me back word. And he sent him out of the dale of Hebron, and he went to Shekem. 15. And a man found him, and, lo, he was wandering in the field: and the man asked him saying, What seekest thou? 16. And he said, My brethren seek I: tell me now where they are herding. 17. And the man said, They have set out hence; for I

heard them say, Let us go to Dothan. And Joseph went after
his brethren, and found them in Dothan.

18. And they saw him afar off: and before he came near
unto them, they plotted against him to kill him. 19. And
they said one to another, Behold, this master of dreams cometh,
20. And now come, and let us slay him and cast him into one
of the pits, and we will say, An evil beast hath devoured him;
and we shall see what will become of his dreams 21. And
Reuben heard, and delivered him out of their hand: and he
said, Let us not strike at his life. 22. And Reuben said unto
them, Shed not blood; cast him into this pit that is in the
wilderness, and lay no hand on him: that he might deliver
him out of their hand, to restore him to his father. 23. And
it came to pass when Joseph was come to his brethren, that
they stripped Joseph of his coat, the coat of many colors, that
was on him. 24. And they took him, and cast him into the
pit; and the pit was empty: there was no water in it.

25. And they sat down to eat bread; and they lifted up
their eyes, and looked, and, behold, a caravan of Ishmaelites
came from Gilead, and their camels bare spicery and balm and
myrrh, going to carry down into Mizraim. 26. And Judah
said unto his brethren, What profit that we slay our brother
and cover his blood? 27. Come, and let us sell him to the
Ishmaelites, and let not our hand be upon him; for our brother
is our flesh. And his brethren hearkened. 28. And there
passed by Midianite merchants, and they drew and lifted up
Joseph out of the pit, and sold Joseph to the Ishmaelites for
twenty silver pieces: and they brought Joseph to Mizraim.
29. And Reuben returned unto the pit; and, behold, Joseph
was not in the pit; and he rent his clothes. 30. And he re-
turned to his brethren and said, The lad is not, and I, whither
shall I go?

31. And they took Joseph's coat, and killed a kid of the
goats, and dipped the coat in the blood. 32. And they rent
the coat of many colors, and carried it to their father, and

said, This we have found: know now whether it be thy son's coat or not. 33. And he knew it, and said, It is my son's coat; an evil beast hath devoured him: torn, torn in pieces is Joseph. 34. And Jacob rent his garments, and put sackcloth on his loins, and mourned for his son many days. 35. Then arose all his sons and all his daughters to comfort him; and he refused to be comforted, and said, For I will go down to my son mourning to the grave. And his father wept for him. 36. And the Midianites sold him into Mizraim unto Potiphar, an officer of Pharoh, captain of the guards. ¶ 35.

The sketch of the race of Edom, given in the preceding piece, we have seen, reaches down to the time of Moses. Accordingly, the history of Jacob's seed, which is brought before us in the present document, reverts to a point of time not only before the close of that piece, but before the final record of that which precedes it. The thread of the narrative is here taken up from the return of Jacob to Hebrōn, which was seventeen years before the death of Isaac.

1–5. Joseph is the favorite of his father, but not of his brethren. *In the land of his father's sojournings.* This contrasts Jacob with Esau, who removed to Mount Seir. This notice precedes the phrase, "These are the generations." The corresponding sentence in the case of Isaac is placed at the end of the preceding section of the narrative (xxv. 11). *The son of seventeen years;* in his seventeenth year (v. 32). *The sons of Bilhah.* The sons of the handmaids were nearer his own age, and perhaps more tolerant of the favorite than the sons of Leah the free wife. Benjamin at this time was about four years of age. *An evil report of them.* The unsophisticated child of home is prompt in the disapproval of evil, and frank in the avowal of his feelings. What the evil was we are not informed; but Jacob's full-grown sons were now far from the paternal eye, and prone, as it seems, to give way to temptation. Many scandals come out to view in the chosen family. *Loved Joseph.* He was the son of his best-loved wife, and of his old age; as Benjamin had not yet come into much notice. *A coat of many colors.* This was a coat reaching to the hands and feet, worn by persons not much occupied with manual labor, according to the general opinion. It was, we conceive, variegated either by the loom or the needle, and is therefore well rendered χιτὼν ποικίλος, a motley coat. *Could not bid peace to him.* The partiality of his father, exhibited in so weak a manner, provokes the anger of his brothers, who cannot bid him good-day, or greet him in the ordinary terms of good-will.

5–11. Joseph's dreams excite the jealousy of his brothers. 5–8. His frankness in reciting his dream to his brothers marks a spirit devoid of guile, and only dimly conscious of the import of his nightly visions. The first dream represents by a figure the humble submission of all his brothers to him, as they rightly interpret it. *For his dreams and for his words.* The meaning of this dream was offensive enough, and his telling of it rendered it even more disagreeable. 9–11. A second dream is given to express the certainty of the event (xli. 32). The former serves to interpret the latter. There the sheaves are connected with the brothers who bound them, and thereby indicate the parties. The eleven stars are not so connected with them. But here Joseph is introduced directly without a figure, and the number eleven, taken along with the eleven sheaves of the former dream, makes the application to the brothers plain. The sun and moon clearly point out the father and mother. The mother is to be taken, we conceive, in the abstract, without nicely inquiring whether it means the departed Rachel, or the probably still living Leah. Not even the latter seems to have lived to see the fulfilment of this prophetic dream (xlix. 31). The second dream only aggravated the hatred of his brothers; but his father, while rebuking him for his speeches, yet marked the saying. The rebuke seems to imply that the dream, or the telling of it, appears to his father to indicate the lurking of a self-sufficient or ambitious spirit within the breast of the youthful Joseph. The twofold intimation, however, came from a higher source.

12–17. Joseph is sent to Dothan. Shekem belonged to Jacob; part of it by purchase, and the rest by conquest. Joseph is sent to inquire of their welfare (שָׁלוֹם *peace,* v. 4). With obedient promptness the youth goes to Shekem, where he learns that they had removed to Dothan, a town about twelve miles due north of Shekem.

18–24. His brothers cast him into a pit. *This master of dreams;* an eastern phrase for a dreamer. *Let us slay him.* They had a foreboding that his dreams might prove true, and that he would become their arbitrary master. This thought at all events would abate somewhat of the barbarity of their designs. It is implied in the closing sentence of their proposal. Reuben dissuades them from the act of murder, and advises merely to cast him into the pit, to which they consent. He had a more tender heart, and perhaps a more tender conscience than the rest, and intended to send Joseph back safe to his father. He doubtless took care to choose a pit that was without water.

25–30. Reuben rends his clothes when he finds Joseph gone. *To eat bread.* This shows the cold and heartless cruelty of their deed. *A caravan,*—a company of travelling merchants. *Ishmaelites.* Ishmael left his father's house when about fourteen or fifteen years of age. His mother took him a wife probably when he was eighteen, or twenty at the furthest. He had arrived at the latter age about one hundred and sixty-two years before the date of the present occurrence. He had twelve sons (xxv. 13–15), and if we allow only four other generations and a fivefold increase, there will be about fifteen thousand in the fifth generation. *Came from Gilead;* celebrated for its balm (Jer. viii. 22, xlvi. 11). The caravan road from Damascus to Egypt touches upon the land of Gilead, goes through Beth-shean, and passes by Dothan. *Spicery.* This gum is called tragacanth, or goats-thorn gum, because it was supposed to be obtained from this plant. *Balm,* or balsam; an aromatic substance obtained from a plant of the genus Amyris, a native of Gilead. *Myrrh* is the name of a gum exuding from the balsamodendron myrrha, growing in Arabia Felix. *Lot,* however, is supposed to be the resinous juice of the cistus or rock rose, a plant growing in Crete and Syria. Judah, relenting, and revolting perhaps from the crime of fratricide, proposes to sell Joseph to the merchants. *Midianites* and *Medanites* (v. 36) are mere variations apparently of the same name. They seem to have been the actual purchasers, though the caravan takes its name from the Ishmaelites, who formed by far the larger portion of it. Midian and Medan were both sons of Abraham, and during one hundred and twenty-five years must have increased to a small clan. Thus Joseph is sold to the descendants of Abraham. *Twenty silver pieces;* probably shekels. This is the rate at which Moses estimates a male from five to twenty years old (Lev. xxvii. 5). A man-servant was valued by him at thirty shekels (Ex. xxi. 32). Reuben finding Joseph gone, rends his clothes, in token of anguish of mind for the loss of his brother and the grief of his father.

31–36. The brothers contrive to conceal their crime; and Joseph is sold into Egypt. *Torn, torn in pieces is Joseph.* The sight of the bloody coat convinces Jacob at once that Joseph has been devoured by a wild beast. *All his daughters.* Only one daughter of Jacob is mentioned by name. These are probably his daughters-in-law. *To the grave.* Sheol is the place to which the soul departs at death. It is so called from its ever craving, or being empty. *Minister.* This word originally means *eunuch*, and then, generally, any officer about the court or person of the sovereign. *Captain of the guards.* The guards are the executioners of the sentences passed by the sovereign on culprits, which were often arbitrary, summary, and extremely severe. It is manifest, from this dark chapter, that the power of sin has not been extinguished in the family of Jacob. The name of God does not appear, and his hand is at present only dimly seen among the wicked designs, deeds, and devices of these unnatural brothers. Nevertheless, his counsel of mercy standeth sure, and fixed is his purpose to bring salvation to the whole race of man, by means of his special covenant with Abraham.

LXVI. THE FAMILY OF JUDAH. — Gen. xxxviii.

1. עֲדֻלָּם ʿAdullam, *righteousness.* חִירָה Chirah, *nobility?*
2. שׁוּעַ Shuaʿ, *luck, riches, cry.*
3. עֵר ʿEr, *watching.*
4. אוֹנָן Onan, *strong.*
5. שֵׁלָה Shelah, *request? rest.* כְּזִיב Kezib, *falsehood.*
6. תָּמָר Tamar, *palm.*
12. תִּמְנָה Timnah, *counted* or *assigned.*
14. עֵינַיִם ʿEnaim, *two fountains.*
29. פֶּרֶץ Perets, *breach.*

XXXVIII. 1. And it came to pass at that time, that Judah
went down from his brethren, and turned in to a certain Adul-
lamite, whose name was Hirah. 2. And Judah saw there a
daughter of a certain Kenaanite, whose name was Shua; and
he took her and went in unto her. 3. And she conceived and
bare a son; and he called his name Er. 4. And she conceived
again and bare a son; and she called his name Onan. 5. And
she added again and bare a son, and called his name Shelah:
and it was at Kezib that she bare him. 6. And Judah took
a wife for Er his first-born, whose name was Tamar. 7. And
Er, Judah's first-born, was evil in the sight of the Lord; and
the Lord killed him. 8. And Judah said unto Onan, Go in

unto thy brother's wife, and be a husband to her, and raise up seed to thy brother. 9. And Onan knew that the seed should not be his; and it came to pass, if he went in unto his brother's wife, that he spilt it on the ground, lest he should give seed to his brother. 10. And that which he did was evil in the eyes of the Lord, and he killed him also. 11. And Judah said to Tamar, his daughter-in-law, Dwell a widow in thy father's house, till Shelah my son be grown. For he said, Lest he also die, as his brethren. And Tamar went and dwelt in her father's house.

12. And many were the days, and Shua's daughter, wife of Tudah, died; and Judah was comforted, and went up unto his sheep-shearers, he and Hirah his friend the Adullamite, to Timnah. 13. And it was told Tamar, saying, Behold thy father-in-law goeth up to Timnah to shear his sheep. 14. And she put the garments of her widowhood off her, and put on a veil, and wrapped herself up, and sat at the gate of Enaim, which is on the way to Timnah: for she saw that Shelah was grown, and she was not given to him to wife. 15. And Judah saw her, and thought her to be a harlot, because she had covered her face. 16. And he turned unto her by the way, and said, Pray now, let me come in unto thee. For he knew not that she was his daughter-in-law: And she said, What wilt thou give me, that thou mayst come in unto me? 17. And he said, I will send thee a kid from the flock. And she said, if thou wilt give me a pledge, till thou send it. 18. And he said, What pledge shall I give thee? And she said, Thy signet, and thy lace, and thy staff that is in thy hand. And he gave her them, and went in unto her, and she conceived by him. 19. And she arose, and went, and took her veil off her, and put on the garments of her widowhood. 20. And Judah sent the kid by the hand of his friend the Adullamite, to receive the pledge from the woman's hand; and he found her not. 21. And he asked the men of her place, saying, Where is the courtesan that was in Enaim by the way? And they

said, There was no courtesan here. 22. And he returned to Judah, and said, I found her not; and also the men of her place said, There was no courtesan here. 23. And Judah said, Let her take them, lest we be shamed: behold, I sent this kid, and thou hast not found her.

24. And it came to pass, after three months, that it was told Judah, saying, Tamar thy daughter-in-law hath played the harlot; and also, behold she is with child by whoredom. And Judah said, Bring her forth, and let her be burnt. 25. She was brought forth, and she sent to her father-in-law, saying, By the man whose these are, am I with child. And she said, Discern now, whose are these, the signet and the laces and the staff. 26. And Judah acknowledged them, and said, She hath been more righteous than I; for therefore I gave her not to Shelah my son. And he knew her again no more. 27. And it came to pass in the time of her bearing, that, behold, twins were in her womb. 28. And it came to pass in her bearing, that one put forth a hand; and the midwife took and bound on his hand a scarlet thread, saying, This came out first. 29. And it came to pass, as he drew back his hand, that, behold his brother came out: and she said, How hast thou made for thee a breach? And she called his name Perez. 30. And afterwards came out his brother, that had on his hand the scarlet thread: and his name was called Zerah. § 40.

This strange narrative is an episode in the history of Joseph; but an integral part of the "generations" of Jacob. It is loosely dated with the phrase "at that time." This does not indicate a sequel to the preceding record, the proper phrase for which is "after these things" (אַחַר הַדְּבָרִים הָאֵלֶּה xxii. 1). It implies rather a train of events that commenced at least in the past, some time before the closing incident of the previous narrative (xxi. 22). But the sale of Joseph, which alone is recorded in the last chapter, only occupied some few weeks or months of a year. Hence the circumstances contained in this memoir of Judah's family must have taken their rise before that event. The date "at that time," is rendered indefinite also by being attached to the phrase, "And it came to pass," which covers at least all the events in the first eleven verses of the chapter. All this is in accordance with the customary mode of arranging parallel lines of events in Hebrew narrative. We shall see reason afterwards for placing the birth of Er at as early a date as possible in the life of Judah (xlvi. 12). Now Judah, we conceive, was born when his father was eighty-seven, and Joseph when he was ninety-one, and hence there is a difference of about four years in their ages. We suppose Er to have been born in Judah's fourteenth year, when Joseph and Dinah were in their tenth, and therefore about three years before the rape of Dinah, and shortly after Jacob arrived at the town of Shekem. The dishonor of Dinah, and the cruel treatment of Joseph, being of essential moment in the process of things, had to be recorded in the main line of events. The commencement of Judah's family, having no particular influence on the current of the history, is fitly reserved till the whole of the circumstances could be brought together into a connected narrative. And the private history of Judah's line is given, while that of the others is omitted, simply because from him the promised seed is descended. As soon as Jacob is settled in the promised land, the intercourse with Hebron and its neighborhood seems to have commenced. A clear proof of this is the presence of Deborah, Rebekah's nurse, in Jacob's family (xxxv. 8). The great thoroughfare from Damascus to Egypt runs through Shekem and Hebron, and we know that when Jacob was residing at Hebron, his sons fed their flocks at Shekem and Dothan, and the youthful Joseph was sent to inquire after their welfare.

1–11. Judah marries and has three sons. *Went down from his brethren.* This seems to have been an act of wilful indiscretion in Judah. His separation from his brethren, however, extends only to the matter of his new connection. In regard to property and employment there seems to have been no long or entire separation till they went down into Egypt. He went down from the high grounds about Shekem to the lowlands in which Adullam was situated (Jos. xv. 33–35). *A certain Adullamite.* He may have become acquainted with this Hirah, when visiting his grandfather, or in some of the caravans which were constantly passing Shekem, or even in the ordinary wanderings of the pastoral life. Adullam was in the Shephelah or lowland of Judah bordering on Philistia proper. *A certain Kenaanite.* This connection with Shua's daughter was contrary to the will of God and the example of his fathers. *Onan* was born, we conceive, in Judah's fifteenth year, and Shelah in his sixteenth.

At Kezib. This appears the same as Akzib, which is associated with Keilah and Mareshah (Jos. xv. 44), and therefore lay in the south of the lowland of Judah. This note of place indicates a change of residence since her other children were born. In the year after this birth the dishonor of Dinah takes place. 6. *Took a wife for Er.* Judah chose a wife for himself at an early age, and now he chooses for his first-born at the same age. *Was evil in the eyes of the Lord.* The God of covenant is obliged to cut off Er for his wickedness in the prime of life. We are not made acquainted with his crime; but it could scarcely be more vile and unnatural than that for which his brother Onan is also visited with death. *And be a husband to her.* The original word means to act as a husband to the widow of a deceased brother who has left no issue. Onan seems to have been prompted to commit his crime by the low motive of turning the whole inheritance to his own house. At the time of Er's death Judah must have been in his twenty-seventh year; Joseph was consequently in his twenty-third, and Jacob had for ten years past had his headquarters at Hebron. Hence the intercourse with Timnah, Adullam, and Enaim was easy.

12–23. Judah now comes into criminal, and, though unknown to him, incestuous intercourse with Tamar. *And many were the days*, a year or somewhat more. *To Timnah.* This town is about twenty miles northwest of Hebron. There is another, however, in the hills about seven miles south of Hebron. *Put on a veil;* to conceal her face from Judah, or any other beholder. *The gate of Enaim.* This is supposed to be the same as Enam (Jos. xv. 34). *And thy lace.* This is the cord by which the signet was suspended round his neck. *Courtesan.* The original word (קְדֵשָׁה) means one consecrated to the worship of Ashtoreth, in which chastity is sacrificed.

24–30. Tamar bears Perez and Zerah to Judah. *After three months* her pregnancy was manifest. *Let her be burnt.* It is manifest Judah had the power to execute this punishment. The life of the widow of his son was in his hands. Stoning was the mode of punishment by the law of Moses (Deut. xxii. 20–24); burning, only in aggravated cases (Lev. xx. 14, xxi. 9). He is a severe judge in a case where he is equally criminal. *She hath been more righteous than I.* Tamar was less culpable in this matter than Judah. For he was moved by lust to commit fornication, and was the indirect occasion of Tamar's conduct by withholding Selah. But Tamar, though wronged, was not free from blame in her mode of righting herself. The youthful indis cretion of Judah in forming an intermarriage with a Canaanitish family, without the concurrence of his brothers or his father, has been fruitful of crime. If this intercourse go on, the chosen family will be speedily absorbed in the surrounding heathenism. Hence we begin to see the necessity of an immediate removal to another land, where they may be kept more distinct from the native superstition. By the disclosure of Tamar Judah is brought to acknowledgment of his fault, and, we may infer, to repentance. His abstaining from all further intercourse with her may be accepted as a proof of this. *A scarlet thread.* The right of primogeniture here manifests its importance. *Perez,* — a breach. Slight incidents become the foundation of names, and are often the hinges on which great events turn. The minutest circumstances connected with the progenitors of the promised seed have a lasting interest.

Judah was at the close of his twenty-ninth year when Perez and Zerah were born. The dates in his family history may be arranged as underneath, on the supposition that the first child was born when the father was in his fourteenth year. This hypothesis is fairly allowable when we take into consideration not only other cases, but the early wilfulness of Judah, and the example he gave to his children. The command also to be fruitful and multiply (xxxv. 11), which was given specially to Jacob, may have had a tendency to encourage early marriages. It is certain that the Jewish rabbis considered a man to have transgressed a divine precept who passed the age of twenty without being married. They also fixed the marriageable age for males at thirteen years and a day. King Ahaz was the father of Hezekiah when he was not more than twelve (2 Kings xvi. 2, xviii. 2); and King Josiah the father of Jehoiakim, when fourteen years of age (2 Kings xxii. 1, xxiii. 36).

Judah	13	years	6	months	when Er was born.
"	14	"	4½	"	when Onan was born.
"	15	"	3	"	when Shelah was born.
"	28	"	9	"	when Perez was born.
"	42	"	3	"	when Hezron born to Perez.
"	43	"	2	"	when Hamul born.

LXVII. JOSEPH IN POTIPHAR'S HOUSE.—Gen. xxxix.

XXXIX. 1. And Joseph was brought down to Mizraim; and Potiphar, an officer of Pharoh, captain of the guards, a Mizrite, bought him of the hand of the Ishmaelites, who brought him down thither. 2. And the LORD was with Joseph, and he was a prosperous man; and he was in the house of his master the Mizrite. 3. And his master saw that the LORD was with him, and all that he did the LORD made to prosper in his hand. 4. And Joseph found favor in his eyes, and he served him: and he set him over his house, and all that he had he put into his hand. 5. And it came to pass, from the time that he set him over his house, and over all that he had, that the LORD blessed the Mizrite's house for Joseph's sake; and the blessing of the LORD was upon all that he had in the house, and in the field. 6. And he left all that he had in Joseph's hand; and he knew not aught with him, save the bread which he did eat. And Joseph was beautiful in form and look.

7. And it came to pass after these things, that his master's wife cast her eyes upon Joseph: and she said, Lie with me. 8. And he refused, and said unto his master's wife, Behold, my master knoweth not what is with me in the house, and all that he hath he hath put into my hand. 9. There is none greater in this house than I, and he hath not kept back from me aught but thee, because thou art his wife: and how can I do this great evil, and sin against God? 10. And it came to pass, as she spake to Joseph day by day, that he hearkened not unto her, to lie by her to be with her.

11. And it came to pass at this day, that he went into the house to do his business; and there was none of the men of the house there within. 12. And she caught him by his garment, saying, Lie with me: and he left his garment in her hand, and fled, and came out of the house. 13. And it came to

pass when she saw that he had left his garment in her hand, and fled out of the house, 14. That she called unto the men of her house, and said unto them, saying, See, he hath brought in to us a Hebrew to mock us; he came in unto me to lie with me, and I cried with a loud voice. 15. And it came to pass when he heard that I lifted up my voice and cried, that he left his garment by me, and fled, and went out of the house. 16. And she laid up his garment by her, until his master came home. 17. And she spake unto him according to these words, saying, the Hebrew servant, whom thou hast brought in to us, came in unto me to mock me. 18. And it came to pass, as I lifted up my voice and cried, that he left his garment by me, and fled out of the house.

19. And it came to pass, when his master heard the words of his wife, which she spake unto him, saying, After this manner did thy servant unto me, that his wrath was kindled. 20. And Joseph's master took him, and put him into the prison, the place where the king's prisoners were bound: and he was there in the prison. 21. And the Lord was with Joseph, and showed him mercy, and gave him favor in the eyes of the keeper of the prison. 22. And the keeper of the prison put into Joseph's hand all the prisoners that were in the prison; and of all that they did there he was the doer. 23. The keeper of the prison looked not to aught in his hand, because the Lord was with him, and that which he did the Lord made to prosper. ¶ 36.

According to our reckoning, Perez and Zerah were born when Judah was in his twenty-eighth year, and therefore Joseph in his twenty-fourth. Here, then, we go back seven years to resume the story of Joseph.

1–6. Joseph fares well with his first master. *Potiphar.* This is a racapitulation of the narrative in ch. xxxvii. *The Lord;* the God of covenant is with Joseph. *In the house.* Joseph was a domestic servant. *And his master saw.* The prosperity that attended all Joseph's doings was so striking as to show that the Lord was with him. *Set him over*, — made him overseer of all that was in his house. *The Lord blessed the Mizrite's house.* He blesses those who bless his own (xii. 3). *Beautiful in form and look* (xxix. 17). This prepares the way for the following occurrence.

7–10. Joseph resists the daily solicitations of his master's wife to lie with her. *None greater in this house than I.* He pleads the unreserved trust his master had reposed in him. He is bound by the law of honor, the law of chastity *(this great evil)*, and the law of piety *(sin against God)*. Joseph uses the common name of God in addressing this Egyptian. He could employ no higher pleas than the above.

11–18. *At this day*, — the day on which the occurrence now to be related took place. *To do his business.* He does not come in her way except at the call of duty. *He hath brought in.* She either does not condescend, or does not need to name her husband. *A Hebrew to mock us.* Her disappointment now provokes her to falsehood as the means of concealment and revenge. *A Hebrew* is still the only national designation proper to Joseph (xiv. 13). Jacob's descendants had not got beyond the family. The term *Israelite* was therefore not yet in use. The national name is designedly used as a term of reproach among the Egyptians (xliii. 32). *To mock us*, — to take improper liberties, not only with me, but with any of the females in the house. *I cried with a loud voice.* This is intended to be the proof of her innocence (Deut. xxii. 24, 27). *Left his garments by me;* not in her hand, which would have been suspicious.

19–23. Her husband believes her story, and naturally resents the supposed unfaithfulness of his slave. His treatment of him is mild. He puts him in ward, probably to stand his trial for the offence. The Lord does not forsake the prisoner. He gives him favor with the governor of the jail. The same unlimited trust is placed in him by the governor as by his late master.

LXVIII. JOSEPH IN PRISON. — Gen. xl.

XL. 1. And it came to pass after these things, that the butler of the king of Mizraim and the baker had sinned against their master, the king of Mizraim. 2. And Pharoh was wroth against two of his officers, against the chief butler, and against the chief baker. 3. And he put them in ward, in the house of the captain of the guards, in the prison, the place where Joseph was bound. 4. And the captain of the guards charged Joseph with them, and he ministered to them, and they were some days in ward.

5. And they dreamed a dream, both of them, each his dream in one night, each according to the interpretation of his dream, the butler and the baker of the king of Mizraim, who were bound in the prison. 6. And Joseph went in to them in the morning, and looked upon them, and, behold, they were sad. 7. And he asked Pharoh's officers that were with him in the ward of his master's house, saying, Why are your faces bad to-day? 8. And they said unto him, A dream have we dreamed, and there is no interpreter of it. And Joseph said unto them, Do not interpretations belong to God? Tell them now to me.

9. And the chief butler told his dream to Joseph, and said unto him, I was in my dream, and, behold, a vine was before me; 10. And in the vine three branches: and as it budded, its blossom shot up, and the clusters thereof yielded ripe grapes. 11. And Pharoh's cup was in my hand: and I took the grapes, and pressed them into Pharoh's cup, and gave the cup into Pharoh's hand. 12. And Joseph said unto him, This is the interpretation of it: The three branches are three days. 13. In yet three days shall Pharoh lift up thy head and restore thee unto thy place; and thou shalt give Pharoh's cup into his hand, after the former manner when thou wast his butler. 14. But remember me when it shall be well with thee, and show unto me kindness, and mention me unto Pharoh, and bring me out of this house. 15. For stolen, stolen was I from the land of the Hebrews, and also here I have not done aught that they should put me into the pit.

16. And the chief baker saw that the interpretation was good, and he said unto Joseph, I also was in my dream, and, behold, three baskets of white bread on my head. 17. And

in the uppermost basket all manner of baked meats for Pharoh; and the birds did eat them out of the basket on my head. 18. And Joseph answered and said, This is the interpretation thereof: The three baskets are three days. 19. In yet three days shall Pharoh lift up thy head from upon thee, and shall hang thee on a tree: and the birds shall eat thy flesh from upon thee.

20. And it came to pass on the third day, the birthday of Pharoh, that he made a feast unto all his servants: and he lifted up the head of the chief butler and of the chief baker among his servants. 21. And he restored the chief butler to his butlership; and he gave the cup into Pharoh's hand. 22. And the chief baker he hanged: as Joseph had interpreted to them. 23. And the chief butler remembered not Joseph, and forgot him. 10 ¶¶¶ 37.

An unmurmuring patience and an unhesitating hopefulness keep the breast of Joseph in calm tranquillity. There is a God above, and that God is with him. His soul swerves not from this feeling. Meanwhile, new and distinguished prisoners are introduced into his place of confinement.

1–4. The chief butler and chief baker, high officials in Pharoh's court, come under the displeasure of their sovereign. *In the house of the captain of the guards.* It appears that this officer's establishment contained the keep in which Joseph and these criminals were confined. *Charged Joseph with them.* As Joseph was his slave, and these were state prisoners, he appointed him to wait upon them. It is probable that Joseph's character had been somewhat reëstablished with him during his residence in the prison.

5–8. These prisoners dream, *each according to the interpretation of his dream,* the imagery of which was fitted to indicate his future state. *They were sad,*—anxious to know the meaning of these impressive dreams. *Why are your faces bad to-day?* Joseph keeps up his character of frank composure. *Do not interpretations belong to God?* In his past history he had learned that dreams themselves come from God. And when he adds, *Tell them now to me,* he intimates that God would enable him to interpret their dreams. Here again he uses the general name of God, which was common to him with the heathen.

9–15. The chief butler now recites his dream. *Pressed them into Pharoh's cup.* The imagery of the dream is not intended to intimate that Pharoh drank only the fresh juice of the grape. It only expresses by a natural figure the source of wine, and possibly the duty of the chief butler to understand and superintend the whole process of its formation. Egypt was not only a corn, but a vine country. The interpretation of this dream was very obvious and natural; yet not without a divine intimation could it be known that *the three branches were three days.* Joseph, in the quiet confidence that his interpretation would prove correct, begs the chief butler to remember him and endeavor to procure his release. *Stolen, stolen was. I.* He assures him that he was not a criminal, and that his enslavement was an act of wrongful violence — a robbery by the strong hand. *From the land of the Hebrews;* a very remarkable expression, as it strongly favors the presumption that the Hebrews inhabited the country before Kenaan took possession of it. *I have not done aught.* Joseph pleads innocence, and claims liberation, not as an unmerited favor, but as a right. *The pit.* The pit without water seems to have been the primitive place of confinement for culprits.

16–19. The chief baker is encouraged by this interpretation to tell his dream. *I also.* He anticipates a favorable answer, from the remarkable likeness of the dreams. *On my head.* It appears from the monuments of Egypt that it was the custom for men to carry articles on their heads. *All manner of baked meats* were also characteristic of a corn country. *Lift up thy head from upon thee.* This part of the interpretation proves its divine origin. *And hang thee,* — thy body, after being beheaded. This was a constant warning to all beholders.

20–23. The interpretations prove correct. *The birthday of Pharoh.* It is natural and proper for men to celebrate with thanksgiving the day of their birth, as life is a pure and positive blessing. The benign Creator gives only a happy and precious form of existence to those whom he endows with the capacity of estimating its value. A birthday feast cannot be without a chief butler and a chief baker, and hence the fate of these criminals must be promptly decided. *Lifted up the head;* a phrase of double meaning. The chief butler remembers not Joseph. This is a case of frequent occurrence in this nether world. But there is One above who does not forget him. He will deliver him at the proper time.

LXIX. JOSEPH EXALTED. — Gen. xli.

1. יְאֹר *river, canal,* mostly applied to the Nile. Some suppose the word to be Coptic.

2. אָחוּ *sedge, reed-grass, marsh-grass.* This word is probably Coptic.

8. חַרְטֻמִּים ἐξηγηταὶ, ἱερογραμματεῖς, *sacred scribes, hieroglyphs.* חֶרֶט *stylus,* a graving tool.

43. אַבְרֵךְ *bend the knee.* In this sense it is put for הַבְרֵךְ imp. hiph. of בָּרַךְ. Those who take the word to be Coptic render it variously, — *bow all, bow the head, cast thyself down.*

45. צָפְנַת פַּעְנֵחַ Tsaphenath-pa'neach, in the Septuagint ψονθομφανήχ. *Revelator occulti,* Kimchi. This is founded on an attempted Hebrew derivation. Σωτήρ κόσμου in Oxf. MS., *servator mundi,* Jerome. These point to a Coptic origin. Recent Egyptologists give P-sont-em-ph-anh, *the-salvation-of-the-life* or *world.* This is a high-flowing title, in keeping with Eastern phraseology. אָסְנַת Asenath, perhaps belonging to Neith, or worshipper of Neith, a goddess corresponding to Athene of the Greeks. פּוֹטִי פֶרַע Potiphera', seems to be a variation of פּוֹטִיפַר Potiphar (xxxvii. 36). אֹן or אוֹן On = Oein, *light, sun*; on the monuments TA-RA, *house of the sun.* בֵּית שֶׁמֶשׁ (Jer. xliii. 13), Heliopolis, north of Memphis, on the east bank of the Nile.

51. מְנַשֶּׁה Menasheh, *causing to forget.*

52. אֶפְרַיִם Ephraim, *double fruit.*

XLI. 1. And it came to pass at the end of two years of days, that Pharoh dreamed, and, lo, he stood by the river. 2. And, behold, from the river came up seven kine, fine-looking and fat-fleshed; and they fed on the green. 3. And, behold, seven other kine came up after them from the river, ill-looking and lean-fleshed, and stood by the other kine on the bank of the river. 4. And the ill-looking and lean-fleshed kine did eat up the seven fine-looking and fat kine. And Pharoh awoke. 5. And he slept, and dreamed a second time: and, behold, seven ears of corn came up on one stalk, rank and good. 6. And behold seven ears, thin and blasted with the east wind, sprang up after them. 7. And the thin ears devoured the seven rank and full ears. And Pharoh awoke, and, behold, it was a dream. 8. And it came to pass in the morning that his spirit was troubled; and he sent and called for all the scribes of Mizraim, and all the sages thereof: and Pharoh told them his dream; and no one interpreted them to Pharoh.

9. Then spake the chief butler unto Pharoh, saying, My sins do I remember this day. 10. Pharoh was wroth with his servants; and he put me in ward in the house of the captain of the guards, me and the chief baker. 11. And we dreamed a dream in one night, I and he: each according to the interpretation of his dream dreamed we. 12. And there with us was a Hebrew lad, servant to the captain of the guards; and we told him, and he interpreted to us our dreams: to each according to his dream he interpreted. 13. And it came to pass that, as he interpreted to us, so it was: me he restored to my office, and him he hanged.

14. Then sent Pharoh and called Joseph, and they brought him hastily out of the pit: and he shaved, and changed his garments, and went in unto Pharoh. 15. And Pharoh said unto Joseph, A dream have I dreamed, and no one can interpret it: and I have heard say of thee, thou canst hear a dream to interpret it. 16. And Joseph answered Pharoh, saying, Not I: God shall answer to the peace of Pharoh. 17. And Pharoh spake unto Joseph: I was in my dream, and, behold, I stood upon the bank of the river. 18. And, behold, from the river came up seven kine, fat-fleshed and fine in form: and they fed on the green. 19. And, behold, seven other kine came up after them, poor and very ill-formed and lean-fleshed: I have seen none like them in all the land of Mizraim for bad ness. 20. And the lean and bad kine did eat up the first seven fat kine. 21. And they went into them, and it could not be known that they had gone into them; and their look

was bad, as at the beginning: and I awoke. 22. And I saw in my dream, and, behold, seven ears came up on one stalk, full and good. 23. And, behold, seven ears, withered, thin, blasted with the east wind, sprang up after them. 24. And the thin ears devoured the seven good ears: and I told the scribes, and no one showed it to me.

25. And Joseph said unto Pharoh, The dream of Pharoh is one: what the God is about to do hath he shown to Pharoh. 26. The seven good kine are seven years; and the seven good ears are seven years: it is one dream. 27. And the seven thin and bad kine coming up after them are seven years; and the seven empty ears blasted with the east wind: they shall be seven years of famine. 28. This is the word that I have spoken unto Pharoh: what the God is about to do he hath shown Pharoh. 29. Behold, seven years come of great plenty in all the land of Mizraim. 30. Then shall arise seven years of famine after them, and all the plenty shall be forgotten in the land of Mizraim: and the famine shall consume the land. 31. And the plenty shall not be known in the land by reason of that famine afterwards; for it shall be very grievous. 32. And because the dream was repeated to Pharoh twice, the thing is established by the God, and the God hastens to do it. 33. And now let Pharoh look out a man discreet and wise, and set him over the land of Mizraim. 34. Let Pharoh proceed and appoint overseers over the land: and take the fifth of the land of Mizraim in the seven years of plenty. 35. And let them gather all the food of those good years that come, and lay up corn under the hand of Pharoh, food in the cities, and let them keep it. 36. And the food shall be for store for the land, for the seven years of famine that shall be in the land of Mizraim, and the land shall not be cut off by the famine.

37. And the thing was good in the eyes of Pharoh, and in the eyes of all his servants. 38. And Pharoh said unto his

servants, Can we find a man like this, in whom is the Spirit of God?

39. And Pharoh said unto Joseph, After God hath shown thee all this, none is so discreet and wise as thou art. 40. Thou shalt be over my house, and according to thy mouth shall all my people behave: only in the throne will I be greater than thou. 41. And Pharoh said unto Joseph, See, I have set thee over all the land of Mizraim. 42. And Pharoh took his ring from his hand and put it upon Joseph's hand, and arrayed him in vestures of fine linen, and put a gold chain about his neck. 43. And he made him ride in the second chariot which he had; and they cried before him, Bow the knee. And he set him over all the land of Mizraim. 44. And Pharoh said unto Joseph, I am Pharoh, and without thee shall no man lift up his hand or foot in all the land of Mizraim. 45. And Pharoh called Joseph's name Zaphenathpaneah; and he gave him Asenath, daughter of Potiphera, priest of On, to wife. And Joseph went out over the land of Mizraim. 46. And Joseph was the son of thirty years when he stood before Pharoh king of Mizraim. And Joseph went out from the face of Pharoh, and passed through all the land of Mizraim.

47. And the land yielded in the seven years of plenty by handfuls. 48. And he gathered all the food of the seven years which were in the land of Mizraim, and laid up food in the cities: the food of the field which was around every city laid he up therein. 49. And Joseph gathered corn as the sand of the sea very much, until he left numbering, because there was no number.

50. And unto Joseph were born two sons before the year of the famine came, whom Asenath, daughter of Potiphera, priest of On, bare unto him. 51. And Joseph called the name of the first-born Menasseh: For God hath made me forget all my toil and all my father's house. 52. And the name of the

second called he Ephraim: For God hath made me fruitful in the land of my affliction.

53. Then were finished the seven years of plenty that was in the land of Mizraim. 54. And the seven years of famine began to come, according as Joseph had said; and there was famine in all the land, and in the land of Mizraim there was bread. 55. And all the land of Mizraim famished, and the people cried to Pharoh for bread; and Pharoh said unto all Mizraim, Go unto Joseph: what he saith to you, do. 56. And the famine was over all the face of the land; and Joseph opened all places in which there was food, and sold unto Mizraim; and the famine was severe in the land of Mizraim. 57. And all the land came into Mizraim to buy, unto Joseph; for the famine was severe in all the land.

Here we have the double dream of Pharoh interpreted by Joseph, in consequence of which he is elevated over all the land of Egypt.

1–8. The dreams are recited. *By the river.* In the dream Pharoh supposes himself on the banks of the Nile. *On the green.* The original word denotes the reed, or marsh grass, on the banks of the Nile. The cow is a very significant emblem of fruitful nature among the Egyptians, the hieroglyphic symbol of the earth and of agriculture; and the form in which Isis the goddess of the earth was adored. 5–7. *Dreamed a second time.* The repetition is designed to confirm the warning given, as Joseph afterwards explains (v. 32). *Corn* is the natural emblem of fertility and nurture. *Blasted with the east wind.* The east wind is any wind coming from the east of the meridian, and may be a southeast or a northeast, as well as a direct east. The Hebrews were wont to speak only of the four winds, and, therefore, must have used the name of each with great latitude. The blasting wind in Egypt is said to be usually from the southeast. *And, behold, it was a dream.* The impression was so distinct as to be taken for the reality, until he awoke and perceived that it was only a dream. 8. *His spirit was troubled.* Like the officers in the prison (xl. 6), he could not get rid of the feeling that the twofold dream portended some momentous event. *The scribes,* — the hieroglyphs, who belonged to the priestly caste, and whose primary business was to make hieroglyphic and other inscriptions; while they were wont to consult the stars, interpret dreams, practise soothsaying, and pursue the other occult arts. *The sages;* whose chief business was the cultivation of the various arts above mentioned, while the engraving or inscribing department strictly belonged to the hieroglyphs or scribes. *His dream;* the twofold dream. *Interpreted them,* — the two dreams.

9–13. The chief butler now calls Joseph to mind, and mentions his gift to Pharoh. *My sins.* His offence against Pharoh. His ingratitude in forgetting Joseph for two years does not perhaps occur to him as a sin. *A Hebrew lad.* The Egyptians were evidently well acquainted with the Hebrew race, at a time when Israel had only a family. *Him he hanged.* The phrase is worthy of note, as a specimen of pithy breviloquence. Him he declared that the dream foreboded that Pharoh would hang.

14–24. Pharoh sends for Joseph, who is hastily brought from the prison. *He shaved.* The Egyptians were accustomed to shave the head and beard, except in times of mourning (Herod. ii. 32). *Canst hear a dream to interpret it,* — needest only to hear in order to interpret it. *Not I: God shall answer.* According to his uniform habit Joseph ascribes the gift that is in him to God. *To the peace of Pharoh,* — so that Pharoh may reap the advantage. *In form.* This takes the place of "in look," in the former account. Other slight variations in the terms occur. *And they went into them,* — into their stomachs.

25–36. Joseph now proceeds to interpret the dream, and offer counsel suitable to the emergency. *What the God is about to do. The* God, the one true, living, eternal God, in opposition to all false gods. *And because the dream was repeated.* This is explained to denote the certainty and immediateness of the event. The beautiful elucidation of the dream needs no comment. 33–36. Joseph now naturally passes from the interpreter to the adviser. He is all himself on this critical occasion. His presence of mind never forsakes him. The openness of heart and readiness of speech, for which he was early distinguished, now stand him in good stead. His thorough self-command arises from spontaneously throwing himself, with all his heart, into the great national emergency which is before his mind. And his native simplicity of heart, practical good sense, and force of character break forth into unasked, but not unaccepted counsel. *A man discreet,* — intelligent, capable of understanding the occasion; *wise,* prudent, capable of acting accordingly. *Let Pharoh proceed,* — take the following steps: *Take the fifth* of the produce of the land. *Under the hand of Pharoh.* Under his supreme control. The measures here suggested to Pharoh were, we must suppose, in conformity with the civil institutions of the country. The exaction of a fifth, or two tithes, during the period of plenty, may have been an extraordinary measure, which the absolute power of the monarch enabled him to enforce for the public safety. The sovereign was probably dependent for his revenues on the produce of the crown lands, certain taxes on exports or imports, and occasional gifts or forced contributions from his subjects. This extraordinary fifth was, probably, of the last description, and was fully warranted by the coming emergency. The "gathering up of all the food" may imply that, in addition to the fifth, large purchases of corn were made by the government out of the surplus produce of the country.

37–46. Pharoh approves of his counsel, and selects him as "the discreet and wise man" for carrying it into effect. *In whom is the Spirit of God.* He acknowledges the gift that is in Joseph to be from God. *All my people behave,* — dispose or order their conduct, a peculiar meaning of this word, which usually signifies *to kiss.* *His ring.* His signet-ring gave Joseph the delegated power of the sovereign, and constituted him his prime minister or grand vizier. *Vestures of fine linen.* Egypt was celebrated for its flax, and for the fineness of its textures. The priests were arrayed in official robes of linen, and no man was allowed to enter a temple in a woollen garment (Herod. ii. 37, 81). *A gold chain about his neck.* This was a badge of office worn in Egypt by the judge and the prime minister. It had a similar use in Persia and Babylonia (Dan. v. 7). *The second chariot.* Egypt was noted for chariots, both for peaceful and for warlike purposes (Herod. ii. 108). The second in the public procession was assigned to Joseph. *Bow the knee.* The various explications of this proclamation agree in denoting a form of obeisance, with which Joseph was to be honored. *I am Pharoh,* the king (xii. 15). *Without thee shall no man lift up his hand or foot.* Thou art next to me, and without thee no man shall act or move. *Zaphenath-paneah.* Pharoh designates him the preserver of life, as the interpreter of the dream and the proposer of the plan by which the country was saved from famine. He thus naturalizes him so far as to render his civil status compatible with his official rank. *Asenath.* The priests were the highest and most privileged class in Egypt. Intermarriage with this caste at once determined the social position of the wondrous foreigner. His father-in-law was priest of On, a city dedicated to the worship of the sun.

With our Western and modern habit we may at the first glance be surprised to find a stranger of a despised race suddenly elevated to the second place in the kingdom. But in ancient and Eastern governments, which were of a despotic character, such changes, depending on the will of the sovereign, were by no means unusual. Secondly, the conviction that "the Spirit of God was in" the mysterious stranger, was sufficient to overbear all opposing feelings or customs. And, lastly, it was assumed and acted on, as a self-evident fact, that the illustrious stranger could have no possible objection to be incorporated into the most ancient of nations, and allied with its noblest families. We may imagine that Joseph would find an insuperable difficulty in becoming a citizen of Egypt or a son-in-law of the priest of the sun. But we should not forget that the world was yet too young to have arrived at the rigid and sharply-defined systems of polytheism or allotheism to which we are accustomed. Some gray streaks of a pure monotheism, of the knowledge of the one true God, still gleamed across the sky of human memory. Some faint traces of one common brotherhood among mankind still lingered in the recollections of the past. The Pharoh of Abraham's day feels the power of him whose name is Jehovah (xii. 17). Abimelek acknowledges the God of Abraham and Isaac (xx. 3–7, xxi. 22, 23, xxvi. 28, 29). And while Joseph is frank and faithful in acknowledging the true God before the king of Egypt, Pharoh himself is not slow to recognize the man in whom the Spirit of God is. Having experi enced the omniscience and omnipotence of Joseph's God, he was prepared, no doubt, not only himself to offer him such adoration as he was wont to pay to his national gods, but also to allow Joseph full liberty to worship the God of his fathers, and to bring up his family in that faith.

Joseph was now in his thirtieth year, and had consequently been thirteen years in Egypt, most part of which interval he had probably spent in prison. This was the age for manly service (Num. iv. 3). He immediately enters upon his office.

47–49. The fulfilment of the dream here commences. *By handfuls.* Not in single stalks or grains, but in handfuls compared with the former yield. It is probable that a fifth of the present unprecedented yield was sufficient for the sustenance of the inhabitants. Another fifth was rendered to the government, and the remaining three fifths were stored up or sold to the state or the foreign broker at a low price. *He left numbering because there was no number.* This denotes that the store was immense, and not perhaps that modes of expressing the number failed.

50–52. Two sons were born to Joseph during the seven years of plenty. *Menasseh.* God made him forget his toil and his father's house. Neither absolutely. He remembered his toils in the very utterance of this sentence. And he tenderly and intensely remembered his father's house. But he is grateful to God, who builds him a home, with all its soothing joys, even in the land of his exile. His heart again responds to long untasted joys. *Fruitful in the land of my affliction.* It is still, we perceive, the land of his affliction. But why does no message go from Joseph to his mourning father? For many reasons. First, he does not know the state of things at home. Secondly, he may not wish to open up the dark and bloody treachery of his brothers to his aged parent. But, thirdly, he bears in mind those early dreams of his childhood. All his subsequent experience has confirmed him in the belief that they will one day be fulfilled. But that fulfilment implies the submission not only of his brothers, but of his father. This is too delicate a matter for him to interfere in. He will leave it entirely to the all-wise providence of his God to bring about that strange issue. Joseph, therefore, is true to his life-long character. He leaves all in the hand of God, and awaits in anxious, but silent hope, the days when he will see his father and his brethren.

53–57. The commencement and the extent of the famine are now noted. *As Joseph had said.* The fulfilment is as perfect in the one part as in the other. *In all the lands,*—all the lands adjacent to Egypt; such as Arabia and Palestine. The word *all* in popular discourse is taken in a relative sense, to be ascertained by the context. We are not aware that this famine was felt beyond the distance of Hebron. *Go unto Joseph* (40–44). Pharoh has had reason to trust Joseph more and more, and now he adheres to his purpose of sending his people to him. *All the face of the land* of Egypt. *And Joseph opened all places in which there was food,*—all the stores in every city. *And sold unto Mizraim.* The stores under Pharoh's hand were public property, obtained either by lawful taxation or by purchase. It was a great public benefit to sell this grain, that had been providently kept in store, at a moderate price, and thus preserve the lives of a nation during a seven years' famine. *All the land.* This is to be understood of the countries in the neighborhood of Egypt. Famines in these countries were not unusual. We have read already of two famines in Palestine that did not extend to Egypt (xii. 10, xxvi. 1).

The fertility of Egypt depends on the rise of the waters of the Nile to a certain point, at which they will reach all the country. If it fall short of that point, there will be a deficiency in the crops proportioned to the deficiency in the rise. The rise of the Nile depends on the tropical rains by which the lake is supplied from which it flows. These rains depend on the clouds wafted by the winds from the basin of the Mediterranean Sea. The amount of these piles of vapor will depend on the access and strength of the solar heat producing evaporation from the surface of that inland sea. The same cause, therefore, may withhold rain from central Africa, and from all the lands that are watered from the Mediterranean. The duration of the extraordinary plenty was indeed wonderful. But such periods of excess are generally followed by corresponding periods of deficiency over the same area. This prepares the way for the arrival of Joseph's kindred in Egypt.

LXX. JOSEPH AND TEN OF HIS BRETHREN.—Gen. xlii.

1. שֶׁבֶר *fragment, crumb*, hence *grain.* בַּר *pure, winnowed*, hence *corn.*

6. שַׁלִּיט *ruler, governor*, hence Sultan. Not elsewhere found in the Pentateuch.

25. כְּלִי *vessel*, here any portable article in which grain may be conveyed. שַׂק *sack*, the very word which remains in our language to this day. אַמְתַּחַת *bag.*

XLII. 1. And Jacob saw that there was grain in Mizraim,
and Jacob said unto his sons, Why do ye look one at another?
2. And he said, Behold, I have heard that there is grain in
Mizraim: go down thither, and buy for us thence; and we
shall live and not die. 3. And Joseph's ten brethren went
down to buy corn in Mizraim. 4. And Benjamin, Joseph's
brother, Jacob sent not with his brethren; for he said, Lest
mischief befall him. 5. And the sons of Israel went to buy
among those that went; for the famine was in the land of
Kenaan.

6. And Joseph was the governor over the land, that sold to all the people of the land: and Joseph's brethren went and bowed down to him with their faces to the earth. 7. And Joseph saw his brethren, and knew them; and he made himself strange unto them, and spake unto them roughly, and said unto them, Whence are ye come? And they said, From the land of Kenaan, to buy food. 8. And Joseph knew his brethren; and they knew not him. 9. And Joseph remembered the dreams which he had dreamed of them; and he said unto them, Spies are ye: to see the nakedness of the land are ye come. 10. And they said unto him, Nay, my lord; but thy servants are come to buy food. 11. All of us sons of one man are we; true men are we: thy servants are not spies. 12. And he said unto them, Nay; for to see the nakedness of the land are ye come. 13. And they said, Twelve brethren are we thy servants, sons of one man in the the land of Kenaan: and, behold, the youngest is with our father this day, and one is not. 14. And Joseph said unto them, This is what I spake unto you, saying, Spies are ye. 15. Hereby ye shall be proved: by the life of Pharoh ye shall not go hence, unless your youngest brother come hither. 16. Send one of you, and let him fetch your brother; and be ye bound, and let your words be proved if the truth be in you; and if not, by the life of Pharoh, spies are ye. 17. And he put them all together in ward for three days.

18. And Joseph said unto them on the third day, This do and live: the God I do fear. 19. If true men be ye, one brother of you shall be bound in the house of your ward; and ye go, carry grain for the famine of your houses. 20. And your youngest brother bring ye to me, and your words shall be verified, and ye shall not die. And they did so. 21. And they said one to another, Verily guilty are we concerning our brother, because we saw the distress of his soul when he besought us and we would not hear: therefore come upon us is this distress. 22. And Reuben answered them, saying, Said

I not unto you, saying, Sin not against the lad, and ye would not hear: and behold also his blood is required. 23. And they knew not that Joseph heard them; for the interpreter was betwixt them. 24. And he turned about from them, and wept: and he returned to them, and spake unto them, and took from them Simon, and bound him before their eyes. 25. And Joseph commanded to fill their vessels with corn, and to restore every man's silver into his sack, and to give them provision for the way. And it was done to them so.

26. And they put their grain upon their asses, and went thence. 27. And one opened his sack to give provender to his ass in the inn: and he saw his silver, and, behold, it was in his bag's mouth. 28. And he said unto his brethren, My silver is restored, and also, behold, it is in my bag: and their heart failed, and they trembled, saying one to another, What is this God hath done unto us? 29. And they went unto Jacob their father to the land of Kenaan, and told him all that befell them, saying, 30. The man who is lord of the land spake with us roughly, and took us for spies of the land. 31. And we said unto him, True men are we; we are not spies. 32. Twelve brethren are we, sons of one father; one is not, and the youngest is this day with our father in the land of Kenaan. 33. And the man, the lord of the land, said unto us, Hereby shall I know that ye are true; one brother of you leave with me, and for the famine of your houses take ye and go. 34. And bring your youngest brother to me: and I shall know that ye are not spies, that ye are true men: your brother will I give you, and in the land ye shall traffic.

35. And it came to pass, as they emptied their sacks, that, behold, every man's bundle of silver was in his sack: and they saw the bundles of their silver, they and their father, and they were afraid. 36. And Jacob their father said unto them, Me have ye bereaved; Joseph is not, and Simon is not, and Benjamin ye will take: all these things are against me. 37. And Reuben said unto his father, saying, Slay two of my sons if

I bring him not unto thee: give him into my hand, and I will restore him unto thee. 38. And he said, My son shall not go down with you; for his brother is dead, and he is left alone: and mischief shall befall him by the way in which ye go, and ye shall bring down my gray hairs with sorrow to the grave.

Twenty years, the period of Joseph's long and anxious waiting, have come to an end. The dreams of his boyhood are now at length to be fulfilled. The famine has reached the chosen family, and they look at one another perplexed and irresolute, not knowing what to do.

1–5. The aged Jacob is the only man of counsel. *Behold, I have heard there is grain in Mizraim:* go down and buy. The ten brothers are sent, and Benjamin, the youngest, is retained, not merely because of his youth, for he was now twenty-four years of age, but because he was the son of his father's old age, the only son of Rachel now with him, and the only full brother of the lost Joseph. *Lest mischief befall him,* and so no child of Rachel would be left. *Among those that went.* The dearth was widespread in the land of Kenaan.

6–17. The ten brothers meet with a rough reception from the lord of the land. *The governor,* — the sultan. This, we see, is a title of great antiquity in Egypt or Arabia. Joseph presided over the corn-market of the kingdom. *Bowed down to him with their faces to the earth.* Well might Joseph think of those never-to-be-forgotten dreams in which the sheaves and stars bowed down to him. *And knew them.* How could he fail to remember the ten full-grown men of his early days, when they came before him with all their peculiarities of feature, attitude, and mother tongue. *And he made himself strange unto them.* All that we know of Joseph's character heretofore, and throughout this whole affair, goes to prove that his object in all his seemingly harsh treatment was to get at their hearts, to test their affection toward Benjamin, and to bring them to repent of their unkindness to himself. *They knew not him.* Twenty years make a great change in a youth of seventeen. And besides, with his beard and head shaven, his Egyptian attire, his foreign tongue, and his exalted position, who could have recognized the stripling whom, twenty years ago, they had sold as a slave? *Spies are ye.* This was to put a color of justice on their detention. To see the nakedness of the land, not its unfortified frontier, which is a more recent idea, but its present impoverishment from the famine. *Sons of one man are we.* It was not likely that ten sons of one man would be sent on the hazardous duty of spies. *And behold the youngest is with our father this day.* It is intensely interesting to Joseph to hear that his father and full brother are still living. *And one is not.* Time has assuaged all their bitter feelings, both of exasperation against Joseph and of remorse for their unbrotherly conduct. This little sentence, however, cannot be uttered by them, or heard by Joseph, without emotion. *By the life of Pharoh.* Joseph speaks in character, and uses an Egyptian asseveration. *Send one of you.* This proposal is enough to strike terror into their hearts. The return of one would be a heavy, perhaps a fatal blow to their father. And how can one brave the perils of the way? They cannot bring themselves to concur in this plan. Sooner will they all go to prison, as accordingly they do. Joseph is not without a strong conviction of incumbent duty in all this. He knows he has been put in the position of lord over his brethren in the foreordination of God, and he feels bound to make this authority a reality for their moral good.

18–25. After three days Joseph reverses the numbers, allowing nine to return home, and retaining one. *This do and live.* Joseph, notwithstanding the arbitrary power which his office enabled him to exercise, proves himself to be free from caprice and unnecessary severity. He affords them a fair opportunity of proving their words true, before putting them to death on suspicion of espionage. *The God do I fear.* A singular sentence from the lord paramount of Egypt! It implies that the true God was not yet unknown in Egypt. We have heard the confession of this great truth already from the lips of Pharoh (xli. 38, 39). But it intimates to the brothers the astonishing and hopeful fact that the grand vizier serves the same great Being whom they and their fathers have known and worshipped; and gives them a plain hint that they will be dealt with according to the just law of heaven. *Carry grain for your houses.* The governor then is touched with some feeling for their famishing households. The brothers, though honoring their aged father as the patriarch of their race, had now their separate establishments. Twelve households had to be supplied with bread. The journey to Egypt was not to be undertaken more than once a year if possible, as the distance from Hebron was upwards of two hundred miles. Hence the ten brothers had with them all their available beasts of burden, with the needful retinue of servants. We need not be surprised that these are not specially enumerated, as it is the manner of Scripture to leave the secondary matters to the intelligence and experience of the reader, unless, as in the case of Abraham's three hundred and eighteen trained servants, they happen to be of essential moment in the process of events. *Your youngest brother.* Joseph longs to see his full brother alive, whom he left at home a child of four summers. *Verily guilty are we concerning our brother.* Their affliction is beginning to bear the fruit of repentance. *Because we saw the distress of his soul when he besought us, and we would not hear.* How vividly is the scene of Joseph's sale here brought before us. It now appears that he besought them to spare him, and they would not hear! *This distress.* Retribution has come at last. *His blood is required.* Reuben justly upbraids them with their hardness of heart. Their brother's blood is required; for murder was intended, and when he was sold his death was pretended. *The interpreter was betwixt them.* The dragoman was employed in holding intercourse with them. But Joseph heard the spontaneous expressions of remorse, coming unprompted from their lips. The fountain of affection is deeply stirred. He cannot repress the rising tear. He has to retire for a time to recover his composure. He now takes, not Reuben, who was not to blame, but Simon, the next eldest, and binds him before them: a speaking act. He then gives orders to supply them with corn, deposit their money in their sacks without their knowledge, and furnish them with provision for the way. Joseph feels, perhaps, that he cannot take money from his father. He will pay for the corn out of his own funds. But he cannot openly return the money to his brothers without more explanation than he wishes at present to give.

26–34. The nine return home and record their wonderful adventure. *In the inn;* the lodge or place where they stopped for the night. This place was not yet perhaps provided with even the shelter of a roof. It was merely the usual place of halting. They would probably occupy six or seven days on the journey. Apparently at the first stage one opened his sack to give provender to his ass. The discovery of the silver in its mouth strikes them with terror. In a strange land and with an uneasy conscience they are easily alarmed. It was not convenient or necessary to open all the bags on the way, and so they make no further discovery.

35–38. On emptying the other sacks all the silver turns up, to their great amazement and consternation. Jacob laments the loss of his son. Reuben offers two of his sons to Jacob as pledges for Benjamin, to be slain if he did not bring him back in safety. The sorrowing parent cannot yet bring himself to consent to Benjamin's departure on this hazardous journey. *And ye shall bring down.* Jacob either speaks here in the querulous tone of afflicted old age, or he had come to know or suspect that his brothers had some hand in the disappearance of Joseph.

LXXI. JOSEPH AND HIS ELEVEN BRETHREN. — Gen. xliii.

11. דְּבַשׁ *honey,* from the bee, or sirup from the juice of the grape. בָּטְנִים *pistachio nuts.* שָׁקֵד *almond tree;* r. *awake.* The tree is also called לוּז. Some refer the former to the fruit, the latter to the tree.

XLIII. 1. And the famine was sore in the land. 2. And it came to pass, when they had eaten up the grain which they had brought from Mizraim, that their father said to them, Return: buy us a little food. 3. And Judah said unto him, saying, The man solemnly protested unto us, saying, Ye shall not see my face, except your brother be with you. 4. If thou wilt send our brother with us, we will go down and buy thee food. 5. And if thou wilt not send him, we will not go down; for the man said unto us, Ye shall not see my face, except your brother be with you. 6. And Israel said, Why have ye done me evil, to tell the man whether ye had yet a brother? 7. And they said, The man straitly asked of us and of our kindred, saying, Is your father yet alive? Have ye a brother? And we told him according to these words. Could we certainly know that he would say, Bring your brother down? 8. And Judah said unto Israel his father, Send the lad with me, and we will arise and go; and we shall live and not die, both we and thou and our little ones. 9. I will be surety for him; of my hand shalt thou require him. If I bring him not unto thee, and set him before thee, then let me have sinned against thee all my days. 10. For unless we had lingered, surely now we had returned this second time.

11. And Israel their father said unto them, If so now, this do: take of the best of the land in your vessels, and carry down the man a present, a little balm and a little honey, spices and myrrh, nuts and almonds. 12. And second silver take in your hand: and the silver that was returned in the mouth of your bags take back in your hand; mayhap it was a mistake. 13. And your brother take: and arise, return to the man. 14. And God Almighty give you mercy before the man, and he shall send you your other brother and Benjamin. And I, if I am bereaved, I am bereaved. 15. And the men took this present, and double silver took they in their hand, and Benjamin; and rose up, and went down to Mizraim, and stood before Joseph.

16. And Joseph saw with them Benjamin, and said to him that was over his house, Bring these men in, and slay and make ready; for these men shall eat with me at noon. 17. And the man did as Joseph said; and the man brought the men to Joseph's house. 18. And the men were afraid because they were brought to Joseph's house; and they said, On account of the money that was returned in our bags at the first are we brought in; to overbear us, and fall upon us, and take us for servants, and our asses.

19. And they came near to the man who was over Joseph's house, and they spake to him at the door of the house. 20. And said, O my lord, we came down indeed at the first to buy food. 21. And it came to pass, when we came to the inn, that we opened our bags, and, behold, every man's silver was in the mouth of his bag, — our silver in full weight: and we brought it back in our hand. 22. And other silver have we brought down in our hand to buy food: we know not who put our silver in our bags. 23. And he said, Peace be to you; fear not: your God, and the God of your father hath given you treasure in your bags: your silver came to me. And

he brought out unto them Simon. 24. And the man brought the men into Joseph's house, and got water, and they washed their feet; and he gave provender to their asses. 25. And they made ready the present for Joseph's coming at noon; for they heard that there they should eat bread.

26. And Joseph came home, and they brought him the present which was in their hand into the house, and they bowed to him to the earth. 27. And he asked them of their welfare; and he said, Is it well with your father, the old man of whom ye spake? Is he yet alive? 28. And they answered, It is well with thy servant, our father; he is yet alive. And they bent the head and bowed down. 29. And he lifted up his eyes, and saw Benjamin his brother, his mother's son, and said, Is this your youngest brother of whom ye told me? And he said, God be gracious unto thee, my son. 30. And Joseph hastened away; for his bowels yearned upon his brother, and he sought to weep; and he went into his chamber and wept there. 31. And he washed his face, and came out, and refrained himself, and said, Set on bread. 32. And they set for him by himself, and for them by themselves, and for the Mizrites who ate with him by themselves; because the Mizrites might not eat bread with the Hebrews; for that is an abomination to the Mizrites. 33. And they sat in his presence, the first-born according to his first birth, and the youngest according to his youth: and the men marvelled one at another 34. And he sent messes from before him unto them: and Benjamin's mess exceeded the messes of them all five times. And they drank and were merry with him.

The eleven brothers are now to bow down before Joseph.

1–10. The famine was sore. The pressure began to be felt more and more. The twelve households had at length consumed all the corn they had purchased, and the famine still pressed heavily upon them. Jacob directs them to return. *And Judah said.* Reuben had offended, and could not come forward. Simon and Levi had also grieved their father by the treacherous slaughter of the Shekemites. Judah therefore speaks. *Is your father yet alive? Have ye a brother?* These questions do not come out in the previous narrative, on account of its brevity. But how pointed they are, and how true to Joseph's yearnings! They explain how it was that these particulars came out in the replies of the brothers to Joseph. For the charge of being spies did not call for them in exculpation. Judah now uses all the arguments the case would admit of, to persuade his father to allow Benjamin to go with them. He closes with the emphatic sentence, *If I bring him not unto thee, and set him before thee, then let me have sinned against thee all my days;* that is, let me bear the blame, and of course the penalty of having sinned against thee in so tender a point. Both Judah and his father knew that this was a matter that touched the interest of the former very deeply. Reuben was bearing the blame of a grievous sin, and had no hope of the birthright. Simon and Levi were also bearing blame, and, besides, had not the natural right, which belonged only to Reuben. Judah came next, and a failure in securing the safe return of Benjamin might set him also aside. He undertakes to run this risk.

11–15. Jacob at length reluctantly sends Benjamin with them. He employs all means, as is usual with him, of securing a favorable result. *The best of the land,* — the sung or celebrated products of the land. *A little honey.* Palestine abounded with bee honey. A sirup obtained by boiling down the juice of the grape was also called by the same name, and formed an article of commerce. *Nuts.* These are supposed to be pistachio nuts, from the pistacia vera, a tree resembling the terebinth, a native of Anatolia, Syria, and Palestine. *Almonds.* The almond tree buds or flowers earlier in the spring than other trees. It is a native of Palestine, Syria, and Persia. For the other products see xxxvii. 25. *Other silver;* not double silver, but a second sum for the new purchase. *God Almighty,* — the Great Spirit, who can dispose the hearts of men as he pleases. Jacob looks up to heaven for a blessing, while he uses the means. *If I am bereaved, I am bereaved.* This is the expression of acquiescence in whatever may be the will of Providence. *Double silver,* — that which was returned and that which was to pay for a second supply of corn.

16–18. The invitation into Joseph's house fills the brothers with alarm. *Saw with them Benjamin.* This was an unspeakable relief to Joseph, who was afraid that his full brother, also the favorite of his father, might have incurred the envy and persecution of the brothers.

Brought the men to Joseph's house. This he eventually did, but not till after the conference between him and them took place. *The men were afraid* of a plot to rob them of their liberty and property.

19–25. They are encouraged by the steward of Joseph's house to lay aside their fears, and prepare their present. *Spake to him at the door of the house.* This was, of course, before they entered. *When we came to the inn.* The relater is prone to lump matters in the narration, for the sake of brevity. They began to "open their bags" at the first lodging-place, and finished the process at the last when they got home. *Other silver.* This explains the phrase "second silver" in v. 12. *Peace be to you.* Be at rest. All is well. *Your God.* The steward of Joseph expresses himself as one who fears and trusts God, the God of the Hebrews, who had displayed his omniscience and omnipotence in Egypt. *He brought out unto them Simon.* While they still linger at the entrance, the considerate steward bethought himself of bringing out Simon to them, which reassured their hearts, and induced them to enter willingly. He now succeeds therefore in bringing them in, and then bestows upon them the usual attentions of Eastern hospitality. They now "make ready their present."

26–34. They are now entertained by Joseph. They brought the present, and made a lowly obeisance before him. *They bent the head.* See xxiv. 26. *God be gracious unto thee, my son.* His kind treatment of Benjamin, on whose presence he had so much insisted, was calculated to reassure the brothers. The latter was born in his thirteenth year, and therefore he was entitled to assume the paternal style in regard to him. Joseph still appeals with a natural and unconstrained reverence to his own God. *And Joseph hastened away.* The little touch of tenderness he had involuntarily thrown into his address to Benjamin, is too much for his feelings, which yearn towards his brother, and he is obliged to retreat to his chamber to conceal his tears and compose his countenance. *They set for him by himself.* As the governor, or as connected by affinity with the priestly caste, Joseph does not eat with the other Egyptians. The Egyptians cannot eat with the Hebrews. *That is an abomination to the Mizrites.* For the Hebrews partook of the flesh of kine, both male and female. But Herodotus informs us (II. 41), that "male kine, if clean, are used by the Egyptians, but the females they are not allowed to sacrifice, since they are sacred to Isis." And he adds that "a native of Egypt will not kiss a Greek, use his knife, his spit, or his cauldron, or taste the flesh cut with a Greek knife." They considered all foreigners unclean, and therefore refused to eat with them (see Rawlinson's Herod. on p. q.). *They sat in his presence;* arranged according to the order of their birth, to their great amazement. Egypt was to them a land of wonders, and Egypt's sultan a man of wonder. *Benjamin's mess.* The honored guest was distinguished by a larger or daintier portion of the fare (1 Sam. ix. 23, 24; Homer, Il. 7, 321). A double portion was assigned to the Spartan kings. The fivefold division was prominent in Egyptian affairs (xli. 34; xlv. 22; xlvii. 2, 24, 26). *And were merry.* They drank freely, so as to be exhilarated, because their cares were dissipated by the kindness they were receiving, the presence of Simon, and the attention paid to Benjamin.

LXXII. THE TEN BROTHERS PROVED.—Gen. xliv.

XLIV. 1. And he commanded him that was over his house, saying, Fill the men's bags with food, as much as they can carry, and put the silver of each in his bag's mouth. 2. And my cup, the silver cup, put in the bag's mouth of the youngest, and the silver for his grain. And he did according to the word of Joseph which he spake. 3. The morning shone; and the men were sent away, they and their asses. 4. They had come out of the city not very far, and Joseph said to him that was over his house, Up, follow after the men; and overtake them, and say unto them, Why have ye requited evil for good? 5. Is it not this in which my lord drinketh, and whereby indeed he divineth? Ye have done evil in so doing.

6. And he overtook them, and spake unto them these words. 7. And they said unto him, Why speaketh my lord according to these words? Far be thy servants from doing according to this thing. 8. Behold, silver which we found in our bags' mouths we brought back to thee from the land of Kenaan: and how should we steal from thy lord's house silver or gold? 9. With whomsoever of thy servants it be found, both let him die, and also we will be servants to my lord. 10. And he said, Now also according to your words let it be: he with whom it

is found shall be my servant, and ye shall be blameless. 11. And they hasted, and laid every man his bag on the earth, and opened every man his bag. 12. And he searched, beginning at the eldest and ending at the youngest, and the cup was found in Benjamin's bag.

13. And they rent their garments, and laded every man his ass, and returned to the city. 14. And Judah went and his brethren to Joseph's house, and he was yet there: and they fell before him on the earth. 15. And Joseph said unto them, What deed is this that ye have done? Wot ye not that such a man as I doth certainly divine? 16. And Judah said, What shall we say unto my lord? What shall we speak? And how shall we clear ourselves? The God hath found out the iniquity of thy servants: behold, we are servants to my lord, both we, and he in whose hand the cup is found. 17. And he said, Far let me be from doing this: the man in whose hand the cup is found, he shall be my servant; and ye go up in peace to your father. 11 §§§ 41.

18. And Judah came near unto him, and said, O my lord, let thy servant now speak a word in the ears of my lord, and let not thine anger burn against thy servant: for so art thou as Pharoh. 19. My lord asked his servants, saying, Have ye a father or a brother? 20. And we said unto my lord, We have an aged father, and a young lad of his old age; and his brother is dead, and he is left alone of his mother, and his father loveth him. 21. And thou saidst unto thy servants, Bring him unto me; and let me set mine eyes upon him. 22. And we said unto my lord, The lad cannot leave his father: and he shall leave his father, and he shall die. 23. And thou saidst unto thy servants, Except your youngest brother come down with you, ye shall see my face no more. 24. And it came to pass that we went up unto thy servant my father, and told him the words of my lord. 25. And our father said, Return, buy us a little food. 26. And we said, We cannot go down: if our youngest brother be with us, then will we go down; for we

may not see the man's face, except our youngest brother be with us. 27. And thy servant my father said unto us, Ye know that my wife bare me two sons. 28. And the one went out from me, and I said, Surely he is torn in pieces; and I have not seen him since. 29. And ye shall take this also from before me, and evil shall befall him, and ye shall bring down my gray hairs in evil to the grave. 30. And now when I go unto thy servant my father, and the lad is not with us, and his soul is bound up in his soul, 31. Then it shall come to pass when he seeth that the lad is not, that he will die: and thy servants shall bring down the gray hairs of thy servant our father in sorrow to the grave. 32. For thy servant became surety for the lad with my father, saying, If I bring him not unto thee, then let me have sinned against my father all my days. 33. And now let thy servant now abide instead of the lad a servant to my lord; and let the lad go up with his brethren. 34. For how shall I go up to my father, and the lad not with me, lest I see the evil that shall come upon my father.

Joseph has had the satisfaction of seeing his brother Benjamin safe and well. He has heard his brothers acknowledging their guilt concerning himself. He resolves to put their attachment to Benjamin, and the genuineness of their change of disposition, to a test that will at the same time expose Benjamin to no hazard.

1–5. *And my cup.* Besides returning each man's money as before, a silver cup of Joseph's is put in Benjamin's bag, after which, when daylight comes, they are dismissed. They are scarcely out of the town when Joseph's steward is ordered to overtake them, and charge them with stealing the cup. *And whereby indeed he divineth.* Divining by cups, we learn from this, was a common custom in Egypt (Herod. II. 83). It is here mentioned to enhance the value of the cup. Whether Joseph really practised any sort of divination cannot be determined from this passage.

6–12. The cup is found in Benjamin's bag. *Spake unto them these words.* The words of Joseph, supplying of course the mention of the cup which is expressed in the text only by the pronoun *this.* *We brought back to thee.* Silver that we might have retained, and to which you made no claim when we tendered it, we brought back. How or why should we therefore steal silver? *Now also according to your words let it be.* He adopts their terms with a mitigation. He with whom the cup is found shall become a slave for life, and the rest be acquitted. The steward searches from the eldest to the youngest. The cup is found where it was put.

13–17. *They rent their garments;* the natural token of a sorrow that knows no remedy. *And Judah went.* He had pledged himself for the safety of Benjamin to his father. *And he was yet there;* awaiting no doubt the result which he anticipated. *They fell before him on the earth.* It is no longer a bending of the head or bowing of the body, but the posture of deepest humiliation. How deeply that early dream penetrated into the stern reality! *Wot ye not that such a man as I doth certainly divine?* Joseph keeps up the show of resentment for a little longer, and brings out from Judah the most pathetic plea of its kind that ever was uttered. *The God,* the great and only God, *hath found out the iniquity of thy servants;* in our dark and treacherous dealing with our brother. *Behold, we are servants to my lord.* He resigns himself and all to perpetual bondage, as the doom of a just God upon their still-remembered crime. *He shall be my servant; and ye, go up in peace to your father.* Now is the test applied with the nicest adjustment. Now is the moment of agony and suspense to Joseph. Will my brothers prove true? says he within himself. Will Judah prove adequate to the occasion? say we. His pleading with his father augured well.

18–34. *And Judah came near unto him.* He is going to surrender himself as a slave for life, that Benjamin may go home with his brothers, who are permitted to depart. *Let thy servant now speak a word in the ears of my lord.* There is nothing here but respectful calmness of demeanor. *And let not thine anger burn against thy servant.* He intuitively feels that the grand vizier is a man of like feelings with himself. He will surmount the distinction of rank, and stand with him on the ground of a common humanity. *For so art thou as Pharoh.* Thou hast power to grant or withhold my request. This forms the exordium of the speech. Then follows the plea. This consists in a simple statement of the facts, which Judah expects to have its native effect upon a rightly-constituted heart. We will not touch this statement, except to explain two or three expressions. *A young lad,* — a comparative youth. *Let me set mine eyes upon him,* — regard him with favor and kindness. *He shall leave his father and he shall die.* If he were to leave his father, his father would die. Such is the natural interpretation of these words, as the paternal affection is generally stronger than the filial. 33, 34. *And now let thy servant now abide instead of the lad a servant to my lord.* Such is the humble and earnest petition of Judah. He calmly and firmly sacrifices home, family, and birthright, rather than see an aged father die of a broken heart.

LXXIII. JOSEPH MADE KNOWN TO HIS BRETHREN. — Gen. xlv.

10. גֹּשֶׁן Goshen (Γεσὲμ Αραβίας; r. perhaps גֶּשֶׁם *rain, shower*), a region on the borders of Egypt and Arabia, near the gulf of Suez.

XLV. 1. And Joseph could not refrain himself before all
that stood by him, and he cried, Have every man out from me.
And there stood no man with him, when Joseph made himself
known unto his brethren. 2. And he lifted up his voice in
weeping: and Mizraim heard, and the house of Pharoh heard.
3. And Joseph said unto his brethren, I am Joseph; is my
father yet alive? And his brethren could not answer him; for
they were troubled at his presence. 4. And Joseph said unto
his brethren, Come near unto me. And they came near: and
he said, I am Joseph, your brother, whom ye sold into Mizraim.
5. And, now, be not grieved, nor angry with yourselves, that
ye sold me hither; because to save life God sent me before
you. 6. For these two years hath the famine been in the land:
and there are yet five years, in which there shall be neither
earing nor reaping. 7. And God sent me before you, to leave
to you a remnant in the land; and to save you alive by a great
deliverance. 8. And, now, not ye have sent me hither, but
God: and he made me father to Pharoh, and lord to all his
house, and ruler in all the land of Mizraim. 9. Haste ye, and
go up to my father, and say unto him, Thus saith thy son Joseph, God hath made me lord of all Mizraim: come down
unto me, stay not. 10. And thou shalt dwell in the land of

Goshen, and thou shalt be near me, thou, and thy sons, and thy sons' sons, and thy flock and thy heards, and all that thou hast. 11. And I will sustain thee there; for yet five years is the famine; lest thou come to poverty, thou, and thy house, and all that is thine. 12. And, behold, your eyes see, and the eyes of my brother Benjamin, that it is my mouth that speaketh unto you. 13. And ye shall tell my father all my glory in Mizraim, and all that ye have seen: and ye shall haste and bring down my father hither. 14. And he fell upon Benjamin his brother's neck and wept; and Benjamin wept upon his neck. 15. And he kissed all his brethren, and wept upon them: and after that his brethren talked with him.

16. And the voice was heard in Pharoh's house, saying, Joseph's brethren are come. And it was good in the eyes of Pharoh, and in the eyes of his servants. 17. And Pharoh said unto Joseph, Say unto thy brethren, This do ye: lade your beasts, and go, get you unto the land of Kenaan. 18. And take your father and your houses, and come unto me: and I will give you the good of the land of Mizraim, and eat ye the fat of the land. 19. And thou art commanded, this do ye: take you out of the land of Mizraim wagons for your little ones, and for your wives, and bring your father and come. 20. And let not your eye care for your stuff: for the good of all the land of Mizraim is for you.

21. And so did the sons of Israel; and Joseph gave them wagons, at the mouth of Pharoh, and gave them provision for the way. 22. And to all of them he gave changes of raiment each; and to Benjamin he gave three hundred silver pieces, and five changes of raiment. 23. And to his father he sent thus: ten asses laden with the good of Mizraim, and ten she-asses laden with corn and bread and food for his father by the way. 24. And he sent his brethren away, and they went; and he said unto them, Do not fall out by the way.

25. And they went up out of Mizraim, and came unto the land of Kenaan, unto Jacob their father. 26. And they told

him, saying, Joseph is yet alive, and he is ruler over all the land of Mizraim. And his heart fainted, for he believed them not.
27. And they spake unto him all the words of Joseph, which he spake unto them: and he saw the wagons which Joseph had sent to carry him, and the spirit of Jacob their father revived.
28. And Israel said, Enough: Joseph my son is yet alive: let me go and see him, before I die.

The appeal of Judah is to Joseph irresistible. The repentance of his brothers, and their attachment to Benjamin, have been demonstrated in the most satisfactory manner. This is all that Joseph sought. It is evident, throughout the whole narrative, that he never aimed at exercising any supremacy over his brothers. As soon as he has obtained an affecting proof of the right disposition of his brothers, he conceals himself no longer. And the speech of Judah, in which, no doubt, his brothers concurred, does equal credit to his head and heart.

1–15. Joseph now reveals to his brothers the astonishing fact that he himself, their long-lost brother, stands before them. *He could not refrain himself.* Judah has painted the scene at home to the life; and Joseph can hold out no longer. *Have every man out from me.* Delicacy forbids the presence of strangers at this unrestrained outburst of tender emotion among the brothers. Besides, the workings of conscience, bringing up the recollections of the past, and the errors, to which some reference is now unavoidable, are not to be unveiled to the public eye. *He lifted up his voice in weeping.* The expression of the feelings is free and uncontrolled in a simple and primitive state of society. This prevails still in the East. *And Mizraim heard.* The Egyptians of Joseph's house would hear, and report to others, this unusual utterance of deep feeling. *I am Joseph.* The natural voice, the native tongue, the long-remembered features, would, all at once, strike the apprehension of the brothers. The remembrance of their crime, the absolute power of Joseph, and the justice of revenge, would rush upon their minds. No wonder they were silent and troubled at his presence. *Is my father yet alive?* This question shows where Joseph's thoughts were. He had been repeatedly assured of his father's welfare. But the long absence and the yearning of a fond heart bring the question up again. It was reassuring to the brethren, as it was far away from any thought of their fault or their punishment. 4. *Come near unto me.* Joseph sees the trouble of his brothers, and discerns its cause. He addresses them a second time, and plainly refers to the fact of their having sold him. He points out that this was overruled of God to the saving of life; and hence, that it was not they, but God who had mercifully sent him to Egypt to preserve all their lives. *For these two years.* Hence we perceive that the sons of Jacob obtained a supply, on the first occasion, which was sufficient for a year. *To leave to you a remnant in the land.* This is usually and most naturally referred to a surviving portion of their race. *Father to Pharoh;* a second author of life to him. Having touched very slightly on their transgression, and endeavored to divert their thoughts to the wonderful providence of God displayed in the whole affair, he lastly preoccupies their minds with the duty and necessity of bringing down their father and all their families to dwell in Egypt. *In the land of Goshen.* This was a pasture land on the borders of Egypt and Arabia, perhaps at some distance from the Nile, and watered by the showers of heaven, like their own valleys. He then appeals to their recollections and senses, whether he was not their very brother Joseph. *My mouth that speaketh unto you;* not by an interpreter, but with his own lips, and in their native tongue. Having made this needful and reassuring explanation, he breaks through all distance, and falls upon Benjamin's neck and kisses him, and all his other brothers; after which their hearts are soothed, and they speak freely with him.

16–20. The intelligence that Joseph's brethren are come reaches the ears of Pharoh, and calls forth a cordial invitation to come and settle in Egypt. *It was good in the eyes of Pharoh.* They highly esteemed Joseph on his own account; and that he should prove to be a member of a respectable family, and have the pleasure of again meeting with his nearest relatives, were circumstances that afforded them a real gratification. *The good of the land of Mizraim.* The good which it produces. *Wagons;* two-wheeled cars, fit for driving over the rough country, where roads were not formed. *Let not your eye care for your stuff;* your houses, or pieces of furniture which must be left behind. The family of Jacob thus come to Egypt, not by conquest or purchase, but by hospitable invitation, as free, independent visitors or settlers. As they were free to come or not, so were they free to stay or leave.

21–24. The brothers joyfully accept the hospitable invitation of Pharoh, and set about the necessary arrangements for their journey. *The sons of Israel;* including Joseph, who had his own part to perform in the proposed arrangement. *At the mouth of Pharoh;* as he had authorized him to do. *Changes of raiment;* fine raiment for change on a high or happy day. To Benjamin he gives special marks of fraternal affection, which no longer excite any jealous feeling among the brothers, as the reasonableness of them is obvious. *Fall out.* The original word means to be stirred by any passion, whether fear or anger, and interpreters explain it as they conceive the circumstances and the context require. The English version corresponds with the Sept. (ὀργίζεσθε) and with Onkelos. It refers, perhaps, to the little flashes of heat, impatience, and contention that are wont to disturb the harmony of companions in the East, who behave sometimes like overgrown children. Such ebullitions often lead to disastrous consequences. Joseph's exile arose from petty jealousies among brethren.

25–28. The returning brothers inform their father of the existence and elevation of Joseph in Egypt. The aged patriarch is overcome for the moment, but at length awakens to a full apprehension of the joyful news. *His heart fainted;* ceased to beat for a time, fluttered, sank within him. The news was too good for him to venture all at once to believe it. But the words of Joseph, which they recite, and the wagons which he had sent, at length lead to the conviction that it must be indeed true. He is satisfied. His only thought is to go and see Joseph before he dies. A sorrow of twenty-two years' standing has now been wiped away.

LXXIV. JACOB GOES DOWN TO EGYPT. — Gen. xlvi.

9. פַּלּוּא Pallu, *distinguished.* חֶצְרֹן Chetsron, of the *court*, or *village.* כַּרְמִי Karmi, *vine-dresser.*

10. יְמוּאֵל Jemuel, *day of El.* יָמִין Jamin, *right hand.* אֹהַד Ohad, *joining together.* יָכִין Jakin, *he shall establish.* צֹחַר Tsochar, *whiteness.*

11. גֵּרְשׁוֹן Gereshon, *expelling.* קְהָת Qehath, *assembly.* מְרָרִי Merari, *flowing, bitter.*

12. חָמוּל Chamul, *pitied, treated with mercy.*

13. תּוֹלָע Tola', *worm, scarlet.* פֻּוָּה Puvvah, *mouth?* יוֹב Job, *enemy?* שִׁמְרֹן Shimron, *watch.*

14. סֶרֶד Sered, *fear.* אֵלוֹן Elon, *oak.* יַחְלְאֵל Jachleel, *El shall sicken* or *inspire with hope.*

16. צִפְיוֹן Tsiphjon, *watcher.* חַגִּי Chaggi, *festive.* שׁוּנִי Shuni,

quiet. אֶצְבּוֹן Etsbon, *toiling?* עֵרִי ʻEri, *watcher.* אֲרוֹדִי Arodi, *rover?* אַרְאֵלִי Areli, *lion of El?*

17. יִמְנָה Jimnah, *prosperity.* יִשְׁוָה Jishvah, יִשְׁוִי Jishvi, *even, level.* בְּרִיעָה Beriʻah, *in evil.* שֶׂרַח Serach, *overflow.* חֶבֶר Cheber, *fellowship.* מַלְכִּיאֵל Malkiel, *king of El.*

21. בֶּלַע Belaʻ, *devouring.* בֶּכֶר Beker, *a young camel.* אַשְׁבֵּל Ashbel, *short?* גֵּרָא Gerah, *a grain.* נַעֲמָן Naʻaman, *pleasant.* אֵחִי Echi, *brotherly?* רֹאשׁ Rosh, *head.* מֻפִּים Muppim, חֻפִּים Chuppim, *covering.* אַרְדְּ Ard, *fugitive, rover.*

23. חֻשִׁים Chushim, *haste.*

24. יַחְצְאֵל Jachtseel, *El will divide.* גּוּנִי Guni, *dyed.* יֵצֶר Jetser, *form.* שִׁלֵּם Shillem, *retribution.*

XLVI. 1. And Israel set out with all that he had, and went to Beer-sheba, and offered sacrifices unto the God of his father Isaac. 2. And God said to Israel in the visions of the night, and he said, Jacob, Jacob! And he said, Here am I. 3. And he said, I am God, the God of thy father: fear not to go down to Mizraim; for a great nation will I make thee there. 4. I will go down with thee to Mizraim, and I will also surely bring thee up: and Joseph shall put his hand upon thine eyes.

5. And Jacob rose up from Beer-sheba: and the sons of Israel carried Jacob their father, and their little ones, and their wives, in the wagons which Pharoh had sent to carry him. 6. And they took their cattle, and their goods, which they had gained in the land of Kenaan, and went into Mizraim, Jacob, and all his seed with him; 7. His sons, and his sons' sons with him, his daughters, and his sons' daughters, and all his seed brought he with him into Mizraim. § 42.

8. And these are the names of the sons of Israel, who went into Mizraim, Jacob and his sons: Jacob's first-born, Reuben. 9. And the sons of Reuben: Henok and Pallu and Hezron and Karmi. 10. And the sons of Simon: Jemuel and Jamin and Ohad and Jakin and Zohar, and Saul son of a Kenaanitess. 11. And the sons of Levi: Gershon, Kohath and Merari. 12. And the sons of Judah: Er and Onan and Shelah and

Perez and Zerah; and Er and Onan died in the land of Kenaan; and the sons of Perez were Hezron and Hamul. 13. And the sons of Issakar: Tola and Puah and Job and Shimron. 14. And the sons of Zebulun: Sered and Elon and Jahleel. 15. These are the sons of Leah, whom she bare to Jacob in Padan-aram, and Dinah his daughter: all the souls, his sons and his daughters, were thirty and three. 16. And the sons of Gad: Ziphion and Haggi, Shuni and Ezbon, Eri and Arodi and Areli. 17. And the sons of Asher: Jimnah and Jishvah and Jishvi and Beriah, and Serah their sister; and the sons of Beriah, Heber and Malkiel. 18. These are the sons of Zilpah, whom Laban gave to Leah his daughter; and she bare them to Jacob, sixteen souls. 19. The sons of Rachel, Jacob's wife: Joseph and Benjamin. 20. And born to Joseph in the land of Mizraïm were those whom Asenath, daughter of Potiphera, priest of On, bare unto him, Menasseh and Ephraim. 21. And the sons of Benjamin: Bela and Beker and Ashbel, Gera and Naaman, Ehi and Rosh, Muppim and Huppim and Ard. 22. These are the sons of Rachel, who were born to Jacob: all the souls were fourteen. 23. And the sons of Dan: Hushim. 24. And the sons of Naphtali: Jahzeel and Guni and Jezer and Shillem. 25. These are the sons of Bilhah, whom Laban gave to Rachel his daughter: and she bare these to Jacob; all the souls were seven. 26. All the souls that went with Jacob into Mizraim, who came out of his loins, besides the wives of Jacob's sons; all the souls were sixty and six. 27. And the sons of Joseph, that were born to him in Mizraim, were two souls. All the souls of the house of Jacob which went into Mizraim were seventy.

§ 43.

28. And Judah he sent before him to Joseph, to lead the way before him to Goshen; and they went into the land of Goshen. 29. And Joseph yoked his chariot, and went up to meet Israel his father to Goshen; and he appeared to him, and fell on his neck, and wept long on his neck. 30. And Israel said unto Joseph, Let me die now, after I have seen thy face,

that thou art yet alive. 31. And Joseph said unto his brethren, and unto his father's house, I will go up and tell Pharoh; and I will say unto him, My brethren, and my father's house, that were in the land of Kenaan, are come unto me. 32. And the men are shepherds, for men of cattle have they been; and their flocks, and their herds, and all that they have, they have brought. 33. And it shall come to pass that Pharoh shall call you; and he shall say, What is your occupation? 34. And ye shall say, Men of cattle have thy servants been from our youth even until now, both we and our fathers: that ye may dwell in the land of Goshen; for every shepherd is the abomination of Mizraim.

The second dream of Joseph is now to receive its fulfilment. His father is to bow down before him. His mother is dead. It is probable that also Leah is deceased. The figure, by which the dream shadows forth the reality, is fulfilled, when the spirit of it receives its accomplishment.

1–4. Jacob arriving at Beer-sheba is encouraged by a revelation from God. Beer-sheba may be regarded as the fourth scene of Abraham's abode in the land of promise. *Offered sacrifices.* He had gathered from the words of the Lord to Abraham (xv. 13), and the way in which the dreams of Joseph were realized in the events of Providence, that his family were to descend into Egypt. He felt therefore that in taking this step he was obeying the will of Heaven. Hence he approaches God in sacrifices at an old abode of Abraham and Isaac, before he crosses the border to pass into Egypt. On this solemn occasion God appears to him in the visions of the night. He designates himself El the Mighty, and the God of his father. The former name cheers him with the thought of an all-sufficient Protector. The latter identifies the speaker with the God of his father, and therefore with the God of eternity, of creation, and of covenant. *Fear not to go down into Mizraim.* This implies both that it was the will of God that he should go down to Egypt, and that he would be protected there. *A great nation.* Jacob had now a numerous family, of whom no longer one was selected, but all were included in the chosen seed. He had received the special blessing and injunction to be fruitful and multiply (xxviii. 3, xxxv. 11). The chosen family is to be the beginning of the chosen nation. *I will go down with thee.* The I is here emphatic, as it is also in the assurance that he will bring him up in the fulness of time from Egypt. If Israel in the process of growth from a family to a nation had remained among the Kenaanites, he would have been amalgamated with the nation by intermarriage, and conformed to its vices. By his removal to Egypt he is kept apart from the demoralizing influence of a nation, whose iniquity became so great as to demand a judicial extirpation (xv. 16). He is also kept from sinking into an Egyptian by the fact that a shepherd, as he was, is an abomination to Egypt; by his location in the comparatively high land of Goshen, which is a border land, not naturally, but only politically, belonging to Egypt; and by the reduction of his race to a body of serfs, with whom that nation would not condescend to intermingle. *Joseph shall put his hand upon thine eyes.* His long-lost son shall be present to perform the last offices to him when deceased.

5–7. The descent into Egypt is now described. *His daughters, and his sons' daughters.* In the following list only one daughter of Jacob is mentioned, Dinah, and only one son's daughter, Serah. It is possible, but not probable, that there were more daughters than these at the time in his family. But even if there were no others, the plural is adopted in order to correspond with the general form of classification, from which the one daughter and the one granddaughter are merely accidental deviations. The same principle applies to the sons of Dan (v. 23), and to other instances in Scripture (1 Chron. ii. 8, 42).

8–27. The list here given of the family of Jacob as it came down into Egypt is not to be identified with a list of their descendants two hundred and fifty years after, contained in Num. xxvi., or with another list constructed after the captivity, and referring to certain of their descendants in and after the times of the monarchy. Nor is this the place to mark out or investigate the grounds of the diversities from the present which these later lists exhibit. Our proper business here is to examine into the nature and import of this ancient and original list of the family of Jacob. It purports to be a list of the names of the sons of Israel, *who went into Mizraim.* This phrase implies that the sons of Israel actually went down into Egypt; and this is accordingly historically true of all his immediate sons, Joseph having gone thither about twenty-two years before the others. And the word "sons" is to be understood here in its strict sense, as we find it in the immediate context (v. 7) distinguished from sons' sons and other descendants. *Jacob and his sons.* From this expression we perceive the progenitor is to be included with the sons among those who descended to Egypt. This also is historically exact. For the sake of clearness it is proper here to state the approximate ages of these heads of Israel at the time of the descent. Jacob himself was 130 years of age (xlvii. 9). Joseph was in his thirtieth year when he stood before Pharoh to interpret his dreams and receive his commission as governor-general of Egypt, (xli. 46). At the end of the second year of the famine nine full years were added to his life. He was therefore, we may suppose, 39 years old when Jacob arrived in Egypt, and born when his father was 91. As we conceive that he was born in the fifteenth year of Jacob's sojourn in Padan-aram, and Reuben in the eighth, we infer that Reuben was at the time of the descent into Egypt seven years older than Joseph, or 46, Simon 45, Levi 44, Judah 43, Dan about 43, Naphtali about 42, Gad about 42, Asher about 41, Issakar about 41, Zebulun about 40, Dinah about 39, Benjamin about 26. *Jacob's first-born Reuben.* This refers to the order of nature, without implying that the rights of first-birth were to be secured to Reuben (1 Chron. v. 1, 2).

9–15. The sons of Leah and their descendants are here enumerated. Reuben has four sons, who appear without variation in the other two lists (Num. xxvi. 5, 6; 1 Chron. v. 3). Of the six sons of Simon, Ohad appears in the other lists, and Nemuel and Zerah appear as colloquial variations of Jemuel and Zohar. Such diversities in oral language are usual to this day in the East and elsewhere. *Son of a Kenaanitess.* This implies that intermarriage with the Kenaanites was the exception to the rule in the family of Jacob. Wives might have been obtained from Hebrew, Aramaic, or at all events Shemite tribes who were living in their vicinity. The three sons of Levi are common to all the lists, with the slight variation of Gershom for Gershon. The sons of Judah are also unvaried. We are here reminded that Er and Onon died in the land of Kenaan (v. 38), and of course did not come down into Egypt. The extraordinary circumstances of Judah's family are recorded in ch. xxxviii. In order that Hezron and Hamul may have been born at the arrival of Jacob's household in Egypt, Judah's and Perez's first sons must have been born in the fourteenth year of their respective fathers. For the discussion of this matter see the remarks on that chapter. The four sons of Issakar occur in the other lists, with the variation of Jashub for Job. The three sons of Zebulun recur in the book of Numbers; but in the list of Chronicles no mention is made of his posterity. Dinah does not appear in the other lists. The descendants of Leah are in all thirty-two; six sons, one daughter, twenty-three grandsons, and two great-grandsons. *All the souls, his sons and his daughters, were thirty and three.* Here "all the souls" include Jacob himself, and "his sons and his daughters" are to be understood as a specification of what is included besides himself.

16–18. Next are enumerated the sons of Zilpah, Leah's handmaid. The seven sons of Gad recur in Num. xxvi., with the variants Zephon, Ozni, and Arod, for Ziphion, Ezbon, and Arodi; but they do not occur in Chronicles. Of Asher's five children, Jishuah is omitted in Numbers, but appears in Chronicles. This seems to arise from the circumstances that the list in Numbers was drawn up at the time of the facts recorded, and that in Chronicles is extracted partly from Genesis. The other names are really the same in all the lists. The descendants of Zilpah are sixteen, — two sons, eleven grandsons, one granddaughter, and two great-grandsons.

19–22. The sons of Rachel. It is remarkable that she alone is called the wife of Jacob, because she was the wife of his choice. Yet the children of the beloved, we perceive, are not placed before those of the less loved (Deut. xxi. 15, 16). Joseph's two sons are the same in all lists. Of the ten sons of Benjamin only five appear in Numbers (xxvi. 38–41), Bela and Ashbel being the same, and Ahiram, Shupham, and Hupham, being variants of Ehi, Muppim, and Huppim. In two hundred and fifty years the other five have become extinct. Naaman and Ard seem to have died early, as two sons of Bela, named after them, take their places as heads of families or clans. In Chronicles (vii. 6–12) we have two lists of his descendants which do not seem to be primary, as they do not agree with either of the former lists, or with one another, though some of the names recur. The descendants of Rachel are fourteen, — two sons and twelve grandsons.

23–25. The sons of Bilhah, Rachel's handmaid, come last. Hushim, the son of Dan, appears in Numbers (xxvi. 42) as Shuham, and perhaps in Chronicles (vii. 12) in an obscure connection. The four sons of Naphtali occur in all the lists, Shallum being the variant in Chronicles (vii. 13) for Shillem. The descendants of Bilhah are seven, — two sons and five grandsons.

26, 27. All the souls that went with Jacob into Egypt, *that came out of his loins*, were eleven sons, one daughter, fifty grandchildren, and four great-grandsons; in all, sixty-six. Jacob, Joseph and his two sons, are four; and thus all the souls belonging to the family of Jacob which went into Egypt were seventy. This account, with its somewhat intricate details, is expressed with remarkable brevity and simplicity.

The Septuagint gives seventy-five as the sum-total, which is made out by inserting Makir the son, and Gilead the grandson of Menasseh, Shuthelah and Tahan, sons, and Edom or Eran, a grandson of Ephraim (Num. xxvi.). This version has also the incorrect statement that the sons of Joseph born to him in Egypt were nine; whereas by its own showing they were seven, and Jacob and Joseph are to be added to make up the nine. Some suppose that Stephen's statement — *ἀποστείλας δὲ Ἰωσὴφ μετεκαλέσατο τὸν πατέρα αὐτοῦ Ἰακὼβ καὶ πᾶσαν τὴν συγγένειαν ἐν ψυχαῖς ἑβδομήκοντα πέντε* — is founded on this version. If Stephen here quoted the Septuagint as a well-known version, he was accountable only for the correctness of his quotation, and not for the error which had crept into his authority. This was immaterial to his present purpose, and it was not the manner of the sacred speakers to turn aside from their grand task to the pedantry of criticism. But it is much more likely that the text of the Septuagint has here been conformed in a bungling way to the number given by Stephen. For it is to be observed that his number refers, according to the text, to Jacob and all his kindred, *exclusive of Joseph and his sons*. They could not therefore amount to seventy-five, but only to sixty-seven, if we count merely Jacob and his proper descendants. It is probable, therefore, that in the idea of Stephen the "kindred" of Jacob included the eight or nine surviving wives that accompanied the children of Israel. Judah's wife was dead, and it is probable that Reuben's was also deceased before he committed incest with Bilhah. If there were two or three more widowers the number of surviving wives would be eight or nine.

The number of the children of Israel is very particularly noted. But the Scripture lays no stress upon the number itself, and makes no particular application of it. It stands forth, therefore, on the record merely as a historical fact. It is remarkable that it is the product of seven, the number of holiness; and ten, the number of completeness. It is still more remarkable that it is the number of the names of those who are the heads of the primitive nations. This is in accordance with the fact that the church is the counterpart of the world, not only in diversity of character and destiny, but also in the adaptation of the former to work out the restitution of all things to God in the latter. The covenant with Abraham is a special means by which the seed may come, who is to give legal and vital effect to the old and general covenant with Noah the representative of the nations. The church of God in the world is to be the instrument by which the kingdom of the world is to become the kingdom of Christ. "When the Most High bestowed the inheritance on the nations, when he separated the sons of Adam, he set the bounds of the peoples according to the number of the sons of Israel" (Deut. xxxii. 8). This curious sentence may have an immediate reference to the providential distribution of the human family over the habitable parts of the earth, according to the number of his church, and of his dispensation of grace; but at all events it conveys the great and obvious principle that all things whatsoever in the affairs of men are antecedently adapted with the most perfect exactitude to the benign reign of grace already realized in the children of God, and yet to be extended to all the sons and daughters of Adam.

28–34. The settlement in Goshen is now narrated. *Judah he sent before him.* We have already seen why the three older sons of Jacob were disqualified for taking the lead in important matters relating to the family. *To lead the way before him into Goshen,* — to get the requisite directions from Joseph, and then conduct the immigrants to their destined resting-place. *And went up.* Egypt was the valley of the Nile, and therefore a low country. Goshen was comparatively high, and therefore at some distance from the Nile and the sea. *And he appeared unto him.* A phrase usually applied to the appearance of God to men, and intended to intimate the unexpectedness of the sight, which now came before the eyes of Jacob. 31. *I will go up.* In a courtly sense, to approach the residence of the sovereign is to go up. Joseph intends to make the "occupation" of his kindred a prominent part of his communication to Pharoh, in order to secure their settlement in Goshen. This he considers desirable, on two grounds: first, because Goshen was best fitted for pasture; and secondly, because the chosen family would thus be comparatively isolated from Egyptian society. The two nations were in some important respects mutually repulsive. The idolatrous and superstitious customs of the Egyptians were abhorrent to a worshipper of the true God; and "every shepherd was the abomination of Egypt." The expression here employed is very strong, and rises even to a religious aversion. Herodotus makes the cowherds the third of the seven classes into which the Egyptians were divided (Her. ii. 164). Others include them in the lowest class of the community. This, however, is not sufficient to account for the national antipathy. About seventeen or eighteen centuries before the Christian era it is probable that the Hyksos, or shepherd kings, were masters of the southern part of the country, while a native dynasty still prevailed in lower Egypt. The religion of these shepherd intruders was different from that of the Egyptians, which they treated with disrespect. They were addicted to the barbarities which are usually incident to a foreign rule. It is not surprising, therefore, that the shepherd became the abomination of Egypt.

LXXV. JACOB IN GOSHEN.—Gen. xlvii.

11. רַעְמְסֵס Ra'meses, *son of the sun.*
31. מִטָּה *bed.* מַטֶּה *staff.*

XLVII. 1. And Joseph went and told Pharoh: and he said, My father and my brethren, and their flocks and their herds, and all that they have, are come out of the land of Kenaan: and, behold, they are in the land of Goshen. 2. And of the whole of his brethren he took five men, and set them before Pharoh. 3. And Pharoh said unto his brethren, What is your occupation? And they said unto Pharoh, Shepherds are thy servants, both we and our fathers. 4. And they said unto Pharoh, To sojourn in the land are we come; for there is no pasture for the flock of thy servants; for sore is the famine in the land of Kenaan: and therefore let thy servants now dwell in the land of Goshen. 5. And Pharoh said unto Joseph, saying, Thy father and thy brethren are come unto thee. 6. The land of Mizraim is before thee; in the best of the land settle thy father and thy brethren: let them dwell in the land of Goshen; and if thou knowest and there be among them men of ability, then make them masters of my cattle. 7. And Joseph brought Jacob his father, and set him before Pharoh: and Jacob blessed Pharoh. 8. And Pharoh said unto Jacob, What are the days of the years of thy life? 9. And Jacob said unto Pharoh, The days of the years of my pilgrimage are thirty and a hundred years: few and evil have been the days of the years of my life, and they have not attained unto the days of the years of the life of my fathers in the days of their pilgrimage. 10. And Jacob blessed Pharoh, and came out from before Pharoh. 11. And Joseph settled his father and his brethren; and gave them a possession in the land of Mizraim, in the best of the land, in the land of Rameses; as Pharoh had commanded. 12. And Joseph sustained his father, and his brethren, and all his father's house with bread, according to the little ones.

13. And there was no bread in all the land; for the famine was very sore; and the land of Mizraim and the land of Kenaan fainted by reason of the famine. 14. And Joseph gathered up all the silver that was found in the land of Mizraim and in the land of Kenaan, for the grain which they bought: and Joseph brought the silver into Pharoh's house. 15. And the silver was spent from the land of Mizraim, and from the land of Kenaan; and all Mizraim went to Joseph, saying, Give us bread, for why should we die in thy presence? for silver faileth. 16. And Joseph said, Give your cattle; and I will give you for your cattle, if silver fail. 17. And they brought their cattle unto Joseph: and Joseph gave them bread, for the horses and for the cattle of sheep, and for the cattle of oxen, and for the asses: and he provided them with bread for all their cattle that year. 18. And that year was ended; and they went to him the second year, and said unto him, We will not hide from my lord that the silver is spent, and the cattle of beasts belong to my lord: there is naught left before my lord but our bodies and our soil. 19. Wherefore shall we die before thine eyes, both we and our soil? Buy us and our soil for bread: and we and our soil will be servants unto Pharoh; and give seed, and we shall live and not die, and the soil shall not be waste. 20. And Joseph bought all the soil of Mizraim for Pharoh; for Mizraim sold every man his field, because the famine had laid hold on

them: and the land became Pharoh's. 21. And the people he removed into the cities, from one end of the border of Mizraim unto the other end thereof. 22. Only the soil of the priests bought he not: for the priests had a stated rate from Pharoh; wherefore they sold not their soil. 23. And Joseph said unto the people, Behold, I have bought you this day and your soil for Pharoh: here is seed for you, and ye shall sow the soil. 24. And it shall come to pass in the increase, that ye shall give the fifth to Pharoh: and four parts shall be your own, for seed of the field, and for your food, and for those in your houses, and for your little ones to eat. 25. And they said, Thou hast kept us alive: let us find grace in the eyes of my lord, and we will be servants to Pharoh. 26. And Joseph made it a statute unto this day over the soil of Mizraim, that Pharoh should have the fifth: but the soil of the priests alone became not Pharoh's.

27. And Israel dwelt in the land of Mizraim, in the land of Goshen: and they were possessed thereof, and grew and multiplied exceedingly. 12

28. And Jacob lived in the land of Egypt seventeen years: and the days of Jacob, the years of his life, were seven and forty and a hundred years. 29. And the days of Israel drew nigh to his death; and he called his son Joseph, and said unto him, If now I have found grace in thine eyes, put now thy hand under my thigh: and do with me kindness and truth; bury me not now in Mizraim. 30. And I will lie with my fathers, and thou shalt carry me out of Mizraim, and bury me in their burying-place. And he said, I will do according to thy word. 31. And he said, Swear unto me. And he sware unto him: and Israel bowed himself on the head of the bed. ¶ 37

Arrangements are now made for the settlement of Israel in Goshen. The administration of Joseph during the remaining years of the famine is then recorded. For the whole of this period his father and brothers are subject to him, as their political superior, according to the reading of his early dreams. We then approach to the death-bed of Jacob, and hear him binding Joseph by an oath to bury him in the sepulchre of his fathers.

1–12. Joseph announces to Pharoh the arrival of his kindred. *Of the whole of his brethren,* more exactly from the end of his brethren. *Five men,* a favorite number in Egypt. *Shepherds,* owners and feeders of sheep and other cattle. 5, 6. *Pasture.* Hence it appears that the drought had made the grazing extremely scanty. *Men of ability,* competent to take the oversight of others. 7–10. *Jacob his father,* he presents before Pharoh, after he has disposed of all business matters. *Jacob blessed Pharoh.* This is the patriarch's grateful return for Pharoh's great kindness and generosity towards him and his house. He is conscious of even a higher dignity than that of Pharoh, as he is a prince of God; and as such he bestows his precious benediction. Pharoh was struck with his venerable appearance, and inquired what was his age. *Pilgrimage,* — sojourning, wandering without any constant abode or fixed holding. Such was the life of the patriarchs in the land of promise (Heb. xi. 13). *Few and evil.* Jacob's years at this time were far short of those of Abraham and Isaac, not to speak of more ancient men. Much bitterness also had been mingled in his cup from the time that he beguiled his brother of the birthright and the blessing, which would have come to him in a lawful way if he had only waited in patience. Obliged to flee for his life from his father's house, serving seven years for a beloved wife, and balked in his expected recompense by a deceitful father-in-law, serving seven long years more for the object of his affections, having his wages changed ten times during the six years of his further toil for a maintenance, afflicted by the dishonor of his only daughter, the reckless revenge taken by Simon and Levi, the death of his beloved wife in childbed, the disgraceful incest of Reuben, the loss of Joseph himself for twenty-two years, and the present famine with all its anxieties — Jacob, it must be confessed, has become acquainted with no small share of the ills of life. *Blessed Pharoh.* It is possible that this blessing is the same as that already mentioned, now reiterated in its proper place in the narrative. 12. *According to the little ones.* This means either in proportion to the number in each household, or with all the tenderness with which a parent provides for his infant offspring.

13–26. Joseph introduces remarkable changes into the relation of the sovereign and the people of Egypt. *There was no bread in all the land.* The private stores of the wealthy were probably exhausted. *And Joseph gathered up all the silver.* The old stores of grain and the money, which had flowed into the country during the years of plenty, seem to have lasted for five years. *And Joseph brought the silver into Pharoh's house.* He was merely the steward of Pharoh in this matter, and made a full return of all the payments that came into his hands. 15–17. *The silver was spent.* The famishing people have no more money; but they must have bread. Joseph is fertile in expedients. He proposes to take their cattle. This was really a relief to the people, as they had no means of providing them with fodder. The value of commodities is wholly altered by a change of circumstances. Pearls will not purchase a cup of water in a vast and dreary wilderness. Cattle become worthless when food becomes scarce, and the means of procuring it are exhausted. For their cattle Joseph supplies them with food during the sixth year.

18–20. The seventh year is now come. The silver and cattle are now gone. Nothing remains but their lands, and with these themselves as the serfs of the soil. Accordingly they make this offer to Joseph, which he cannot refuse. Hence it is evident that Pharoh had as yet no legal claim to the soil. In primeval times the first entrants into an unoccupied country became, by a natural custom, the owners of the grounds they held and cultivated. The mere nomad, who roamed over a wide range of country, where his flocks merely cropped the spontaneous herbage, did not soon arrive at the notion of private property in land. But the husbandman, who settled on a promising spot, broke up the soil, and sowed the seed, felt he had acquired by his labor a title to the acres he had cultivated and permanently occupied, and this right was instinctively acknowledged by others. Hence each cultivator grew into the absolute owner of his own farm. Hence the lands of Egypt belonged to the peasantry of the country, and were at their disposal. These lands had now become valueless to those who had neither provisions for themselves nor seed for their ground. They willingly part with them, therefore, for a year's provision and a supply of seed. In this way the lands of Egypt fell into the hands of the crown by a free purchase. 21, 22. *And the people he removed into the cities.* This is not an act of arbitrary caprice, but a wise and kind measure for the more convenient nourishment of the people until the new arrangements for the cultivation of the soil should be completed. The priestly class were sustained by a state allowance, and therefore were not obliged to alienate their lands. Hence they became by this social revolution a privileged order. The military class were also exempted most probably from the surrender of their patrimonial rights, as they were maintained on the crown lands.

23–26. *I have bought you.* He had bought their lands, and so they might be regarded, in some sort, as the servants of Pharoh, or the serfs of the soil. *In the increase ye shall give the fifth to Pharoh.* This explains at once the extent of their liability, and the security of their liberty and property. They do not become Pharoh's bondmen. They own their land under him by a new tenure. They are no longer subject to arbitrary exactions. They have a stated annual rent, bearing a fixed ratio to the amount of their crop. This is an equitable adjustment of their dues, and places them under the protection of a statute law. The people are accordingly well pleased with the enactment of Joseph, which becomes henceforth the law of Egypt.

27–31. *And they were possessed thereof.* They become owners or tenants of the soil in Goshen. The Israelites were recognized as subjects with the full rights of freemen. *They grew and multiplied exceedingly.* They are now placed in a definite territory, where they are free from the contamination which arises from promiscuous intermarriage with an idolatrous race; and hence the Lord bestows the blessing of fruitfulness and multiplication, so that in a generation or two more they can intermarry among themselves. It is a remarkable circumstance that until now we read of only two daughters in the family of Jacob. The brothers could not marry their sisters, and it was not desirable that the females should form affinity with the heathen, as they had in general to follow the faith of their husbands. Here the twelfth section of the Pentateuch terminates.

28–31. Jacob lives seventeen years in Egypt, and so survives the famine twelve years. *He called his son Joseph.* Joseph retained his power and place near Pharoh after the fourteen years of special service were completed; hence Jacob looks to him for the accomplishment of his wishes concerning the place of his burial. *Put thy hand under my thigh* (xxiv. 2). He binds Joseph by a solemn asseveration to carry his mortal remains to the land of promise. *And Israel bowed himself on the head of the bed.* On receiving the solemn promise of Joseph, he turns towards the head of the bed, and assumes the posture of adoration, rendering, no doubt, thanks to God for all the mercies of his past life, and for this closing token of filial duty and affection. The Septuagint has the rendering ἐπὶ τὸ ἄκρον τῆς ῥάβδου αὐτοῦ, "on the top of his staff," which is given in the Epistle to the Hebrews

(xi. 21). This is obtained by a mere change in the vowel pointing of the last word.

LXXVI. JOSEPH VISITS HIS SICK FATHER.—Gen. xlviii.

XLVIII. 1. And it came to pass after these things, that one said to Joseph, Behold, thy father is sick. And he took his two sons with him, Menasseh and Ephraim. 2. And one told Jacob, and said, Behold, thy son Joseph cometh unto thee: and Israel strengthened himself and sat upon the bed. 3. And Jacob said unto Joseph, God Almighty appeared unto me at Luz in the land of Kenaan, and blessed me; 4. And said unto me, Behold, I will make thee fruitful, and multiply thee, and make thee a multitude of people: and I will give this land to thy seed after thee as a perpetual possession. 5. And now thy two sons that were born to thee in the land of Mizraim are mine: Ephraim and Menasseh, as Reuben and Simon, shall be mine. 6. And thy issue which thou begettest after them shall be thine; after the name of their brethren shall they be called in their inheritance. 7. And as for me, in coming from Padan, Rachel died upon me in the land of Kenaan, by the way when there was a stretch of land to go to Ephrath: and I buried her there in the way to Ephrath, which is Bethlehem.

8. And Israel beheld Joseph's sons, and said, Who are these? 9. And Joseph said unto his father, They are my sons, whom God hath given me here. And he said, Bring them now unto me, and I will bless them. 10. And the eyes of Israel were dim from age; he could not see: and he brought them near unto him; and he kissed them, and embraced them. 11. And Israel said unto Joseph, To see thy face I had not thought: and, lo, God hath showed me also thy seed. 12. And Joseph brought them out from between

his knees, and bowed with his face to the earth. 13. And Joseph took the two, Ephraim in his right hand towards Israel's left, and Menasseh in his left toward Israel's right: and brought them near unto him. 14. And Israel stretched out his right hand, and laid it on Ephraim's head, who was the younger, and his left hand upon Menasseh's head: he guided his hands wittingly, for Menasseh was the first-born. 15. And he blessed Joseph, and said, The God before whom walked my fathers, Abraham and Isaac, the God who fed me from my being unto this day, 16. The Angel, that redeemed me from all evil, bless the lads; and let my name be put upon them, and the name of my fathers, Abraham and Isaac: and let them grow into a multitude in the midst of the land.

17. And Joseph saw that his father laid his right hand upon Ephraim's head, and it displeased him: and he held up his father's hand to remove it from Ephraim's head to Menasseh's head. 18. And Joseph said unto his father, Not so, my father: for this is the first-born; put thy right hand upon his head. 19. And his father refused, and said, I know, my son, I know: he also shall become a people, and he also shall be great: but truly his younger brother shall be greater than he; and his seed shall be the fulness of the nations. 20. And he blessed them in that day, saying, In thee shall Israel bless, saying, God make thee as Ephraim and as Menasseh. And he set Ephraim before Menasseh. 21. And Israel said unto Joseph, Behold, I die; and God will be with you and restore you to the land of your fathers. 22. And I have given thee one share above thy brethren, which I took out of the hand of the Amorite with my sword and with my bow. § 38.

The right of primogeniture has been forfeited by Reuben. The double portion in the inheritance is now transferred to Joseph. He is the first-born of her who was intended by Jacob to be his first and only wife. He has also been the means of saving all his father's house, even after he had been sold into slavery by his brethren. He has therefore undeniable claims to this part of the first-born's rights.

1–7. *After these things.* After the arrangements concerning the funeral, recorded in the chapter. *Menasseh and Ephraim.* They seem to have accompanied their father from respectful affection to their aged relative. *Israel strengthened himself,* — summoned his remaining powers for the interview, which was now to him an effort. *God Almighty appeared unto me at Luz.* From the terms of the blessing received it is evident that Jacob here refers to the last appearance of God to him at Bethel (xxxv. 11). *And now thy sons.* After referring to the promise of a numerous offspring, and of a territory which they are to inherit, he assigns to each of the two sons of Joseph, who were born in Egypt, a place among his own sons, and a separate share in the promised land. In this way two shares fall to Joseph. *And thy issue.* We are not informed whether Joseph had any other sons. But all such are to be reckoned in the two tribes of which Ephraim and Menasseh are the heads. These young men are now at least twenty and nineteen years of age, as they were born before the famine commenced. Any subsequent issue that Joseph might have, would be counted among the generations of their children. *Rachel died upon me,* — as a heavy affliction falling upon me. The presence of Joseph naturally leads the father's thoughts to Rachel, the beloved mother of his beloved son, whose memory he honors in giving a double portion to her eldest son.

8–16. He now observes and proceeds to bless the two sons of Joseph. *Who are these?* The sight and the observant faculties of the patriarch were now failing. *Bring them now unto me, and I will bless them.* Jacob is seated on the couch, and the young men approach him. He kisses and folds his arms around them. The comforts of his old age come up before his mind. He had not expected to see Joseph again in the flesh, and now God had showed him his seed. After these expressions of parental fondness, Joseph drew them back from between his knees, that he might present them in the way that was distinctive of their age. He then bowed with his face to the earth, in reverential acknowledgment of the act of worship about to be performed. Joseph expected the blessing to be regulated by the age of his sons, and is therefore careful to present them so that the right hand of his dim-sighted parent may, without any effort, rest on the head of his first-born. But the venerable patriarch, guided by the Spirit of him who doth according to his own will, designedly lays his right hand on the head of the younger, and thereby attributes to him the greater blessing.

The imposition of the hand is a primitive custom which here for the first time comes into notice. It is the natural mode of marking out the object of the benediction, signifying its conveyance to the individual, and implying that it is laid upon him as the destiny of his life. It may be done by either hand; but when each is laid on a different object, as in the present case, it may denote that the higher blessing is conveyed by the right hand. The laying on of both hands on one person may express the fulness of the blessing conveyed, or the fulness of the desire with which it is conveyed.

15–16. *And he blessed Joseph.* In blessing his seed he blesses himself. In exalting his two sons into the rank and right of his brothers, he bestows upon them the double portion of the first-born. In the terms of the blessing Jacob first signalizes the threefold function which the Lord discharges in effecting the salvation of a sinner. *The God before whom walked my fathers*, is the Author of salvation, the Judge who dispenses justice and mercy, the Father, before whom the adopted and regenerate child walks. From him salvation comes, to him the saved returns, to walk before him and be perfect. *The God, who fed me from my being unto this day*, is the Creator and Upholder of life, the Quickener and Sanctifier, the potential Agent, who works both to will and to do in the soul. *The Angel that redeemed me from all evil*, is the all-sufficient Friend, who wards off evil by himself satisfying the demands of justice and resisting the devices of malice. There is a beautiful propriety of feeling in Jacob ascribing to his fathers the walking before God, while he thankfully acknowledges the grace of the Quickener and Justifier to himself. The *Angel* is explicitly applied to the Supreme Being in this ministerial function. *The God* is the emphatic description of the true, living God, as contradistinguished from all false gods. *Bless the lads.* The word *bless* is in the singular number. For Jacob's threefold periphrasis is intended to describe the one God who wills, works, and wards. *And let my name be put upon them.* Let them be counted among my immediate sons, and let them be related to Abraham and Isaac, as my other sons are. This is the only thing that is special in the blessing. *Let them grow into a multitude.* The word *grow* in the original refers to the spawning or extraordinary increase of the finny tribe. The after history of Ephraim and Menasseh will be found to correspond with this special prediction.

17–22. Joseph presumes that his father has gone astray through dulness of perception, and endeavors to rectify his mistake. He finds, however, that on the other hand a supernatural vision is now conferred on his parent, who is fully conscious of what he is about, and therefore abides by his own act. Ephraim is to be greater than Menasseh. Joshua, the successor of Moses, was of the tribe of Ephraim, as Kaleb his companion was of Judah. Ephraim came to designate the northern kingdom of the ten tribes, as Judah denoted the southern kingdom containing the remaining tribes; and each name was occasionally used to denote all Israel, with a special reference to the prominent part. *His seed shall be the fulness of the nations.* This denotes not only the number but the completeness of his race, and accords with the future preëminence of his tribe. 20. *In thee*, in Joseph, who is still identified with his offspring. 21, 22. At the point of death Jacob expresses his assurance of the return of his posterity to the land of promise, and bestows on Joseph one share or piece of ground above his brethren, which, says he, *I took out of the hand of the Amorite with my sword and with my bow.* This share is, in the original, שְׁכֶם Shekem, a shoulder or tract of land. This region included *the parcel of the field where he had spread his tent* (xxxiii. 19). It refers to the whole territory of Shekem, which was conquered by his sword and his bow, inasmuch as the city itself was sacked, and its inhabitants put to the sword by his sons at the head of his armed retainers, though without his approval (xxxiv.). Though he withdrew immediately after to Bethel (xxxv.), yet he neither fled nor relinquished possession of this conquest, as we find his sons feeding his flocks there when he himself was residing at Hebron (xxxvii. 13). The incidental conquest of such a tract was no more at variance with the subsequent acquisition of the whole country than the purchase of a field by Abraham or a parcel of ground by Jacob himself. In accordance with this gift Joseph's bones were deposited in Shekem, after the conquest of the whole land by returning Israel. The territory of Shekem was probably not equal in extent to that of Ephraim, but was included within its bounds.

LXXVII. JACOB BLESSES HIS SONS. — Gen. xlix.

5. מְכֵרָה *weapon;* r. כָּרַר or כָּרָה *dig.* *Device, design?* r. מָכַר *sell,* in Arab. *take counsel.* *Habitation.*

10. מְחֹקֵק *lawgiver, judge, dispenser of laws.* This word occurs in

six other places, — Num. xxi. 18; Deut. xxxiii. 21; Jud. v. 14; Ps. lx. 9; cviii. 9; Isa. xxxiii. 22; in five of which it clearly denotes ruler, or judge. The meaning *sceptre* is therefore doubtful. שִׁילֹה Shiloh, a softened form of שִׁילוֹן, a derivative of שׁל, the ultimate root of שָׁלָה, שָׁלַם, and possibly שָׁלַט, and hence denoting *the peacemaker*, *the prince of peace*. It is not employed as an appellative noun. But it is used afterwards as the name of a town, now identified as Seilun. This town probably had its name, like many other ancient places, from a person of the same name who built or possessed it.

XLIX. 1. And Jacob called his sons: and he said, Gather yourselves together, and I will tell you that which shall befall you in the after days. 2. Assemble yourselves, and hear, ye sons of Jacob; and hearken to Israel your father.

3. Reuben, my first-born art thou, my might and the beginning of my strength: the excellency of dignity, the excellency of power. 4. Boiling over as water, thou shalt not excel, because thou wentest up to thy father's bed: then didst thou defile it, to my couch he went up. ¶ 39.

5. Simon and Levi are brethren: instruments of violence are their weapons. 6. Into their counsel let not my soul enter, in their congregation let not mine honor join; for in their anger they slew a man, and in their self-will they houghed an ox. 7. Cursed be their anger, for it was fierce: and their wrath, for it was cruel: I will divide them in Jacob, and scatter them in Israel. ¶ 40.

8. Judah, thee shall thy brethren praise; thy hand shall be on the neck of thine enemies: thy father's sons shall bow down to thee. 9. A lion's whelp is Judah; from the prey, my son, art thou gone up: he stooped down, he couched as a lion and as a lioness: who shall rouse him up? 10. The sceptre shall not depart from Judah, nor the lawgiver from between his feet; until Shiloh come, and unto him be the obedience of the peoples. 11. Binding unto the vine his ass, and to the choice vine his ass's colt, he hath washed in the wine his garments, and in the blood of grapes his mantle.

12. Red are his eyes from wine, and white his teeth from milk. ¶ 41.

13. Zebulun shall dwell at the haven of seas; and he shall be at the haven of ships, and his flank toward Zidon. ¶ 42.

14. Issakar is an ass of bone, couching between the hurdles.
15. And he saw rest, that it was good, and the land, that it was pleasant: and he bowed his shoulder to bear, and became subject to tribute. § 44.

16. Dan shall judge his people, as one of the tribes of Israel.
17. Dan shall be a serpent on the way, an adder on the path: that biteth the horse's heels, and its rider falleth backward.
18. For thy salvation have I waited, O LORD. § 45.

19. Gad, a troop shall press on him: and he shall press on the heel. § 46.

20. Of Asher, fat shall be his bread; and he shall yield royal dainties. § 47.

21. Naphtali is a hind let loose; he giveth goodly words. § 48.

22. Son of a fruitful tree is Joseph, son of a fruitful tree by
a well, whose daughters run over a wall. 23. And masters
of arrows grieved him, and shot at him, and hated him. 24.
And his bow abode in strength, and the arms of his hands
were firm; from the hands of the Might of Jacob, from him,
the Shepherd, the Stone of Israel, 25. From the God of thy
father who shall help thee, and the Almighty who shall bless
thee, are blessings of heaven above, blessings of the deep that
lieth beneath, blessings of the breasts and of the womb. 26.
The blessings of thy father have prevailed over the blessings
of my progenitors unto the bound of the perpetual hills: they
shall be on the head of Joseph, and on the brow of him who
was distinguished from his brethren. ¶ 43.

27. Benjamin shall ravin as a wolf; in the morning he shall devour the prey, and in the evening he shall divide the spoil.

28. All these are the twelve tribes of Israel: and this is

that which their father spake unto them, and blessed them; each according to his blessing blessed he them. 29. And he commanded them, and said unto them, I am to be gathered unto my people: bury me with my fathers, in the cave that is in the field of Ephron the Hittite; 30. In the cave that is in the field of Makpelah, which is before Mamre, in the land of Kenaan, which Abraham bought with the field from Ephron the Hittite for a possession of a burying-place. 31. There they buried Abraham, and Sarah his wife; there they buried Isaac, and Rebekah his wife; and there I buried Leah. 32. The purchase of the field and of the cave that is therein was from the sons of Heth. 33. And Jacob made an end of commanding his sons, and gathered up his feet into the bed, and expired, and was gathered unto his peoples.

From the special conference with Joseph we now pass to the parting address of Jacob to his assembled sons. This is at the same time prophetic and benedictory. Like all prophecy, it starts from present things, and in its widest expanse penetrates into the remotest future of the present course of nature.

1, 2. *And Jacob called his sons.* This is done by messengers going to their various dwellings and pasture-grounds, and summoning them to his presence. *And he said.* These words introduce his dying address. *Gather yourselves together.* Though there is to be a special address to each, yet it is to be in the audience of all the rest, for the instruction of the whole family. *That which shall befall you in the after days.* The after days are the times intervening between the speaker and the end of the human race. The beginning of man was at the sixth day of the last creation. The end of his race will be at the dissolution of the heavens and the earth then called into being, and the new creation which we are taught will be consequent thereupon. To this interval prophecy has reference in general, though it occasionally penetrates beyond the veil that separates the present from the future creation. The prophet has his mind filled with the objects and events of the present and the past, and from these he must draw his images for the future, and express them in the current language of his day. To interpret his words, therefore, we must ascend to his day, examine his usage of speech, distinguish the transient forms in which truth may appear, and hold fast by the constant essence which belongs to all ages. *Hear, ye sons of Jacob; and hearken to Israel your father.* This is a specimen of the synthetic or synonymous parallel. It affords a good example of the equivalence, and at the same time the distinction, of Jacob and Israel. They both apply to the same person, and to the race of which he is the head. The one refers to the natural, the other to the spiritual. The distinction is similar to that between Elohim and Jehovah: the former of which designates the eternal God, antecedent to all creation, and therefore equally related to the whole universe; the latter, the self-existent God, subsequent to the creation of intelligent beings, and specially related to them, as the moral Governor, the Keeper of covenant, and the Performer of promise.

3, 4. Reuben, as the first-born by nature, has the first place in the benedictory address. *My might.* In times and places in which a man's right depends on his might, a large family of sons is the source of strength and safety. *The excellency of dignity, and the excellency of power,*— the rank and authority which belong to the first-born. *Boiling over as water.* That which boils over perishes at the same time that it is pernicious. This is here transferred in a figure to the passionate nature of Reuben. *Thou shalt not excel.* There is here an allusion to the excellency of dignity and power. By the boiling over of his unhallowed passions Reuben lost all the excellence that primogeniture confers. By the dispensation of Providence the double portion went to Joseph, the first-born of Rachel; the chieftainship to Judah; and the priesthood to Levi. The cause of this forfeiture is then assigned. In the last sentence the patriarch in a spirit of indignant sorrow passes from the direct address to the indirect narrative. *To my couch he went up.* The doom here pronounced upon Reuben is still a blessing, as he is not excluded from a tribe's share in the promised land. But, as in the case of the others, this blessing is abated and modified by his past conduct. His tribe has its seat on the east of the Jordan, and never comes to any eminence in the commonwealth of Israel.

5–7. *Simon and Levi are brethren,* by temper as well as by birth. *Their weapons.* This word is rendered *plans, devices,* by some. But the present rendering agrees best with the context. Weapons may be properly called instruments of violence; but not so plots. "Habitations" requires the preposition *in* before it, which is not in the original, and is not to be supplied without necessity. *Into their counsel.* This refers to the plot they formed for the destruction of the inhabitants of Shekem. *They houghed an ox.* The singular of the original is to be understood as a plural denoting the kind of acts to which they were prompted in their passion for revenge. Jacob pronounces a curse upon their anger, not because indignation against sin is unwarrantable in itself, but because their wrath was marked by deeds of fierceness and cruelty. *I will divide them in Jacob, and scatter them in Israel.* He does not cut them off from any part in the promised inheritance; but he divides and scatters them. Accordingly they are divided from one another in their after history, the tribe of Simon being settled in the southwest corner of the territory of Judah, and Levi having no connected territory, but occupying certain cities and their suburbs which were assigned to his descendants in the various provinces of the land. They were also scattered in Israel. For Simon is the weakest of all the tribes at the close of their sojourn in the wilderness (Num. xxvi. 14); he is altogether omitted in the blessing of Moses (Deut. xxxiii.), and hence obtains no distinct territory, but only a part of that of Judah (Jos. xix. 1–9); and he subsequently sends out two colonies, which are separated from the parent stock, and from one another (1 Chr. iv. 24–43). And Levi received forty-eight towns in the various districts of the land, in which his descendants dwelt, far separated from one another. This prediction was therefore fulfilled to the letter in the history of these brothers. Their classification under one head is a hint that they will yet count but as one tribe.

8–12. Judah, the fourth son of Jacob, comes in for the supremacy after the three former have been set aside. His personal prowess, the perpetuity of his dominion, and the luxuriance of his soil are then described. 8. *Thee shall thy brethren praise.* This is an allusion to his name, which signifies praise (xxix. 35). As his mother praised the Lord for her fourth son, so shall his brethren praise him for his personal excellence. Ardor of temperament, decision of character, and frankness of acknowledgment are conspicuous even in the blemishes of his early life. Tenderness of conscience, promptitude in resolve, capacity for business, and force of eloquence come out in his riper years. These are qualities that win popular esteem. *Thy hand shall be in the neck of thine enemies.* They shall flee before him, but shall not escape his powerful grasp. They shall be compelled to yield to his overwhelming power. *Thy father's sons shall bow down to thee.* Not only his enemies, but his friends, shall acknowledge his sway. The similar prediction concerning Joseph (xxxvii. 6–8) was of a personal nature, and referred to a special occasion, not to a permanent state of affairs. It had already received its main fulfilment, and would altogether terminate with the lifetime of Joseph. The present announcement refers to Judah not as an individual, but as the head of a tribe in Israel, and will therefore correspond in duration with that commonwealth.

9. *A lion's whelp is Judah.* In physical strength Judah is compared to the lion, the king of beasts. At first he is the lion's whelp, the young lion, giving promise of future vigor; then the full-grown lion, exulting in his irresistible force, seizing and overmastering the prey, and after reaping the fruits of his victory, ascending to his mountain lair and reposing in undisturbed security. The lioness is brought into the comparison with propriety, as in defence of her cubs she is even more dangerous than the male to the unwary assailant. After being satiated with prey, the lion, reposing in his majesty, will not disturb the passer-by; but who shall rouse him up and escape?

10. From his physical force we now pass to his moral supremacy. *The sceptre,* the staff of authority. *Shall not depart from Judah.* The tribe sceptre did not leave Judah so long as there was a remnant of the commonwealth of Israel. Long after the other tribes had lost their individuality, Judah lingered in existence and in some measure of independence; and from the return his name supplanted that of Israel or Jacob, as the common designation of the people. *Nor the lawgiver from between his feet.* This is otherwise rendered, "nor the judicial staff from between his feet;" and it is argued that this rendering corresponds best with the phrase "between his feet" and with the parallel clause which precedes. It is not worth while contending for one against the other, as the meaning of both is precisely the same. But we have retained the English version, as the term מְחֹקֵק has only one clear meaning; "between the feet" may mean among his descendants or in his tribe; and the synthetic parallelism of the clauses is satisfied by the identity of meaning. Lawgiver is to be understood as judge, dispenser or administrator of law. Judah had the forerank among the tribes in the wilderness, and never altogether lost it. Nahshon the son of Amminadab, the prince of his tribe, was the ancestor of David, who was anointed as the rightful sovereign of all Israel, and in whom the throne became hereditary. The revolt of the ten tribes curtailed, but did not abolish the actual sovereignty of Rehoboam and his successors, who continued the acknowledged sovereigns till some time after the return from the captivity. From that date the whole nation was

virtually absorbed in Judah, and whatever trace of self-government remained belonged to him until the birth of Jesus, who was the lineal descendant of the royal line of David and of Judah, and was the Messiah, the anointed of heaven to be king of Zion and of Israel in a far higher sense than before. *Until Shiloh come.* This is otherwise translated, "until he come to Shiloh," the place so called. This is explained of the time when "the whole assembly of the children of Israel was convened at Shiloh, and set up the tent of meeting there" (Jos. xviii. 1). We hold by the former translation — 1. Because Shiloh has not yet been named as a known locality in the land of promise. 2. Judah did not come to Shiloh in any exclusive sense. 3. His coming thither with his fellows had no bearing whatever on his supremacy. 4. He did not come to Shiloh as the seat of his government or any part of his territory; and 5. The real sovereignty of Judah took place after this convention at Shiloh, and not before it. After the rejection of the second translation on these grounds, the former is accepted as the only tenable alternative. 6. Besides, it is the natural rendering of the words. 7. Before the coming of Shiloh, the Prince of Peace, the highest pitch of Judah's supremacy in its primary form has to be attained. 8. On the coming of Shiloh the last remnant of that supremacy was removed, only to be replaced by the higher form of preëminence which the Prince of Peace inaugurates. *And unto him be the obedience of the peoples.* "Unto him" means naturally unto Shiloh. "The obedience" describes the willing submission to the new form of sovereignty which is ushered in by Shiloh. The word is otherwise rendered "gathering;" but this does not suit the usage in Prov. xxx. 17. "The obedience" intimates that the supremacy of Judah does not cease at the coming of Shiloh, but only assumes a grander form. *Of the peoples.* Not only the sons of Israel, but all the descendants of Adam will ultimately bow down to the Prince of Peace. This is the seed of the woman, who shall bruise the serpent's head, the seed of Abraham, in whom all the families of the earth shall be blessed, presented now under the new aspect of the peacemaker, whom all the nations of the earth shall eventually obey as the Prince of Peace. He is therefore now revealed as the Destroyer of the works of evil, the Dispenser of the blessings of grace, and the King of peace. The coming of Shiloh and the obedience of the nations to him will cover a long period of time, the close of which will coincide with the limit here set to Judah's earthly supremacy in its wider and loftier stage. This prediction therefore truly penetrates to the latter days.

11, 12. The exuberant fertility of Judah's province is now depicted. We now behold him peacefully settled in the land of promise, and the striking objects of rural plenty and prosperity around him. The quiet ass on which he perambulates is tied to the vine, the juice of whose grapes is as copious as the water in which his robes are washed. The last sentence is capable of being rendered, "Red are his eyes above wine, and white his teeth above milk." But a connection as well as a comparison seems to be implied in the original. Judea is justly described as abounding in the best of wine and milk. This fine picture of Judah's earthly abode is a fitting emblem of the better country where Shiloh reigns.

13. Zebulun means *dwelling*, to which there is an allusion in the first clause of the verse. *At the haven of seas.* This tribe touched upon the coast of the sea of Kinnereth and of the Mediterranean. It probably possessed some havens for shipping near the promontory of Karmel: and its northwestern boundary touched upon Phœnicia, the territory of Zidon. He is placed before Issakar, who was older, because the latter sank into a subordinate position.

14, 15. *An ass of bone*, and therefore of strength. *Couching between the hurdles,* — the pens or stalls in which the cattle were lodged. Rest in a pleasant land he felt to be good; and hence, rather than undertake the struggle for liberty and independence, he became like the strong ass a bearer of burdens, and a payer of tribute. He is thus a hireling by disposition as well as by name (xxx. 18).

16–18. The sons of the handmaids follow those of Leah. *Dan shall judge his people as one of the tribes of Israel.* He will maintain his position as a tribe in the state. When threatened by overwhelming power he will put forth his native force for the discomfiture of the foe. The adder is the cerastes or horned serpent, of the color of the sand, and therefore not easily recognized, that inflicts a fatal wound on him that unwarily treads on it. The few facts in the history of Dan afterwards given correspond well with the character here drawn. Some of its features are conspicuous in Samson (Judg. xiii.–xvi.). *For thy salvation have I waited, O Lord.* The patriarch, contemplating the power of the adversaries of his future people, breaks forth into the expression of his longing desire and hope of that salvation of the Almighty by which alone they can be delivered. That salvation is commensurate with the utmost extent and diversity of these adversaries.

19. Gad also shall be subject to the assaults of the enemy. But he

shall resist the foe and harass his rear. This brief character agrees with his after history. He is reckoned among the valiant men in Scripture (1 Chr. v. 18).

20. Asher shall have a soil abounding in wheat and oil. He occupies the low lands along the coast north of Karmel. Hence the products of his country are fit to furnish the table of kings. Gad and Asher are placed before Naphtali, the second son of Bilhah. We cannot tell whether they were older, or for what other reason they occupy this place. It may be that Naphtali was of a less decisive or self-reliant character.

21. Naphtali is a hind let loose. The hind or gazelle is agile and nimble. When free on its native hills, it roams with instinctive confidence and delight. It is timid and irresolute in confinement. This is probably the character of Naphtali. *He giveth goodly words.* Here we pass from the figure to the reality. Eloquence in prose and verse was characteristic of this particular tribe. The only important historical event in which they are concerned is the defeat of Jabin's host, which is celebrated in the song of Deborah and Barak (Judg. iv. 5). In this passage we may study the character of the tribe.

22–26. Jacob had doubtless been made acquainted with the history of his beloved son Joseph from the time of his disappearance until he met him on the borders of Egypt. It had been the meditation and the wonder of his last seventeen years. When he comes to Joseph, therefore, the mingled emotions of affection and gratitude burst forth from his heart in language that cannot be restrained by the ordinary rules of speech. The first thing connected with Joseph in the patriarch's mind is fruitfulness. The image is vivid and striking. *Son of a fruitful tree.* A branch or rather a shoot transplanted from the parent stem. *By a well;* from which it may draw the water of life. *Whose daughters,* — luxuriant branches. *Run over a wall,* — transcend all the usual boundaries of a well-enclosed garden. This fruitfulness attaches to Joseph in two respects. First, he is the prudent gatherer and the inexhaustible dispenser of the produce of Egypt, by which the lives of his father and brethren were preserved. And then he is in prospect the twofold tribe, that bursts the bounds assigned to a twelfth of the chosen people, and overspreads the area of two tribes.

23, 24. The memory then reverts to the past history of Joseph. A new figure is now called up. A champion is assailed by a host of archers. They vex him, shoot at him, and in every way act the part of an enemy. But his bow continues elastic, and his arms are enabled to bend it, because he receives strength from the God of his fathers, "the Might of Jacob, the Shepherd, the Stone of Israel." Such is the rich and copious imagery that flows from the lips of Jacob. "The Might," the exalted upholder; "the Shepherd, the Stone," the fostering guardian as well as the solid foundation of his being. His great hands upheld Joseph against the brother and the stranger. *From him.* This seems the free rendering of the word requisite to bring the two members of the parallel into harmony.

25, 26. These two thoughts — the peaceful abundance of his old age, which he owed to Joseph, and the persecutions his beloved son had endured — stir the fountains of his affections until they overflow with blessings. *From the God of thy father,* — the Eternal One who is the source of all blessing. *And the Almighty,* who is able to control all adverse influences. *Blessings of heaven above,* — the air, the rain, and the sun. *Blessings of the deep,* — the springs and streams, as well as the fertile soil. *Blessings of the breasts and the womb,* — the children of the home and the young of the flocks and herds. *Have prevailed.* The benedictions of Jacob pronounced upon Joseph exceed those that came upon Jacob himself from his fathers. To Joseph is given a double portion, with a double measure of affection from a father's heart. *Unto the bound of the perpetual hills.* Like an overflowing flood they have risen to the very summits of the perpetual hills in the conceptions of the venerable patriarch. *Of him who was distinguished from his brethren;* not only by a long period of persecution and humiliation, but by a subsequent elevation to extraordinary dignity and preëminence.

It is to be noted that this benediction, when fairly interpreted, though it breathes all the fondness of a father's heart, yet contains no intimation that the supremacy or the priesthood were to belong to Joseph, or that the Messiah was to spring from him. At the same time Joseph was in many events of his history a remarkable type of the Messiah, and by intermarriage he, as well as many foreigners, was no doubt among the ancestors of the Messiah (2 Kings viii. 18, 26).

27. Benjamin is described as a wolf who is engaged morning and evening, that is, all day long, in hunting after prey. He was warlike by character and conduct (Judg. xx., xxi.), and among his descendants are Ehud, Saul, and Jonathan.

28–33. After the benediction Jacob gives directions concerning his burial. *All these are the twelve tribes.* This implies that the benedictions refer not to the heads only, but to the whole tribes. *Each according to his blessing.* All are blessed, but the form of the blessing is suited to the character of the individual. 29–32. *Bury me with my fathers*, —with Abraham and Sarah, Isaac and Rebekah, and Leah. This dying command he now lays on the twelve, as he had before bound Joseph by oath to its performance. 33. *Gathered up his feet into the bed.* He had been sitting upright while pronouncing the benedictory address and giving his last directions. He now lies down and calmly breathes his last.

LXXVIII. THE BURIAL OF JACOB.—Gen. l.

10. אָטָד Atad, *the buck-thorn.*
11. אָבֵל מִצְרַיִם Abel-Mitsraim, *mourning of Mizraim*, or *meadow of M.*

L. 1. And Joseph fell upon his father's face, and wept
upon him, and kissed him. 2. And Joseph commanded his
servants, the physicians, to embalm his father: and the phy-
sicians embalmed Israel. 3. And they fulfilled for him forty
days; for so they fulfil the days of the embalmed: and Miz-
raim mourned for him seventy days.

4. And the days of mourning for him were past, and Joseph
spake unto the house of Pharoh, saying, If now I have found
grace in your eyes, speak now in the ears of Pharoh, saying,
5. My father made me swear, saying, Lo, I die; in my grave
which I have digged for me in the land of Kenaan, there shalt
thou bury me. And now let me go up now, and bury my
father, and return. 6. And Pharoh said, Go up, and bury
thy father, as he made thee swear.

7. And Joseph went up to bury his father; and with him
went up all the servants of Pharoh, the elders of his house,
and all the elders of the land of Mizraim. 8. And all the
house of Joseph, and his brethren, and his father's house:
only their little ones and their flocks and their herds left they
in the land of Goshen. 9. And with him went up both
chariots and horsemen; and the camp was very great. 10.
And they went to the threshing-floor of Atad, which is beyond

Jordan, and they held there a very great and sore lamentation: and he made for his father a mourning of seven days. 11. And the Kenaanite dwelling in the land saw the mourning in the threshing-floor of Atad, and they said, A sore mourning is this to Egypt: wherefore the name of it was called Abel-Mizraim, which is beyond Jordan. 12. And his sons did unto him according as he commanded them. 13. And his sons carried him into the land of Kenaan, and buried him in the cave of the field of Makpelah; which Abraham bought, with the field for a possession of a burying-place, from Ephron the Hittite, before Mamre. 14. And Joseph returned to Mizraim, he and his brethren, and all that went up with him to bury his father, after he had buried his father.

15. And Joseph's brethren saw that their father was dead, and they said, Mayhap Joseph will hate us, and surely requite us all the evil which we did unto him. 16. And they sent unto Joseph, saying, Thy father commanded before his death, saying, 17. So shall ye say unto Joseph, Ah, now! forgive now the tresspass of thy brethren and their sin; for they have done thee evil: and now forgive now the trespass of the servants of the God of thy father. And Joseph wept when they spake unto him. 18. And his brethren also went and fell down before him: and they said, Behold, we are thy servants. 19. And Joseph said unto them, Fear not, for am I in God's stead? 20. And you, ye meant evil against me: God meant it for good, to do as it is this day, to save much people alive. 21. And now fear not: I will sustain you and your little ones. And he comforted them, and spake to their heart.

22. And Joseph dwelt in Mizraim, he and his father's house: and Joseph lived a hundred and ten years. 23. And Joseph saw of Ephraim the children of the third generation: the children also of Makir the son of Menasseh were borne upon Joseph's knees. 24. And Joseph said unto his brethren, I die: and God will surely visit you, and bring you up from this land which he sware to Abraham, to Isaac, and to Jacob. 25.

And Joseph took an oath of the sons of Israel, saying, God will surely visit you, and ye shall carry up my bones hence. 26. And Joseph died, the son of a hundred and ten years; and they embalmed him, and he was put in a coffin in Mizraim.

This chapter records the burial of Jacob and the death of Joseph, and so completes the history of the chosen family, and the third bible for the instruction of man.

1–3. After the natural outburst of sorrow for his deceased parent, Joseph gave orders to embalm the body, according to the custom of Egypt. *His servants, the physicians.* As the grand vizier of Egypt, he has physicians in his retinue. The classes and functions of the physicians in Egypt may be learned from Herodotus (ii. 81–86). There were special physicians for each disease; and the embalmers formed a class by themselves. *Forty days* were employed in the process of embalming; *seventy days*, including the forty, were devoted to mourning for the dead. Herodotus mentions this number as the period of embalming. Diodorus (i. 91) assigns upwards of thirty days to the process. It is probable that the actual process was continued for forty days, and that the body lay in natron for the remaining thirty days of mourning. See Hengstenberg's B. B. Mos. u. Aeg., and Rawlinson's Herodotus.

4–6. Joseph, by means of Pharoh's courtiers, not in person, because he was a mourner, applies for leave to bury his father in the land of Kenaan, according to his oath. This leave is freely and fully allowed.

7–14. The funeral procession is now described. *All the servants of Pharoh.* The highest honor is conferred on Jacob for Joseph's sake. *The elders of Pharoh, and all the elders of the land of Mizraim.* The court and state officials are here separately specified. *All the house.* Not only the heads, but all the sons and servants that are able to go. *Chariots and horsemen* accompany them as a guard on the way. *The threshing-floor of Atad*, or *of the buck-thorn.* This is said to be beyond Jordan. Deterred, probably, by some difficulty in the direct route, they seem to have gone round by the east side of the Salt Sea. *A mourning of seven days.* This is a last sad farewell to the departed patriarch. *Abel-Mizraim.* This name, like many in the East, has a double meaning. The word Abel no doubt at first meant mourning, though the name would be used by many, ignorant of its origin, in the sense of a meadow. *His sons carried him.* The main body of the procession seems to have halted beyond the Jordan, and awaited the return of the immediate relatives, who conveyed the body to its last resting-place. The whole company then returned together to Egypt.

15–21. His brethren supplicate Joseph for forgiveness. *They sent unto Joseph*, commissioned one of their number to speak to him. *And now* that our common father has given us this command. *And Joseph wept* at the distress and doubt of his brothers. He no doubt summons them before him, when they fall down before him entreating his forgiveness. Joseph removes their fears. *Am I in God's stead?* that I should take the law into my own hands, and take revenge. God has already judged them, and moreover turned their sinful deed into a blessing. He assures them of his brotherly kindness towards them.

22–26. The biography of Joseph is now completed. *The children of the third generation*,— the grandsons of grandsons in the line of Ephraim. We have here an explicit proof that an interval of about twenty years between the births of the father and that of his first-born was not unusual during the lifetime of Joseph. *And Joseph took an oath.* He thus expressed his unwavering confidence in the return of the sons of Israel to the land of promise. *God will surely visit.* He was embalmed and put in a coffin, and so kept by his descendants, as was not unusual in Egypt. And on the return of the sons of Israel from Egypt they kept their oath to Joseph (Ex. xiii. 19), and buried his bones in Shekem (Jos. xxiv. 32).

The sacred writer here takes leave of the chosen family, and closes the bible of the sons of Israel. It is truly a wonderful book. It lifts the veil of mystery that hangs over the present condition of the human race. It records the origin and fall of man, and thus explains the coexistence of moral evil and a moral sense, and the hereditary memory of God and judgment in the soul of man. It records the cause and mode of the confusion of tongues, and thus explains the concomitance of the unity of the race and the specific diversity of mode or form in human speech. It records the call of Abraham, and thus accounts for the preservation of the knowledge of God and his mercy in one section of the human race, and the corruption or loss of it in all the rest. We need scarcely remark that the six days' creation accounts for the present state of nature. It thus solves the fundamental questions of physics, ethics, philology, and theology for the race of Adam. It notes the primitive relation of man to God, and marks the three great stages of human development that came in with Adam, Noah, and Abraham. It points out the three forms of sin that usher in these stages, — the fall of Adam, the intermarriage of the sons of God with the daughters of men, and the building of the tower of Babel. It gradually unfolds the purpose and method of grace to the returning penitent through a Deliverer who is successively announced as the seed of the woman, of Shem, of Abraham, Isaac, Jacob, and Judah. This is the second Adam, who, when the covenant of works was about to fall to the ground through the failure of the first Adam, undertook to uphold it by fulfilling all its conditions on behalf of those who are the objects of the divine grace. Hence the Lord establishes his covenant successively with Adam, Noah, and Abraham; with Adam after the fall tacitly, with Noah expressly, and with both generally as the representatives of the race descending from them; with Abraham specially and instrumentally as the channel through which the blessings of salvation might be at length extended to all the families of the earth. So much of this plan of mercy is revealed from time to time to the human race as comports with the progress they have made in the education of the intellectual, moral, and active faculties. This only authentic epitome of primeval history is worthy of the constant study of intelligent and responsible man.